#3137

WEAVER
820 MAIN STREET
FORD CITY PA 16226

FEB 1 0 1994

MAX WEBER:
A BIOGRAPHY

D1571092

Max and Marianne Weber as newlyweds, 1893.

MARIANNE WEBER

MAX WEBER:
A BIOGRAPHY

With a new introduction by

Guenther Roth

Translated and Edited by

Harry Zohn

Transaction Books
New Brunswick (USA) and Oxford (UK)

Copyright © 1988 by Transaction, Inc.
New Brunswick, New Jersey 08903

All rights reserved under International and Pan-American Copyright Conventions. No part of this book may be reproduced or transmitted in any form or by any means, electronic or mechanical, including photocopy, recording, or any information storage and retrieval system, without prior permission in writing from the publisher. All inquiries should be addressed to Transaction Books, Rutgers—The State University, New Brunswick, New Jersey 08903.

Library of Congress Catalog Number: 88-11611
ISBN 0-88738-702-0
Printed in the United States of America

Library of Congress Cataloging-in-Publication Data

Weber, Marianne, 1870-1954.
  [Max Weber. English]
  Max Weber ; a biography / Marianne Weber ; with an introduction by
Guenther Roth ; [translated from the German and edited by Harry Zohn].
     p.   cm.
  Reprint. Originally published: New York : Wiley, 1975.
  Includes bibliographical references and index.
  ISBN 0-88738-702-0
  1. Weber, Max, 1864-1920. 2. Sociologists—Germany—Biography.
  3. Sociology—German-History. I. Zohn, Harry. II. Title.
[HM22.G3W467513 1988]
301'.092'4—dc 19
[B]   88-11611
                                                                CIP

TRANSLATOR'S PREFACE ⸺⸺⸺⸺

It is a privilege to be associated with the first publication in English of
a book which Peter Gay has referred to as "an important biography," Robert
Nisbet has described as "a moving and deeply felt biographical memoir," and
Gerhard Masur has called "one of the most moving biographies ever written
by a wife about her husband" and "the foundation for all further inquiries
[concerning Weber]."

Marianne Schnitger Weber was born at Oerlinghausen on August 2, 1870,
and died at Heidelberg on March 21, 1954. She wrote *Max Weber, ein Lebensbild* in the years following her husband's untimely death in 1920. Her book
was first published in 1926 by the house of J. C. B. Mohr (Paul Siebeck),
Tubingen. A second edition was issued in 1950 under the imprint of Lambert Schneider, Heidelberg; it was slightly abridged and combined Chapters
19 and 20 of the first edition. Both editions have long been out of print
and are hard to find on the secondhand book market. My translation is
based on the 1926 edition, but it also takes cognizance of the minor emen-
dations and corrections of the 1950 edition. It is thus the most complete,

the most accurate, and perhaps even the clearest version of this work that has ever been published. Certainly there is no comparable "Life and Works" of Max Weber on the international book market.

Neither German edition is annotated. Presumably out of consideration for people then still alive, Marianne Weber chose not to identify many of the persons she wrote about, and occasionally her biography reads like a *roman à clef*. The 1950 edition does contain an index, the work of Pastor Bruno Goldschmit, but even this generally helpful list of persons and places is incomplete and sometimes faulty and misleading.

The present edition is copiously annotated, though it has not been possible to give information on every person mentioned or even to identify everyone to whom Marianne Weber refers as Herr X, Dr. Y, or Professor Z. Also, it is often difficult to tell whether sentences or phrases that Marianne or Max Weber put between quotation marks are more or less famous quotations or simply the kind of reminiscences, witticisms, or other allusions that lead a private life in every family. I hope that erudite readers with long memories will come forward with further identifications, notes, or corrections for a possible second edition of this book. With a few exceptions, notes on persons, places, and events may be found on the page where these are first mentioned. My notes are labeled as editor's notes, to distinguish them from those of the author. For purposes of reference, or if certain chapters are read out of turn or skipped, the index may be consulted for the first occurrence of someone or something glossed.

If certain mysterious references proved tantalizing and required some sleuthing on the part of the translator and his informants, Marianne Weber's style posed a problem of another sort. Frau Weber, a noted feminist, was an accomplished writer in her own right; in addition to several books about women's problems, she published an autobiography in 1948. Her biography of her husband is a great panorama of German and European life during more than a century and sheds much light on the social, political, intellectual, academic, and cultural life of Germany in that period. It is replete with detail and written in a leisurely fashion. The author's German is often colorful, evocative, ornate, metaphorical, soulful, highflown, and occasionally even overblown; her flavorful language frequently reflects her unabashed enjoyment of luxuriant imagery. It has been my aim to produce a faithful translation within the framework of reasonably clear and idiomatic English, but I have tried to resist the translator's itch to sacrifice an author's characteristic style on the altar of readability. If Count de Buffon's dictum *"Le style c'est l'homme même"* has any validity, at least some of Marianne

Weber's stylistic peculiarities must be allowed to shine through in the English translation, for certainly this author's style reflects her personality and her special way of looking at the world. An attempt has been made to tone down some of her more purple passages and modify some of her stylistic quirks. But apart from the fact that stylistic homogeneity is hard to achieve in a work of this type and length, to eliminate all of Marianne Weber's stylistic mannerisms, however antiquated or quaint some of them may sound today, would have been an act of denaturization of the kind that theorists and practitioners of translation from Goethe to Walter Benjamin and Vladimir Nabokov have decried. I am not persuaded by the argument that it is desirable, or even permissible, to rewrite and thus "improve" a work in the process of translation. I find the following statement by Nabokov (from his *Congeries*) far more convincing: "We must dismiss once and for all the conventional notion that a translation 'should read smoothly' and 'should not sound like a translation.' In point of fact, any translation that does *not* sound like a translation is bound to be inexact upon inspection, while on the other hand, the only virtue of a good translation is faithfulness and completeness. Whether it reads smoothly or not, depends on the model, not the mimic." Thoughtful readers will, I hope, agree that in trying to be both faithful and complete I have served both them and the author well by producing a version that reflects most of the virtues, though of necessity also some of the deficiencies, of Marianne Weber's magnum opus and, above all, conveys its special flavor.

I wish to express my gratitude to Professor Johannes Winckelmann of the Max Weber Institute of the University of Munich, to Professor Wolfgang J. Mommsen of the University of Düsseldorf, to Dr. Michael Baumann of the University of Heidelberg, and to Georg Bangen of the Free University of Berlin for their willingness to answer my questions and help me with the difficult task of annotating this volume. I am indebted also to Professors Reinhard Bendix (University of California, Berkeley), Robert Lilienfeld (City University of New York), and Egon Bittner and Kurt H. Wolff (Brandeis University) for their helpful interest in this project. A special word of appreciation is due Eric Valentine of John Wiley & Sons and Christine Valentine for being such ideal editors.

HARRY ZOHN

Brandeis University
Waltham, Massachusetts
December 1974

CONTENTS

ILLUSTRATIONS _____

AUTHOR'S PREFATORY NOTE ———

Friends and colleagues of Max Weber have made available his letters to them for use in this biography. Only by integrating numerous passages from letters into the narrative has it been possible to let Max Weber speak directly in this book and to illustrate his reactions to, and impact upon, everyday life as well as to the intellectual and political movements of his time. The author would like to thank them all, particularly the friends and colleagues who did not withhold even those letters Weber wrote them in cases of conflict and who permitted their partial publication. But she owes particular thanks to those friends who gave her inestimable help and encouragement by their personal interest and their counsel.

Das war der Mann, der immer wiederkehrt
wenn eine Zeit noch einmal ihren Wert,
da sie sich enden will, zusammenfasst.
Da hebt noch einer ihre ganze Last
und wirft sie in den Abgrund seiner Brust.

Die vor ihm hatten Leid und Lust;
er aber fühlt nur noch des Lebens Masse
und dass er alles wie *ein* Ding umfasse,—
nur Gott bleibt über seinem Willen weit:
da liebt er ihn mit seinem hohen Hasse
für diese Unerreichbarkeit.

This is the man who always will emerge
at moments when an era on the verge
of termination will assess once more
its value. He will lift its load before
he hurls it down the caverns of his heart.

Before, men had of bliss and pain their part;
but he feels nothing but life's total weight
and that all things are joined in one estate—
only the span to God he cannot breach:
and yet he loves Him with heroic hate
for being utterly beyond his reach.

From Rilke's *Das Stundenbuch* [*The Book of Hours*], Part I. The reference is to Michelangelo ["Das waren Tage Michelangelos"].—Ed.

—Rainer Maria Rilke, translated by Max Knight

MARIANNE WEBER
AND HER CIRCLE

INTRODUCTION TO THE TRANSACTION EDITION

Guenther Roth

When Marianne Weber (1870–1954) began editing her husband's voluminous literary remains in the early 1920's, Othmar Spann (1878–1950), the
once famous sociologist of an "organic" theory of society, remarked that
Max Weber had been "a demonic, restless person, who was capable of
affecting others through the strength of his personality, but to whom it was
denied to leave behind a life's work that could last. . . . His time is over, his is
a dead science."[1] Few judgments have been more mistaken. Max Weber has
turned out to be the one German economist and sociologist who is still
widely read today, the only one who became "influential" worldwide many
years after his death.

In his lifetime, Weber was only one member of a galaxy of brilliant scholars, and it was far from obvious that his voice would penetrate the din of
battle and be heard in the future. We like to believe that Marx, Durkheim,
and Weber survived their times because of the intrinsic quality of their

achievement, but their vaunted "influence" has been very much dependent on our own receptivity and our own orientations. Yet it is also fair to say that without Marianne Weber her husband's oeuvre might not have gained its later importance for the course of social science. Ultimately, she was not interested in his contribution to sociology; only a few pages of the biography deal with it. But she never wavered in her faith in his greatness as a human being and a scholar. After completing the editions and biography, she wrote to Paul Honigsheim (1885-1967) in 1926: "In my judgment Weber's fame is only at its very beginning. People will be stupefied when they put their hands on his work (ten to twelve volumes). I live for his immortality on earth."[2] In fact, before and after Weber's death she lived for much more, although her "companionship" with him, lived and remembered, remained the bedrock of her life.

Biographical Genres: Dutiful Wives and Pious Daughters

Marianne Weber is today recognized as the wife of a famous man and as a feminist of sorts. In her biography of Weber she casts herself very much as the heroine at her husband's side. But even though she reveals much—shockingly much for many of her first readers—about their troubled lives and the doomed world in which they lived, we can understand her story better if we ask beforehand what kind of wife and feminist sat down at her husband's desk to produce such an extraordinary biography (*Lebensbild*).

For a long time, women had written diaries to monitor their spiritual growth and had composed family chronicles for private circulation. Now they published what they wrote. Many of the women and men in Marianne Weber's circle and academic milieu left us biographies or autobiographies. Theirs was the high point of this literary mode of expression. Some of these biographies, which often rely heavily on letters, may appear to us stilted and sentimental. Yet they treat vexing moral issues that remain pertinent to the present intellectual and political situation, when liberalism is on the defensive and a counterrevolution has been mounted against the counterculture. Marianne Weber and most of her liberal political friends were spokeswomen for an ethical rigorism that is echoed in some of the neoconservative literature today. But several of her close friends also followed, in theory and practice, the "new ethic," as the morality of sexual liberation was called. The counterculture before World War I played through many themes that were resurrected in the 1960's and 1970's.

The Webers tried hard to grapple with the moral antinomies and personal

Looking back as a septuagenarian, Marianne recounted the balance of benefits and burdens in her life at the time: "Life offered me rich opportunities for fulfilling myself (*Selbstverwirklichung*), my hunger for learning was undiminished and could be combined with public activities. . . . Max Weber also took a very warm interest in my work in the women's movement and offered gallant help, whenever difficulties arose. . . . My life was so rich in the personal and public realm that there remained no room for unattainable wishes in the reproductive sphere. This very richness gave me the strength to help Max Weber, my life's lodestar, endure and overcome the fate of a severe neurosis of many years' duration" (L 56).

In retrospect, too, the biographical significance of the book that established Marianne Weber's scholarly reputation, *Wife and Mother in Legal Development*, is easy to see.[7] Written "during [my] husband's severe illness but under his supervision, I managed to finish it after a seven-year effort" (L 124). Thus, the work was begun only two to three years after the fateful showdown over Helene between Max Weber senior and junior in Heidelberg in 1897, the confrontation that was followed by the father's death and the son's breakdown (see ch. 8 below). Marianne openly acknowledged that this time her husband not only suggested the project but also advised her closely and took a strong hand in the final editing (L VIf.). This certainly makes it a joint Weberian enterprise.

The lengthy historical survey was meant to be an introduction for women and men interested not in the logical structure but in the practical significance of legal norms for the condition of women, a sociological approach Weber later also adopted for his chapter on law in *Economy and Society*. But unlike the latter work, Marianne's was not a dispassionate handbook. Dedicated to "Helene Weber née Falkenstein in grateful love," her book contains a strong attack on patriarchy and a vigorous plea for equality in marriage. In addition to the familial motivation, however, it should also be recalled that Marianne began writing her book just when the new civil code was introduced in 1900. This new code was opposed by the women's movement because it preserved the husband's privileges almost completely, although it conceded to women limited legal agency.

Before Marianne launched her attack on patriarchy, she criticized matriarchal theories from Bachofen to Engels and tried to sketch a historically adequate "developmental history" (*Entwicklungsgeschichte*) of modern marriage. She agreed that familial patriarchalism was not a natural given, but declared completely untenable the socialist assertion that the development of private property brought forth the forms of patriarchal marriage. Legitimate marriage appeared to her the product of a long development: "Women were interested in having their children recognized as the man's 'legitimate' heirs and becoming themselves 'legitimate,' that means, protected against absolute arbitrariness. This interest finally became strong enough to force patriarchalism into making concessions."[8] In the Weberian vein, she also argued that the interests of advanced capitalism in exploiting cheap female labor do not determine any particular social or legal form of marriage but instead are relatively indifferent to them.

Marianne Weber waxed most eloquent in passages that can be read as a general indictment of German law and German husbands, as well as a thinly disguised account of what went wrong between Max senior and Helene. She detailed the many ways in which husbands are motivated to crush any attempt at external and internal independence on the part of their wives. Against this prevalent state of affairs she set her own ideal of ethical individualism and mutual responsibility on an equalitarian basis: "Let us state once more our case against the ideal of patriarchalism, which gave birth to our marriage laws, by summarizing the general ethical and psychological consequences that must result for the woman and conjugal life if the husband indeed exercises his legal authority over her person and property and thus makes dominance his duty, yet often without the magnanimity demanded by Fichte. . . . [Subordination] diminishes not only the woman's happiness but also the ethical value of the conjugal relationship. . . . If, according to the authority principle, the husband's subjective wishes become orders, the wife has not much left to offer him out of 'free love.' The mutual education in selflessness is falling away, all those inner tasks that married life renews daily and that makes it so wonderfully satisfying if meeting the challenges can be taken more and more for granted."[9]

Two pillars of the French and German educational establishment, Emile Durkheim (1858-1917) and Friedrich Paulsen (1846-1908), responded critically to Marianne's book and illustrate the resistance she met despite her relative moderation. Complimenting the "good judgment and critical acumen" with which she handled the secondary literature, Durkheim yet found that she gave Engels more attention than the scientific value of his theory warranted. He criticized her view that the patriarchal family had completely subordinated the woman, arguing that, on the contrary, it had enhanced her place in the home and brought her closer to the man. Although he commended Marianne's "conservative prudence" in opposing marriage as a completely free contract, he was dismayed by her advocacy of divorce by mutual consent; this threatened "the organic unity of the conjugal union and of the family." Durkheim's strongest objection had to be directed against Marianne's ethical individualism, which made her demand complete legal equality between wife and husband. In his eyes, this undermined "the religious respect the hearth inspires."[10]

Durkheim's review proves not only that he was willing to take note of a woman scholar, but also that he could have answered a question often asked by later scholars puzzled by his almost total disregard of his German adversary: "Who is that Max Weber anyway?" "Oh, he's Marianne's guy." As Marianne recounts anecdotally, that was an exchange, in Baden dialect, between two craftsmen in Heidelberg at the time when she was publicly much more visible than her husband (407).

Friedrich Paulsen, whose *Introduction to Philosophy* Max had given his bride to read, reviewed her book in seventeen pages of the prestigious *Preussische Jahrbücher*.[11] Writing in the year of his death, Paulsen took the patronizing approach of an older generation that liked to appeal to "the nature of things" against the demands of the women's movement. Like Durkheim, Paulsen applauded Marianne's critique of the socialist theories of an original state of matriarchy. Lauding her rejection of the sexual liberation movement, he gave her credit for highminded ethical idealism in the tradition of Kant and Fichte, but at this point also started his critique. Law should follow custom, not ethical ideals, which easily blind their adherents to the wisdom of slow historical progress. Just as Durkheim viewed her as something of a "terrible simplificatrice," Paulsen considered her impractical. He conceded that he could not prevail over her in matters of conscience, but he appealed to the status quo, the willingness of most women to subordinate themselves. Marianne's proposal to give marriage partners equal rights of decision-making appeared to him totally infeasible: "That was the constitutional principle of the kingdom of Poland, and we all know what happened to it!" He also considered impractical Marianne's plea for separate property management and for improving the conditions of illegitimate children by forcing fathers to accept financial and educational responsibility. In his view, legalizing "concubinage," thus tolerating unmarried couples, was only going to increase the number of illegitimate children and general sexual license.

Whereas Durkheim and Paulsen admitted that women's dignity could be enhanced under a cautiously reformed patriarchal law, Georg Simmel (1858–1918) pursued a philosophical argument about the inherent value, if not the superiority, of "female culture," an argument that alternatively attracted and repelled support within the women's movement.[12] From the beginning of his career in the 1890's, he wrote more seriously than any other male of his generation about women's psychology (from anti-militarism to coquetry), female culture, prostitution, and the women's movement. These topics were discussed in his Berlin salon no less than in the Webers' Heidelberg salon, which he visited several times with his wife Gertrud (1864–1938), who wrote on sexual ethics under the pen name Marie Luise Enckendorf.

Marianne Weber responded as early as 1904 to Simmel's 1902 essay on female culture, but without yet naming him. In her first feminist essay "The Participation of Women in Science," which paralleled her husband's 1904 essay on "The 'Objectivity' of Knowledge in Social Science and Social Policy," she stressed, in good Weberian fashion, the novel evaluative viewpoints that women could bring to bear on scientific issues, rather than the absolute gender differences that Simmel emphasized.[13] In 1911, Simmel published a quite different version of his essay "Female Culture" in Weber's *Archiv für Sozialwissenschaft* and included it in the same year, with "The Relative and the Absolute in the Problem of the Sexes," in his collection *Philosophical Culture*.[14] Two years later, Marianne Weber responded to these essays with "Women and Objective Culture" in *Logos*, the philosophical house journal of Heinrich Rickert and Max Weber.[15] As is well known, Simmel considered the "tragedy of culture" to lie in the fact that the general accumulation of knowledge and of artifacts outpaced the individual's capacity to catch up with this expansion: "objective culture" outraced "subjective culture." Man's creativity was inherently self-defeating. Simmel welcomed the efforts of modern women to advance their subjective culture. But objective culture was mainly a product of male externalization, whereas female nature was self-contained. The objectification of female nature was therefore a contradiction in terms.

Marianne Weber acknowledged that Simmel meant to create a "progressive" gender ontology of female culture in order to elevate women onto a higher pedestal. Thereby women would constitute a value sphere in their own right. But she bluntly declared this metaphysical rescue attempt another discrimination against women and insisted on women's ability to contribute to objective culture. She admitted only historical and psychological, not ontological differences. Thus, she rejected Simmel's assertion of an "ultimately self-contained completeness of being which constitutes the meaning of life for the female type."[16] She also denied the "typical tragedy" of each of the two sexes, distinguishing instead between jobs and vocations. Most men and women hold jobs only for the sake of making a living, but a minority of both sexes lives for a vocation. Women, too, Marianne told Simmel, can experience that deep satisfaction that comes from "complete objectification of the subject." Hence, the very advance of objective culture appeared to her truly progressive: it enabled women to transcend their "special female mission" (of female reproduction) and to contribute to cultural production.[17]

If Marianne Weber followed Simmel to heights of philosophical abstraction, she also engaged for a number of years in down-to-earth organizational activities. Shortly after moving to Heidelberg in 1897 she reestablished and directed a branch of a national association dedicated to the promotion of women's education, "Frauenbildung-Frauenstudium."[18] The local organization presented lectures on women's issues, sometimes given by prominent members of the movement, and courses on academic subjects given by faculty members. The audience consisted of men and women.

Following the example of women like Marie Stritt in Dresden, in 1901 Marianne also was instrumental in setting up a legal aid office for the "socially disprivileged," especially waitresses and servant girls. (There was no industrial proletariat in Heidelberg, a small university town of 25,000 inhabitants.) She managed to persuade Georg Jellinek, the renowned constitutional theorist of the state, to allow his wife Camilla (1860–1940) to run the advisory service. Camilla quickly underwent a radicalization and ended up as a champion of abortion rights. Marianne Weber also started and lost a campaign to win voting rights for women in the Protestant state church of Baden. But she could exult at the appointment of Else von Richthofen as the first female factory inspector of the state of Baden in 1900, an event that served "to strengthen the faith of the women's movement" (230). She had established her intimate friendship with Else, which was to last almost sixty years, in Freiburg. Max engineered the appointment of Else, his first female doctoral student, just as he later took up cudgels for her successor, Dr. Marie Baum, when she found her chances of advancement blocked in her office, which she held from 1902 until 1907. Marie Baum (1874–1964)—affectionately called "Bäumchen" (Little Tree) in Marianne's letters—also became a lifelong friend during her long career as welfare official, officer in the Women's Federation, Reichstag deputy (1919–1921), and university teacher.[19]

The last progressive role Marianne Weber played in the Heidelberg of the prewar years was her involvement in a new kind of "academic sociability," in which women and men shared intellectual and artistic interests at private gatherings, outside the authority structure of the university and outside the status hierarchy of the old professoriate. Actually, the first step toward private intellectual exchange, in opposition to the formal dinner parties of the older generation, was not propitious. In 1904, the theologian Gustav Adolf Deissmann founded the Eranos circle for the study of religious history by inviting Max Weber and his friends Gothein, Jellinek, and Troeltsch. Weber soon took a commanding part in a setting congenial for testing his ideas about the Protestant ethic and the comparative study of the economic ethics of world religions. Today, such a group most likely would meet as a faculty seminar on campus; then it met in turn at the home of each participant. Marianne Weber and Marie Luise Gothein resented their exclusion. Marianne allowed herself a rare sarcasm in observing that "Max is taking care of 'Protestant asceticism,' I am in charge of 'ham in burgundy'" (356). Gothein complained: "Especially when the Eranos group met, I often felt painful regret that I was not a man, and this all the more so because at the time I too was very much occupied by issues in religious history."[20] At a different occasion, her husband had explained to her the exclusion of women: "It is shameful that one must say it, but the absence of women raises the intellectual level of the conversation. When women are present, most men become either glib and bored or, what is worse, charming and lively in a phony way, in short, insufferable. Is it the women's fault or the men's? I prefer to think the latter. The men could, after all, behave differently toward women."[21]

In time, such a change seems to have become possible in a conducive setting. The situation was not changed at first by the still-ailing Max Weber, but by the arrival of his brother Alfred, who joined the faculty in 1908. In the following year, he organized the Janus circle, in which men and women discussed philosophical and scientific issues (cf. 413 below). Marianne and Max attended, but after 1910 their own Sunday teas (called "jours") became the major attraction (see ch. 13). Although the now-recuperating Max was the dominant figure, Marianne could play the role of a hostess who was nationally known in her own right.

Marianne's national visibility was enhanced by the fact that the 1910 convention of the German Women's Federation took place in Heidelberg (Oct. 6-11). In its aftermath, a faculty member attacked Marianne and her collaborators as a bunch of "unmarried women, widows, Jewesses, sterile women" (430). This led to one of Weber's famous feuds that involved points of honor and complicated legal maneuvers. While Marianne reports on the matter at great length to demonstrate Weber's chivalry, the convention itself is mentioned in only a few uplifting sentences. She kept silent about the bitter infighting within the women's movement. In fact, the 1910 convention marked the ascendancy of the more conservative over the more progressive wing in the BDF under the new presidency of Dr. Gertrud Bäumer (1873–1954), whose close political ally Marianne was.

The factional struggles were paralleled, in Marianne's immediate social circle, by the explosive personal effects of the "new ethic" of sexual liberation. Marianne Weber responded by fusing her progressive role with a conservative stance in her public pronouncements, while mitigating her ethical rigorism in judging her friends.

The Conservative Battle Against Sexual Liberation

From the very beginning of her career in the women's movement, Marianne Weber fought not only patriarchy but also feminist ideas that appeared to threaten the institution of legitimate marriage, either directly by advocating "open" forms or indirectly by advocating women's full economic independence. As she recalls in her autobiography, "it was truly aggravating for conscientious leaders of their sex that the changes in women's social position also produced side-effects that made it necessary to do battle in their own ranks" (L 236). From the outset, she was in disagreement with Marie Stritt (1855-1928), second president of the BDF from 1899 to 1910 and editor of its official journal *Centralblatt*, in which they took issue with one another. As early as 1901, Stritt had translated Charlotte Perkins Stetson's *Women and Economics* as a programmatic statement of her own position. Without identifying any names, Marianne Weber attacked the Stetson-Stritt position in her 1905 essay "Vocation and Marriage," which Friedrich Naumann (1860-1919) published as a pamphlet in 1906, together with her essay "The Participation of Women in Science."[22]

Charlotte Perkins Stetson (1860-1935), better known today as C. P. Gilman, advocated the complete economic independence of women in the face of irresistible social and technological developments that separated women from the household. Predictably, this appeared to Marianne a kind of economic determinism and materialism. Arguing against her opponents in the name of "ethical values and general *Kulturwerte*," she declared that "it cannot be the goal of our movement to replace the mother at home by the working wife, especially one whose working time would be approximately as long as the husband's." She reasoned that the majority of women forced to join the labor force earn relatively little, and certainly not enough to pay for services that would relieve them of the double role of wage earner and homemaker. Fresh from her visit to the United States, where she had met Jane Addams and Florence Kelley, Marianne Weber related how much more women were esteemed there, even though the percentage of married women in the work force was much lower than in Germany. The explanation seemed to lie "not in the quantity but the quality of female professional work." Crucial, then, was not economic independence as such, but having a vocation "as an objectively valuable task."

Marianne Weber pursued a double strategy. Since most women could not be emancipated by entering the labor market, marriage law had to guarantee legal equality and economic rights vis-à-vis the husband. While rejecting the working wife as a general ideal, she insisted, however, that all young women prepare themselves for employment: "Our elevated view of marriage makes us treat training for employment as an unconditional moral duty."[23] Young women should not regard marriage as an institution that takes care of them and should not accept personal subordination in turn. Especially women from the propertied strata should be willing to develop their ethical personality through "methodical, premeditated conduct" (*methodische planvolle Lebensführung*). The argument, then, culminates in a Weberian promotion of inner-worldly asceticism. Marianne's appeal appeared very shortly after her husband's "The Protestant Ethic and the Spirit of Capitalism," a "best-selling" essay that made him once more familiar to a broad audience. But where Weber had concluded his historical study with only a few cryptic—if by now world-famous—remarks on the spiritual state of the present, Marianne presented a normative program.

This program made Marianne Weber attractive as a candidate to those groups that wanted to replace Marie Stritt. Gertrud Bäumer reported to Marianne in 1906 that "the Hamburgers, together with many other associations, would like to elect you president. Please don't keel over in the face of this request. . . . This would be an ideal solution in a matter that weighs very much on the associations. They don't want Stritt anymore. I have been asked to urge the proposal on you as a matter of salvaging the Federation."[24] As it turned out, it was Bäumer, not Weber, who became the next president, from 1910 to 1919, when the former handpicked the latter as her successor (1919-1923).

Before Bäumer established her reign, libertarian forces almost prevailed in the BDF. The challenge came from the League for the Protection of Motherhood and Sexual Reform (*Bund für Mutterschutz und Sexualreform*), which was founded in Leipzig in 1904. Since it proposed to alleviate the fate of unmarried mothers and illegitimate children, it was at first joined even by Friedrich Naumann, Werner Sombart, and Max Weber—and hence presumably also supported by Marianne. But the league was soon captured by Dr. Helene Stöcker (1869-1943), another follower of Charlotte Perkins Stetson. She came out of the Abolitionist movement, but developed her own idiosyncratic Nietzschean "transvaluation of all values." Prostitution, she had come to believe, could not be overcome by moral repression but only by moral libertarianism.[25] That was part of the "new ethic," which was also heavily influenced by the Swedish writer Ellen Key (1849-1926). The Webers quickly turned against the messengers of "free love." Marianne quotes one of Max's more brutal outbursts, utterly devoid of the chivalry she so often attributes to him: "This specific *Mutterschutz* gang is an utterly confused rabble. After the babble of [Helene Stöcker] I dropped out. For women to aim at crass hedonism and an ethics that would benefit only men . . . that is simply rubbish" (373).[26]

Marianne Weber first took up arms against the "new ethic" before a male audience, largely composed of Protestant ministers. Adolf Harnack, president of the Evangelical–Social Congress, invited her to deliver a speech on "Basic Questions of Sexual Ethics" at the Strasbourg meetings on Pentecost 1907. This was one of the first occasions when a woman could address a public assembly; previously men had to read papers written by women, who had to sit in a segregated corner and keep silent, if they did not want the police to dissolve the meeting.[27] In her biography Marianne merely mentioned, somewhat disingenuously, that "Max stood by her" (373), but in her autobiography she admitted to a conflict: "The invitation to speak before a circle familiar to me through Max Weber's membership made me proud and anxious. The difficult speech was written in the beautiful springtime setting of Lake Como. Max Weber insisted on conceptual clarity and rejected any kind of pathos. I rebelled against his corrections, but finally submitted to his superiority. I travelled alone to Strasbourg. . . . I felt protected by Adolf von Harnack's chivalry. He exuded benevolence and indicated agreement. For me it was an important and encouraging event" (L 239). One can easily imagine that Max Weber was worried what Harnack would think of him if he had not properly coached Marianne to articulate just the right kind of progressive and conservative mixture.

Marianne Weber echoed her husband's general clamor against naturalism and materialism, reiterating that "our humanity" (Menschentum) depended on ethical integrity. She conceded to modern relativism that the violation of sexual morality through grand passion no longer ethically disqualified a person, but only if he or she retained a sense of guilt. By contrast, notions of healthy sex promoted by medical doctors imbued with a naturalist ideology were indications of spiritual decay (seelische Unkultur). Marianne interpreted the present "period of strong sexual tension" and "sexual libertinism" as part and parcel of the "social question," caused not only by the urban masses' distress but also by the spread of late marriage in the educated strata. She objected most strongly to what we call today serial monogamy. At the same time, she demanded not only the possibility of divorce by mutual consent but also an end to the criminal prosecution of "wild marriages," the German phrasing for unmarried couples. She even favored sex education for the young, of course, in ethical no less than physiological respects. Finally, she insisted that women defend not only their moral self-respect but also force the males to improve themselves by forsaking the double standard.

In 1908, the polarization in the women's movement was discussed at great length by one of Marianne's friends, Alice Salomon (1872-1948), in the *Archiv für Sozialwissenschaft*.[28] Under the patronage of Gustav Schmoller and Max Sering, Alice Salomon had received a doctorate from the university of Berlin in 1906, when this was not yet generally possible for women, and for a dissertation that may well have been the first German study of "The Causes of Unequal Wages for Male and Female Work." Also in 1908, Salomon founded the *Soziale Frauenschule* in Berlin, a private welfare academy for women, which was to make her internationally famous and help her become secretary of the International Council of Women in 1909.

Like Gertrud Bäumer, Marie Baum, Agnes Harnack and Marianne Weber, Salomon considered herself "liberal with regard to individual rights, progressive with regard to social justice, and conservative in ethical matters."[29] Salomon, a member of the BDF's national board since 1902, contrasted the two wings of the women's movement in terms of a generational difference. While women of different ages and different persuasions often managed to work together on the practical level, two broad ideological clusters could be distinguished. One postulated the natural equality of the sexes, the other probed their natural difference; the old program of the women's movement concerned unmarried women, the new one focused on the family; the older idealism tended to weaken the family, the new moralism tried to strengthen it. Salomon asserted that the very influx of women into the universities, especially the new social sciences, undermined the old Enlightenment radicalism and replaced it with a reformism that was instructed by the findings of empirical social research. In her survey, Gertrud Bäumer and Marianne Weber stood united against Charlotte Perkins Stetson and Heinrich Braun's wife Lily Braun, whose massive 1901 study, *The Women's Question, Its Historical Development and Economic Aspect*, had provided spur and foil to Marianne's own big study. An exponent of the "new ethic" of sexual liberation in word and deed, Lily Braun was an ally of Stöcker and Stritt, whom Salomon also criticized extensively.[30]

Within the BDF these political conflicts came to a head when the abortion issue was discussed at the 1908 general assembly. Under the leadership of Camilla Jellinek and Marie Stritt, a commission came out in favor of abolishing Section 218 of the German Criminal Code, which then outlawed abortion outright and which in spite of its attenuation is still bitterly divisive today. But on the executive committee, Marie Baum prevailed over Stritt, the president, and had the committee's recommendation rejected in favor of a rather limited modification of Section 218. Whereas Stöcker's *Mutterschutz* League had been denied admission to the BDF, which accepted only corporate, not individual membership, the conservative German Evangelical Women's League had been permitted to join against Stritt's opposition and helped reverse several years of progressive advance. Although the vote on the abortion issue was close, the setback was permanent and Stritt's downfall became inevitable. Thus, Gertrud Bäumer came to replace her at the Heidelberg convention in 1910.[31]

Beneath this political level, the new ethic created great turmoil in the Weber circle. In a delicate balance of frankness and discretion, Marianne Weber describes the invasion of Heidelberg. To restore a passage somewhat truncated below: "Young people placed a different life–style, one that was beyond convention, alongside the firmly established structures of the older generation. Freedom from convention began to emerge in a manner previously limited to artistic circles in Munich. New types of persons, akin to the Romantics in their intellectual impulses, once again called into question bourgeois modes of thinking and living. In the name of personal freedom they fought for old as well as new ideals of conduct." The "old" ideal apparently refers to the individualist romanticism of the circle around Caroline Schlegel–Schelling (1763–1809), whom Helene Stöcker extolled in her writings.[32]

As Marianne tells the reader, her Strasbourg speech already reflected the profound impact made on friends by the Freudian psychiatrist Otto Gross (1877–1920), who was soon to be repudiated by his master for his sexual and political anarchism. She reprinted most of a blistering letter (dated Sept. 13, 1907), in which Weber rejected an essay by Gross for publication in the *Archiv*: "His entire essay fairly bursts with value judgments. . . . in a scholarly journal there is no place for an essay that wants to be a sermon" (380). Yet, as we have seen, Weber was soon to accept, if he had not in fact commissioned it, Alice Salomon's value–laden and partisan defense of the ethical position taken by Marianne and her allies in the women's movement. Marianne did not identify the actual recipient of the letter: Else von Richthofen.[33] Else, whose career plans had developed under "the dominating influence of Marianne Weber" (as she wrote in an unpublished autobiographical statement), had resigned her position as factory inspector after a short time, since she did not feel up to the task—to the great disappointment of Alice Salomon.[34] In 1902, she married Edgar Jaffé (1866–1921) in a loveless match, following the not infrequent pattern of gentile aristocracy marrying Jewish money. Jaffé not only built a beautiful villa for her at a choice spot in Heidelberg, but also bought the *Archiv für Sozialwissenschaft* for Max, "the happy idea of creating a new form of activity for Weber," as Marianne put it (277).

When Weber rejected Gross's essay in 1907, he knew the psychiatrist was not only the father of Else's new son Peter, but had subsequently even converted Jaffé to his message of sexual liberation. This did not, however, prevent Weber from becoming Peter's godfather. In spite of the principled position he shared with Marianne, his very commitment to "responsibility in all human relationships" (388) made it possible for him to come to the aid of women friends who had opted for the new ethic. But he also seems to have felt a certain fascination.

In 1910, Otto Gross returned to the rural mecca of the new counter-culture, the Swiss village Ascona, which competed for popularity with the old headquarters of the German bohemia, the Munich suburb of Schwab-ing.[35] Three years later, the peripatetic Gross abandoned Ascona and left his wife Frieda with the anarchist Ernst Frick. As the niece of the philosopher Alois Riehl, Frieda Schloffer was an old friend of the Webers and of Else from their Freiburg years. When, in the same year, Otto's father, the influen-tial criminologist Hanns Gross, had his son arrested and started legal action to take Frieda's children away, Max Weber went into action. In the spring of 1913 and 1914, he spent several weeks in Ascona and expended much effort on helping Frieda, the "Dora" of Marianne's account (488–494). Thus, in-stead of finishing *Economy and Society*, long past several deadlines, he found himself dictating legal briefs to the legendary Franziska zu Reventlow (1871–1918), while assuring Marianne that "the countess is utterly uninteresting to me. Regards to Mother, my darling child; wonder what she would say!" (491). For the sake of his distressed women friends he even missed his mother's seventieth birthday in April 1914.

Otto Gross converted not only Else to his message, but also, somewhat later, her sister Frieda, who had married the English scholar Ernest Weekley after meeting him in Freiburg in 1896. After her experience with Gross, Frieda in turn converted D. H. Lawrence, for whose sake she abandoned her husband and three children in 1912. The lovers were given refuge by the Jaffés, who to Marianne's and Max's great regret had moved to Munich in the preceding year. Marianne did not reveal, of course, that before leaving Heidelberg, Else had yielded to Alfred Weber's entreaties and become his lover. It was not until 1984 that D. H. Lawrence's barely disguised auto-biographical novel *Mr. Noon* (Part II) appeared, which celebrated the attrac-tiveness of the two sisters while satirizing Edgar Jaffé and Alfred Weber as ridiculous German professors.[36]

In the chapter of the biography called "Travel Pictures," Marianne also does not mention explicitly a joint trip with the Jaffés to Italy in the spring of 1910, from which she had to return early, perhaps because of the impending

Heidelberg women's congress. It was in Venice that Max supposedly declared himself to Else. Whatever the significance of this obscure episode, Alfred clearly resented his brother's "meddling," and Max's eagerness to provide legal and other advice to Else finally backfired and led to a break between him and her that seems to have lasted until 1917.

In the deliberate jumble of fragments from the correspondence out of which Marianne pieces together the mosaic of her biography, she admits that Max felt attracted by "that world full of enchantresses, charm, trickery, and hunger for happiness" (491), although he seemed to draw a firm line: "I could under certain circumstances be quite fond of specifically 'erotic' women," he reported having told Frieda Gross, "but I would never form any inner attachment to one or count on her friendship. For it had turned out that I was not a suitable friend for such women, for in truth only an erotic man was of value to them" (492). Marianne approved of Max's general "human" interest in women and quoted a seemingly harmless, if somewhat condescending remark: "How boring life would be without you little women (*Frauchen*); something always happens to you" (369). She did not relate a somewhat less trivial and franker remark from a letter to Frieda: "How much beautiful women complicate life's problems! And yet, what would life be without them!"[37] But Marianne came to understand the power of "enchantments" (*Verzauberungen*), as she liked to call them, and revealed with relative openness the importance to Max of the Swiss pianist Mina Tobler (1880-1967), whom he contrasted with the Ascona enchantresses as "this child who is different but seems so 'noble' in her reserved and delicately rapturous way" (491). For her sake Weber wrote the unfinished study on "The Rational and Social Foundations of Music" and planned a sociology of arts.

If, in the political realm, the "new ethic" was held at bay by the conservative majority of the women's movement, not to mention the vilification and persecution from the male establishment, the new currents were very much a reality in the Weber circle. Although the Weber receptions were sometimes called "tea with morality," to others it appeared that Marianne Weber was keeping a strange menagerie. Many years later, Marianne was able to concede in her autobiography that "at the time my generation's principled rigorism was still in my blood, although attenuated by empathy with individual fates. It was so much simpler . . . to stick to the universal validity of high ideals than to risk complicated dialectical discussions about the possible autonomous value (*Eigenwert*) of 'free love'. . . . Later I was not spared the experience of having to come to terms, in a more differentiated fashion, with the hot issues of eroticism. I felt forced to suspend judgment not only in individual cases but also to listen more closely to the defenders of a new, freer sexual ethic" (L 239 f.).

World War I: Women and Nationalism

The outbreak of the World War I put an end to "the good life" (the title of ch. 13). Suddenly, the human entanglements among the friends as well as the lonely scholarly work of which Weber was intermittently capable paled into insignificance. Never again would nationalism be so intensely felt in Europe. Ultimately, the Webers compromised themselves less than hundreds of other professors and their wives, but their stand is hard to accept today. For that matter, nothing separates the majority of the old German women's movement so much from today's feminism as the nationalism affirmed in 1914, when the labor movement too was submerged in the all-embracing national community. Very few men and women could resist the charismatic excitation: "The hour had come, and it was of undreamed-of sublimity" (518). A Weber intimate, the young Georg von Lukacs, who was to make his political mistakes at a later time, remembered after half a century: "My own deeply personal attitude was one of vehement, global, and especially at the beginning, scarcely articulate rejection of the war, and particularly of enthusiasm for the war. I recall a conversation with Frau Marianne Weber in the late autumn of 1914. She wanted to challenge my attitude by telling me of individual, concrete acts of heroism. My only reply was: 'The better, the worse.'"[38]

At first, the emotional exaltation could help people get over the beginning of the slaughter. The Webers quickly lost Max's brother Karl, brother-in-law Herman Schäfer, and their close friend Emil Lask, who went to his death "inwardly without illusions" but only out of ethical conviction (530).[39] But the political excitement could also easily damage or ruin old personal relationships, sometimes irrespective of the political spectrum. Marianne Weber does not mention Weber's quarrel with his left-wing friend Robert Michels, who made critical remarks about Germany from abroad and finally agreed to resign as co-editor of the *Archiv*. With a disapproving undertone toward both, she recounts how Weber and Troeltsch (unnamed in the text), though living in the same house, did not talk with one another for several years in the wake of a disagreement over visiting policy for wounded French prisoners (524). The severity of this break may indicate that long-standing tensions erupted at this occasion. When the National Liberal Eberhard Gothein came out for the annexation of the French iron-ore region of Briey-Longwy,

Marianne recalls in her autobiography, Max also broke with him, until Gothein reformed himself into a democrat at the war's end (L 89).

Within the women's movement the nationalist fervor exacerbated differences of opinion, even in the BDF. Bäumer's relations with her deputy Alice Salomon deteriorated from the very beginning. In August 1914, Salomon found herself marooned in Ireland at the home of Lady Aberdeen (1857-1939), president of the International Council of Women and wife of the viceroy. There she converted to Christianity under the shock of events; she had been born into a secularized Jewish family. Meanwhile, Bäumer began to suspect that Salomon did not try hard enough to return as quickly as possible.[40] Although Salomon joined her political friends in the newly established "National Women's Service," which combined welfare relief for hundreds of thousands of women with mobilizing them for the war economy, her difficulties were only beginning.

Marianne Weber is silent about her husband's war-time contribution to the leading women's journal *Die Frau*, which was edited by Bäumer together with her mentor and life companion Helene Lange (1848-1930). Coming to Bäumer's aid in a dispute with the Swiss pacifist Gesine Nordbeck in February 1916, Weber struck a tough macho stance and affirmed "our responsibility before history" as a great power. In his letter to the editor, he adumbrated his incipient distinction between the ethic of responsibility and the ethic of conviction and fended off the pacifist viewpoint with the argument that "there is only Tolstoy's consistency, nothing else." Whoever does not absolutely follow the Sermon on the Mount "should be reminded that he is tied to the rules of this world, and that includes for an unforeseeably long time the possibility and the inevitability of war."[41]

From the beginning of his career in Freiburg, Weber had publicly condemned the Ethical Culture Society, then a new undertaking, and the various efforts at organizing an international peace movement. His intransigence was aggravated by the considerable overlap of personnel between these groups and the promoters of the "new ethic," such as Helene Stöcker.[42] Also, from the 1890's, Weber had been the intellectually superior adviser to Pastor Friedrich Naumann, whose National Social journal *Die Hilfe* advocated economic expansionism, "world politics," and social reform. Now Bäumer echoed his line in her double role as staff member of both Naumann's and Helene Lange's journals.[43]

In 1915, Bäumer forbade official BDF participation in a pacifist women's congress that met in The Hague in April under the aegis of Jane Addams. Stöcker went, as did the suffragists Dr. Anita Augspurg (1857-1943) and her companion Lida Gustava Heymann (1868-1943), Bäumer's strongest opponents on the left wing of the bourgeois women's movement.[44] "I am certain," Alice Salomon remarked later, self-critically, "that the women who sub-jected themselves to the BDF's order, as I did, acted wrongly."[45] Salomon was, however, able to arrange an audience for Addams with Chancellor Beth-mann-Hollweg. Although the Webers had visited Jane Addams in Chicago, they obviously did not want to have anything to do with her at this moment. It is unclear to what extent Weber had such pacifist initiatives in mind when he wrote ungallantly in his letter to Bäumer: "The pacifism of American 'ladies' (of both sexes) is truly the most deadly cant that was ever professed, in all subjective sincerity, on the intellectual level of tea talk, propounded as it is with the pharisaical attitude of the parasite, who pockets the high war profits, toward the [German] barbarians in the trenches."[46]

In her war chapters, Marianne Weber chose to dramatize her husband's increasingly vociferous Cassandra role, which gave him a national audience by 1917, the high point of his political influence, before the rush of revolu-tionary and counter-revolutionary events pushed him to the sidelines again. In time, she herself sobered up. A limited transformation can be seen in the change of tone from her essay "War as an Ethical Problem," which appeared in *Die Frau* in September 1916, to the 1918 essay on "The Special Cultural Tasks of Women." In the former, Marianne hews very closely to Weber's argument in "Between Two Laws," if he himself did not "edit" the text again. Harking back to the subject of her earliest book, Johann Gottlieb Fichte, and emphasizing his notion of the nation's ethical "autonomy," she glorified war as the supreme opportunity for a modern ethical heroism that transcends the ethos of the ancient Germanic warriors. The new military technology required a new type of ascetic heroism. Marianne concluded that "one can feel the duty and the ardent desire to do everything in one's power so that such global catastrophes can be prevented in the future, and can yet feel even as a woman that mankind would be emptied without the opportunity for, and challenges inherent in, such tests of ethical greatness."[47]

After two years of war, Marianne Weber was, however, already very wor-ried about the loss of sexual self-discipline among many soldiers and also women at home, with the army promoting prostitution while trying to contain the epidemic spread of venereal disease. Toward the end of the war, Marianne could no longer play the role of the female cheerleader: "All our experience has thoroughly destroyed the illusion that such catastrophes, which tear apart the customary fabric of everyday life, can permanently exalt the essence of humanity and bring clear moral gains." Following Weber's distinction between the charismatic qualifications of the few and the or-dinariness of the masses, she came to recognize that the average person is likely to be morally diminished by the deprivations of war. Although she declared herself surprised by the "massive decay of morals (*innere Kultur*) at home," she was even more concerned about the war's brutalizing impact on countless male *Volksgenossen*, who might be hard to integrate into civilian life. Here she glimpsed, if indistinctly, the origins of the "trench swine" (*Frontschweine*), who in the Weimar years were to carry violence into the streets and beerhalls until it engulfed all of political life. In view of these dangers, Marianne assigned to the "cultured" woman the special task of "rebuilding morality and shaping the immediacy of existence through love and beauty, balance and harmony, dignity and gentility."[48]

Apart from genuine nationalist fervor, the BDF's active support of the war effort had been calculated to gain the suffrage for women at the hour of victory, just as the Social Democrats had hoped that the returning workers would be rewarded by the abolition of the three-class suffrage in Prussia. Imperial Germany's collapse suddenly threw the suffrage into women's laps and confronted them with many practical political tasks. When Stefan George, ever the misogynist and esthete, heard that Marianne Weber had triumphantly welcomed the right of women to run for office, he supposedly had Friedrich Gundolf convey to her his sentiment: "God be thanked. Now men can turn to better things."[49] In fact, vast numbers of women voted and many stood for office. Most prominent BDF leaders joined forces with the Weber brothers, Friedrich Naumann, Theodor Heuss (1884–1963), Gustav Radbruch (1878–1949) and other men to organize a new party, the German Democratic Party (DDP), as the left wing of liberalism. Bäumer and Baum went to the Weimar Constituent Assembly and on to the Reichstag, the former until 1932, the latter until 1921. Marianne and Max Weber threw themselves into the rough and tumble of electoral politics, but only Marianne managed to get herself elected as a member of the constituent assembly in the state of Baden, where she was her party's single female deputy, in contrast to several women from the Social Democrats and Catholic Center Party.

Curiously, in her biographical account, Marianne Weber mentions neither her political activities nor her election to the BDF presidency in 1919. We only find a sudden reference to "getting rid of her office in the women's movement" (696). After all, it would have been appropriate for her to call attention to it, since it was the culmination of a career that Max had supported from early on. Instead, she focused on his futile efforts to oppose the extreme Right and Left and to find a viable position on the Versailles treaty negotiations. Weber accompanied the German delegation to Versailles as an adviser, but he too ran out of advice on how to come to terms with a treaty that more than any other factor doomed the Weimar Republic from the very beginning. Struggling hard against complete discouragement, he withdrew to his last scholarly labors. Marianne wants the reader to share her own deep disappointment that the country failed to call her husband to a charismatic role in its hour of greatest need, albeit she is not completely blind to Max's self-defeating propensities.

In the aftermath of Imperial Germany's self-destruction, nationalism and anti-Semitism began to race out of control. While the Webers' own patriotic feelings reached a high point, they vigorously opposed anti-Semitism, but in a manner that was not completely free of awkwardness. Max Weber pushed through the appointment of Franz Eulenburg (1867-1943), who later became a Nazi victim, at the University of Munich, although "the academic mood has become extremely reactionary and radically anti-Semitic," as he reported to Georg von Lukacs' father. At the same time, he seems to have counselled against electing or appointing Jews to highly visible positions, since anti-Semitism had intensified so much in the wake of their prominence among revolutionary leaders (cf. 648).[50]

Paradoxically, one practical reason for Marianne Weber's elevation to the BDF's presidency seems to have been the anti-Semitism of the federation's right-wing corporate members, such as the German Evangelical Women's League. In her autobiography published in 1933 Gertrud Bäumer provides a highfalutin rationale that glossed over the underlying realities. The very granting of women's suffrage had blurred the purposes of the women's movement and therefore "Marianne Weber's election as president of the BDF expressed the feeling that . . . the personal embodiment of the female mode of action should be emphasized prominently. Now that the external barriers had fallen, we wanted to demonstrate concretely the spirit with which we intended to transfuse the newly opened realm through the spiritual (*geistig-seelische*) transformation of man."[51] In turn, Marianne only recalled her anxiety about the challenge and said nothing about the political context in the very brief mention of her election in her own autobiography: "Again I faced a task that appeared to me too difficult in that phase of my life. But the leader (*Führerin*) and friend Gertrud Bäumer commanded me. Once again it turned out that a person can do more than she thinks possible, if she wills what she ought to do" (L 112).

Whatever other factors went into Marianne Weber's election, we now know that as early as Jan. 30, 1914, Bäumer wrote in a confidential letter to the BDF's Jewish executive secretary Alice Bensheimer that, because of the Protestant conservatives, she had come to settle on Marianne Weber as her successor instead of Alice Salomon, with whom she would have preferred to work.[52] This must have been before the personal difficulties between the two women. In old age, Alice Salomon remembered the story somewhat differently: "Up until the end of the war I had never encountered anti-Semitic statements. ... Gertrud Bäumer told me early in the war that I should become her successor. She told me that I had the duty to take over the office, since I held a prominent position longer than any other woman. ... But the election was postponed until after the war. Now, however, I was told that members hesitated to elect somebody president who had a Jewish name or Jewish ancestors, since popular attitudes had become so unreliable."[53]

Salomon's international connections continued to give her troubles. Upon her return from a first postwar meeting with Lady Aberdeen in Switzerland, Marie Baum criticized her friend: "You know, Alice, that I don't approve of Germans cheapening themselves that way."[54] Salomon earned outrage from other women she considered good friends when she dared to welcome Jane Addams in English upon her first postwar visit in Berlin. Ironically, Jane Addams, sent by Hoover on a mercy mission, had by that time fallen from her American pedestal as a saint of charity and had been declared the country's most dangerous woman by a U. S. government agency.

In the meantime, Marianne Weber, paralleling her husband's line, had criticized the "Pan-German" and anti-Semitic excesses of right-wing women's groups and had herself been sharply attacked by them. Under the impact of these attacks, but also because of her own wounded patriotic feelings, she came to disagree with Alice Salomon on the advisability of attending the first postwar congress of the International Council of Women in Norway. Defensively, she argued against participating, "since, without being able to promote the German cause, we would give the German-National and conservative agitation, which is based on our alleged internationalism and pacifism, the best ammunition."[55] In the ensuing struggle, recalls Alice Salomon, the BDF—Marianne?—"sent a liberal woman [Marie Baum] instead of a power politician [Gertrud Bäumer] to me to demand that I not go to Norway."[56] Salomon went ahead anyway and on June 30, 1920, tendered her resignation to Marianne Weber as the BDF's deputy chairperson and as member of the executive board (*Engere Vorstand*). By that time, however, Marianne Weber had collapsed in grief over Max's death on June 14.

Weimar: Guarding Max Weber's Legacy and Coming Into Her Own

According to Marie Baum, Marianne Weber suffered a serious breakdown in reaction to Max's death.[57] For many years, Marianne had coped with her husband's isolating illness in part by taking an active role in the women's movement. Now she withdrew from public life for several years and continued to act merely as BDF figurehead, while Bäumer remained dominant and Emma Ender did much of the executive work before formally taking over as president from 1923 to 1931. Pointedly, Bäumer calls Ender the "energetic and organizationally gifted successor to Marianne Weber."[58]

Although some of Marianne's friends were clearly disappointed about her withdrawal, her own way of coming to terms with her life's ultimate disaster was to concentrate completely on editing Weber's fugitive literary remains and on writing the biography. One of her feminist friends tried to call her back from her relentless widowhood: "Return to yourself. Every human being is supposed to be whole. You have propagated the autonomy of your sex, you have demanded of women to rest in themselves. Now show that you can do it" (L 114). Marianne conceded that this was wisely spoken, but insisted on bringing Weber back to life for herself and posterity: "After I had saved the works of the departed, I was allowed to begin my own work, my husband's *Lebensbild*. I was passionately devoted to depicting his human greatness and richness. The first seeds of the task grew in me when I immersed myself in his letters immediately after his death. The intellectual creation was his, but now I had to give birth to him out of my own powers. Can a person of modest gifts portray a great human being? Well, that happens often. . . . Insofar as possible, not I but he should speak out of my pages through the most characteristic passages of his letters. I also wanted the shadows of the dead who belonged to him, especially of his mother Helene Weber, to come to new life" (L 125).

Worshipful communion with the dead—"Max Weber's desk is my altar, a place consecrated by him" (L 115)—was not Marianne's only motive in her dedicated labors. Because she was convinced of his greatness, she had smarted for many years under what she considered slights to Weber from the Heidelberg faculty and other universities in the wake of his illness. Her bitterness was not assuaged until, with a mixture of pride and regret, she accepted the honorary law doctorate from Heidelberg in 1924 in recognition of her own legal study and her editorial work. Marianne's portrayal of Max as a figure of "unimpaired genius" (L 124) despite serious illness was meant to impress not only doubtful academic colleagues, but even more a reading public that adulated gurus such as Oswald Spengler (1880–1936), Count Keyserling (1880–1946) and his Darmstadt "School of Wisdom," and especially Stefan George.

The George cult was the toughest competition for Weber's reputation as "the myth of Heidelberg." Before the war three circles had flourished in Heidelberg, the Wagnerians, the Weberians and the Georgians.[59] While there was no overlap between the Weberians and the group around the Wagnerian art historian Henry Thode and his wife Daniela—a natural daughter of Richard Wagner and Cosima von Bülow—what Simmel called the "crossing of social circles" (die Kreuzung sozialer Kreise) led to close, if often rather tense relations with the Georgians. In spite of George's increasing misogyny, which began with the requirement that women publish only under male pseudonyms and ended with their banishment from the cult, Else Jaffé and Marie Luise Gothein played key roles in the Heidelberg circle around Friedrich Gundolf (1880-1931),[60] just as did Gertrud Simmel and Gertrud Kantorowicz (1876-1945), Georg Simmel's secret lover, in Berlin. In the two intersecting circles, George embodied art, Weber scholarship. Whereas the two "giants" treated one another with great circumspection at their two well-staged personal meetings (in 1910 and 1912), followers either took ardent sides or felt pulled hither and thither. Just after Weber's death Erich von Kahler (1885-1970) launched a frontal attack from the Georgian camp on Weber's "Science as a Vocation." Soon Arthur Salz (1881-1963) countered with a pamphlet "For Science. Against the Educated Who Disdain It."[61] Edgar Salin (1892-1974), a major Georgian figure in Heidelberg, who combined economic history with esthetic interests, conceded in his memoirs that "apart from George, nobody among the Germans surpassed Max Weber in the powerful impression he made on people," but added that "compared to his brother, Weber was profoundly insensitive to the arts (amusisch). His spirit was awake enough to feel the greatness of music, architecture, and poetry, but he had no direct access to art. Instead, he created his 'sociology' in order to approach through conceptual means phenomena that he could not reach by way of experience (Erlebnis)."[62] It was against this diminution on the part of apolitical literati, whom Weber could so cordially detest, that Marianne went out of her way to describe Weber's involvement with the arts and artists.

Given the dramatic climax of the biography—the defeated country losing one of its greatest political minds, the university losing a scholar who was just at the point of bringing long labors to fruition—Marianne could not be expected to undermine her construction by confessing a private crisis. Quite apart from any other reasons for her reticence, she would have spoiled her hero's appeal to the anticipated audience by revealing that her ethically sanctified marriage was in trouble at the end, an all-too-human occurrence. The fact is that in his fifties Weber was overwhelmed by his old affection for Else Jaffé, his and Marianne's closest friend. For Else's sake he turned down several enticing academic opportunities and took Lujo Brentano's prestigious chair in Munich: "The wonderful, familiar city and the friends living nearby beckoned" (646), a clear reference, if in plural disguise, to Else's residence outside the city. Weber fell in love as never before, with a woman in her forties whom he had known for twenty years. Thus, he finally experienced a passionate relationship with one of the "erotic women" and "enchantresses" against whom he had warned himself, but one who was reassuring through long familiarity and could be trusted to do right by his wife and his brother in spite of it. In a passage in "Politics as a Vocation," on which he worked in 1919, Weber inserted an ill-fitting generalization that may have disguised a very personal confession: "Rarely will you find that a man whose love turns from one woman to another feels no need to legitimate this before himself by saying: she was not worthy of my love, or she has disappointed me, or whatever other like 'reasons' exist. This is an attitude that, with a profound lack of chivalry, adds a fancied 'legitimacy' to the plain fact that he no longer loves her and that the woman has to bear it."[63] While Weber did not blame Marianne, he admitted neither the strength of his feelings for Else to her nor the fact of their sexual consummation.

There is a parallel here to Georg Simmel, who hid before his wife and the world the fact that he had a daughter with Gertrud Kantorowicz. Here, too, reality and appearance differed. Gertrud Simmel and Gertrud Kantorowicz continued to grace by their presence the weekly "jours" in Simmel's salon, "the purpose of which was to cultivate that which is most singular. Conversation took a form that forbade all participants to refer to their own person, their problems and anxieties. Freed from all human burdens, discourse was elevated to an atmosphere of intellectuality, charm, and tact . . . Only select, highly intellectual persons were admitted. At the 'jours' there was, of course, always Gertrud Kantorowicz, a name intimately tied to Simmel's life and my own." Thus Margarete Susman (1872–1966) introduced her description of Simmel's salon. But when Gertrud Kantorowicz told her secret to Margarete immediately after Simmel's death, the latter recoiled: "I should have embraced her lovingly and rejoiced about the love child. But the lie she had lived so long with me proved too painful."[64] In contrast to Marianne, Gertrud Simmel had always maintained a greater critical distance from her husband, sharing Marianne's critique of "Female Culture" and exclaiming to her: "I am very impatient with all men say about us, and that includes Georg" (L 383). And again unlike Marianne, Gertrud Simmel later turned with unrestrained fury on Simmel in a *roman à clef* unpublished to this day.

In the last months of Weber's life, Marianne had to cope with plenty of

family troubles in addition to her political and organizational responsibilities. In the fall of 1919, Helene Weber, whom she considered her true
mother, died. At Easter 1920, the widowed Lily Schäfer, Max's favorite sister,
committed suicide, feeling betrayed by one of the charismatic males prominent in the educational reform movement. Lily left behind four young
children, and Marianne suddenly found herself on the road to adoptive
motherhood. Weber welcomed the idea of this role for her much more than
any paternal role for himself. Quite realistically, Else seems to have reinforced his own doubts about dealing with children. While away on a speaking tour for the BDF, Marianne wrote a letter (on April 30, 1920) in which
she revealed her comprehension of the marital dangers facing her. She worried about her qualifications for motherhood and conceded that she did not
have "the productivity of the moment that Else possesses in such incomparable manner," a phrase ostensibly referring to children but possibly also to
Else's greater power vis-à-vis Weber. For, she continued, objecting to
Weber's proposal that she should spend several months of every year apart
with the children: "Only you can separate me from you—and only if I feel
that the power has left me to assure your happiness."[65] A few days later, Else
shared with Marianne the wait at Max's deathbed, as thirty-four years later
she would hold the dying Marianne's hands.

Just before the end, Weber seems to have dedicated *Economy and Society*
to his mother and the first volume of *Collected Essays in the Sociology of
Religion* to Marianne. She in turn dedicated "Hinduism and Buddhism" to
Mina Tobler and "Ancient Judaism" to Else. Thus, for all the world to see,
Weber's major works were linked to the four women most significant in his
life.

After several years of unflagging concentration on the editions and the
biography, Marianne freed herself from her preoccupation and returned to a
public role. Having moved back to Heidelberg in 1921 and a year later into
the ancestral Fallenstein mansion, she reestablished her salon in the mid-
1920's. Her circle differed, however, significantly from the prewar years.
With thousands of women studying at the universities, the salon no longer
had a "progressive" function. Now women constituted two thirds of the
thirty to forty participants at each meeting. The challenge, as Marianne saw
it, lay in maintaining a precarious gender balance to retain enough males to
avoid the drift toward a mere women's club.

Else Jaffé and Marie Baum were faithful regulars, but Marianne deliberately excluded "the women in the women's movement who were close to me,
for such a female inundation could have swept away the male element. . . .
How satisfying it was that the men were not the exclusive carriers of the

xliv   Transaction Introduction

intellectual substance. Thanks to our intellectual emancipation, Heidelberg was enriched by a new type of woman who combined intellectual activity with the special female mission" (L 206). Letting Alfred Weber take his brother's place as the first discussant, Marianne managed to attract some of the best-known scholars from Heidelberg and elsewhere to talk about a wide range of ancient, medieval, and modern topics. The number of women speakers remained, however, very small: Marianne herself; Marie Luise Gothein, whose two-volume *History of Garden Art* was reprinted in English as late as 1979;[66] Marie Baum, since 1928 a lecturer on welfare policy at the University of Heidelberg; Luise Klebs, holder of an honorary doctorate for her work on hieroglyphics; and two or three others. (Lists were kept only from 1930 on, and then only incompletely.) Camilla Jellinek, holder of an honorary doctorate in law since 1930, also took part, but did not speak formally. With the exception of the unmarried Marie Baum, the four well-known women were widows. At her Sunday teas, which took place every three or four weeks, Marianne participated "passionately and not always fairly, as her own memoirs show, but she always tried to be just," reminisced Baum, who continued: "At her sixtieth birthday party, we spoofed the little authoritarian (*herrscherliche*) proclivities that we knew well and liked about her."[67] Else play-acted Marianne as mother superior in a nunnery who to her horror is proposed for the papacy by her faithful daughters.

When the biography appeared in 1926, Otto Gradenwitz (1860-1935), a Heidelberg law professor, declared it historically valuable because it helped modern people better understand the justification for the legal institution of suttee! But no less a historian than Friedrich Meinecke (1862-1954) defended Marianne against the charge of indiscretion and read her family drama in the light of Greek tragedy.[68] Gertrud Bäumer lamented again the loss of a potential national leader and answered the often-asked question "Why did the people not call him as their political leader?" by suggesting that such an election was possible only in a rare "great moment when pettiness and hesitation fall away and fate fires up the will to pursue the essential. It was hardly possible under the conditions of everyday life."[69]

From the Left, Käthe Leichter, the leading woman of her generation in the Austrian Social Democratic Party, wrote much more skeptically. As the founder of a revolutionary, pacifist student group in Heidelberg during the war, she had seen Weber reject her group's appeal for political support and found him unwilling to help even when she was ordered out of the country, although he later came to the rescue of Ernst Toller (1893-1939), the group's go-between. Leichter recalled that Weber had never conceded that, for socialists, the ethic of responsibility and the ethic of conviction must coincide. She judged that, "despite his great gift for leadership, it was not given him to affect the course of events in such a way that his death made a difference in the shape of German history. Alas, the earth has not changed. What probably has changed is the world of scholarship, the German university. Through Weber's death it lost perhaps the last great bourgeois fighter for the integrity and objectivity of scholarship and teaching."[70]

The most renowned woman among novelists and historians at the time, Ricarda Huch (1864-1947) had still another reaction from the corner of romantic idealism. In 1919, she had listened to Weber's "Politics as a Vocation," and the young Max Rehm, carried away by his appeal, had presumed that she, "knowledgeable about the psyche and steeped in history, understood the significance of the historical moment of which we other witnesses had only an inkling."[71] After reading the biography, however, Huch wrote to Marie Baum: "It would be better to talk rather than to write about it, but I could not help feeling again that Max Weber was an actor. I had that feeling quite spontaneously the only time I ever heard him give a speech, and I expected something quite different. The wellspring of his instincts did not flow, I think, and he substituted for them his rational awareness, something against which I react. . . . I always notice immediately if something comes from conscious awareness when it should be rooted in the depth of the unconscious."[72]

There had indeed been a histrionic element in Weber's two famous speeches: he had taken a deliberate stance of toughmindedness in the face of youthful idealism and exaltation, appealing to cool heads and not to fast heartbeats. But Huch's challenge was more basic. As a romanticist historian with anarchist leanings, she wanted her heroes to be in touch with their feelings and not be tortured rationalists. On this score, however, Baum remained closer to Marianne's perception than to that of her old intimate, Ricarda.

Finally, seventy-six-year-old Helene Lange recognized that the biography was as much about women as about Weber. In a letter to her protégée Emmy Beckmann, her successor as president of the General German Association of Women Teachers, she observed somewhat caustically: "I have just read Max Weber's biography by his wife. . . . Max is less important to me than Marianne. Of course, this is a terrible heresy, but it is the truth. There is so much for women in this book—quite unintentionally and unconsciously, but all the more insistently. His mother was one of the most extraordinary human beings I ever met. I say human beings advisedly, for she also towered over most men. Her daughter-in-law has brought this out clearly. . . . Of course, Weber's sociology and the rest of his scholarly work are very important, but

every movement that furthers humanity directly appears to me more important. This too is a great heresy."[73]

In the waning years of the Weimar Republic, Marianne Weber reached the
height of her popularity as a public speaker on social and sexual ethics,
appearing before youth groups, students, theologians, and adult education
audiences. She still campaigned against "free love," but to the dismay of the
theologian Otto Baumgarten (1858-1934), a cousin of Max, she refused to
advocate its legal suppression (L 176). She called for tolerance toward the
lifestyles of individuals, but rejected demands for the legal recognition of
relationships that were not meant to endure and be ethically binding. She
therefore opposed (L 174) the much debated proposal for a "companionate
marriage" on a trial basis, as advocated by Judge Benjamin Lindsay (1869-
1943).[74] For her, this was typically American utilitarianism and hedonism
deficient in ethical challenge, just as the world of the flapper girls appeared to
her utterly vacuous and decadent.

These activities ended in 1933, but substantively they paralleled Marianne's most popular book, *Women and Love*, begun before the Nazi seizure
of power but published only in 1935.[75] It appeared in the famous series "The
Blue Books," cheap volumes of high culture for a mass market; 30,000 copies
were printed by 1936. The publisher had persuaded a reluctant Marianne
Weber to come once more to the rescue of sexual morality. Reversing the
title and thrust of Helene Stöcker's book of 1905, Marianne set out to
compose a normative work that used exemplary lives to make its general
points. Yet the mixture of exemplification and evaluation created a certain
tension, since Marianne tended to allow extraordinary individuals the freedom to transcend rules that ordinary mortals should obey.[76]

Relying on the writings of Charlotte Bühler (1883-1974) and Eduard
Spranger (1882-1963), she dealt derivatively with child psychology and adolescent development, but her heart was set on the biographical cases, which
made up two thirds of the book. Indeed, in significant respects the volume
can be read as a companion piece to Max's biography. It compensates for the
male-centeredness of the latter by moving further in the direction of a
feminine perspective. Thus, after writing a biography that seemingly centered on one man, but actually gave much space to two women, Helene and
herself, Marianne elaborated the theme of women and love, treating not only
relations with men but also of women with one another and exploring the
varieties of mothering. The book contrasts the "free" aristocratic marriage
of Karoline and Wilhelm von Humboldt with the closed bourgeois marriage
of their daughter Gabriele to Heinrich von Bülow, compares the failure of
Richard Wagner's marriage to Wilhelmine Planer with his extramarital rela-

tion to Mathilde Wesendonck, and scrutinizes Cosima Wagner's powerful roles as mistress, wife, and widow. A chapter on free love as adventure pronounces judgment on the countess Franziska zu Reventlow, whom Weber, in violation of his own military ideals, had helped in her effort to keep her son out of the draft. At several places, the experience of having lived with Max comes through clearly. When she compares, for example, women's luxurious capacity for friendship with the much more restricted and instrumental male mode, she seems to think of Max, who never had close male friends. It appears to me that Marianne's own marital history and that of her friends provide an unspoken rationale for the parade of historical figures.

By the time she wrote the book, Marianne was, however, not only Max's widow—an experience clearly reflected in the chapter on widowhood—but also had adopted Lily's four children and taken into her home various younger members of the Baumgarten and Mommsen families, as well as a number of unrelated younger women. (The functioning of the household depended, of course, on the stalwart maids to whom Marianne devoted a whole chapter in her autobiography.) In an episode about which she showed some embarrassment later on, she even became a kind of "protective madonna" to the temporarily lapsed Catholic philosopher Peter Wust (1884-1940), one of Max Scheler's followers.[77]

Marianne's closest relationships, however, were with women. After Max's death, Marianne was comforted by the intense presence of Marie Kaiser and Anna Neumeyer, friendships that lasted until death. Speaking through their letters, these two women and Gertrud Simmel appeared later prominently in the autobiography.

In *Women and Love* Marianne fashioned a typology based on such personal experiences and on her literary knowledge: the personal friendship of women, the personal mothering of younger women and men, the impersonal social mothering of official welfare work, and impersonal religious charity. Parallel to Weber's notion of elective affinity (*Wahlverwandtschaft*), she employed the terms *Wahlmutterschaft* and *Wahltochterschaft*, which denote the taking of a mother or daughter role on the basis of mutual attraction. Her primary contemporary example was the bond between Gertrud Bäumer and Helene Lange, the two most influential leaders of the German women's movement. Around the turn of the century, Lange chose Bäumer, who was twenty-five years younger, and lived with her until her own death in 1930. Marianne Weber, herself for fifty years a close friend of Gertrud, described how the younger woman gradually became not only more successful and powerful than the older in the world outside but eventually also took over the mothering role. At the same time that Marianne approved of older women mothering younger men and women, she had a sharp eye for sexual harassment and denounced "the reckless hedonism of married men, especially of professors, who try to drag their women students into 'free' relationships" (L 174).

Marianne's last type, impersonal religious charity—that is, help given irrespective of the recipient's personal qualities—was familiar to her through Helene Weber's inclinations. She chose as her example Eva von Tiele-Winckler (1866-1930), a figure straight out of the universe of medieval saints. Born into a wealthy aristocratic family in Silesia, her mother a Catholic, her father a Protestant Prussian officer, Eva grew up reading Thomas à Kempis and Tauler. At the age of eighteen, she decided never to marry but to dedicate her life to the poor, whether German or Polish. Turning more and more to asceticism and mysticism, while afflicted with debilitating illness, she spent her large fortune on the care of the poor and sick, especially children, and at the age of twenty-seven founded a house for Protestant deaconesses.[78]

Eva von Tiele-Winckler and Helene Lange, inner-worldly ascetics of contrasting kinds, died at the beginning of the Great Depression. The country plunged into an abyss of despair and poverty and became ripe for the triumph of Nazism, which swept away Christian charity as well as secular women's emancipation. The liberal German Democratic Party shrank to insignificance, and an ill-advised effort by Bäumer and others to fuse it with a nationalist youth order failed. The BDF was torn apart by political conflict and became much weaker than other women's organizations. Ardent patriot that she was, Helene Lange proved herself in dying a child of the revolutionary year 1848, her birthyear, and a committed republican, for she ordered her coffin draped with the old democratic colors Black-Red-Gold, in protest against the Right's Black-White-Red. Alice Salomon suffered the next step in her persecution and was denied the presidency of the International Council of Women when Emma Ender declared to Lady Aberdeen that the BDF could not support her candidacy because of the anti-Semitic groundswell. But the BDF's last president, Agnes von Zahn-Harnack, closed ranks with Bertha Pappenheim of the League of Jewish Women and in 1932 campaigned against anti-Semitism. A year later, she succeeded, against Bäumer's advice, in dissolving the organization before it could be taken over by the Nazis.

Meanwhile, in 1929, Marianne Weber had joined one of the many life-reforming groups that searched for the moral rebirth of self and nation. The nonpartisan *Gemeinschaft* (*die Köngener*, as usual for such groups named after a castle) had a majority of women members but was directed by troubled or lapsed theologians, who tried to create the role of secular "life counselors," for which Marianne felt herself highly qualified. Nothing became of these plans when the group's leader, an Indologist, turned into a prominent religious Nazi collaborator in 1933 and the young members were inducted into the Hitler youth. After the leader's defection, the group was permitted to linger on and to meet once a year for a discussion of strictly ethical and religious, not political issues. Whereas Marianne Weber had been a major speaker at the annual workshops in 1929 and 1931, she does not seem to have lectured after 1933. Instead, Gertrud Bäumer spoke in 1938 and 1939 about "The Meeting of the German Soul with Christianity" and "German Lay Piety" in a rarefied spiritual atmosphere that Marianne considered inherently oppositional to the Nazi regime.

The Nazi Years and Their Aftermath: Opposition and Survivor's Guilt

In 1933, Marianne Weber's salon changed its function once more. Her first had sometimes looked like a *salon des refusés* (as Max quipped). The second salon, resumed after an interruption of about seven years, no longer attracted political outsiders and the literary and philosophical avantgarde. After a short suspension, Marianne's circle was able to meet throughout the Nazi period, but now more than ever as a dwindling and aging band of banished, oppositional academics. In a postwar memoir about the salon, Marie Baum claimed that during the Nazi regime "this social circle was perhaps the only one in our city in which full trust and silent agreement were taken for granted in spite of the large number of participants. There were no political discussions. Those who did not like the aura of liberty or considered it too dangerous excluded themselves."[79] As the university was "switched to the same current" (*gleichgeschaltet*), there were fewer and fewer possibilities for intellectual exchanges. That made the Weber circle all the more important: "Thus it happened," Marianne remembered, "that our Sunday meetings became precious as a remnant of an earlier, richer intellectual community. Basically, the circle was now reduced to members of the same cohort, who had very different inclinations but were united in their attitude to the new state and could trust one another" (L 214).

Before they fled, the sociologist Karl Mannheim and the economist Jakob Marschak appeared as speakers as late as the summer of 1933. They were followed into exile by other speakers: Otto Meyerhof, the Nobel-prize-winning biochemist; E. Täubler, the classicist; Arnold Bergsträsser, the political scientist; Kurt Hahn, the educator; Heinrich Zimmer, the Indologist. Emil Lederer, editor of the now defunct *Archiv für Sozialwissenschaft* and an old friend of the Webers, had also had to leave. Whereas Alfred Weber immediately retired in 1933,[80] other speakers were fired or forced into early retirement: Gustav Radbruch, jurist and minister of justice in two Weimar governments; Otto Regenbogen, the classicist; Hans von Eckart, Else Jaffé's son-in-law; Gustav Hartlaub, the art historian; Willy Hellpach, the social psychologist; and also Marie Baum and Karl Jaspers (1883-1969). Thus, about half of all speakers—from a list beginning in 1930—were exiled or dismissed, and the proportion is higher if only the immediate circle is considered. Ricarda Huch joined the inner circle from 1932 to 1934, when she came to live with Marie Baum, for whom she was for over fifty years "the dearest person in whose love I rested."[81] When the Prussian Academy of the Arts ousted Heinrich Mann, Käthe Kollwitz, and Alfred Döblin in 1933, Huch declared her own resignation in an outraged letter: "What the present government prescribes as the proper national attitude is not my *Deutschtum*. The centralization, the compulsion, the brutal methods, the defaming of those who hold other views, the bragging self-praise I consider *undeutsch* and unsavory."[82]

Whereas political debate was impossible at the Sunday meetings, Huch, Baum, and Weber often talked politics behind closed doors. Talk was, however, different from action. Sooner or later, personal tests of strength and courage became unavoidable for most of the women. Huch had spoken up early and in 1936 was threatened with criminal prosecution when her son-in-law lost his academic position. Marie Baum became very active in helping Jewish families emigrate. The Nazis had dismissed her from the University of Heidelberg upon discovering that her Christian grandmother was no less than a Mendelssohn-Bartholdy. After several subpoenas, the Gestapo raided her house in 1941 but did not find incriminating documents she carried on her body. She suffered great anguish over her ultimate unwillingness to join the deportations voluntarily: "That is an example of our failure in the light of an absolute divine imperative."[83]

When Alice Salomon had to follow the other Jewish BDF leaders Alice Bensheimer and Bertha Pappenheim into exile in 1937—their old gentile antagonists, Augspurg, Heymann, and Stöcker, had left in 1933—Agnes von Zahn-Harnack, an active helper, cried out: "I was so grateful to hear your voice over the telephone. Your soul is sound, but we run around like dumb dogs. I want to write to you, but how can I express myself? My pain, my tears, my shame, my gratitude, my veneration, my admiration, my powerlessness, my weakness, my deep sorrow, my heartfelt wishes. God be with you, God protect us."[84] Toward the end of the war, her brother Ernst von Harnack (1888–1945), her cousin Arvid Harnack, and his American wife Mildred Fisher were executed for their participation in the resistance movement, as was Elisabeth von Thadden (1890–1944), a close friend of hers, Baum, and Huch.

Marianne Weber apparently was not involved in any active rescue effort. She maintained her intimate friendship with Anna Neumeyer, the wife of a well-known scholar of international law, both of whom were Jewish. By 1938, Anna tried to assuage Marianne's guilt feelings. In August 1940, Marianne celebrated her seventieth birthday with the Neumeyers and Else Jaffé at the country house of the former BDF leader Dorothee von Velsen (1883–1970), by that time an illegal gathering. Karl Neumeyer, like his wife an admirer of Max Weber, made a speech about him. When the deportation order came a year later, the Neumeyers took their lives after careful deliberation. Marianne went into a depression "the like of which I had never experienced before. It was my soul's answer, my penitence. This death was a severe reproach—to survive it meant being guilty" (L 443).[85] At the time, two of Marianne's adoptive children faced grave danger. The husband of her daughter Klara, a minister in the Confessing Church (the Lutheran opposition to Nazi cooptation), was jailed for refusing an oath. The wife of her son Albert was Jewish, but in the end she turned out to be one of the few Jewish survivors in Berlin, giving birth to a child just as the Red Army forced its way into the capital.[86]

In contrast to those who left or went into "internal exile" (*innere Emigration*), Gertrud Bäumer chose a highly ambiguous and ultimately self-defeating strategy. As one of the highest female officials in the Weimar Republic (in the Ministry of the Interior), she was fired immediately in 1933. By cultivating contacts with high-ranking men and women in the Nazi hierarchy, however, she survived ouster from the writers' union, an injunction against public speaking, and an arrest warrant. In this manner, she managed to continue her journal *Die Frau* until 1943 and to publish weighty novels on medieval female rulers. She glorified the Christian idea of the *Reich* as the fulfillment of occidental history, compared to which the Nazi *Reich* had to appear as an inferior emanation. In a 1936 letter, she criticized Marianne Weber: "In my opinion, you totally overlook what is essential in Christianity, the idea of the *Reich*, so long as you consider its meaning to be the individual soul."[87] When, after the outbreak of World War II, Marianne cautiously signaled that her circle had now "completely distanced itself from what is going on," Gertrud, recalling Max Weber's "Between Two Laws," invoked his memory against her and insisted that the political and the moral can never coincide: "Nobody has seen this clearer than Max Weber. I cannot find persons who say that they are not going to sacrifice themselves for this government any more moral than those who say: we sacrifice ourselves for Germany. Here it is really true: 'Right or wrong, my country.' I don't want to excuse the wrongs, but I cannot escape from my country's fate by draping myself in the mantle of virtue. Since my country's guilt is my own, I must shoulder it, if the nation's existence is at stake."[88]

This dialogue, from which Marianne Weber's letters are missing, is the only indirect evidence we have of her actual thinking at the time, in contrast to her postwar recollections.[89] Overall, Marianne's mode of opposing the Nazi regime was more a matter of persistence than of resistance. She continued what she could do best. Apart from keeping her salon going, she tried to go on publishing and to uphold her ethical worldview.[90]

In the wake of Marianne's success with *Women and Love*, the publisher asked her for a work of philosophical life guidance (*Lebenslehre*). Composed as a series of letters to a young man, it dealt with the ethical structure of existence (good and evil, duty and happiness, rules and exceptions, freedom and restraint, personality and community, vocation and marriage); cultural fulfillment (culture and nature, beauty and art); and religion and religiosity (Christianity and non–Christian religiosity). In her autobiography, Marianne confessed that the philosophical demands of the topics taxed her capacities severely. Written with declining powers, it was the weakest of her works. But it is also true that by its remoteness from the reigning ideology it simply did not fit the Nazi agenda in the later years. The first publisher's rejection was followed by half a dozen others, until the manuscript was finally typeset illegally and rescued from destruction in 1944.[91] It was published as early as 1946 with a postscript on the meaning of the German catastrophe and a confession of collective and personal guilt. Gertrud Bäumer also rushed into print with a pamphlet on "The New Road for the German Woman," in which she blamed the demonic Hitler and the susceptible German people, men, women, and youth, for the evils of the Third Reich—everybody but herself.[92]

A few weeks after the occupation of Heidelberg in 1945, two GI's, students of Talcott Parsons at Harvard, sought out and queried Marianne Weber. Asked whether she considered herself guilty, she replied: "I did not sacrifice my life, but survived through silence, when masses of innocent people were destroyed. That I recognize as my personal transcendental guilt, a failure before my own highest values" (L 486). In a review of her last book, Paul Honigsheim, recipient of her 1926 letter and a voluntary exile after 1933, gallantly acquitted her of any guilt.[93]

After the war, Marianne continued her meetings until about 1952. Indeed, honoring her memory with a picture surrounded by flowers, the circle carried on at least until the end of the 1950's. When Alfred Weber died in 1958, Alexander Rüstow (1895–1963), who had returned from Turkish exile, took over the role of the Weber brothers. By then, members of the circle had done their part in the democratic renewal of the university of Heidelberg, foremost Gustav Radbruch, Alfred Weber, Hans von Eckardt, Otto Regenbogen, Karl Jaspers, and Marie Baum, who also supervised the restoration of Elisabeth von Thadden's private secondary school, which is today named after its founder. In 1949, Theodor Heuss, to the last an admirer of Max Weber and a longtime collaborator of the old Heidelberg liberals, became the first president of the Federal Republic of Germany, supported by Elly Heuss–Knapp (1881–1952), another highly accomplished member of the first generation of academic women. Marianne Weber took great satisfaction from these new beginnings.

Four years before her death in 1954, Marianne republished her biography in a slightly abridged version. But in the quarter century since its first appearance, she had moved a long way from the spirit and content of Max Weber's work to that of his brother, becoming more Alfred's echo than Max's mouthpiece. Ever since the end of World War I and Max's death, ethical and philosophical interests had become increasingly more important to them than the empirical tasks of social science. Alfred Weber hit the table with his fist when the political scientist Arnold Brecht, another famed emigré, told him in 1950 that he taught American students his brother's "relativist" philosophy of science (Wissenschaftslehre): "What! You tell this old nonsense to the Americans? The first thing I tell my students is what the highest values are." He meant the spiritual values. Under the impact of Nazi nihilism, men like Alfred Weber and Gustav Radbruch turned even more resolutely from scholarship back to speculative philosophy or theology in search of unchanging values.[94] Max had taught Marianne to be a scholar, but she had preferred to see him first of all as a great man. On this score, she had the avid support of Karl Jaspers, for whom Weber was the greatest living philosopher of the century because he lived truthfulness. An idol crashed for Jaspers when he finally learned after Marianne's death that Max had not solved his own ethical quandaries and had apparently felt moved to protect his wife from hurtful revelation.[95] Whatever the truth may have been, however, Marianne Weber made a good choice when she had Max Weber's grave stela inscribed. In phrases that speak of human greatness as well as human limitation, she chose to place on opposite sides the words:

"We shall never see his like"

"Everything temporal is only a likeness"

Acknowledgments

I am grateful for the support of my wife Caroline Walker Bynum, who shared my intellectual interest in the topic and gave me a personal sabbatical as a "scholar's spouse" at the Getty Center for the History of Art and the Humanities in Santa Monica. I would like to thank Steven Wight, who took time from his medieval studies to put the manuscript in the computer. Finally, I would like to thank Irving Louis Horowitz for having persuaded me to write the introduction.

Notes

Numbers in parenthesis refer to pages in the biography. I have sometimes changed the wording in the translation. Capital L with number in parenthesis refers to Marianne Weber's autobiography, *Lebenserinnerungen* (Bremen: Storm, 1948).

1. Othmar Spann, "Bemerkungen über Max Weber," *Tote und lebendige Wissenschaft* (Jena: Fischer, 1925), sec. ed., p. 140; reprinted in *Gesamtausgabe*, W. Heinrich et al., eds. (Graz: Akademische Druckanstalt, 1969), vol. 7, p. 200.
2. Quoted in Eduard Baumgarten, ed., *Max Weber. Werk und Person* (Tübingen: Mohr, 1964), p. 605.
3. Marie von Bunsen, *Georg von Bunsen. Ein Charakterbild aus dem Lager der Besiegten gezeichnet von seiner Tochter* (Berlin: Hertz, 1900); Margaret Münsterberg, *Hugo Münsterberg* (New York: Appleton, 1922); Grete Ostwald, *Wilhelm Ostwald. Mein Vater* (Stuttgart: Berliner Union, 1952); Agnes von Zahn-Harnack, *Adolf von Harnack* (Berlin: Bott, 1936), repr. 1951; see also id., *Die Frauenbewegung. Geschichte, Probleme, Ziele* (Berlin: Deutsche Buchgemeinschaft, 1928); Marie Luise Gothein, *Eberhard Gothein. Ein Lebensbild, seinen Briefen nacherzählt* (Stuttgart: Kohlhammer, 1931); Julie Braun-Vogelstein, *Ein Menschenleben. Heinrich Braun und sein Schicksal* (Tübingen: Wunderlich, 1932); repr. as *Heinrich Braun. Ein Leben für den Sozialismus* (Stuttgart: Deutsche Verlagsanstalant, 1967); see also id., *Was niemals stirbt. Gestalten und Erinnerungen* (Stuttgart: Deutsche Verlagsanstalt, 1966).
4. Marianne Weber's relative frankness contrasts, however, with the determination of unmarried feminist leaders, such as Jane Addams and Helene Lange, not to reveal anything about other women in their lives. Focusing on the cause and the movement, they wanted to render a strictly impersonal account of their struggles. See Helene Lange, *Lebenserinnerungen* (Berlin: Herbig, 1927).
5. See Baumgarten, *op. cit.*, p. 635.
6. See Marianne Weber, *Fichtes Sozialismus und sein Verhältnis zur Marxschen Doktrin* (Tübingen: Mohr, 1900) p. VI.
7. Marianne Weber, *Ehefrau und Mutter in der Rechtsentwicklung. Eine Einführung* (Tübingen: Mohr, 1907), repr. Allen: Scientia Verlag, 1971.
8. *op. cit.*, p. 79.
9. *op. cit.*, p. 495f.
10. Emile Durkheim, review in *L'Année sociologique*, vol. 11: 363-369, repr. as id., *Journal sociologique* (Paris: Presses Universitaires, 1969), pp. 644-649. As against

Marianne and Max Weber, Durkheim discounted the historical origins of "legitimate" marriage as a device to protect women against male caprice and emphasized instead the psychological benefits of marriage to males. Frankly conceding that indissoluble marriage was often a burden for a woman, he firmly believed that men needed the institutional restraint of lifelong monogamy to rein in their potentially anarchic sexual drives.

11. Friedrich Paulsen, "Die Frau im Recht der Vergangenheit und der Zukunft," *Preussische Jahrbücher*, vol. 132 (1908): 396–413.

12. For a basically positive discussion of Simmel, see Helene Lange, "Steht die Frauenbewegung am Ziel oder am Anfang?," first published in *Die Frau*, Nov. 1921, repr. in id., *Kampfzeiten* (Berlin: Herbig, 1928), vol. 2, pp. 251–272.

13. Marianne Weber, "Die Beteiligung der Frau an der Wissenschaft," in id., *Frauenfragen und Frauengedanken* (Tübingen: Mohr, 1919), pp. 1–9.

14. Georg Simmel, "Weibliche Kultur," *Archiv für Sozialwissenschaft und Sozialpolitik*, 33 (1911): 1–36; also in id., *Philosophische Kultur* (Leipzig: Klinkhardt, 1911), pp. 278–319; "Das Relative und das Absolute im Geschlechter-Problem," pp. 67–100. In English, the essays are now available in Georg Simmel, *On Women, Sexuality, and Love*, tr. and introduced by Guy Oakes (New Haven: Yale University Press, 1984), pp. 65–132.

15. Marianne Weber, "Die Frau und die objektive Kultur," *Logos*, 4 (1913): 328–363; repr. in *Frauenfragen*, op. cit., pp. 95–133.

16. *On Women*, op. cit., p. 112.

17. For Simmel's reply to Marianne, see his letter of Dec. 14, 1913, in Kurt Gassen and Michael Landmann, eds., *Buch des Dankes an Georg Simmel* (Berlin: Duncker, 1958), p. 132. See also L 382.

18. On the Heidelberg women's movement around 1900, see the forthcoming essay by Ingrid Gilcher-Holtey, "Modelle moderner Weiblichkeit. Diskussionen im akademischen Milieu Heidelbergs um 1900." See also her radio essay, "Max Weber und die Frauen," *Norddeutscher Rundfunk*, April 2, 1987.

19. For Baum's appreciation of Max and Marianne Weber, see her autobiography, *Rückblick auf mein Leben* (Heidelberg: Kerle, 1950), p. 132f.

20. Gothein, op. cit., p. 151.

21. loc. cit.

22. Reprinted in *Frauenfragen*, op. cit., p. 20–37. On the contrasting positions of Weber and Stritt, see Barbara Greven-Aschoff, *Die bürgerliche Frauenbewegung in Deutschland 1894–1933* (Göttingen: Vanderhoeck, 1981), p. 63ff and 216f. See also Richard J. Evans, *The Feminist Movement in Germany 1894–1933* (London: Sage, 1976). Evans treats Weber only tangentially, referring to the *Centralblatt's* refusal "to review a conservatively inclined book on marriage by Marianne Weber" in 1906 (p. 150). Since Weber's book did not appear until the second half of 1907, it is possible that the earlier pamphlet, which anticipated the arguments of the book, was at issue. That Marie Stritt did not like Marianne's essay on "Vocation and Marriage" is confirmed in Marianne's own correspondence. (Stritt translated Stetson's book under the title *Mann und Frau*, Dresden: Minden, 1901).

23. The quotations are from *Frauenfragen*, op. cit., pp. 27–34.

24. Letter to Marianne Weber, April 6, 1906, in Gertrud Bäumer, *Des Lebens wie der Liebe Band. Briefe*, ed. Emmy Beckmann (Tübingen: Wunderlich, 1956), p. 17.

25. On Stöcker's role, see the extensive treatment in Evans, op. cit., 116–143. See also Ann Taylor Allen, "Mothers of the New Generation: Adele Schreiber, Helene Stöcker, and the Evolution of a German Idea of Motherhood, 1900–1914," *Signs*, 10:3 (1985): 418–438, and Amy Hackett, "Helene Stöcker: Left-

Wing Intellectual and Sex Reformer," in Renate Bridenthal, Atina Grossmann, and Marion Kaplan, eds., *When Biology Became Destiny. Women in Weimar and Nazi Germany* (New York: Monthly Review Press, 1984) pp. 109–130.
26. I am reasonably certain the woman was Helene Stöcker, author of *Die Liebe und die Frauen* (Minden: Brun, 1905).
   It turns out that Weber's fulmination (which I have restored to its ferocity) is from a letter of Jan. 11, 1907, to Robert Michels, who had published observations on love and prostitution in Germany, France, and Italy in the first volume of Stöcker's *Mutterschutz*. From this time on, Weber was to have many discussions with Michels, sometimes during his visits in Turin, on empirical and ethical questions of sexuality and eroticism. See Wolfgang Schwentker, "Passion as a Mode of Life: Max Weber, the Otto Gross Circle and Eroticism," in Wolfgang J. Mommsen and J. Osterhammel, eds. *Max Weber and His Contemporaries* (London: Allen and Unwin, 1987), p. 496.
   In the same year in which Michels published his famous book on political parties and the iron law of oligarchy, he also brought out *Die Grenzen der Geschlechtsmoral* (Munich: Frauenverlag, 1911), which appeared in a series edited by Havelock Ellis as *Sexual Ethics: A Study of Borderland Questions* (London: Scott, 1914). While Michels was co-editor of the *Archiv für Sozialwissenschaft*, his book was reviewed by his Turin colleague Rodolfo Mondolfo, 36 (1913): 920–926. See also Weber's letter to Marianne, April 22, 1911, below 481f.
27. Actually, Weber was preceded in 1906 by Gertrud Bäumer, who spoke about "The Social Demands of the Women's Movement in the Context of the Economic Position of Women." See Harry Liebersohn, *Religion and Industrial Society: The Protestant Social Congress in Wilhelmine Germany. Transactions of the American Philosophical Society*, vol. 76, pt. 6 (1986), p. 39. On the (mal)treatment of women at public meetings, see also Marie-Elisabeth Lüders, *Fürchte Dich nicht. Persönliches und Politisches aus mehr als 80 Jahren. 1878–1962* (Cologne: Westdeutscher Verlag, 1963), p. 55. (Like Bäumer, Lüders (1878–1966) represented the German Democratic Party in the Reichstag from 1920 until 1932. In 1957, she was president pro tem of the Federal Republic's Bundestag.)
28. Alice Salomon, "Die Entwicklung der Theorie der Frauenbewegung," *Archiv für Sozialwissenschaft*, 26 (1908): 451–500.
29. Alice Salomon, *Charakter ist Schicksal. Lebenserinnerungen*, Rüdiger Baron and R. Landwehr, eds. (Weinheim: Beltz, 1983), p. 128. (The unpublished English original was written in New York City in the 1940s.)
30. Lily Braun, *Die Frauenfrage. Ihre geschichtliche Entwicklung und ihre wirtschaftliche Seite* (Leipzig: Hirzel, 1901). On Braun's significance, see Alfred G. Meyer, *The Feminism and Socialism of Lily Braun* (Bloomington: Indiana University Press, 1985). For Braun's clash with spokeswomen of the BDF over the issue of ethical marriage and free love, see her barely fictionalized autobiographical account in *Memoiren einer Sozialistin. Kampfjahre* (Berlin: Klemm, 1923), p. 442ff.
31. See Evans, *op. cit.*, ch. 5, and Greven–Aschoff, *op. cit.*, pp. 107–117.
32. On the relation between the Romantic movement, especially Caroline Schlegel-Schelling, and the "new ethic," see Dr. Marie Bernays, *Die deutsche Frauenbewegung* (Leipzig: Teubner, 1920), p. 16f., 62f. Bernays (1883–1939) was a close ally of the Webers and in her empirical studies followed up Max's interest in the "psychophysics" of industrial labor.
33. See Martin Green, *The von Richthofen Sisters. The Triumphant and the Tragic Modes of Love* (New York: Basic Books, 1974), p. 55f.
34. *op. cit.*, p. 23.

35. See Martin Green, *Mountain of Truth. The Counterculture Begins: Ascona 1900–1920* (Hanover: University of Massachusetts Press, 1986).
36. D. H. Lawrence, *Mr. Noon*, ed. Lindeth Vasey (Cambridge: Cambridge University Press, 1984); see also Frieda Lawrence, *Nur der Wind* (Berlin, Rabenpresse, 1936).
37. Cited in Wilhelm Hennis, *Max Webers Fragestellung* (Tübingen: Mohr, 1987), p. 202.
38. Georg Lukacs, *Die Theorie des Romans* (Darmstadt: Luchterhand, 1963), p. 5; now cited in Judith Marcus and Zoltan Tar, eds., *Georg Lukacs. Selected Correspondence 1902–1920* (New York: Columbia University Press, 1986), p. 17f.
39. In Berta Lask's *roman à clef*, *Stille und Sturm* (Halle: Mitteldeutscher Verlag, 1955), the Webers, who appear as Helene and Max Wormann, are blamed for Emil Lask's death. See vol. I, p. 598.
40. See Salomon, *Charakter, op. cit.*, p. 142f. and 146.
41. "Zwischen zwei Gesetzen," Wolfgang J. Mommsen and Gangolf Hübinger, eds., *Max Weber, Zur Politik im Weltkrieg*, vol. 15 of the *Max Weber Gesamtausgabe* (Tübingen: Mohr, 1984), p. 97f.; see also my essays "Max Weber's Ethics and the Peace Movement Today," *Theory and Society*, 13 (1984): 491–511, and "Weber's Generational Rebellion and Maturation," in Reinhard Bendix and G. Roth, *Scholarship and Partisanship* (Berkeley: University of California Press, 1971), p. 25ff.
42. On the peace movement, see Roger Chickering, *Imperial Germany and a World Without War. The Peace Movement and German Society 1892–1914* (Princeton: Princeton University Press, 1975).
43. An example of Bäumer's early wartime writings is *Der Krieg und die Frau* (Stuttgart: Deutsche Verlagsanstalt, 1914). See also Agnes von Zahn-Harnack, "Der Krieg und die Frauen" (1914), repr. in id., *Schriften und Reden 1914–1950*, eds. Marga Anders and Ilse Reicke (Tübingen: Hopfer, 1964), pp. 9–19.
44. See Lida Gustava Heymann and Anita Augspurg, *Erlebtes—Erschautes. Deutsche Frauen kämpfen für Freiheit, Recht und Frieden. 1850–1940*, ed. Margrit Twellmann (Meisenheim: Hain, 1977), ch. 5.
45. Salomon, *op. cit.*, p. 154.
46. "Zwischen zwei Gesetzen," *loc. cit.*
47. Marianne Weber, "Der Krieg als ethisches Problem," repr. in *Frauenfragen, op. cit.*, p. 178.
48. Marianne Weber, "Die besonderen Kulturaufgaben der Frau" (1918), repr. in *op. cit.*, p. 250f.
49. Kurt Hildebrandt, *Erinnerungen an Stefan George und seinen Kreis* (Bonn: Bouvier, 1965), p. 228.
50. See Wolfgang J. Mommsen, *Max Weber and German Politics 1890–1920* (Chicago: Univ. of Chicago Press, 1984), pp. 310 and 325ff. The quotation is from p. 328.
51. Gertrud Bäumer, *Lebensweg durch eine Zeitenwende* (Tübingen: Wunderlich, 1933), p. 432f.
52. See Greven-Aschoff, *op. cit.*, p. 112, 238 n. 33.
53. Salomon, *op. cit.*, p. 186f. During the war Helene Lange's and Gertrud Bäumer's insensitive handling of the League of Jewish Women, an early corporate member of the BDF, led its president Anna Pappenheim—Freud's erstwhile Anna O.—to lead the league out of the National Women's Service and to charge the two leaders with "hatefulness toward Jewish women and Judaism." The long-range difficulties were not resolved through Bäumer's letter of apology. See Marion Kaplan, "Sisterhood under Siege: Feminism and Anti-Semitism in Weimar and

Nazi Germany," in Renate Bridenthal et al., *op. cit.*, p. 187. See also Kaplan, *The Jewish Feminist Movement in Germany. The Campaigns of the jüdische Frauenbund, 1904-1938* (Westport: Greenwood, 1979). On Bäumer's excessively tactical reaction to anti-Semitism in 1933, see the evaluation in Greven-Aschoff, *op. cit.*, p. 186.

54. Salomon, *op. cit.*, p. 188.
55. Cited in Greven-Aschoff, *op. cit.*, p. 113.
56. Salomon, *loc. cit.* The German editors misidentified Baum as Zahn-Harnack. In the meantime, Prof. Joachim Wieler, who wrote the postscript to the autobiography, made available to me a copy of Salomon's letter of resignation, together with Bäumer's very hostile reply to the executive board. These clearly identify Baum. In her own autobiography, Bäumer played down the incident, without naming Salomon; *Lebensweg, op. cit.*, p. 435f.
57. Marie Baum in her edition of Ricarda Huch, *Briefe an die Freunde* (Zurich: Manesse, 1986), p. 213.
58. Bäumer, *op. cit.*, p. 434.
59. See Paul Honigsheim, *On Max Weber*, tr. Joan Rytina (New York: Free Press, 1968), pp. 79-86 et passim; Helene Tompert, *Lebensformen und Denkweisen der akademischen Welt Heidelbergs im Wilhelminischen Zeitalter* (Lübeck: Matthiesen, 1969), p. 41ff.
60. See Edgar Salin, *Um Stefan Georg. Erinnerung und Zeugnis* (Munich: Küpper, 1954) p. 111; see also his comparison of the Weber brothers in id., *Lynkeus. Gestalten und Probleme* (Tübingen: Mohr, 1963), p. 66f.
61. Erich von Kahler, *Der Beruf der Wissenschaft* (Berlin: Bondi, 1920); Arthur Salz, *Für die Wissenschaft gegen die Gebildeten unter ihren Verächtern* (Munich: n. n.: 1921).
62. Salin, *op. cit.*, p. 108f.
63. H. H. Gerth and C. Wright Mills, *From Max Weber* (New York: Oxford University Press, 1946), p. 117.
64. Margarete Susman, *Ich habe viele Leben gelebt. Erinnerungen* (Stuttgart: Deutsche Verlagsanstalt, 1964), p. 53f.
65. Baumgarten, *op. cit.*, p. 635.
66. Marie Luise Gothein, *A History of Garden Art*, ed. Walter P. Wright (New York: Hacker Art Books, 1979).
67. Marie Baum in her introduction to *Der Marianne Weber-Kreis. Festgabe für Georg Poensgen*, privately printed for the members (Heidelberg: Kerle, 1958), p. 11.
68. Friedrich Meinecke, review in *Historische Zeitschrift*, 135 (1927), repr. in René König and J. Winckelmann, eds., *Max Weber zum Gedächtnis* (Cologne: Westdeutsher Verlag, 1963), pp. 143-147.
69. Gertrud Bäumer, "Persönlichkeit und Lebenswerk von Max Weber," *Die Hilfe*, 10/11 (1926), repr. in König, *op. cit.*, p. 124.
70. Käthe Leichter, "Max Weber als Lehrer und Politiker," *Der Kampf*, 19: 9 (1926), repr. in König, *op. cit.*, p. 142.
71. Max Rehm, "Erinnerungen an Max Weber," in König, *op. cit.*, p. 25.
72. Letter of Oct. 22, 1928 in Baum, ed., *Ricarda Huch Briefe, op. cit.*, p. 172f.
73. Letter of April 10, 1926, in Emmy Beckmann, ed., *Helene Lange, Was ich hier geliebt. Briefe* (Tübingen: Wunderlich, 1957), p. 271f.
74. See also Marianne Weber, *Die Idee der Ehe und die Ehescheidung* (Frankfurt: Societätsdruckerei, 1929), p. 42; Benjamin B. Lindsey, *The Companionate Marriage* (New York: Boni, 1927).
75. Marianne Weber, *Die Frauen und die Liebe* (Königstein: Langewiesche, 1935).

76. See also *Die Idee der Ehe, op. cit.*, p. 44.
77. The Wust/Weber correspondence was not published until 1951. Wust addressed Marianne as "my dear little mother" and signed himself "your son"; she wrote to her "dear son" and signed "your foster mother." See Walter Theodor Cleve, ed., *Wege einer Freundschaft. Briefwechsel Peter Wust—Marianne Weber 1927–1939* (Heidelberg: Kerle, 1951). For Marianne's later recollection and Marie Kaiser's warning, see L 144f. and 363.
78. For more than four decades, Tiele-Winckler vacillated between periods of great organizational activity on the local and national level and periods of withdrawal from the world. As in so many medieval cases, her fortitude and obedience were tested severely by her father and her spiritual guide, Friedrich von Bodelschwingh (1831–1910), the founder of Bethel, to this day the most renowned of the Protestant welfare facilities. For medieval parallels, see Caroline Walker Bynum, *Holy Feast and Holy Fast. The Religious Significance of Food to Medieval Women* (Berkeley: University of California Press, 1987).
79. Marie Baum in *Der Marianne Weber-Kreis, op. cit.*, p. 10.
80. Eberhard Demm, "Zivilcourage im Jahre 1933. Alfred Weber und die Fahnenaktionen der NSDAP," *Heidelberger Jahrbücher*, 26 (1982): 69–80.
81. A testimonial of their relationship is Marie Baum's biography, *Leuchtende Spur. Das Leben Ricarda Huchs* (Tübingen: Wunderlich, 1950).
82. Huch to the president of the Prussian Academy of the Arts, Max von Schillings, in *Briefe an die Freunde, op. cit.*, p. 225f.
83. Baum, *Rückblick auf mein Leben, op. cit.*, p. 284.
84. Harnack to Salomon, June 12, 1937, reprinted in Joachim Wieler, *Er-Innerung eines zerstörten Lebensabends. Alice Salomon während der NS-Zeit und im Exil* (Darmstadt: Lingbach, 1987), p. 183.
85. On the Neumeyers' suicide, see also Dorothee von Velsen, *Im Alter die Fülle. Erinnerungen* (Tübingen: Wunderlich, 1956), p. 338.
86. Among the countless victims were Käthe Leichter und Gertrud Kantorowicz. Leichter, who in the mid-1930's had become one of the leaders of the socialist underground in Austria, managed to write her autobiography secretly in prison, recalling her Heidelberg student days, before she was among the first to be gassed in a trial series.
  After taking great risks and freeing Friedrich Gundolf's brother from Buchenwald through an elaborate ruse, Gertrud Kantorowicz tried to flee across the Swiss border in 1942, leading Margarete Susman's sister, Ernst Kantorowicz's mother, and another aged woman. Only one made it across. Susman's sister was killed, and Gertrud was dragged back to Berlin. Recognized by one of her interrogators as the nurse who had taken care of him in Turkey during World War I, he engineered to have her sent to Theresienstadt instead of Auschwitz. There she nursed the sick and invalid, read Homer in Greek and wrote poems in the Georgian style, until she died a few hours before the camp's liberation. See Herbert Steiner, ed., Käthe Leichter, *Leben und Werk* (Vienna: Europaverlag, 1973); Michael Landmann, postscript to Gertrud Kantorowicz, *Vom Wesen der griechischen Kunst* (Darmstadt: Deutsche Akademie für Sprache und Dichtung, vol. 24, 1961).
87. Letter of May 23, 1936, Bäumer, *Des Lebens wie der Liebe Band, op. cit.*, p. 92.
88. Letter of Dec. 27, 1939, Bäumer, *op. cit.*, p. 128f. Recently, Bäumer, Zahn-Harnack and Weber were treated as precursors of fascism in a Marxist dissertation by Christine Wittrock. Postulating that fascism was the last stage of capitalism, she views the image of women under fascism as the last stage of a development that began with the bourgeois women's movement. The analysis

focuses on written statements and leaves out any personal conduct. See *Weiblichkeitsmythen. Das Frauenbild im Faschismus und seine Vorläufer in der Frauenbewegung der 20er Jahre* (Frankfurt: Sendler, 1983). See now also Claudia Koonz, *Mothers in the Fatherland: Women, the Family and Nazi Politics* (New York: St. Martin, 1987).

89. The cumulative evidence of post-war memoirs confirms, however, Marianne's basic opposition to the Nazi regime. For example, Dorothee von Velsen, who felt suicidal in 1933, recalled that at the time she fled to Marianne Weber, "who followed the course of events with a magnificent sense of equanimity, and to Marie Baum, who was deeply wounded." When she vacationed with Marianne in 1940, she reminisced, "we whispered every evening: 'Another day is gained!' As long as England held out, freedom had a refuge. But we did not gloat." (Velsen's sister lived in England.) See Velsen, *op. cit.* p. 346.

90. In *Women and Love*, Marianne's strenuous opposition to "free love" led her to a moral lapse with regard to Nazi repression. Attacking sexually explicit literature, she mentioned as a sorry example of permissive sex education the advice given by a Marxist medical doctor in a published correspondence with young male and female workers. In a one-line footnote she added: "It is right that such publications are outlawed today" (p. 35). I am reasonably certain that she referred to Max Hodann's *Sexualelend und Sexualberatung* (Rudolfstadt: Greifenverlag, 1928). In suppressing much of German literary life, the Nazis made unrestrained use of the 1926 "law against trash and smut" that Gertrud Bäumer and Theodor Heuss had helped pass in the Reichstag for the sake of protecting young readers and of elevating popular taste.

91. Marianne Weber, *Erfülltes Leben* (Heidelberg: Lambert Schneider, 1946). In 1936 she finally managed to get out the long-delayed *Jugendbriefe* (Tübingen: Mohr), the letters of the young Max Weber, with the editorial help of Georg Kunze, a secondary school teacher, who had refused to take the civil service oath to the new regime and, being unemployed, lived for some time under her roof. A second volume of letters was apparently typeset but too controversial to be printed and was subsequently lost.

92. Gertrud Bäumer, *Der neue Weg der deutschen Frau* (Stuttgart: Deutsche Verlagsanstalt, 1946). For her unrepenting apologia pro sua vita see her public declaration of 1947 in Bäumer, *Des Lebens wie der Liebe Band, op. cit.*, p. 339ff.

93. Paul Honigsheim in *American Journal of Sociology*, 55 (1949): 102ff.

94. Arnold Brecht, *Mit der Kraft des Geistes. Lebenserinnerungen*, vol. 2: 1927-1967 (Stuttgart: Deutsche Verlagsanstalt, 1967), p. 394f.

95. See Dieter Henrich, "Karl Jaspers: Thinking with Max Weber in Mind," in Mommsen and Osterhammel, *op. cit.*, p. 539ff.

Postscript. Errata in original text of biography.

p. 310 below: read Carl Menger (1840-1921) instead of Anton Menger. p. 386: read *lo scoppio del carro*. According to Gianfranco Poggi, this is a Holy Week ritual exclusive to Florence. A mechanical dove carrying a lit taper flies along a wire toward a cart full of firecrackers. It is a good omen if the dove sets off an explosion.

Biographical data

I have tried to provide year of birth and death for most persons mentioned in the introduction, but there is a good deal of incorrect information in the literature, including handbooks and encyclopedias. This is also true of Marianne Weber's dates. She was born on Aug. 2, 1870, and died on March 12, 1954, contrary to the translator's preface (p. v.) and several other sources.

MAX WEBER:
A BIOGRAPHY

1

ANCESTORS

I

Max Weber's maternal grandparents were such unusual people and imparted such clearly recognizable elements of their own makeup to their grandchild's personality that the outlines of their lives belong at the beginning of his story.

The Fallenstein family can be traced back to the middle of the seventeenth century in Thuringia. Georg Friedrich Fallenstein's father and grandfather could already be described as intellectuals.[1] Fallenstein's grand-

---

[1] According to a German-American relative, who shares the American penchant for genealogical studies, the originally aristocratic Hessian family was named Wallenstein, constituting a Protestant branch of Albrecht Wallenstein's family. [Albrecht Wenzel Eusebius von Wallenstein, Duke of Freidland, 1583–1634, Austrian general in the Thirty Years War.—Ed.] He established that a lieutenant colonel named Wilhelm von Wallenstein served in the Swedish army and received some estates from Gustavus Adolphus as a fief, but sold these some years later. The researcher surmises that this officer came to Germany with Gustavus Adolphus in 1631 and left some offspring there when he fell in battle. Since the Swedish language has no W, his name was written with a V, and since that letter has an F-sound in Germany, that is how it came to be spelled. *Se non è vero è ben trovato.* [If it is not true, it is cleverly invented.] Gervinus gathered authentic information on the family and preserved it in his "Recollections of G. F. Fallenstein," the source of the data given above.

father, a native of Witzelrode near Meiningen, was assistant principal of the Gymnasium at Herford, and his father was the sometime director of the pedagogical seminary at Kleve. There is a certain amount of information about the latter, Max Weber's great-grandfather. He was a highly gifted man with an overabundance of undisciplined energy. He lived in near poverty with a wife who was descended from a Huguenot family and who, like him, was passionate, impetuous, and inclined to be adventurous.

G. F. Fallenstein, born as their eldest son in 1790, was his parents' darling and bone of contention. He preserved the painful childhood recollection of fleeing from their squabbles. But the situation deteriorated further. His father, a philologist of repute, began drinking, and suddenly deserted his family. He was never heard from again, and it was never known whether he had emigrated or had drowned on his way overseas. His wife was left in dire poverty with several children.

Like an orphan, her son Friedrich grew up with strangers, but he overcame all hardships. The Duke of Meiningen made it possible for him to study at the university, but the youth did so only in a desultory way. He studied botany, zoology, and medicine. His poetical side made him turn to philology. He translated classical writers, wrote Romantic poetry under the name of Frauenlob, and authored stories and essays.

When he was still a young man, he found his mother and several of his brothers and sisters living in great poverty in a squalid building in Berlin. He himself had nothing and was nothing, and yet he wanted to help. Despite everything he became engaged at the age of nineteen to a beautiful fifteen-year-old girl [Betty] of no means. When her grandfather for financial reasons refused to give them permission to marry, the desperate young man suffered a nervous breakdown that lasted for several months. After his recovery, friends found him a job as a private secretary. At the age of twenty he managed to get permission to marry. His lovely, gentle wife was his good angel; he loved her dearly and remained faithful to her throughout his eventful life. She bore him six children. They constantly struggled to make ends meet, and for years husband and wife had to live apart. At first Fallenstein was able to earn a living only for himself—as a tutor, a county secretary, a writer and poet. His wife and his children lived with friends. But his energy, his sense of duty, and his lofty ambition enabled him to weather even the greatest hardships. In fact, the overcoming of obstacles gave him pleasure. He had an abundance of manly strength, a dynamic spirit, a puritanical outlook, and a crusty frankness, coupled with a passionate, easily inflamed temper, which was, however, controlled by chivalry and a childlike soft-heartedness toward weaker persons, particularly women and children.

His patriotism, kindled by his personal acquaintance with Friesen, Luden, and Jahn,[2] stood every test. In 1813 he anticipated the Prussian king's call to arms. Without much reflection he joined Lützow's volunteer corps and, poor as he was, had two fellow volunteers outfitted at his expense. He divided his remaining funds between his wife and the regimental treasury, confident that the state would take care of his family. But without the help of friends, his wife and two small children would have been in terrible straits. As it was, she lost one child because of malnutrition; for this Fallenstein held Napoleon personally responsible and felt burning hatred for him as long as he lived. Life in the camp and on the battlefield inspired Fallenstein's muse. He struck up a rapturous friendship with Theodor Körner,[3] and together they wrote battle songs and libertarian poems that were sung and recited by their comrades in arms. His mind was filled with the Teutonic and libertarian ideals of the time. He collected old German literary documents, gave his sons old German names, hated everything wälsch,[4] and in his social relationships affected an "unvarnished crustiness" [hanebüchene Knorrigkeit].

After his return he suffered greatly because of the political fruitlessness of the war. He was personally affronted at the ingratitude of the Prussian government which, despite the king's promises, offered the returning soldiers no adequate employment. Therefore, when the war broke out again in 1815, he joined the army for the second time and went to Paris. There he was given a well-paid job with the military police. For the first time he was able to relax and enjoy life. But he was so used to privation that he now became intoxicated with the joy of making lavish gifts. To his beloved wife, who was doing without necessities at home, he sent silver plate, silk dresses, and morocco slippers, as well as what he himself called "junk and frippery": a silver rattle for the youngest boy. This was typical of the contradictions of his personality. A woman friend wrote about him: "There are certainly many who knew him only to be proud and severe, but anyone who

---

[2]Karl Friedrich Friesen, 1784–1814, was an aide-de-camp of Adolf Freiherr von Lützow, who in 1813 founded Lützow's Free Corps, a national legion known as Die Schwarze Schar [The Black Corps] and Lützows Wilde Jagd [Lützow's Wild Huntsmen]. Friesen, who fell in France in 1814, also assisted Friedrich Ludwig ("Turnvater") Jahn, 1778–1852, in founding the gymnastic movement and the Burschenschaften, fraternities designed to disseminate nationalism in the academic world. Heinrich Luden, 1780–1847, a nationalist historian at the University of Jena, also took an active part in these movements.—Ed.

[3]Karl Theodor Körner (1791–1813), libertarian poet and dramatist, fell while serving in Lützow's Free Corps. His poem Lützows wilde Jagd was set to music by Robert Schumann.—Ed.

[4]Wälsch or welsch refers to things Italian or French, sometimes to foreign or "un-German" influences generally.—Ed.

was close to his heart was surrounded by a veritable profusion of love. And
I noticed in him the full wealth of a beautiful human soul when he had the
meagerest means at his disposal." All his life Fallenstein displayed a magnificent generosity and helpfulness toward needy people; yet he was also constantly governed by the uneasy frugality that he had had to practice in
times of need. For example, when he became the owner of a beautiful house,
he did not allow a cake to be baked in it, even for guests.

In 1816 he went to Düsseldorf as a government secretary and became an
employee of exemplary conscientiousness and prudence, an indefatigable and
self-sacrificing man who was always ready to exert his uncommon energy in
the public interest far beyond the call of duty. Consequently a tremendous
work load was soon placed upon his shoulders; with the title and the salary
of a secretary, he performed the functions of a councillor. His superiors fully
appreciated and praised his extraordinary talents, his unflagging energy, and
his extensive knowledge. "He had the ambition and the dynamism of those
thoroughbred horses which use their strength without moderation until
they break down" (Gervinus).[5]

Despite all this, he was deliberately and disgracefully slighted by the ministry in Berlin; he was not promoted and received such pitiful remuneration
that, as his family grew, he found it necessary to work as a writer in addition to his regular employment. Why was this? One reason was his democratic and libertarian disposition. He saw "the spirit of the times moving
through all peoples and civilizations at an unrestrainable pace, like a joyful
child of God and of freedom, like the God that walked ahead of Moses." Because of this, he was enthusiastic about equality for all citizens and, together with Jahn and his circle, inveighed against reactionaries. But he was
also troublesome in other ways. He criticized an action of the government
with a vehement article, written in the martial style of the wars of liberation, in which he protested against the presentation of an estate to a
French nobleman. He even appealed to the king, and was brought to court.
Although he was acquitted, he was threatened with a disciplinary transfer,
and only the unanimous protest of his superiors prevented this. Afterward
he lived in Berlin under a cloud. Following several deliberate official snubs,
he bitterly planned to escape this "servitude" by emigrating. When he was
able to breathe freely for a change, he felt his existence to be a "miserable

---

[5]Georg Gottfried Gervinus, 1805–1871, literary critic, historian, and publicist, professor at
Göttingen and Heidelberg, elected to the National Assembly in 1848. Author of commentaries
on Shakespeare (1849–52), a history of German literature (1835–42), and a history of nineteenth century Germany (1856–66).—Ed.

life of drudgery" and sighed, "May God relieve me of this feeling if He cannot give me another life to live." Finally, in 1832, after fourteen years in the employment of the state, he took an examination and was given a suitable position as a government counselor at Koblenz.

Before moving to Koblenz he suffered a terrible blow, the loss of the beloved wife who had always made him happy. He was left with a houseful of underage children. The vehement yet kindly man stood before a chasm, and on his children, some of whom he sent away, the troubled father may have had an even more oppressive effect than before. It had always been hard for them not to be crushed by him. The old Lützow corpsman was a stern moralist and believed unconditionally in the maxim *"Du kannst, denn du sollst."* [6] Anger frequently made the veins on his forehead stand out. Toward his sons in particular he was a strict, demanding father. The little girls, like all weaker persons, usually found him gentle, yet he also tried to toughen them, using educational methods that today seem barbaric. To cure a headache, for example, he would hold their heads under the cold stream from the water pump early in the morning; in winter he made them walk around without warm underclothes; in the blazing summer sun he did not let them wear a hat. He was especially strict at the table; the children were given large helpings of the less popular dishes, and woe to them if they did not clean their plates! The punishment for lying was a sound thrashing, and this was administered even to the small girls. Yet they loved their father more than they feared him.

The sons, however, escaped his rule as soon as they could; three went overseas, and another ran away. Their father never saw them again. A letter written by Fallenstein when one of his sons was confirmed shows the extreme ethical demands he thought he could bring to bear on his children's development, and the heroic severity with which he judged their inadequacies. As he saw it, adolescents could choose one of two paths: either "onward and upward," or perdition.

June 9, 1835

Dear Otto,

The few lines you added to your aunt's letter gave me the unexpected but welcome news that you are to be confirmed, and by now have been confirmed. May God grant, my son, that you have a proper

---

[6] Attributed to Immanuel Kant: "I ought, therefore I can."—Ed.

appreciation of the importance of this chapter in your life, and that
the resolutions and decisions that you have made for your own good
here and in the hereafter, as well as the assurances and promises that
you have made at the altar, will endure and be fulfilled. All your life
you should have God and the honor of a righteous German in mind. Be
and remain true, faithful, and confident of your good conscience and of
Christ, and you will relate to the world confidently and securely. Despite some bad habits that you have unfortunately displayed, you have
given your father pleasure as a loyal, truthful, diligent, and good-
natured fellow. Retain these qualities and increasingly give up bad habits, especially incivility, impetuousness, self-righteousness, and the
like. Be more industrious, my son, in the tasks leading to your goal in
life, and above all bear in mind that one is, and achieves, little or
nothing if one is not outstanding or does not do outstanding work.
In all things try to emulate the best, the highest, and the finest,
for mediocrity is bad in everything, not worthy of honor or of life. In
particular remain truthful and morally pure; then you will be worthy
of us and cling to God and not consider, do, or tolerate anything
dishonorable. Guard your tongue, but always act as though the doors
and windows were open; whatever you have to be ashamed of before men
is at the same time a sin before God. Preserve your faith; be helpful
and obliging to everyone and, above all, be grateful. Forget yourself, but
never forget those who have befriended you and yours and have helped
you. Preserve your innocence, and do not judge others irreverently. Do
no injustice, but do not wittingly suffer any to be done to you. Bear
in mind three things at all times: fear God, honor women, love your
neighbor. And remember as a fourth point that I would rather see you
dead than have anyone call you a scoundrel and a coward. Fear no one
but God, but hate evil, lies, and impurity. Honor women in thought
and deed, for your mother's sake and to guard against sin. Love your
neighbor, and remember that no one exists merely for his own sake.
Each person is there for his fellowman, and no love or loyalty surpasses
the kind that makes a man give up his life for his brothers. You belong
completely to your duty; never forget that. No earthly gain is worth
anything as compared to the honor of being loyal, true, and valiant.
Let these words be your life's companion, my dear son Otto, and may
they remind you of your father, your late mother, and your newly acquired mother, all of whom will think of you with love if you remain
worthy of them. You know what sorrow other people have caused me;
see to it that nothing like that ever comes to me from you. You are
a Fallenstein, and I have entrusted you with an honest name. Keep it

free of any blemish. Let people esteem it because of you as well, and God grant that they may never curse or revile it. For this you should work, live—or die! . . .

And now to your future and your destiny. I am not unaware that you have little inclination for your studies and no dedication to them. Your lukewarm attitude and lack of diligence are in every way unjust, particularly so far as I am concerned, and I was very sorry that your latest school report was a bad one too. I deserved better of you and did not expect this, especially after our last conversation. I do not wish to force you to devote yourself to a task against your will and inclination, but I *do* demand that you now decide, and in an honorable manner, what position you want to fill in life with seriousness and a sense of duty. I have taken care of you to the best of my ability. From your early boyhood it has been your wish to go to sea, and as far as I know this has remained your fondest hope. Very well; if you are serious about it, if after mature deliberation this is still your resolute, manly, and firm desire, then I shall have an opportunity, through the good offices of your mother's brothers who live here, to place you on a Liverpool boat under very favorable conditions. Consider carefully what you do, and above all remember that the step you take is a decisive one, that you cannot go back and that here as everywhere the only motto for an honest fellow is "onward and upward!" If you make your decision, you will leave immediately for Genoa to board the ship; it is called Rabb (?) and you will live on it for five years or go down with it. I shall write you more about it later; I also hope to see you first and commend you to God's mercy and to your fortune with the blessing of a fatherly kiss and a handshake. But do not talk about this to anyone, and when I come, tell me truthfully what is innermost in your own heart. Farewell, my son! Your mother will now add a few lines. Farewell, and in all you do think of your devoted father.

It was fortunate for the children, including those who had already left their father's house, that after four years as a widower their difficult father met a gentle girl who so strikingly reminded him of his late wife that she won his heart at first sight. This girl was Emilie Souchay, the daughter of a refined, wealthy, patrician Frankfurt family. Her father, Karl Cornelius Souchay, the founder of a commercial firm in Frankfurt, Manchester, and London, was descended from a Huguenot family, Souchay de la Doboissière, which had owned an estate near Orleans and had renounced its aristocratic privileges when the family fled to Germany. Some of the refugees settled in Hanau as goldsmiths; others went to Frankfurt. K. C. Souchay's grand-father was a goldsmith in Hanau, his father a minister at the French Reformed Church in Frankfurt.

K. C. Souchay (Max Weber's great-grandfather) was a cheerful, amiable, and cultured man. By his own efforts and by his marriage he acquired consid-erable wealth which he spent generously. He regarded himself only as the administrator of his property, an attitude he imparted to his children. He lived in a beautiful, elegantly furnished house at the Fahrtor; its wide, sun-ny front looked over the Main River and the Sachsenhausen hills beyond. This kindly, cheerful man liked to live happily and let others live in the same way. He smilingly said about himself: "I have always lived like a rich man, and I have managed to do so with God's help. The skinflints around me have always thought I was rich, even when that was not yet true." To enhance this good life he married a girl of entirely German descent and from a good family. Helene Schunck, the daughter of Major Schunck from Schlüchtern, bore him seven children. She created a harmonious atmosphere around herself and was so lovely that the painter Stieler[7] said she was the most beautiful woman in Germany and offered to capture her charm in a portrait that is still owned by the family. It may therefore be assumed that the grace and noble beauty of Max Weber's mother, qualities she passed on to several of her children, were more a German than a French heri-tage.

Emilie Souchay, Weber's grandmother, however, was not so endowed. She was remarkably small and very plain; she was intelligent and profound, but had a delicate constitution and was shy and withdrawn. Her strength lay in her deeply religious nature, angelic goodness, and devotion to everything great and beautiful. In her memoirs, which she wrote for the benefit of her family, she said this about herself:

> The greatest—indeed, I am inclined to say, the only—sufferings of my childhood and early youth grew out of my constitution. Not that I can remember ever having been sickly, but an indescribable timidity lay in my bones and often gripped my heart. . . . In many an anxious hour the longing for inner freedom became my fervent prayer. When I opened my Bible one day, these words caught my eye: "My grace is sufficient for you." [2 Cor. 12:9] I have reflected a great deal about the deep meaning of these words and have found in them the most beautiful in-terpretation of the parable of the talents. [Luke 19:11–27]

---

[7]Josef Karl Stieler, 1781–1858, from 1820 on court painter in Munich.—Ed.

As an old lady she summed up the experiences of a person whose modest energies were always threatened by feelings of inadequacy in these words:

We should like so much to go through life in our own way and we do not understand that our own nature has set us a goal that we cannot lose from sight with impunity. To contemplate the limits of our nature with courage, to guard against false ambition, but to do whole-heartedly what we are charged with doing and to trust humbly in God's help—this, to my mind, is the task whose fulfillment will bring God's blessings upon us.

When Fallenstein met Emilie Souchay, she was already thirty years old and had never thought of marrying. She seemed by nature destined far more for the quiet, gentle, contemplative life of a nun than for life at the side of an energetic man who never stopped striving. All she knew about marriage was that it was a spiritual communion and an affectionate friendship between a man and a woman. Nevertheless, Fallenstein's intensive courtship brought her into conflict with herself, and she requested time for reflection. When she made an affirmative decision in spite of her misgivings, it was because her goodness had overcome her anxieties. She felt that God Himself had called her to be a helpmate to Fallenstein and a mother to his orphaned children. "It was hard for him to have to place such a burden upon me, and at first this kept him from expressing himself. But I felt strong in my awareness that God had given me such a great and beautiful task and in my confidence that He would help me to see it through."

The letters exchanged by Fallenstein and Emilie Souchay are characteristic of the style of the time (1835) as well as of the writers' personalities.

With the perplexity of a deeply moved heart, I, a man whom you, dear madam, may hardly have noticed, dare to take a step prompted by an inner necessity that sweeps away conventional considerations; and yet I struggle to find the words to tell you what has become a dear consciousness for me since the moment you came into my life. May the kindly graciousness that your blue eyes and your entire appearance betoken permit to speak without a further struggle for expression.

It is the confession of a heartfelt love ventured with anxious embarrassment by a man to whom life has brought many trials and who has faced humanly more dangerous things with greater equanimity than he now faces you.

The one I embraced twenty-five years ago with the first ardor of young love, the faithful, gentle woman whose first love I was, who shared my life in hard times over a period of twenty-one years, who was my very own, who calmly and trustingly lay in my arms from her fifteenth year on through all the vicissitudes of life, the dear mother of my six children whom I buried four years ago, suddenly stood before me again as though brought back to life in her full individuality, her entire inner and outer being and life, when I suddenly caught sight of you on that evening at your brother's house. The impression stirred me to the innermost fibers of my being, and the surprise was not entirely without pain. A further consequence is this step that I am taking, and I feel that my future, madam, depends on its result—all the more so because your appearance has so wondrously intertwined my entire past with the future destined for me by God that I can, in truth and before God, offer to you, my gentle, amiably quiet Emilie, with my hand the love of my youth and of my life, cleansed and beautified by what I have lived through and lost. Before taking this step I have conscientiously searched my soul. If you, dear lady, could like God look into my heart, if I could bare it to you through speech as it lies before our Creator at this moment, you would trust the simple, sensible words of an honest man who assures you that what he expresses to you is a deep-rooted sentiment—not a love born of passion, but one based on the most sincere and most steadfast devotion, one that has been transfigured from profound mourning over what has been lost into the most heartfelt joy at what has been regained.

I realize, dear lady, what I am demanding by imploring you to be not only the second mother of my children, but their regained mother, and to become the greatest treasure of my life. I have nothing to offer in return but an honest, faithful heart, but at the same time I am offering you my life in heartfelt devotion. Wonderful Emilie, as dear to me as my blessed Betty: I have only been able to say simple, religiously composed words, for my heart is wondrously stirred and yet solemnly serene. It is now exactly twenty-five years since I became engaged to my dear departed Betty, and just four years since she slipped out of my arms and into the grave. At a time of such commemoration the human heart does not lie. Decide now between us; no matter how you may decide, my worshipful love for you is my property and will be my companion even in renunciation.

To this Emilie Souchay replied:

I do not know whether it will be possible for me today to answer a letter that moved me to the bottom of my heart the way I ought to and should like to. But I will try to tell the noble man who has opened his heart to me with a hitherto unsuspected wealth of love what my feelings are, even though as yet I do not understand them myself. It is my solemn resolution to be quite frank with you, because I feel that this will be a blessing for you and for me; but only God, who knows me better than I know myself, knows whether I shall be able to tell the truth, even with the best of intentions. Until now my life, viewed externally, has been a very happy one, and it would be ungrateful of me not to make a joyous acknowledgment of the favorable circumstances in which I have lived. Nor have I, particularly in recent years, had any desire to leave my station in life—especially since I believed that my character was not suited to giving anyone happiness, at least not in a situation where great demands were made of me. Those who know me more intimately will verify this for you better than I can.

My mother has promised me to inform you of all my faults and weaknesses. Give credence to her and be assured that no one feels the truth of her words more than I do. At first I could not suppress the thought that you were simply mistaken in me because I evoked such a dear image in your soul. My sister confided this to me, and you can imagine how moved I was bound to be when I saw you again. Only my firm resolve not to destroy this dear memory willfully could give me some composure—or, rather, it put me in a mood of such exaltation that I seemed to be a different person.

When you left, a vision of possible happiness laid hold of me, but at the same time I had a feeling of total inability to fill such a place, and since then this feeling has oppressed me in many a difficult hour. Then my heart grew lighter again, and I felt confident of being able to place my future and yours in the hands of the eternal Father. Everything in me was confused, and only one thing became ever clearer: that I must heed the pure voice of my heart and be truthful toward you and toward myself. Believe me, as soon as I clearly recognize it as the will of God, I shall leave the circle which is so dear to me—not without a struggle, but yet with joyous courage—in order to fulfill an even finer calling. But how could I ever have dreamed that such a fate was in store for me, of all people? Give me some time to regain my full senses after the first excitement, and consider how greatly your happiness, too, depends on the decision that I shall make. In any case, the memory of those beautiful days will accompany me through life and give me happiness, and may God grant that it will be a blessing for you as well in one way or another.

It was high time for Fallenstein to glide into a more peaceful port on his life's journey on the gentle arm of a new wife. His energies, which had been taxed to their limits so early in life, were beginning to diminish and he was subject to depressions. The fact that he was finally free from financial worries was a great relief. The Souchay family had the same generous impulses as he had, as well as the means to indulge them. He was now able to gratify his desire to help others generously. But he also had to suffer many disappointments, personal as well as professional. The disappearance of his sons, whom he never saw again, must have upset him a great deal. When the overworked man requested an assistant, his application was rejected. He then tendered his resignation and was hurt by the reproaches with which it was accepted. In 1842 he was transferred to the Ministry of Finance in Berlin as an official making reports [Vortragender Rat], but was unable to adapt to the very different conditions and assignments there. The man who had done extraordinary things for so many years now candidly acknowledged the bitter experience of not being equal to the new job. Fortunately he was able to leave the post after a few years.

He moved to Heidelberg, and in 1847 built himself a spacious house of quiet elegance opposite the castle on the Neckar River. He himself planned the large rock garden, which extended all the way up to the Philosophenweg. His house and garden, with its bubbling spring that blended with the rushing of the Neckar River, became an island of beauty which was home to his children and grandchildren and a pleasure for countless others. For the rest, he kept the stoical simplicity and naturalness of his way of life, and he demanded these qualities of his family as well: rising early, washing with cold water, every kind of hardihood, the utmost exertion of willpower, and self-control. All these principles were adopted by his daughter Helene for her own life and the rearing of her children, even though her delicate constitution suffered when she was a child.

Fallenstein remained tirelessly active. In public life he was particularly interested in the promotion of peace among the different creeds as well as the retention of the Code Napoléon in the Rhineland. His hatred of Napoleon did not prevent him from preferring Napoleon's institutions to those prevalent in Prussia at the time. He was particularly convinced that the forcible removal of the Napoleonic institutions would alienate the Rhineland from Prussia. In addition to his political interests he was active in charitable work of all kinds; for example, with the aid of the Souchay family he organized systematic relief through loans of money or cattle for the small farmers of Schönau, one of the starving villages in the Odenwald.

He also started writing again, collecting German proverbs and working as an industrious contributor to Grimm's Dictionary.[8] In Heidelberg he joined the "Historical Circle" that had formed around Schlosser and Häusser,[9] and he struck up a friendship with Georg Gervinus, the historian, who moved into his house. With a true official's loyalty Fallenstein clung to his fatherland Prussia, but around 1848 he completely abandoned his monarchist cult and began to love Germany more than Prussia. In the balmy southern air he returned to the libertarian ideals of his youth.

Although not in perfect health, Fallenstein still seemed to have the strength of a giant once he acquired an aim in life. He died at the age of sixty-three as he had always wanted to die: "young," that is, before the infirmities of old age could beset him. His young daughters from his second marriage "remembered as in a beautiful dream" their father "whose warm hands we still felt in ours and whose kind heart was always alive to a child's questions and joys."

In the memory of those who had known him, he lived on as a man who was equipped with an abundance of physical and moral strength, who had grown tough in the school of life, who was passionately excitable, strong in love as in hate, but at the same time most kindhearted and chivalrous toward the weak. He lacked moderation and balance, and he was often irksome and burdensome in everyday life, but in his work his devotion and self-abnegation overcame his impetuosity. In the judgment of Gervinus, "Because of his abundance of strength, everything about him verged on the excessive—the emotion of the moment as well as the well-reflected "permanent principle." (These words apply to Fallenstein's grandson, Max Weber, as well.) His survivors inscribed these words on his tombstone: "All who are led by the Spirit of God are sons of God." [Rom. 8:14]

* * *

But how did delicate Emilie Souchay fare at his side? According to a letter she wrote to a friend long after her husband's death, she was denied the profound happiness of complete spiritual harmony and communion. Her husband's vigorous nature—which made him think that he could demand and obtain everything from himself and others and evidently never left any

---

[8]Jacob and Wilhelm Grimm began publishing their *Deutsches Wörterbuch* in 1852.—Ed.
[9]Friedrich Christoph Schlosser, 1776–1861, Heidelberg historian; Ludwig Häusser, 1818–1867, historian and politician.—Ed.

doubt that he, Friedrich Fallenstein, correctly saw what should be done—
prevented him from understanding her constant inner struggles. He was impatient with Emilie's permanent sense of inadequacy and her pious acceptance of the limitations nature had imposed upon her and others. She was
so good; why, then, did she torment herself so? And although he himself
remained rooted in the faith of his fathers, her religious depth remained inaccessible to him. He was a rigorous moralist who wanted, and was able, to
do what he ought to do and who was convinced that it was the same with
others; she was a submissive soul, lacking confidence yet trusting in God;
they were bound to talk past each other.

Thus, long after her husband's demise, Emilie summed up her married life
in these words:

The hardest struggle of my life is behind me (or so I believe): the impos-
sibility of communicating my true self to my late husband. His great
overestimation of me made him regard my failure to attain the ideal
that was in my heart—a failure inherent in my individual capacity—as
a kind of recalcitrance. He lacked any appreciation of this, and my sorrow over it seemed weakness to him. It was indeed hard for me to bear
the fact that he did not understand this, that he could not imagine
that despite a sadness about one's own imperfections one can still cling
to *hope,* that it is possible to acquiesce in the limits of one's nature
and still strive, within these limits, to attain what God has bidden
us to do, confident that He will lead us to the goal (for it is said
that *God* is powerful within the weak, and to me these are words of
truth which have comforted me on a thousand occasions). In short, it
was hard for me that he could not grasp what to me seemed the very
foundation of Christianity, and this came between us just when daily
life brought us sorrows. The way in which he rejected me irritated me
and kept me from pouring my heart out; otherwise we should have
adapted to each other much better and in all things. As it was, the
treasures of his mind and heart became clearly visible to me only on occasion, and his religious views in particular, and how these views affected his life, remained a mystery to me. I did always sense that he
was a much warmer person than Gervinus and thus more farsighted. For
example, he agreed to my going to church; afterward he liked to have
me retell him the sermon, and he did not pour cold water over me,
as G. did with his wife. But he did not consider it important to have
an exchange of ideas about it with me, and yet pure Christianity was
the essence of my life and all my longing was directed toward fathoming
it. —Where has all this taken me? I merely wanted to clarify in my

mind what made me very unhappy, more so than I now understand, over a period of years, without my having been able to blame either myself or Fallenstein for it. It simply seemed to me—and seems to me now—that a woman should be very close to her husband in all things if the marriage is to be a blessed one.

Emilie Souchay passed on her ideas about the spiritual foundation of conjugal life to her daughters; like her, some of them were unable to realize this ideal. But in spite of her resignation her life was blessed, for the promise of her favorite biblical saying was fulfilled. She gave birth to seven children, of whom four daughters and a son lived to maturity. And under the burden of her tasks the timid, shy woman became a giant in moral strength. Her saintly kindness, gentleness, and self-denial gave her strength for everything that was asked of her. Her stepsons found her a loving, understanding mother who valiantly protected them from their noble-minded but all too violent father. They thanked her with respect and devotion. Time and time again she must have brought out the chivalry, tenderness, and kindness that lay dormant in her husband. In her self-abnegation she was a model of religious, moral living and spiritual depth to her daughters, who were endowed with far greater vigor than she. They felt that their mother's mere existence was a decisive influence on them. The impression she made on her descendants even in her old age has been described by one of her granddaughters:

When I think of Grandmother Fallenstein, I am reminded of the biblical passage about the grain of mustard seed which is the smallest of seeds and yet produces a tree in which the birds of the air have nests. One could hardly be "smaller," and not merely in stature, than this wealthy patrician daughter. She was shy, without any external brilliance or self-assurance, and completely oblivious of her own self. She had no desire to assert herself. But none of her grandchildren would ever have wanted her to be different. A child cannot be misled; it heads toward what is important. Grandmother was good, always good, at whatever hour we came to see her; that was definite, and this is why it was always good to be with her. Everyone agreed on that: big and small, poor and rich. We usually were wild boys and tomboys, but I don't remember that we ever took our wildness into Grandmother's blue room, which was like heaven to us. I never saw her unfriendly, ill-humored, or impatient. Nor did I ever think that she might be so. I am convinced that she kept the boys in check as she did me. One

could not help being well-behaved in the face of such tenderness. I was
no paragon of virtue, but whenever I opened the door to her room, I
stepped into an atmosphere of quiet goodness which mysteriously embraced me, covered me like something gentle and cozy, and penetrated
deeply into me. . . . I never even saw Grandmother weep, but I often
saw her comfort others—for example, my mother when she had lost one
of my little brothers—and I sensed her power over people's minds and
hearts even when I did not understand it. But she knew nothing of
her quiet power. Grandmother's joy in nature was infinitely deep, but
it was as quiet as her whole being. She reverently absorbed all beauty,
just as she listened to good music almost as though she were dead to
the world. She was utterly lost in thought when, in the evening, she
would look at the brilliant lights reflected in the water, or at the
moonlit river and mountain landscape. Later I found such pure enjoyment echoed in a number of little poems. Calmly and joyously she
viewed all earthly beauty, which always was only the outer covering of
the divine. What I received from her, and mysteriously and amorphously
absorbed in my childhood, I was able to see in clear outline only when
she had long since been taken from us. On the day of my confirmation
it rushed in upon me from the words with which she prefaced her book
of memoirs and which sum up my fragmentary recognition of her personality, that her quiet, trusting self-denial combined with a profound
religiosity to produce not resignation but the most beautiful inner
harmony.

Before we leave Emilie Souchay, let us read her words that provide a bridge
between the unending suffering of the world and God's love, the bridge of
a faith constantly regained by struggle:

Our last conversation was so brief and yet so full of substance! All the
pain that pervades the world and the human heart was in it. In the
end I can say only one thing: that without a fight, a life-and-death
struggle, no true peace may be obtained. Why there must be such a
fight is the great unsolvable riddle. It is an impenetrable secret for us
that from the hands of the all-loving Creator there could emanate a
world which by its entire organization causes the creatures living in it
unspeakable suffering. And because of the spirit of knowledge which God
Himself has breathed into him, the greatest pain of all is given to man.
. . . Nevertheless, it has been engraved on our hearts that God is everlasting love: again and again, out of our profound spiritual distress, we
raise our eyes to Him as the Savior and Redeemer. When a new day
dawns after the dark night and the early light lies over the fields, we

feel blessed. Then all of us who have in so many dark hours struggled in vain for comfort and strength are suddenly flooded by the radiance of the sky and feel that we too are in the heart of the great Father and that these beautiful words are true: "Blessed are those who hunger and thirst for righteousness, for they shall be satisfied." [Matt. 5:6]

II

Of the surviving children of this couple, different in so many ways and yet harmonious in noble-mindedness, we are here concerned only with Helene, Max Weber's mother. But all four Fallenstein sisters[10] had unusual qualities of mind and heart. All of them were endowed with an emotionality that made their lives at once rich and difficult, and with a courage that let them face their futures without fear or constraint. They mastered life equally by virtue of their religious resources and their store of energy, with an ethical passion and selfless kindness shaping their daily lives. As consubstantial flowers from the same stem, they were very close to one another all their lives.

Born in 1844, Helene Fallenstein grew up in the house on the Neckar into a young woman of captivating sweetness. She had grateful and affectionate memories of her father, with whom the little girls had played fearlessly before losing him at an early age. Although in her youth she was delicate and subject to frequent headaches, she adopted his principles early in life and lived by them the rest of her life. An iron will, activity, a heroic moral stance, excitability, fiery dynamism: these she inherited from her father. But her mother, so delicate and helpless toward life, made an equally deep imprint upon Helene's character. It was not hard for Helene to make her mother's unearthly goodness, purity, and selflessness the yardstick for her own behavior, because her mother was profoundly religious and utterly unselfish.

Helene's sisters remembered various incidents that were characteristic of the growing girl's courage and impulsive kindness. One summer day around

[10]Ida, the eldest daughter from the second marriage, became the wife of the Strasbourg historian Hermann Baumgarten; one of their sons was Otto Baumgarten, the well-known professor of theology. Henriette married the church historian and poet Adolf Hausrath in Heidelberg. Emilie was married to the Strasbourg professor of geology, E. W. Benecke. The only brother, Eduard Fallenstein, a student, died in France in 1870 from the hardships of the war. [Hermann Baumgarten, 1825–1893, also taught history at Karlsruhe. Otto Baumgarten, 1858–1934, was a professor at Kiel from 1894 to 1926. The geologist and paleontologist Ernst Wilhelm Benecke, 1838–1917, was a professor at Heidelberg (1869) and Strasbourg (1872).—Ed.]

noon, when her mother was resting, a rat strayed into the living room. Since the gardener was not around and the sleeping mother was not to be disturbed, Helene herself killed the horrible animal by skillfully grabbing it around the neck and drowning it in the well outside. Another time a wo-man peddling apples came into the house. While they were bargaining, the woman collapsed on the floor. The young girls saw immediately that it was not a simple fainting fit. A doctor was sent for, who told them: "The woman is dying. Someone will have to get a carriage immediately and take her to the hospital." But young Helene, her eyes flashing, declared: "If the woman is dying, she will not be taken away; she'll die in our house!" And this is just what happened.

Helene, unaware of her own inner beauty, once mentioned the sensitivity that she and her sisters had inherited from their mother: "It often makes life hard, but I enjoy it with humble gratitude as a God-given treasure."

Life smiled from all sides upon the lovely rosebud of a girl. She was exceed-ingly charming, as beautiful as she was good, and she had a fiery, receptive spirit. People enjoyed being with her and loved her. But her conscience kept her from getting a false sense of security. On the contrary, the more ap-proval came her way, the more she searched her soul for a right to it. In retrospect she wrote about her development:

> The view of the intellectual world around me as well as my increasing understanding of the selfless work of our mother then brought me a period of brooding self-torment as I thought about the sources and manifestations of the egotism which is present in everything, even the noblest stirrings of men. Yet I did not wish to tell anyone about this, out of a not entirely unfounded concern that this too might have been caused by an urge to be regarded as fascinating and important. But Ida must have noticed it at some time. After all, she herself had too much of a tendency to brood, and, as on many other occasions in my life, she showed me a goal when she said, "You know, you are so busy wondering where and when the devil called 'egotism' will make an ap-pearance that you miss the best opportunity to overcome him by thinking, acting, and caring for others. Try to think of this every eve-ning and give thanks to God when you know that you have done something kind, good, and useful for someone." It worked.

When, later, the exuberance of youth and the good fortune of being loved by people heightened her self-awareness, the words of a motherly friend, Mrs. Gervinus, gave her inner direction:

I was becoming accustomed to accepting quite superficially, as something quite natural, all the beautiful things that life gave me. . . .
We had been dancing at a large party for the first time, and I told
Mrs. Gervinus how much I had danced, how nice the people, whom I
hardly knew, had been to me, and how annoyed I had been that Emilie
H., who was much smarter than I and the sweetest person in the
world, had been a wallflower. —"Well, my child," so she said, "let that
be a lesson in modesty and humility to you. You are lively, you like to
chat, and you have a friendly face. That is why people are so obliging
to you and give you credit for things even without knowing whether
they are really there. Let that motivate you every time really to accomplish something, to show yourself worthy of this trust."

As an old woman, Helene added to this memoir, which was intended for
her children: "Even today I am deeply embarrassed when people who hardly
know me give me credit for something."

The religious atmosphere that permeated Helene's home was a free and
completely undogmatic one, as was true even then of southern Protestantism in contrast to the tradition-bound North German *Rechtgläubigkeit*
[orthodoxy]. And this freeing of Christianity from the obligation of believing in the divinity of Christ, His vicarious suffering, and the Apostles'
Creed appeared to that circle as a rescue, as the only means of preventing
the age from abandoning its "character" and halting the destruction of
community consciousness. This "liberal" Christianity, which desired to overcome the *credo quia absurdum*[11] in order to reconcile faith with reason,
had much militant pathos in those days.

One of the leaders of this movement in Heidelberg was Pastor Karl Zittel.[12] His gentle, cheerful piousness evoked not a self-righteous God but
a loving God the Father, and he did not torture himself by pondering the
unknowable. When asked his views on immortality, he would cheerfully reply:
"Children, I am willing to be surprised." Helene was confirmed in his church
and was grateful to him for the rest of her life. In addition to the quiet
depth of her mother, Zittel's pure figure instilled in her soul the value of
religion.

But the intellectual struggle, from which Zittel's nondogmatic doctrine
had for a time saved her, was touched off by influences from someone else.

---

[11]"It is to be believed because it is absurd"—from Tertullian's *De Carne Christi,* one version
of "Tertullian's rule of faith."—Ed.

[12]1802–1871, theologian and politician, city parson in Heidelberg from 1848 on.—Ed.

Gervinus, Fallenstein's friend, lived on the upper floor of the house. After the latter's death, Gervinus became the daughters' fatherly friend and teacher, a man they adored. His wife, too, was one of the persons whom the sisters regarded as higher beings. The childless couple became particularly close to Helene. The "aunt" took care of the girls' musical training and the "uncle" gave them an appreciation of classical civilization. He read Homer with them, and that poet became Helene's enduring possession. "Our lessons in Homer again came to mind; and I remembered how for years we really were completely filled with his ideas and views and saw our ideals embodied in an Athena or an Apollo. It again became quite clear to me how beautiful those days were and that what Gervinus gave us was really the best, for even today I get a very wonderful feeling when I read a bit of Homer." When Helene, approaching old age, visited Rome for the first time, she owed her appreciation of the ruins to those lessons.

During her childhood and adolescence, to be sure, she had to pay dearly for this expansion of her mind. She was too thoughtful and profound not to be shaken by the conflict between the Christian and the classical view of life. She was aware of her respected teacher's inclination toward the world of temporal beauty and earthliness and felt it as a "temptation" to apostasy from her own self. The certainty of her childhood faith crumbled, and it took severe struggles for her to feel religiously sheltered again. At the age of seventeen she wrote about this:

I remember that once I had frequent, long conversations with the Good Lord in which I asked him about *everything* and received answers; I can still clearly hear the inner voice that answered me. That gave me an inward peace that I no longer know. Certainly this childlike faith that accepts everything without examining it cannot endure, nor should it endure. Actually, everyone fashions his own religion for himself. But everything was taken away from me by the lessons of the uncle who wanted to explain everything rationally and who always advised me to fashion religion for myself by means of reason; but with one's reason one cannot find a faith. At that time I was not aware of what I was losing. I just lived from day to day, although my relationship with Gervinus often caused me severe crises of conscience.

Dealing with the gods struggling in her own heart was of little significance, however, when compared to other dangers and storms that Gervinus caused her delicate soul and for which she felt ill-prepared, all the more so because of her religious uncertainties. When she was sixteen, a chaste, closed bud of a girl, Gervinus, whom she respected as a teacher, loved like a father, and had trusted for years, one day lost control of himself. The aging man suddenly engulfed the unsuspecting girl with the searing heat of a passion beyond control. She was torn by horror, disgust, pity, and her old grateful devotion to her fatherly friend and teacher. Because her nerves were delicate, she came close to a breakdown. Helene never got over this shock. From that moment on she regarded physical passion as guilt-laden and subhuman. Even when she was an old woman, the memory of that experience would bring an expression of horror to her face. The incident was particularly disastrous because Helene felt the man's passion was a great injustice to his wife, whom she respected and loved. Helene now had to keep her distance from her without being able to tell her the reason. At first the secret was so well kept that Mrs. G. did not understand the change in the girl's behavior, and for a long time resented what she took to be Helene's ingratitude. As for the demon-ridden man, he continued to feel entitled to Helene's confidence, even to the control of her mind and her future, and expected her to show him her usual openness after a short separation. He even made plans for her future, choosing one of his students for her husband.

But things happened differently. Helene went to Berlin to see her sister Ida, who meant so much to her and who had recently married the historian Hermann Baumgarten. There she met his friend and political partisan Max Weber, a doctor of laws. At the age of twenty-four he was intelligent, promising, and very attractive because of his sunny disposition, his joy of life, his unsullied purity and buoyant warmth. They soon fell in love. Helene was only sixteen and a half. Despite generally voiced reservations about their youth, and after only weeks of acquaintance, they made plans to marry. Helene returned to her parental home secretly engaged. This event seemed to be a divine dispensation. The young man recognized the value of the treasure he had found and gave to the beautiful, sensitive girl the controlled, chaste love of unspent youth, a love she returned with increasing affection. Her fiancé brought her not only a sun in which she bloomed magnificently, but also freed her from a painful situation that she could not handle. He became "home" to her, her protection from the tempest of an uncontrolled passion that had loosened the still tender roots of her life. There was profound gratitude in her love, and in keeping with her nature she repaid her beloved with humble devotion, and was ready to make any sacrifice. The young girl was jubilant:

Oh Max, my dearest, only Max, look, whenever I am alone like this and think of your love, imagining you the way you really are, your whole dear personality, I always have the feeling that I cannot grasp it, cannot believe it. I am beguiled by a dream (and what Chamisso expresses so beautifully and *truthfully* certainly is no exaggeration).[13] And yet I also feel that we were bound to find each other, for I can achieve complete happiness only through a firm, close union with *you*.

Her fatherly friend's reaction to her engagement once again brought her great distress. When she visited him for the first time after her engagement, she found him inconsolable. In a violent outburst of despair and rage, he accused her of being ungrateful and of deceiving him by blocking his marital plans for her. Helene felt that she was at the end of her strength.

If I did not have my Max, Mother, and you, my sisters and brother, I think I would jump in the Neckar at the thought that it is now all over between uncle and me. You cannot imagine how hard it has been for me to bear this, particularly because of the way he looks at these things. He is bound to despise me completely, and despise me he does. You did write me what he thinks about it, but he cannot have told it to you in such harsh terms as he did to me. Each of his words was a stab in the heart, and I can still feel the pain. And yet I cannot be angry with him; rather, I regret with all my heart that he is inflicting such terrible pain upon me and himself, for he was terribly emotional about it and cried like a child. Oh, Ida, seeing the strong man weep and being unable to console him, because he did not want any comfort from me, made me suffer terribly. When I left him, the world at first seemed like a tomb; and if later I had not realized that so many people love me so much and that the fight I could have fought would not have been a good one, I don't know what might have happened. But I was thinking of Max, the man whose big heart full of love belongs to me.

Weber was equal to the situation, and he was quite prepared to stay with his betrothed through this great crisis. His attitude inspired her complete confidence:

For me it is a boon to hear from you as much as possible about your relationship with Gervinus. I truly yearn for a chance to bear *everything*

---

[13]*Ich kann's nicht fassen, nicht glauben, es hat ein Traum mich berückt*—the beginning of the third song in Adelbert von Chamisso's poetic sequence, *Frauenliebe und -leben* [Woman's Love and Woman's Life], set to music by Robert Schumann (1840) and also by Carl Loewe.—Ed.

together with you. You need not fear that anything will distress me, nor should you think that I shall reproach myself unduly with having caused all these bitter experiences. Of course, I should lack any understanding of the closest, most intimate relationships between people if the entire occurrence had not profoundly moved me, if I did not regret the disruption of such a fine relationship from the depth of my soul and for the sake of the entire family, for your sake and mine, and especially for the sake of Gervinus, who is not only your respected and beloved fatherly friend but also the man with whose name I have associated a certain enthusiastic admiration since my boyhood, whom I have always regarded with pride as one of the foremost men of our fatherland.

Helene needed his assurance to escape lasting injury. She was still young and weak, and her nerves were severely shaken. The first picture she gave her fiancé shows not a happily engaged sixteen-year-old, but a beautiful woman made mature by sorrow. Weber wrote about it: "Your dear, dear face looks at me so seriously that I could almost get worried if I did not know all the things it expresses. . . ."

The proximity to an uncontrollable man remained so unbearable that soon after the engagement Helene went away for several months. Even after her return a satisfactory relationship with Gervinus could not be restored. A full year after her engagement she had to tell Weber that she got frightened during a chance encounter with Gervinus at a concert:

How I should have liked to feel your dear, faithful hand gripping mine, or your arm about me; then I should once again have had the blissful feeling that in these faithful arms, on this warm and loving bosom I am safe and protected and that this is the place for me. And I would also have liked to show you off, my magnificent Max; I am so terribly proud of you and conceited about you.

With the transfiguring strength of her adoring love, Helene even regarded her unproblematical fiancé as a religious rock where she could take refuge from her inner struggles. She took everything seriously; even love was not able to displace her constant struggle for God.

Things do not always go as smoothly for me on the inside as it may look, and in matters of faith and religion, the firm trust in God, I can still learn a great deal from you, for in these things I have by no means attained clarity. In all this I was disturbed and deprived by my association with Gervinus, and it is very hard to regain it. . . . When I vainly tried to find a way out of all the entanglement, when I was about to despair at the seemingly insurmountable obstacles that arose between my love, between you and me, the scales fell from my eyes. Where was my support? I did believe in God's omnipotence, in His dispensation, but I could not surrender to Him trustingly, I was not able to say from the depths of my heart, "Father, not as I will it but as thou wilt," and even after our betrothal I had not yet learned to place my confidence in God again. Then you came along with your pure, believing heart, and although you may not have known how things were with me in that respect, you did set me on the right path with some of the things you said. You have no idea how happy you have made me with this, but you must believe me when I say that I owe it largely to you if I have come closer to finding God again. But my dearest, only Max, you will also help me, won't you, not to lose courage if I find out, as I recently have, that I have forgotten how to seek and probe; I know you will help me to go on trying all the same!

III

But what was the family background of this young man? He too had a very valuable heritage, although a less unusual one than Helene's. His father, Karl August Weber, was a linen dealer in Bielefeld. The family had belonged to the commercial upper class for several generations, and it was held together by a proud sense of kinship. The ancestors were said to have been expelled from Salzburg because of their evangelical beliefs, and to have introduced the linen trade in their new home. Weber's grandfather, David Christian Weber, was co-founder of Weber, Laer, & Niemann, the first big firm through which Bielefeld linen became famous. As co-owner of this firm, Karl August married Lucie Wilmanns, the daughter of a distinguished physician from a respected family. At first the couple lived in an elegant house built in the Empire style. In this house, which is still standing today, they led a life of intellectual stimulation. Later the business declined because of technical innovations to which the old directors could not adapt, and they had to content themselves with a more modest standard of living.

Everyday living harmoniously followed the firmly established cultural norms of bourgeois notables. This life reflected the comfortable small town with its industrial future, on which the nation's intellectual and political life made little impact. When Helene and her mother called upon Weber's family for the first time, Bielefeld seemed to the girl "like a little town in Goethe's time, when he wrote about Hermann and Dorothea."[14]

In those days the linen trade was still carried on by home labor in "early capitalist" fashion: making money was neither an end in itself nor a sign of success, but was primarily a means to a comfortable life that was appropriate to one's class. Accordingly the pace of work was slow. As a man getting along in years but still not old, Father Weber would rise at six in the morning following a time-honored custom, and then work in his large garden for several hours. He would often give a "leisurely" reading for the women who were busy preparing vegetables. He did not walk to his office until around eleven o'clock. Going to the club for a drink in the late afternoon and enjoying a bottle of good Bordeaux were part of his day. He later lived in the memory of his grandson Max as a most amiable, kindly, and refined old gentleman whose type he preserved in his book about the "spirit" of capitalism. The grandmother looked at the world through beautiful, alert eyes; her fine features indicated a lively intelligence. The atmosphere of the house was a religious one. The women in particular were under the influence of the Protestant orthodoxy prevalent in Westphalia and displayed a sterner moralistic attitude than the more flexible men.

The visitors, Helene and her mother, who were also profoundly religious but who were far more liberal and had no dogmatic ties, noticed that the inhabitants of the house assembled for morning and evening prayers. Emilie Fallenstein commented on this: "I confess that this is very much to my liking, and I am deeply touched when dear Max looks at his Helene so lovingly and obviously with the most beautiful and sacred intentions for the future, and I feel that we belong to one another in time and eternity."

When Helene's fiancé came to visit her, he gave in without resistance to the religious rhythm of her home, and in this harmony Emilie saw the surest guarantee for her child's happiness, a happiness that she herself had been denied. "I suppose I have always felt it, but with each day it has become clearer to me and made me more happy: our deepest inner striving is the same, thank God! And in this certainty I confidently commend my child's happiness to your care. I know that your life will praise God and please men. There can be no greater happiness for a mother."

Helene effortlessly adapted herself to the customs of her new family,

---

[14]Goethe's idyllic verse epic *Hermann und Dorothea* appeared in 1798. Contrasting peace and revolution, it tells the story of a refugee girl who is wooed and won by Hermann, a noble-minded youth from a small town that has the virtues of unspectacular industriousness and moral decency.—Ed.

loved her future parents-in-law dearly, and was loved by them in return. From them she devotedly learned all the hallowed rules of bourgeois housekeeping. These had more weight here than at home in Heidelberg, for her mother-in-law was a housewife of uncommon worldly wisdom, and of course her sons held her up to their young wives as a model of excellence. Learning the special family style of cooking and baking to which the men were accustomed was in those days regarded as one of the most indispensable foundations of marital happiness, a happiness that seemed to depend decisively on the man's comfort. Helene was willing to acquire whatever could assure the well-being of her future husband.

Everything seemed to combine into a joyous harmony, and no one who saw the beautiful, affectionate young couple had any doubts that they had been destined for each other to all eternity. Astute observers saw only an overeager obligingness and submissiveness on the part of the girl and an excessive readiness on the part of the young man to accept her services and let himself be spoiled without limit. But a shrewd psychologist who could have compared the documentation of Helene's inner struggles with the man's philosophy of life as expressed below might have been able to notice that the apparent harmony of the personalities of the couple was really an illusion, one of those self-deceptions typical of happy lovers who make Eros harmonize with each personality, with each other, and with the whole world. "I hope that you will in all that life may bring adopt this principle of mine: let no real *worries* arise (in our weakness we all too easily create worries for ourselves); instead, do at all times what is right and be firm in your confidence that everything will happen the way it is best for ourselves and for all. I have always had this firm belief and shall not let anyone deprive me of it."

* * *

The twenty-four-year-old lawyer was employed by the Berlin municipal government, edited a liberal weekly, and soon became active in politics. The times were extremely eventful and exciting. When Prince Regent Wilhelm had taken over the government, he had appointed predominantly Liberal ministers in order to show that he took the constitution seriously. "The new Liberal era" was supposed to begin; the Liberals had reason to hope for great times in which they would finally make their political ideals prevail. But after promising beginnings everything bogged down again; the elected representatives of the people had only modest power, the *Herrenhaus* [upper house] remained a stronghold of the Conservatives, and the movement toward parliamentarianism was opposed as a revolutionary development. The most important constitutional right was fiscal control. In the spring of 1862 the House demanded a more effective method of approving and supervising the governmental budget. The crown wanted just the opposite, for King Wilhelm I wished to double the standing army. There was a grave constitutional crisis. The Liberal ministers were dismissed, the *Landtag* [Regional Diet] was dissolved, and the king found himself at the end of his political resources. At that point he called upon the man whom he had rejected for years: Bismarck became Prime Minister and dared to govern without a budget for seven years. Under him the Prussian state prepared for military expansion, great-power politics, and German unification under the leadership of Prussia. The country was greatly agitated. To true patriots Bismarck appeared to be the evil demon of the fatherland, the corrupter of liberty and unity.

Weber experienced this exciting period as an impressionable young man to whom any occasion for fighting and action meant an enhancement of life. He was no more of a democrat than Hermann Baumgarten, but he was decidedly liberal. As a twelve-year-old boy he had lived through the days of 1848, and their fervor was still burning within him: "The magnificent impressions that those tumultuous years, so singularly splendid in their wealth of ideal hopes and enthusiasm, made upon my youthful spirit will be alive in me for as long as I live."

He now belonged to the Constitutional Party, one of the parliamentary factions on the right wing of the Liberal Party. Its aims were both "a strong Hohenzollern kingdom and full recognition of the rights guaranteed the people." When the new elections to the *Landtag* were being prepared, he became secretary of the central election committee in Berlin and thus established an early contact with important and experienced politicians.

You can imagine that I am having a most interesting time here. I come into contact with almost all areas of the state and am establishing close relationships with a number of the most respected and most capable political experts in the entire country. I often feel quite strange when I find myself in the company of all those dignified old gentlemen who have been known as champions of our constitutional way of life for decades. . . . In short, I must say that I really am in my element, and all this activity, which has by no means supplanted my work for the city, gives me exceptional pleasure.

* * *

When the young people were able to be united in marriage after a two-year engagement, they were radiantly happy. They loved each other with all their hearts, and the young wife was effusively grateful. After several years of marriage she wrote to her husband:

> None of my sisters is as well off as I am, none can be one heart and one soul with her beloved as I can, except when I am being "foolish." Recently, when Ida happened to say, "Well, you see, the ideals one dreams of are never fulfilled," I could barely keep from telling her how *my* ideal has come true—the way I had never imagined and believed that such wealth could be in store for a foolish young thing like myself in the shape of you!

Weber now occupied the post of magistrate in Erfurt. The comfortable pace of life in the provincial town and the modest style of their household gave the couple enough leisure to be heartily young and gay. A circle of good friends gathered about them, and everyone was captivated by Helene's charm and Max's fresh, unpretentious *joie de vivre*. When Emilie Fallenstein visited her children, she gained a most favorable impression. "As a housewife Helene is really in her element. However, up to now she has taken things a bit too seriously, especially domestic economy. But that will pass; it really is only her exaggerated conscientiousness, because she *is* practical by nature."

Regarding the cultivation of their intellectual interests, the young people were on their own. As compared with the breezy Heidelberg atmosphere, in Erfurt there was an intellectual calm. At Ida Baumgarten's suggestion, Helene studied the writings of the undogmatic Anglo-American theologians Parker and Channing,[15] and in the early years of her marriage she occasionally managed to draw her husband into the depths of her inner life. In 1867 she wrote to Ida:

> Max and I celebrated Easter by reading some of Parker's speeches, and Max too liked them extremely well—the one about the ideal of a Christian church; then the one about belief in immortality, which really is especially beautiful and convincing; and the one about Jesus' relationship to his time and all times. Max is always so busy and he

---

[15]Theodore Parker, 1810–1860, Unitarian preacher, theologian, and reformer. His *Works* appeared in 14 volumes between 1863 and 1870. William Ellery Channing, 1780–1842, clergyman, abolitionist, and writer, founder of the American Unitarian Association. (*Works*, 6 volumes, 1841–43).—ED.

has to read newspapers and such; that is why he has little chance to take up anything else, no matter how much it may interest him. . . . Erfurt is quite dead in this respect. Nobody is interested in such things, except for a very small circle to which the theologians, however, do not belong. People know nothing about the efforts of the Protestant Congress, and many do not *want* to know anything about it, for they regard it as radical and incompatible with their views. I tell you, all the theologians in your city and in Heidelberg are a pure delight compared to the ones here. There is life there, they do their own work and research and do not merely hash over the old things like the theologians here. . . . We need a powerful man for our time who will awaken the dreamers . . . and Parker could have the same relationship to him as John the Baptist [had to Jesus], paving the way for him.

It is evident that the twenty-three-year-old woman, who was now leading a richly fulfilled worldly life at the side of a beloved husband and with two small children, had the same intensive religious interests as before. The following lines addressed to her trusted sister show that in other respects, too, she was not changed by the abundance of her happiness and the atmosphere of affection and admiration around her.

I think I would be terribly discouraged even today to see all the things that can be accomplished by strength of will and then not feel strong enough to emulate them. Sometimes I think that I have advanced in some things, made a little progress since my wedding, but then there are always days when it is evident that despite all those good intentions everything remains the way it has been. But Max must not know about such moods; he does not laugh at me, but he thinks it is quite unnecessary to have such thoughts, and will not admit their validity.

Strange! Despite her wonderful talent for being good—or perhaps because of it—her life, like that of her far more delicate mother, was marked by great inward struggles. Helene always applied absolute standards and in every situation demanded the utmost from herself. Therefore, she was never satisfied with herself and always felt inadequate before God. Always ready to take the responsibility for everything that did not go the way it should have, she took all failures to heart, though the reason for them was never moral inadequacy but only lack of prudence or nerve.

The woman who won everyone's heart had a favorite verse that she often quoted to express what she thought of herself: *"Bist du am Stock ein Röschen,*

*Gott danke für und für; bist du am Stamm ein Mööschen, so dank' ihm auch da-
für.*"[16] Helene, who to others was a magnificent rose, saw herself as only
a little bit of moss when she compared her achievements with those of
others. Instead of enjoying her beauty and abundant capacity for love to
the full, with humble resignation she kept coming up against the limitations of her personality. It also seems strange that, as a woman of twenty-
four, she expressed a wish that she was to repeat on many occasions: "Ida,
I was so pleased that you share my views about the attractiveness of *old
age*; I cannot get this out of my mind, and yet they laughed at me for
expressing such a fantastic idea."

Why was it that in the midst of happiness and with her rising strength,
this young woman frequently yearned for the quiet of old age? Later evidence enables us to surmise the reason. Whether it was because she, like
her mother, was unsensual by nature, or because her religious feeling rebelled,
or because the terrible experience in her youth had sullied that emotion
for her forever—for whatever reason, the physical aspect of marriage was to
her not a source of joy but a heavy sacrifice and also a *sin* that was justified
only by the procreation of children. Because of this, in her youthful happiness she often longed for old age to free her from that "duty." But old age
was still far off. In the meantime, motherhood gave her temporal happiness
again and again. Each child was to her a gift of God, and each one made
her love bloom more luxuriantly.

---

[16]"If thou art a little rose on a bush, thank God forever; if thou art a little moss on a
tree, thank Him for that, too"—apparently one of the album verses that were popular at
the time.—Ed.

2

PARENTAL HOME
AND YOUTH _____

One year after their wedding, on April 21, 1864, the Webers' first son was born at Erfurt. He received his father's name and he was followed, at intervals of two years, by seven brothers and sisters. Two of the little girls died, but four sons and two daughters grew to maturity. The eldest son later remembered that in his childhood he had had the feeling of being the "son and heir" and a profound sense of the privilege of "primogeniture," which soon gave him a feeling of responsibility for his younger brothers and sisters.

His birth was very difficult. The child's head was too large, Helene contracted a fever, and she was not able to breast-feed him, as she did her later children. This was done by another woman, the wife of a Social Democratic carpenter, and the boy dreamed his first weeks away in a laundry basket under a carpenter's bench. When later his social and democratic views developed in opposition to the political heritage of his ancestors, the family used to joke that "Max drank in his political views with his nurse's milk."

His mother and grandmother were astonished at the early self-sufficiency and playful absorption of the little boy, who did not seem to need anyone. Emilie told a graphic story about the boy of two and a half:

> He usually plays by himself, but his playthings—or, rather, the remnants thereof: little balls of yarn, pieces of wood, and suchlike—keep him company in a way that I have seen with no other child. For example, this morning he first built a railroad station with his blocks, put in a train with little carriages filled with freight and passengers, and placed on the locomotive a long strip of paper that was wide at the top and narrow at the bottom, to indicate the smoke; then he expressed surprise at the long, thick smoke and invited us to be surprised as well. Afterward, with the aid of a footstool and the strips of paper, the blocks turned into a salt mine with many flags on top—all of it an original invention interwoven with memories of Pyrmont.[1] He will play like that for hours, chattering almost incessantly.

On his walks the child frequently went by a railroad overpass and was mysteriously enveloped by white smoke from the locomotives being shunted below. Playing with trains occupied him for a long time, and when at the age of four he traveled to Belgium with his mother, the sight of a derailed locomotive made a lasting impression upon him. When he passed that spot on a later occasion, he described his impression as follows: "In connection with Verviers I remember the first 'jolting' experience of my life, a train derailment thirty-five years ago. What jolted me was not only the event itself, but the sight of something so exalted to a child as a locomotive lying in the ditch like a drunk—my first experience of the transitoriness of the great and the beautiful on this earth."

Soon the boy became dangerously ill with unilateral meningitis, which left him susceptible to cramps and congestion for years. He now slept in a bed with padded sides. The danger of dying or of becoming an imbecile cast a shadow over the life of the weak child and over Helene's happiness. Looking back to that period, she wrote: "It marked the end of any lighthearted enjoyment; but on the other hand, I was vouchsafed the profound joy of striving to perform my maternal duties to the neglect of everything else." The young mother now tended her child constantly and never left the house without leaving word as to where she might be found. She had always been uncommonly conscientious, and several years of caring for her firstborn

---

[1] Bad Pyrmont: town in Lower Saxony, a health resort with brine springs.—Ed.

child made her totally self-sacrificing with all her younger children as well. She was never again able to understand that a mother could entrust her small children to strangers for more than an hour during the day, let alone at night. She regarded trips taken by parents without their children as frivolous "temptations of God." Despite this, two of her children died—fateful events, as we shall see.

During his illness, little Max's head grew conspicuously, while his limbs remained girlishly small. The doctor predicted either hydrocephalus or room for a great many things under the arching cranium. Max suffered all kinds of nervous anxieties as an aftereffect of the disease. Helene reported about the four-year-old child:

> His nervous peculiarities and anxieties are gradually decreasing a bit. When I ask him to get something, he now goes up to the house from the garden and back down again all by himself. Just a few weeks ago he refused to do so, especially because he has to pass the chicken yard, and he seems to see something uncanny about the chickens . . . he now gets along better with other children too.

At Borkum she used to carry the five-year-old boy into the ocean, thinking that this would make him stronger. But every day there was so much screaming that the bathers demanded a stop to the treatment. Even as a grown man, Max Weber did not forget the terrors of this procedure.

* * *

In 1869 a new phase began.

The senior Weber received a call to Berlin as a salaried municipal councillor, and soon after he began his parliamentary career as a National Liberal deputy. At times he was a member of the Landtag [Regional Diet] and the Reichstag [Imperial Parliament]. At first the family lived in a rented apartment, but soon it moved into an attractive small house at 19 Leibnizstrasse, Charlottenburg. The house was located on the outskirts of the city and included a garden about two-thirds of an acre in size. There the children were out of the metropolis and grew up with sunshine and plenty of elbowroom, almost as though they were living in the country. The garden with its lovingly and carefully tended fruits and vegetables, and with chickens and cats, was a source of enjoyment. The family grew, and the life in which there pulsated the rhythm of the metropolis and of politics quickly turned into a broad, quickly flowing stream in which peaceful hours were to be had only by an extreme exertion of willpower.

Helene found it increasingly difficult to make her husband share her own intellectual and religious interests, for they were not really vital necessities to him. His public life, his position, his politics, and his social life claimed his attention. He was busy with meetings all day, went on election trips, and often spent his vacations traveling alone, or, later, with the children. He regarded himself as the natural center of his family life, and at home he expected to find happiness in love as well as comfort and service.

Helene had more than enough work to do. There was always a "little one" in the cradle, and her physical strength seemed to increase with each new task. She did not let anyone else take care of the babies, and superconscientiously watched over the development of the schoolchildren. She was incapable of turning heavy work over to the servants, since she lacked both organizing talent and the desire: "I cannot let other people work for me." As a young housewife she was up at six in the morning to wash the children's diapers, and even in her old age she burdened herself with domestic chores of all kinds. She could even be found on the roof when snow had clogged the gutters. She knew everything and was able to do any job. Her limbs moved with joy and graceful strength, and her striding gait was especially beautiful. But at home she did not simply walk; she jumped upstairs and downstairs to serve her husband and her children, Mary and Martha in one. In the city she used to jump onto the horse-drawn trolley as it rushed past and then jump off again, so as to save the horses the strain of setting the carriage in motion. (She expected her nieces to follow this practice as well, which gave their mothers some misgivings.) Because of Helene's dynamism, the servants under her benevolent tutelage seldom had the satisfaction of doing anything on their own responsibility.

The difficulties of the household increased, because the senior Weber came to dinner at very irregular hours. Their social obligations grew; regular invitations to the deputies were among the father's professional duties. Every day Helene spent her unusual energy to the point of exhaustion. In countless letters she wrote that "in the evening my head always reels." When the children were beyond the preschool stage, she used to content herself with five or six hours of sleep, but during the day she frequently had an irresistible desire to sleep.

In 1875, when she was thirty-one and had already borne six children, she described her day as follows:

So we rise at six, eat breakfast shortly after seven, after (little) Max has practiced. By the time he has had his breakfast and has been taken to school, by the time the sandwiches have been made for the other children and my big Max, the lamps have been prepared and the food has been put out, it is about nine o'clock. Then I put the baby girl, who came to me for her meal at six, into her bath. When I come down, Father Max usually is at breakfast. I have another cup with him, and take a peek at the paper, because this is my only chance to see him now when there are so many meetings. Then I go to the kitchen again, or there is something else to do around the house. At twelve o'clock the baby is fed, and the boys too get the first installment of our late dinner, which we eat at three or four o'clock. But Father Max usually comes home much later, and then I whip up something for him as best I can. At seven the children get their supper. By the time Max (Jr.) is in bed and we have finished our supper, it is nine, and then I am no longer fit for anything sensible, especially if my husband is not at home. So the day passes, and then I ask myself: What have you accomplished other than taking care of food and drink and tending the baby?

A few years later she gave a most charming description of her life with the six children then alive:

The children are all asleep—except for Max, Jr., who is still practicing next door, and I want to use the quiet period before bedtime to write you a few lines again. A little thing like my Lili keeps one on the move all day long, especially if one has to satisfy her hungry stomach every two hours. When she has drunk her fill, she lies quietly in her carriage, plays with her little fingers, and in her zeal sticks her tongue way out. She already has a firm grip and is able to scratch; the other day Arthur proudly showed me the scar of a scratch she had given him on the cheek. The fat little stump is awfully amusing and gentle with the baby; he can hardly keep from kissing her little hands all the time and sings the loveliest songs to her. Yesterday, for example, he sang: "You are my little darling, my little sweetheart, my little kitten, you are true to me!" And two days ago, when she was crying, he tried to calm her by repeating to her in a soothing tone of voice, "Yes, my little sister, you are a good girl, and even when you scream or wet yourself, you are a good girl"—probably mindful of the fact that *he* is not considered a good boy when *he* does such things. Mädi [Klara] already regards herself as something of a big sister. She helps lull the baby to sleep, handles her swaddling clothes nicely, and appropriates all the little jackets that the baby has outgrown or the little shirts that can no longer be mended for the time "when I shall have a live doll myself." Max now looks more and more like a university student-to-be. To my great joy he associates a bit more with boys of his own age, and a few of them occasionally drop in for dinner or afternoon coffee. Twice a week he has fencing practice, and even though I am hardly in favor of this preparation for dueling, it is very good for his health, especially since he dislikes all other kinds of physical training, such as swimming, gymnastics, and skating. Karl is the same harum-scarum as always, but at least he does his homework with a little more care and thus no longer makes life so hard for me. He still has such funny notions and excuses at the strategic moment that one is disarmed even if one is very angry. The other day, for example, when he showed up with the seat of his pants torn for the unpteenth time and I finally got angry, he said, full of indignation: "It's not my fault. The schoolbenches are so worn that I get splinters in my legs. When you have to take a back seat,[2] you always have to slide very quickly, while those who move up can take their time. When we don't know something, we are always told 'Quick, move back a seat,' and that's how the pants are worn out. You might go to the principal and complain about it." Since having to move back looms so large in his school life, I would certainly have every right to complain! Alfred is the nicest child at home and the most useful. He does quite well with the baby and is very proud that recently he rocked her to sleep . . .

In the whirl of work, however, Helene never lost her need for inner composure and regarded as her main maternal task not the physical care of her children but their intellectual guidance. But how difficult it was to wrest this from each hectic day, how hard even to enjoy the children!

Oh, if I could only have more quiet moments for enjoying the children! But now I am going to work for this with all my strength, for one thing that you said has stirred me: that one ought to give the *moment* its due and not always live and work only for the future. I have always labored in the hope of achieving a time of rest and enjoyment of my husband and my children, and how discouraged I felt in those days before Christmas when in the midst of our irregular life and the numerous tasks I always looked forward to Christmas and the holidays on which I would really enjoy the children once again. And then . . .

---

[2]The reference is to the flexible seating order in German classrooms, based on academic ratings—from *Primus* to *Ultimus.* —Ed.

Well, and then, right after Christmas of 1876, a four-year-old daughter, an exceptionally lovely girl, died. It was the first deadly sorrow to afflict Helene after thirteen years of a happy marriage.

* * *

Helene had already lost a child in the first years of her marriage. Infant Anna was on this earth only so long as a small snowflake that quickly melts, and she therefore left but light traces in her mother's soul. The four-year-old daughter named Helenchen was already an enchanting human being, and her days of suffering lent her an early perfection. On Christmas Eve the child recited a little verse, in a somewhat husky voice. The next day a malignant diphtheria appeared. The hours spent at the bedside of the little darling, who died resigned to the will of God, were indelibly engraved on the mother's heart. She did not rebel; she was too pious for that. She submitted, but the earth, of which the child no longer was part, changed. "Spring brings me no blossoms, for my rosebud is crushed." She suffered profoundly and longingly. She yearned to follow the child to eternal rest, but for the sake of the others she did not give herself the right to do so.

In still another respect this event was a fateful chapter in their lives. Although her husband had at first shared her profound shock, he soon left the mother alone in her life-and-death struggle. It was part of his nature, typical of countless men, to evade prolonged personal sorrow and not to let his *joie de vivre* be disturbed for long: "He did not go with me." Thus Helene for the first time became aware of a distinct rift in their spiritual community, a rift that was never to close again. The struggling woman was too selfless and did not believe that she could draw her husband into her world of grief. She veiled her feelings from him and shared her sorrow with her distant sisters. She now became aware of something that must have been growing within her: the clear realization that her husband, the love of her youth, was spiritually entirely different from her and that neither she nor fate would be able to transform him. Though she was modest to the point of self-disparagement, she instinctively applied unshakable standards to the emotional life of others, standards her husband did not meet. Helene wrapped herself in renunciation and inner loneliness, and the inevitable estrangement from her husband began. Her mother's belief that there was a spiritual bond between the couple turned out to have been a delusion, as was true of the mother's own marriage. Over the years, particularly after the money Helene inherited from her mother improved their material lot,

Weber *père* came to share his circle's desire for inner and outer well-being, for a comfortable bourgeois standard of living, social status, and the like. He did not want to suffer. But the woman at his side slowly grew away from him, withdrawing into herself and acquiring new interests that he did not share. At first he did not notice that she was living on another plane, for she continued to serve him with loving submissiveness.

As an old woman Helene blamed herself for not having taken her husband along into her world. Long after his death she wrote to her grown children:

> There came the deaths of the children which I had to bear all by myself, partly because of the circumstances, partly because it was repugnant to my husband's personality, so full of health and lightheartedness, to share the pain of death with me. In so doing I had to fight for my belief in God and my interest in all religious development, an interest he did not share. In those days I regarded it as being considerate, as God-ordained resignation, that I bore my sorrow alone and did not force him against his nature to go along—and yet it was cowardice, fear of being misunderstood in these most difficult and most private concerns. I had no idea that the consequence would be our growing apart inwardly. For at that time I was, despite everything, so happy that often I did not comprehend how the people around me could look so gloomy and serious. My own demeanor was supposed to tell everyone that life was not like that.

Helene's vitality and religious humility enabled her to weather the sorrows of those days. After all, new and promising life kept blossoming all about her—six well-developed, gifted children—and since she also loved her sisters' children as though they were her own, her love was able to expand to wider fields. But she knew what life had in store, and from then on she extracted some significance from every death. Whenever she was shaken by the sorrows of others, she found consolation in the knowledge that her little darling was sheltered from life's struggle.

> If one sees such terrible suffering and the even more terrible things that one man does to another—often merely because he is incapable of empathizing with his thoughts and feelings, and how this destroys the best in human beings and in what they desired and were meant to do in this world—the thought of a young life dedicated only to happiness and joy of living which was removed from earth with this dedication still intact can be a real comfort to us. The memory of the

calm, peaceful face of my little Helene has always accompanied me as a comfort in times of inner distress. And yet I have so little reason to complain that life is being made hard for me, except for the feeling that I am incapable of fulfilling and being what I demand of myself. This is especially difficult for me now in the face of my son Max.

The meaning of this reference, made in 1880, to her relationship with her eldest son will become clear when his development has been described. Let us return to him now.

* * *

After the family moved to Charlottenburg, the atmosphere of the parental home was increasingly rife with political interests, which were eagerly absorbed by the young sons. As a Berlin municipal councillor, their father was now in charge of construction, and he was instrumental in getting beautiful trees planted to line the streets. In the Prussian Diet he was a specialist in the cultural division of the Budget Committee. He had no oratorical ability and therefore was not a leading politician, but he was an intelligent and judicious one. The leaders of the National Liberal Party frequented his house, some coming as friends, some attending the usual social gatherings: the noble-minded Bennigsen and the agile Miquel[3] as well as other important political personalities, including the deputy Rickert;[4] Friedrich Kapp,[5] a democratic-liberal politician of the older school whose death left a painful gap in the circle of friends; Hobrecht, the Minister of Finance and his brother, an important architect attached to Weber's office;[6] Legation Counselor Aegidi,[7] who was also a professor and Bismarck's secretary in the Foreign Office; Julian Schmidt,[8] the creative literary historian and a close friend; and Dilthey, Goldschmidt, Sybel, Treitschke, and Mommsen, all stars in the academic firmament.[9] A few of the men from this group were among the leading figures who determined the intellectual contours of their time.

[3]Rudolf von Bennigsen, 1824–1902; Johannes von Miquel, 1828–1901.—Ed.
[4]Heinrich Rickert, Sr., 1833–1902.—Ed.
[5]1824–1884.—Ed.
[6]Artur Hobrecht, 1824–1912, and James Friedrich Ludolf Hobrecht, 1825–1902.—Ed.
[7]Ludwig Karl Aegidi, 1825–1901.—Ed.
[8]Heinrich Julian Schmidt, 1818–1886.—Ed.
[9]Wilhelm Dilthey, 1833–1911; Levin Goldschmidt, 1829–1897; Heinrich von Sybel, 1817–1895; Heinrich von Treitschke, 1834–1896; Theodor Mommsen, 1817–1903.—Ed.

The sons of the house—in whom the closer friends of the parents, particularly Kapp, Julian Schmidt, and Aegidi, took a lively interest—were stimulated in various ways by their association with these men. Even as adolescents they were permitted to pass out cigars at dinners for the deputies, and they picked up whatever they could of the political disputes. The two eldest boys in particular, Max and Alfred, became familiar with political problems at an early age and received a graphic presentation of the special character of political life. Added to this were their father's daily stories about what happened in parliament and in the party, and about the leaders of high politics, especially Bismarck, who was greatly admired by the National Liberals at the time.

The knowledge of world history in the making that young Max acquired in this manner remained vividly in his mind for forty years. Even the outbreak of the War of 1870 made a lasting impression on him. The six-year-old boy experienced it in the same place where he later experienced the outbreak of the World War—in his grandparents' home on the Neckar, where his parents spent their vacation. The tremendous tension before the decision; the naive belief in the justice of the German cause; the joyful seriousness of a belligerent nation willing to make sacrifices in order to gain the position of a great power; then the overwhelming victory celebration and the proud exultation over the finally achieved unity of the Reich—all this the child absorbed alertly, and he was shaped by it for life.

Then came his school years at Charlottenburg. The aftereffects of his illness were over, but little Max was a rather weak, small boy, shy and clumsy in all physical exercise. His neck seemed too thin to support his large, pear-shaped head. He had no trouble, however, with his schoolwork, and beyond that his intellectual activity and an independent thirst for knowledge early asserted themselves. His mother reported about the nine-year-old: "Max is engrossed in history and genealogy." And his grandmother wrote:

Max already aspires to higher things. Latin greatly appeals to him. Every day he enjoys the words, and he is happy if one hears him recite his lesson. He has never confused one word with another. But he is now bored with writing. He does his share of scribbling, getting a lot of it on his hands, and it does not seem to matter to him what impression his outward appearance makes. This is gratifying, as is the fact that he is romping about with the neighbors' children and getting his cheeks red. Yet he still finds time to practice his piano for half an hour in the afternoon. He started lessons with a local teacher a short time ago and is enthusiastic about it; his fingers are nimble and his ear seems good.

The boy evidently did not mind writing letters. When his parents were away, they received chroniclelike reports, and when he traveled with his father, his mother got detailed descriptions. Already writing was the form in which he preserved and presented what he had seen and experienced. His childhood letters very seldom contained anything about himself, but a great deal about domestic life and the beautiful outside world which he was eagerly absorbing. In his letters one can hear the ingenious, charming sayings of his young siblings, one can accompany them to school, and smell the scent of the summer garden in which the lovingly tended fruit is ripening, the chickens are clucking, and the countless feline families are disporting themselves. The twelve-year-old writes:

> Important news! Kittens!! Two weeks ago the red and yellow cat had a litter of four kittens on Zerbe's bed (!!). Then the gray one had four under the staircase leading to Miss Blum's veranda; one of these, a black tomcat, is our particular guest. Then the "old one" had three in Dad's john—a black tomcat, a gray one, and a gray cat. The kittens of the red and yellow one have been drowned; the others were much too big for that when they were first noticed. So, another seven cats (!!!!).
>
> Max.

One can also share in the summer outings to the Havel lakes, and in winter one can see a giant snowman intently staring at the frozen landscape with his eyes of coal. From letters to a cousin, who will be discussed shortly, we learn how Max, as the eldest son, followed an old family custom and hung nuts (which he had gilded himself) and cookies on the Christmas tree, with an old-fashioned Christ Child enthroned on the top; how Helene, for whom this festive period had been tinged with profound sorrow since the death of her daughter, after tireless activity finally sat with her flock before the closed door in the magically darkened room and sang the beautiful old songs; and how the children's paradise then opened up, how the little ones were enchanted by the radiance of the Christmas tree, and slowly found their way back from the sacred miracle to their own more prosaic selves. In describing what went on, Max already used a variety of technical terms:

> The doll you sent for Klara has been appropriated [annektiert] by Arthur, and he remained in possession of it despite most emphatic protests from Klara and a number of attacks amidst loud yelling from both parties [Fraktionen]. He so fell in love with the doll that he wouldn't

let it out of his hands, and finally it even had to go to bed with him. Klara, to be sure, attempted its recapture [*Rückeroberung*], but she did not succeed and realized the futility of her intentions. Thus the doll will probably become Arthur's property by virtue of the statute of limitations [*Verjährungsrecht*].

In summer the father frequently took the three oldest boys along on his trips, and on long hikes he showed them the magnificent German countryside. A nephew made these remarks about it: "An accomplishment for which not every father would have the patience and the nerves! Words cannot describe the mischief the three rascals are capable of and all the roughhousing they must have every day to be happy." Long, diarylike epistles from the fourteen-year-old Max take us through Thuringia's towns and forests as far as the Rhine. They show how the boy, who was not at all occupied with himself, reverently absorbed the beauty of the earth and everything that satisfied his historical imagination. We can hear the merry laughter of the traveling companions when the eight-year-old Karl makes his droll remarks. And we can experience the reverential awe the older boy felt when he was first surrounded by the halls of the Cologne cathedral.

Paulinzella, August 1, 1878

Dear Mama,

I promised I would write you a letter from Erfurt, but we have time to spare now, so don't be offended if I already give you some news about us. On the train Karl[10] remarked: "Papa, there must be a city called Paris around here; it says something about it in the station." After we had explained to him where Paris was located, he said: "I don't know that either, I haven't got a photo yet." In Kösen we left our things at the station and went to the Wirtshaus "Zur Katze" [Cat Inn]. While we were having lunch there, a gray and white cat came near our table. "Aha," said Karl, "there's the famous cat the inn is named after." Then we took a ferry over the clear water of the Saale to get to the Rudelsburg. . . . The old castle is perched boldly and handsomely on a ledge overlooking the Saale. You probably know it, for if I remember correctly, Papa told me that you two have been there. Anyway, they have excellent beer and good coffee up there. The view over the Saale Valley is not particularly extensive, but it is very pretty. One wooded peak after another comes into view; woody heights and cultiva-

---

[10]Eight years old.

ted valleys with little towns and villages may be seen. While we were having coffee, Karl suddenly disappeared. We looked for him and found him sitting in a room by the window and looking down at the valley. He said he was watching the railroad trains. "Why do you suppose the ancient knights weren't able to do that?" Papa asked him. The answer: "Because they didn't have the time." We left the Rudelsburg and got onto a path that ran alongside a corn field and a narrow trench that was about twenty feet deep. We jumped down into this trench and invited Papa to come down too, because it was much easier to walk there. To everyone's amusement he really came down. Soon, however, the ditch narrowed to a rocky gorge on both sides of which rose steep rock walls about twenty feet high. At length we came to a barrier of rocks that we climbed over. After a lot of climbing we finally got out of the gorge. "Papa," asked Karl, "how did you get over those rocks, anyway?!" And Alfred said: "We sure got Papa into a tight spot there!" Then we came to a pretty place underneath a big linden tree. On it there was a sign that said: "Fowling Place. The Kösen Municipal Council Apologizes for Having Forgotten the Benches." From there we went to see the saltworks. When Papa explained these to Karl and spoke of *Soolbäder*[11] [salt-water baths], Karl said: "Oh sure, I know about those, they're spelled with two o's." Then we walked across the town and went on a pretty, wooded, uphill path to the Kaiser-Wilhelmsburg, which, by the way, is very modern. We heard the pealing of the church bells. "Oh," Karl said, "that stupid church really could stop tinkling; now the locomotive might think the station was ringing and might come roaring up." . . .

From Naumburg we traveled up the beautiful Saale Valley to Jena. You probably know how it is surrounded on all sides by cultivated mountains. From the train one sees the Fuchsturm rising up on the left, while the city is on the right. . . . As soon as we entered the city we saw several fraternity taverns with the appropriate flags. Then came a monument to some professor, followed by the house in which Goethe and the two Schlegels[12] once lived. Finally we came to the crown of all fraternity facilities, the Burgkeller. This is where Uncle Baumgarten used to carouse, and even now one can see students' caps flashing and two fraternities' flags fluttering overhead . . . Jena certainly is a very pretty and friendly place, a real student town, like Heidelberg. From the center of the city we walked steeply uphill on the right

[11]This spelling is now obsolete.—Ed.
[12]The brothers August Wilhelm Schlegel, 1767–1845, and Friedrich Schlegel, 1772–1829, were among the leading figures of German Romanticism.—Ed.

bank of the Saale, and after walking through a pine forest, some of which was beautiful, and along almost dangerous precipices we came to the Fuchsturm, the remnant of an old fortress which, like so many others, was destroyed in the well-known fratricidal war.[13] . . . [There follows a detailed description of the Fuchsturm.] When we arrived in Schwarza, the weather was very nice, and we immediately headed for Schwarzburg. For the first three-quarters of an hour the road was sunny but not particularly pretty as far as Blankenburg. From there, however, it makes a left turn and leads into the picturesque Schwarza Valley, always along the bank of the river. We first went to the Chrysopas, an inn on the road, then farther up the Schwarza Valley through one of the most beautiful parts of Thuringia. On both sides rise steep walls which, however, are timbered with pine trees, and on the left the Schwarza River turbulently roars along. Now and then some slate rocks appear, arrogantly and provocatively jutting out into the fine forest air. There were a lot of strawberries too. After three hours, at five in the afternoon, we arrived at Schwarzburg, and you probably know its pretty location and appearance. We spent a very nice evening sitting on the terrace of the Hotel "Zum Hirschen" [Stag Hotel] and looking down at meadows with herds of stags, at calm treetops, and at the rushing Schwarza . . .

On the return trip he wrote:

At nine in the morning we left Mainz and sailed down old Papa Rhine on an express boat that called only at Biebrich, Koblenz, and Bonn, and we reached Cologne as early as half past four. . . . The trip was delightful and gave all of us much pleasure. Only at the end did Alfred and Karl seem to get bored. They began to fool around, danced up and down with their deck chairs, and rolled over each other, or they sat by the engine or down by the paddlebox and watched the motion of the wheel and the resultant waves. [There follows a description of the boat ride.] So we arrived in Cologne at four-thirty. An enormous crowd of people stood on the shore. No sooner had the boat landed when a lot of porters and baggage handlers rushed up, grabbed bags indiscriminately, and carried them off. Naturally, everybody started shouting for his suitcases. *"Na, was hat'n Sie 'n?"* [Well, what've you got?], a porter

---

[13]The tower referred to is the sole remnant of castles once located on the Hausberg, the Greifberg, the Kirchberg, and the Windberg, all of which were destroyed in 1304. The *Bruderkrieg* to which Weber refers was fraternal strife in the princely house of the Wettins.—Ed.

asked Papa. "These two cases here, to the main railroad station." "You go ahead, I'll be there before you, *young* man!" But we did not leave right away; we waited for quite a while, at least a quarter of an hour. Then a cab came along, with three gigantic trunks loaded on the coach box; on the topmost one sat the coachman, and he looked very brave: "*Vorsüüücht!*" [Look ouuut!] The trunk lying on top started to wobble and lay at an angle. Monsieur Coachman slid back and his legs landed on the coach box; he had trouble resuming his proper position. From the railroad station we went to the cathedral. We entered through the future main portal and immediately were under the full, truly overwhelming impression of the magnificent edifice. Such enormous height, such pillars! If one looks at these, the building strikes one as an enormous, fantastic structure, but if one observes the majestic Gothic arches, an indescribable feeling of repose and security takes hold of one. Saturday services were in progress, so the ambulatory was closed. We shall have to postpone this for some favorable future occasion, and this also goes for a closer examination of the entire cathedral of which we only tried to get an impression. Then we climbed up. Only from the top can one see the whole wealth of the architecture and the sculpture, and survey the basic design of the entire edifice. More than on the surrounding countryside, which one can see for miles as far as the Siebengebirge,[14] more than on the city, one's eyes rest on the two tremendous towers that are now no longer fragments looking into the future like question marks, but are finished except for four small sections, the towers' future being decided with complete assurance . . .

* * *

But books were the most important thing in his rich boyhood. At an early age Max studied on his own whatever he could get his hands on, history and the classics above all. But he also read philosophy. In *Sekunda* he read Spinoza and Schopenhauer; in *Prima* he especially read Kant.[15] At the age of twelve he told his mother that someone had lent him Machiavelli's *The Prince,* and that he was going to read the *Antimachiavell*[16] and also look

---

[14]"Seven mountains" or hills, including the celebrated Drachenfels, on the right bank of the Rhine, several miles southeast of Bonn.—Ed.
[15]*Sekunda* is the penultimate year, *Prima* the last year in a German Gymnasium or school preparing for study at a university.—Ed.
[16]A polemical work in opposition to Machiavelli written in 1739 by Frederick the Great.—Ed.

into Luther's works. That same year he asked his Heidelberg grandmother whether his cousin Hausrath would enjoy a homemade genealogical table of the Merovingians or Carolingians in return for his gift of a butterfly collection. The fourteen-year-old Max told her that he was busy making a historical map of Germany in 1360: "This map costs me a lot of effort, because I have to gather the material for it from all sorts of genealogies, territorial histories, and encyclopedias. I often have to spend a long time consulting the encyclopedia to get information about the most insignificant village. I am finally finishing it, and I think that once I have mastered the history with the aid of the map, I shall enjoy it very much." In a letter to his mother, the fifteen-year-old boy makes this very characteristic statement: "I don't daydream, I don't write poetry, so what else shall I do but read? So I am doing a thorough job of that." Around that time he was already taking notes on his reading.

At the beginning of 1877, before his fourteenth birthday, Max wrote—evidently as a belated Christmas present—two historical essays "after numerous sources," one "About the Course of German History, with Special Regard to the Positions of the Emperor and the Pope," the other "About the Roman Imperial Period from Constantine to the Migration of Nations"; the latter was "Dedicated by the Author to His Own Insignificant Self as well as to His Parents and Siblings." The text of the second essay is illustrated with a sketch of Constantinople, the family tree of Constantius Chlorus,[17] and daintily drawn heads of the *Caesares* and *Augusti*, apparently copied from antique coins the boy was collecting at the time.

Two years later, again around Christmas, he wrote "Observations on the Ethnic Character, Development, and History of the Indo-European Nations." This essay already incorporates the results of original thought—in the "philosophy of history," so to speak. It aims at an understanding of the entire history of civilized nations and seeks to clarify "the laws governing their development."

He starts out by describing the "nature" and the cultural level of the most important nations, using the distinction between "national emotions" [*Volksgemüt*] as the source of religions and folk poetry and "national spirit" [*Volksgeist*] as a form of intellectual activity that gives rise to "culture" in the true sense. His meaning is made clear by a comparative analysis

---

[17]Constantius I, "The Pale," ca. 250–306, Augustus since 305, father Constantine the Great. —Ed.

of various literary works, philosophies, and religions, drawing on the Orient and the Occident, and in particular on the works of the Greeks. The contrast between Homer and Ossian[18] evidently made a deep impression upon Weber. He gives a detailed comparison of their different ideals of life and attitudes toward death, expressing himself on these points not only in the essay but in letters from which we shall quote shortly. In the second part of his essay the future scholar attempts to show the "laws" governing the political history of nations from the beginnings of civilization to the present. He is convinced that such laws exist, just as they do in nature: "Nations cannot completely abandon the course on which they have set out any more than celestial bodies can leave their orbits—provided that there are no external disturbances, something that also modifies the orbits of the stars." He explains the thousands of years of fluctuating struggle between East and West by the fact that the two main branches of the Caucasian race, the Semitic and the Indo-European, have been divided by insurmountable antipathy. In his view, this antipathy, which can no longer be explained, determined in particular ancient history down to the Middle Ages. And again and again the intermingling of the two elements seemed to him to have led to "Semiticization," that is, the defeat of the Aryan culture. Semitic despotism and religious fanaticism, he says, have repeatedly endangered the Indo-European realms. Even the Battle of Salamis, which assured Aryan rule in the West for a millenium, did not separate them forever. The ancient culture was ruined by the renewed penetration of Semitic influences—among other things, the Christianization of the Occident. From this Max drew a political conclusion: the Indo-Europeans could bear neither an intellectual intermixture nor the "despotic" forms of government peculiar to the Semites. To be sure, the republican form would not have been desirable for them either; "the only political condition beneficial to them, and therefore the desirable kind, is a constitutional government."

The adolescent did almost no work for school, and only occasionally paid attention in class. In *Tertia*,[19] for example, he secretly read all forty vol-

---

[18]The Scottish writer, historian, and politician James Macpherson, 1736–1796, freely edited some Gaelic poems and published them, together with his own insertions, as *Fingal* (1762), *Temora* (1763), and other works purporting to be translations from a Celtic warrior and bard named Ossian, said to have lived in the third century. The first German translation of these supposed relics of a fascinating ancient northern culture appeared in 1764, and Goethe and other writers of the *Sturm und Drang* period participated in a veritable Ossian cult.—Ed.
[19]The third highest class in a Gymnasium.—Ed.

umes of the Cotta edition of Goethe during class hours. He was always the youngest and the weakest in class. He remembered being "lazy as sin" [sünden-faul], devoid of any sense of duty or ambition. He despised any kind of "position hunting." He was not uncivil to his teachers, but he did not really respect them, and he often discomfited them by asking questions they were unable to answer. The friends with whom he used to smoke a pipe and play skat (these included K. Mommsen,[20] W. Dieterici, and F. Cohn) received much help from him with their schoolwork. If there was a gap in his knowledge, he went to the root of the matter and then gladly shared what he knew. Because he was such a good companion and was in no way arrogant, his contemporaries considered him a "phenomenon."

Later his memories of his behavior in school led him to feel that he had been a moral problem child for his mother, even though she smilingly denied it. Some of her letters, however, show that the personality of her precocious eldest son and his increasing reserve and aloofness did cause her sorrow. Once she wrote to Ida Baumgarten, who kept in close contact with her grown sons: "I envy you the inner relationship that impelled Otto to write you such a letter. Will my sons too come to their mother some day, seeking counsel and support in this way? I fear I am too much of a Mööschen[21] for that also."

In those days Helene had to look into the soul of her child by means of a reflected light. In the summer of 1877 and the following winter, Ida's eldest son Fritz was a student in Berlin. Helene took the sunny, amiable, and warmhearted youth into her heart like a son, and delighted in his charming, radiant, youthful freshness. He came and went freely, had an open, sociable disposition, and adored his aunt. His young cousins soon became attached to him. He was studying to be a teacher, and Helene consulted him about the children. The student became completely wrapped up in the Charlottenburg family life and gave his mother a graphic description of the people and characteristic little happenings.

Now that I have been in Charlottenburg for several consecutive days, I am getting to know the people from an entirely different angle. I

---

[20]Karl Mommsen, in later life a bank director, was the son of the scholar Theodor Mommsen.—Ed.
[21]See page 30.—Ed.

understand now why you easily get into fights with Uncle; if he were not my uncle, I would fight with him too. His Helene treats him far better than he deserves. He is a real despot. But he has a rich mind and heart and cares a great deal about the people around him; I already owe him a lot. But I get along even better with my aunt. She has a marvelous way with the children, and yet she always complains that she isn't as good at it as you are. She doubts if her sons would ever come to her the way we come to you, "and even if they came, I couldn't advise them the way your mother does. I don't have the gift of gab." . . .

In Charlottenburg, Uncle received me by lecturing me: How could I be so unpedagogic as to give little Max Grandfather Fallenstein's biographical sketch (for the big genealogical table on which Max is working). What I had always secretly criticized—namely, that Max manages to read so many unsuitable things—had now happened to me! After dinner we took a four-hour walk in the Grunewald, enjoying the wonderful echo along a charming lake in the middle of a pine forest. Max and Alfred came with us, and from time to time Max brought us a clump of earth or a pine cone. Alfred was jovial and shouted with delight. When it got dark, my aunt sang one song after another with her beautiful voice. A full moon appeared, the stars glittered, and uncle and aunt, nephew and son joyfully walked and sang through the forest. Max simply won't sing, but Alfred is an enthusiastic singer. You won't soon find brothers as fundamentally different as these two. On the way home Max told me, not without self-congratulation, about his trip to Strasbourg, and Alfred pricked up his ears. I had a hard time trying not to laugh at the two of them. The parents behind us were giggling too. Alfred was especially funny when he believed every word of the hunting stories I told him.

When Fritz left Berlin again, Max, now fourteen and a half, wrote him regularly, often giving him lengthy reports about everything that went on at home and about what occupied his thoughts. Helene was grateful that the grownup nephew was drawing Max out of his shell. She hoped that this would be a salutary influence and asked Fritz for permission to read her son's letters. These letters show what filled his mind in his fifteenth and sixteenth years: Curtius' *Geschichte der Griechen* [History of the Greeks], the works of Mommsen and Treitschke, a history of the United States, Hehn's *Kulturpflanzen und Haustiere* [Cultivated Plants and Domestic Animals]. He made this incidental remark about his reading habits: "My progress is slow, because

I make many notes as I read." Of fiction writers, he particularly enjoyed W. Alexis[22] and Walter Scott:

> In recent weeks I spent much time on Scott's *Kerker von Edinburg* [*The Heart of Midlothian*]. I don't know whether you have read this book, but it is one of the most stirring novels I know. I always wonder about my schoolmates who devour all sorts of penny dreadfuls and completely ignore these solid old novels. It is a strange phenomenon encountered especially in the upper classes of the Gymnasium that these young people feel far above all sensible novels, although they don't even know some of them. Instead, as I have said, they get pleasure only from sensational little stories. I imagine the reading of aristocratic Rome under the early emperors was like this. It may sound presumptuous of me, one of the youngest and greenest students in *Sekunda*, to make such statements. But this situation is too blatant for me to keep quiet for fear of saying something wrong. There are always exceptions, of course. . . .

His judgments on the Greek and Latin classics—Homer, Herodotus, Virgil, Cicero, Sallust—show precocious, independent mental activity and astounding intellectual intensity. A comparison between Homer and Ossian also shows that he was receptive to poetry and sensitive to the "ultimate realities." For months he occupied himself with Cicero, whom he found "insufferable" because of his braggadocio, phrase mongering, and political vacillation. Apparently he thought that the picture presented of him in school was a false one, and he read all sorts of things by and about Cicero. Roman historical figures and the motivation of their actions came to life for him in all their immediacy. These firm critical judgments from a boy of fourteen and a half began to bother his cousin, Fritz, a student six years his senior, and when he intimated to Max that he had probably copied his views from somewhere, the boy defended himself both modestly and firmly. Helene was not sure whether she should be glad about the young eagle raising his wings or whether his unchildlike scholarship and dialectics were presumptuous and should sadden her. After all, she was still quite young, and his letters were already completely beyond her judgment. Thus she was genuinely happy when he occasionally managed to write a real child's letter, such as a detailed, vivid description of Kaiser Wilhelm's ceremonious entrance into Berlin after the attempted assassination. Here are some excerpts from his letters:

---

[22]Willibald Alexis, pseudonym of Georg Wilhelm Heinrich Häring, 1798–1871, German writer of historical fiction influenced by Sir Walter Scott.—Ed.

You ask me to tell you how I liked the various writers.

Regarding Homer, I am sure you know that I like him best of all the writers I have ever read. The reason for this is really not so easy to find. I think it is not merely because of the beautiful sounds of the Greek language in themselves, but especially because of the great naturalness with which all the actions are related. At least I cannot claim that while reading Homer I have ever had that feeling of suspense which is the basis of novels read for enjoyment and the greatest fascination of dramas. Dramas, to be sure, do not merely aim to arouse suspense and fascination; if they did, they would not be such an important educative force for young and old; yet I find that a drama, in particular a tragedy, would not make much of an impression if it did not arouse suspense. In Homer such suspense is almost entirely lacking. That is why it is much easier to break away from him than from a novel. When I read a novel, I have a hard time putting it down. I should like to go on reading, and when I stop I always have a certain feeling of discomfort. But if one reads Homer, one can stop at any time, put it aside, and start all over again another time—simply because it is not a lively presentation but a story, because Homer does not present a chain of successive actions but describes the origin and the calm sequence of the actions. If a catastrophe occurs, one has long since been prepared for it—for example, Hector's death—while the catastrophe in *Ekkehard,* in *Die Ahnen*[23] and in most other novels, with the possible exception of Scott's, occurs suddenly. In Homer everything has for a long time been unalterably determined by fate, and this greatly diminishes the suspense and the pain in the reader.

I do not like Virgil nearly so well as Homer. In Virgil's *Aeneid* he seeks to arouse a certain suspense, but one hardly feels it, or, if one does, it is not a pleasant sensation. This clearly comes out in Book Four, where the catastrophe of Dido is described. He succeeds in part, but the feeling it gave me was not a pleasant one—because the tension does not arise naturally from the material itself but is artificially created by means of various devices. To be sure, little bourgeois epics like Goethe's *Hermann und Dorothea* would be pointless, they would be idylls rather than epics if there were no suspense, but they simply are middle-class epics. Their subject matter is, as a rule, limited and deals with only one episode from the life of the hero. The real purpose of a

---

[23]*Ekkehard:* 1855 novel by Joseph Viktor von Scheffel, 1826–1886. *Die Ahnen* [The Ancestors]: series of novels (1872–80) by the novelist and dramatist Gustav Freytag, 1816–1895. All these historical works once enjoyed a wide readership.—Ed.

heroic epic like the *Aeneid,* on the other hand, is the utmost glorification of the hero; in addition, it should give pleasure with its beautiful
depiction of details. For that reason it really is permitted to arouse
only a little suspense. . . .

Regarding Herodotus, I can say that I have every respect for him and
his utterly incredible diligence. One can tell from his historical writings that he went everywhere and made the most minute investigations. This fully makes up for his credulity—something for which he can
hardly be faulted if one considers the educational level of his time.
Herodotus was no critic. He did criticize upon occasion, but if one
reads his critiques from our point of view, they frequently are even more
nonsensical than the theories and opinions he criticized. He does not
go more deeply into the inner causes of events. Where he seems to do
so, his explanations usually are products of his own imagination and are
determined by his religiosity and the superstitiousness that sprang
from it. Of course, he is not a completely reliable historian. It is true
that he researched and produced everything with great zeal, but he
particularly wanted to demonstrate the course of fate and the unalterable thoughts of the deity which repeatedly find their expression
in history and by which everything is determined. His manner of narra-
tion is a wholly poetic one. He is close to Homer. His history is an
epic transcribed into prose. He makes very pleasant reading, especially
because of his invariably beautiful, calm language and the enthusiasm
that occasionally breaks through in his books about the Persian wars.

Although Livy lived 400 years after Herodotus, he has the same
faults but not the same merits. He too is a bad critic; what sources
he used and how he used them is difficult to determine, I believe. He
can hardly have used all the old documents that were probably still
available at that time. It was, at any rate, too much effort for him.
He certainly was not as diligent as Herodotus, and since he also lacked
his naiveté and enthusiasm, I have very little incentive to read Livy.

As for Cicero, I cannot say that I particularly like him. I find, for
example, that his first Catilinarian oration lacks fire and decisiveness.
In almost every book about Cicero that I have read so far, I have seen
him praised, but I really don't know what this praise is based upon. It
is certain that he was a person of great moral purity, and he probably
remained quite untouched by all the wild debauchery and hedonism.
But the literature on him makes no reference to this, or mentions it
only incidentally. But his first Catilinarian oration and his vacillating
and unstable policies in general do not impress me at all. He did not
reach a definite decision, even though the danger to the state confronted him in the shape of one man. His entire Catilinarian oration

is really just one long whimper and lamentation. And this in the presence of the most dangerous man, the head of the conspiracy! After all, in the same speech he accused Catiline of immorality, etc.! Did he perhaps believe that if he complained that the state was in danger, an immoral and indifferent man would heed these complaints and abandon his plans because of this lamentation? I do not think so; on the contrary. When he spoke to Catiline about the anxieties and fears of the senate and the citizenry, was he not bound to confirm him in his plans? After all, the substance of his speech was a plea to Catiline for God's sake to leave town. Did he perhaps think Catiline would pay any attention to him? No, on the contrary; if Catiline saw this vacillation on the part of the senate and the consul, if he was able to think that Cicero had lost hope to such an extent that he had to beg him, Catiline, in person, then he and his cohorts were bound to gain that much more confidence. And what about Cicero's shortsighted policy of attempting to remove only Catiline from Rome? If he thought that he would then be able to deal more easily with the other conspirators, he was mistaken. Among the conspirators there were men who displayed energies and intellectual abilities far superior to those of Catiline. And Cicero himself said that he knew the conspirators, so he could not have been mistaken on this score. But even if he was, he did know about Mallius's uprising near Fasulae.[24] If he really managed to get Catiline out of the city, what did it avail him? Catiline then went straight to Mallius's camp, and then presumably the danger to the state was even greater than if Catiline had remained in the city. Could he not have detained him in the city and had him "bumped off"? After all, the conspiracy was evident. No one would have blamed him; he said so himself. What, then, was the reason for his hesitation? He said he wanted to wait until there was no one left who could defend Catiline, and then he was to die. What does that mean? It is not clear to me. Did he think that Catiline's adherents would defect and no longer defend him if he waited a good long time? In this he was really mistaken! On the contrary, the number of his adherents was bound to grow every day, and this too Cicero said in his speech. In short, I find his first Catilinarian speech extremely weak and pointless, his entire policy vacillating with regard to its ends. I find Cicero without appropriate resolve and energy, without skill, and without the ability to wait for the right moment. For if he had arrested and strangled Catiline at the proper time and had nipped Mallius's preparations in the bud, the Roman state would have been spared the tre-

---

[24]The correct names are (Gaius) Manlius and Faesulae.—Ed.

mendous, bloody battle of Pistoria in which so many thousands died in
a civil war. Are you of a different opinion? Should you ever have the
time, write me what you think and what your reasons are. If I have
sometimes gone a bit too far afield or have gotten too excited in the
heat of argument, or have not made myself clear, please excuse me, for
since it is quite late, I have written this rather long epistle very
quickly and hastily. (September, 1878)

Many thanks for your last letter, in which you say that I was too rash
with my remarks about Cicero. Maybe so, but this is what you asked
for. What you said about the influence of bookreading on a person is
very true. Yet I don't know whether you are right to apply it to me in
this particular case, for what you have written sounds as if you believe
that I got some book and copied from it, or at least reproduced the contents of a book read earlier. For isn't that the gist of your long lecture?[25]
You seek to express this main point as vaguely as possible, because
you are of the opinion—an erroneous one, so far as I know myself—that
I would take this sort of thing amiss. Although I have summoned all
my self-knowledge, I have not been able to admit thus far that I have
let myself be overly swayed by any book or any words from the mouth
of our teacher. To be sure, I wrote very fast, and my pen put down
some things that were certainly not my intellectual property; but it
is generally true that we younger ones profit in large measure from the
treasures that you seniors—and you certainly are to be regarded as
one—have accumulated. But I don't remember ever having heard any
important statement about Cicero's character or policy from my Latin
teacher. Nor can I have drawn much from books, for I have only recently
looked this period up in important works, such as Mommsen's history
of Rome. I admit that everything may indirectly stem from books.
What are books for but to enlighten people about things that are not
clear to them and to instruct them? It is possible that I am very sensitive to books, that is, their comments and deductions; this you can
judge better than I, for in certain respects it really is easier to know
a person other than oneself. Yet the content of my—perhaps completely untrue—statements does not directly come from any book. For
the rest, I cannot resent any of your criticism, for I have now found
out that quite similar things are contained in Mommsen. At any rate,
I believe that what I said about Cicero may be derived from a mere

---

[25]Weber here adapts a line from Schiller's *Die Piccolomini*—"*Was ist der langen Rede kurzer
Sinn?*"—which S. T. Coleridge translated as "What's the short meaning of this long ha-
rangue?"—Ed.

knowledge of Roman history of the period. If one reads the first three Catilinarian orations and at each sentence asks himself why Cicero spoke it, one comes to the identical conclusion. With all due respect for Cicero's eloquence, his fine turns of phrase, and his great linguistic and philosophical significance, I don't like him at all in other respects, least of all since reading his third oration against Catiline. Considering the conditions of the time, moral purity is something to be greatly appreciated, even if it is not unblemished. But a comparison between him and Catullus or Cato gives the same result as a comparison between Pompeius or Bibulus and Caesar . . . (October 25, 1878)

Fortunately this obligatory reading (Wieland's[26] poem about the nature of things) is not the only reading I am doing. I have read at least a few other things that were very interesting and enjoyable. These include, first of all, several pieces by Ossian,[27] his most beautiful poems which I had not read before. I don't know if you have read him; not too many people do nowadays. But with respect to language and poetry his work is among the most beautiful imaginable. I am almost inclined to place him above Homer, but surely he is his equal, although he is infinitely far removed from him. His wild poetry seizes hold of the reader from the first moment, and if the reader tries to be receptive to it, it goes round in his head for a long time. I shall not soon forget a *memento mori* like "Death duskily stands behind thee, like the dark side of the moon behind its growing light."[28] Sad to say, I am not, generally speaking, very receptive, but despite this I have never read anything with such pleasure as I did *Fianghal* [*Fingal*] earlier and *The Songs of Selma, Carthoun* [*Carthon*], *Oghthama* [*Oithona*], and others now. When the poet lets us fly over the misty waters in swift sailboats, when he makes us roam about in the roaring forest beneath flashes of lightning or lets us ride over the steaming heath in a raging storm, we get as much pleasure, albeit of a very different kind, as we do when Homer takes us over the blue seas amidst gentle zephyrs and along verdant coasts or lets us sit cozily over a meal in a warm room. Both poets speak about youth from the vantage point of old age, but in very different ways. Homer takes a joyful view of youth, while Ossian offers the viewpoint of a wise old man. He regards young people as happy only in

---

[26]Christoph Martin Wieland, 1733–1813, German writer of prose and poetry. His didactic poem *Die Natur der Dinge* appeared in 1751.—Ed.

[27]See footnote 18, this chapter.—Ed.

[28]This passage could not be located in *The Poems of Ossian*, so a literal rendition of the German translation has been given.—Ed.

the sense that their lives are dreams. Thus he says in a gloomy mood at the beginning of a battle poem:[29]

> Our youth is like the dream of the hunter on the hill of heath. He sleeps in the mild beams of the sun; he awakes amidst a storm; the red lightning flies around: trees shake their heads to the wind! He looks back with joy on the day of the sun, and the pleasant dreams of his rest!

This poem quite clearly shows the sentimental, misty, stormy outlook of the aged poet of the northland, in contrast to the naive, sunny, calm writings of the old southerner. There is another, touching place where Ossian complains that he, the blind old man, can no longer see the beautiful light of the sun. But he bemoans this least of all. His real complaint is that he is no longer able to see wild Fingal, that he has lost the youthful strength of his arms and his youthful courage. What a contrast to the south! There a man knows nothing higher than life, than seeing the beautiful light of the sun ($o\rho\alpha o\sigma$ H$\epsilon\rho\iota o\lambda o$). To a Hellene the beyond is gray, gloomy, and full of terror. To rule over the shades in the dark underworld is the lot of the dead heroes. To the ancient inhabitants of Italy death at least did not appear to be so terrible. Unlike the cattle-raising Hellenes, they were used to receiving all good things from the earth. To the Nordic peoples, however, death seemed to harbor neither terror nor suffering: it frequently seemed desirable to them. This explains the descriptions of battle in the writings of the two poets. While in Homer flight is not deemed disgraceful if a life can be saved by it, Ossian views death as a necessity if flight would be the only escape from it. —Forgive me, dear Fritz, if I have done some blathering again; as I have indicated, it is because I have scribbled so much, have lost control of myself, and simply go on and on . . . (December 19, 1879)

Reading such letters gave Helene an idea of her eldest son's intellectual life, but she continued to be distressed at the veil that was between her and the young soul—particularly at the time of his confirmation, when she tried even harder to communicate with him. His schooling was conventionally dogmatic and offered nothing to his hungry intellect; Max endured it not without respect, but with apparent indifference. A year later he listened with fascination to the lectures of a venerable "liberal" teacher on

---

[29]Weber here quotes from the versified German translation of *The War of Inis-Thona.* —Ed.

the history of religion, and of his own accord he learned Hebrew in order to study the Old Testament in the original language.

Before his confirmation his mother tried to make him appreciate her own religious excitement: "Last Sunday I had some quiet hours with the children, and I asked Max, Jr., to read to me a sermon entitled 'Sunday' by Pastor Riff, an ingenious Alsatian. At first he said he did not feel like it and would prefer something historical or Homer or Dante, but then he started and I noticed how the realistic, forceful style clearly gripped him and made him think." Thus she anxiously tried to interest her son in the world in which she was at home. Yet she had to realize painfully that the fifteen-year-old boy did not experience any deeper religious excitement and, above all, that he resisted her maternal influence. She felt helpless and suffered a great deal because of it:

> The closer Max's confirmation approaches, the less can I see that this whole period of his development has any deeper influence on him that might make him reflect about the things that he is to say in front of the altar as his own conviction. The other day, when I was alone with him once again, I tried to draw him out on what he thinks and feels about the main questions of Christian consciousness. At first he seemed quite astonished at my assumption that the consideration and self-clarification of such questions as belief in immortality, the Providence that directs our destinies, etc., ought to be the result of confirmation lessons for every thinking person. I had such a warm inner feeling of what has become the most vital conviction for me, although it is not dependent on any form, and yet—dearest Ida!—it was not possible for me to express it to my child in such a way that it would make any impression upon him! It is easy enough for Fritz to praise the old saying, "One can quench one's thirst at small fountains, too." But the fountains have to flow! . . . And it has not been easy for me to give up in this instance too, to leave the influence to others or to the times or to experience.

Max's older friend Fritz also tried to penetrate Max's closed mind, apparently at Helene's request, and the boy's answer, which shows that he knew his own nature and was aware of what made him so difficult for his mother, may have reassured Helene a little:

> You ask me about my confirmation lessons and tell me about the good impression yours made upon you. We have a pastor who is in the prime

of life, but this does not really benefit the instruction, because what an older gentleman might lack in energy, he would probably compensate for in venerability. For there are always fatuous fellows who get enjoyment from disrupting the class with their childish behavior. I don't think they would dare do this to an older, awe-inspiring gentleman. Another strange thing is that we have almost no homework, with the exception of a few Bible verses that most students take care of rather superficially. What you say about those who scoff at religion is certainly quite correct, for I really believe that a man who could honestly say he had absolutely no conviction or hope of a hereafter must be an extremely unhappy creature. To wander into life without any hope and in the belief that every step only brings one closer to utter disintegration, a dissolution that ends existence forever, must truly be a terrible feeling and deprive a man of all hope in life. That every man may harbor doubts goes without saying, and I believe these very doubts may serve to make his faith all the more firm once they are overcome. You write about the tremendous impression your confirmation made upon you. Believe me, I too am aware of this important turning point in my life. Do not believe that just because I have not written you or said anything about it my feelings are less great. I believe it is in my nature that I seldom share my feelings with others; I often have to make a great effort to do so. As a rule I keep every joy to myself, but that does not mean that my feelings are slighter. As I have said, it is hard for me to discuss these things with others. I usually keep even my thoughts to myself—at the risk of being considered to have no thoughts at all. For the same reason I am a bad companion too, and, as I am painfully aware, quite inept in conversation—a failing which thus far I have been unable to correct even with the best will in the world.

A later document, a letter about the confirmation of his younger brother, shows that Max was impressed with the solemnity of the *Jugendweihe*,[30] though not in the way his mother would have wished:

There is something peculiar about a confirmation. The solemn ceremony as such really stirred me, because at the time I regarded it as a kind of chapter in my life. But the nature of this chapter was not clear

---

[30]Literally "youth consecration," a term usually applied to the ceremony that replaces the confimation communion in free churches, or to the manhood rites of primitive peoples. In the former sense this ceremony is still practiced in the German Democratic Republic.—Ed.

to me, nor was I able to figure out wherein its essence lay, for of course no noticeable change had occurred in my life. . . . Therefore it is not an easy task to make the sense and the significance of his confirmation clear to a boy from our social class. To me it meant my official entrance into a great community with whose theoretical teachings and views I had become familiar long before my confirmation classes. One naturally seeks the significance of this ceremony in the *practical* sphere. However, for one thing, at this age one is certainly not qualified to be active in this sphere . . . and for another, an *understanding* of the practical meaning of Christianity in one's daily life is something that one can attain only upon another occasion. Thus it surely is no easy matter for a candidate for confirmation to appreciate the significance this day is supposed to have for him, and one can definitely make only modest demands in this regard.

The confirmation text that Weber received was "Now the Lord is the spirit, and where the spirit of the Lord is, there is freedom." [2 Cor.3:17] Hardly any other biblical text could have better expressed the law that governed this child's life.

* * *

With her younger sons Helene experienced the same sorrow of a futile effort to root them in the soil of her own life. Once she wrote about Alfred:

He is having a very hard time. This I notice by the vehemence and stubbornness with which he seizes upon every opportunity to prove that every other view has at least the same justification and probability as the Christian religion. Then he cites Strauss's *Das Leben Jesu*[31] and the philosophy of Kant. I stand there and feel sorrowful and sad tht I cannot help him, because I lack the right words at the right time. And then he too gets the feeling that I do not understand and cannot help him, and this is very hard for me to bear . . . But he is much more approachable in other matters, and sometimes he comes and reads something to me, the only misfortune being that I am so terribly tired in the evening.

The younger son at least consulted his mother about the difficulties of his growing years. The older son by nature endured everything by himself and

---

[31]David Friedrich Strauss's *Life of Jesus* appeared in 1835. Its rejection of traditional dogma and advocacy of an unorthodox liberalism raised a storm of controversy.—Ed.

did not let others notice his inner struggles. It seemed that the more conscious he was of Helene's efforts, the more harshly he withdrew. As he put it later on, his heart in those days was defiant and dismayed. But Helene would not be deterred:

> I am keeping the hours before and after teatime free in order to encourage Max, to whom I cannot give any time during the day, to speak with me or read to me and thus give me some insight into his interests. He hardly feels the need to do so, and considering our very different natural dispositions I must study ways of preventing an inner estrangement between the boy and myself. To my joy it now seems to me as though he has somewhat modified his principle of never saying anything sensible to me, and I am now trying to make him stick to this without his being aware of it. (1880)

Why was it that this charming, graceful, loving woman, so strikingly valiant, humorous, and joyful despite her inner seriousness and so devoted to her children, had no communication with them in their years of development? For the others did not really see in her a companion and a confidante either. Max—she called him "Grosser" [big boy]—preserved a distinct memory of his relationship to her in those years. According to him, one reason for his defensiveness was his secret intellectual arrogance. His mother really had nothing to offer to his precocious, superior mind, and his heart remained a tightly closed bud. He was not yet able to appreciate his mother. And besides, both parents evidently made mistakes in raising their children. They were still too young and too closely attached to the authoritarian tradition to find the right attitude toward this precocious son who had greater intellectual gifts than they had. Firstborn children frequently are the object of excessive moralizing and ill-tempered censure. When Fritz Baumgarten gave his Heidelberg grandmother his impressions of the various members of the family and mentioned that Max, Jr., was still a mystery to him, she replied:

> I was sure in advance that you would like it in Charlottenburg. Helene really is all kindness. Even as a three-year-old child she literally enchanted me with her grace, and she has remained the same both spiritually and physically, except that she has become even more sensible as she has grown older. I can also picture Uncle in his heartfelt goodness and the liveliness with which he argues and *manages* the boys, including yourself. Everything is so simple there, and yet not only the parents

but the children as well are quite different from one another. Regarding Max, Jr., I think he is an inwardly *vehement* person, and somewhat *reserved*. Yet he has a good mind and also goodwill (that is, if someone else's will has not annoyed him). When we were there last summer, it was his job to bring the table wine up from the cellar, and he did it gladly; yet when he had not brought quite the right kind and was scolded, he became somewhat morose. But this will surely change in time. When he was a little fellow in Erfurt, I saw him play by himself for hours; at that time he was indescribably sweet. We took a walk every day, and he had the most original ideas. I believe (and I tell you this in confidence) he needs to be treated with a little more *love* so he can break away from himself.

Weber, Sr., claimed intellectual authority and did not really like young people to hold different opinions. When there were conflicts, he always felt he was in the right. Helene was different; she always saw the reason for failure in herself and this greatly oppressed her: "My migraine was caused in part by my inner despondency—was I taking the right course in many things?—and an inward fatigue that brings to mind the line '*Ach, ich bin des Treibens müde*' . . ."[32]

A statement about her relationship with one of her younger sons shows how she was going wrong without realizing it: "I always ask myself: Am I again going about it the wrong way if I struggle against some things that I would like to change in him? Is he going to withdraw the same way as Max?" The point was that she wanted to change many things about her children. Without being aware of it, and in all humility, she struggled like her father to shape the young souls in her own image. Her justification for this was her consciousness of an absolute, of a divine law that she was executing.

Thus she imposed upon her children, by example as well as by express demand, a way of thinking and a moral attitude they could neither understand nor achieve at their age and with their personalities.. She expected fruit of a certain kind from weak little trees that may have been meant to bear fruit of a different quality. Moreover, she tended to moralize and sometimes rebuked the children in front of strangers—something that her sensitive eldest son greatly resented. She provoked his secret opposition, because she took all faults and undesired events too much to heart. And

---

[32]"Oh, I am tired of this hustle and bustle." From Goethe's *Wandrers Nachtlied* ["*Der du von dem Himmel bist . . .*"].—Ed.

finally, her own exemplary character was a burden. The children secretly measured themselves against her and recognized this ideal as unattainable. Thus the adolescents adopted attitudes of opposition to escape their feelings of inferiority. A strange thing happened: It was not given to this woman, who so enchanted others, young and old alike, to make her own children truly happy in their growing years or to communicate with them. The aloofness of her eldest son in particular seemed to dam up the flow of her love and render it ineffective.

Yet Max's soulful disposition already showed itself from time to time. He dearly loved his youngest brothers and sisters, followed their activities with interest, and wrote his mother letters about them that must have pleased her. For example, he wrote her in 1879, while she was spending her summer vacation in Heidelberg with her two youngest children:

> I greatly miss Klara and Arthur now. Sometimes when I am sitting down here in my room, I seem to hear their cheerful bawling, but it is only the Charlottenburg children playing in the street who give me this agreeable-disagreeable illusion. The house always seems dead to me now; when you come to think of it, a few small lungs can make an awful lot of noise. Of course, Alfred is trying to make up for the noise with his own rooster's voice. Otherwise all is well. We go to school, fool around, and live like clockwork—more quietly, if I may say so. Things have become more idyllic around here, provided that Charlottenburg harbors any poetic, idyllic treasures. . . . I for my part would prefer being with you in Heidelberg amidst noise and uproar to being here in Charlottenburg in poetic peace.

* * *

In those years it was not clear whether the "big boy" would decide in favor of his father's or his mother's type. He already had an obscure feeling that such a choice would have to be made someday—as soon as he got hold of himself and consciously began to develop his own personality. There was his mother, in whom the powers of the gospel were active, to whom loving service and self-sacrifice to the last were second nature, but who also lived in accordance with burdensome heroic principles, performed her inordinate daily tasks with a constant expenditure of moral energy, never "left well enough alone," and quietly placed every significant event in the context of eternity. She was dynamic in all she did, energetic in coping with her everyday chores, joyously open to everything beautiful in life, and had a liberating laugh. But every day she plunged into the depths and was anchored in the supernatural.

Max's father was totally honorable, utterly unselfish in politics and in his job, intelligent, good-natured, warmhearted, and amiable so long as things went his way, but a typical bourgeois, at peace with himself and with the world. He categorically refused to recognize the serious problems of life. In his mature years he loved inner comfort, closed his eyes to suffering, and did not share the sorrows of others. His liberal political ideas could not be put into practice. New ideologies, which might have inspired him to sacrifice himself in some direction, did not kindle his enthusiasm. His cheerful openness to the world, enthusiasm for nature, and the capacity for unpretentious enjoyment; his feeling of being a fortunate person for whom everything worked out, on whose every journey the sun smiled; his ability and desire to look on the bright side of everything—all these qualities predestined him to be a good companion to his growing sons. Although he left their upbringing largely to their mother, he hiked and traveled a great deal with his children and thus offered them a stimulation that is given to few. He was at his most charming on trips; on such occasions he gave up his wonted comforts for his children and was young with them.

Did these parents not complement each other in the best possible way? And was it not natural that the son should have become attached to his father whose nature spared him the uncomfortable feeling of his own inadequacy? Of course, Weber was not very good at being a "good companion" to the precocious boy. He was too much the traditional, patriarchal paterfamilias, too convinced of his own superiority and his inalienable right to respect and authority. Some of his peculiarities—such as the way he let his wife wait on him—drew secret criticism from the children, although they followed his example. Differences of disposition and style soon became apparent. For example, when Max went to Italy with his father for the first time at the age of seventeen, the boy suddenly wanted to leave Venice and go home by himself; he could not bear the way his father expected him to express his enthusiasm. Nevertheless, at that time the youth felt that he had far more in common with his father than with his mother.

3

STUDENT LIFE AND
MILITARY SERVICE

In the spring of 1882, Max Weber took his final examinations [*Abitur*] at the Gymnasium and he also helped his friends to cheat their way through. His teachers certified his outstanding knowledge, though it had unfortunately not been acquired through traditional academic industriousness. But they expressed doubts about the *moral* maturity of the troublesome, inwardly disrespectful youth. Lanky and skinny, a "candidate for consumption" with his delicate limbs and sagging shoulders, Weber, then barely eighteen, enrolled at the University of Heidelberg, animated equally by a thirst for knowledge and the desire to become a robust, vigorous *Kerl* [fellow]. He found a room facing the Castle at the Waldhorn (now called the Scheffelhaus),[1] right next to the familiar property of his grandparents. There he

[1] An inn on the right bank of the Neckar that was the meeting place of the writer Joseph Viktor von Scheffel and his friends from the late 1840s on. It is the scene of Meyer-Förster's novel *Alt Heidelberg* [The Student Prince]. The Scheffelhaus was razed several years ago.—Ed.

happily but quite unsentimentally inhaled beauty and freedom. His letters to his parents contain earthy Berlin humor and reflect a receptive joy of living.

Like his father he chose jurisprudence as his major subject and professional training. He also studied history, economics, and philosophy, and soon began to study everything in liberal arts that was being given by professors of some distinction. He took Roman Law: Pandects and Institutions with Immanuel Bekker,[2] who was at the zenith of his fame, and by his own efforts worked his way into the *corpus juris*—"very hard work at first." The neophyte, who was initially looking for established and demonstrated truths rather than ingenious hypotheses in the realm of empiric-dogmatic science, found the critical skepticism of the legal scholar disturbing. Bekker gave

> too many controversies and doubts, too few firm points. At each point he has to observe that the system's implementation is completely in arrears there and that the courts have not followed any definite practice, that Winscheid holds this view and Ihering[3] believes such-and-such, etc.—all without presenting his own views, which would be something to hold on to until one became familiar with the sources. This makes the law appear much more fluid than it can be, and the great work of legal evolution seems considerably diminished if at the very points where the first great decisions ought to be made one is put off with the explanation that a great gap still exists there.

Nor could Weber stand the extremely dry economics lectures by the veteran professor Knies.[4] Instead he acquired the fundamentals of the subject by reading Roscher[5] and Knies. On the other hand, he was fascinated by Erdmannsdörfer's[6] course on medieval history and his historical seminar, for which Weber soon undertook to present a paper. On the side he read Ranke's *Geschichte der romanischen und germanischen Völker* [History of the Romance and Germanic Peoples] as well as his *Kritik neuerer Geschichtsschreiber* [Critique of Modern Historians]: "Both of these works are written in such a peculiar style that I was at first incapable of reading them; if I were not

---

[2]Ernst Immanuel Bekker, 1827–1916, professor of Roman law at Halle, Greifswald, and Heidelberg (from 1874 on; Rector after 1886).—Ed.
[3]Rudolph von Ihering, 1818–1892, jurist and professor at Göttingen from 1872 on.—Ed.
[4]Karl Knies, 1821–1898, professor at Heidelberg from 1865 to 1896.—Ed.
[5]Wilhelm Roscher, 1817–1894, professor at Göttingen and Leipzig.—Ed.
[6]Bernhard Erdmannsdörfer, 1833–1901, professor at Heidelberg from 1874 on.—Ed.

acquainted with the facts, I would not understand them. Their language is reminiscent of the language of *Werther* and *Wilhelm Meister.* "[7]

Through Kuno Fischer's[8] lectures Weber sought to increase his knowledge of philosophy, for which he had laid the foundations during his years at the Gymnasium. He attended Fischer's course in logic at 7 A.M., but he found that his absorption of Hegel's conceptual realism was not sufficient compensation for the expenditure of energy required by this early start: "I hate the man who forces me to get up at a quarter past six in the morning." The young student was also extremely sensitive to any trace of vanity that might lead lecturers to show off their own personalities. Only when he took history of philosophy in the second semester was he appreciative as well as critical.

Weber's thirst for knowledge did not prevent him from being open to the other side of academic life as well. He was courted by various students' associations. But the *Korps* [students' corporations] immediately repelled him by promising to help him with his "career." At first he was open to all of them, accepted their invitations, and enjoyed himself in their midst. He used the fencing room of the *Alemannen* [Alemanni], his father's fraternity, and had a workout there in the morning between logic and pandects. He accepted the hospitality of the Alemanni and made observations that he later utilized, but for the time being he felt no desire to make any commitments.

He had many other opportunities for social contact. The Hausrath family now lived in his grandparents' house next door. His very gifted and distinguished, albeit misanthropically inclined uncle, who was becoming more and more of a recluse, became interested in the bright student and liked to discuss with him the failings of disliked colleagues or the ills of the times. His wife Henriette, the sister of Weber's mother and like her a wonderfully rich, warm, and deep personality, soon instilled love and sympathetic understanding into him. There were also the Hausrath cousins, male and female, the playmates of his childhood, as well as a cousin who was several years older than Max—Otto Baumgarten, Ida's second son, who was spending the last semester of his theology studies in Heidelberg. Otto belonged to the school of theologians that was free from dogma. Intellectually very active, well or-

---

[7]Prose works by Goethe (1774 and 1795f., respectively).—Ed.
[8]1824–1907, neo-Kantian philosopher, professor at Jena and Heidelberg, author of a ten volume History of Modern Philosophy (1852–77).—Ed.

ganized, and mature, he immediately drew his younger cousin into the sphere of his religious interests. For the second and last time Weber found himself under the influence of an older, superior friend. They would meet over lunch and in the evening read theological and philosophical works together: Lotze's *Mikrokosmos*, Plato, Biedermann's *Dogmatik*, Strauss's *Der alte und der neue Glaube* [The Old Faith and the New], Pfleiderer's *Paulinismus*, Schleiermacher's *Reden über Religion,*[9] and so on. Max attended Otto's practice sermons and even read the sermons of his fellow students with him. He wrote home about these joint readings:

> Strauss's *Der alte und der neue Glaube* does not contain very much that is new, nothing that one would not approximately know oneself. It is simply intended to be a brief encyclopedic survey of the freethinkers' *Weltanschauung* and therefore it is bound to appear rather superficial in many places. Schleiermacher's *Speeches on Religion,* which I have not really got into yet, have made no impression on me so far. On second thought, they made quite a disagreeable impression upon me. Or rather, although I have a fair idea of the man's intentions, they remain incomprehensible to me in their Old Franconian, Ciceronian style. But I am anxious to get to the point and am by no means unaware of the great kindheartedness of the man which often comes through. Pfleiderer's *Paulinismus* is, in any event, very interesting, and even its Introduction promises something significant.

The reading of Lotze was abandoned after a few weeks "full of anger at his unscholarly quality, his fatuous poeticizing, and his tedious emotional philosophizing." Instead, they started reading Lange's *Geschichte des Materialismus*[10] "whose eminently sober mode of development was refreshing after Lotze's *Wust* [mess]—this is the only word for this kind of system, apart from a few outstandingly beautiful sections."

Jurisprudence, economics, history, philosophy, theology—this wide range of intellectual projects had to be fitted into the student's day. That is why Weber soon made regulations for his day which, however, were frequent-

---

[9]Rudolf Hermann Lotze, 1817–1881, philosopher and physiologist; Gustav Biedermann, 1815–1890, philosopher and physician; Otto Pfleiderer, 1839–1908, Protestant theologian; Friedrich Schleiermacher's work has appeared in English translation as *On Religion: Speeches to Its Cultured Despisers.* —Ed.

[10]The full title of the work by Friedrich Albert Lange, 1828–1875, is *Geschichte des Materialismus und Kritik seiner Bedeutung in der Gegenwart* [History of Materialism and Critique of Its Present Significance], 1866.—Ed.

ly broken as he participated increasingly in the life of the uniformed students' associations:

> The logic course at seven in the morning forces me to rise early. Then
> I rush around in the fencing hall for an hour each morning and conscientiously sit through my lectures. At half past twelve I eat next door
> for one mark, sometimes drinking a quarter liter of wine or beer with
> my lunch. Then I often play a solid game of skat with Otto and Herr
> Ickrath, the innkeeper, until two o'clock (Otto cannot live without
> skat), whereupon we withdraw to our respective lodgings. I look
> through my notes and read Strauss's *Der alte und der neue Glaube*. In the
> afternoon we sometimes go hiking in the mountains. In the evening
> we are together again at Ickrath's, where we get a pretty good supper
> for eighty pfennigs, and afterward we regularly read Lotze's *Mikrokosmos*,
> about which we have the most heated arguments.

Occasional invitations to professors' homes provided welcome material for his gift of mimicking characteristic qualities in people and events and shaping them into lively anecdotes.

During the Pentecost vacation Weber accompanied his cousin Otto to the latter's home in Strasbourg. In those days he formed an intellectual bond with the Baumgarten family. A long letter to his mother about the Pentecost sermon of Pastor Riff—the same clergyman whose sermon the boy had once had to read to his mother—shows how firmly Otto had tied him to religious interests. However, it is not clear whether he really was religiously moved or whether he absorbed everything with the detachment of a man who has a burning interest in the intellectual phenomenon of religion but is not under its spell. A sidelight on what he regarded as the "essence" of religion in those days is provided by another document. At about that time his Bielefeld grandmother died, leaving behind a lonely, aging, unmarried, orphaned daughter. The eighteen-year-old student was profoundly moved by her fate and wrote to his mother:

> On such infinitely sad occasions when a human being has buried his own
> life, at least his inner life, together with another, what can one say
> to this person except to assure him of one's sympathy and respect?
> And what else should I say to my aunt who is so far above me in age,
> experience, and cultivation of the heart? One can only express the
> hope that such a person's faith will give him composure, that his hope,

whatever it may be like, will give him comfort. One can also call out to him the beautiful words which for me express the quintessence of Christianity and true tolerance: "As thou hast believed, so be it done unto thee." [Matt. 8:13] This, this is the only thing that I wish for my aunt, and I know that I have thereby wished her everything, for she carries a faith in her heart which is in itself a mighty fortress against everything that comes to her from the outside as weakness.

* * *

In Weber's second semester at Heidelberg, Otto was no longer there. Plainer people and more mundane interests occupied Weber's leisure hours; in fact, the other side of his personality now seemed to come to the fore. He established a closer relationship with the *Alemannen*, took lunch with them, attended the obligatory drinking parties two evenings a week, and increasingly lived the life of a fraternity brother. In his third semester he fought the customary duels and received the ribbon. He now indulged wholeheartedly in the gaiety of student life, became a jolly fellow, and soon distinguished himself by his outstanding capacity for alcohol. This was of no small significance in those days, because it was part of a brother's education for manhood that he should be able to pour in the greatest amount of alcohol without losing his self-control. Moreover, the food, which got worse every week as the semester wore on, forced people to drink more beer. This way of life soon completely changed Weber's physical bearing, and the desire with which he had come to the university was fulfilled. The increase in his physical girth was even more striking than the expansion of his intellect: the lanky youth became broad and strong, and he inclined toward corpulence. When his mother first saw him so changed, with a dueling scar across his cheek, the vigorous woman could think of no other way to express her astonishment and fright than to give him a resounding slap in the face.

In other ways, too, the metamorphosis of their oldest child may not have pleased the parents completely, although he did not appreciably neglect his studies. The fraternity "obligations," the red caps, the gala dress, the beer parties and songfests, the dueling trips, and a healthy appetite devoured considerably more than his monthly allowance. The student, who had no talent for saving money, repeatedly had to ask his father for additional sums, much to the latter's annoyance. Nevertheless, running up debts was the only thing to do, and it carried on the old tradition. While

contributions had to be made to pay for what the *"alte Herren"*[11] enjoyed at founder's day celebrations and the like, the credit that was extended everywhere to the student corporations made borrowing almost a
Standessitte [class custom]. Lunches, caps, and carriage rides were, as a rule,
paid for only years later, and then with usurious compound interest. Weber
managed in the same way and so he could not balance his budget even in
his later student years, when he was no longer active in the fraternity.

But fraternity life greatly influenced his inward disposition as well as his
outward demeanor. The corporation was small, and every individual felt
responsible for its reputation. The brothers did not associate with friendly
warmth, but were cold as ice toward one another. Friendships were regarded
as unmanly. Everyone kept his distance but paid close attention to what
the others were doing. There was mutual criticism as well as friction—all
decreed by an ideal of manliness that attached the greatest importance to
formal bearing. The only poetic element was the choral singing of those
magnificent student and patriotic songs; their melodies accompanied Max
Weber to the end of his life. Anyone who managed to hold his own within
this community felt extremely secure, superior, and blasé toward the rest
of the world. The corporation had its regulations for every situation:
"There were no *problems* for us; we were convinced that we could somehow
solve everything that arose by means of a duel." Looking back on the influence of those years, Weber remarked: "The customary training for 'snappi-
ness' in fraternity life and as a noncommissioned officer undoubtedly exerted
a great influence on me and removed the pronounced inner shyness and insecurity of my boyhood years."

II

In the fall of 1883 Weber moved to Strasbourg in order to serve his year
in the army. The Baumgarten and Benecke families may have had something
to do with this choice of place. Of course, after three semesters of marvelous fraternity freedom this new manly form of existence at first had no
attraction whatever, particularly since military duty and drill put a considerable strain on the nineteen-year-old student. With the exception of fenc-

---

[11]The "old boys" or alumni who had once belonged to a corporation and still influenced its
practices.—Ed.

ing, he was not skilled in physical exercise, and he was so stout that none of the uniforms in the clothing depot would fit him properly. He finally had to be squeezed into a mess sergeant's uniform. His delicate feet and ankle joints had trouble supporting his heavy body and broke down during the hours of military drill. To a leading question from his mother—whose noble nature demanded to see the good side not only of every "thou shalt" but also of every "thou must," simply because it was a "must," and who never wanted to admit that necessities could really be unpleasant—he replied rather testily: "For the time being, your confidence that I may already have some feeling that my present way of life is somehow beneficial meets with stubborn disbelief on my part. In any case, any feeling of that nature which may be present is bound to be stifled by another sensation, which is caused by the swollen and painful ankle joints on which one runs around seven hours a day."

More oppressive, however, than the physical discomfort were the monstrous stupidity of the drill in the barracks yard and the subjection to the bullying of junior officers. Moreover, it soon became apparent that a systematic continuation of his studies was out of the question. "When I get home at nine o'clock, I usually go to bed soon. I have trouble falling asleep, though, because my eyes are not tired and the intellectual part of a man is not being occupied at all. The feeling that I am slowly sinking into the night of profoundest apathy, a feeling that begins in the morning and keeps growing until I go off duty, is really the most disagreeable part of it all." He managed to get permission to attend only H. Baumgarten's historical seminar, and that was an oasis in the desert.

How was he to cope with this meaningless and seemingly endless existence? At first there appeared to be no other choice but to cast out the demons by Beelzebub. The one-year volunteer therefore adopted a strange and rather unwholesome way of life. Instead of going to bed early, as he used to do in the early weeks, Weber would spend his evenings in taverns with his fellow sufferers, drinking until midnight, and then fall into a deep sleep. In the morning he ran to report for duty on an empty stomach, and then a dreamlike, semiconscious state of mind, the so-called *Kater* [hangover], helped him endure "the not thousandfold but millionfold repetition of the many purely mechanical skills. The hours fly by in a trice, because nothing, not one thought, stirs in one's head." At home his landlady was ready to serve him strong black coffee which temporarily turned him into a human being again, until the afternoon drill swallowed up the rest of his resuscitated mental energies. When his parents reproached him with the fact that his letters were becoming less frequent, he excused himself by referring to the peculiar mental and physical condition that military life had produced in him,

> a condition which simply makes any thinking faculty disappear. After five to six hours of field drill in the morning with field pack, coat, and mess kit, I always lie down in the afternoon. In the evening I am physically exhausted, but I have still been able to read with enjoyment Buckle, Gibbon, or Biedermann. But if we have "manual of arms" and marching exercises for three hours in the morning and two in the afternoon, which is now the regular practice, and if there also are roll call, rifle cleaning, instruction, and that sort of maddeningly superfluous stuff, this is not an excessive physical strain for me, but I am simply incapable of any intellectual activity. Any remnant of mental energy has vanished. For no money in the world could I rouse myself to write a letter or make an attempt to work. So I sit in my armchair, smoke one cigar after another, and think of nothing—really nothing at all; it has happened that after I had been sitting there for what I thought was a short time, my watch told me that I had spent a full three hours without thinking one thought.

But one can learn to do anything. When Weber's time as a recruit was over, his body was used to military service, and he displayed more endurance than most one-year men. He was an utter failure in the gymnasium, however. *"Mensch, dat is ja als ob 100 Hektoliter Pschorr am Reck baumelten"* ["Man, it's like a couple o' thousand gallons o' Schlitz swingin' from the horizontal bars], said a noncommissioned officer from Berlin. On the other hand, Weber pleased even higher superior officers with the impeccable elegance of his goose step—something he related not without pride—and he distinguished himself on marches. Night duty, to be sure, was very hard for him: "Running around at night at very low temperatures and with sopping wet clothes is unbearable. It always makes me feel that I am running a very high fever, and afterward I am so limp that I go on duty doubting whether I shall be able to endure it."

What he rebelled against the most, and time and time again, was "the tremendous waste of time that is used to turn thinking beings into machines that react with automatic precision upon command."

Involving the one-year volunteers in all sorts of pointless activities where they have nothing to do but stand around idly for forty-five minutes or an hour and look on—that is called "military training." This is supposed to teach one patience, as though—good gracious!— after three months of going through the manual of arms for hours every day and after being forced to pocket countless insults from the most miserable scoundrels anyone could ever be suspected of suffering from a lack of patience! As a matter of principle the one-year men are to be cut off from any opportunity to occupy themselves intellectually during their military service, and this supposedly works to the advantage of the military.

Despite his anger Weber was objective enough to admit that the mechanism of the body does work most accurately when all thinking power has been eliminated.

At any rate, Weber's resilient sense of humor and delight in observing unfamiliar procedures and new human types helped him, even in that condition, to store up experiences that his hunger for reality later would have regretted having missed. Every incident supplied him with a graphically presentable perception of human characteristics and the way they were shaped by prevailing systems and ideas. Moreover, from many things he was able to extract material for amusing anecdotes. The types of the Prussian noncom, the lieutenant, the Polish recruit, the three-year man with a working-class background, life in the barracks and on guard duty, field practice—the characteristic features of all these were recorded briefly in his letters and stored up in the chambers of a hungry mind.

February 6, 1884

Having just returned from drill I found your letter, and consequently I am starting a fresh letter rather than finishing the one I started a week ago and continued, paragraph by paragraph, up to page three. Today, thank God, I have a free day ahead of me, except for Uncle's seminar, and thus there is a chance that I shall finish the letter this time. The past week and a half has been extremely crowded with exercises and field practice. At the mere thought of several field practice sessions of five or six hours each, some of them held miles from Strasbourg, I am again quite weary and crushed. Such a field practice may be quite nice and pleasant as a change. But in the long run it is some-thing which, as a foretaste of maneuvers and war itself, uses to a very great extent all the qualities one associates with a soldier. Field prac-tice goes something like this: In the morning, in almost complete darkness, the men line up with helmets, field packs, mess kits, haver-sacks, and coats, and march off. At first everything goes quite well. One is used to the helmet, which was quite bothersome in the first weeks, and to the army boots, which weigh a ton. If you wear a cap instead of a helmet and ordinary boots rather than the army kind, you always have the feeling—at least I do—that you are walking around bareheaded and in your stocking feet. Similarly, at first the field pack—still empty—is hardly noticed. But as time goes on, you become unpleasantly aware of the coat, which is wound around your chest and the field pack like a sausage. If you are at all broad-chested, the coat passes directly below your right shoulder and greatly impedes breathing, in addition to making it very hard to carry your rifle on the left shoulder. Then you begin to notice the two pouches filled with blank cartridges, which press hard against your groin with every step. Finally, the pressure of the lower edge of the field pack against your lumbar re-gion also is a very annoying sensation when you walk for hours.

In addition there are some extraspecial pleasures, such as when during field practice not only the lieutenant of your own company is present, but also a first lieutenant from another company, who is in charge—and the two lieutenants cannot stand the sight of each other. Then the first lieutenant rides along on the right, the second lieutenant on the left, and the man on the left says: "The one-year man there on the flank—take bigger steps." And from the right: "The one-year man there—don't run like that, my horse is having trouble keeping up with you . . ." From the left: "That one-year man—damn it all, your nose is dragging in the mud!" From the right: "Volunteer Weber, con-found it, how are you holding your head? Are you trying to let your nose dry in the sun?" From the left: "The one-year man there—your side arm is hanging down from your navel again! The devil take you by the pound—push it back!" From the right: "*Heiliges Rattenbeafsteak* ["Holy rat beefsteak"]—that one-year man there, your side arm is hang-ing down behind you like a white elephant's tail"—etc., etc. And so it goes; the two gentlemen settle their skirmishes in this fashion. At least, this is what happened to us a number of times in the beginning, but now we get fairly decent treatment.

At any rate, everyone is quite cheerful when we are finally out of the gate, where we "break step," that is, march at ease. Having gone without breakfast, the men gradually dig out their food. In the haversack there are sandwiches, in the rice bag there is a bottle of schnapps, and in the cartridge pouches there are, space permitting, cigars. Naturally, the musketeers want their share, too, and gradually they become more lively. The majority of them are people from the Erfurt and Schwarzburg region, and there are also many Poles, some of whom have had the German language beaten into them only here by the noncommissioned officers. After some time one gets to hear one of the specific soldiers' songs in which "German Rhine" [*Deutscher Rhein*] always rhymes with "brandywine" [*Branntwein*] and "fatherland" [*Vaterland*] with "schnapps in hand" [*Schnaps zur Hand*].

Finally we have reached our destination. After some patrols have ascertained the position of the enemy, we begin our advance, and after we have gone up to a certain distance, the whole column breaks up into a so-called *Schützenlinie* [line of skirmishers], a *Schwarm* [extended order]. We advance at a lively pace until the command "Down!" is given, whereupon—squish!—everyone flops down on his belly in the deepest mud, packs and all. Now begins the large-scale popping of blank cartridges, and it is always a pleasant thought that the German Reich must still have a lot of money left for such expensive amusements. Then we run forward a stretch at top speed, only to throw ourselves down again—naturally, once more into a puddle or a mud pile or some other unmentionable object of an unclean nature—and then the crackling starts up again. An attack by enemy cavalry is brilliantly repulsed and a terrific salvo is fired: "Aim! Fire! Bang!" In the same instant you are deaf in both ears, for the men behind you, a couple of raw recruits, have put the muzzles of their rifles right on your shoulder. Now the lieutenants can give all the commands they want; they just sound like the unarticulated, distant whining of a dog.

After alternately trotting and rolling in the filth for a while longer, we finally advance to the point where we can fall in for the attack with fixed bayonets under the cover of the fire. To the monotonous beat of a drummer—boom, boom, boom!—we go forward, first slowly, then more quickly. Finally, the whole line rushes at the enemy with fixed bayonets, howling like beasts (these are supposed to be shouts of "Hurrah"). In the process, of course, one is regularly knocked down or gets one's hands stepped on or is hit over the head with a gun barrel or is stabbed in the hollow of the knee by the bayonet of the man behind. The officers involved ride in the rear and give a thousand fast and furious commands which, of course, are not understood, and this finally degenerates into a horrible, elephantine roar. Naturally, the result is that the attack is repulsed and the whole spectacle starts all over again.

After a few hours of such fun the march back finally is begun—
everyone completely deaf in both ears, with one black eye and a buzzing,
spinning, battered head, blistered feet, scratched and bleeding hands,
body bruised all over, trampled half to death, bathed in perspiration,
muddy water, and—if lucky—liquid manure, the individual parts of
one's uniform hardly distinguishable from the muck, and with legs
which, like those of a hippopotamus, become thicker toward the bottom and end in a lump of hardened mud. After the worst stuff has
been scraped off with sticks, the men are taken back to the city in
this condition and displayed to the male and female inhabitants of
Strasbourg.

The big maneuvers out in the country, in the beautiful Vosges valleys and
around the little villages of Northern Alsace and Lorraine, afforded Weber,
interesting impressions "of the effect which the Prussian military of the
time had upon a foreign population that maintained a largely negative attitude."

It is a real pity that the people of Alsace do not readily make friends
with us Prussian military men and that they treat us with such indifference. Only mothers who have sons in the German army are different.
Once, for instance, we were on the march and my captain sent me back
to give a message to a detachment that was following behind us.
While I was waiting for these men at a farmhouse near Pfalzburg, the
farmer's wife brought me a washbasin full of coffee as well as bread and
wine. Afterward she would not accept any payment, because, as she said
with tears all over her face, she thought that if she was good to me,
there might be people back in Prussia who would be good to her son,
who was serving there as a recruit. I wonder whether the Poles in Upper Silesia [Wasserpolacken], the Silesians, and the people in other places
where Alsatian regiments are stationed are fulfilling the hope of that
poor woman. Who knows?

His ability to associate with plain people in a spirit of affable camarade-
rie, and at the same time to be like a sovereign, stood Weber in good
stead. Wherever he might be, he quickly added the local flavor to his language. Without compromising himself, he was a peasant when in the company of a peasant; people opened their hearts to him, and he found out
what he wanted to know.

In the second half of his year of military service Weber became a Korporal-
schaftsführer [squad leader] and had new experiences. The responsibility and

the fact that he now had some say filled him with satisfaction, but his new post took even more time and energy. He had nothing but "domestic" duties, for which he had no natural talent. For example, he had to watch over the cleanliness of both the military garb and the birthday suits [Adamskostüm] of "Polish pigs," and supervising all aspects of his charges' lives kept him busy all the time. "After one has *felt* important as a superior for three days, one ends up with stomach cramps and loss of appetite as the only results of the conscientious leadership of a squad. Thank God, this cup [of sorrow], too, will pass. For the time being I am a veritable service machine, and my off-duty occupations are eating+drinking+sleeping+0."

When the end of that period was finally in sight and a return to his books became a probability, Weber once more summed up the condition and the experiences of his military training:

> This military existence is gradually getting too stupid and loathsome, especially since in recent weeks it has left no room whatsoever for anything else. The days of my squad leadership are now numbered, I hope. I spent the past four weeks in the barracks from early till late, and yet I was not able to prevent things from being stolen on a number of occasions. To avoid having this reported and possibly being punished, I had to have these things replaced at my expense. . . . One's capacity for self-sacrifice really should not be affected by whether one sacrifices oneself for a great, breathtaking idea or for dirty foot-rags. "Sacrifice" is the right word, for there hardly is a more ignominious way to crucify oneself than to submerge oneself in the profoundest mental stupor. In any case, as one makes this sacrifice on the altar of humanity it is disturbing to see that one is doing it far more maladroitly than any noncommissioned officer and that it has no great value for oneself or for the German Army. Nor is there a great deal to be learned from it, for we can learn but not use the only skill in which the noncoms are superior to us: to beat people, kick them, etc. (May 30, 1884)

Weber's military education assumed another aspect, however, when he was no longer at the receiving end and entered the executive circle. A year later, in the spring of 1885, when he returned to Strasbourg for his first officer's exercises, he began to like things: "My position really is different now from what it used to be, and if, as I confidently hope, I am promoted in two or three weeks, I shall experience the pleasant as well as the useful side of the military establishment." He had innate qualities of leadership and the ability to give commands and instructions. In addition, his storytelling skill and his superior sense of humor made him a desirable comrade in the eyes of the officers. Soon he was able to write home:

> As I already wrote you, I am doing quite well here, and I am pleased with my landlord and landlady. Military life has been quite strenuous in the last few days, but in general it is really very nice now and not without interest. As I have said, my superiors seem to be very well satisfied with me. Thank God, the captain has not seen me do gymnastics as yet, and by now I can do the other stuff tolerably well. Generally speaking, the attitude of the younger officers is kind and comradely. The captain thought that I ought to regard the eight weeks as a rest cure, and he is right, for I have had to tighten my belt by at least three holes and am so slim that no one classes me among the fat people any longer. The captain is very pleased that the company is now able to dress ranks properly, for, so he says, my belly always used to be in the way and caused the whole damn mess in the company. Without any doubt I am now considered to be a good soldier, and my captain seems to be extremely well satisfied with me and convinced of my absolute diligence. Yesterday he returned my visit and spoke in the most flattering terms of my excellent training.

The result of Weber's military training was a great admiration for the "machine" as well as a martial and patriotic mentality that made him long for an opportunity someday to take to the field at the head of his company.

* * *

The year at Strasbourg in which Weber was so intellectually starved now began to influence his inner development in the opposite direction. His close association with his relatives, the families of the geologist E. W. Benecke and of the historian Hermann Baumgarten, was his spiritual sustenance in those days and prevented the young man from devoting all his free hours to tavern life.

> My Sundays, of course, are the bright spots in this stable and riding-school existence of a horse which is to be broken in. What would they be without an opportunity to spend the afternoon in one of the charming houses of my relatives! Family get-togethers as such have never been my ideal. But here, where I am treated as a son of the house and also like any other student who is a frequent visitor, the fact

that I am a relative is only a bridge that enables us to speak about a thousand things that could not otherwise be discussed, and in a way that would otherwise be impossible. (October 22, 1883)

The two scholars' wives were the sisters of Weber's mother. Ida, the older one, has already been mentioned as Helene's trusted friend and adviser. Helene felt a profound relationship with Ida and placed her above herself as a model of religious and moral life. Emilie, the youngest sister, was the vibrant focus of a family with many children and the sunshine of her noble-minded husband, who was handicapped by his defective hearing. Selfless kind-heartedness and lofty noble-mindedness prevailed in both families. Weber's male and female cousins, whom he knew from the vacations they had spent together in Heidelberg, had grown up in these households. Of the Baumgarten children, he had been friends with Fritz and Otto for some time. Otto's early marriage to Emily Fallenstein—the daughter of one of the sons from Weber's grandfather's first marriage, a son who had gone overseas—interested Weber a great deal and afforded him for the first time a profound insight into difficult psychological problems.

The girl was unusual in every respect. She was much older than the young Baumgartens, not good looking, sickly, and with a history of nervous disorder, but she was genuinely religious and possessed a magic power, the gift of clairvoyance. She was talented in many other ways, too. She wrote poetry and sang, had keen powers of reasoning, and such intensity of intellect that she dominated not only Ida and her children but also the group of outstanding young people who frequented the Baumgarten home. Both brothers loved the much older girl. The father and other relatives, however, were untouched by her religious genius and saw her primarily as a sinister and ailing person.

When Otto, at twenty-four, insisted on a permanent union with the girl, who was seven years his senior, his father was violently opposed to the idea. This woman, who was sick to the core, would she not be a misfortune for his son? Ida, who had her son's confidence, took a different stand. She believed in the inspired powers of the girl, and felt that a spiritual communion was the only thing that mattered. She felt, too, that Otto was irresistibly drawn by his destiny and would leave his father and mother sooner than renounce this marriage. This grave conflict left deep marks on everyone involved in it and temporarily separated father from son and father from mother. But after a short time they accepted the inevitable and were reconciled; the marriage took place.

The couple moved into a quiet parsonage at Waldkirch. One year later death ended the marriage for which they had had to fight so hard. Emily died while giving birth to a malformed child. For the young husband, however, she had not died; she was merely transformed. He was even capable of speaking to her at the open grave, while the others shuddered.

Even after the ecstasy of death had faded, he continued to live in spiritual communion with her, in the ways she had shown. For the rest of his life she remained completely real to him. The youthfully warm, sociable, open-minded, devoted man remained a widower and henceforth distributed the outpourings of his inexhaustible loving heart among countless "poor souls." He gave brotherly help wherever he could, to the point of self-deprivation. He became a second father to his brothers' children. Who, then, was right—the people who regarded the marriage of a vigorous young man to a moribund woman as a misfortune, or the husband, who saw her as his eternal destiny?

Weber followed the fate of his friend with deep sympathy. Even when he was visiting from Heidelberg, he became the confidant of all those involved, since he was able to empathize with each individual's point of view. He, too, had a burning interest in the remarkable woman, but inwardly he agreed with the father's concern. Even before moving to Strasbourg, then, he was a friend not only to the sons but to their parents as well. The communicative but isolated scholar felt a need to discuss political events with his nephew as though they were the same age, and he instilled into Weber his frequent agitation over the political course of the eighties. He undoubtedly influenced Weber with his way of looking at things. It is appropriate, therefore, to say something at this point about H. Baumgarten, since he was—like Max Weber after him—both a scholar striving for an unqualified exploration of truth and a fiery politician.

* * *

Baumgarten was a remarkable man[12] then approaching old age, already a bit wearied by life's struggles and a heavy burden of personal sorrows. He was more interested in observing public affairs in a critical and scholarly way than in shaping them actively. In his youth and his prime he had fought

---

[12]I have drawn the following data from the fine biography by his student Erich Marcks. [Introduction to Baumgarten's *Historische und politische Aufsätze,* 1894.—Ed.]

with moral and political passion—in the company of Dahlmann, Duncker, Gervinus, Jolly, Sybel, Treitschke,[13] and others—for the unification of Germany and its position as a great power under the leadership of Prussia. The national struggle obsessed and inspired that generation, and when the dream of a new German grandeur was coming true, Baumgarten was jubilant: "What have we done to deserve the grace of God in being permitted to witness such great and mighty things?" With a premonition he added these words: "At my age, where shall one get something new to fill one's life?" That was the tragedy: the task that would have been proper for this generation of liberal, middle-class patriots—participation in the internal development of the Reich, whose external form they had helped to create—was denied them. Bismarck alone was at the helm, and as for Emperor Friedrich, whose era had been the hope of the liberals, the days of his rule were numbered.

Baumgarten, who had no access to political participation, saw the shadows accompanying the new situation with all the more shrewdness and clarity. He realized that power pragmatism and the deification of the state along with their consequence, *militarism*, not only were a danger to the *mind* of the Germans, but that the predominance of the Prussian mentality had led to fateful errors in the political arena as well. He was able to observe at first hand the incessant blunders that were committed in the case of the Alsatians, and they made him give up all hope that this ethnic group would ever be regained for German civilization. In addition, the imperilment of his constitutional ideals by the colossus Bismarck filled him with mounting discomfort. In the young generation's unconditional, idolizing devotion to this genius he saw a dangerous excess that would take its toll in the loss of judgment for other values. "The great man will leave us in great distress."

All this came to a head in a sensational literary feud with his former friend Treitschke. As an advocate of the southern German petty states and of liberal ideals, Baumgarten made a harsh attack upon Treitschke's one-sided glorification of the Prussian spirit and the Hohenzollern dynasty. But since Treitschke's *Geschichte des 19. Jahrhunderts* [History of the Nineteenth Century] had tremendous impact because of the "shining splendor" of its presentation and its passionate affirmation of what had come into being

---

[13]Friedrich Christoph Dahlmann, 1785–1860, historian and politician; Max Duncker, 1811–1886, historian and politician, professor at Halle and Tübingen; Julius Jolly, 1823–1891, Baden statesman and Heidelberg professor, H. Baumgarten's brother-in-law; Heinrich von Sybel, 1817–1895, historian, professor at Bonn, Marburg, and Munich.—Ed.

after 1870, not even the old partisans were ready in any appreciable number to listen to irksome warnings. The aging Baumgarten felt isolated, even ostracized, and he suffered greatly because of it.

In those years the new ideals of social justice and reconciliation of the classes were burgeoning among a section of middle-class youth. They filled Baumgarten's wife and son with enthusiasm, but Baumgarten himself was no longer receptive to them. The older he became, the more somber were the hues that veiled public affairs from him. His youthful nephew did not share his uncle's pessimism and constantly sought to modify it, but he largely agreed with Baumgarten's judgment of Bismarck's policies, for this was in keeping with his parents' political convictions. He no doubt owed a great deal to his uncle's pronouncements and to his conversations with him. This is apparent in the political letters that Weber started writing him from Berlin at Baumgarten's request and continued for a prolonged period of time, and of which more will be said later.

* * *

The soul of the Baumgarten house at that time was Ida, a most remarkable woman. Her husband, who was so absorbed in his political and scholarly interests, had an attachment to the Protestant church which seemed inherited (he was a pastor's son) rather than voluntary; at any rate, it no longer had much inner meaning for him as he grew older. Ida, to be sure, shared his intellectual interests, but her real life took place in profound inwardness, before the countenance of her God. She measured all activity by the inexorable standards of Christian ethics. For that reason she was never satisfied with herself and constantly exerted her will. Increasingly she rejected self-sufficient scholarship and the typical scholar, finding the frequent divergence between thought and action offensive. Measured by the evangelical ideals of brotherhood, her academic surroundings seemed socially unkind, arrogant, and selfish, and often woefully small in human terms, being marred by vanity and jealousy. What good was a steadily growing library if knowledge did not also augment wisdom and kindness and daily actions were not sustained by the soaring of the intellect?

In the cultural atmosphere of her household she sought to live the gospel, and often she suffered greatly because it was unrealizable. Was it really impossible to fashion an undivided world in accordance with the teachings of the Sermon on the Mount? Her ever-vigilant, acute sense of social responsibility impelled her to make expenditures for needy persons that her husband often found most disquieting. However, he loved Ida dearly and cherished her so much that she usually was free to follow the voice of her conscience. In other ways, too, she often undertook tasks which, in the opinion of others, overtaxed her and her family. She lost a dearly beloved daughter because she took into her house the sister of a child who was ill with scarlet fever. For years she gave a home to an orphaned relative, although the child's problem personality was a great burden on her and her own children. Her strong soul, confined to a delicate body, was engaged in a lonely struggle with the demons of an unfathomable depression. But she did not make others suffer because of this; to them she always appeared cheerful and composed. "Self-conquest" was her daily watchword. Later in life Ida realized that her husband lived by a law that differed from her own. She withdrew into herself and carried on her inner struggles alone. She shared her religious and social interests with her son and younger friends. Ida and her sister Helene had very similar natures. They both preserved the undiminished moral and religious heritage of their mother. In Ida, however, everything was more austere and somber.

The atmosphere of the Baumgarten home was an aristocratic and intellectual one. Young Weber soon felt impelled to come to terms inwardly with the view of life that prevailed there—that is, Ida's view, which his mother regarded as absolutely superior to the view prevalent in her own house. After all, Helene was much weaker than her sister, and the ways of her husband made themselves felt more than Baumgarten's ways. As a result Weber, who was serious-minded but also lighthearted and above all open-minded, felt some opposition to the enormous moral tension that prevailed in the everyday life of the Baumgarten home. He shared his father's view that it was "eccentric" to judge every action by a moral law and try to measure it by absolute standards. He rejected the rigorism that left no room for smiling tolerance of one's own weaknesses and that, with its "all or nothing," seemed to do violence to human nature. He regarded this "overtension" [*Überspannung*] as inimical to any form of unconstrained happiness, something that he demanded of life at that time:

> What fault do I find with Baumgarten's view of life? No fault, surely, although it is not really compatible with certain convictions that I hold, at least for the time being. I have said only that there seems to be some danger that this view of life will lead to certain eccentricities which *may*—but need not—impair the happiness of those involved. . . . A main characteristic of these people is their disregard of reality

and their disdain for those who take it into consideration. I would go
so far as to say that the Baumgartens do not treat people as they are
but as they *ought* to be, or, in other cases, as they must be imagined
to be according to logical deductions.

He supports this view by referring to Otto's marriage: "I believe that given
the spirit of the house no other development was possible, and therefore
I think that certain dangers and weaknesses are inherent in this spirit too,
like any other view of life which may seem less profound and is less finished,
but does not harbor those dangers."

A year later his conscious point of view had not changed:

I never leave the Baumgarten house without having gained a great deal
from it, even though what I derive from it rarely agrees with the
thinking of the majority of the members of this household. To certain
basic views that prevail there I am in a very conscious and very definite
opposition. *I could not abandon this opposition without changing completely,*
and I must not give it up because so far nothing has convinced me
that it is not justified. I have never attempted to make a secret of
this situation, and almost all those concerned treat me with amiable
tolerance.

However, although he rejected the rigorism that he believed to be inimical to life and remote from reality, he felt at home among the Baumgartens, and without his being quite aware of it, Ida's influence on his inner
development increased. Later, he was everlastingly grateful to her for teaching him to understand his mother. He was now removed from the pressure
of his mother's moral example and demands, and even though she could not
speak on her own behalf, Weber's contact with Ida and his understanding
of her character now revealed Helene's nature to him as well. As he sensed
that Ida's increasing inner loneliness was largely determined by her own hard
life, he realized why Helene was bound to become inwardly lonely at his
father's side.

Above all, under Ida's influence he became conscious of what he had only
dimly sensed before: that he had to choose between his parents—if not between the different ideas they expressed, then between the personality
types they represented—and that this choice was less an emotional matter
than a *moral* decision, one that would be decisive for the future of his soul
and the formation of his own personality. All his life Weber vehemently rejected the notion that nature preshapes us in accordance with inevitable

laws; he was convinced that in him either of two polar tendencies could have prevailed. For example, he might have become a confirmed egotist, an essentially amoral hedonist who by virtue of his intellectual superiority would have appropriated for himself the right to force others to serve his purposes. Or he might have become a man who gives up intellectual activity early in life and is content with a comfortable position, such as that of a district judge in a small town. Those who knew Weber only as someone whose intellectual and moral character was already established at an early age cannot know whether he was right about himself. At the age of twenty-four he was a man whose basic structure was complete and self-contained, a man whom insights and experiences could enrich but no longer remold.

* * *

What the young man owed to Ida Baumgarten for his inner development he acknowledged after her death in the following lines addressed to her daughter:

When I say that your mother was a second mother to me as well, you, my dearest friend, know more than anyone else how profoundly sincere I am. Today I cannot even imagine my life without the deep and indelible impressions and pesonality-forming moral influences, with all their aftereffects, that I received in your Strasbourg home. Without them, everything that I hold dear and cherish today would start crumbling. I first learned to suspect dimly under the impression of your mother's personality that there are other things and tasks than the fulfillment of duty in the *external* profession of a man. Only later, when I saw the light in the circle of my family, did I comprehend it fully. I wouldn't know where to begin if I wanted to try to put on paper how much I, and through me others who are dear to me, owe to her. When she told me on numerous occasions that her life had been a hard one, this was not a lament; rather, she meant to indicate that she had fought a good fight. Her fight was not in vain. This will be borne out by the large circle of her children's friends, all of whom have absorbed some of the serious and pure atmosphere that she disseminated in your house.

* * *

In those days, at the age of twenty, Weber did not realize that Ida was more and more inspiring him with secret reverence for a way of thinking and standards that conflicted with certain aspects of his personality. When during his military year he was laid up for several weeks with inflamed tendons and had a chance to occupy his mind, Ida provided him with religious books, among other things, and he gave his mother a detailed account of them.

> The only thing I did while I was in sick quarters, and at other times, was to read some philosophy and also a little volume of Channing's writings. The latter, which Aunt Ida kindly lent me, was of particular interest to me because of the extraordinary and, in its way, unassailable loftiness of its sentiments. Channing's entirely original and often magnificent view of the nature of religion—which, incidentally, is hardly to be called Christian—combined with an unusually charming personality, makes this somewhat older contemporary and compatriot of Parker an even more likeable figure than the latter. He is, in any case, considerably more universal, if only because he does not concern himself so passionately with the solution of the theoretical and religious-philosophical problems that are so important to Parker. Thus he has more time for, and a clearer vision of, the solution and psychological motivation of ethical and moral questions, and a small number of philosophical propositions suffice him for this. The point of view expressed in these theoretical sections is a rather naive one and may be described as childlike. But some of the practical results he derives from it make so much sense, and the clear, calm idealism he draws from the observation of "the infinite worth of the human soul" is so refreshing and so comprehensible to everyone, even those who do not share his way of looking at things, that there can be no doubt that his views are universal and based on real needs of the spiritual life. *This is the first time* within my memory *that something religious has had a more than objective interest* for me, and I believe that in becoming acquainted with this great religious figure I have not spent my time quite uselessly after all. (July, 1884)

This is the only extant document from that period which indicates religious excitement on the part of the young man. It is therefore worth outlining at this point a few of the basic ideas of Channing, who meant so much to Ida and Helene as well. Channing was active as a preacher in the eastern part of the United States in the first third of the nineteenth century. Thus, he was a contemporary of Schleiermacher and German idealistic philosophy. His conception of Christianity and of religion in general is set down in a number of extraordinarily spiritualized yet crystal clear, gentle, and joyous lectures and essays; compared with the theology prevalent at the time, it is undogmatic and impartial. He counted himself among the community of free spirits and believed in the harmony between reason and revelation and in a Christianity that is not opposed by the intellect, the conscience, and the love of any man. In his view, religion and morality are identical. We grasp God not in ecstatic emotionalism, but in the fulfillment of clear and simple duties. The sacrificing of a desire to God's will is, he says, more important than all delights. The greatest good is the moral energy of a sacred decision, its spiritual freedom. The essence of this freedom is mastery over one's senses and over matter, mastery over fate, all fears, and custom, as well as independence of any authority:

> I call that mind free which jealously guards its intellectual rights and powers, which calls no man master, which does not content itself with a passive or hereditary faith . . . which receives new truth as an angel from heaven . . . which devotes itself faithfully to the unfolding of all its powers, which passes the bounds of time and death, which hopes to advance forever, and which finds inexhaustible power, both for action and suffering, in the prospect of immortality.[14]

Channing also concerned himself with man's relationship to the state. The development and protection of godlike human beings is the objective of all social institutions. The human spirit is greater and more hallowed than the state and must never be sacrificed to it. Civil and political liberty is at the service of intellectual freedom. There is no conflict between Christian individual ethics and political ethics. The life of communities is subject to the same moral law as the life of individuals. There is no room for an affirmation of the state's power for its own sake; a power struggle at the expense of individuals is evil, war is reprehensible, etc.

Of these ideas culled from Channing's writings it may have been the expression of the doctrine of freedom that inwardly stirred the young man. In its strictly logical form he was already familiar with it from his reading of Kant. But Channing's religious certitude did not go beyond the area in which the hard struggle between perception and idea, between the demands of the intellect and those of reason, was carried on. He presented the ex-

---

[14]"Spiritual Freedom. Discourse Preached at the Annual Election, May 26, 1830." *The Works of William E. Channing, D.D.*, Boston, 1875, p. 174f.—Ed.

alted claims simply as the ultimate insights of a soul with self-knowledge, insights that did not require logical proof, and he bathed them in the warmth of a free-flowing religiosity which regarded fulfillment not only as obedience to a strict commandment, but as a path of the soul to God, as its road to likeness to God.

Whatever Max Weber's attitude to these teachings may have been, intellectual and moral freedom, "self-determination" of the personality by a *Soll* [moral obligation] remained a basic law for him all his life, a law to which he consciously subjected himself and of which he constantly assured himself by testing his practical observance of it.

Another conviction that remained with Weber all his life was also expressed by Kant and the earlier Fichte and either taken over by Channing or independently derived by him—namely, that the purpose of political and social institutions is the development of an autonomous personality. However, he did not regard this as their only purpose, as will soon be shown. For that reason he rejected Channing's view of the state and, above all, his pacifism. In December of 1885 he wrote to Helene:

What do I do on Sundays? . . . If I don't get up too late, I have a chance (before starting to work) to read some Channing or Spinoza. Regarding the former, I didn't take along a particularly suitable volume. An essay on war[15] contained in it seems to me not only most impractical and a pure theory, but simply *reprehensible* it its endeavor to classify all persons and actions that relate to war and are concerned with it as ranking far *below* the office of a hangman. I utterly fail to see what moral elevation is to result from placing professional military men on the same level with a gang of murderers and having them stigmatized with public contempt. If this were done, war would certainly not gain in humaneness.

Channing, to be sure, prepares a popular way out for himself when he says that war is permitted as an extreme expedient, but that this must be decided by the conscience of each individual who is asked to go to war. Here he wants to apply these very dubious words from the New Testament: "We must obey God rather than men." [Acts 5:29][16] (He even regards it as a "moral" honor from the standpoint of early Christian martyrdom if someone whose conscience has stirred is

---

[15]Channing's "Lecture on War," 1838 (*op. cit.*, pp. 664ff).—Ed.

[16]Channing's words are "No outward law is so sacred as the voice of God in [the citizen's] own breast" (*op. cit.*, p. 676).—Ed.

shot as a deserter or put in the house of correction.) Well, if it were not obvious that Channing knows absolutely nothing about such things and has in mind the conditions of the American hired armies with which the predatory wars of the democratic American federal government against Mexico, etc., were fought, then this reasoning— provided he himself believes that individuals could ever put it into practice—would have to be called a highly frivolous one.

As it is, however, it is simply a fault in *reasoning* to present as a general basic Christian view a doctrine that may be comprehensible under American conditions, even though it is not justified or even harmless, but is only the speculation of a man who is in this respect far removed from practical life. This may work on a number of occasions, but putting forth such theories is not without dangers, because it may easily produce a rift in people's sentiments between the supposed demands of *Christianity* and the consequences and conditions that are created by the social order of the states and the world. In some instances such a rift has already been produced. The whole misery of the Middle Ages was based on this constructed chasm between the supposedly divine and the human order.

These lines reflect the student's agitation over Channing's irksome doctrine of the incongruity between the commandments of the gospel and any use of violence, especially war, which is not exclusively an act of self-defense but also serves for the expansion of a national state based on power politics. Weber had recently endured great suffering during military drill, but he recognized the need for it and himself had a certain martial spirit. He was as sensitive to the greatness of an ethic of active heroism and a spirit of patriotic sacrifice as he was to the greatness of the ethic of brotherhood and sacrifice for one's fellowmen. He considered the realization of a culture pertaining to this world and transcending the individual to be just as much an indisputable "law" as the perfection of an individual's soul in the Christian sense. He regarded the national power state as the indispensable servant of this culture. Moreover, the reputation and power of his own fatherland were to him indisputable values that overshadowed most others.

At that time, however, he still did not recognize the antinomy between the different values, and he would presumably have been unable to bear it. Instead, he believed that Channing "constructed" a "chasm" between the divine and the human order of things as an unjustified "consequence" when he made the state the servant of individuals and espoused a strict pacifism in the name of the gospel. Three decades later, before and during the World War, Weber expressed himself on this problem on several occasions. By that time he had thought through the incompatibility of the postulates derived from those scales of values with inexorable acuity and rejected as self-deception any attempt to reconcile these different "laws":

> The attitude of the Gospels toward war is absolutely unequivocal in the decisive places. They are opposed not only to war, which is not even specifically mentioned, but, in the final analysis, to any and all laws of the social world—if it wants to be *a world of this-worldly "culture,"* that is, one of beauty, dignity, honor, and greatness of "living creatures." Anyone who does not draw these conclusions . . . should know that he is bound to the laws of this world which include for as long as can be foreseen the possibility and inevitability of wars based on power, and that he can satisfy the "demands of the day"[17] only *within* these laws.

From this insight Weber drew different conclusions from those of Channing and the far more radical Tolstoy. He never lost his profound reverence for the gospel of brotherhood, and he accepted its demands relating to personal life. But he also accepted the inner values: a feeling of unassailable dignity, an active heroic ethic, service to suprapersonal cultural values that enhance life in this world. For him, the God of the Gospels did not have any claim to exclusive dominion over the soul. He had to share them with other "gods," particularly the demands of the fatherland and of scientific truth.

> Anyone who lives in the "world" (in the Christian sense) can experience nothing else than the struggle between a number of sets of values each of which, if viewed separately, appears to be binding. He must choose which of these gods he wants to and ought to serve, and *when* he will serve one or the other. But then he will always find himself in conflict with one or more of the other gods of this world, and above all he will always be far removed from the God of Christianity—at least from the one who is proclaimed in the Sermon on the Mount. (1916)

* * *

---

[17]*"Forderung des Tages,"* from Goethe's *Maximen und Reflexionen.* —Ed.

Let us return to young Weber. Because of Ida's influence and his distance from Helene, Weber's relationship to his mother changed during his years in Strasbourg Helene, to whom the inacessibility of her "big boy" was such a source of suffering, must have been deeply moved when he first expressed what her view of life and, far more than that, her very existence meant to him:

> When you write—and not for the first time—about your "inability" to do something for our intellectual and emotional development, to be a mother to us spiritually as well, I must state emphatically that this is entirely based on a misconception. But I frankly admit that I am partly to blame for the development of this idea, because of my ina-bility to express myself orally about all sorts of things and to communi-cate with precisely those people who are closest to me, to be cordial or even kind in associating with them—in a word, because of my *Zuge-knöpftheit* [uncommunicativeness] and surly demeanor. I can only assure you in all honesty, dear Mother, that in spite—or because—of the fact that it has not always been clear to you, your influence upon us has been greater than that of most parents on their children; I can now speak from experience. If I have often been unfriendly and unkind, this was due to the fact that I was greatly—perhaps overly—occupied with myself. At such times I was at odds and dissatisfied with myself, yet I was incapable of either confessing this openly or concealing it completely. My thoughts often followed quite eccentric paths, and I must attribute it mainly to your influence that I have now attained to a calmer way of looking at things and am able to view the ideas and personalities of others without prejudice and to learn from them. In my years at the university thus far I have done what I now recognize as some very careless things, but they were not *evil* pranks, and if I have not committed any such acts—young as I was and am, I was often tempted to do so—it was because I was thinking of you.

Certainly, as a student he had abandoned himself to the vulgar high spir-its of fraternity life. He had done a lot of drinking, spent far more money than was necessary and than his parents expected him to spend, and had had companions in Strasbourg who gratified all their sensual appetites in a coarse, irresponsible, and mindless manner. But his mother had reason to be thankful. Without using words—for in those days the dark substrata of life and their menacing problems were left under thick wraps—and only through the holy purity of her being, she had implanted in him indestructible inhi-bitions against a surrender to his drives. He withstood the example of the others and thought it better to struggle more and more painfully against the demonic temptations of the spirit by a robust corporeality than to give nature its due.

* * *

In this he was aided by his capacity for a profound, sensitive enjoyment of the pure magic of feminine grace, a grace in which sexuality is dormant or has been completely transformed into spiritual energy. His friendships with contemporaries of his own sex were comradely and without rapturous emotionalism. For a time he had affectionate feelings only for two young fellow one-year men at Strasbourg. Except for his relationship with Otto Baumgarten, he was always intellectually superior to his friends, and to his mother's sorrow he never felt any need to attach himself to a leader. He remained alone and coped by himself. Anyone who sought him out, however, found him ready to understand him and to empathize with him. Even at an early age nothing human was alien to him.

It was not his style to look for gratification of his emotional needs outside the family circle, for example in contacts with women. He maintained friendships only with relatives, with whom he was familiar and had had naturally cordial relations since childhood. There was no lack of such natural relationships with both old and young people. The large family offered every age group. As the sons grew up, week-long visits from female cousins of the same age often enriched the hospitable Charlottenburg house. Helene surrounded her nieces with motherly love, and their uncle found their youth refreshing and joined them in enjoying the stimulation of the big city. The sons took a lively interest in the special character of each cousin and felt more attracted to these girls, who had grown up mostly in the south, than to the frequently "odorless" metropolitan flowers of Berlin. For the young nieces, this house with the epicurean uncle, the divinely kind and vibrant aunt, the uncommonly impressive and handsome sons, and the distinguished friends was an intoxicating experience. They felt at the center of events, and the excitement was almost unbearable. Young Weber enjoyed the company of each girl and gave his affectionate friendship to a few, without, however, being captivated by them or letting them distract him from his work. Only in his last year at the Gymnasium was he genuinely in love with one of his young cousins for a while.

The charm of the Baumgarten home was further enhanced by two fine daughters. When Weber came to Strasbourg, the older one, eighteen-year-old Emmy, had blossomed into a girl of great loveliness. She was remarkably dainty and delicate, intelligent and lively, a young madonna with a crown of blonde tresses above her narrow, oval face. Her soul and her heart were entirely in the Fallenstein manner: absolutely pure and self-denying, profound and unselfish. But she had also inherited the nervous problems of her mother and grandmother, and at an early age exhaustion and melancholia began to overshadow her youth.

The young one-year soldier was profoundly touched by her loveliness, charm, and animation, and he confided in her in a tender, brotherly friendship. Without suspecting it, she was one of his guardian angels in those days. Military exercises took him back to Strasbourg on several occasions—first in the spring of 1885, then in 1887. In the meantime he cultivated his relationship with the Baumgarten house by corresponding with Hermann and Ida. In 1886 he began exchanging letters with Emmy as well, and when the young people met again during the second officers' exercises, a restrained affection sprang up between them. Weber was now twenty-three years old and had just become a *Referendar* [junior barrister]; for the first time Eros had touched him deeply.

Ida's motherly heart sensed what was going on with conflicting emotions. She loved this unusual nephew like a son, as did her husband, but she feared the disaster of a love match between such close relatives. And besides—was her delicate daughter not an entirely too fragile instrument for the hands of this young colossus, gentle though they might be? Would he not crush her spiritually? Moreover, he was still so young, only at the beginning of his career, and marriage was in the distant future. And so, to forestall danger, Ida sent Emmy to Waldkirch to stay with her brother Otto for a while. But Weber followed her there, and the young people spent a few days of sweet closeness in the poetry of spring. They felt that they were in love with each other, but no word was spoken, and they remained at a chaste distance. Only at parting did a warm stream of tears moisten the young man's eyes for an instant. Otherwise everything remained veiled; even the knowing mothers kept silent.

At that time Weber hoped to be able to endure the seemingly endless expanse of time until he achieved professional independence and to marry Emmy at a later date. In addition to this hope, of course, there were whispers of doubt: Would he be strong enough to overcome all the obstacles to such a marriage? Would he be able to assume the responsibility for her delicate life? He avoided a decision and left everything in abeyance. The shadows over Emmy thickened; her condition worsened progressively. Yet there remained a secret hope that there would be a change in their fortunes.

III

Weber's military service came to an end. At his parents' request the twenty-year-old Weber resumed his studies at the University of Berlin (fall of 1884) and spent one year at his parents' home. The idea was, above all, to recoup the great expenses of his fraternity life and military period. Helene found that her son had developed. She particularly noticed that his heart had been enriched and had become more mature. This was the most important thing to her, and she credited it to the influence of her sisters. For this reason the cost of his years in Heidelberg and Strasbourg did not seem inordinate to her:

> How much it is worth to me that Max has become closer to Henriette and to the old house and was treated like your own child! I should like to express my gratitude to you again and again, and it is a consolation to me whenever my husband says that it was a mistake to let him go to Heidelberg and to expensive Strasbourg where he adopted a rather grandiose style of life. Yes, he squandered an unconscionable amount of money, and in Tübingen he would have kept away from many things, but nowhere else would he have been able to find the enrichment of mind and heart that the two years have brought him.

Above all, Helene felt grateful that her son had now really turned toward her and endeavored to share her inner world and give her an insight into his.

Max has become acclimated again very nicely, and his inner development during the past year is a great joy to me. He is so much more understanding and communicative, and I suppose he is fully aware that this gives me pleasure. Before he had to attend lectures we read Channing for an hour each morning, if I was able to manage it, particularly his addresses on adult education and self-culture.[18] This greatly interested and delighted us, although Max and I proceed from very different points of view, since I cannot share his theory that some people exist only to work for others and mechanically earn their daily bread.

Helene was unable to agree with an idea that reflected an unqualified affirmation of a culture which as a matter of course demands the sacrificing of the masses for its purposes. Individual souls were too important to her for that, and she felt too deeply and painfully that the "masses" consisted of struggling, suffering individuals. In those years Channing's teachings and Ida's influence may have further developed her basic disposition. She let the misery of the big city knock on her door and she looked those in distress in the face; what she saw burned itself into her conscience.

Often all the misery that exists around us unseen and unheard, as well as the helplessness with which we face this misery, weigh so heavily on my mind that any enjoyment, any possession appears to me like an injustice. I must so often think of our mother, and I am glad that she did not have any real insight into conditions and spiritual filth such as surround us in Charlottenburg because of the proximity of the big city. She would not have been able to bear it.

This sense of social responsibility was now ever more deeply engraved upon her soul.

Helene had the impression that her "big boy" was comfortable at home. He kept to a strict schedule, to be sure, but as yet his pace was not breathless and he also devoted himself to his family,

even though we always have to lecture him on self-restraint in work. He is now concentrating on jurisprudence as his professional field of study. He is taking German Civil Law with Beseler, "whose sound scholarship makes up for the dryness of his lectures," International Law with

---

[18]Presumably "On the Elevation of the Laboring Classes" (1840) and "Self-Culture" (1838).— Ed.

Aegidi, German Constitutional Law and Prussian Administrative Law with Gneist, and History of German Law with Brunner and Gierke.[19] In addition, he attended Mommsen's and Treitschke's lectures on history. "Speaking of lecture courses, let me assure you right away that in this respect I have become a really diligent student here."

Gneist's lectures were of particular value to him: "I find them true masterpieces . . . . I was really surprised at the way in which he even goes into current political problems in his lectures and at the vigorously liberal views he expresses without propagandizing or agitating, which is what Treitschke is doing once again in his lectures about state and church." The impressions gathered from the lectures of this historian who revealed his whole political self on the rostrum and made passionate evaluations influenced Weber's later views about the rights of a university teacher, which will be discussed later.

Young, fresh, but obviously unsophisticated friends from Weber's Strasbourg period came to the house. Helene enjoyed them, but she wrote to Ida:

> I only wish I could add a bit more substance to this relationship; you managed to do this with Max, and it is apparent at all times. But with the exception of Sch——[20] no one desires it, and this is what I regret about Max's social life in general. He has a really affectionate relationship with the two Strasbourg friends, but it is a kind of paternal relationship, because the two are below him in age but even more in interests. With the exception of your Otto, it has always been thus; Max does not want to look up to anyone, and this surely is a great weakness.

Did Helene use the right term for her son's lack of desire for support and guidance? It may have been the strength of a young titan who simply did not find in his age group anyone he could have regarded as superior; in his early self-sufficiency, to be sure, he may not have looked for such a person. Besides, associating with simpler people who made demands upon his heart

---

[19]Georg Beseler, 1809–1888, professor at Berlin from 1849; Rudolf von Gneist, 1816–1895, professor at Berlin from 1844; Heinrich Brunner, 1840–1915, at Berlin from 1872; Otto von Gierke, 1841–1921, at Berlin from 1867 to 1872 and again from 1887 on.—Ed.

[20]Karl Schellhass, b. 1862, professor of history at Munich and author of books on the Counter-Reformation.—Ed.

rather than his mind meant a rest for him, and his innate chivalry made him interest himself in weaker persons. Thus his little brothers and sisters were a source of life to him. Even at the age of fifteen he had missed their "cheerful bawling." Now his charming little sisters Klara and Lili were his playthings and his joy. He began to spoil them exceedingly and at the same time imperceptibly to guide them. On them he lavished his secret affection and tenderness. Helene described this as follows: "Lili (four years old) has been reinstated in all her rights and duties. Tomorrow she has to take over the difficult task of waking people up. She hops up and down on Max until he decides to get up, and she sits with him when no one else has time to look after her." Max's power of concentration was so great that his brothers and sisters could do as they pleased around him without disturbing him in his work. His charming little sisters were an inexhaustible source of joy to him. On the occasion of her fifth birthday he wrote the following letter to the little girl in Heidelberg:

July 25, 1885

Dear Lili:

It just occurred to me that the day after tomorrow is your birthday, and that you will then be five years old and a really big Lili and won't cry anymore and will want to eat your soup quite fast, without Mama having to feed you, and that you will always listen nicely when you are told something, so that Papa and Mama and everybody will like you very much and enjoy you, and that you will want to be a really big and sensible Lili from the day after tomorrow on. So I went to see the Birthday Man and told him everything and asked him to give me something very nice for my little sister so that I might have a present for her—a ball, or a tobacco pipe, or a new left leg for your blonde doll, or a few hairs for poor Golderschatz,[21] or a little sponge to wash his dirty face with, or a new back for the new china doll's head, because it has only had a face and no head for such a long time, or some other nice thing. But the Birthday Man laughed at me and said: "What are you thinking of, you stupid student, Lili already has a ball, and she won't like a pipe anymore, and the doll's left leg is still around and will be sewn on again, and Golderschatz is so dirty only because he is kissed so much, and that's just what is nice about him, and the other doll doesn't need a back to her head, because she is already used to running

---

[21]Evidently the name of a doll.—Ed.

around like that. And anyway, Lili is in Heidelberg now, and they have a Birthday Man there too, and he will bring Lili something if she is good. Besides, Lili doesn't want any presents from you, because she forgot you long ago. You just go and sit in your smoking room and light yourself a pipe. Lili doesn't even know who you are; otherwise, she would probably have taken you along to Heidelberg."

Then I got very sad and sat down on my sofa and really lit a pipe for myself and thought: But now I've really got to find out whether Lili doesn't know about me anymore and whether she won't come again soon, and if the Birthday Man doesn't give me anything that I can present to her, then I've got to write her a letter on real nice paper that she can later use to make a little boat for the fountain out in the garden, and I've got to try real hard to write nicely and without inkblots, so that she might almost be able to read it if she were even bigger. And look, here is the letter, and there is an ink spot on it after all, though only a small one. So, and now I'm anxious to see when you come again how much you've grown now that you're five, and I'm wondering whether or not you're almost as big as I am, and whether you would still like to be a boy, but not such a naughty boy as Arthur. But now I've got to go to bed.

Your terribly tall brother Max.

As far as his brothers were concerned, Weber now shared his mother's solicitude. He worked with them and concerned himself with their adolescent problems. He was especially close to Alfred, who was next to him in age and his junior by four years. Alfred gladly took the advice of his admired, precocious brother. The two brothers were similar in some respects, dissimilar in others. The younger boy had depth of spirit and, like Max, early on struggled for an intellectual existence. He had many kinds of interests. Because he had some poetic ability of his own, he was very receptive to artistic things. It was more difficult for him than it had been for Max to choose among his various talents, and his struggle to become a complete personality was harder. He first studied history of art and then, like Max, jurisprudence and economics. The oldest existing document concerning their relationship is a long letter by the twenty-year-old student Max from his Strasbourg period that deals with Alfred's confirmation. Max supposes that his brother, who tended to meditate more than Max did, would require an interpretation of his *Jugendweihe* in addition to the one that his mother and the minister would be able to give him. His endeavor to help his

brother, racked by doubts, towards a positive attitude throws some light
on his own attitude toward Christianity.

As children of their time and their family, Helene's growing sons did not
find it easy to make up their minds about that ritual. They were gifted
with intelligence and had depth as well as a meditative disposition. In
their home they absorbed the evangelical religious spirit of their mother,
a spirit that was always reconfirmed by struggles, and they realized how dear
the transmission of this treasure to them was to their mother's heart. On
the other side they felt the cosmopolitan coolness of their father, who respected religion but had less and less personal use for it as time went on.
Then there was also the influence of their environment: the decline of the
church's power to create a community among intellectuals and the working
class; the gradual disappearance of a basis for a uniform *Weltanschauung*; and
the cynicism of schoolchildren in the big city. Active intelligence negated
the dogmas of the church and refused to sacrifice the mind; there were not
yet any new forms for expressing the eternal in transitory things.

Weber's long letter sounds somewhat labored and is addressed to his
brother's mind rather than to his heart. What he tries to make him understand is not the religious substance of Christianity for the individual,
but its general cultural significance as a world power shaping all of Western
life, thought, and feeling. At the same time he wants to make him realize
that it would be presumptuous to resist integration into the great brotherhood simply because one's reason faces insoluble riddles.

Dear Brother,

My intention today is first to thank you at last for your two letters, and then—and primarily—to write you at least a few words as
a brother and a Christian concerning the significant turning point in
your life that you have reached. I do this in order to show you how
I view this important step and what significance it has in my estimation for the one who is taking it. And finally, I write to offer you
my warmest congratulations on this occasion.

You have become familiar with the doctrines of Christianity as they
have been observed and believed in our church from time immemorial.
You will not have failed to notice that the conception of the true
meaning and inner significance of these teachings differs greatly among
different people and that each person attempts to solve in his own
way the great riddles that this religion poses for our mind. Like any

other Christian, you are now being asked to develop your own views as a member of the Christian community. This is a task that everyone must solve and everyone does solve in his own way—not at one stroke, but on the basis of many years of experience in the course of one's life. You will be responsible only to yourself, to your conscience, to your mind, and to your heart for the way in which you perform the task that you are now facing for the first time.

I believe the greatness of the Christian religion lies in the very fact that it is available in equal measure to every person, old and young, happy and unhappy, and that it is understood, and has been understood for almost two thousand years, by everyone, albeit in different ways. It is one of the chief foundations on which everything great that has been created in our time rests. The nations that have come into being, all the great deeds they have performed, the great laws and regulations they have recorded, even science and all great ideas of mankind have developed primarily under the influence of Christianity. Within the world's memory the thoughts and the hearts of men have never been so filled and stirred by anything as by the idea of the Christian faith and of Christian charity. The more you look at the tablets of history, the more clearly will you see this . . . .

It is this community of mankind that you are now entering as a member of the Christian community, and you will be aware—at least to a certain degree, but increasingly so, as has happened to me—that by your confirmation, by reciting the creed, by expressing the desire to be admitted into this great, worldwide brotherhood, you have imposed certain rights and duties upon yourself. As a member of the Christian community you assume the right and the duty to do your share toward the development of all of mankind. Sooner or later every one of us realizes that it is a necessary prerequisite for his happiness to set this duty and task for himself and to fulfill it to the best of his ability. The sooner we recognize that our own contentment and inner peace are indissolubly bound up with the endeavor to fulfill this duty, the sooner we have the joyous feeling that we have been placed on this beautiful earth as collaborators in a great project, the better it will be for us. And so I will close by expressing the wish that you may have an increasing recognition of the fruit of true Christianity—giving pleasure to our parents and peace to yourself.

On this occasion Weber answered the question of the reason for his own existence—the problem that torments every young, thoughtful person—not in religious but in historical terms, by referring to the cultural significance of Christianity and the duty of each individual to all mankind. A subsequent letter, written when his brother entered the last class of the Gymnasium (1885), shows that in the meantime he has also grasped the significance of the very different immediate personal duties:

> Besides, this very period, the last before one transfers the center of one's existence away from the circle of one's family for a long time, gives one an opportunity to know and fulfill the first real duties that one faces. Even though these family duties, which relate to the very narrowest of a man's circles, may appear to be simple and small, it is difficult to do full justice to them. I know from experience how easy it is to deceive oneself, for these seemingly small duties become a constant burden because of their very smallness and obviousness, and the obligation to put up with them seems extremely trivial. But if one believes that one does not have to pay any attention to these demands, one really furnishes proof that one is unable to do justice to them and is not equal to the task. As I have said, in this respect, too, this period in one's life is very useful for learning, because it is not as easy as one thinks to do the right thing in this particular situation, and often one does not have the proper awareness and feeling until much later . . .

Six months later (the spring of 1886), Alfred read Strauss's *Life of Jesus* and became involved in severe struggles and doubts. When he wrote to his older brother, Max took the time to answer him in great detail, even though he was just about to take the examination qualifying him to be a *Referendar*. He tried to help Alfred by demonstrating that the conceptual basis of Strauss's philosophy had already been rendered obsolete by later scholarship. His letter is a full-length essay, and only excerpts from it are given here:

> I would have answered your very nice letter much earlier if I had not been busy working and waiting for my written exam to begin at long last. Now I am at least sufficiently organized again to find a quiet evening hour.
>
> You certainly wrote me about all sorts of important questions, and I was all the more interested to hear about them because I was your age when I occupied myself with them for the first time and in much the same way. That was some time ago, but I still remember very vividly the extraordinary impression that Strauss's *Life of Jesus* made upon

me when I first became acquainted with it. This work surely was quite a coup, and it is written with a frankness and honesty of conviction which seems to place a pistol against every person's chest: "Be my follower or you are a hypocrite!" With such a peremptory "either-or," to be sure, great questions of the intellectual and moral history of mankind can seldom be finally disposed of, but the pioneering work of the spirits that have the courage to raise such questions endures nevertheless. This is what happened to Strauss's ideas as well; they swept away many incomplete things that had previously existed, and created clarity. But on the other hand, scholarship has taken a different course since then. Against Strauss's expectations, it by no means accepted his views as a final result, but only as the inspiration for fresh and much more profound questions. It was simply discovered that Strauss's book contains not an *answer* but a *question*—or, rather, numerous questions—that no light is shed on other and more important aspects of the subject, and that one would have to base oneself on concepts that differed from those Strauss used or was able to use.

I hope we shall soon have an opportunity to discuss this in person, because it really is worth being clear about what matters here. There is always a danger, especially in this instance, that one will become one-sided, treat everything in the same way, and consequently gloss over all the difficult problems that face us with a concept whose meaning one knows only approximately or not at all. A case in point is the concept of "myth" which Strauss advances and which, as I noticed and well understand, you like very much, because it seems to offer an easily comprehensible key for the explanation of that which gripes our mental concepts and our logic. Upon closer examination, however, this concept is utterly meaningless, does not clarify matters at all, in no way explains the connection between Jesus as a concrete individual and the Christ of history, and is basically inapplicable to the transformations of the human spirit and of human culture with which we are here concerned. [There follow explanations of the nature and the origin of myths on the one hand and the creation of Christianity by Jesus as a historical personality on the other.]

If one wanted to treat the myth of Heracles or Persephone (the product of a highly gifted, settled people's poetic view of nature) in the same way as that which was alive in the minds of the early Christian communities (a motley group of people from all over the world who were mostly homeless and who for a long time struggled with poverty), this would be like equating a newspaper editor who described the misery of the working classes and the consequences of alcohol consumption on the basis of statistics and added benevolent, or possibly polemical or satirical, remarks about these conditions and those whom he regarded as responsible for them with a man who at the very same moment had to contend with extreme destitution and with the observations and fantasies that might be in his head. There are many similar examples—for instance, if a nursemaid stoppers an ink bottle in the evening and puts two matches diagonally across it because she is of the opinion that Satan is contained in the black liquid and now cannot get out, we laugh at her; if at a time that was one of the hardest of his life, Luther hurled an inkwell at the Evil One in the Wartburg, one may also laugh at this—but this is a different kind of laughter. And if we think of witchcraft trials, we stop laughing altogether—and yet the same thing, superstition, seems to be involved in all cases. But each time a different side of the human spirit is involved, and in each case the meaning is different.

You have written me about many other things that could be discussed, for example, concerning the value of knowledge gained "only by experience and reason." Surely no one was more inclined to have a high estimation of the value and scope of these than the ancients, but they never attained clarity about the conditions and the real basis of knowledge and our capacity for it. . . . We have now deepened the question somewhat—that is, we do not content ourselves with speaking of "experience," but go on to ask why experience gives us truth and to ask about the nature and the value of the kind it gives us and the kind it cannot give. . . . Nor is the "incomprehensibility" of religious matters to which you refer a settled question by any means, for now we must ask ourselves: What is my attitude toward these incomprehensible things? What *value* did they have for people in the past and what value do they have for me? Or do they perhaps have no meaning for me whatever, because of their very incomprehensibility? To my way of thinking, this last question should definitely not be answered in the affirmative, but an individual will not find an instant answer to the question about their meaning. (March, 1886)

When his brother's process of disengagement from traditional Christian thought and his struggle for clarity about metaphysical problems took the form of Cartesian doubt and self-despair, Max handled him more roughly in an effort to straighten him out:

Although I am generally not in favor of discussing fundamental matters, I was rather pleased with your letter in more than one respect, although some things in it struck me as strange. To begin with these things, I cannot really understand why you seem to be constantly trying to convince yourself that, as you put it, it is all over with you and you have to despair of yourself. I can only ask: Why? And since I can see no other reason than difficulties with certain general theoretical concepts—this is all I can discern—I can see in this only an enormous overestimation of what theory means in the world and to an individual. That someone who does not proceed from eternal damnation or the like should, for the sake of theoretical views, seriously hold the opinion that he cannot exist or that life is a burden to him is, if you look at it closely, utterly absurd. I know very well that a man can have a very hard time with this. But it will never occur to anyone who has any appreciation of what is, if viewed absolutely, the minimal value and the weakness of our tools of cognition and bears these limitations in mind to give up striving for knowledge itself if he is confronted with the possibility of an error in theories about things that will never underlie our experience. I would really take a very close look at this kind of thinking to establish whether it does not include a measure of self-deception and perhaps also involves the attraction that pessimism has and to which almost everyone succumbs at one time or another. The tremendous power such thoughts have over you has, to be sure, put you on the wrong track, and this is where I have sometimes found you. It is indeed a wrong track, for it does not lead anywhere. In general, however, I am not absolutely certain that you are so very far off the course that would seem the right one to me.

These thoughts as set down in the summer of 1887 suggest the assumption that at the age of twenty-three Weber had long since fought his way to a recognition of the limits of intellectual power and had for the time being cast anchor in a silent veneration of the unexplorable. But the fact that he refrained from lifting the veil that shrouds the divine did not paralyze his urge for knowledge. In the realm of scientific thought, to be sure, he limited it to that which could be experienced.

4

INITIAL SUCCESS _____

I

Before the examination that would qualify him to be a *Referendar* [junior barrister] (winter, 1885–86) Weber spent his last semester at Göttingen. He continued his strict work routine, regulated his life by the clock, divided his day into exact segments for the various subjects of instruction, and "saved" after his fashion by preparing his evening meal in his room—a pound of chopped raw beef and four fried eggs. The last hour of his day was reserved for a game of skat with a very simple friend who had failed his examination and whom Weber was preparing for a second attempt. For the rest, he was tempted neither by the winter fun that jingled past his windows nor by spring wanderlust; from the time he stopped dueling, he got no exercise of any kind. Even during his vacation he wanted not a restful enjoyment of nature—provided that his father wished to travel with him—but impressions to satisfy his thirst for knowledge:

> The North Sea and nature are not going to run away and will be there to enjoy later, but the time is passing during which I can occupy myself with other things in addition to jurisprudence. I am not disposed to

regard the enjoyment of nature as an invention of modern times, and I do not lack the capacity for it, but I do know other and equally great enjoyments that I must prefer to the enjoyment of nature *as such*, because I shall be able to enjoy nature at a later date, and possibly to a greater degree, if I have really done a lot of hard work, whereas it will be harder and harder for me to find the time for intellectual enjoyment . . .

Having decided in favor of an asceticism of work, Weber gave up the great variety of intellectual interests and concentrated on his immediate goal. In doing so he experienced for the first time the satisfaction of a complete "fulfillment of duty," and he wrote a jocular report about this condition: "In general, I strike myself as a greatly improved edition of myself." Even when he spent his vacation at home he did not let himself be distracted. Helene was astonished at the intensity with which her "big boy" was now devoting himself to the "demands of the day," and because of her womanly feeling that life should be harmoniously integrated, she immediately saw a new problem in his single-mindedness:

Now the *Referendar* examination has to be passed, and given his nature, Max is now in the midst of it and looks straight ahead; to my genuine surprise he has pushed aside almost all other literary matters while he is here. In the morning, when he had to wait too long for Papa to come down to breakfast, he always pulled out a pocket edition of *Maritime Law* or *Law of Exchange* and became absorbed in it as though it were a novel. Next summer he wants to take his doctorate here, and I think that then his other interests will again prevail over this dry-as-dust legal stuff, for which I have no feeling whatever. He is by no means practical and organized enough in his everyday doings to be an official; also, he has always been more interested in the historical development of the law than in its application.

Despite all this, Weber remained a good companion who enjoyed intelligent or amusing talk over a good drink and equally loved simple, intimate gatherings. He certainly did not think of himself as an eccentric who wanted to escape from the normal way of life, and he did not need to oppose traditional behavior to be aware of his own strength. Certainly he derived no pleasure from the festivities, particularly dancing, that were arranged with a great expenditure of time for young people of both sexes. And anyone who looked at the young colossus in this light and with no regard for convention would probably have exempted him from dancing, an exercise that was so unsuited to him. Helene, however, did not feel this, and there are various statements about his attitude toward it, for it was the subject of frequent discussions between mother and son. She was serious-minded but also vibrantly open to the world, and so she could not understand her son's early rejection of what to her was simply part of being young. In fact, she thought that young men had a human and Christian duty to give young ladies a pleasure that was so important to them. Naturally, the more she emphasized the obligatory character of this activity, the more stubborn did her son's resistance to it become. For a time this resistance was also passed on to his younger brothers, who had different personalities. That form of youthful togetherness evidently never raised his spirits, and he never found young girls less captivating than when he had to hold them in his arms, detached from their everyday existence, decked out in their holiday best or half undressed, with no opportunity for an intellectual or heart-to-heart exchange. He was equally unreceptive to something else that young people unconsciously seek in such entertainments: flirtation, which lends a secret charm even to the most banal conversation. After attending a dance at Göttingen he tried to convince his mother that his disinclination was justified by giving a humorous, detailed account of the time expended as against the pleasure obtained:

> I have not answered your letter as yet, because during the past week I lost much time because of one and the same event. To wit: (1) was invited to a ball at von Bar's[1] and got annoyed (¼ hour); (2) went out and bought a *chapeau claque* [opera hat] (½ hour and a fortune); (3) forgot gloves, went out and bought same (½ hour and more money); (4) dressed up, with x number of shirt studs departing this life, a vest button turning out to be loose, and even the Argosy suspenders breaking (almost a full hour!); (5) had previously sewed one sleeve of the dress suit where the seam had split (¼ hour); (6) went and had my hair combed, getting a whole pharmacy of salves and scents installed on my head (¼ hour); (7) ran to Herr von Bar's house, believing I was ½ hour late; (8) was much too early (¼ hour); (9) chatted for ½ hour, much idle talk; (10) feeding time (1¼ hours); (11) trampled, chatted, and sweated (from 10 P.M. to about 3 A.M., 5 hours); (12) overslept and missed Dove's[2] lecture (1 hour); (13) had to make it up (1 hour)—a

---

[1] Karl Ludwig von Bar, 1836–1913, professor of law at Göttingen from 1879 on.—Ed.
[2] Alfred Wilhelm Dove, 1844–1916, professor of history.—Ed.

total of about 12 hours, a whole day! Hold it! (14) visited the toilet, which happened today; almost forgot about that. In this period of time one can work through all of the general part of the German Criminal Code and the specific part at least up to the "criminals dangerous to public welfare." You can say what you will about dancing and its merits. It may possibly be worth the tenth part of the time to someone who is so inclined and has a slim figure, but neither is the case with me. "No one lives by another law but the one under which he was born"—so it aptly says in the *Sachsenspiegel*.[3] But unfortunately we no longer live by the law of our fathers, and Roman law says much more unmercifully: *Ultra posse nemo obligatur* [No one is obliged to do more than he can]. Thus one is allowed to stop only when one *cannot* go on, and even this limit is not always respected by the young ladies, who, in view of their trampling ability, are very unjustly called the "weaker sex."

Incidentally, I did have a better time than I thought I would. I had passable conversations with a few of the young ladies, and as time went on I gradually acquired a thorough acquaintance with several subjects as they were illuminated from various sides by various ladies: skating rink, choral society, betrothal of an assistant librarian, cotillion, heat in the room, meteorological possibilities, etc. In sum: I wouldn't mind 1–1½ hours of dancing if one participated as a sensibly dressed person and not in tails, top hat, white gloves, black trousers, and accessories to go with these, plus yakanism.[4]

So that his mother would not worry that he was about to become a recluse, Weber shortly afterward examined "sociability" from its positive side. After receiving an invitation to have lunch with a family, he wrote her as follows:

If I wanted to grumble about this, too, your reproaches would certainly be justified. In my opinion, however, a so-called ball does not nearly compare in value and civilizing substance with such a very cosy get-together or even the most trivial morning pint that is drunk together with a sensible person. Herr and Frau von Bar were extremely charming; Herr von Bar displayed his excellent sense of humor and in the course of the afternoon expatiated upon almost the entire field

---

[3] Important code of Saxon law written in the first half of the thirteenth century by Eike von Repgow.—Ed.

[4] *Sprechanismus*—a punning combination of *sprechen* (talk) and *Mechanismus* (mechanism).—Ed.

of politics. It seemed to me that with this procedure—*sine figura et strepitu* [without formality and noise], as the *Corpus juris canonici* [body of canon law] has it, without "tails and trampling"—which meant that having heard all sorts of things of general and particular interest, having had an excellent time and even eaten my fill, and having gone home contentedly after three hours and lit my pipe, I was considerably better off than when I had to work hard for a piece of meat by making kangaroolike leaps and had to sneak out into the entrance hall in order to enjoy a cigar and a glass of beer.

A year later, when he was a Berlin *Referendar*, he once more discussed seriously the typical city social life of the time, and what he wrote to his Strasbourg girl friend remained his opinion in later years too:

To the detriment of all involved, we view our social life only as a "duty" that is sugar-coated as much as possible. This may be seen in the makeup of parties. A widely quoted proverb says that *after* the work is done, repose is sweet. There is no reason to associate this only with daily work; it applies equally well to one's life work. One would have thought, then, that the main element in parties would be furnished by those who already have a good day's work behind them and can look back on some achievements in their life. Social life ought to revolve around *them*. They ought to be the center and all others only appendages.

But no, here it is different! At the center of the greatest and most extensive forms of social life are the interests of young people. Everything revolves about them: their interest in amusing themselves determines the scope and the kind of social organizations. Since social life cannot mean for these young people a rest after the day's heat and burdens, it is bound to be an end in itself, an institution that exists for its own sake and which they must, willy-nilly, make the best of. No one can deny this: An interest in people as human beings drives no one from the bosom of his family, where there are plenty of opportunities for inexhaustible studies of human nature, to a ball, where a person may exchange a few superficial phrases—almost always the same ones—with someone else, but will, in any case, not increase his knowledge of human nature, although he may increase his knowledge of clothes. This purpose of a conversation results in an effort to acquire a certain facility in it, and this is simply the performance of a duty, for the social amenities require that a conversation take place. In other words, snottiness is cultivated, and here in Berlin the results have been splendid, and particularly among ladies, that is, the very ones who are paraded as jewels of any social organization. But this can easily change the entire position of the sexes. In the face of such a critically tinged girl with a fabulous yakanism someone like myself can feel *Verlegenheit* [self-consciousness] . . . but not the *Befangenheit* [constraint] that is an awareness of the *limits* within which the social intercourse of the sexes must take place.

It may seem strange that the twenty-three-year-old Weber should complain so vigorously that the needs of *young* people determine the character of the festivities to such a great degree. In contrast to the self-evaluation of today's young people, who nurture feelings of superiority as "youth," Weber was particularly attracted by social intercourse with mature people as the bearers of knowledge and practical experience. He did express himself about older people in humorous terms, but he very seldom said anything irreverent about them. A chivalrous civility and amiable deportment were characteristic of him, but he always kept his distance. However, when he was overcome by passionate zeal during a scholarly or political discussion, he would express his opinions with heedless frankness, on occasion even to authorities whom he respected, a frankness that indicated a great inner certainty.

* * *

Even at that early age Weber viewed women and even girls primarily as human beings and only secondarily as members of the opposite sex. He expected them to display an animated grace and a reserve designed to serve as a guide for a man's behavior. "It is an old tradition that in a conversation a male generally takes the initiative and a female then sets the limits; *therefore it entirely depends on the girl* whether a young man is once and for all trained . . . to observe these limits himself." He took seriously any sign of a scholarly interest on the part of a woman and was pleased when it was expressed graciously. On the other hand, he was irritated by the *"Berlinertum"* [Berlin style], meaning a certain kind of forced self-assurance and social "routine" that manifested themselves in pseudoclever or witty altercations and robbed a rosebud of a girl of her fragrance even before she had fully opened up. He spoke with interest and benevolence about the new type of woman that was coming into being, the first female university students he met in Berlin.

One of them was a *Fuchs* [freshman] in her third semester, the other one a *bemoostes Haupt* [veteran student] like myself. Both of them were studying medicine, and the *Füchsin*[5] was also a student of the natural sciences. The latter had a certain energy in her movements that was not always esthetically pleasing; besides, she had a scholarly way of expressing herself even when the conversation was about very unscholarly subjects—something that is frequently encountered among ambitious freshmen. The old student, however, met with my full approval. (December 3, 1885)

Weber's approval of the new type was not unqualified, to be sure. Female students were fighting hard for recognition, and so they tended to display a combative spirit. Moreover, Weber's attitude at that time was unconsciously determined by a young man's great need for a woman's care and help as the foundation of his intellectual existence. Thus he expressed a preference for the traditional type in a letter to his girl friend, who herself was a most charming personification of the typically feminine.

The other type to which I really am even more attracted and which has the additional advantage of not being a product of modern times is the *Studentenmutter* [students' landlady]. One of the outstanding representatives of this type is my local landlady, "Tante Töne" [Aunt Töne], the subject of numerous reminiscences from my father's Göttingen period, when, strangely enough, she is supposed to have looked exactly as she does today, thirty years later. Although from an esthetic point of view she had the same ineradicable frightfulness that she has always had, I have hardly ever had such good accommodations as I have in her house.

Even in those early years he regarded the inner freedom and independence of women, even married women, as an "inalienable human right" fully equal to that of a man. He imperceptibly tried to make his mother more aware of her right—nay, duty—to assert herself. In the summer of 1885 he commented in detail on her anxiety about the marriage of a close friend of hers whose emotional stamina was in danger of being exhausted by the tyranny of her husband, who was a distinguished man but had pathological tendencies. In writing about this Weber may have wished to tell Helene some-

---

[5]This slightly jocular neologism, derived from *Fuchs*, normally means "vixen" (an animal, not a woman. —Ed.

thing between the lines that his filial piety did not permit him to express
in any other way.

I did imagine conditions in the home of the Xes to be something like
that, and I was quite well acquainted with the poor woman's anxiety
and, as it were, intimidation. But I am not at all sure that if the
woman could manage to display a bit less anxiety and to assert and
practice a certain amount of freedom of movement as something natural, her husband would regard his tyrannical treatment of everybody—
which has by now become a habit with him—as something less natural.
For I have always had the impression that, given his keen eye for such
things, he sees everything that is done secretly against his mind and
his prejudices as clearly as though it were being done openly.
　　Far be it from me to judge whether such a behavior toward him is feasible. But an outsider cannot help thinking that an openly independent
action may give the husband the vague feeling that he is attempting
to suppress a moral right, the right of freedom of thought and of speech,
of personality in general; and the husband might clearly realize that he
is not being confronted with all sorts of machinations and conspiracies
directed against him, as he imagines in his morbid stupor, but with
the simple awareness of a personal right.

In later years Weber frequently expressed what he implied here: that a
married woman should be very firm and impose limits upon a husband who
tends to deprive her of her freedom and to exploit her for his purposes
beyond the necessary division of labor. He regarded this as necessary not only
for the woman's sake, but also for the sake of the husband and the marriage.
He thought that a woman with a fully developed life of her own enriched
the household; besides, a husband must not be put in the wrong by a wife
who sacrifices herself beyond her natural duty, a sacrifice which is in the
long run impossible for her without secret rebellion.

II

In May of 1886 Weber took the examination qualifying him to be a *Referendar* and thereby moved one step nearer to independence. At the age of
twenty-two he had long since outgrown student life. Shortly before completing his studies he wrote to his mother: "These years will never return,
that much is certain; yet I have the feeling that it is time for them to

end, and I cannot regret this." But his eyes did fill with tears when the only fraternity brother from his Heidelberg period, a man with whom he had spent his last hour of relaxation before his examination in Göttingen after working hard all day, saw him off and, following a fine old student custom, sang the sentimental *"Bemooster Bursche zieh' ich aus"*[6] to him at the railway platform. It was a kind of farewell to youth. An endless road still stretched before him; his goal, the fruitful exertion of all his faculties and outward independence, was still shrouded in darkness.

Weber returned to his family home and, since he had no income as yet, lived there for seven years, until his marriage. He still had six long years of professional preparation before reaching all his goals. He now planned to take his law degree, for which the requirements were high in Berlin at that time. Consequently, in addition to being active as a junior barrister [an unsalaried trainee], Weber continued his studies, particularly in the seminars of Goldschmidt and Meitzen.[7]

His voluminous doctoral dissertation, *Zur Geschichte der Handelsgesellschaften im Mittelalter* [On the History of Trading Companies in the Middle Ages], which he dedicated to Goldschmidt, was in the border area between legal and economic history. It gave him "an inordinate amount of trouble" and developed into a work of genuine scholarship whose results Weber incorporated even in his last sociological work.

> I had to read hundreds of Italian and Spanish collections of statutes, and first I had to master both languages sufficiently for me to read books in them after a fashion; in the case of Spanish, this was somewhat time-consuming. Then, too, most of the stuff was written in disgusting ancient dialects, and one is surprised that the people understood that gibberish! Well, I had plenty to do, and if the results are meager rather than copious, it is less my fault than that of the Italian and Spanish city councillors who failed to put in the statutes precisely those things that I was looking for.

Weber's graduation was ceremonious and a true *Rigorosum.*[8] The candi-

---

[6]"I leave as an old student," the opening line of A. Methfessel's *Lied eines abziehenden Burschen.* —Ed.

[7]Levin Goldschmidt, 1829–1897, professor of law at Heidelberg and Berlin; August Meitzen, 1822–1910, economist and statistician, professor at Berlin from 1875 on.—Ed.

[8]*Rigorosum*, "rigorous examination," usually denotes the oral examination of a doctoral candidate.—Ed.

date was examined in seven juridical subjects, and the examination included a public debate about three theses propounded by the candidate, his friends being invited to take the opposite view. Weber had asked Theodor Mommsen, Otto Baumgarten, and Walter Lotz.[9] The last-named gave the following report:

> After we had been disposed of, tradition required Max Weber to ask in Latin whether, now that he had refuted all opponents and successfully defended his theses, there was anyone in the audience who dared to oppose him. At that point an old gentleman, scrawny as a spider, with wonderful smooth white hair and an impressive profile, stood up in the audience. It was Theodor Mommsen, whom I saw and heard for the first time on that occasion. He remarked in connection with Thesis Number Two that the candidate had made statements about the concepts *colonia* [colony] and *municipium* [town] that seemed surprising to him, who had occupied himself with these problems all his life, and he requested further clarification of these views. There began an extensive discussion between Mommsen and young Weber. Mommsen concluded by saying that he was still not entirely convinced of the correctness of Weber's thesis, but that he did not wish to impede the candidate's progress and would withdraw his opposition. The younger generation, so he said, often had new ideas that the older one could not immediately embrace, and that might be so in this instance. "But when I have to go to my grave someday, there is no one to whom I would rather say, 'Son, here is my spear; it is getting too heavy for my arm'[10] than the highly esteemed Max Weber." With these words Theodor Mommsen concluded the public debate, which had been followed most attentively by the audience, and Max Weber was graduated with due ceremony.

As soon as Weber had finished his first treatise, he began to prepare his *Habilitationsschrift*.[11] "One of my most highly esteemed and most amiable teachers, the well-known agrarian historian Meitzen, is needling me about a study—which, I am convinced, is not yet ready to be discussed—of the Roman distribution of land and the colonate." These beginnings expanded

---

[9] 1863–1941, economist and professor at Munich.—Ed.

[10] "*Sohn, da hast du meinen Speer!/Meinem Arm wird er zu schwer*"—the opening lines of *Lied eines alten schwäbischen Ritters an seinen Sohn* [Song of an Old Swabian Knight to His Son], a poem (1774) by Friedrich Leopold Graf zu Stolberg, 1750–1819.—Ed.

[11] A second dissertation required of those aspiring to faculty status at a German university.—Ed.

into a work about the agrarian history of imperial Rome which involved him in lively literary polemics and frequent verbal disputes with Mommsen.

With this study Weber qualified at Berlin in the spring of 1892 to teach Roman, German, and commercial law. He barely allowed himself any breathing spell at all. Around that time he accepted an assignment from the *Verein für Sozialpolitik* [Social Policy Association] to study the situation of agricultural workers east of the Elbe River, a project combining economic research and legal studies. However, this will be discussed later after another aspect of Weber's development has been dealt with. In addition to his scholarly concerns, he was passionately interested in political events. His reactions have been preserved in a series of letters to Hermann Baumgarten from the years 1884 to 1892, and it will be appropriate to pursue these threads in the fabric of his life first.

* * *

The basis for Weber's political judgments was the National Liberal attitude of his father which was, to be sure, soon amalgamated with new elements that appeared in the course of his development.

Let us first look at the significant political events of the eighties[12] about which there are statements by Weber. These events took place under Bismarck who was in increasingly exclusive control of the destinies of the nation. The great era of liberalism was past. Its left wing, the Progressive Party under the leadership of Eugen Richter,[13] was usually in opposition, while the National Liberals under Bennigsen and Miquel as a matter of principle wished "not to follow or fight, but to influence" the chancellor. They made the *Kulturkampf* [struggle between the state and the Catholic church] possible for him and also supported the *Sozialistengesetz* [antisocialist law], which suppressed the political rise of the socialist-led masses of workers. In so doing they abandoned their libertarian ideals in order to stand at Bismarck's side.

Yet Bismarck found them troublesome. When he no longer needed them in his struggle with the Catholic church, he sought to weaken their power by bringing about a further split in their own ranks, and he succeeded in doing so when the question of protective tariffs versus free trade was agitating people. Bennigsen approved of Bismarck's protectionist policy but

---

[12]Here I have used Hermann Oncken's *Rudolf von Bennigsen* and Otto Schulthess's *Geschichts-Kalender*.

[13]1838–1906, member of the Reichstag from 1867 on.—Ed.

balked at the Franckenstein clause.[14] As a consequence some of his followers, among them Treitschke, turned to the right and joined the Free Conservatives. Above all, however, a left-wing group under the leadership of
Forckenbeck, Rickert, Lasker, and Bamberger[15] broke off as the "Secession," which soon (1884) combined with the "Progressives" to form the
Deutsch-freisinnige Partei [German Liberal Party]. The new party was in opposition, rejected protective tariffs and the extension of the antisocialist law,
and opposed the way in which Bismarck concluded the *Kulturkampf* in an effort to bring the *Centrumspartei* [Catholic Party] into line. This meant the
splintering of liberalism, which Bismarck desired. He was not able to choose
between carrying out his policies with the aid of the Centrists and the Ultracon-
servatives on the one hand and the National Liberals and Free Conservatives on
the other, and he could play off one group against the other at will. The
diminished [Catholic] Center Party tried to maintain the old National Liberal
line of supporting Bismarck in specific instances and representing moderately
liberal principles. It was also ready to participate in the social policies initiated
by the "imperial message" of 1881 about the social duties of the state, but it
refused to go along with Bismarck's financial policies. Bennigsen withdrew for a
few years.

Bismarck was in sole control and tolerated only minions or willing tools
around him. The National Liberals increasingly came under the spell of his
political views; the old individualistic libertarian ideals faded among them,
and they left this banner to the German Liberal Party, which pinned its
hopes on a change on the throne and in the chancellor's office. They
adapted themselves to the fact "that in contrast to their dream of a parliamentary government Bismarck forcibly and craftily pushed through a new
type of monarchic constitutional state."[16] Thus they came closer and
closer to Bismarck's policies, approved the extension of the antisocialist
law, supported his new social policy, retained the tariffs, and approved an
increase in the army under the impression of a threat of war with France—
in short, they ended up where Bismarck had wished them to be: a government party "of the second order," by the side of the moderate Conserva-

---

[14]A stipulation by Georg Arbogast Baron von Franckenstein, 1825–1890, a Bavarian politician, Reichstag delegate, and leader of the Center Party, that some surplus revenues be returned to the individual states, making it impossible for the Reich to stand on its own feet
financially.—Ed.

[15]Maximilian von Forckenbeck, 1821–1892, a founder of the National Liberal Party, president
of the Reichstag from 1874 to 1879; Eduard Lasker, 1829–1884, German-Jewish jurist and leader
of National Liberals; Ludwig Bamberger, 1823–1899, German-Jewish Reichstag deputy.—Ed.

[16]H. Oncken, *Rudolf von Bennigsen*, vol. 2, p. 576.

tives. The liberal ideals no longer counted among them. Emperor Friedrich III, the hope of the Liberals, died after a short time on the throne, and, as Gustav Freytag complained, "with his death the complementary color to the nature of his father disappeared." The bourgeoisie did not attain to political power. Of the leaders of liberalism, only the adaptable Miquel became a Minister. The young ruler Wilhelm II displayed ecclesiastic-feudal inclinations. The extreme conservative and high-church circles—Stöcker and Hammerstein[17]—tried to ensnare him. But Bismarck's countereffect was stronger. Wilhelm II declared that he wished to adhere to the old course, and he expressed himself in favor of Bismarck's cartel policy.

* * *

The deputy Max Weber, Sr. was one of Bennigsen's followers, which meant that he adhered strictly to a middle course, deplored the split in the left wing as a disaster for liberalism, and worked for unity in the party. The son evidently agreed with his father in essence, but did not tie himself down to party lines. He did not have a one-sided liberal orientation, for a firmly established *national power state* appeared to him as the necessary basis of everything else. Nor did he subscribe to a glorification of the idea of the state at the expense of intellectual freedom and the rights of the individual. For the time being he was primarily interested in learning, observing, assessing, and understanding the various currents. His reports to Hermann Baumgarten do not reflect even a trace of one-sided partisanship or youthful stubbornness; rather, they are indicative of an endeavor to understand events on their own terms, to grasp them objectively, and to do justice to the various motives of political action. And he tried to lead his uncle, who was able to take only a disappointed and critical view of the Bismarck era, to a more positive evaluation of it.

This wait-and-see attitude is exemplified by a statement he made when he was twenty about the *Sozialistengesetz*, for the extension of which the National Liberal Party was responsible:

> If one wants to justify it, one probably has to take the point of view (which may not be entirely incorrect) that without this law a very

---

[17]Adolf Stöcker, 1835–1909, pastor, Berlin court chaplain, politician, and anti-Semitic agitator; Wilhelm Baron von Hammerstein, 1838–1904, Conservative leader, Reichstag deputy, editor of the reactionary *Kreuzzeitung.*—Ed.

considerable curtailment of many achievements of public life—freedom
of speech, rights of assembly and of association in general—would be inevitable. After all, with their style of agitation, the Social Democrats were about to compromise profoundly some fundamental institutions of public life. Should there now be a general restriction on these
basic rights, which are considered indispensable for public freedom, or is
it better to experiment with the two-edged sword of repressive exceptional laws? There probably was justification for such an experiment.
Privately, it sometimes seems to me that universal, equal rights for all
should take precedence over everything else, and that in the final analysis it would be better to muzzle all than to fetter some. The cardinal
fault really is the Greek gift of Bismarck's Caesarism, universal sufferage,
the veriest murder of *equal rights for all in the true sense of the word.*

Weber's sense of justice reacted against exceptional laws that impeded
the fight of the proletarians (who were becoming more demanding) for their
interests. On the other hand, he disapproved of the symbol of political
equality of rights—apparently because it was Bismarck's original plan to use
universal suffrage in the Reich to keep liberalism in check. The entire situation inevitably led to continual conflicts with the powerful man who was
ruling Germany. Weber's judgment of him was in the same vein in those early years as it was thirty years later: admiring recognition of his incomparable
political genius and his policy that aimed at Germany's power and unity,
but also a rejection of uncritical devotion and deification. *"Bismarck sans
phrase"* [Bismarck without question], the slogan that was forced upon
so many of his generation, to him seemed not simply a way of clouding political judgment but also meant the adoration of ruthlessness in military and
other matters and inner coarseness and shallowness. Then, too, the concrete parliamentary experience of his father convinced Weber at an early age
that the demigod was not only making political mistakes but also had
human weaknesses which he would pay for on his own account and on behalf
of the nation.

What Weber disapproved of more than anything else was Bismarck's way
of dealing with people—that he tolerated no strong, independent political
minds around him so that his power might be absolute, that he played off
his officials one against the other, doing them moral harm in the process
and making it impossible for men of integrity, such as Bennigsen, to take
over responsible posts. Such men came to expect that even as they started
in office the confidence of their fellow workers had already been so under-

mined that a small matter was enough to bring the office holder down again—without outsiders realizing who was pulling the strings. "It is becoming more and more apparent how well Bismarck has succeeded in either destroying all truly independent and important political associates and possible successors or in sidetracking them completely. Under such circumstances, who can be surprised if a great number of people who originally had different views are now interested only in him?"

Then as later, Weber regarded as a particularly reprehensible aspect of Bismarck's behavior his insatiable lust for power, which led him to tolerate no important personalities around him, thus making himself ever more indispensable and accustoming the nation to his political guardianship. To be sure, Weber did not consider Bismarck solely responsible for this situation, of which the disastrous effects became increasingly apparent in the crucial years of a change in emperors; he also blamed the nation which put up with the arbitrary rule of a strong-man. "The terrible destruction of independent opinion which Bismarck has caused among us is, of course, the main reason, or one of the main reasons, for all the flaws in our present situation. But are we not at least as much to blame for this as Bismarck himself?"

Even as a young man Weber regarded the education of the nation to independence of political thought and intellectual freedom as being of paramount importance; that is why he repeatedly took issue with Treitschke's teaching method. The circles influenced by this brilliant teacher believed that history extending up to the present should be regarded as a tool for political education and therefore, in contrast to the study of past history, can dispense with scholarly objectivity. Treitschke acted in accordance with this belief. He politicized his students, filled them with enthusiasm for Bismarck and the Hohenzollern dynasty, and stirred up anti-Semitism among them. The twenty-three-year-old Weber, who abhorred "the anti-Semitic battle cries of the conservatives" as much as he detested the Hohenzollern legend, decried "the decidedly disagreeable effect this personal influence has on the students' modesty of judgment, their judiciousness and sense of justice." Weber regarded this way of influencing young people at a time "when a man is supposed to be looking for a point of view of his own" as pernicious. The impressions he gained in Treitschke's course probably helped to convince him that an intentional molding of those in process of development by forcing political value judgments upon them has no place on the rostrum and that a teacher who tries to influence docile youth as a demagogue or "prophet" in the lecture room is overstepping his authority.

Weber tried nevertheless to be fair even to the passionate and fervent historian, as he did to Bismarck, by attributing his effectiveness not to him alone but to his environment as well. To enable H. Baumgarten to understand Treitschke's "idealism," Weber sent him a little volume of poems with these words:

> If certain things were not already current among my contemporaries—a veneration of militaristic ruthlessness and other kinds of inconsiderateness, the culture of so-called realism, and a philistine disregard of all those endeavors that hope to reach their goal without an appeal to the bad qualities of people, particularly brutality—then the countless, often glaring instances of one-sidedness, the vehemence of the struggle against other views, and the predilection for what is today called Realpolitik—a predilection caused by the powerful impression of success—would not be the only things that students derive from Treitschke's lectures. They would reserve their judgment on such things, or they would regard them as disagreeable excesses; but in all this, and sometimes even in these very excesses of political passion and one-sidedness, they would discern the man's great and ardent striving for an idealistic basis, and some of this they would carry away with them. The way things are now, to be sure, serious, conscientious work, work that is not concerned with results and is done only in the interest of *truth*, is held in low esteem, and a boorish self-conceit, which often is unbearable even in conversation, as well as a singular crudity of judgment toward all "nonopportunistic" views hold sway. (1887)

Weber always judged political events on the basis of one thing to which he clung all his life: *Intellectual freedom* was to him the greatest good, and under no circumstances was he prepared to consider even interests of political power as more important and attainable for the individual. Not for reasons of political expediency, but only in the name of *conscience* does a man have the right to oppose the conscientiously held different beliefs of others. On this basis he rejected the *Kulturkampf*, just as he later opposed the Prussian language policy for the Germanization of the Poles. To be sure, he could not rejoice when Bismarck ended the *Kulturkampf* in his favorite way by yielding to the Curia suddenly and completely, for this was tantamount to a confession that an injustice had been done to the Catholics.

The bill relating to ecclesiastical policy has now been passed; parts of Bismarck's speeches on that occasion once more had some of the breadth of world history about them, and now that this matter was to be brought to a conclusion, it contrasted favorably with what had been said by most people. Still, this unceremonious "peace" is sad, and in any case it is a confession of an injustice, a grievous injustice, if one says today that there were only "political" reasons for the struggle on our side. If it is true that for us it was not a matter of conscience but only one of expediency, then we really have done violence to the conscience of the Catholic people, as the Catholics say we have, for reasons that were of an external nature. For most of the Catholics it surely was a matter of conscience, and in that case it was not a matter of conscience against conscience, as we always reminded them. We have acted *without conscience*, then, and are the losers morally as well. This is the worst part of our defeat, for it prevents us from ever resuming the struggle the way it must be resumed if it is to lead to victory. (1887)

Nevertheless, Weber was unable to agree with the policies of the liberal left of the time, a group that represented the old libertarian ideals of personality with greater vigor than the right wing. He deplored the split and regarded the chronic opposition of the *Freisinn* [Left-Wing Liberal] Party to Bismarck, particularly in the approval of the budget, as unfruitful and injurious to liberalism. "For what shall one say about a party which has for years rejected every request for expenditures that was made of the Reich, on the grounds that the resources had not been substantial, and now that the means are to be provided, rejects this by saying expressly that no need for it has been established—an amusing dilemma" (1887, on the occasion of the financial bills).

And then, the Liberals lacked great leaders: "The thought that these people could be called upon some day to take Bismarck's place always gives one the shivers . . ." He criticized the hope of the left wing that Bismarck would resign while Friedrich was on the throne, for it made him conclude that the leadership lacked some sound political judgment.

For this very reason one must completely abandon any thought of a future positive policy in concert with these people, and this perpetuates the split of liberalism as well as the spectacle of liberalism being compromised by stereotyped, fanaticized demagogues on the one hand and by blind Bismarckites on the other. Yet one had to hope that in time some of the once-united elements would come from the left and return to positive participation. (1888)

* * *

The events of the year 1888—the death of the old emperor and particularly the tragedy of Emperor Friedrich[18]—profoundly shook young Weber: "I am continually thinking of public affairs." He felt profound compassion for the unfortunate empress, who was unpopular both as a foreigner and an uncommonly distinguished woman.[19] She was involved in a conflict with Bismarck—which humanly speaking was by no means to her discredit—having to sacrifice her daughter's happiness to the interest of the state,[20] and this earned her the animosity of the conservative press.

When after Friedrich's short reign Wilhelm II mounted the throne, Weber was particularly interested in seeing him removed from high-church and feudal influences, and he viewed the preservation of Bismarck's position of power as the only effective counterbalance to such influences:

> There were other indications, too, that Bismarck's influence upon him has more and more become so exclusive that checking the truly reactionary tendencies the Crown Prince [Wilhelm II] has probably absorbed is largely a matter of how much longer he will live. For there is no doubt that Bismarck is not favoring these tendencies for their own sake. He is aware of the danger they pose; the only precarious feature of his policy was that he tried to *use* them for his purposes and that he was not quite able to do this without being used by them. (April 30, 1888)

It seemed decisive to him for the future of the state

> whether Bismarck will, just as soon as the situation is normalized, think it is time to give some thought to his successor and will reestablish contact with the really statesmanlike elements. If that is not done, a serious danger may be posed by radical countercurrents and, if the banner of the Reich is to be carried by the Prussian Junkers in concert with the ultramontanists, by the decline of the national elements in Central Germany. This is something that no one will deny.

---

[18]Friedrich III, who had succeeded Wilhelm I, died of cancer of the throat after three months on the throne.—Ed.

[19]Victoria Adelaide Mary Louise, 1840–1901, a daughter of Queen Victoria of England.—Ed.

[20]Princess Victoria was engaged to Prince Alexander of the Hessian collateral line of Battenberg, who incurred the disfavor of the Russians as ruler of Bulgaria.—Ed.

Weber soon saw the possible dangers of Wilhelm II's will to power and particularly of his quickly apparent need to assert himself in public. At the end of 1889 he expressed himself about this as follows: "These Boulangist-Bonapartist proclamations are by now unwelcome. It is as though one were sitting in a railway train proceeding at a great speed, wondering whether the next switch will be placed properly." A year and a half later, after Bismarck's fall, he wrote:

What is beneficial about this situation is that it was not simply a matter of one Caesar, the Kaiser, succeeding the other, Bismarck, but that both are in conflict with each other, which has prevented people from dispensing with their own judgment. In almost no case can one speak of such a dispensation as far as the Kaiser is concerned. . . . Even those who judge him most favorably have an open mind, and so far one has nowhere encountered that fanatical support of his person as of a dogma, which always characterized the adherents of Bismarck. From *this* point of view it is a commendable quality of the Kaiser that he does not fully please any faction—and has thus far affronted one after another on some occasion or other. (1891)

One year later (1892) even this indirect merit of the monarch has been cancelled out for Weber by the faults of his policies. The following judgment remained definitive and was only strengthened by subsequent political events:

The most unfavorable opinions of him keep gaining ground. He evidently treats politics only from the point of view of an ingenious lieutenant. No one will deny that he vigorously does his duty in the sense of service. But the wrongheadedness that prevails in between times and the uncanny consciousness of power which animates him have brought such an unprecedented disorganization to the highest places that it is bound to have an effect upon the administration as a whole. For example, he has gradually reduced Caprivi,[21] who is humanly so estimable, to a caricature, and by now one can hardly speak of an authority of the Reich government. We are currently escaping diplomatically truly serious situations as if by a miracle. But there can be no doubt that European politics are no longer directed from Berlin. (1892)

---

[21]Count Georg Leon von Caprivi, 1831–1899, German imperial chancellor (1890–94) and Prussian prime minister (1890–92).—Ed.

III

But in spite of the fact that the horizon of foreign and domestic politics was increasingly clouding over, Weber was unable to share the pessimism of Hermann Baumgarten's old age. He was young, and he could see hopeful signs of a promising future beyond the fading glories of dynastic policies. During his period as a *Referendar* (from 1886 on) Weber associated with a circle of young people—economists, officials of various political hues interested in social welfare, some of them students of the *Kathedersozialisten* [academic socialists]—who had an interest in social ideas. These people no longer subsisted on the political heritage of their fathers; there was a new Spring of political interests and objectives.

As Weber saw them, they were not the "disagreeable types" of anti-Semites, nationalistic fanatics, supposed realists, or gentlemanly windbags. They had

> a basis substantially different from that of the National Liberalism of the seventies, but one that is equally free of class desires and high-church tendencies, and they are completely above any suspicion of careerism and other subjective considerations. In short, I am not in a position to dispute their intellectual freedom. They too view the period between 1867 and 1877 in a substantially different light from what has been customary. Most of them are primarily economists and social reformers, and so it is not surprising that the state's intervention in the so-called social question should seem more important to them than will seem justified to others on the basis of present conditions.

The awakening of these social and sociopolitical interests, the first traces of which may be found in a letter dating from 1887, removed Weber from the National Liberal politics of his father, policies that were increasingly used by the big industrial entrepreneurs to press their economic demands.

> The incontrovertible facts that the liberalism of the seventies subordinated the social tasks of the state to other things more than can be justified or, at any rate, more than what we now regard as normal; that social legislation is even now endured by the liberals with an almost entirely passive distrust, which may often be quite justified, instead of acting and removing the really considerable reservations by

making some modification; that, generally speaking, the liberals are not exclusively interested in legislative projects (and justifiably so, in my opinion)—this is what causes these politicians to regard the National Liberal era merely as a transition to greater tasks of the state . . . (April 30, 1888)

Weber's first trip to the ballot box was not made in the interest of the candidate of the National Liberal Party; he voted the Free Conservative ticket instead. It may have been because he expected a greater understanding of the representation of social interests from that quarter and at the same time was attracted by the party's attitude in questions of power politics. However, he did not become a partisan of any political group. Later he often referred to that first vote, but never to his motives for it.

The "shift in generations" had taken place. The sun of culture had moved on; other problems were illuminated for the young generation than had been exposed to their fathers, and with them they received different impulses for action and investigation. *"Der neue Trieb erwacht . . ."* [The new impulse awakens . . .][22]

* * *

From the beginning these interests of Weber's had a twofold character: they were shaped by national-political ideals on the one hand and by his newly awakened feeling of social responsibility and justice on the other. In assessing the economy, technology, and political institutions, he asked to what extent they were suitable pillars for Germany's position as a great power, and to this question he added another: What arrangements could be made to assure a dignified, cheerful, and healthy existence for the Germans, who, be they farmers or industrial workers, were creating the substructure of national power with their hands?

Weber's passion for the national power state evidently sprang from an innate instinct that could not be affected by any reflection: The powerful nation is the extension of the body of a greatly gifted person, and to endorse it is to endorse oneself. His growing social interest was made more vibrant by the fact that it was so dear to the hearts of people to whom he felt close—his mother, Ida Baumgarten, and her son Otto.

---

[22]From Goethe's *Faust I*, line 1085: "The newborn impulse fires my mind" (Bayard Taylor's translation).—Ed.

Weber worked on a new periodical founded by Otto Baumgarten that was devoted to the social enlightenment of clergymen. They were to be put in touch with social reformers and officials in an effort to increase mutual understanding of their different worlds. Weber sought to interest Hermann Baumgarten in this project as well, and wrote him about it as follows:

It will surely be salutary for the theologians and will promote respect for their profession if they are, as in this case, obliged to speak with relative sobriety in the language of other mortals. Conversely, laymen, especially younger officials and those with a lively interest in social policy, are accustomed to a very serious degree to respecting the church in a superficial and conventional way. Leaving aside those who are totally indifferent, these men have serious doubts of the clergy's practical abilities. It seems useful to me—if only in view of the young social reformers' judgment of the social scale of values and the capacity of the Catholic church as compared to the Protestant church—to get these circles accustomed to the idea of joining forces with the blackcoats, whom they have placed *ad acta* [written off]. (1891)

* * *

Social questions had been in the air for some time; the practical problems of modern industrialism kept them in the minds and on the consciences of thinking people. As early as the seventies it again became clear to small groups of the bourgeoisie that if imminent misfortune was to be averted they would have to concern themselves with social questions. The *Gründerphase*[23] [founding phase], which favored ostentation, the creation of new wealth by the development of heavy industry, and the free sway of the acquisitive urge, separated the life-styles of the property owners and the masses of manual workers more conspicuously than ever before. The brilliant thinkers of socialism had forged intellectual weapons for the unpropertied to use in their fight against a social order that chained millions to machines for the benefit of a minority, without offering them more than the barest subsistence in return. The Social Democrats, as the party of those who had nothing to sell but their labor and "nothing to lose but your chains," shook the foundations of a propertied and legal order that sanctified this situation. At the same time, by means of a new scale of values, they sought to free the masses from the spell of a church that left

---

[23]*Gründerphase, Gründerjahre, Gründerzeit* commonly refer to the period of expansion and reckless financial speculation that followed the Franco-Prussian War in the early 1870s.—Ed.

the propertied their good conscience, referred those without property to the hereafter, and thus functioned as a "black police" for the state.

A number of outstanding scholars in the field of economics, such as Adolf Wagner, Schmoller, Brentano, Knapp,[24] and others, as well as teachers of law like Gneist, understood the reasons for a socialist critique of society. A few of them assigned some of the blame for the exacerbation of class conflicts to the laissez-faire, laissez-passer [lack of restraint] of the free-trade doctrine and to the followers of the Manchester School with their approval of a ruthless pursuit of profit. They demanded that economics orient itself to ethical ideals again and that the state regulate free work contracts. These men, whom their opponents mockingly called *"Kathedersozialisten,"* influenced students with their lectures and their writings. In order to gain influence over wider circles and the state as well, they founded the *Verein für Sozialpolitik* (1873), which was joined by businessmen, industrialists, and officials.

At a preliminary discussion in Eisenach, in which men of every political persuasion participated, the interest centered on the labor question. Gustav Schmoller outlined a program to which the Association substantially adhered, although there were numerous additions. He espoused a view of the state that was "equally far removed from the glorification of the individual under natural law with all its capriciousness and the absolutistic theory of the all-devouring power of the state." While he acknowledged the splendid progress of technology and its accomplishments for the economy, he was also aware of the serious situation that had been produced by the mounting inequality in property and income and its effects upon morality. He saw as the main cause of these ills the fact that all advances in the division of labor and in legislation were invariably concerned with an increase in production rather than with their effect upon human beings. The Association, so he said, did not want a leveling of society. It rejected socialistic experiments and recognized the existing forms of production and property, but it fought for an improvement in the situation of the working classes.

The initial demands of this circle were that the government regulate work contracts, enact factory laws, control banks and commerce, provide better education, training, and housing for workers, etc. The Association brought together scholars and practical men and placed scientific work in the service of life. The joint exploration of social and economic "questions"

---

[24]Adolf Wagner, 1835–1917, professor at Dorpat, Freiburg, and Berlin; Gustav von Schmoller, 1838–1917, professor at Halle, Strasbourg, and Berlin; Lujo Brentano, 1844–1931, professor at Breslau, Strasbourg, Vienna, Leipzig, and Munich; Georg Friedrich Knapp, 1842–1926, professor at Leipzig and Strasbourg.—Ed.

was organized to that end; the material gained in this way was to serve as a basis for verbal discussion. In the first decade of its existence, the Association submitted its proposals directly to the legislators. In those days its meetings were filled with lively propaganda designed to interest people in all walks of life in social welfare. But when at the beginning of the eighties Bismarck started to engage in social politics, thus reducing the prospects for a direct influence upon the governmental machinery, the Association gave up its activities of agitation and replaced propagandistic with academic discussion. The accent was shifted to strictly scientific investigations of current problems.

It was at this stage that Weber joined the Association, and he remained a permanent member. At that time the agrarian question was a burning problem, for the landed proprietors—hitherto a class that had always claimed to have a special mandate to protect the state—now requested special governmental protection of their economic interests by an increase in the duties on grain, a prohibition of transfers, and the like.

On assignment from the Association, around 1890–91, Weber began investigating the condition of agrarian workers. An inquiry was organized, and Weber designed the questionnaire that was sent to the landowners. The material that came in was distributed among several young social reformers. Weber himself worked on the most important part: *The Situation of Farm Workers in Germany East of the Elbe River.* This first work of his in the field of political economy, almost 900 pages in length, was written with lightning speed within a year, while he was giving his first law courses. It immediately established the young scholar's reputation in a discipline that was outside his field. From that time on he was regarded as an expert in agrarian matters.

One of the masters of political economy, especially agrarian history, G. F. Knapp, gave a report on the results of the inquiry at the Association's convention in the spring of 1893. "Finally," he said, "a monograph has been written by Dr. Max Weber about the situation of the workers east of the Elbe which has astounded all readers with its wealth of thought and profundity of insight. This work more than anything else has given me the feeling that our expertise is at an end, that we have to start learning afresh."

This was the first occasion on which Weber addressed a larger group of scholars and social reformers. Speaking plainly and without notes, he gave an account of the results of his work.[25] The situation was as follows: The landed nobility was beginning to feel a labor shortage. The most vigorous and best-paid elements of the peasant population, who had for many years

---

[25]Cf. *Gesammelte Aufsätze zur Wirtschaftsgeschichte,* pp. 444ff.

rendered statute service with hand and horse for remuneration in kind, were leaving their home soil and going overseas or overcrowding the big cities. Poles and Russians by the thousands were flooding the eastern boundaries, which Bismarck had opened only to migratory workers and closed to settlers. His successor was not strong enough to resist pressure from the landed nobility. Now the foreigners came in unimpeded, initially as seasonal workers. But some of them stayed put and in this way occupied the eastern borderlands that the Germans had wrested from these people centuries before. What was the reason for that? Where did the danger lie and how could it be met? These were not only questions for those directly involved; they must also be of interest to politicians.

First of all, what was the reason for it? The inquiry revealed as the most important reason for the depopulation of the eastern rural regions the dissolution of the old collective agrarian system in favor of large-scale farming. The landowners acquired more and more land, replaced the old privileges and payments in kind of their tenant farmers with money wages, and managed things with an eye to the market, thus changing from a patriarchal, seignorial class to a commercial, entrepreneurial class and destroying the former community of interest with their workers. The workers, who no longer had a share in the yield of the soil and no hope of independence in the form of land of their own, left their masters' employment—not for material reasons, for the best-paid people in particular did so, but for idealistic reasons, in order to be free. "Their illusions are evidence that in economic life, too, there are ideals with a power that is greater than that of the bread-and-butter question." A person's subservience to a master cannot be maintained if the master's personal responsibility for the individual worker dwindles. The consequence of this was the landed nobility's interest in cheap and tractable labor. Poles and Russians were brought into the country by the thousands. Precisely in the east that meant a serious national danger. The immigration of foreigners increased the desire to emigrate; moreover, the nutritional and cultural level of the German rural population was reduced to that of an inferior eastern civilization.

Weber looked at this entire process, which he had illuminated, from an austere, statesmanlike point of view. "I regard the question of farm labor merely as one of political common sense—neither as the question of whether the farm workers are badly off or well off, nor as the problem of how the landed proprietors may be provided with cheap labor." He felt that agrarian policy must be determined not by production interests but by the interests of the *state*, the interest in the preservation of a dense, vigorous, loyal rural population as a reservoir for national armed forces and the peaceful defense of the eastern borderlands. Therefore: close the border again; prevent the farmland from being swallowed up by the large estates; colonize systematically. "We wish to weld the small farmers to the soil of the fatherland, not with legal but with psychological bonds. I say it openly: we wish to exploit their land hunger in order to tie them to the homeland. And even if we had to ram a generation into the soil in order to guarantee the future of Germany, we would shoulder this responsibility."

It was in a peculiarly resigned mood that Weber viewed the tasks of his time.

I do not know whether my contemporaries share my feeling of the moment with equal intensity: It is the cruel curse of epigonism which burdens the nation, from its broad ranks up to the very top. We can no longer revive the naive, enthusiastic vigor that animated the generation before us—because the tasks we face are different in nature from those that confronted our fathers. . . . We cannot appeal to great emotions shared by the whole nation, as was the case when it was a question of creating a unified nation and a free constitution.

But he nevertheless had a vision of a national future that would make worthwhile the work done on domestic problems, tasks that appeared small by comparison with the work of the previous generation.

When we look back someday, we hope to be able to say: at this point the Prussian state recognized its social mission in good time. To be sure, we make greater claims on the future. We believe that it will honor the bills of exchange we are drawing on it. We hope that at the end of our days we shall be granted what youth has denied us: to look calmly into the future of the nation and to be able to proceed on the basis of a firm social organization of the state and of the people to solve the *cultural tasks* we shall face at the time.

"At evening time there shall be light" [Zech. 14:7]—this was Weber's hope as a young man endowed with political instinct and acute judgment who was already greatly concerned about the conduct of the nation's responsible leaders. However, the end of his life was to be a time of deepest darkness.

* * *

At the same time as the *Verein für Sozialpolitik* gave Max Weber the impe-

tus for expanding his work into the field of political economics, his sociopolitical interests were stimulated in yet another, neighboring field. The activity of social agitation that the above-mentioned association had abandoned was now taken up by a group of Protestant theologians who had been
inspired by the ideas of the *Kathedersozialisten* and worked in close collaboration with them. Like the Catholic church, the Protestant church had
realized that mere *charitable activity* was insufficient in the face of proletarian
misery. It also recognized the danger to its own existence. The disturbing
growth of Social Democracy led to an intellectual "revolution" and brought
the defection of the masses from Christianity and their emancipation from
the traditional authorities dangerously close. This danger opened people's
eyes. They recognized the effects of the machine age and were shocked as
they confronted phenomena that they had been unable or unwilling to see
before. They took a fresh look at the Bible and found that some of the
socialist demands were justified by the Gospels.

Some clergymen joined with socialist professors to form an association
that demanded from the church "resolute support of the justified demands
of the fourth estate" and from the government "a vigorous initiative in
support of workingmen for a policy of sweeping social reforms." Stöcker called
upon the clergymen to study the social question and join together in a
Christian Social party. State socialism seemed to that circle to be the economic system appropriate to Christianity. The court preacher, who was
greatly gifted as an agitator, reminded the Christian state of its duties,
called upon the propertied to meet the just demands of the unpropertied,
and founded a workers' party on a monarchic-Christian basis by means of
which he hoped to wrest the masses from the Marxist-oriented Social Democrats. It was in vain. His party had no success among the workers, and
hence it became a party of "little people," with an agrarian and middle-class
orientation and a markedly conservative bent. It was pointedly opposed to
the Jews and the nonchurchgoing liberals, and this diminished its effectiveness among the bourgeoisie as well. From the outside it was checkmated
by Bismarck's cartel policy. The church authorities warned against mixing
religion with politics. However, the attempt to bring the church close to
the life of the people and to make the idea of state socialism palatable to
conservative circles was of lasting significance.

Stöcker now sought a sphere of influence in foreign policy. In 1890 he convened the first Evangelical-Social Congress. It was intended to be a nonpartisan meeting place and forum for theologians of various persuasions, socially conscious officials, politicians, and political economists, a place for

the joint discussion of burning social and moral questions. The first convention took place in 1890 at Whitsuntide. Those invited were men of every political and ecclesiastic orientation "who believed in preserving the state and were favorably disposed toward the church." Prominent personalities of many types—particularly theologians, including many church dignitaries—were in attendance. The imperial message of February 4, 1890, which called for more laws for the protection of the working class, reassured the rightists that in participating in the Congress they were not on the wrong track. Moreover, the abrogation of the antisocialist legislation was imminent; something had to be done to forestall the danger of a revolution. Thus there was an agreement between high-church authorities like Stöcker, Nathusius, Cremer, Dryander,[26] and undogmatic, research-minded theologians like Kaftan, von Soden, von Harnack, and, among younger men, Rade, Baumgarten, Göhre, and Bonus.[27] Some high officials and politicians attended as well. Among the rightists, the pure figure of the aged Pastor von Bodelschwingh[28] was touching. His simple religious spirit and brotherly love breathed the spirit of a genuine discipleship of Jesus. Theological disputes and arguments on church policy between the orthodox and the liberal authorities at first took up a great deal of time. People predominantly spoke "the language of Canaan," avoided any radical note, and had harsh words for Social Democracy, which was robbing the shepherds of their flock in order to lead it into the desert of unbelief and hostility to authority. But the gathering also was genuinely eager to help, and it was willing to examine the fateful causes for the rise of Social Democratic power in greater depth than had been done before.

As to the religious and economic crisis, the Congress spoke of collective guilt, and it resolved to work "to make the classes conscious of their social obligations toward one another and get them to fulfill them, and in particular to make employers acknowledge the morally equal value of labor." In

---

[26]Martin von Nathusius, 1843–1906, professor at Greifswald from 1888 on; Hermann Cremer, 1834–1903, professor at Greifswald from 1870 on; Ernst von Dryander, 1843–1922, chief court preacher in Berlin from 1898 to 1918.—Ed.

[27]Julius Kaftan, 1848–1926, professor at Basel and Berlin; Hermann von Soden, 1852–1914, New Testament scholar, professor at Berlin from 1893 on; Adolf von Harnack, 1851–1930, Protestant theologian, professor at Leipzig, Giessen, Marburg, and Berlin, president of the *Evangelisch-Sozialer Kongress* from 1903 to 1911, author of *Das Wesen des Christentums* and other works; Martin Rade, 1857–1940, professor at Marburg from 1904 on; Paul Göhre, 1864–1928; Artur Bonus, 1864–1941, author of *Von Stöcker zu Naumann* (1896).—Ed.

[28]Friedrich von Bodelschwingh, 1831–1910, founder of the church-supported Bethel Heilstätte (sanatorium) near Bielefeld.—Ed.

order to familiarize himself with the inner life and the milieu of the industrial proletariat, P. Göhre went to work in a factory for a few months and then published his impressions, which caused a sensation.[29] The Second Congress featured a discussion of the new "religion" of the workers, the materialistic view of history, and it was stated that the church's most important social task was to overcome this view. At the same time it was decided that the economic goals for which the workers were striving under the leadership of Social Democracy could not and must not be opposed in the name of the church.

In the audience were Helene Weber and her eldest son Max, who wrote: "It always gives my mother a lot of pleasure to listen to the wrangling among the pastors, who are often somewhat naive but are usually ingenious. There really is something refreshing about the enviable ease with which, trusting in the better understanding of the Good Lord, they surmount economic problems over which we wrack our brains; and yet one cannot really accuse them of being superficial."

When around that time an orthodox Konsistorialrat [consistorial councillor] attacked Göhre's publication and person, Weber came to his defense in Die christliche Welt [The Christian World]: "Göhre's study—this I, and not I alone, can certify from personal experience—has built a bridge to an understanding between the young theologians and the social reformers and future officials . . ." At the same time Weber rejected the authoritarian view, still prevalent among the older theologians, of the workers' intellectual quest to be emancipated from the domination of the creed. "Modern workingmen want more than forbearance, compassionate understanding, and charity; they demand the recognition of their right to reflect about the same things, and in the same way, as the so-called educated people. . . . Their intellect has emancipated itself from bondage to tradition, and we should not only understand this and view it with indulgence, but take it into account and recognize it as something justified."

Among those in attendance at the Third Congress was Friedrich Naumann,[30] who was at that time chaplain to the inner mission in Frankfurt am Main and already known as the "poor people's pastor" and leader of the younger members of the Christian-Social movement. In that circle he was the fiery storm-and-stress man whose social fervor transformed the slow-

---

[29]*Drei Monate Fabrikarbeiter* [Three Months as a Factory Worker], Leipzig, 1891.—Ed.

[30]1860–1919, theologian and politician, founder of the *Nationalsozialer Verein* and of the periodical *Die Hilfe.* —Ed.

moving theological casuistry of more scholarly minds and cooler heads into an unreserved recognition of social distress and of the obligations of Christian circles.

At first Naumann considered himself exclusively as an advocate of the proletarians. He was a democrat by conviction and genuinely religious, but he did not feel bound by any dogma and was indifferent to church politics. He did not pursue any personal or partisan power, but merely wished to help the unpropertied secure their temporal rights and at the same time to fill them with new hope and faith. Only his religious beliefs kept him from joining the Social Democrats. He hoped that Marxism would be conquered from within by a living and developing Christianity and that a Christian-Social era would replace Social Democracy. "The Christian-Social movement is to us something evolving, a dynamic spring song that fills our souls." In concrete matters he, like Stöcker, proceeded from the hope that it would be possible to place alongside the Social Democratic workers' movement an equally well-prepared Christian movement that would not be tied down by Marxism and international connections. Jesus was to be resurrected as a man of the people, and the Christian ethos was to have a regenerative effect.

Naumann characterized socialism as inner-worldly chiliasm—though sin militated against its realization. However, "Christians must believe that they are making progress in their efforts to bring about earthly happiness; otherwise there will be nothing moral and enthusiastic about their work." Of course, he found no instructions for an ideal economic system in the Gospels, but he did discover guidelines there: "According to the New Testament, the conquest of poverty is an immediate task of Christianity." The theological authorities reacted to such interpretations and theses with disagreement and disapproval, but his way of thinking particularly inspired younger people; they joined him in rejecting the edifying way in which their elders sought to gloss over class differences. "We wish to shine the bright, clear light of the Gospels on our economic conditions and by this light seek a way to improve them and remedy our moral defects." Naumann was joined by the theologians Otto Baumgarten, the editor of *Evangelisch-Soziale Zeitfragen* [Modern Evangelical-Social Problems]; Martin Rade, whose weekly, *Die christliche Welt*, reflected an undogmatic religiosity; Paul Göhre, the first man to become personally familiar with the outward and inward fate of proletarians; and others—a circle of enthusiastic, high-minded people, united by exalted aims.

Naumann's and Göhre's hope that the workers would join together in a party other than Social Democracy proved to be unrealizable for them, as it had for Stöcker. However, Naumann and his friends had a more lasting influence upon the social thinking of the middle classes than the older movement had been able to achieve, for Naumann's effect was a wholly positive rather than a polemical one. He was not only an inspiring prophet, but also had that "holy sobriety" which always tries to grasp and shape concrete matters in accordance with their own possibilities. He was a thinker who unceasingly strove for an unbiased knowledge of reality and was always ready to adjust his views, who always sought the advice and instruction of scientifically trained men.

Naumann and Weber met at one of the first Evangelical-Social congresses. Their acquaintance soon blossomed into friendship and became important for Naumann in particular. He sensed in the younger man an innate political instinct that he himself lacked, and he soon chose the young expert as a source of knowledge and guidance in political and economic matters. From the beginning, they shared a positive attitude toward mechanization and industrialism as a sine qua non for a great power with a growing population. They did not wish to turn back the wheel of history, but they wanted to fight the defects of the modern capitalistic system from within. On the other hand, both men regarded the capitalistic development of the large estates in the provinces east of the Elbe as a national and social disaster.

The main idea that Naumann derived from Max Weber was the latter's evaluation of national power. Under Weber's influence Naumann recognized that the preservation and advancement of Germany's position as a great power was not only a duty dictated by the past but also a prerequisite for a decent life for the masses. The goal of both men's political action was a fatherland organized along the lines of a power state with a growing, hardworking population whose complete political maturity would enable it both to protect its own rights and to share in the responsibility for the fate of the nation. At a later date Naumann's phrase for this was *Demokratie und Kaisertum* [democracy and imperial rule],[31] in the hope that Wilhelm II would decide to become a "social-minded emperor."

At the suggestion of Göhre and Weber, who had also become friends, a discussion of the agrarian question was planned for the Fifth Evangelical-

---

[31]*Demokratie und Kaisertum: Ein Handbuch für innere Politik* is the title of a book by Naumann (1900).—Ed.

Social Congress. The friends joined together to make another survey of the situation of the farm workers. The questionnaires of the *Verein für Sozialpolitik* had previously gone to the employers, but this time the questionnaires were sent to the country parsons. These men were a more impartial group; besides, they were to be aroused to social activity in this manner.

This time the intention was to determine not only the economic situation of farm workers, but also their intellectual, religious, and moral condition as well as the effect of one upon the other. Again, voluminous material was gathered, and Göhre and Weber reported about it at the Fifth Congress in Frankfurt am Main (1894). The results did not substantially differ from those of the earlier inquiry, but they furnished a valuable supplement to it.

Of the viewpoints from which Weber dealt with his subject the following is of interest: *He used concrete material to illustrate the limitations of the economic view of history.* The "ironclad wage law" was not observed in the country; low wages went hand in hand with high food prices, a low living standard of the workers was found side by side with a high quality of land, and vice versa. The decisive factor for the fortunes and the general situation of the farm laborers was not the general economic condition of their environment, but the traditional social stratification. In rural regions the latter was determined not by the technical and economic conditions, but by the way in which the population was grouped, the distribution of establishments and lands, and the legal aspects of the work contract.

Behind Weber's remarks there again was, as an undertone, the strict subordination of individual lives to national interests. Disagreeing with Naumann before this forum, he explicitly rejected the notion of being able or anxious to bring about the *happiness* of the masses.

We are not engaging in social politics in order to create human happiness. . . . Last night Pastor Naumann's address reflected an infinite yearning for human happiness, and I am sure all of us were moved. But our pessimistic attitude leads us, and me in particular, to a point of view that seems of incomparably greater importance to me. I believe we must forgo the creation of a positive feeling of happiness in the course of any social legislation. We desire something else and can only desire something else. We want to cultivate and support what appears to us as *valuable* in man: his personal responsibility, his basic drive toward higher things, toward the intellectual and moral values of mankind, even where this drive confronts us in its most primitive form.

Insofar as it is in our power, we wish to arrange external conditions not with a view toward people's well-being, but in such a way as to preserve—in the face of the inevitable struggle for existence with its suffering—those physical and spiritual qualities that we would like to maintain for the nation.

5

DOMESTIC LIFE
AND PERSONAL
DEVELOPMENT

We shall now return to other aspects of Weber's development, going back
to the year 1886 and showing first of all the domestic background of his
life.

Outwardly the family's way of life changed when, after the death of her
mother, Helene received what was then a substantial inheritance. To be
sure, they did not live pretentiously—that was impossible with such a large
household—but in 1885 the modest villa on Leibnizstrasse was enlarged for
the second time and a few drawing rooms were added. This obligated them
to lead an even more active social life. To the extent that this took the
form of a casual coming and going of old and young friends, it meant an
enrichment to most members of the family, particularly to Helene, for she
really enjoyed the good things of life only when she was able to share them
with others.

She liked nothing better than to fill her house and garden with young people her sons' age on Sundays, and so she opened her home to all sorts of persons without families of their own; young girls who were studying in Berlin she called her "Sunday daughters."

I only wish people had the time and the general willingness to open their homes to as many as possible on such days. This would be so much better for our young people than an uncritical reading and discussion of all the things that the newspaper drivel puts into their youthful minds. Then they would hear something sensible from time to time. And I see again and again that it does not take much effort to make everyone comfortable: some cold meat, a cup of tea, and beer.

Young friends of both sexes attended at will, and they usually showed up at the family table in the afternoon for these Sunday parties, which became a wonderful asset as the sons grew up.

People gathered about Helene who was so gracious and vibrant, so enthralled by everything that concerned the world around her. Her eyes shone with pure kindness and sympathy. She never sought out her own kind, but her most loving care was reserved for the disadvantaged. If the party was small, there was an hour of music making or reading aloud in the afternoon. She or the "big boy" brought to life simple, universally comprehensible pieces of literature, such as the works of Fritz Reuter.[1] The parties were not at all "literary." Most of the time, however, there was a lively exchange about political, social, and human subjects, and soon the *Referendar*, without wanting to, became the intellectual focus of the young people. In the evening, of course, it was not "some meat" that disappeared, but huge roasts and yards of sausages. So that the servants might have a day off, Helene prepared everything herself, together with her young female protégées; they had fun bustling about the big kitchen. Let Weber himself describe what happened on a Sunday when his parents were absent:

The two Sundays here were very lively. On the first I had lunch alone with Otto [Baumgarten] in the afternoon. Dr. Walter Lotz was the first to show up, as always laden with a lot of books on economics for me, and later he was followed by Hagen[2] and Karl Mommsen. A proper distribution between billiards and skat was made, and this really chewed up the afternoon. After dinner, to Mommsen's distress, there

[1]1810–1874, Low German storyteller and poet.—Ed.
[2]Hagen was the son of a city councillor.—ED.

developed instead a very animated political discussion about strikes, the anti-Socialist law, Stöcker, etc., with those opposing the Reich being in an alarming majority. This discussion lasted so long that Otto had trouble catching the last train and the others making the last streetcar.

The second Sunday went more according to plan, with Nasse[3] and Lotz present at noontime and in the afternoon. Nasse cleverly steered the conversation to questions of banking and currency, which are of no concern to him but are the special field of Lotz, whereupon Nasse enjoyed something that was much to his taste: he relaxed on the deck chair on the veranda and listened. He is a strange fellow; although he understood only half of it, he still enjoyed it. Toward evening, Greber, Homeyer, and of course Karl Mommsen joined us for a game of skat, made obligatory by the fact that Nasse had come for no other purpose. Otto showed up too, having just returned from Hamburg and Kiel. You see, this cannibal fodder, those six hapless male nurses in East Africa, had written him the most pitiful letters from Lower Italy: their funds are completely exhausted, and since they are too embarrassed to do so (!), he should intercede with Herr Wichern[4] on their behalf for that which the whole world screams for. This is what happens when one gets involved in paying for someone else's beer without any need to do so! . . . There seems to be a hair-raising confusion as well as a horrible ineptness on the part of the young people. If they continue to behave like that in Africa, they will probably soon wind up in the larder of some black chieftain as "cold missionary," like that nice picture in *Fliegende Blätter*. [5]

At a later date Karl Helfferich[6] was among the young people who were brought into the house by the sons. At that time it was mainly a shared interest in banking and the stock market that linked the promising young political economist to the sons, and they introduced him to the *Staatswissenschaftliche Gesellschaft* [Political Science Society], a circle of young people with political and social interests who met regularly on Thursday evenings.

* * *

---

[3]Dirk Nasse, a medical student.—Ed.
[4]Johann Hinrich Wichern, 1808–1881, theologian and educator, founder of the *Innere Mission*. —Ed.
[5]An illustrated comic magazine.—Ed.
[6]1872–1924, politician and economist, treasurer and deputy chancellor during World War I.—Ed.

As has been said, Helene needed this kind of informal hospitality as a fulfillment of a mission that was important to her. But the enlarged scope of their life also increased their obligation to give formal *Gesellschaften* [social gatherings] for older dignitaries, at which a long sequence of foods and drinks had to be served carefully and in accordance with social etiquette. This became an additional load and gave Helene even less leisure than before: "If I could have the feeling just once that my day's work is half way done, and if I could just read, write, and do things in peace without harming anyone! But I still can't accomplish even the barest necessities . . ." And then: was it right to spend money for such luxuries—stag dinners with choice wines—if one could not reserve at least an equal amount for those in need? But she would never have dared to discuss this with her husband, and she really could not give in to her impulses. As it was, he was beginning to regard her increasing urge to share a great deal of her prosperity with others as an eccentricity that he attributed to Ida's influence.

For this reason he did not even think of giving Helene the right to dispose of her own property. Instead, he was typical of the husbands of the time who needed to determine by themselves how the family income was to be used and left their wives and children in the dark as to how high the income was. That generation defended its patriarchal need for power on the grounds that women knew nothing about financial matters anyway, and that it was not part of their "nature" to concern themselves with them. In keeping with this tradition, then, Helene in her forties had neither a definite housekeeping allowance nor a special fund for her personal needs. Instead she had to go, on each occasion, clutching her cashbooks which were never entirely accurate, and request what she needed for the household and for herself. She was thus subject to constant control and, typically, to frequent criticism and surprise from her husband at the great expenditures, although he certainly was in no position to judge whether they were necessary. When more than half of the family income came from her own property, she began to feel that this situation was increasingly illogical and irksome.

The situation might have improved if Helene had earlier mustered the courage to risk a fight and simply demand a different order of things. But although in other ways valiant, she was too soft for that—something with which she reproached herself later; after all, it was a matter of self-interest, and even at that time she had not abandoned the idea of her God-ordained subordination and indulgence. She did not hide the fact that she suffered, but her husband disregarded it. He deemed it his duty as a paterfamilias to keep the property together and to hold his unbusinesslike and overgenerous wife in check. He simply did not have a charitable disposition and viewed his own considerable extravagance as that of a man of means, with the clear conscience of his class.

Helene realized too late that in every respect it would have been better to fight him than to suffer, for now the pressure she felt frequently became so severe that she had to unburden herself to her grown son. In doing so, however, she unintentionally made him side against his father. At the same time the son realized that it was a mistake to keep putting the husband in the wrong because of his wife's suffering. Since Helene was seldom able to follow her heart, she gradually lost her natural attitude toward her way of life and was constantly tormented by the feeling that too much was being done for her own comfort and "not enough for others." She now began to economize on herself wherever she could. She also undertook, in addition to her usual work load, certain domestic chores for which she would otherwise have hired outside help, in order to create with these "wage earnings" a secret fund for her poor. When she lay in bed at night her body ached at the thought that hundreds of thousands in the big city had no warm resting place, and in place of every major present that her husband gave her she would much rather have had the money for the poor. In short, the more she felt her charitable activities to be restricted, the more strongly did the Franciscan side of her nature come out. Her heart went out to her brethren, and it would have been a liberating boon rather than a sacrifice to her if she had been permitted to give up all luxury. She now felt the disharmony between the teachings of the Gospels and the way of life of the upper middle class as a constant irritant, just as her sister Ida did. Everything that so deeply moved her now flowed into what was then in her circle a mightily surging stream of *social* interests.

For a long time Helene had shared the young theologians' and political economists' concern with the causes of the growing proletarianization on the one side while wealth increased on the other, and with the apostasy of the masses from Christianity. Now all this was being recognized and labeled by the young generation and by her sons! This made her happy, and she fervently hoped that their recognition of the causes would enable the young people to find means to remedy the situation as well. She would gladly have given all she had for it. The religious-social interests she shared with Otto Baumgarten, Göhre, Naumann, and Rade were a source of energy to her in the incipient autumn of her life. Her husband, however, did not join these young people; he remained what he was, a liberal bourgeois.

In our house an interest in precisely these things is particularly difficult to express. The free thought of the older generation is generally accompanied by intolerance, and everything that does not fit in with its pattern not only repels it but causes a kind of nervous condition. Then there are inner conflicts and attempts at oppression. Dread of the "black man" simply is in the blood of our liberals, and it really makes them suspect that every pastor has at least the makings of a hypocrite.

The elder Weber also shut himself off from other modern currents to which Helene was open. Along with the social issue, the question of women's rights was beginning to excite people. It could no longer be overlooked that thousands of middle-class girls could no longer be certain that they would be given happiness and fulfillment by a man. The training of young men for the professions, including the period of obligatory military service, took a very long time, and they often did not marry until their thirties. The girls had to wait, and the number of those who did not get married at all steadily increased. The lives of most of these girls remained without purpose or independence unless they learned to give them substance by their own efforts through satisfying work.

Helene was among the first who appreciated the painful difficulties of a contemporary girl's existence without having experienced them herself. She was able to understand that idle waiting for a man in the dependent state of a *Haustochter* [live-in maid who is regarded as one of the family] was threatening thousands with fruitless suffering and stagnation. As soon as the common struggle of women for a higher intellectual level and an expansion of activity came to her attention, she was moved and gripped by it. She immediately supported the first tentative steps of female joint action. This was brought home to her by a friend, the wife of Deputy Rickert, whose fragile body sheltered a great, free spirit:

A few days ago Frau Rickert sent me the memorandum and petition regarding the admission of female teachers to the universities, and I signed it, too, although my husband refused to have anything to do with it. . . . The proposal that the training should be geared more to independent thinking and concentration on a small number of subjects, depending on talent and inclination, made a great deal of sense to me.

But her own experience as a mother showed her an even more comprehensive meaning of the question of women's education. She was always supervis-

ing the intellectual development of her schoolchildren, and if she had had
to forgo this very early in the case of her uncommonly gifted older sons, she
now felt that her youngest son and her daughters were quickly outgrowing
her tutelage as well:

> I ought to pay much more attention to Arthur's schoolwork, so that
> he does not adopt Karl's loafing. And now Klara, too, is coming more
> and more under my care, and day after day it is hard for me to realize
> how little positive knowledge I have acquired. I have no firm knowledge
> of anything—neither of grammar nor of orthography nor of history. If
> I had my way, the girls ought to take a final examination. But my
> husband has absolutely no use for this. (1888)

As we have seen, her eldest son, Max, grew into those social interests
during his period as a *Referendar,* and he became her expert for all social questions. Soon Alfred, too, gave her the same kind of pleasure.

Around that time she came into close contact with a young theologian
who came into her house for a year as the mentor of her third son Karl.
What her own sons had denied her was now granted her by him: a full insight into a struggling young soul of great purity. Here she was able to influence the growth of a young man whose religious gifts made him more akin
to her than her own children. For the first time she shared everyday life
with someone who had the same spirit as she. She also shared with him her
constant worries about Karl, for whose guidance he had come into the house
after numerous other attempts.

As he grew up this third son was markedly different from his older
brothers. He was richly gifted, handsome and charming, precocious in his
ability to express himself, endowed with an artistic temperament—an attractive lightweight who knew how to charm everyone. In school he was
lazy and ready to be led astray by flighty schoolmates. Thus he did not fit
into the family. His mother already saw him as a "prodigal son" and pursued
him with anxious love. As always when things did not work out with the
children as she had wished, she regarded as her personal failure a situation
that sprang from the innate disposition of others and the unavoidable influences of the surroundings. The young theologian managed with great tact
to keep a rein on the colt, and Helene was very grateful to him for that.
But her enjoyment of this domestic community with a young man whose
soul was on the same wavelength as her own did not last long. Her husband,
given his nature, could not let the woman whom he passionately loved and

wished still to dominate to slide further into interests that he found distasteful and to come into close contact with people who meant nothing to him. He dismissed the young man before his task was completed—an incident that Helene regarded as an injustice to both the young man and her son and did not get over for a long time.

* * *

Family life with three grown sons, each with his own sphere of interests and circle of friends, and three younger children was thus extremely rich but not harmonious, and in the nature of things it became increasingly difficult to attune the different elements to one another. Outsiders, to be sure, did not become aware of any problems; they saw only the humor and the freshness, the circle's full range of important interests, and Helene's all-enveloping kindness. To please her, the family frequently gathered in the "old German" room to spend an evening reading together. They treated one another with kindness and self-restraint, and there was a great deal of teasing and joking. But the underlying mood was one of somberness, and Helene's loving heart was heavy because she did not succeed in creating an atmosphere of sympathy in which the differences between the father and his grown sons would disappear and all dissonances would be resolved. The real tragedy was that she and her suffering in her marriage—something that could no longer be concealed from the older children—finally became the focal point of all their problems. She took everything harder than she had before, because she no longer had an inexhaustible vigor to pit against the disharmony.

The day of her silver wedding anniversary, an occasion which for many couples ushers in the difficult transition to the autumn of life, was overshadowed for Helene by a secret, resigned melancholy, although husband and wife were surrounded by six lively, gifted children. Certainly the countless friends who joined in the celebration received the impression of great, unflawed happiness and great abundance. But Helene's greatest joy was a painting given by her sisters, which showed the balcony of the Heidelberg house with their dead parents looking onto a landscape transfigured by moonlight. Her "big boy" hung it in her room that morning, and when the hustle and bustle of the festivities that she had prepared for others permitted her a free moment, she slipped in there to satisfy her yearning for those far away from her, her bygone youth, and her spiritual home.

* * *

What all this and his own unsatisfying way of life meant to the eldest
son shines through his letters to his close friend Emmy Baumgarten. In his
years of work as a *Referendar*, mechanical activities—simple clerical tasks—
took up a lot of his time. The court very often used the young people to
keep the records, and Weber naturally hated that. In the process his hand-
writing deteriorated to the point of such hieroglyphic illegibility—
sometimes the examination of witnesses had to be repeated—that it soon
appeared advisable to put him to some other use. Yet this activity seldom
satisfied him. In retrospect he explained the reason for this:

> I can look back on part of my period as a *Referendar* only with horror.
> There is hardly anything more painful than years of having only half or
> even less of one's energy used, while one has such hours that it is impos-
> sible to find some additional permanent employment, and yet being
> unable to change this or shorten this horrible four-year pilgrimage by
> even one minute by working harder. One has the feeling that lead
> weights are pulling one down on the couch of intellectual stagnation
> and indolence. . . . In those years I really envied every manual worker his
> honestly earned living, even though my mind told me that as compared
> to the millions who do not even know the concept of "profession" I
> was infinitely privileged.

Weber saved himself from intellectual tedium and indolence by intensively
continuing his studies. He first worked for a degree from the School of Law,
for which the requirements were then very high at the University of Berlin.
The only vacations of any length for his constantly working mind were the
repeated officers' exercises, which lasted about two months each time. He
then got a good workout after his desk-bound life, and, astonishingly
enough, although he was so heavy and out of training, he proved equal to
it all. At first the exercises brought Weber into welcome contact with
the familiar households of his Southern German relatives, but when his regiment was transferred to Posen [Poznan] in 1888, this source of sentimental
pleasure dried up. Instead the new situation catered to his need for observation and direct experience. He observed the social conditions with interest
and recognized that in this eastern border region the Prussian spirit had
the same difficulties as in Alsace in amalgamating a foreign people with German things and in making "moral" conquests keep pace with political con-

quests. At the end of an exercise in 1888 Weber toured the estates of the Prussian settlement commission, "where an attempt is being made to establish German farming villages on manorial estates that have been bought with state funds." From that time on he felt one of the most important political problems was the winning of the East by a policy of settlement.

During one of the last exercises he wrote to Helene from Schrimm:

For once my duty is over so early, and I am so caught up with my proof sheets, that I have a chance to write you a letter. The most striking change that has occurred in the general conditions of my military service since I was called up the last time is a considerable increase in duty, particularly for the officers. The only great distance that exists for us here is that to the rifle range—about three-quarters of a mile—and this I have to cover both ways almost every day *per pedes* [on foot], which prolongs my period of duty by about two hours and once again satisfies my desire to take walks for the next ten years.

Otherwise I cannot complain about the conditions of my service. I have drawn a very pleasant company commander, who is, above all, not nervous, and since I am the oldest officer in the company, the captain evidently does not deem it appropriate to give me more disagreeable and less independent assignments than the other active officers— which is more than what usually happens. These officers are actually quite easy to live with, although I cannot deny that I prefer our "Thursday evenings" to their company. There are very few of them, of course; ten of us eat together in the officers' mess. It is decidedly more comfortable than the mess at Posen, which gives the impression of being a banquet room and yet is only too commonplace. In the evening I am more frequently at home than I had thought I would be. As a result, of course, quite often one or two or several people drop in on me, which is neither more advantageous financially nor more timesaving than having dinner in a restaurant.

My daily schedule, of course, is quite different from what it was in Berlin. I get up at about the same time that I used to go to bed in my last weeks there. I cannot say that I am sleeping more than in civilian life. My duty is not strenuous for me in any way; this includes even major maneuvers and marches, although from the standpoint of pleasure I have little use for the "sand-slogging." Nor can I really say that I have lost any weight thus far. On the contrary, my appetite has about quadrupled, so the officers' mess is losing money on me and I shall probably be counted as two persons soon. They are seeking to indemnify themselves by as draconian an application of a system of fines as possible; this system is based on an unwritten, highly intricate code that is incomprehensible to the uninitiated, even jurists, and is used by the mess for rendering moral judgments. Since the proceeds are used to buy communal punch, this jury box is rather fiscally oriented, and this aspect of our life here is almost the most expensive. Otherwise things really are much cheaper than in Strasbourg and in Posen, and at this cheap rate the rations are no worse and, above all, no less plentiful.

On the whole, then, life here is certainly bearable and actually extremely comfortable. The orderly in particular is a great luxury. I am forgetting how to dress and undress by myself and to move from the spot without the most compelling reason, especially since my orderly—a very bright *Bildhauer* [sculptor], as he calls himself—does an excellent job of taking care of all my needs without my having to give him orders. He even keeps my manuscripts, proof sheets, and papers in order—something that I never manage to do at home—and within the framework I have established he provides me with an imaginative variety of sausages and other domestic delights. Freed from all worry about the necessities of life, I really could devote myself to scholarly activity in my off-duty hours. To some extent this has already been done, though by no means on as large a scale as I had planned, for these intervals are always interrupted by duty. Thus, for example, not too much can be done with my off-duty hours today: 11–1, 1–3, 5–6:30, and from 7:30 on, especially since it starts up again at 5:30 tomorrow morning. I have always taken care of the proof sheets of my Roman agrarian history immediately; but the manuscript was finished quickly, and since I am making extensive changes in the scholarly apparatus, this is quite a lot of work.

I am no longer able to make my book the way I would like it. I did get around to a few studies on the history of commercial law, but I did not start a real monograph leading to the acquisition of the *venia docendi* [authorization to teach at a university] in the field of commercial law as well, a work that would contain more than a critique of Goldschmidt's polemic against me. I would not be averse to launching a review of Oldenberg's[7] book somewhere. That would not be a time-consuming task, for one only has to think of an appropriate point of view and the whole thing is finished in a few hours. This is why I have always found that the best way to write reviews is to utilize complete

---

[7]Karl Oldenberg, 1864–1936, at that time a lecturer in political science at the University of Berlin, later a professor at Marburg, Greifswald, and Göttingen.—Ed.

leisure while lying on the sofa. But if I were to lie down on my sofa here, I would fall asleep without fail.

. . . . Among the subjects of my activity in the last two days there were one hour (!) of instruction in *Vaterländische Geschichte* [national history] and one hour's (!) instruction on the *K.K. Haus*.[8] It is a pity that the six princes are not married yet, for otherwise a discussion of their six wives would offer so much material that one could fill one hour with it about as well as with "National History" . . .

* * *

At home, in addition to his law practice, Weber immersed himself more and more deeply in his books. For one thing, his scholarly interests were asserting themselves more and more, and for another, he did not want to lose any time in reaching his goal. It was a matter of necessity. His part in family life, with its daily rhythm determined by the head of the house, and his enforced, prolonged financial dependence on a father from whom he became more estranged every year made his life increasingly constrained and gloomy. It is true that his humor and youthful vigor repeatedly managed to dispel this gloom, but they were never able to do so completely—especially since Weber was reserved and never relieved himself by a frank discussion of the problems. He repressed everything. Even his girl friend received only intimations, and then only if she occasioned him to explain to her his attitude to the parental home. He now enjoyed his periods of solitude even more than previously: "I am contemplatively sitting here in my room in philosophical solitude as a one-man family. This has its good points; one can arrange one's day as one wishes, gets in no one's way, and always has the feeling of accomplishing more and having much more time. So my fate is not lamentable after all; on the contrary, I would not want this solitude to end too soon."

He had a perfect understanding of Helene's situation and displayed great solicitude and sympathy for her. A female cousin who came for a visit wrote: "Max is a charming 'eldest daughter.' " After all, his practical interests had developed in the same direction as hers, even though their points of departure were different. His new interest in the situation of the working classes, unlike his mother's, was not determined by charitable impulses but

[8]*K.K.* stands for *Kaiserlich-Königlich* (Royal-Imperial) and refers to the House of Habsburg, the dynasty of the Austro-Hungarian Empire.—Ed.

primarily by political motives—an interest in making the masses favorably disposed toward the state and wresting them from the clutches of socialism. But these motives were directed toward the same goal: a reconciliation of class differences and a more just distribution of burdens and properties. Soon there was also a warm feeling for the mental and spiritual fate of those chained to joyless mechanical labor.

The twenty-three-year-old junior barrister also shared his mother's grave worries about her seventeen-year-old son Karl and concerned himself intensively with the question of how this talented and attractive but flighty brother could best be handled and what approach he ought to recommend to his mother. Remembering his own behavior toward her, he felt that neither her solicitous love nor her moralizing exhortations were appropriate. His advice was to keep Karl "on short rations," but to do less preaching, and when during his mother's absence he took his brother in hand himself for a prolonged period of time, he tried to show his mother a more indirect method of education. A letter to his girl friend reflects his thinking and at the same time sheds light on his mother, his brother, and himself:

It's a nasty business with Karl. Unfortunately, I know the whole nature of the boy quite well from my own experience—particularly his kind of windbaggery, how one gets started and keeps foundering in it—and know it better, I fear, than my mother, who always holds the view that with the wealth of love which she shows this problem child she can and should keep him on a high level and protect him from emotional desolation and impoverishment. I am firmly convinced of the powerful effect this has upon a person, and I believe I experienced it firsthand as soon as I became conscious of such things; if I wanted to, I could even specify the form this took with me. But depending on the soil in which this anchor is implanted, it is not entirely free from danger.

As far as I can see, Karl is still living spiritually from hand to mouth. When he is at home and sees my mother's continued worry and loving solicitude toward him, I believe he enjoys this with genuine, momentary gratitude and sometimes shows it very attractively in the way he acts—by courtesy and the like. When he goes to school on the next day, he finds there the same bunch of boys—light-minded, blasé, and, out of sheer frivolity, capable of anything, even the worst—who simply regard him as one of them. Now, it would take a great deal of moral courage not to join them in everything they do. But quite apart from that, he fashions the simple argument for himself that what so many others do cannot be bad for him. If the others perform stupid and ugly pranks and yet want to and will make their way in the world, why shouldn't he? So he joins in, and more than that: in order to be in their good graces, he even outdoes them. Often, after he has made the best resolutions at home—or so I think—and, in the nature of things, has thus gained the pleasant feeling that he has made tremendous progress toward becoming a better person, in school he gets the feeling of some kind of heroism, a very special emancipation. So he uses the situation of the moment both in school and at home to achieve a temporary well-being and anxiously guards against any second thoughts that might spoil the enjoyment of the moment for him.

This is the altogether trivial fact of the matter, and who knows how frequently this happens with adolescents. The problem is what one accomplishes with persons at this stage if one tries to appeal to their conscience. I believe that this approach is not successful and that one would be building on quicksand. In the case of Karl, at least, the only result is that he gets the feeling of being able to do whatever he wants without having to bear the consequences, and this is something rather serious with such people, who live only for the moment. I believe one should go only up to the point where he does not completely lose a feeling of confidence and retains the awareness that others care about him, regard him as one of them, and want to help him. For the rest, however, one must be consistent in showing him one's displeasure at every rascality, possibly in a severe form, and in keeping him aware of the fact that with this sort of behavior he has no chance of winning the respect of others. After all, for some years to come he will not be mature enough to have a real appreciation of his mother's love and care. This is why he makes use of the benefits of this love, but in general shoves it aside as something burdensome to him, and this produces in him an utter insensitivity, a kind of hardening in his view of these things that renders him incapable of acquiring at some time in the future the understanding that he now lacks.

It is the same as with the love of truth and its treatment in education. Even though I am not in favor of making a liar out of someone by mistrusting him constantly, it still is not right to give him one's unwarranted trust and thus seduce him into using this confidence to practice deceit, bringing him to the point where he gets accustomed to replacing lying, which may be a product of imprudence, with a breach of confidence, which always has an element of meanness. It is now quite hard for my mother to think that the boy is not inwardly accessible to her at this time, and she has the feeling that she is not doing

her job. I know that this feeling has greatly troubled her for a long
time—without justification, I believe, for the importance of her influence is inestimable, and it has a slow but lasting effect. But the difficulty about the position of mothers in our education and way of life
is that the beginning of this influence has, and can have, so few visible
manifestations; that is why it is so hard to overcome that feeling.
(1887)

* * *

The young theologian's participation in Karl's education was very welcome
to the older brother, because it relieved the mother. Also, he felt attracted to the unpretentious young man who knew how to fit into the
complicated domestic situation, and he regretted his premature departure.
The theologian, for his part, placed great trust in the *Referendar*, who was
not much older than he, and sought his advice in his inner struggles. The
atmosphere of the house may at times have shaken his spiritual world,
which was based on a belief in dogmas; in any case, he was forced to come
to terms with Helene's liberal views, and there, too, he turned to Weber.
The mother was pleased that her son had such a sympathetic attitude
toward her protégé and saw in this a new bond between her and him:

Our points of view are much more in harmony now, and he is so toler-
ant and clear in what he says. But what pleased me most was to see
how V.,[9] a short time before he left us, always approached Max
straightforwardly with all his questions and doubts, whether it was
the answering of prayers, ecclesiastical discipline, or the Apostles'
Creed: "Tell me, Herr Referendar, what about this, what is your stand
on that?" And once he went so far as to say, "Max really is a splendid
fellow, nothing human is alien to him."

An echo of the conversations of these young men may be found in a letter to Weber's girl friend, which is more characteristic of the writer than
of its subject. It shows Weber's precocious ability to sympathize and empathize even with qualities that were far removed from his own nature, and
it reflects, above all, his respectful solicitude for a developing, struggling
human being. His feeling of responsibility toward a younger man prohibited

[9]In her edition of Max Weber's *Jugendbriefe* (Tübingen, 1936, pp. 224ff.), Marianne Weber gives
the full name: Voigt.—Ed.

him from impugning a faith for which he was unable to substitute anything better. He avoided forcing his own value judgments upon him and was equally careful not to put the other man in a position where he would have to commit himself prematurely. His later scholarly attitude seemed prefigured in the fact that he wished only to help the other man attain greater *clarity* about the various possibilities of thinking and believing, thus guiding him to the point where he could make a choice of his own.

> The fact that Herr V. really left us at the beginning of April has brought about a great change. I am especially sorry about this for my mother's sake, for there was a meeting of the minds between them in many interests that are really not so close to us, particularly of an ecclesiastical nature. But it is also a genuine loss for all of us, because he was really a man of rare tact and honest aspiration, free from affectation and phrase mongering, so that one could only learn something from him, especially from the manner in which he worked his way into a situation that was fraught with many difficulties. Although we two will probably take very different roads, it often gave me pleasure to discuss many things with him. I will not deny that presumably this was particularly due to the fact that I felt honored by the confidence shown me by the younger man—a feeling that was all the stronger because I know from experience that at a stage of inner doubt and a gradual development of a point of view of one's own, a person has very little inclination to trust others . . . especially those people who are closest to him by nature. I regarded it as all the more of an honor because it gave me a certain feeling of responsibility. For every observation shows that precisely in this situation, where it is making a serious effort to be on its own, the human mind is peculiarly manageable in a certain respect—because it does not know that it is being directed. Thus it is easily steered in a certain direction by some influence, be it from an experienced or an inexperienced person. Then it goes on in this direction because it is earnestly striving to get a firm foothold, and in this way an individual is apt to make a decision that may be decisive for his entire future intellectual course without having completely surveyed the question, to make a choice without even knowing that he is choosing. Even though I am not certain what a theologian would say to the answers I gave Herr V. to his very varied questions—some of them floored me at first, such as, "What do you think of baptism?" or "If you were a preacher, would you recite the creed?"—still, I think that in each case I pointed out to him to the best of my ability the *different points of view* from which such questions can be answered.

Regarding my own viewpoint I always told him the plain truth; on the other hand, even in our most extensive discussions I avoided asking him point-blank what *he* thought about this or that important point—and I think I was right in this. Here is my reason for this: I know—also from experience—that if at Herr V.'s stage of development a man is goaded into taking a stand on a point he has not yet worked out in his own mind and expresses an opinion, he is apt not to continue his dispassionate quest for truth—naturally, a man feels bound, as it were, to something that he has once said—but, without knowing it, to look only for reasons that justify what he once said. Thus he is nailed down to his own statement, which often was made only under a momentary impression . . . (1887)

* * *

Thus everyone who was seriously worried by profound problems and who opened his heart to Weber met with his sympathetic interest. It gave him pleasure to help younger people attain greater clarity, and he always took time to do so. To the extent that this ability showed itself in his letters to his girl friend, we are given further insight into his own evaluations of that time. We have, for example, a statement about Goethe that is characteristic of that period (1887), when he was twenty-three:

I was very pleased that you so greatly enjoyed the performance of *Die Jungfrau von Orleans*[10] by the Meiningen troupe.[11] I am sure it was excellent. This pleased me all the more because nowadays it is not given to everyone to enjoy Schiller's dramas. People, particularly those who occupy themselves with literature a great deal, are having their taste for Schiller spoiled by the exaggerated exclusive adoration of Goethe, and this makes them so unjust toward everyone else that I have often had occasion to be annoyed, for example with Alfred and people his age. For what good is it to me if people tell me today how all-encompassing Goethe's poetic conception is and how one can find in it the entire contents of human life from A to Z, if afterward I find one side, and the most important one, hardly touched? For in general people's conception of life is not that the only thing that mat-

---

[10]Friedrich Schiller's play about Joan of Arc (1801).—Ed.
[11]An ensemble of the court theater at Meiningen that made numerous tours between 1874 and 1890 under the direction of Duke George II—Ed.

ters is for them to have a sense of well-being and to find a side of life
that they can enjoy. Nor do people face *only* the question as to the
road on which they can or cannot find happiness and inner satisfaction.
But if one looks at things soberly and closely, this question is the deepest that one can derive from Goethe's works, including *Faust,* and everything, even the knottiest ethical problems, is illuminated from this
standpoint.

For look, it surely is peculiar that Goethe should have perceived vile-
ness for what it was only if it was at the same time ugliness and pettiness, and that he had no clear perception of it if it confronted him
in the guise of certain beautiful feelings—see *Die
Wahlverwandtschaften*[12]—or in monumental greatness—see his encounter with Napoleon. To him form was all, and form in his writings,
too; that is, by "form" I mean not only the beauty of verses, but the
form in which things are imagined. And that is why he was a great artist, for he mastered form like few others, and by means of form an artist makes whatever he wants out of his subject. But as poets and
writers, I think, others can be placed beside him . . . (1887)

The mature Weber admired in Goethe the all-encompassing genius and
recognized that the primary determinant of his life was not a need for "happiness" but a titanic struggle for perfection in the exertion of his own enormous creative powers and a reverent sense of oneness with the laws of the
universe. But later, too, he refused to venerate Goethe as an untouchable
sphere removed from moral judgment, and Goethe never embodied for him
the *totality* of the human; he missed the heroic elements in him. When
young, ordinary persons presumed to justify their own striving for happiness
by pointing to this model, he derided them by saying that one had to be
Goethe to live like Goethe. He did not accept the idea of a special "morality of genius." Although he felt no need to moralize about creative people,
he stood his ground when such discussions arose: what is "sin" for Müller and
Schulze [Smith and Jones] must be so for Goethe. He considered that
there was a difference only if the consequences of culpable conduct were *different* for the total personality of a genius from what they were for ordinary
people. He admitted that guilt and punishment could be the basis of creative achievement and of the development of inner wealth and sovereignty
in a personality—particularly when guilt is recognized and expiated as such.
But he did not abandon the principle of measuring even the "superman" by

---

[12]*The Elective Affinites,* a psychological novel by Goethe (1809).—Ed.

the norms he deemed universally valid and on which he based his own conduct.

* * *

Another letter shows that Weber's *Weltanschauung* at that time was influenced by Kant—as a result of a prolonged struggle that had begun in his last years at school, in the *Sekunda*, with an exclusive affirmation of Spinoza: "Years ago I honestly struggled with all that conceptual confusion; it leads to very little, that I now know for certain, but from time to time one gets carried away again."

This time the occasion for philosophizing was a very simple one: disapproving statements by his cousin about a young man she disliked gave him an opportunity to give her a graphic explanation of the doctrine of the "freedom and necessity" of the responsibility of a person who acts and of his natural constraint. His activity at court, which every day subjected the actions of antisocial persons to his judgment, made it natural for him to reflect about these questions.

Who is it that implants in the criminal's soul the idea that leads to action? Certainly not he himself; he has been led to it by circumstances, by conditions that were inherent in him and not of his own making. It could not have happened any other way; in other words, he cannot be held responsible for what he did, because he is not free. His inner being is as much subject to a necessary development as any product of nature. The human intellect simply cannot comprehend why what he does and what we call bad should not be just as "natural" and therefore justified as what another man does and calls "good" . . . a very plausible argument, isn't it? And if viewed rationally, quite correct, too. . . . But now we much first examine our intellect to see whether it has the right to judge these questions, whether it is even capable of penetrating them with its concepts, whether it has not presumed to do something that it is incapable of achieving, because it lacks the concepts for it. The latter seems to me to be the case. For it is easy to see that with our good old intellect we can by no means . . . discover what the meaning of "good and evil" is, for otherwise the most intelligent people would have to be best informed about this, and everyone knows that unfortunately this is not always the case. Besides, with the same resource the world would constantly have to make new discoveries and inventions in the field of morality that would be as great as those made in other areas with the aid of the intellect, and as quickly in this area as in the others, which is not the case. And finally: No one will succeed in explaining to me with the aid of intellectual concepts and definitions wherein the difference between "good" and "evil" lies—which means that the intellect lacks the concepts for it. . . . The consciousness of the individual's responsibility for his actions does not rest on intellectual concepts and can be neither constructed nor refuted by the intellect. That is why one is wrong if one believes it to be an old preconception that was inculcated in us in our youth. Moral judgments cannot be inculcated unless the ability to grasp them, *the faculty for making moral distinctions,* is there, and this in turn is based on the antithesis between good and evil. This antithesis, then, must be presupposed to make an education possible and is inherent in man; education can develop it, sharpen it, give it practical substance, but it cannot create it.

To this exposition he adds some information about the special quality of ethical, esthetic, and taste judgments, and then returns to the problem of responsibility:

That is why it is not enough to say of a man that circumstances have made him reach such and such a state; this only gives the intellect a clue for making the development of that person's moral condition *plausible* to itself . . . but there is no moral judgment as yet. It can, to be sure, prevent us from condemning the man; in this I agree with you (but only because I am against condemnation generally). But the judgment as to whether what he did was good or bad and our judgment as to his responsibility for it are not touched by this; I cannot consult my intellect about it, for in this regard it faces an insoluble riddle. . . . Here we simply are at the limit of our intellectual capacity and step into an entirely different world in which an entirely different side of our mind undertakes to judge things and everyone knows that its judgments, though they are not based on intellectual concepts, are fully as sure and clear as those of any logical chain of reasoning . . .

* * *

Each year Helene increasingly felt that her "Grosser" was burying himself in his books too much. Evidently she wanted her eldest son to be an even stronger support to her in her sad state of mind. She unburdened herself to her niece, who was close to both of them, and the niece then admonished Weber. His answer indicated that he recognized his filial duties and wanted to fulfill them, but found it hard to do so in addition to the ever-increasing pressure of work. He felt he was caught up in a severe conflict of duties, of the kind that is usually experienced only by daughters, and he tried to make it clear to his girl friend that a satisfactory solution was impossible. The very fact that at this stage of his life he was still part of his parents' and brothers' and sisters' life as a son of the house was an impediment on the way to his own goal:

At home one simply gets done only half of what one does elsewhere. I am often sorry to see that my mother apparently has the impression that I no longer care about anything except heaven knows what ambitious plans and that I keep aloof from my family. But that's the way it is. I work slowly, and it may be that I missed a great deal in the past. . . . It is simply a question of which obligation comes first, and this is what I regard as my obligation: to learn something to the best of my ability—all the more so when I consider how few people in other classes are in a position to think of anything but their daily toil and labor, something that, relatively speaking, really is not great in my case and, unlike what is true of the others, is not a matter of my daily bread. (1887)

But his self-interest did not blind him to his mother's situation and her legitimate claims. Yet he did not know how to do them full justice; the bonds that kept him in the house and that he was unable and, for his mother's sake, unwilling to break constricted him more every year:

I can assure you that the thought that here in my mother's house I am not offering what one really should expect is not a pleasant one for me, and it certainly does not facilitate my work. You are now telling me how I should act and what I should do differently, and you are probably right . . . but it isn't that easy for me to do things differently. Do you really refuse to believe that I still have *a great deal* to do before I have accomplished anything?

Now you tell me that there is no hurry. But I have not been in a hurry. And this summer I had a most peculiar experience. It was as if my family had gone to Heidelberg only to bombard me with heavy artillery from that range: when am I going to take my doctoral examination? I know quite well that my failure to accomplish this sooner is secretly a bit of a disappointment to my father. I don't want to be

found wanting in this respect, do I? And then it is often quite difficult to manage with the time one has. Here it is especially hard for
me occasionally to do something together with my mother, because
both of us can usually do it only in the evening; at that time—and
this is the main trouble—she is invariably so dead tired that it seems
to me as though she has to make a great effort to listen and does so
only to please me.

Thus he stood by his mother in times of difficulty—she always found him
ready when she expressly turned to him with her worries and questions—but
because of the strain of work he was unable to offer her a spiritual atmosphere that could have supported and warmed her in her everyday life. And
although inwardly he took Helene's side, he did not blame his father for all
her difficulties. She was getting older and did not conserve her strength;
thus she was less flexible in coping with the frictions of married life:

All this—and I could say this over and over again—would not be of
such great importance if my mother did not take some things much
more to heart as time goes on. To give but one example: My father
has always been sanguine, and his mood is often subject to abrupt
changes, even if the outward occasion is a slight one. In contrast to
earlier years, such a change now often makes a really profound, painful
impression upon my mother, one that she does not easily get over,
even if the annoyance that occasioned it was only a fleeting one. I am
a son of the house, and you will perhaps admit that it would not be
in keeping with this position and would not be beneficial to family life
if I were to interfere in anything but an indirect way.

He also saw more general causes for Helene's vulnerability, viewing it as
the typical fate of the delicate soul of a woman whose life revolves around
the assimilation of complex emotional experiences, whereas a man's work
obliges him to deal with far more robust problems every day.

The daily work of people is differently constituted, and one can experience this firsthand when one works in an office and deals more or less
intensively with the numerous, infinitely changing human relationships
which on paper and in the files have a peculiar kind of spectral life, as
though one saw the silhouettes of living persons performing a dance on
a curtain. One notices that what is involved here is the existence of
those who carry on behind the curtain the daily struggle for what is

mine and what is yours. It becomes apparent that the very fact of being occupied with these phantoms and with the interests of external life—some small, some big—makes it harder for us to understand that other people, whose calling lies more on the *inner* side, are apt to take some remark that was made only on the basis of a momentary mood to heart and that it therefore makes a more lasting impression upon them than such a momentary impulse would deserve to make. I am saying this only because I would not want to give the impression that I feel entitled to make reproaches in any direction.

* * *

Not only his empathy with his mother's spiritual life but the fate of his girl friend as well gave Weber a deeper understanding of the special problems of a woman's life, a life in which service to others does not produce objective achievements, but is constantly obliterated by the passage of time. During those years the depression and physical exhaustion from which his girl friend suffered more frequently and more acutely oppressed him too. She suffered all the more from the limitations imposed upon her by illness because, like Helene and Ida, she was naturally inclined to serve and help others.

Just a year after the beautiful spring they had spent together, she decided to give up the man she secretly loved. She could not even be sure that he still loved her. His letters, which were intimate in a brotherly way, did not give her an unequivocal answer. But even if he did, she came to doubt more and more whether she would get well and be a worthy life's companion to him. Under no condition would she tie him down or give him any indication that she was waiting for him. She was out of his sight, and for years the two young people made no attempt to see each other again. Their exchange of letters became less frequent, and the image of the girl friend faded. But Weber did not break away from her inwardly. After all, there still was hope that one day she would reemerge in good health and, with her old charm, give him a radiant smile. He left everything in abeyance. Because the nature of such illnesses was then little known, he secretly had the guilty feeling that his own indecisiveness was the cause, that she was withering away because of unrequited love. And with every year he became more convinced that if he could not cure the girl and make her happy, he had no right to full human happiness either. There also gradually developed a mysterious feeling, from his innermost being, that it was not given to him to make a woman happy.

The friendship took its course. In his letters, which grew less frequent, he tried over and over again to revive the girl's self-confidence and make her feel important to him and to others:

> Don't take on too much, dear Emmy. That is what you used to do, for as I still remember quite well, you always thought you were not to others what you ought to be, and yet being together with you did all of us so much good. In a different way you are faring as my mother did, who never realized how much her devoted love *indirectly* meant to us at times when we needed an *inner* protection from many things, and when this protection lay in the thought of her.

He did not accept her self-torment at the idea that she was not able to do enough for her family, and interpreted her dismay as a consequence of the special fate of women:

> It almost reminds me of some thoughts my mother sometimes has. In this I simply recognize again and again that what makes the duties imposed upon women by nature so arduous is that these duties culminate not so much in individual questions, externally great ones in particular, which may be solved by a conscious decision, but, much more essentially, demand to be solved by constant self-conquest, and that the success of this fulfillment of duty may far less often be seen in concrete and palpable form: instead, its fruits ripen in what appears to be the natural course of everyday living.

When a few years later he gained an insight into the inner distress of the new generation of young girls, he found an even more precise expression for the special quality of a woman's lot:

> This again makes me see clearly how infinitely easier nature has made life for us men. Even in the most unsatisfying occupation we can *see* the external success of our doings and dealings. A woman, on the other hand, whether she is a mother, daughter, or sister, sees nothing of what her life actually means to others; often, in fact, it must seem to her as though she were nothing but one more worry and burden to others. It simply cannot be expressed what a tremendous inward enrichment it is to have someone who freely undertakes to care for us as a matter of course and thereby demonstrates a feeling of being part of us. But we simply feel a need to find outward manifestations of this,

and precisely in these external regards we men have been given an unfair
advantage by nature; to be sure, we pay for this preferential treatment
with greater inner poverty.

The extent to which his material dependence upon a father from whom he
felt estranged was a burden to Weber is indicated by the following lines
which, however, express his feelings about this situation with a reserve dictated by filial piety:

> You know, it is a peculiar feeling when one gradually outgrows one's stu-
> dent shoes and yet has to wait for years before one can stand on one's
> own feet; at least this is how I feel, and I simply have to swallow the
> idea almost every day. Nor can I convince myself that this feeling is
> not justified, for *earning his own bread is the foundation of happiness for a
> man,* and for the majority of people it is the object of their lifelong
> striving. This is still far away from me, and nothing can be changed for
> the time being; but I miss it greatly, more than others do, and that
> is why I am very reluctant to lose more time. (1887)

* * *

Was there for Weber no shorter road to his desired independence? Was
it necessary for this extremely gifted man, who at an early age had a wide
range of abilities in a number of fields and for whom all his teachers predicted a distinguished future, to devote so much of his youthful energy to
a protracted legal career? Surely he could have switched to some other, freer
profession? His teachers saw the future scholar in him and could not imagine
any better employment for this eminent intellect. Hermann Baumgarten
in particular suggested *Habilitation* to him even before his graduation from
the university. But Weber himself vacillated, and evidently he did not dare
to deviate from the course he had embarked upon, for even as a docent he
would presumably have had to wait for an indefinite period of time before
he could have earned "his own bread."

Above all, Weber's disposition was unmistakably toward an *active* rather
than a contemplative life. Scholarly work, possibly within the framework of
jurisprudence, attracted him as an interesting sideline but not as the substance of his life, for political and social interests were equally strong in
him, and as a strong-willed person he longed for great responsibilities, for *Le-*

bensfluten und Tatensturm[13] [the flood of life and the tempest of action]. Even at a later period he envied the ship's captain who has human lives in his hands hour after hour. When toward the end of his legal training he substituted for an important Berlin attorney for a few months, he found such satisfaction in an activity that demanded at the same time ingenuity, resoluteness, and a fighting instinct that even after his *Habilitation* he planned to establish himself as an attorney as well. When his uncle urged him to obtain a *Dozentur* [university lectureship], he wrote him:

> At times . . . a purely scholarly activity, too, had almost lost its attraction as compared to the impression that practical interests, the regulation of which is the primary task of legal development, offered many combinations which, so it seemed to me, could not be grasped with the resources of our scholarship. Thus the urge to occupy myself with our scholarship for its own sake appreciably diminished.

When Weber nevertheless decided during his period as a junior barrister to aim for an academic career in addition to the practical legal profession, he evidently was guided primarily by his new view that he could reach his goal more quickly on this track:

> Ever since I have known for certain that I am able to accomplish something in my legal practice which is not certain in an academic career, it has been clear to me that I would never abandon this practice if under the present conditions it did not get me farther away from this goal [of earning my own bread] and there were no prospect of making more progress on the other road in this respect as well. Therefore I believe I should at least try it. Now, this does not appear to be an idealistic point of view at all, but I regard it as justified. The fact remains that I have often been unable to recognize properly and fulfill other duties that are incumbent on me in the house and to which I must attempt to do justice, even if I don't really feel up to it.

Before qualifying for university teaching he made one serious attempt to break loose. He applied for the position of a legal counselor to the city of Bremen, and went there to make a personal call on the municipal notables.

---

[13]"*In Lebensfluten, im Tatensturm*"—from Goethe's *Faust I*, l. 501 (in Bayard Taylor's translation, "In the tides of life, in action's storm").—Ed.

A local man was given preference. He later wrote his uncle, who had disapproved of this step:

> I have an extraordinary longing for a practical position, and this longing might have been fulfilled and thus disposed of there. I confess that even though a scholarly career appeals to me otherwise, I think of the transition from an expectant, unsalaried junior barrister and assessor to an equally expectant and unsalaried *Privatdozent* [adjunct lecturer] only with reluctance. I believe that a position that made me financially independent would give me less outward peace, but incomparably more inner peace for scholarly work.

For the time being this decided his professional fate. He prepared himself for Roman, German, and commercial law and began lecturing in the spring of 1892. At the same time a legal career was open to him, and he considered setting up as an attorney or forming a partnership with some outstanding man. But he was pushed the other way: His respected teacher of commercial law, Goldschmidt, took seriously ill and became an invalid. He appointed Weber as his substitute in the second semester, and the young docent now had to lecture to a large group of students on commercial law and the law of exchange. The powerful head of the university system, Althoff,[14] became interested in him and had him in mind to succeed the famous scholar. At first, in 1893, he entrusted him with an associate professorship in hopes of keeping him in Berlin. This meant that suddenly a great career was opening up to him, but Weber's interests had already shifted too much to the area of political economy.

For this reason he did not want to tie himself down to teaching law, for there were already preliminary discussions with a view to giving him a chair in the field of political economy. At the age of twenty-nine he was close to his goal; on the basis of his three books[15] he already enjoyed a reputation as a scholar. In Evangelical-Social circles he was viewed as a future politician. At that time he wrote:

---

[14]Friedrich Althoff, 1839–1908, jurist and high official in the Prussian Ministry of Culture.—Ed.

[15]*Zur Geschichte der Handelsgesellschaften im Mittelalter* (1889), *Die römische Agrargeschichte in ihrer Bedeutung für das Staats – und Privatrecht* (1891), and *Die Verhältnisse der Landarbeiter im ostelbischen Deutschland* (1892).—Ed.

I simply am not . . . a real scholar. For me scholarly activity is too much bound up with the idea of filling my leisure hours, even though I realize that due to the division of labor, scholarly activity can be carried on successfully only if one devotes one's entire personality to it. I hope that the *pedagogic* side of my university post, the indispensable feeling of *practical* activity, will give me satisfaction, but as yet I cannot tell whether I have any talent for this aspect of it . . .

His last letter to H. Baumgarten (before the latter's death), written at the beginning of his first semester as a docent, gives an idea of the ceaseless hard work in those years:

The reason for my long silence was that in recent months I suffered from the aftereffects of overestimating my capacity for work. I announced a *Privatkolleg* [lectures to a small group of students], a *Publikum* [public lectures for a larger group], as well as a seminar, and in the meantime I have started teaching. In addition, I have undertaken to participate in an inquiry of the *Verein für Sozialpolitik:* the situation of the farm workers in the east. Finally, I substituted for an attorney at the *Kammergericht* [Prussian supreme court] every day from 9 A.M. to about 7 P.M., working partly at the court, partly in the office. All together this gave me what is basically a very good feeling: to be swamped with work. On top of that I had to write some book reviews, and by the same mail I am sending you an article written *in usum pastorum* [for pastoral use] for the journal of my friend Göhre. It may be of interest to you. I am now having my first experience as a lecturer, and I must say that the continuous preparation from one lecture to another is far more considerable than I had imagined it would be. I believe that in time the seminar in particular will give me much satisfaction and pleasure. . . . In addition I must get ready for a campaign against my critics, present and future, particularly Mommsen, whose substantially very negative, personally quite friendly treatment of my book [on Roman agrarian history] in *Hermes* is occasion for a detailed rebuttal. So the summer will be quite full of work, I think, especially since I have also promised Otto a "blue book" about the farm workers and the landed property in the east.

The price he paid for this rapid advancement, always under the pressure of the domestic situation and his dependence, he indicated in a letter to his girl friend:

In these last years, whose unwelcome barrenness I remember with horror, I had abandoned myself to such utter resignation, a resignation that was not without a certain bitterness, that, apart from a certain melancholy glow that some rich and beautiful memories of earlier years brought into my bookish existence, I was completely absorbed in what I would call the automatic continuation of my obligatory professional work—very much to my mother's chagrin.

All his statements suggest that Weber felt driven toward this goal as if unwillingly. "I simply am not a real scholar," he said at the time of his first great success in the scholarly arena. And anyone who looked at his powerful, athletic figure with this in mind, disregarding the high social rating of the academic profession, was bound to agree with him. It was almost paradoxical to imagine this man spending his life with a pen in his hand, bending over folio volumes at his desk. His thirst for knowledge as well as his desire and ability to impart knowledge to others were, to be sure, strong and deep-seated; they had been apparent since childhood. An insatiable intellect always needs fresh sustenance. But other, active elements of his nature demanded fulfillment too. He believed that the recognition of reality and its domination by the intellect could be only the first step toward the *direct* shaping of reality by action; he seemed to be a born fighter and ruler even more than a born thinker. The question was whether the right form for it would be found, whether his time offered the appropriate material for the crystallization of these forces. He himself thought of becoming a practical politician at a later period.

* * *

Weber's hidden tenderness and his repressed need for elemental happiness and womanly charm had only one outlet at that time: his charming, affectionate relationship with his young sisters. Here he could act freely and animatedly, without inhibitions or conflicts of conscience. The youngest girl, tow-headed Lili, a creature of fairylike grace and daintiness, was now a bright, ingenious, precociously contemplative schoolgirl. At the age of seven she had asked her mother questions such as "What, exactly, do we live for?" and "Why did the Good Lord create bad people, too?" It had not been easy for her alarmed mother to give her satisfactory answers. Fortunately the child's thirst for knowledge was later directed toward more innocuous things as well. Her brother said of her: "Our littlest one recently asked me the meaty question as to the age at which one becomes a *Backfisch* [adolescent girl]. She still has some time to go until then. She has not lost her unquenchable thirst for knowledge. I really have no idea where I shall get enough material for telling her a bedtime story every evening, for not too much has happened in world history." The massive, bearded brother, whom the children disrespectfully called *Dicker* [fatso], came to her bedside evening after evening when she called him, braided her blond pigtail, answered her questions, and gradually told her the entire story of the world, but most of all about Frederick the Great, of whom she could not get enough.

The older Klara, who had already outgrown school, was now exceedingly graceful and lively, a blossoming girl with long brown hair. Her happy-go-lucky *joie de vivre* and natural self-assurance, which indicated that she would find happiness everywhere, especially delighted her brother. This young, unaffected girl who for the time being wanted only to live and thrive—"blissful within herself"[16]—was a beneficial and necessary diversion for him from all the burdens and problems of life. He could tease her, caress her, spoil her, and at the same time educate and dominate her.

My eldest little sister now faces the important moment of leaving school, and next she is to learn housekeeping with a Hessian forester's family that has been recommended to us. She is going out into life under full sail—fortunately with ingenuousness, though there are some rough edges that still have to be polished. Maybe she is my favorite because I recognize in her many traits which—to the extent of my self-knowledge, something that is always particularly imperfect—I remember as having been developed in me when I was her age.

His brotherly education of her consisted mainly in his spoiling her inordinately. He fulfilled all her wishes; Helene watched almost with apprehension. He showered her with presents bought with the first money he had earned; she could not express enough wishes. He also gave her other things, of which she herself wrote:

How he loved nature, and how he could tell stories, teach, and make things beautiful on hikes! What enjoyment he got from music! He ac-

---

[16]*Selig in ihm selbst*—an allusion to the last line of Eduard Mörike's poem *Auf eine Lampe:* *"Was aber schön ist, selig scheint es in ihm selbst."*—Ed.

quainted me with all Wagner operas, and only because of his sensitive understanding and intellectual grasp do they mean so much to me. With his marvelous ear and memory for music he grasped the motifs. I still remember with pleasure our evenings at the opera, when we walked home hand in hand through the Tiergarten [Zoological Gardens] and he always whistled all the themes.

Now and then he also let the young girl look into his heart and told her that for Emmy's sake he did not feel entitled to marry. Besides, there would be no woman who could love him and whom—given his nature—he could make happy. Brother and sister pictured a future life together. "How did you imagine it would be with me? Out with it! I can guess, but I know that it is wrong. For an old bear like me it is best if he trots around in his cage alone."

In the significant years 1892–93, by the end of which he had acquired a scholarly reputation, professional independence, and a wife, the sister was boarding with a family. He sent her all sorts of good things, wrote her affectionate and amusing letters, and requested the same from her:

I'll gladly tell you more, but will you then write me quite often, too? Even if it's only a bit of nonsense, but very often! But I know you! In you there's only "a teeny bit of love and a teeny bit of faithfulness and a big bit of falseness . . . ."[17] I've canceled all dances because of overwork; I won't dance until next winter when I again escort my ugly darling to the ball. But hey, hey! "Was hör' ich hier, was hör' ich da, wer bläst die Ziehharmonika?" [What's that I'm hearing everywhere, who's blowing the accordion there?] "Offsprings" of the male sex wish to go skating with you boardinghouse pancakes [Pensionspfannekuchen]? Just don't come marching in here with a future brother-in-law, because I think I might get jealous and kill him dead as a doornail.

When the sister sent home the fruits of her Swiss schooling in the form of a letter in lamentable French, he censured her in striking jargon. This amusing letter also contains important news about imminent professional decisions, which was intended for their father who was visiting her.

---

[17]". . .a ganz bissele Lieb' und a ganz bissele Treu und a grosses bissele Falschheit"—humorous use of the Swabian dialect and an allusion to the words of Johannes Brahms's song Trennung (op. 97, no. 6)—Ed.

Ma chère petite,

Sois bien remerciée de la lettre suprème, mais—schockschwérenot—qu'est-ce que ce français schaudereux que tu parles?—Oh jéminé—ça semble être un dialect bien paysan qu'on a à Vevey—laendlique—schaendlique, comme nous disons.—Si je deviendrai professeur à Marbourg alors tu veux mourir? Je? pas du tout, mais—tu le peux raconter à papa, mais tout bas, parce que c'est un sécrét *profond*—à Berlin: professeur extra-ordinarius avec un "Lehrauftrag" du droit commercial, comme—tu lui racontras aussi cela—m'ont dit messieurs le Geheimrat Althoff et Geheimrat Eck—peut-être déjà cet été, vraisemblablement vers fin de juillet, certainement pendant l'hiver. La Faculté semble être unisono. Vois-tu cette noblesse magnifique? Il faudra que tu auras beaucoup plus de respect que jadis, mais pas de peur, je te traiterai avec Leutseligkeit et Herablassung. Mes chambres desquelles tu veux être héritier, je te les laisse avec plaisir, parce que je dois me procurer une villa pour moi et deux ou trois dienstbare Geister à moindre . . . .[18]

[My Dear Little One,

Thank you for your last letter. But, damn it all, what is this horrible French that you speak? Good gracious—it seems to be a peasant dialect that is spoken at Vevey; rustic—rusty, as we say. If I become a professor at Marburg, will you want to die? Me? Not at all, but—you can tell Papa, but very softly, because it's a deep secret—I shall be an associate professor at Berlin with an invitation to teach commercial law. As Privy Councillors Althoff and Eck[19] have told me—you can tell Papa this too—it may be as early as this summer, probably toward the end of July, but in the winter semester for sure. The faculty seems to be in full accord. Do you see this wonderful generosity? You'll have to have more respect for me than before, but never fear, I shall treat you with affability and condescension. You'll want to inherit my rooms, and I'll gladly let you have them, because I shall have to get a villa for myself and at least two or three domestic servants.]

Klara was the fresh young fountain at which Weber refreshed himself in the midst of his bookish world. What he meant to the girl and how he appeared to her at that time she retrospectively expressed as follows:

---

[18]The text of this almost Mozartian macaronic letter as given in the original of this biography differs somewhat from the version contained in the *Jugendbriefe*, op. cit., pp. 369ff.—Ed.
[19]Ernst W. E. Eck, 1838–1901, professor of law at the University of Berlin from 1881 on.—Ed.

And how he experienced everything with me, all my friendships, all our little follies! How he enjoyed and understood all that! For me, Max was the soul of the house. We went to him with everything and he was always able to help in one way or another. And despite his excessive modesty, this man, who towered above his companions even in his youth, always managed to add a special touch to our youthful Sunday circle. His talent for imparting knowledge was unique. Even in those days he used to give a lot of background information in his exhaustive and truly enriching answers to our questions, some of which may have been foolish, without making the questioner feel that he was ignorant. I always have to think back to this when I experience him in a different circle where after a while people really listen only to him. This clarity of thought and power of concentration enabled him to do his work at the same table where the family was engaged in lively conversation, reading aloud, and the like. Not only did this not disturb him, but he was able to follow our conversation and often season it with an amusing remark. He must have been a delightful eldest son for Mama, an infinite asset to her even then.

Yes, the presence of this son meant a great deal to Helene. Yet her ardent wish for him was that he would leave the house and get married. He never unburdened himself to her, but she had an idea of the weight that was upon him and why he was burying himself in his work. She saw how by virtue of his intellect and his willpower he refused to succumb to any passion that one might have named. She also realized that behind the walls with which he surrounded himself he had to restrain a demonic passionateness which now and then burst forth with a destructive blaze. Without being aware of it, he made the greatest demands on himself and on others. He was capable of *raging* when he found people petty-minded, unless love made him gentle.

6

MARRIAGE

I

In the spring of 1892 Max Weber, Sr.'s grandniece, Marianne, came to Berlin to be trained for independent professional work. Her grandfather, Karl David Weber, was the older brother of the city councillor, and so her mother was the cousin of his children. After the invention of mechanical weaving had caused a decline of the Bielefeld business, Karl Weber had moved the marketing of linen made by cottage industry to the country, to a beautiful quiet village on the outskirts of the Teutoburger Wald. Oerlinghausen stretches along a ledge on the northern slope of the rampartlike Tönsberg. From the ridge of this mountain there is an incomparable view of the magnificent German landscape. Toward the east and west there are the wooded summits of gently sloping hills, which jut out into the countryside like walls. Toward the south there is the Senne, a broad, lonely expanse of moors with nurseries of pines; its dreamy blue seems to blend on the horizon with a boundless ocean. Toward the north, however, there is a contrast: the undulating Westphalian plain gradually rises up to the mountains; as far as the eye can see there are carefully cultivated fields, set among woods and oaktree nurseries, with the friendly gabled roofs of Westphalian farm houses showing through the treetops—a blooming tapestry of life.

Here Karl Weber, the energetic son of the Bielefeld business house that had suffered because of modern technology, built a new business from scratch. He set the poverty-stricken small farmers of the Senne, who managed to coax only potatoes and buckwheat out of the sand, at looms and provided them with yarn. In marketing the linen produced by domestic diligence he was the first in his circle to use the business methods of modern capitalism, which the older generation had shunned as being "undignified." Instead of waiting for the wholesalers' salesmen to call on him, he traveled around with his samples himself. This created much annoyance among his Bielefeld peers—until they emulated him. Later on, in his book on the spirit of capitalism, his nephew Max analyzed his novel business methods and his personality as an example of modern entrepreneurship.

Slowly and with great effort Karl Weber worked his way up to solid prosperity and acquired a reputation as an important, even brilliant, businessman. He lived modestly. For relaxation he enjoyed hunting and his beautifully kept mountain garden. The children and grandchildren of his large family venerated him as a patriarch and subjected themselves to his authority in all areas of life. In the village, too, he was king—not only because he had more money than the others and provided employment, but especially because of the aristocratic aloofness of his demeanor. He kept away from the villagers, treated his subordinates with a master's condescension, his peers with perfect courtesy, and women with chivalry. Thus people regarded him with respect and secret awe, and as he grew older they surrounded him with a mythological aura. When he was in his prime he lost his much-loved, gifted wife, and thereafter he remained alone. When his eldest daughter, Anna, was eighteen, she married Eduard Schnitger, a young physician who had recently moved there from Lemgo and whose admission to this patrician family was regarded as a great honor for the impecunious young man. His happiness was short-lived. Anna died of puerperal fever while giving birth to their second child; Eduard himself had transmitted the germs from his medical practice.

With this greatly talented young woman an irreplaceable treasure of barely developed powers of love and spirit was lost. The whole village mourned her. But young as she was, she had already experienced great sorrow. Signs of a mysterious mental illness had appeared in her husband, and the situation was aggravated by the fact that illness was not recognized as the cause of his strangeness. After Anna's death the disaster took its course.

Eduard managed to continue in his profession, but the furies of a persecution mania chased him from place to place. From time to time he regarded his closest relatives as the cause of all his fright and torment. The family, too, was in despair over Anna's death.

Eduard soon entrusted his little daughter to his aged mother, the widow of a Gymnasium director in the small Lippe town of Lemgo, where beautiful old gabled houses bear witness to a distinguished past. Life imposed one burden after another upon Eduard's mother. Living in the most meager circumstances and beset by much sickness and hardship, she had finally managed to raise six children. Now, one after another, three of her sons were afflicted with severe mental disturbances. Only one son and the two daughters were well, and they were intelligent and courageous. The girls earned a living as teachers and shared the burden of an unkind fate with the frail old woman. In this they were all aided by their humor, generosity, frugality, and an unshakable, humble piety which made them try to interpret all visitations as "trials" and signs that they were God's children in particular measure. They struggled and suffered a great deal, but without bitterness. Their lives were limited and hard, yet each spring brought new blossoms as well as the love and devotion of others.

Anna's daughter Marianne grew up under the care of these women. Her aunt was strict and demanding in addition to being constantly worried and overburdened. But Marianne was gratefully aware of the love as well as the quiet grandeur of these women who bore their sorrows cheerfully. She lived through all the grievous events, among them the outbreak of madness in two uncles in the small apartment and the distress and anxiety of the women. Hidden horrors and terrible sounds and visions were engraved on her mind.

However, because of her youthful *joie de vivre* she was soon able to assimilate all these impressions without suffering any perceptible harm. After all, the earth was new and beautiful and, despite everything, full of love. And in the background there was her Oerlinghausen grandfather who was said to be rich and through whom she was part of a respected family. One day she would have access to a wider, brighter existence. Only when her childhood was over did her past experiences return to weigh upon her. Now she rapidly grew to be a meditative, questing personality, receptive to joy and eager for living, but no less sensitive to suffering.

When Marianne was sixteen, Grandfather Weber thought it was time to remove his granddaughter from small-town life and have her acquire an education appropriate for her class by spending several years in a fashionable institute in a larger city. Marianne studied eagerly and learned a great deal; she developed intellectual appetite and ambition, heard and saw genuine works of art, and compared herself with others. When she left Hannover at the age of almost nineteen, she had become a cultured person with exacting standards in every respect and was alienated from the limited conditions of a provincial city. She no longer belonged in that framework; when her grandmother died, no one wanted to keep her in that town, for there was nothing to satisfy her lust for life. Her former schoolmates were already struggling with the barrenness of an unfulfilled youth, slowly wasting away with unsatisfied longing for fulfillment in marriage, something achieved by only a few in that small-town society. For the young men went away, often for good, or else they returned with a wife. The girls remained at home with their aging parents, and only the strongest broke away to look for satisfying work in the outside world, like their brothers. Lemgo, once a Hansa town, was like a beauty forgotten by the modern age, and its life was like a quiet pond without a fresh influx, from whose muddy bottom bubbles of ugly gossip and malicious intrigue rose from time to time.

Now Marianne was homeless. She was not able to share Eduard's difficult life. The Oerlinghausen family tried to make her settle with them. Anna's younger sister Alwine, a kindly, serious woman with many children, whose husband had become a partner in the family business, lovingly took Marianne in. In this very harmonious family circle she was supposed to prepare herself for the future tasks of being a housewife and mother by helping around the house. It seemed to be high time for this. She was sure to find a suitable husband some day, even though in the country the prospects were not exactly favorable for a girl with her high intellectual standards. But Marianne's disposition was not typical, and she inwardly rebelled against the traditional fate of girls. The small domestic duties in a household that did not really need her help seemed unimportant to her. She had no capacity for this kind of work, and to help by serving others was an effort for her.

The smooth but uneventful flow of rural life in which the men devote themselves to their businesses and the women to the home and the children offered nothing to her aspiring intellect and passion for life. There was nothing to develop her own strength, and she felt that her life was condemned to stand still. The days did not stream by, they crept by. She was almost sick with boredom and was profoundly unhappy, but felt guilty about it. The family sensed her alienation with mounting discomfort and would have liked to help, but did not know how. Unfortunately the girl did not at all conform to the hallowed ideal of femininity that the men believed in, an ideal that had shaped all the women of this group, and evidently her stay at the institute, with its highly organized work and all its stimulation, had also spoiled her for country living!

What now? A career? Surely that was not necessary. A profession for a woman made sense only if she was poor and had to forgo all prospects of marriage. Karl Weber's granddaughter need not and must not earn any money; what would people think? Marianne was at her wit's end. Should she become a teacher, like her always overburdened aunts, or perhaps a nurse? No, that did not appeal to her, and there really was no need for it. Perhaps she could attend the university. A few energetic women were studying medicine in Switzerland. But that was something far too unusual, and besides she recoiled from the demands of that profession. She was courageous, but she was also nervous and did not have a heroic disposition.

When Marianne was twenty-one, the Charlottenburg family took pity on her and invited her to spend a few weeks with them during the winter. Now she could get her fill of the intellectual atmosphere of their house and the cultural treasures of the big city. The quick rhythm of Berlin life surged through her veins; *this at last was living!* She could hardly take everything in. The assessor, Max, took her to her first ball and benevolently uncled [beonkelt] her. For the first time she met a group of lively young men. Of them all, her three grown cousins seemed to her to be the most impressive and the most distinguished. The two younger cousins were extremely handsome, but the assessor was not. He did not attach any importance to his appearance. He was corpulent, his pear-shaped head bore fencing scars, and his hair was cut short. His delicately curved lips were in strange contrast to his large, unshapely nose, and his dark eyes were often hidden by his overlapping eyebrows.

No, this colossus was neither handsome nor youthful, but in his every gesture he was powerful and manly, and despite his massiveness he had a subtle grace of movement. What elasticity in his stride, what expressiveness in his hands! Now and then his eyes would show flashes of kindness, anger, or mischief, and occasionally his peculiar aloofness gave way to liberating humor, sympathetic understanding, and chivalrous kindness.

What meant more to the girl than the young people and all that intoxicating life was Helene's motherly love. To be sure, Helene referred her new niece to "faithfulness in that which is least" [Luke 16:10] and the value of helping and serving, but at the same time she conceded her the right to work outside the house and disengage herself from her family. For the first time the girl felt that her individuality was not regarded as unfeminine and egotistical, but was accepted the way it was. She returned to the Oerlinghausen circle with firm resolutions, reassured by the knowledge that at some future time she would be allowed to seek her own road in life. As yet Eros had not touched her. But at home, in the stillness of rural life, she remembered her remarkable cousin, and his figure secretly assumed ever greater dimensions. He had acted in such a modest, unpretentious, almost austere way; he did not seem "demonic" at all, and yet he engaged her imagination. She could hardly fathom his intellect and could know nothing of his future, but from a distance she responded to the substance of his character.

After much deliberation, and because after a year nothing else had happened, the patriarch [Karl Weber] consented to Marianne's plan to develop her modest artistic talent. In the spring of 1892 she went to Berlin. There she finally found what she needed: a strict discipline of work directed toward achievement, and then, the house at Charlottenburg. She could permit herself all these riches only if she toiled away outwardly and inwardly, and there always was an opportunity to do so. While her personality was still developing, she was rarely capable of natural enjoyment of the moment. She was too preoccupied with herself, and she had not yet fully absorbed the misfortune of her youth and the sufferings of her family. Thus she was very sensitive to the sufferings of others. She understood Helene in particular, divined her fate, sensed her unattainable goodness and purity, revered and loved her devotedly, and willingly let herself be educated by her, although she immediately realized that she herself was made of entirely different material from this saintly woman, and would always remain so. "When one is with you, one's heart always opens up to all humanity!" Helene's daughters were still too young, and besides, the mother could not share her domestic difficulties with them. Thus Marianne became her confidante even before Helene had any idea that she would some day become a daughter to her.

When after an interval of a year and a half Marianne saw the assessor again, she immediately knew how she felt, and she also knew that she would be able to stay near him only if no one suspected that she was in love. She also heard about the delicate, lovely Emmy, her mysterious illness, and her closeness to Helene. The rest she surmised. The secret did not bother her at all; for the time being, all she wanted was to be near the man she loved.

In the fall of 1892 Weber traveled south for the first reunion in five years with his girl friend, who had found a second home in a beautiful sanatorium.

She could increasingly bring her illness under control and was now able to help other patients. When he told Marianne about this, she felt that he had visited Emmy in order to find out how they felt about each other—and that he was finished with the past. She could not help but ask herself why this had happened at that particular time. Now her feelings were beginning to assume a clearer outline and she began to hope for fulfillment.

But the road there went along an abyss. A friend of Max, whom Helene was mothering, courted Marianne. The girl was too dazed to be aware of this; she noticed only that her cousin was changing and withdrawing into his shell again. Helene ardently wanted her young friend and Marianne to marry, a union in which she saw great happiness for both. And her "eyes were holden" [Luke 24:16], all the more so because she was still hoping for a marriage between Max and Emmy. After all, Max had visited Emmy, and this had been followed by the news that the girl was slowly getting well. Marianne was given away without being asked. Hopeless confusion ensued. Helene felt responsible to her young friend, and her guilty feelings toward him brought her to the point of a nervous breakdown. The situation demanded renunication all around, which seemed to be the only dignified and bearable thing to do. Weber wrote a letter to Marianne which like no other document illuminates the fate of his youth and his nature in those years.

Read this letter, Marianne, when you are calm and composed, for I have things to tell you that you may not be prepared to hear. You believe—I think—that we are through with each other and that I shall banish you to the still, cool harbor of resignation in which I myself have lain at anchor for years. But that is not so.

First this: If we understand each other at all, I need not tell you that I shall *never* dare to offer a girl my hand like a free gift. Only if I myself am under the divine compulsion of complete, unconditional devotion do I have a right to demand and accept it for myself. I am telling you this so that you will not misunderstand what follows. And now listen.

As you yourself realize, I have known you for only a very short time, for you have been a mystery to me in many respects which I now understand. But you do not know me, you cannot possibly know me. You do not see how I try, with difficulty and varying success, to tame the elemental passions with which nature has endowed me. But ask my mother; I know well that her love for me—which forces me to silence, because I cannot repay it—is rooted in the fact that morally I used to be her problem child. For years the idea that the rich heart of a girl could come close to my sober nature never occurred to me. This is why I was blind and certain of my opinion even in your case.

When I watched my friend's affection for you grow and thought I saw signs of your returning it, I was not able to understand why more than once an obscure oppressive feeling—something like sadness—came over me when I looked at you and thought that I would have to see you go through life at his or another man's side. I took it for the selfish feeling of someone who has given up at the sight of another person's happiness, and I suppressed that feeling. But it was something else. You know what it was. The word must not pass my lips, for I have a double debt to pay to the past and do not know whether I am able to do so. You know about both, but I have to speak about this nevertheless.

First, the events of the last difficult days. Both of us, although the guilt is mine alone, have impaired my friend's happiness, and more severely than you are able to fathom now. His pure figure stands between us. He knows what I am writing you now, and he is manly and rational. But I do not know if and when the time will come when he could look into your eyes without embarrassment or a feeling of resignation, and with lively sympathy, if you stood before him as the wife of another man. For as long as this is not so, I could never build my own life's happiness on his resignation, for a shadow from the past would fall over the feelings that I would be able to offer to the wife at my side.

But I must speak of even more difficult matters.

From my mother you know that six years ago I came close to what I now regard as the pure heart of a girl who resembles you in some respects and is dissimilar in others. But you do not know the full weight of the responsibility that I assumed when I was still half a boy in my relationship with girls. I did not recognize it myself until late, and it is a lifetime responsibility. *She* knew better than I what my situation was; I did not realize this until later. For a long time I was not sure whether we were through with each other. In order to know it for certain I went to Stuttgart last fall. I saw her, the appearance and voice of old, and it was as if some invisible hand were extinguishing her image deep in my heart, for the figure that approached me was different from the one that had lived in me, as though it were from another world. Why that was so I do not know. We parted—so I thought—for life.

Then, at Christmastime, I heard that the doctors were not able to find the cause of her continuing illness and had come to the conclusion that she was *still* secretly in love. So I am searching *my* heart in vain for a definitive answer to this question: Is it possible that when I thought I was helping her overcome her feeling for me (provided it existed), I was actually arousing hopes in her? Now comes the news that she is beginning to get well, and believes that she is, and I am doubly oppressed by the uncertainty as to whether it is hope or renunciation that is strengthening her nerves. Whatever the reason, I could not accept cool renunciation or resignation from her either. I cannot be dead for her if I am to live for another, and that is why I must look into her eyes and see whether her heart beats sympathetically when I receive from another girl the happiness that she would have given me if prejudices, my outward hopelessness in my tedious period as a *Referendar*, and also my weakness had not intervened. But when will that day come? I do not know.

And now I ask you: have you inwardly renounced me in recent days? Or resolved to do so? Or are you doing it *now*? *If not, then it will be too late*, we shall then be bound to each other, and I shall be hard toward you and not spare you. I say to you: I shall take the course that I must and which you now know. And you will take it with me. Where it will lead, how far it is, whether it will lead us together on this earth, I do not know. And even though I now know how great and strong you are, you proud girl, you may still succumb, for if you go with me, you will not only bear your burden but mine as well, and you are not used to taking such paths. Therefore, test both of us.

But I believe I know how you will decide. The tidal wave of passion runs high, and it is dark around us—come with me, my high-minded comrade, out of the quiet harbor of resignation, out onto the high seas, where men grow in the struggle of souls and the transitory is sloughed off. But *bear in mind*: in the head and heart of the mariner there must be clarity when all is surging underneath him. We must not tolerate any fanciful surrender to unclear and mystical moods in our souls. For when feeling rises high, you must control it to be able to steer yourself with sobriety.

If you will go with me, then do *not* answer me. In that case I shall quietly press your hand when I see you again and not cast down my eyes before you, something that you should not do either.

Farewell; life is coming down hard on you, you misunderstood child. This is all I shall say to you now: I thank you for the wealth you have brought into my life, and my thoughts are with you. And now once more: Come with me, I know that you will come.

When Marianne read this letter, she was profoundly shaken by a sense of the ineffable and eternal. She asked nothing further. From then on her life was to be a thanksgiving for the gift of this hour. But oh, how hard it was to wait when the ecstasy had subsided, for now renunciation had been transformed into hope. There was an exchange of letters between Ida and Helene. A few months after the event—the time seemed long—Max and Marianne were permitted to become engaged. Helene was still heartsick, but she was now able to bear the new development, for she had long since taken the girl into her heart as a daughter. Thus she began gently and self-lessly to look forward to the future of her children.

When Max went to call upon his fiancée in the home of their common relatives, she gave him the following blessing and greeting to take along:

> Max, who is leaving right away, is bringing you only a heartfelt greeting. It is with a joyous and grateful heart that I am letting my "big boy" go. I know that I am not losing him but getting him back with doubled wealth, and therefore the hour of parting will not be hard for me, as it is for many a poor mother. Everything that I have missed doing or have done wrong—you know it and so does he—you two will bring to completion as you educate each other and bear things together. And learn one thing, dear children, as a warning example: Bear joy *and grief* together. It is God's will that if something is hard for one, the other should help and not be cravenly and falsely discreet out of love or fear. Max knows that he still has a lot to learn in this regard, and he will keep it in mind for my sake. God be with you! Love is eternal.
>
> Your Mother

Their incipient happiness was still shadowed by the grief they had experienced, their own and that of others. The couple was not able or allowed to shake anything off. Being young was still ahead of them, and slowly they learned how to be young. In Max in particular the life that was now streaming toward him only gradually removed the crusts which feelings of guilt, renunciation, and repressions of all kinds had deposited on his nature. He did not spare himself anything. Immediately after their engagement Weber went to Strasbourg to have a heart-to-heart talk with Ida, who had been a second mother to him. It turned out that she too had for years wavered between hope and fear for Emmy. Once more Max realized his whole youthful responsibility: he was keeping a tender, loving girl waiting for the decisive word that was never spoken. From this emotional journey he wrote to his fiancée:

While traveling I found in my coat pocket Volume 2 of *Münchhausen*, [1] which I had left there, and instead of the review I had planned to write I read the story of blonde Lisbeth. As I thought of my brunette Westphalian girl, it became clear to me that in some respects you are a Lisbeth, but even clearer that I am not an Oswald in *any* respect. What an old bachelor you have taken for yourself, my child. Sometimes I am still quite depressed, as though I were the object of an enormous aberration of taste on your part that might disappear one fine day. But let me go on. In Heidelberg I was recognized in Benecke's house as I rode by. I went there for supper and was received by these exceptionally kindhearted people with the customary, truly touching joy. Only Dora (Emmy's friend) still seemed to be under the pressure of recent events and was cordial but rather quiet.

The past came to life for me, too, and when I walked home along the Neckar a feeling of mellowness such as I had not known for a long time came over me. The moonlight is refracted into countless shimmering beams on the water that rushes by incessantly, and the castle, illuminated from behind, stands out darkly above it, with the contours of its front as indistinct and tangled as the future. From my bed I had a view of this dark, great, threatening mass standing in the midst of the moonlight; but when I awakened, I saw in the greenery that surrounds it the joyful harbingers of spring . . . It is very warm here, and the trip to Strasbourg was almost summery. My aunt received me very cordially, and after dinner we sat together in the garden for hours and discussed everything. In the main it was just as I had imagined it. I shall write you more about it later, as we haven't quite finished yet. My feeling of responsibility is not diminished; I shall have it permanently, that I can see. But don't worry, my child, I have long since assimilated it and it no longer is a source of excitement to me, although it was in recent days under the pressure of the situation. I am aware that I have made grave mistakes, but I have done nothing that I would have to be ashamed of. In the summer you must meet my aunt and Emmy in Stuttgart; I have requested this, and I know how gladly you will do it for my sake. . . .

Never in my life have I been as tired as I am now. I suppose this is partly due to the days I spent in Strasbourg. I was not used to doing

---

[1] Karl Immermann's comic novel *Münchhausen* (1838–39) contains *Der Oberhof* [The Upper Farm], sometimes printed separately as a prime exemplar of the new genre of the *Dorfgeschichte* [village story]. It is the story of a love match, following some vicissitudes, between Oswald, a noble-minded Count who has come to Westphalia from Swabia, and Lisbeth, a foundling.—Ed.

nothing but sitting quietly so as to continue my intellectual relationship with my aunt and discuss past, present, and future with her, more from the standpoint of sentiment than with any practical goal. That goes strongly against my grain, and from my letter you must have noticed the great exhaustion that it brought me. Nonetheless, it was beneficial to both her and me, and even though I now feel as if I have emerged from a kind of bone-and-soul grinder, you will surely notice, my darling, when I take you in my arms again that I have taken a step forward in assimilating all that the past has imposed upon me. Then you will no longer think, my child, that, as you wrote in your last letter, I have "something to hide" from you. What should that be? Surely you are familiar with the past and my inner relationship to it and know that my concern is directed exclusively at producing the most sincere relationship possible between past and present and thus sparing us any possibility that our happiness might be built on the silent and painful resignation of others.

When Emmy heard about his engagement and wrote him a cordial, sisterly letter, he answered her:

My dear Emmy,

In years a letter has seldom given me such pure joy as your friendly lines on the occasion of my birthday did yesterday, for they showed me what I had hoped for: that we have remained as close to each other as ever and that I shall continue to have in you the sister of my own age whom I have always painfully missed. As you know, I have always measured the women and girls who crossed my path against your personality, and for my roughhewn nature it was a blessing that I felt inwardly constrained to view the opposite sex through your eyes. I have done it in the case of the one for whose happiness I have now assumed the responsibility, and I believe this will remain so. In the autumn we saw each other and spoke to each other but briefly. At that time I had no idea that it might be granted to me to take on such a responsibility for another person's life. I think you recognized from my earlier letters that in these last years, whose disagreeable barrenness I remember with horror, I had abandoned myself to such utter resignation, a resignation that was not without a certain bitterness, that, apart from a certain melancholy glow which some rich and beautiful memories of earlier years brought into my bookish existence, I was completely absorbed in what I would call the automatic continuation of my obligatory professional work—very much to my mother's chagrin, as you can imagine.

I don't know how detailed an account of what led up to my engagement my mother gave you during her short visit, whether you are aware that because of this resignation I have caused grievous suffering to others as well. Incapable of believing that I could be the object of a richly gifted girl's affection, I thought that my Marianne's affection was meant for one of my closest friends who, for his part, had taken a deep interest in her. In doing so I had to overcome something I did not understand at the time. Only the catastrophe that was the result of his courtship as encouraged by me—something that profoundly agitated my mother and Marianne—showed me that my vision had been unnaturally blurred.

I am a man who is strangely given to pondering and a bridegroom who is old beyond his years in many ways. My bride, who after the past and these events will understand this, as you will understand it, will at first have to practice a little forbearance in this regard. But it is certainly true that the world looks very differently to me now than it did last autumn. For I now face hard and great tasks of a purely human nature for which it is worthwhile to exert one's strength, even if outwardly they appear in less impressive guise than the goals usually offered us by a man's profession, which is practiced in the marketplace of life. Particularly last autumn, when I stayed in the Ottilienhaus,[2] unfortunately for but a short time, I learned to appreciate the full inner wealth and the quiet grandeur with which the externally so small and insignificant things and incidents of daily life can be invested. And since I have never had more than a superficial respect for the value of the masculine profession, apart from the obligation to "make the most of one's talent," I have a deep yearning for such everyday, purely human tasks to be given to me. And, the way life is constituted, that is the case for us *men*—in contrast to you—only in one's own house.

It would give me genuine pleasure if we could frequently hear from each other. But I would not urge you to write me more often than your strength, which surely still needs conserving, permits. *Auf Wiedersehen!* In brotherly love and friendship,

Your Max

Shortly before his wedding he addressed the following lines to Emmy:

My dear Emmy,

I would have answered your dear, deeply moving letter long ago if I had not until recently hoped to thank you in person for all the kind

[2]Emmy Baumgarten lived under medical supervision in the so-called Ottilienhaus in Stuttgart.—Ed.

things you have written me. This I shall now have to postpone until my wedding trip, and that is why I am writing you. Now you know the past and realize why it would have been impossible for me *not* to have had a frank discussion with you about everything before I undertake my new task. My belief that I could never belong to a woman nor be capable of coming close to a girl was, as you know, the consequence of my many years of unresolved doubt as to what your attitude toward me was or would be, and I would never have overcome this deep resignation without being certain about our relationship. Now the past is clearly revealed to us. I recognize all the illusions I have created for myself, the mistakes I have made as well as my responsibility, and yet I am inclined to believe that *both* of us would be reluctant *not* to have this past behind us. I would not want to expunge it from my memory for anything in the world, for it has made me realize that there are feelings that change but never get stale and spoil. In the last few years, which were often barren and almost always without prospects, it was your image, next to that of my mother, that gave me the degree of strength to be good which I possessed and have retained. Therefore I also owe it to you if I feel strong enough to assume the great measure of responsibility imposed upon me by the union with a woman who is entrusting her life's happiness to me. With sincere joy my future wife and I look forward to seeing you again.

And now farewell. You know my heartfelt wishes for you. Never before have I thought of any human being with such a strange mixture of a strong sense of responsibility, gratitude, and genuine joy and friendship as I am thinking of you, my darling, in whose friendship I have taken such pride. And that will remain so, I know. And don't worry about the "Sunday clothes"; my future wife knows me, too, only in my holiday best, despite all my efforts against it. As ever with brotherly love,

Your Max

In this way Weber delicately combined the present and the future with the timeless substance of the past, lifting the veil from the past at the threshold of a new life. He gave the friend of his youth the certainty that she had had his love and would remain dear to him. He was not mistaken in his hope that she too would not want to have missed the experience of her youth.

After Weber's death Emmy Baumgarten expressed what this experience meant to her in the following lines:

All those years I was not sure whether Max felt more for me than a cordial friendship, a brotherly affection. In 1887, when he was on officers' practice in Strasbourg, well, at that time it seemed to me as though his entire behavior reflected something more than that. Those days are transfigured in my memory. They were the most beautiful of my youth. Despite the misgivings that appeared even then, I was walking on air. When I recall it to mind, it is always with the greatest gratitude that it was given to me for once to know this most wonderful feeling because of him and to be on top of the world for a short time.

As for her, she had long since found her inner purpose in the devoted care of others.

II

Gradually the present demanded its due. The couple's appreciation of each other grew. The seriousness of their relationship was lightened by their sparkling humor and impish banter. The engagement was still supposed to be kept secret, but as Weber remarked, "Every jackass here gives me a meaningful look and asks me whether something has happened to me. I would never have thought I was beaming so." He was impatient to establish his own household. The appointment to a chair in national economy at Freiburg, which had been pending all summer, did not materialize for the time being. No matter; then he would simply get married while still a lecturer with the prospect of replacing Goldschmidt. He now gave vent to everything he had endured silently in his parental home:

> In the morning I look at your wreath and the green ribbon above me, and then it feels as though I had awakened in a hotel or some other place where I no longer belong. I am really not making any progress in my work. It is a transitional stage, and I am beset by a tremendous mental sluggishness, as you can probably tell from my letters. The reason is a simple one. For years I have realized with infinite bitterness that I was unable to obtain a position that would give me an independent income. I never had any kind of respect for the concept of a "vocation," since I thought I knew that to a certain extent I fitted into a rather large number of positions. The only thing that attracted me was my own bread, and the fact that it was denied me made my family home a torment. But now the end is in sight, and it is different 'from what I, who had seen myself as an itinerant bachelor, had ever hoped for. The upshot is, right now, nothing but an impatient desire finally to reach that goal.

Of course, the young people still had much to do to prepare for their marriage. Above all, Marianne had to learn to cook before she could be entrusted with the physical well-being of a husband. The family was concerned over whether she would duly honor the "linen sacrament," observe domestic propriety, and know how to handle everyday problems. Weber was less concerned. He desired the development of her individuality, her inner freedom, and her independence. Above all, she must not from the outset look up to him humbly as to the "high star of glory"; she was to stand beside him tall and proud:

> I am enclosing two letters from the cousins who next to Emmy are closest to me. . . . The poem that this sensitive girl, who controls her emotional life freely and with singular grace, clearly intended for you is related to our conversation whose substance you will remember. But I believe that she is mistaken about you in one respect—the feeling that she calls "self-debasement." For that does not apply to you, my child, does it? You feel nothing like that, do you? *We stand by each other free and equal.*

But Weber, too, believed that the best way to assure his wife of her equality would be to provide her with a domain of her own within the household that he could not touch. When she wrote him from the place where she was being trained in housekeeping and asked him for instructive reading matter—after all, she was at the very beginning of her intellectual development—Helene was particularly horrified and thought that it would be much more proper and logical if the bride sewed her trousseau in her leisure hours—if only to muse and dream quietly about the future. This was what Helene had done in her engagement period, and she believed that it was still the appropriate preparation for the conjugal fate [*Gattungsschicksal*]. The bridegroom was infected with his mother's misgivings and wrote to Marianne as follows:

> Shall I still send you the Bebel?[3] If you want it, I shall do so right away, for I do not consider myself your guardian. Or shall we read him together at some future time? And do you want more things to read now? I have put aside Paulsen's[4] *Einleitung in die Philosophie* [Introduc-

---

[3] August Bebel, 1840–1913, co-founder of the Social Democratic Party and orthodox Marxist, author of *Die Frau und der Sozialismus* (1883), *Christentum und Sozialismus* (1892), etc.—Ed.
[4] Friedrich Paulsen, 1846–1908, philosopher, author of *System der Ethik* (1889), *Schopenhauer, Hamlet, Mephistopheles* (1900), etc.—Ed.

tion to Philosophy] for you; he had it sent to me, and it is a good, not too difficult book which I usually glance at in bed at night. But above all, take care of your body now. You must get stronger and look outward rather than inward, into your interior as well as mine, and you must not think with such contempt of those who are "only housewives." I mean this in your own interest: There is a necessary *pièce de résistance,* for you must have a domain in which, unlike the field of thought, I do not compete with you. You would never believe how little respect I have for the so-called "intellectual training" ["*geistige Bildung*"]. A vigorous naturalness of feeling and of practical activity is what impresses me—perhaps because I myself lack it—and I feel the need to be impressed.

Look, I am lecturing you again, but don't take it amiss. You know that I fully understand what your individuality is, don't you? I would simply like you to have an area I cannot touch, a housewifely sphere of duty and work, which seems to you to be more than an unavoidable misfortune, for—I can only keep repeating it—you will by no means have as easy a time of it with me as it may seem to you. And then, the more our very own fields of interest coincide and are identical, the less independent of me and the more vulnerable will you be. Do you understand what I mean? But of course, no *artificial* self-limitation.

So my "lecture" did not particularly shock you? Well, so much the better. By saying that I have no respect for intellectual training I meant only that I don't regard it as a good fortune for anyone if he considers the gratification of his thirst for knowledge as the real substance of his life and as that "which makes human beings human," and views the economic tasks he faces only as an unavoidable burden of existence. Emotionally speaking, it makes a tremendous difference to the relationship between a husband and his wife whether this is the case or whether the woman perhaps instinctively seeks the focal point of her existence in her practical position.

As far as I am concerned, my desire has always been for an economically independent and practical effectiveness, something that circumstances have denied me. The scientifically most useful *new* ideas, in my experience, have always come to me when I was lying on the sofa with a cigar in my mouth and was cogitating *con amore*—that is, not as the result of real work. I regard this truly intellectual production in the narrowest sense only as a product of free hours, as a sideline of life, and even now my pleasure in a learned profession would always lie on the practical-pedagogical rather than on the really "scholarly" side. The great marital happiness of our Westphalian relatives is also based on the fulfilling and satisfying *practical* work of the men. Nothing is more horrible to me than the arrogance of the "intellectual" and learned

professions. That was what I meant, and when I said that you would not have
a very easy time of it with me, I meant to say only that my sphere of duty does
not please me sufficiently for me to bring into our house the kind of natural
happiness that comes from the aforementioned work. That is why is is a
problem for you that you are relatively little *naive*—practical, if I may put it
that way.

Has my "lecture" really made you wonder again, my child, whether you
are "the right one," whether I miss something in you? Then I had better keep my mouth shut. You know that one's heart does not ask
about qualities and is unteachable. But my *mind* tells me that in the
future you will have a more secure position, and one that will be easier
for you, if the focal point is not in the purely intellectual-
philosophical realm, to put it that way, but if you have as a basis a
domain of practical activity that is out of bounds to me. I almost fear
you understood me to say that I was taking back or watering down my
earlier request that you should make the greatest possible demands
upon me regarding the discussion and sharing of intellectual interests.

On the contrary, my child, this is the situation: To prevent such
a companionship in the "intellectual" sphere from jeopardizing your position, I must never get the—unconscious—feeling that, because by virtue of
more prolonged efforts in this direction I naturally have richer resources in
this area, you now are dependent on me in every respect. And this very
situation, so it seems to me, could easily arise unless I got the feeling that in
your practical field you have an equally independent sphere of activity that is
controlled by you and fulfills your *practical* interests as much as my teaching
profession or some other vocation that might be in store for me fulfills mine.
My heart says, "It seems to me as though you were placed in the world
especially for me." But my head asks whether I was equally put in the world
for you, and here, I think, you underestimate the difficulty of getting along
with me. That is why you must have a definite sphere of activity that is
valuable to you as such, so that you will not be dependent on the fluctuations
of my temperament.

Marianne, however, did what her own conscience prompted her to do, although she had no idea that in the future the household would not demand much of her, and that the happiness of her marriage would some day
depend to a great extent on her independent intellectual existence.

At that time Weber still had a tremendous amount of work to do: his
lectures, the new investigation of farm workers for the Evangelical-Social
Congress, the preparations for a course on agrarian policy for pastors in the

autumn, accumulated book reviews, and the like. Thus he was glad when the house emptied, as it did every summer:

> I hope to be all by myself soon. Strange how this always affects me. The aversion to work, which has been pursuing me for months, disappears. Today I read 100 pages of physiological psychology, 100 pages of theory of knowledge, and an Italian law book without getting mental indigestion; for the first time in a long while my mental vigor is good. I wonder whether this is not due to the fact that a man of my age no longer belongs in his parents' home. I needed this fresh impetus, for about thirty books for review have been lying around for six months. I have been getting nasty letters, and even though I answered them nastily, I did realize with annoyance that these people really are right.

When Marianne spent a few weeks in Charlottenburg before their marriage, she began to help him eagerly with the processing of the material for the investigation. That kind of work suited her, and above all, it was something she could share with the overworked Weber. It seemed advisable to her to familiarize herself with scholarship as soon as possible if she was to be inwardly close to him and not to be overwhelmed by this insatiable competitor. Helene was both pleased and worried. Ink-stained hands six weeks before the wedding? Would the girl ever be satisfied with the everyday pursuits of a *Hausfrau*, with the "lifting and carrying, preparing and working for others?" Would the *Gattungsdienst* [connubial duties] not be a heavy sacrifice for her? Marianne thought: "Everything in due time."

* * *

In early autumn a great family wedding took place at Oerlinghausen. Wina [Alwine], the loving and graceful mistress of a flourishing clan with whom the bride had spent her tortured girlhood, was delighted to be able to open her beautiful country estate to so many important guests. Since her engagement the local family had been very pleased with Marianne. Helene and her family were dearly loved there, and the *Privatdozent* [adjunct lecturer] was already admired as the distinguished man with a "future." Who would have thought that this peculiar girl would draw such a lot in life?

The rich, romantic countryside and the wonderful gardens artfully inserted into it which usually were so quiet made a fine setting for the celebration. Otto Baumgarten married the couple in the village church: "Love believes all, hopes all, tolerates all." Those who were knowing and mature were deeply moved. There were the bride's relatives on her father's side who would never again be part of such a joyous, broad stream of life. There was her father, the unsociable, lonely Eduard, in whom there were signs of proud happiness, too, for with kindness and an inspired knowledge of human nature his son-in-law had managed to gain his complete confidence. There were the merchants with their large families—all serious people who believed in doing their duty and in aristocratic business ethics, and who combined refinement of character with professional efficiency. There was the Charlottenburg family who added substance and a touch of excitement as well as a high intellectual level to the rustic idyll. Wina adorned the festival with flowers and Helene contributed a profusion of lovely verses. The selfless kindness of these women and the gracious demeanor of the guests brought all the different elements into harmony for the occasion.

There was also some robust humor. The orthodox parson of the village criticized the *Freigeistigkeit* [free thought] of his colleague who had married the couple and made a profession of faith in the cross at the wedding banquet— much to the gratification of those who regarded themselves as part of the "small community." On the other hand, Baumgarten extolled his friend, the bridegroom, as a "merry eater beloved of God."[5] For Helene and the young couple the happiness of that day was made blessed by the suffering they had endured.

---

[5] Presumably a reference to Luke 15:23.—Ed.

7

THE YOUNG TEACHER
AND POLITICIAN
FALL 1893 to 1897 _____

I

"We get along almost too well," wrote the young wife from their wedding trip. But a few critical moments did show her her husband's nervous irritability. She was supposed to decide on their route and did not know which of the various attractive but unfamiliar possibilities she preferred. Weber got seriously annoyed. In fundamental matters he always followed his own conscience, but now for the first time he asked his wife to make a decision for him. This was repeated on later occasions, often when important matters were at stake, such as whether he should accept or decline an offer of a chair.

This first trip together gave Weber only a short break. Immediately after he had moved into his own home, a course in economics for pastors began;

it was sponsored by the leadership of the Evangelical-Social Congress and Weber participated as a teacher. He lectured on agrarian policy, for there was nothing that interested him more. Extensive hospitality was a necessity for the young husband, and it gave him satisfaction to be able to gather his friends around his own table at last.

The question was whether Marianne would be capable of running a household of this kind. The whole family waited in suspense for the domestic accident statistics, and almost every day someone dropped in at mealtime. But nothing unusual happened. On the contrary, like other young wives, Marianne, surprisingly enough, regarded it as a matter of honor to meet all demands, and she was able to manage. Fortunately she had found an East Prussian girl [Bert(h)a] to whom humble service was a God-ordained form of existence which she found completely fulfilling. She attached herself to the couple with devoted loyalty until her death twenty-three years later. Helene, who had secretly feared serious trouble and discomfort during the "years of apprenticeship," got the reassuring impression that her daughter-in-law was doing her best. The latter wrote to her: "Look, you think that I have learned something in the past year—from whom, directly and in a roundabout way? I lack the words to tell you what you mean to us, but you know it yourself."

The life of the young couple still remained under the shadow of the Charlottenburg house and the past. They were especially close to Helene and shared her many and varied difficulties, which were exacerbated by constant overexertion. Weber, Sr., had left his position, and although still fully vigorous, he was now barely half-occupied and stayed home a major portion of his time. How Helene felt and what her close relationship with the young couple meant to her she expressed in delicate occasional verses:

> Frühling ist's worden Kinder auch in Euren Herzen,
> Reich setzt der Baum des Lebens Blüt' und Früchte an.
> Still glücklich seh' ich's wachsen, denn ich weiss, dass was aus Schmerzen
> Geboren ist, kein Sturm des Lebens Euch entblättern kann.
> Was Ihr mir seid, nicht wisst Ihr's ganz, Ihr Beiden . . .
> Doch Kraft und Mut zum Leben kommt mir nur aus andrer Glück.

[Spring has come, my children, into your hearts as well. The tree of life is putting forth blossoms and fruit. In quiet happiness I watch it grow, for I know that what is born of pain cannot be defoliated by any storm of life. What you mean to me you do not fully know, you two. . . . But strength and the courage to live come to me only from the happiness of others.]

Relaxation, enjoyment of the moment, days magnified only by their own happiness were rarely vouchsafed the young people. To the extent that they lived consciously, it was done mainly for "tasks" and for "others." But for the time being they desired nothing else; like ships used to carrying cargo, they needed this ballast to follow a steady course on their new route. Both of them knew that they still had to learn how to live quietly, securely, and with a simple enjoyment of life. To be sure, a robust humor and cheerful comfort, a delight in teasing and being teased, brought sunshine into the seriousness of every day. The drollery and robust humor with which Weber occasionally handled disagreeable situations is indicated by a letter he wrote his wife half a year after their marriage from Posen, where he had had to squeeze into a uniform again for two months:

> Posen, March 11, 1894
>
> I cannot escape the fate of being "invited" today, that is, of having a few active comrades, whom custom obliges to do so, treat me to some of the unspeakably vile "champagne" which is sold here for almost less than Bavarian beer—and under the unfortunate condition that I drink it, too. Because of my basic loyalty to a fundamental tenet of my life, the so-called *Bierehrlichkeit* [beer honesty], whose importance you will be able to appreciate, I usually make this criminal concoction disappear from the face of the earth. Heaven hardly knows what the consequences for my mental condition in the afternoon will be, let alone myself.
>
> Now things are much more livable with me. First of all, you will find the place heated; second, there are a spirit stove (for one mark) and cans of cocoa (I had to stop my orderly from scooping the cocoa out of them with his dirty mitts in the morning); further, you will see in a glass cupboard in my bedroom an array of bottles of Graetz beer and all sorts of delicacies, from a smoked goose (!) down to a common horsemeat sausage, artillery style. My own corpse, newly resuscitated today by a steam bath like a Galatea—or what was that marble woman's name? I am losing my whole classical vein in this pig bay—is even clothed in a linen shirt, which happens only on Sundays. Oh yes, the old, greasy barracks biped remembers that it is human and even is married to a most appetizing little woman and must therefore try to be distinguishable from an ordinary pig, at least under a magnifying glass.

The situation is disastrous only in respect to the beds; my clear conscience is not matched by a soft pillow.[1] On these much-too-short
and much-too-narrow boxes I find no adequate place on which I could
properly lay my tired head and especially my tired little backside. My
predecessor in the apartment, an active comrade, seems to have been
endowed with an extremely meager growth in the latter respect. In
years of activity he pressed an acute angle into the mattress, and I
have not yet succeeded in regenerating it into an obtuse one, something that would be in keeping with my proportions.

While Weber was toiling away in Posen, there was an event in his family
at home that made everyone happy. His sister, the eighteen-year-old Klara,
became engaged to the physician Dr. Ernst Mommsen, a son of the famous
scholar. The families had been friendly for a long time. Theodor Mommsen
felt particularly drawn to Helene and had high hopes for the young researcher and politician Max. He liked to debate with him and bore him no grudge
even after heated encounters. One of his sons, Karl, was Max's friend at
school.
In their intellectual tradition, then, the two families were as well-
suited to each other as the young couple itself. While the aged scholar was
delighted by the fresh grace and exuberant *joie de vivre* of his new daughter,
Helene was enriched by Ernst's spiritual refinement and his empathetic understanding. Weber was moved by his young sister's happiness as though it
affected him directly. He regarded it as the only destiny appropriate for her.
Her personality was so different from his. She was made only for earthly happiness, and he had particularly delighted in her energy and naturalness. Now
he was thankful that she could enjoy a youth different from his, without
spiritual pressure, struggles, and complications:

If I had not given up bawling [*Heulen*], I would have bawled this morning when I received your dear letter with the news of this fabulous
good fortune. The only thing that pains me is that I am away and do
not get to see my little darling as a *secretly* engaged girl—for matters
seem to have progressed to that point, haven't they? From time to
time I fear that you might be practicing mystification upon me, or
that everything could disintegrate in my hands again. It is nice to see
it happening in the world for a change that such sunny natures, un-

---

[1] . . . *meinem guten Gewissen wird kein entsprechend sanftes Ruhekissen geboten*—an allusion to the
proverb *Ein gutes Gewissen ist ein sanftes Ruhekissen* [A clear conscience is a soft pillow].—Ed.

broken in their maidenhood, find the greatest happiness that life has to offer them. There will be plenty of experiences and disappointments in later life; why should a girl be stunted by them in young years? Today I am not in a position to write more about all this; first you will have to let me see once more in black and white that the whole thing is not a belated carnival prank. To imagine Klärchen as a daughter-in-law of "Uncle Theodor," or whatever one is supposed to call him now, for the time being surpasses my powers of comprehension. . . .

After everything that passed through my mind in recent days, this absolutely fabulous and still hardly believable good fortune was a relief that is simply out of this world. But that little one! She wrote me a very cute little card and seems to have adapted to the situation with her characteristic naturalness. Some personalities require a long period of cloudless sunshine before they become weatherproof, and one of those is this child with her still untamed vital energy. After the most careful consideration I can't think of anyone in the whole wide world who would be as well-suited to her as a husband as this one. He will be good and henpecked, of course, and he needs some of that, too.

The hopes placed in this marriage were fulfilled. The new family thrived and led a full life. And just as her brother had expected, Klara grew into a warmhearted and exceedingly energetic, intelligent woman who mastered life in every respect and always made her husband, her children, and a large circle of friends happy with her undiminished vigor and freshness. Her tree of life spread its branches wider and wider, bearing fruit and blossoms at once.

* * *

Weber's way of life in Berlin was sometimes a cause of concern to the women. Was it really absolutely necessary for him to overload himself with work? His teaching assignments—about nineteen hours of lectures and seminars—were enough of a strain by themselves, especially since the young professor, who was replacing his famous teacher, was immediately obliged to take part in the civil service examinations for jurists. And in addition there were so many self-imposed tasks. Hardly was one completed when his restless intellect took hold of a new one. Little time remained for shared leisure. The two months of military practice also had to be made up now. Outside there were the greenery and the profusion of spring, but Marianne rarely succeeded in luring her husband away from his desk and out of doors. The balcony, on which he was easily able to set up another desk, really sufficed him, for it provided fresh air and a piece of sky as well as a few colorful flowers. Otherwise, to be sure, one's eye traveled only over city courtyards with sparse greenery to the metropolitan railway embankment behind which whitish lime works could be glimpsed. A stroll together in the Tiergarten was considered a treat—so the young wife wrote to Helene. "Imagine, Max went walking in the Tiergarten with me for an hour. It was a real sacrifice for him, and yet afterward he enjoyed it, too. Otherwise things are as I imagined they would be. He is up to his neck in work, is awfully quiet, and I have the feeling that I must not disturb him. But since I completely understand him and his nature, it is not hard for me to be patient and wait for better days."

When a few months later Marianne expressed in a letter her apprehension that he was overexerting himself and that his life-style was unhealthy, Weber calmed her with statements that indicate that despite his unusual capacity for work he was subject to occasional nervous strain and by no means felt entirely secure:

My *general* state of health is incomparably better than in previous years—something that I had no longer hoped for, except at a much more advanced age, or expected during our engagement period, which was full of cares for me in this respect. When after years of loathsome torment I had finally achieved an *inner* equilibrium, I feared a profound depression would set in. It did not happen, and I believe it was because I worked constantly and thus did not let my nervous system and my brain get any rest. Quite apart from my natural need to work, this is one reason why I am so very reluctant to make a really perceptible pause in my work. I believe I could not take the risk of letting the incipient relaxation of my nerves—which I am enjoying with the feeling of a truly new happiness—turn into enervation, until I recognize unmistakably that my convalescent stage is definitely over.

He continued to overdo things. The material of the pastoral investigation still had to be processed, but first the project was to be supported by comprehensive computations of the East Elbe population movement in the individual rural districts. And already there was a pressing new project: a specialized study of the stock exchange system. He became an expert in this field, too. The Reichstag was planning a "stock exchange reform," an official survey was published, and Weber began work on a series of essays for

Goldschmidt's *Zeitschrift für das gesamte Handelsrecht* [Journal of General Commercial Law] which dealt particularly with trading in futures. At the same time he wrote, at Naumann's request and for the Göttingen *Arbeiterbibliothek* [Workingmen's Library], *Eine Börsen- und Bankfibel für 10 Pfennige* [A Ten-Pfennig Primer on the Stock Exchange and Banking]; this lively work brought an understanding of the central economic organs within the reach even of laymen. In it he pointed out, among other things, that even purely speculative trading not only served private interests, but also fulfilled important and useful functions in the equalization of prices and the distribution of commodities.

What interested him in this was, as with the agrarian questions, the *political* problem: The accumulation of capital in the hands of the banks and the wholesale merchants must not be prevented *nationally*, for it meant a storing up of strength for the economic competitive struggle of the nation. Moralistically motivated legislation that suppressed certain kinds of speculative deals—particularly, on the urging of the agrarians, trade in wheat futures—would merely shift the market for these articles to other countries and strengthen their financial power at Germany's expense.

> Politically it is not a matter of indifference whether the Berlin or the Paris stock exchange offers foreign powers in need of money, such as Italy and Russia, a better outlet for their debentures. And for economic interests at home it is not a matter of indifference whether domestic or foreign merchants dominate the markets. . . .
>
> As long as the nations carry on the inexorable and inevitable economic struggle for their national existence and economic power, even though they may live in peace militarily, narrow limits will be imposed upon the implementation of purely theoretical and moral demands— because of the consideration that there can be no *unilateral* disarmament in the economic sphere either. A strong stock exchange simply cannot be a club for "ethical culture," and the capital of the big banks is no more of a "charitable institution" than rifles and cannons are. For an economic policy striving for *this-worldly* goals they can be only one thing: *resources* in that economic struggle. This policy will welcome it if "ethical" needs, too, can be satisfied in relation to these institutions, but it is its duty, in the *last* analysis, to guard against fanatical interests or unworldly apostles of economic peace disarming their own nation.[2]

[2]*Gesammelte Aufsätze zur Soziologie und Sozialpolitik*, pp. 256ff.

Two years later, in the autumn of 1896, Weber and his older colleague Lexis[3] were invited to attend the deliberations of the committee on the stock exchange that was charged with assessing the effects of the new laws. Weber was entrusted with making a report on these deliberations to the *Bundesrat.* This was a meeting of the capitalistic and political magnates who were vying for the control of Germany: the representatives of heavy industry and finance were in competition with the landed proprietors. It was of great interest to Weber to be sitting opposite these types, for the idea of fighting their political preponderance and policy of vested economic interests had been preying on his mind for some years.

We meet in the chamber of the *Bundesrat.* The stock exchange people have occupied the entire main table, where Prussia sits, the agrarians have taken over the seats of some medium-sized states, and, scorned by both, my colleague Lexis and I sit off in a far corner in front of the blotters belonging to Reuss, older and younger lineage.[4] The refined type of agrarians—Count Kanitz, Count Schwerin[5]—keep silent, and only the boors let loose. . . .

Things have now become more lively and more interesting, too. To the great annoyance of the agrarians I have been elected to a committee on which I am to deliberate about the future of the German wheat trade together with Count Kanitz and a number of stock exchange fellows. There have already been some spirited clashes with these gentlemen. I, too, have already had a number of run-ins with these desperate customers, but so far the tone has been such a courteous one that there is no danger of people shooting one another dead in pairs in the near future. But as fate would have it, so far I seem to have met with the approval of the millionaires;[6] at least Privy Councillor of Commerce X [*der Geheime Kommerzienrat* X] always squeezes my hand so

---

[3]Wilhelm Lexis, 1837–1914, economist, professor at Strasbourg, Freiburg, Breslau, and Göttingen.—Ed.

[4]Reuss was the name of two former Thuringian German principalities. In 1564 one of these was divided into three dynasties or lineages. The members of the older and the younger lineages were raised to the rank of prince in 1778 and 1806, respectively. The dynasty was dissolved in 1919.—Ed.

[5]Hans W. A. Graf von Kanitz, 1841–1913, whose proposal of 1894–95 that the government buy up all imported wheat and sell it at a uniform price was rejected by the Reichstag; Hans Graf von Schwerin-Löwitz, 1847–1918, member of the Prussian parliament, president of the Reichstag from 1910 to 1912.—Ed.

[6]*Millionen-Knöpfe,* a rather disrespectful colloquial term, was replaced in the 1950 edition by the standard *Millionäre.* —Ed.

vigorously that I am surprised at not finding a check for some 100,000 marks under my blotter, which is otherwise used by the older lineage of Reuss. (November 20, 1896)

* * *

It was probably a good thing in every respect that the *Philosophische Fakultät* [College of Liberal Arts] of the University of Freiburg now resumed the negotiations that had been started a year previously, and that this time the government of Baden took the unusual step of offering the legal scholar a chair in *Nationalökonomie* [political economy]. For Weber this event led to impressive experiences with Privy Councillor Althoff, the head of the Prussian educational system, who dominated the Prussian universities as an "enlightened despot." Since this occurrence and other, similar ones later induced Weber to criticize the "Althoff system" in public, some of these developments will be outlined here.

Althoff was greatly interested in the gifted docent and wanted to keep him in Prussia; he designated him as Goldschmidt's successor, but he did not know whether the faculty of the University of Berlin would be ready to propose such a young scholar as the successor of an old man of high scholarly rank. He therefore tried to do some maneuvering in the expectation of human weaknesses and sought to tie Weber to Prussia by making him all sorts of promises. He also informed his opposite number in the Baden government that such a magnificent legal career awaited Weber in Prussia that he would use Freiburg only as a springboard.

Weber, however, told Althoff that he would never let himself be forced upon the faculty at Berlin or any other university, which caused Althoff to remark: "This Weber is displaying an excessive sensitivity in personal matters." When Althoff one day discussed the matter with Weber's father as a member of the budget commission, the father and the son got quite excited, presumably because they viewed it as an attempt at "horse trading." When the Baden minister of education asked Althoff for information about Weber and informed him that the unusual proposal to the faculty was arousing certain misgivings, Althoff showed the confidential letter to the young man with this remark: "I would certainly not go to a state in which the minister of education so clearly manifests the *animus non possidendi* [spirit of have-nots]." But unless Althoff expressly asked him to stay, Weber wanted to be free to make his own decision. Althoff now promised him in writing that he would propose him to the Berlin faculty, but without any obligation to the docent, and Weber agreed. When Weber opened the envelope at home, however, he noticed a clause that obliged him to decline any offer he might receive. His immediate objection brought a letter by return mail which withdrew that clause as having been in error; the predating of the document made it appear that it had been completed *before* Weber's objection, although Weber remained convinced that this was not so.

This and other occurrences gave Weber the firm impression that Althoff, an important man, would, like Bismarck, employ any means to reach his goal, that he made use of the dependency and moral weakness of people to that end, only to despise them thoroughly afterward. This game of chess with people's characters was reprehensible in Weber's eyes, no matter how positive the aims it served, and he could not forgive it.

To get away from this autocratic personality was a reason in favor of accepting an offer from Freiburg. In addition there was the lure of the south and, above all, of the new subject. He would naturally have to work extremely hard before he could satisfy himself in that subject, but a change of discipline suited him. As a science, economics was still elastic and "young" in comparison with law. Besides, it was on the borderline of a number of scholarly fields; it led directly to the history of culture and of ideas as well as to philosophical problems. Finally, it was more fruitful for a political and sociopolitical orientation than the more formal problems of legal thought. Weber decided quickly, although not without a struggle, for leaving Berlin was going to remove him from the center of political life and from his mother. He knew that the parting would be very hard for her and his wife.

All the various objections that may be raised to my accepting the position at Freiburg arose in me again, and at times it seemed to me as though I were being "pensioned off" upon my departure from Berlin. Well, that is natural if one has lived in Berlin for such a long time, and they have made certain that in Freiburg I shall not have the feeling of being outside the world. I am now "on deck" again and tell myself, first of all, that parting would be even harder for us at a later date and that, second, the position in F. is a clearer one and probably more in keeping with my interests. This means that in the near future you will presumably have a rather hard-working but also a more satisfied and therefore more comfortable and less "irritable" husband. And I believe, too, that in the future it will be more valuable for my mother to have the indisputable right to come for a prolonged stay with us in the south than what she has now: more frequent visits, but hectic and seldom undisturbed hours.

When they left Berlin at the end of their first year of marriage, Weber presented his wife with the almost complete etchings of Max Klinger,[7] whose symbolic content greatly moved both of them at that time. On one of the prints from the cycle *Vom Tode* [On Death] which depicted Death as the Savior, he wrote the following verses:

> *Ich hoffte einst, es wäre mir beschieden*
> *Ein früher Tod in voller Jugendkraft.*
> *Ich wünsch' ihn nicht mehr, denn ich fand hienieden*
> *Was Menschenherzen ewige Jugend schafft.*
> *Naht einst, mein Kind, das Ende unsrer Tage,*
> *So legen wir die Arbeit aus der Hand*
> *Und wandern froh des Todes dunkle Pfade,*
> *Vereint ins unbekannte Land.*

[Once I hoped I would be vouchsafed an early death in the full vigor of my youth. I no longer desire such a death, for I have found here below what gives human hearts eternal youth. When one day the end of our life approaches, my child, we shall lay down our work and cheerfully walk together on the dark paths of death into an unknown land.]

II

In the fall of 1894 they moved to Freiburg. Weber was now greatly looking forward to his new sphere of activity. He was greatly attracted to everything new and unknown, and for the time being his life in Berlin, which was encumbered with so many somber memories, seemed a thing of the past. To be sure, the work load that awaited him was even greater than he had imagined, and it surpassed everything up to then. As he said jokingly, he

---

[7]1857–1920, German etcher, painter, and sculptor whose varied and strikingly evocative art provided a bridge from the *Jugendstil (art nouveau)* to expressionism.—Ed.

was now attending his own big lectures on political economy for the first time.

He immediately lectured for twelve hours a week and conducted two seminars. When in the second semester his friend and colleague G. v. Schulze-Gävernitz[8] went on leave, he felt obligated to assume part of his duties as well. He called himself a hunted animal. Soon he assembled a group of students whose careful introduction to scholarly work gave him the greatest satisfaction. In addition the publisher pressed him for a continuation of his essays on the stock exchange. The investigation of the farm workers now had to wait while he had assistants prepare many thousands of examples. The material grew more and more extensive and actually was no longer of such burning interest to him, for he was convinced that the results would confirm his earlier findings. Above all, there were more urgent tasks. The projected new work was never completed. Some of the valuable statistical material was placed at the disposal of students; other data were used in his later essays on agrarian policy. Some of this material was immediately incorporated as illustrations into the academic inaugural lecture which will be discussed later.

In addition to everything else, Weber gave occasional lectures before scholarly and political groups, speaking among other things about the Polish question before the local chapter of the *Alldeutscher Verband* [Pan-German Union], of which he was a member. He was in demand for lectures out of town as well, for his gifts as a speaker had become known. He yielded to tempting invitations and undertook not only occasional individual lectures but also whole cycles—for example, one at Naumann's request before a Frankfurt evangelical workingmen's association on "The National Basis of Economics." Occasionally he traveled to Frankfurt after his lecture at the university, spoke there in the evening, made the return trip at night, and saw the sunrise as he prepared for the coming day's work at his desk.

His working strength seemed doubled and he was equal to anything. As a rule he worked until one hour after midnight and then immediately fell into a deep sleep. When his wife remonstrated with him, he would say, "If I don't work till one o'clock, I can't be a professor." At the end of the third semester—spring of 1896—he felt that he had mastered his new subject and was in particularly good health. During the Easter recess he went to Berlin for a time and participated in the board meetings of the *Verein*

---

[8]Gerhart von Schulze-Gävernitz, 1864–1943, economist, professor at Freiburg from 1893 to 1926.—Ed.

für Sozialpolitik, worked at the library, and saw friends. This whirl of activity was his relaxation after a semester with three major lecture courses. "The Berlin air agrees with me remarkably well; my nervous system is more productive, for the burden and the toil of the last few days were great, and yet I am completely fresh." (March, 1896).

* * *

Despite the *Hatz* [rat race] Weber enjoyed the lighter side of domestic life. An ordinary little dog, which had been acquired for the emotional needs of the housekeeper, became an amusing plaything for him as well. When Marianne was away, news of the charming animal was woven into his letters:

> Bertha just left and informed me that she was taking little Murcks along, evidently so that I might watch the incident from the balcony. That is really extremely funny. She has him on a blue leash and he angrily yelps at her, lies down, and then skips about like mad, so that she has to jump after him—until she finally releases him. Then he rushes after her with loud yelps, dragging the leash on the ground. But training seems to be hard for him, too. He willfully picks out a room. Presumably a hereditary affliction. . . .

Outwardly the life of the couple was typical of their circle. Yet they attracted attention as being "different." Among other things, they had social views and views of the relationship between the sexes that were unfamiliar to those around them. And on their walls there were Klinger etchings, some of them showing nudes. Was it really possible to sit down on the sofa under a little Eve meditating by a dusky forest pond? Or could one take an unembarrassed look at the nude figure of a male stretching toward the light from a dark ground, which the artist had called *Und dennoch* [And Yet]? Besides, Marianne acted in accordance with her mood at any given time and expressed entirely unusual views. She also occupied herself with social work and, strangest of all, with scholarship. Soon she was the first woman to attend philosophical lectures, as well as H. Rickert's[9] seminar. This really was *very* conspicuous and gave rise to various conjectures and ex-

---

[9]Heinrich Rickert, Jr., 1863–1936, neo-Kantian philosopher, professor at Freiburg (from 1894) and Heidelberg (from 1916).—Ed.

cited arguments about what a woman could, should, and was allowed to do. Could a marriage be happy if the wife had serious interests in addition to her household and her husband? What should be one's attitude toward this irregularity as a matter of principle?

When Helene visited her children in Freiburg, she heard much of what people were thinking, and although her own concern about their domestic happiness was already waning, she now grew alarmed in a different direction. Was it right for the couple to offend people? Perhaps their life-style should conform to the views of others and they should at least remove the Klingers from their walls. This problem seriously agitated her. But the children laughed and stood their ground. They certainly did not wish to be conspicuous or offend anyone, but they did not want to make any concessions to small-town traditionalism, either.

However, those around them soon got used to the Webers. They made close friends, including some who also lived unconventionally. Cordial relations were established from the very beginning with Fritz Baumgarten's large family. He was active at the local Gymnasium as an excellent teacher and was married to a deeply religious, strong-minded, but frequently ailing woman. Their life was not an easy one, and the Webers admired the loving strength with which these people bore each day's burdens. The Baumgartens were a bridge to the past. Ida frequently stayed with her children in Freiburg and also maintained a close friendship with the Webers.

In the house of the philosopher A. Riehl[10] they participated in an intellectually refined social life that was given artistic form by the rare grace and Viennese tradition of a distinguished woman. Their contemporaries, the philosopher Heinrich Rickert the younger and his wife Sophie, offered them a friendship and an intellectual relationship that they valued all their life. Rickert's and Weber's parents had already had a close political and social relationship. The sons, who were almost the same age, had known each other since boyhood, though not intimately. Years previously Weber had studied Rickert's first epistemological writings, *Zur Lehre von der Definition* [On the Doctrine of Definition] and *Der Gegenstand der Erkenntnis* [The Object of Knowledge], and he had admired their acuity of thought and lucidity. When A. Riehl accepted an offer from a Prussian university, Weber overcame all sorts of petty resistance among the faculty to secure the vacant

---

[10]Aloys Riehl, 1844–1924, professor of philosophy at Graz, Freiburg, Kiel, Halle, and Berlin. —Ed.

chair for Rickert. Now Weber of course had no time to occupy himself further with epistemological problems, but Marianne began systematically to
satisfy her desire to think about the meaning of life and the world. She
became Rickert's zealous student and kept her husband informed about
what she was learning. "Max, little Murcks, and 'the object of knowledge'
are my favorite things." There was a close friendship between the two wom-
en. In the sculptress Sophie, Marianne saw for the first time a new type
of woman with an artist's soul, a woman who expended the same emotional
strength on her artistic creation that she did on being a wife and mother.

The circle of friends also included Weber's colleague G. von Schulze-
Gävernitz, the psychologist and philosopher Hugo Münsterberg, and the
learned philologist Gottfried Baist,[11] an eccentric whose astonishing
knowledge had to be elicited by asking questions, for he was incapable of imparting it spontaneously either in writing or in a coherent speech. Weber
found his new colleagues "exceptionally agreeable" and liked to socialize in
his leisure hours. The customary evening parties were important occasions
for putting the new household to the test. Weber's students, too, dined
there frequently, and on Saturday evening a group of unmarried colleagues
gathered for an informal exchange of views—a format that suited everyone
best. Weber sought social relaxation outside the house, too. On the weekly evenings of bowling his anecdotes gave pleasure and his drinking ability
created as much astonishment as his other achievements. People enjoyed his
company, though the young wives complained that their husbands were now
coming home much later than before. In the summertime the Webers made
regular weekly outings—with a few friends and G. Baist as a constant
companion—to a country inn and there enjoyed trout and Markgräfler.[12]
At a banquet at the Leimstollen in honor of the distinguished researcher
v. Kries,[13] who had declined an offer from another university, the golden
wine flowed freely. At an advanced hour Weber wagered that he weighed a
hundred kilograms and committed himself to emptying his glass for every
pound he weighed less. Amidst loud shouting he was weighed on the local
scale, lost the bet, and had to pay the penalty. For the trip home the

---

[11]Hugo Münsterberg, 1863–1916, professor of psychology at Harvard from 1892 to 1895, and 1897
until his death; Karl Gottfried Baist, 1853–1920, professor of Romance philology at Freiburg, author of
books on Spanish language and literature.—Ed.
[12]A well-known wine from the Markgräfler Land, a region on the Upper Rhine south of the
Breisgau.—Ed.
[13]Johannes von Kries, 1853–1928, professor of physiology at Freiburg.—Ed.

whole party climbed up on a rack wagon; only Weber followed on foot, walking with a firm step.

When at a fraternity banquet in honor of the same scholar he won a
fourfold *Bierjunge*[14] from a student, it was the students' turn to be astounded: Was that a hero from the Teutonic woods who had come to life
again and whom an unmartial epoch had provided with a pen rather than
a spear? Or had he once been a duke who used to march off to war at the
head of his vassals? At any rate, his whole appearance did not match the
professorial type. He was still close to some students in age, and when after
each seminar he had a "pint" with them, they could enjoy not only his
knowledge but his storytelling abilities as well. On such occasions he would
discuss any subject and claim no authority whatever. Nevertheless, everyone
felt that there was a difference, and no one thought of not keeping his
distance.

In his hours of relaxation he was a good companion whose behavior was so
down-to-earth and unassuming that no one was overawed. As a colleague,
however, he was frequently troublesome, because he was intolerant toward
"human considerations" in his profession when they conflicted with purely
objective actions—for example, in matters of academic appointments. If
someone had to be helped to get his due—as in Rickert's case—he took vigorous action without sparing anyone. Since he was not averse to doing disagreeable things, his colleagues liked to use him for embarrassing tasks: "In
the meantime I have had all sorts of annoyances. It is as if I were under
a curse to get everywhere just in time to perform a hangman's services. Here
we have to discipline a colleague because of general turpitude, and since the
others feel revulsion, naturally I am stuck with the task of setting things
in motion."

* * *

The stern heights of the Black Forest served as the background to this
busy life. Regular strolls together were, of course, out of the question;
Weber only rushed up the Schlossberg between assignments. The infrequent
hikes were therefore all the more gratefully enjoyed. He loved the fir-
studded mountainous country with the sunny vineyards; everywhere there

---

[14]The word *"Bierjunge"* (beer boy) is used as an invitation to a drinking contest. In this instance
Weber apparently beat a student in the rapid downing of four glasses of beer.—Ed.

were the traces of an old civilization. The city soon seemed like a stone prison, and he did not wish he were back there.

At the end of the second semester Weber allowed himself an extended rest for the first time since his wedding. He took Marianne to the solitude of the Scottish highlands and to the west coast of Ireland. They finally had a delightful chance to rest and recuperate. Weber relaxed completely only when he was traveling and looking. Then he became quite young again, was receptive to all earthly beauty, and could not absorb enough of the world. He would not stay in one place longer than three days at the most. Whatever he saw and experienced gave color and form to the knowledge he already had.

The couple whizzed over the asphalt of London in dainty two-wheel "hackneys"[15] in order to say a quick hello to the historical sites with which they had become acquainted on their first trip together. Then they relaxed in the comfortable leather seats of the "Flying Scotchman." Outside the green landscape flitted by. Weber pointed to lonely churches scattered through the countryside. The village that used to belong to these churches had disappeared; the "landlords" had been appropriating the farmers' land for centuries. Weber was thinking of the possible future of the German East.

They visited Edinburgh, a gray northern city with many historical associations. The cold, gray walls of the castle in particular harbor tragic memories, and the nearby solitude of the highlands gave the city a melancholy atmosphere. Travelers stay there for but a short time and find enjoyment out in the lonely mountain country interspersed with lakes: untouched, secluded nature, at once sublime and lovely, melancholy and cheerful. Almost daily, a cloud cover lends it an acerb solemnity but also an unspoiled freshness, and almost every day a motley, sunny opalescence breaks through the moisture.

Weber described what he had seen in happy letters to Helene. The mother gained the impression that her children now were really being young together. Some of his descriptions follow:

Luss on Loch Lomond, August 14, 1895

Toward evening we took a stroll to one of the small lochs. When we started out the sun was shining—but, as it goes in this country, the next thing you know a few clouds come rushing along over the mountain tops, and then it is as though someone were squeezing out a

---

[15]English terms used in the original have been italicized and put between quotation marks. —Ed.

sponge. However, by now it already is part of the scenery, at least for me. As you walk you hardly pay any attention to whether or not it rains for five minutes, and on one day—almost regularly—one experiences the gamut of weather. The combined effect of the absolute absence of people wherever one goes, apart from a few shepherds' dwellings, and the magnificent severity of this nature is almost touching, despite the simplicity of the means—particularly of the colors—with which the scenery is adorned.

There really are but two basic colors, green and steel gray, but there are countless combinations. The meadows and the ferns that cover the always moist mountain rocks up to the summit, interrupted only by heath, are brownish green, yellowish green, bluish green; the little rivers that flow through the meadows catlike and swift as an arrow are a brownish gray. Lead gray is the color of the lakes, which seem incapable of strong undulation. And on top of it all there is a gentle, variously thick haze through which the sun shines.

But all this is only incidental to the great, wonderful solitude that forces itself into the foreground of feeling and seems to mark the landscape. The very absence of forests and, with the exception of some parts of Loch Lomond and the Trossachs,[16] of almost any trees worth mentioning contributes to that impression. It seems to me that one experiences this solitude of the flat country, which extends to the very gates of the cities, differently from the way one experiences it in England. There one does not see a single farming village on the entire journey from London to Edinburgh, but only an occasional castle in a park, with leaseholders' dwellings and individual farm buildings at some distance. From time to time one also sees churches from the thirteenth and fourteenth centuries which stand among a dozen workmen's huts instead of among fifty to sixty farmhouses, as they once did. These churches have become too big for their congregations, like a consumptive's suit. And in England one gets the feeling that there would be room for hundreds of thousands of farmers, while Scotland simply was made to be a cattle pasture and, even more, a sheep walk.

This morning we traveled by "coach" over the mountains to the Trossachs—the only forest worth mentioning—on Loch Katrine. It is strange how lead gray the foliage of the holm oaks, the chestnuts, the larches, and the plants with thorny leaves are; with their tangle of curiously deformed branches they make up the major part of these bushy

[16]A mountain defile in Perthshire between Loch Katrine, celebrated by Sir Walter Scott in *Rob Roy* and *The Lady of the Lake.*—Ed.

copses. Of course there was a tremendous sudden downpour lasting for fifteen minutes, and then it rained on the trip to Loch Lomond. But when we were on the lake the sun came out, and in the afternoon there even was the rare spectacle of an almost completely blue sky and sunshine, with the kind of heat that is customary here: moderate and wonderfully comfortable, moist and yet fresh. During the trip and on a walk afterward, the lake showed itself to us in its full splendor.

Incidentally, the world is a village in Great Britain, too. Would you believe that we met acquaintances from Berlin here? When we were taking the steamer to Loch Katrine, I suddenly noticed on the *"peer"* [sic], among the pinched English mouths of those hurrying to get aboard, the Germanic bard's face of Gierke. We then traveled together as far as Loch Lomond, where our ways parted. Meeting a compatriot does affect one strangely. Ordinarily we have become acclimated to the point where we have adopted the general custom of speaking in a whisper. We act as if we did not see the people to the right and to the left of us. We answer only when asked, and then briefly and very politely. We always eat less of everything than we would like to, open our mouths as little as possible, and even when our stomachs rumble audibly, we splash about in the soup with our spoons as if we didn't care about the grub.

But no sooner were Germans nearby than there was such an outburst of laughter while we were waiting for the *"coach"* that all the English came rushing up to see the barbarians, and in the *"coach"* I overheard someone say *"merry Germany."* Before we parted we had a *"lunch"* that the waiters there won't soon forget. G. began to eat as though we were in the Teutoburg Forest, and I joined in. When everything kept disappearing, the perplexed *"waiters"* finally brought superhuman quantities of *"roast-beaf"* [sic], salmon, etc., presumably out of fear that otherwise we were going to bite people. Three of them stood around our table, and they stared aghast at the debris of their property. They were obviously relieved when a signal finally came from the steamboat and put a stop to the meal. To the astonishment of the waiters, we also drank—G., the terror of all temperance hotels, out of conviction and I to keep up with him—I don't know how many decanters of water.

Loch Maree, August 17, 1895

The trip here to Gairloch on Loch Maree showed the quite characteristic difference between the northern, real highlands and southern and central Scotland. The character of absolute solitude is here significantly heightened. While in the south a sort of green plaid seems to be spread over the sharp edges of the basalt mountains, the ones here are often so steep that in the spring the thaw tears off all the grass and heather, at least on the peaks, that have grown there the previous summer. Numerous rocks, often in wondrous formations, cover the slopes. In between, in place of the great plains of the south, which are alternately yellowish brown and grayish green, there is a colorful heath that compresses all its hues, from violet to yellowish green, into every tiny space where they then blend to produce a total impression of a brownish radiance. One can look into the *"glens"* between the mountains and see miles of plains interlaced with peat bogs; despite their absolute uniformity they give an impression of variety, much as the sea does.

After a good hour of travel with a steep ascent, the valley of Loch Maree, miles in length, opened wide, and we immediately realized that the stern seclusion of this spot ought to satisfy even Marianne's need for solitude. While traveling for several hours we saw a village consisting of eight scattered little houses and a shelter for hunters. For the rest, one has the feeling that there are no human beings for miles around. The narrow road by the lake, built on basalt, emits a peculiar booming sound, like a distant pealing of bells, as the carriage passes over it—presumably because of the cracks in the rock underneath caused by the water. The afternoon and evening sun produces a strange effect. The veil of thin haze, which always more or less perceptibly envelops the entire landscape from top to bottom, makes the sun's rays somewhat faded, sometimes almost greenish, and only when the sun sets do they change to pink. Wherever the moist mountain ledges are hit by the rays, they blanch in a curious way.

In this rocky wilderness one suddenly comes upon the charming Loch Maree Hotel, situated in a depression by the lake, with a small garden on a green meadow. Next to a central building made of quarry stones there is a one-story wooden building with a number of most comfortable rooms overlooking a grassy courtyard, and we are housed in one of these. This discreet civilization in the midst of an almost complete wilderness—something that we have now encountered three times—is really the most attractive thing about Scotland. The explanation for this evidently lies in the fact that while in Germany the inns were an outgrowth of city and village taverns or of merchants' hostelries and finally were brought up to the usual international standards, here the hunting lodges of the *"landlords"* became inns. While in Germany there was an *upward* development and the clientele became more refined, here the first guests were of the highest stratum of society, and only gradually was there a downward broadening of the circle of guests. Even now the English travel books list the *"earls"* or *"dukes"* to whom they belong. The *"landlords"* start the hotels and lease them out; they own the steamship *"peers"* which they lease; they also lease the steamship traffic on the lochs in northern Scotland. Their hunting grounds are fenced in—for example, across from us there are miles of an enclosed *"Deer Forest"* for the Earl of Ross, which lacks only *trees* to be a forest in the German sense. Except for a diamond-covered, whiskey-drinking lady, the company here—fourteen to sixteen persons—is extremely choice; people are urged to observe the proprieties. Yet the dinner is anything but stiff, the conversation was quite lively (although not with us, we are being excluded as an unknown species of animal), and the old innkeeper who presides at the table is a very agreeable man with exceedingly good manners, and an impassioned huntsman.

Stornoway, Hebrides, August 22, 1895

As you see, we have now arrived in a region that is northwesterly enough to meet all reasonable demands and really could be topped only by a trip to Ireland—and I think Marianne would actually like to take one. From Stornoway we traveled across the island for two hours on a road more desolate than anything we have seen until now: as far as the eye could see, nothing but brown moors. Then, when we already felt somewhat uneasy, we caught sight of a few white specks together with the ocean, and one of these specks turned out to be the one-story *"Temperenz Inn"* [*sic*], where we were given a room in which the most noteworthy thing was a portrait of a locomotive hanging on the wall.

At first Barvas seemed to consist only of the aforementioned light-colored houses. Otherwise one could see only a number of large mole hills along the road. Viewed more closely, these proved to be about a hundred subterranean caves in which as many families had their lodging. Above ground there was only a wall of sandstone, about one meter high, with a roof made of peat and protected against the elements by a cord net weighted down by rocks, with a hole for the smoke. Inside live the Gaelic inhabitants, peat diggers who understand no English. By way of a strange contrast, every family owns a horse and a wagon, their only capital, for transporting the peat to Stornoway. So we had, thank God, really come to the ash gray pitch huts at the end of civilization. On the marshes toward the lake there grazed countless half-wild cattle. Near the huts there were horses, and on the moors sheep were pastured. Some oats were planted around the huts.

After we had noted this condition of paradisiac unculture with satisfaction[17]—that is, in the hotel we were given a rather clean little room on the ground floor in which I bumped my head against the ceiling; the menu had shrunk to mutton chops of giant dimensions and a strange pudding consisting of a violet paste—that did not prevent them from serving these treasures in the style of the great English hotels with five to six vinegars, sauces, big plates and little plates, huge tin covers, and the whole pedantic claptrap that can make your blood boil if you're hungry; nor did it prevent institutions like the one designated in this country by the letters w.c. from being *"in full dress"*— that is, the hotel culture of England sent its rays even into this region of cave dwellers. Anyway, after we had seen all that, we looked for the beach with the *"very strong bathes"* [sic] that had been mentioned to us. Lo and behold: after searching for three-quarters of an hour, with me grumbling and Marianne meekly trotting along beside me—it wasn't there, that is, it was covered with rocks and inaccessible, it started to rain, we lost our way in the dunes—and arrived "home" again, sopping wet, without a dry stitch on our bodies, stinking from the smoke from the caves, and bespattered with mud. We were informed that the beach was farther north.

On the next morning we were off again—but with even less success. In the first place, we found only a high rocky coast with numerous ravines in which the angry ocean surged magnificently; but we almost missed it, because we were frantically searching for a bit of sand. In the second place, we could not even enjoy this spectacle in peace, because two unruly young bulls came galloping toward us, knocked us down, and almost threw us down the coast. Fortunately it was a place where there was a sandy slope before the cliffs. After this delightful experience we had enough of Barvas, and in the evening we traveled by carriage through the fog and the heath back to Stornoway without having seen the Druid stones and other sights. And we traveled on all night to Stromferry, where, restored to human civilization, we cleansed ourselves from all the muck of this Phaeacian journey. Thus, within twenty-four hours we were in two carriages, two boats, on one train, and in five inns. . . .

In Skye there are fully developed hotel and tourist facilities. We first spent a horribly boring Sunday in Portree, enjoying the six churches, with their bells tinkling one after the other; fortunately it rained. On Monday and Tuesday we took a few mountain trips. The most beau-

---

[17]This clause dangles equally in the original.—Ed.

tiful was the one to the Cuchullin Hills toward the south of the island. First we went by carriage, then we rode a pony for several hours, and finally we walked up a steep mountain path. At first it rained, like almost every day in Skye, and I was somewhat annoyed at these eternal douches, but one mustn't let the rain keep one from doing anything here. Afterward the weather became splendid, that is, it matched the landscape: the sun kept breaking through the clouds that were rushing about the jagged crests. From time to time a finely woven white veil descended from the black cliffs into the "glen," approached us, and turned out to be a brief rain shower, as though a watering can were being emptied.

The road from the hotel to the mountains, into the Cuchullin Hills, is absolutely dreadful; I have hardly ever seen such a rough "path"—through torrential streams, foot-deep moors, rubble, and slippery meadows, up and down razor-sharp, smooth rocks. One would call it almost impassable for human beings; but I shall never comprehend how horses negotiate it. I sat on a sturdy little pony, with my legs almost touching the ground, like Jacob the patriarch. Marianne, happy as a lark, sat on a long-legged animal. There also was a guide, and so we set out like the Holy Family on the flight to Egypt. The horses soon were foot-deep in water, wading through brooks several meters wide and with rocky or rubbly bottoms. One moment they were splashing through the moor, the next moment the masses of rubble gave way under them, and sometimes they seemed to be climbing up almost vertically, only to descend the same way later. At first one would have hardly thought it possible that they did not leave a leg among the rocks with each step, but soon we felt quite secure. To be sure, not much is left of my horsemanship, and when "Charlie" started a gentle jog trot on level ground I had to make frequent use of "major's reins."[18] Also, some parts of my body are so banged up that even now I like to have a soft chair. Marianne turned out to be better equipped in this regard. It is marvelous how well the trip is agreeing with her; she sleeps like a log for ten hours. The whole thing is vastly different from our wedding trip with its nervous haste; we have never before known such a feeling of relaxation in every respect.

From the top of the mountains one looks beyond a wild rocky valley and sees far below a lake with an opening at the far end which leads to the rocky bay of the brightly illuminated sea. Over the summits

[18]The term "Majors Zügel" is sometimes applied to a kind of "emergency brake" that an inexperienced rider might apply.—Ed.

and over our heads there was a cloud cover, so that we glimpsed the scenery below as though the curtain of a theater had not risen completely. Some of those rocky formations are incredible, and among those ragged, jagged summits there appear bell-shaped tops that look exactly as though the basalt, welling up like a fountain, had suddenly congealed.

* * *

Killarney, Ireland, September 7, 1895
Even after our brief impression thus far, the place where we are now deserves its reputation of being the most beautiful in the British Isles. The dome-shaped bare mountains of Scotland—although gentler than those on Skye, for example—are here supplemented for the first time by an absolutely wonderful vegetation of ancient trees. The southwestern tip of Ireland, where Killarney is located, is hit by the Gulf Stream first, and thus one finds growing luxuriantly in the open here all the plants that are offered, for instance, by the garden of Villa Carlotta on Lake Como. The hotel garden—an English-style park with isolated, splendidly formed trees on great velvety lawns, as well as flower beds and playgrounds, predominantly without paths (people walk on the grassy carpet)—is the most beautiful thing I have ever seen.

Ireland presents a strange contrast to England and Scotland, even from the window of a train. In Scotland there prevails a majestic wilderness; in the highlands one hardly sees any people. In Ireland one sees man's works every time one looks out the window. For reasons that must be sought in the history of agrarian development, the entire land is settled almost exclusively with individual small farms. One hardly ever sees villages, but while in England the "enclosures" of the "landlords" made them disappear when the peasants were "expropriated," they never existed in Ireland. Each farm is located in a definite, cultivated area. The development since the beginning of the seventeenth century, which meant a confiscation of the land for English lords of the manor, has turned the former owners of the land into small leaseholders living in typical little houses that are painted white and have one door, two windows, and usually a straw roof.

All the land has been distributed among them as fenced-in lots. In the north, around Belfast and Ulster, there are usually quickset hedges; in the west, in Galway county and Connaught [Connacht] province, the soil is terribly rocky. The stones unearthed each year by the plow were piled up at the borders, and later they were used in the building of cyclopean walls, without mortar. Thus, if one travels for some hours, one sees that the entire land is divided like an oblique-angled chessboard right up to its mountains, which are not high. The countless piles of stones in particular give the landscape what is to us a very odd appearance. There are almost no woods, except where we are now and in a few other places.

. . . Today's conversations were the nicest we have had so far with natives. All acknowledged that they are ardent "homerulers," admittedly because they—rightly—see the "landlords" as the root of all evil and then hope to cut them down to size. Of course, the agrarian conditions here are incredible. The detailed figures that I was able to obtain about a few small leased pasturelands up in the mountains indicate usurious practices that can only be called shameless. As the people remarked matter-of-factly and with peculiar resignation, the land is "very quiet" now and "Captain Moonshine," who during the past decade prevented at gunpoint the renewal of expired leases, is at present inactive, and we were shown many expelled leaseholders who are eking out a living as beggars or vendors of refreshments. Yet hunting in the mountains of the "Earl of Kenmare," who owns everything around here, has been leased for £1000, and his estates yield £60,000 a year. On all roads, bridges, "peers," etc., "estate-fees" have to be paid to these robber barons who appear in their wonderful castles only to collect the rent (twice yearly) and to hunt for a few weeks, but the rest of the time spend their money in England.

Evidently nothing stirs the imagination of the people here more than this situation. The results of the last elections, which were unfavorable for "homerule," are apparently driving masses of people overseas again—for example, our horse driver who is about to emigrate to the United States. He asked me whether I believed that Ireland would ever get "homerule"; he does not. I said that I doubted it, too, and could understand the resistance to it, for the country would be handed over to the Catholic priests, and not everyone could stand those. But despite the fact that he joked about churchgoers, our pony driver is a social partisan of the clergy—because, so he said, it comes from among country people and therefore knows what ails the country. Sad enough, these exceptions; handsome fellows with melancholy faces and an air of resignedly merry roguishness illustrate the rule of the type all the more. The horrible moral conditions in the old clan houses, which are shared by sixteen families (!), as well as centuries of oppression, have produced a populace that will not soon change in its essential characteristics.

The ruins in this country are wonderful, at least some of them. Marianne in particular is always spellbound when she sees a crumbling wall, and despite some facility it's hard for me to invent new historical lies for the passable gratification of her desire to know the intimate history of the ruins' inhabitants. Incidentally, there probably is no country as rich in ruins as Ireland, though a good number of them are not particularly romantic. They are the big stone houses of the old clan chieftains who developed into "*landlords,*" as well as the seventeenth century residences of the "*landlords.*" They are now abandoned; nine-tenths of the landlords live in England, and their residences are used as quarries. Their by no means poetic past does not prevent the ivy from garnishing them nicely. Another category of ruins—the numerous abbeys, of which we saw two of the most beautiful today—was created by Cromwell, whose name is attached to all decayed walls around here.

III

At the beginning of his second semester at Freiburg, Weber followed the custom of the time and gave his public inaugural lecture, before a large audience, on *Der Nationalstaat und die Volkswirtschaftspolitik*[19] [The Nation-State and Economic Policy]. The audience and the speaker himself were deeply stirred, for the speech contained both perception [*Erkenntnis*] and an avowal of principles [*Bekenntnis*]. Weber's ideas set off a spirited discussion. "My inaugural lecture aroused horror at the brutality of my views. The Catholics were almost the most satisfied with it, because I gave a firm kick to 'ethical culture.' "

This speech had a definite political influence on young people; of the older generation, Friedrich Naumann and some of his adherents in particular were affected by it when it appeared in print. Weber again discussed the East Elbian agrarian problems and made the same demands on the Prussian state that he had made earlier. He combined his presentation of the concrete situation with the question of the *standards of value* that should guide economic policy—a problem which at that time greatly occupied the economic sciences under the influence of *Kathedersozialismus* [academic socialism]. The question was whether there were *intrinsic* standards for judging and shaping the economic forms of life: perhaps the ideal of technical perfection in the production of commodities, or the ideal of social justice in their distribution. Weber answered this question in the negative—not on the basis

---

[19]*Gesammelte politische Schriften*, Drei-Masken-Verlag, Munich, 1920, pp. 7ff.

of a different ideology, but from concrete experience. What made the economic struggle between the Germans and the Poles so tragic was the very fact that because of technical progress a higher type, the indigenous German farmer, was being displaced by a lower one, the Polish seasonal worker. Therefore, "we must not indulge in the optimistic hope that with the greatest possible development of an economic culture the work is done and that the process of selection in free and peaceful economic competition will then bring victory to the more highly developed type." Or perhaps an increase in the *Lustbilanz* [amount of pleasure] in human life, the *happiness* of the world, could be a standard of value. This, too, was rejected by Weber:

> The somber seriousness of the population problem in itself keeps us from being eudaemonists, from believing that peace and human happiness lie concealed in the womb of time and that elbowroom in earthly life can be gained in any other way but in a hard struggle of men against men.
> As for the dream of peace and human happiness, *Lasciate ogni speranza*[20] is written over the gate to the unknown future of human history.

Political economy is in no position to derive ideals of its own from its material; rather, it is tied to the old general types of human ideals. It is a science that, above all, is concerned with the *quality of the human beings* who are produced by economic and social conditions. But as soon as it makes value judgments, it is "bound to that form of humanness which we find in our own nature. . . ."

> If we were able to rise from the grave after thousands of years, it would be the remote traces of our own nature that we would search for in the face of the future generation. Even our highest and ultimate earthly ideals are changeable and transitory. We cannot wish to force them upon the future. But we can desire that the future recognize in our ways the ways of its *own ancestors*. We, with our work and our nature, wish to be the forefathers of future generations. Therefore the standards of value of German economic policy can only be *German* standards. . . The *power* interests of the nation are, wherever they are in question, the ultimate decisive interests that must be served by that nation's economic policy.

---

[20]*Lasciate ogni speranza, voi ch'entrate!* [All hope abandon, ye who enter here!], the inscription over the gate to hell in Dante's *Inferno*, III, 9.—Ed.

In this connection Weber termed himself an "economic nationalist," and he described economic policy as the servant of the nation-state. He finally measured the importance of the various classes for political leadership by the interests of this state and came to a pessimistic conclusion: Only a class that is capable of placing the political and economic interests of the nation above its own is qualified for leadership. This ceased to be the case with the Prussian Junker class when it changed into an entrepreneurial class; it claimed the support of the state at the expense of the others. As for the bourgeoisie, the Caesarean sun of Bismarck had for the time being burned out its slowly developing political judgment. The working class, too, was not yet on the road to political maturity; "it does not have a spark of that Catilinarian vigor of *action* nor a breath of that powerful *national* passion which prevailed in the halls of the French Assembly." Thus an enormous job of political education had to be done among all groups if Germany wished to maintain itself as a national power state, if the future of a high-class German nationality was to be assured.

Even in the face of the tremendous misery of the nation's masses which burdens the sharpened social conscience of the new generation we must candidly confess: an even heavier burden on us today is the consciousness of our responsibility *before history*. It is not given to our generation to see whether the struggle we are carrying on is bearing fruit, whether posterity will acknowledge us as its ancestors. We shall not succeed in shaking off the curse that is upon us, that of being the epigones of a politically great epoch, unless we are able to become something else: precursors of a greater one.

* * *

Around that time Friedrich Naumann tried to draw Weber more into his sphere of interests. In the spring of 1894 *Die Hilfe* [The Help] was founded; Weber was mentioned among the contributors. The "enlightened despot" of the Saar area, the industrial magnate Baron von Stumm,[21] mounted a campaign against this unusual weekly and declared in a major speech in the Reichstag (January 9, 1895) that Naumann and the social-minded pastors were more dangerous than the Social Democrats. Stumm won great in-

[21] Karl Ferdinand Freiherr von Stumm-Halberg, 1836–1901, owner of mines, steel and iron works, etc., and conservative politician.—Ed.

fluence over the monarch. The *Zuchthausvorlage* [House of Correction Bill]—coercive measures for the suppression of wage disputes—was submitted.[22] All this brought Max Weber into action. He girded his loins, prepared a statement against the coercive laws for the *Frankfurter Zeitung,* and attacked Stumm and the agrarians in the *Kreuzzeitung.* The conservative paper accepted or rejected his articles, depending on how the wind was blowing in high quarters:

> In the meantime you will have noticed that the *Kreuzzeitung* did print my article—after sitting on it for one and a half weeks. H[ammerstein] is really incredible. He evidently attributes the Kaiser's change in attitude toward the agrarians to Stumm; so long as it seemed as though the imperial favor was smiling upon the agrarians as well, he kept his hands off the all-powerful one and deemed it "at this time politically unwise" to take my article, but now he has taken it out of his drawer and flung it in the Kaiser's face! . . . Please watch the *Post* now, too, so that I can immediately fly at its throat if it opens its mouth. (Letter to Alfred Weber, February 27, 1895)

At Whitsuntide, 1895, the Webers again took part in the Evangelical-Social Congress at Erfurt. This time the discussion focused on the question of women's rights, and the speech by Elisabeth Gnauck-Kühne[23] was by far the strongest and most impressive performance. It inspired the women with great enthusiasm for the propagation of their ideals.

Naumann was already planning to found a political organization. For the convention he had written down some thoughts on a Christian Socialist program that bespoke an anticapitalistic attitude. There were no national and constitutional postulates, thus no really political ones, but his ideas reflected a deep concern for the fate of the little people.[24] Hans Delbrück[25] and Weber called Naumann's attention to the importance of the national-political idea. Soon thereafter Weber's inaugural address ap-

---

[22]In his book *Max Weber und die deutsche Politik, 1890–1920* (Tübingen, 1959, p. 114), Wolfgang J. Mommsen points out that Marianne Weber here confuses the *Zuchthausvorlage* of 1898 with the *Umsturzvorlage* (a bill dealing with revolutionary activities) of 1895.—Ed.

[23]1850–1917, founder of the Evangelical-Social women's group (1894) and, after her conversion in 1900, co-founder of the Catholic Women's League; author of *Die deutsche Frau um die Jahrhundertwende* (1904).—Ed.

[24]Cf. Martin Wenck, *Die Geschichte der Nationalsozialen,* Hilfe-Verlag, 1905, pp. 32ff.

[25]1848–1929, historian, professor at Berlin, and editor of the *Preussische Jahrbücher.* —Ed.

peared in print. It brought about a decisive change in the thinking of Naumann and some of his followers. As Wenck put it,

> The impression made by these ideas upon the younger Christian Social-
> ists, particularly Naumann himself, was great. An entirely new perspec-
> tive opened up to them. Before then, proletarian Christianity had
> been the point of departure. Compassion for the little people, and
> hence a sharing of their thinking . . . National considerations were en-
> tertained only for their ethical value, as patriotism which crystallized
> into their attitude toward the monarch and later toward monar-
> chism. But now these national elements as a factor of political power
> entered their thinking and soon filled it completely.

Naumann himself wrote about Weber's thoughts in the July issue of *Die
Hilfe:*

> Is he not right? What good is the best social policy to us if the Cos-
> sacks come? Anyone who wants to conduct domestic policy must first
> secure the people, the fatherland, and its boundaries; he must provide
> for national power. Here is the weakest point of Social Democracy. We
> need a socialism that is capable of governing, capable of carrying out a
> better all-around policy than previously. Such a socialism has not ex-
> isted until now. Such a socialism must be nationalistic [*deutschnational*].

On this subject Wenck remarked: "And from that hour on began the evolution of *national* socialism from Christian socialism." Naumann now
planned to found a daily newspaper as well as a political organization, which
was to prepare a national socialist [*nationalsoziale*] party.

From the beginning Weber counseled against it. Although he felt personally close to Naumann and his immediate circle—Göhre, Rade, Baumgarten,
and others—and greatly enjoyed their youthful enthusiasm, those political
plans seemed to him to be doomed to failure from the start. Most of these
people lacked innate political instincts. A large number of their followers
would continue all the more to be guided by ethical and religious ideals.
And above all, the group lacked the focus of unified economic interests.
From the outset Weber regarded it as highly unlikely that it would be
possible—as Naumann hoped—to wean part of the working class away from
Social Democracy. In his view it would have been preferable to forgo founding a party of their own and instead to be all the more free to make the

bourgeoisie more social-minded and, on the other hand, to lead the workers to a better appreciation of nationalist politics. He tried to dissuade them, but he did not want to withdraw from the common attempt of the friends and joined the committee preparing the newspaper.

In the fall of 1896, Naumann came to Freiburg to discuss everything. Marianne reported: "Naumann asked questions with the aid of notes; Max answered 'from the fullness of his wisdom.' I myself was the audience; I let the household take care of itself, sat in the next room as if rooted to the spot, and listened. I again admired Naumann's tremendous objectivity, sobriety, and the inner modesty with which he took advice." A short time thereafter the paper and the association saw the light of day. The latter was founded in Erfurt (November, 1896). Although Weber had at the same time been called to Berlin for the deliberations of the stock exchange commission, he participated at its founding. The impressions he received at the conference confirmed his misgivings. The mixture of clergymen, professors, and officials on the one hand and craftsmen and a few workingmen on the other did not seem to him to be highly qualified to make political decisions. Naumann's conduct, too, was an annoying beginning:

On Monday, in Erfurt, Naumann bungled things badly in that he submitted in place of the prepared outline of a platform an entirely new draft in which he had *eliminated* the question of women's rights and the opposition against the landed proprietors. The consequence of this was that I sharply attacked him and the entire "party," saying that in this way they would become "political jumping jacks" and that if their present treatment of the Polish question continued, I would neither subscribe to nor support *Die Zeit* but would most vigorously oppose it. The speech-making of the pastors, which made up about three-quarters of the meeting, and the entire spectacle of political children trying to put their hands on the spokes of the wheel of German development, was pathetic in the extreme. Well, I see from the newspaper that they finally dropped the idea of founding a "party" and established an "association" instead. We must wait and see what will come of it. Not much, I believe.

As Weber had feared, these men simply were guided by very different ideals, mostly in the realm of foreign policy; it would take a great deal of effort to amalgamate them. They argued for days and yet could not agree on whether the national or the social idea should open the platform. It was even harder to settle on the relationship between Christianity and politics. Weber himself mercilessly criticized Naumann's program:[26]

Naumann—so Weber says—desires the participation of educated people. But what he offers here is, despite all the nationalist viewpoints, the party of those who labor and are heavy laden, those whom the shoe pinches somewhere, of all those who have no property but would like to have some. By constructing a difference between labor and property the program turns all rising classes of the population who have already acquired some property, including the rising strata of the working class, into natural enemies of the National Socialist movement. Only the dregs of the population will then belong to this movement economically. This party of the weak can never amount to anything. Such a standpoint of wretchedness [*Miserabilitätsstandpunkt*] turns the members of the National Socialist group into political jumping jacks, people who, as the sight of some economic misery gets on their nerves, react with unarticulated movements to the right or to the left, one time against the agrarians, the next time against the stock exchange and heavy industry. This political fuzziness is due to the abandonment of the opposition to the landed proprietors that was contained in the first draft of the program. But the only remaining choice is whether the bourgeoisie or the agrarian-feudal class is to be supported. By its actions against the bourgeoisie Social Democracy has only paved the way for reaction. The same mistake threatens to be made here.

Therefore, they decide to attempt to become a new national party of civil liberty which takes a stand in favor of a bourgeois capitalistic development. For what we lack is a *national democracy* to which we can entrust the leadership of Germany by our votes because we are certain that our national and economic power interests will be safe in its care. The preservation of the national power interests, of course, must be accomplished most vigorously and consistently—for example, in the Polish question. For the national viewpoint, too, is incompatible with the standpoint of wretchedness. Anyone who wants to pursue an earthly policy must be free of illusions and be acquainted with the fundamental fact of the eternal struggle of men with one another.

Wenck adds to this report: "The very sparse applause after what undoubtedly was an excellent speech showed how strong the 'standpoint of wretchedness' was among the overwhelming majority at that time."

---

[26]M. Wenck, *op. cit.*, p. 63.

Despite these basic differences—because for Naumann, too, the national power state remained for the time being a means of social reform, while conversely, Weber demanded social and political justice to safeguard the nation-state—Weber joined the National Socialist Association and supported Naumann whenever and wherever he could, whereas other associates (Paul Göhre and Maurenbrecher,[27] among others) soon defected to the Left. Naumann's first candidacy for the Reichstag was financed by Helene Weber and Ida Baumgarten, both of whom were widows by that time.

Unfortunately Weber's fears came true. The daily stopped publication after a year because of lack of funds. The first campaign for parliamentary representation brought a *succès d'estime,* but the goal was not reached in any election district. The new organization, which did not want to be a bourgeois party and kept equally aloof from the Social Democrats, did attract through the person of its leader a number of important and high-minded personalities from the middle class, but the masses stayed away, and thus it did not become a political "machine." When after five years of continued effort again only one candidate was successful in the election campaign and Naumann was defeated for the second time, the fate of National Socialism [*Nationalsozialismus*] as a separate movement was sealed: "The great wave has swallowed us up." At Naumann's urging the group merged with the left democratic wing of the bourgeoisie, the *Freisinnige Vereinigung,* and together with it formed the liberal *Wahlverein,* thus joining with the bourgeoisie, as Weber had desired five years previously.

* * *

In the years discussed above, Weber's life undoubtedly moved in the direction of practical political activity. His nationalism was too ardent for him to be permanently satisfied with the effectiveness of his writings. His fighting instincts and rhetorical gifts, too, demanded more than a merely literary employment. And even if now he could no longer doubt his talent for teaching and research, he was not sure whether these tasks were the most appropriate form of activity for him. He expressed such doubts to L. Brentano: "If I have achieved success in my academic career to which I did not aspire or lay claim, this leaves me rather cold and in particular gives

---

[27]Max Maurenbrecher, 1874–1930, originally a Protestant pastor, later a Pan-German politician and reformer, author of books on religion, history, and politics.—Ed.

me no answer to the question as to whether *this* career is the activity that is suitable for me."

To be sure, he postponed any attempt to enter practical politics until later. He could have made connections even then. At the beginning of 1897 he accepted an invitation to speak before a liberal political association in Saarbrücken, Stumm's domain. Some time after he was offered a chance to become a candidate for the Reichstag from that district. Weber declined for the time being, because he was once again looking forward to a new sphere of activity. The *Philosophische Fakultät* of the University of Heidelberg had appointed him as the successor of the veteran scholar Knies. At the moment Weber did not regard political activity as compatible with his new assignment.

It really would not have been easy for him to fit into one of the existing political parties. For the time being the National Socialist platform could be given serious consideration. With the Liberal Left he shared the *democratic* ideals, but he missed in them a sense of great national-political feeling; in that respect they were "philistines" to him. He shared the National Liberals' *individualistic* attitude, and he also agreed with their affirmation of industrial capitalism as an organizing force that was indispensable to the national economy. However, their lack of social and democratic convictions and social-political insights constituted an insurmountable barrier for him. What tied him to conservative and Pan-German circles was their *national feeling,* but they were supporting the economic policy of the agrarians at the expense of the German spirit and their fellow Germans. In April, 1899, Weber resigned from the Pan-German Union with the following letter:

Not being certain of the person to whom such a declaration ought to be addressed, I have the honor to inform you of my resignation from the *Alldeutscher Verband.* The reason is the Union's attitude in the question of the *Polish farm workers.* While the Union usually discusses and debates important and unimportant things (often utter trivia) with equal zeal, in a *vital question* for the Germans it did not rise above desires expressed in theoretical terms on a very few occasions. It *never* advocated the complete exclusion of the Poles—which of course can be done only by degrees—with anything like the vigor with which it called for the deportation of Danes and Czechs, which is a matter of utter indifference from the standpoint of nationalist politics and which the government uses to throw dust in the eyes of public opinion. The Union acquiesced in the shameless demand made by the

Königsberg board of agriculture that the Poles be *settled,* in the agrarians' demand in the *Landtag* [provincial diet] that the importation of Poles be facilitated, and in the government's promise to do so if Russia (!) agreed. Consideration for the financial interests of agrarian capitalism, which is represented by the Union's numerous conservative members, is more important to the Union than the vital interests of the Germans.

I am resigning in order to be free to state these things in public when the opportunity arises. I have pleaded this cause within the Union in speeches in Berlin, Freiburg, etc., to the point of *Steckenpferdreiten* [riding my hobbyhorse], but this has failed to influence the attitude of the Union. I am tired of making these pointless efforts, particularly since, as you know, my voice carries absolutely no weight in these matters. I am regarded as an "enemy of the Junkers." This, of course, does not prevent me from being in sympathy with the Union's endeavors, nor does it diminish my sincere personal regard for its leaders. (April 22, 1899).

8

BREAKDOWN _____

I

When Weber was able to cope satisfactorily with all aspects of his Freiburg activities and was beginning to settle down there, he received a call to Heidelberg. A short time before he had declined an offer to direct and organize the *Sozialwissenschaftliches Institut* [Institute of Social Science] at Frankfurt (Merton Foundation[1]), even though the idea of having millions at his disposal for the advancement of science was a temptation. Leaving Freiburg and his local circle of friends, where he had found such summery good cheer, was hard, yet he finally decided in favor of Heidelberg. The city on the Neckar had a mellow, homelike atmosphere and happy memories for him of his childhood and early, carefree student years. Besides, there he would feel less out of touch politically than in Freiburg, and the university had always had the reputation of being particularly stimulating intellectually.

Weber left Freiburg with a feeling of gratitude. The period of his life

----

[1]Wilhelm Merton, 1848–1916, industrialist, founder of the *Institut für Gemeinwohl* [Institute for Public Welfare] in 1890 and co-founder of the *Handelshochschule* [Commercial College] in Frankfurt.—Ed.

which was now finished had been a happy one in every respect. In Freiburg Weber had freed himself of the shadows of the past and had carried an enormous work load with a steadily increasing consciousness of strength. He had become cheerful and free. He had made lasting friendships, especially with the Rickert family. Both he and Marianne were more emotionally and spiritually adaptable than they had been two and one-half years earlier, when they had left Berlin, and they looked forward to their new life in the beloved hometown of Weber's mother. Weber promised his wife that he would take better care of his health, and since he was bound by no obligations, he carried out this resolution overnight: he went out very seldom and got to bed at a reasonable hour.

Weber now became the colleague of his former teachers, for the stars on the scholarly firmament—Kuno Fischer, Immanuel Bekker, Erdmannsdörfer, and others—were still active in Heidelberg at a ripe old age. Academic social life still conformed to the style, views and social customs of the generation of mentally active but elderly privy councillors. Abundant gastronomic joys were part of this. While in Freiburg the older scholars, in accordance with the modest circumstances of the younger men, used to hold unpretentious suppers, here the *diner* still had, in leading circles, the status of a ritual act. Weber was told that accepting an invitation from I. Bekker, the senior member of the *Juristische Fakultät* [School of Law], was an "obligation" that entailed cancelling a seminar if necessary. He protested against this ritual, however, and after he and Marianne had participated in it a few times—behind closed windows and by candlelight, even in early summer, when the most glorious sun was shining outside—they decided, for their part at least, to invalidate this "obligation" and to cultivate only the kind of unpretentious companionship with people their age which they had known in Freiburg.

They soon came to enjoy their rich new life. In place of the mountains of the Black Forest, the gently sloping heights of the Odenwald with their luxuriant southern flora now beckoned for cheerful relaxation. The silvery river which here flows into the broad, smiling Rhine Valley strikingly connects this cozy corner with the larger expanse. New and distinguished friends joined their circle: Georg Jellinek, Paul Hensel, Karl Neumann, and, above all, the theologian Ernst Troeltsch,[2] who was the same age as We-

---

[2]Georg Jellinek, 1851–1911, professor of constitutional law at Basel and Heidelberg; Paul Hensel, 1860–1931, professor of philosophy at Heidelberg and Erlangen; Carl Neumann, 1860–1934, art historian, professor at Heidelberg, Göttingen, and Kiel; Ernst Troeltsch, 1865–1923, theologian and philosopher, professor at Bonn, Heidelberg, and Berlin.—Ed.

ber and became a close friend of the couple. Troeltsch's freedom and breadth of spirit, buoyant vitality, clear and graphic thinking, wide-ranging sense of humor, and directness and warmth made him a companion with whom there was an enjoyable and fruitful scholarly and spiritual exchange. To be sure, in many things—especially politics—Weber and Troeltsch had different ideas. Troeltsch's views at that time made him part of the older National Liberal generation; social and democratic ideals were alien to his strongly bourgeois instincts. He did not believe in many things that the Webers were striving for—neither in the intellectual and political development of the working classes nor in the intellectual development of women. Their temperaments were different, too. For Troeltsch it was enough that he had to fight for intellectual freedom and tolerance within theology. Otherwise, he was not a fighter but was oriented toward reconciliation, adjustment, and acceptance of human weaknesses.

* * *

Professionally there were all sorts of new and urgent tasks to accomplish in Heidelberg. Knies, Weber's predecessor, was old when he retired. The teaching was inadequate; for the time being Weber was the only full professor in his field—a situation he immediately criticized as substandard for a major university. For this reason he urged that a second chair be established. And since the distinguished old Knies had disdained to hold seminars, something that Weber considered of paramount importance, he had to reestablish a seminar and procure a library to go with it.

However, he was quite happy about it, for he had now mastered his discipline and enjoyed the lucid, tight organization of his important lectures on theoretical and practical political economy, agrarian policy, and the labor question. His courses were always carefully planned, but for the rest he surrendered to the inspiration of the moment and spoke without notes. The severe conceptual structure was clothed with a wealth of historical knowledge; his uncommon mental acuity was supplemented by an equally uncommon descriptive power. Thus he made even the most abstract ideas comprehensible by a profusion of examples and the directness of his lecturing style. Each course of lectures seemed to have been freshly produced in the workshop of his mind. For his great course on theoretical political economy he gave his students a printed outline that he intended to expand into a textbook.

In accordance with Weber's wishes, his wife now led a full intellectual life of her own. She attended his lectures on political economy as well as lectures on philosophy, and became engrossed in a research paper for Paul Hensel's seminar. In addition she undertook the leadership of a newly founded society for the propagation of modern feminist ideals. Weber was delighted about her thirst for action and was soon more of a feminist than she was. He eagerly followed the pros and cons of public opinion, helped wherever he could, and stood by with his sword drawn when it was a matter of fighting off hostile acts of the old guard. After one of the first public debates about women's rights with a leading light of the university—an exciting event for the new society—Marianne made the following report:

> The whole mood was dominated by a speech by Max which lasted about a quarter of an hour. He proceeded very diplomatically and framed his arguments as though he merely wanted to give a more detailed interpretation of the views of his *Herr Kollege* [colleague], which we had not properly understood. In doing so, of course, he gave *his* point of view, briefly sketched the whole question of women's rights, and expressed the innermost thoughts of women which, for the time being, they can only stammer indistinctly. He also gave some strong admonitions to old-fashioned women, who—so he said—with their intolerance toward the new type were much more vehement opponents of the entire movement than the men. He compared them to hens that mercilessly peck away with their beaks at a strange hen that has strayed into their barnyard. In short, it was wonderful. I believe the women would have liked to form a thanksgiving procession for him.

Now the first female students were beginning to enter the lecture halls of the university, though still in small numbers. They were concerned not only with their destiny as women but with their generally human destiny as well. Each was aware that she was a pioneer of a new world order and felt that she had to help overcome resistance. The new type was subject to mockery and determined moral opposition, and won tolerance and recognition only slowly.

Among the girls who won approval for the new type because of her attractive personality was Weber's first female student, Else von Richthofen,[3] who studied under him together with Marianne. Delicate and young

---

[3]Born in 1874, she married Edgar Jaffé in 1902. Her sister Frieda married D. H. Lawrence in 1912. (See Martin Green, *The von Richthofen Sisters: The Triumphant and the Tragic Modes of Love*, New York, 1974). Else died in Heidelberg in December, 1973.—Ed.

as she was, she wanted to become a factory inspector. It was part of the women's program to obtain such occupations. They were convinced that they would be fulfilling a necessary social mission as advocates of the female workers. There was soon a close friendship between these two women who had the same aims, and Weber took a lively interest in his student's development. He persuaded the farsighted factory inspector for the state of Baden to add her to his staff at some future date. This was done, and the attractive personality of the young doctor and her graduation with honors dispelled all doubts. This first female official, who performed her arduous duties with courage and circumspection, served to strengthen the faith of the feminist movement.

* * *

Thus the new life quickly put forth rich blossoms. The Webers felt more secure and more buoyant than before. Then, in the early summer of 1897, a great crisis arose, which left an indelible mark on all involved.

Ever since the Webers had left Berlin, it had been a necessity for Helene to spend a few quiet weeks each year with the children, who were so close to her. However, it was never easy to arrange this happy holiday, for her husband was still unable to accept the fact that she shared with others interests that were alien to him and cultivated affectionate relationships from which he felt excluded. He somehow felt that Helene, in spite of her age, still belonged to him, that his interests and desires took precedence over hers and everyone else's, and that he had the right to determine the time and the duration of her vacation. This the Heidelberg children refused to recognize. That year it was particularly difficult to reconcile the various desires. Helene did not have the strength just to do what she liked. She could not cope with discord, and when her desires were involved she never knew how far she could go with her husband. Plans fell through, there were angry discussions by letter, and finally the elder Weber accompanied Helene to Heidelberg, so that her undisturbed rest with the children seemed curtailed or completely frustrated.

Then the long-threatening disaster came to a head. The son was no longer able to contain his pent-up anger. The lava erupted and the monstrous thing happened: a son sat in judgment on his father. The settling of accounts took place in the presence of the women. No one tried to restrain him. He had the clearest conscience and felt better during this row, which marked the end of his previous diplomatic treatment of all family difficulties. His mother's freedom was at stake, she was the weaker one, and no one could violate her spiritual rights. "We demand that Mama should have the right to visit us alone quietly for four to five weeks each year at a time that is convenient for her. As long as this is not done, any family relationship with Papa is meaningless to us and its outward maintenance has no value for us."

The elder Weber had a different nature and came from a different generation; he could not and would not realize and admit—least of all at that moment—that his conduct had been improper. Nor was this vehement attempt to influence him designed to make him do so. He stuck to his point of view, and so the son also remained adamant; only understanding on the part of his father would have made him relent. They parted without a reconciliation. For Helene there followed agonizing days of accusation and self-accusation. The illusion was shattered and the long-concealed truth became severely apparent: a broken marriage, a crumbled pedestal. Helene was crushed by what had happened to her husband, for which she assumed some of the responsibility; yet even to her this long-standing crisis seemed inevitable.

However, Helene still had hope; she hoped for the future understanding of her husband, for a chance to reestablish the partnership that had begun under the bright star of soaring youthful affection, had been blessed with thriving, gifted children, and now was foundering on the rock of renunciation and truth. Alas, spring and summer were long past—but was it not possible that in the autumn of life, grown wise, they would once more clasp hands for a new union in freedom and helping love? Her strong hope and merciful love are movingly expressed in the following lines:

> God will and must give him and me the strength to bear it and to improve things. That is why I have destroyed your kind letters which, however, think only of me. That is why I beg you, by all your love for me, to let me go my way, and *please* try, try to rid yourselves of your bitterness in order to help me. Look, it is *not for nothing* that I vowed before the altar to be faithful and loving in joy and in sorrow. That was not something superficial, and it also applies if the sorrow comes from him—after all, I cause *him* sorrow, too. I cannot, as Ida has done, burn all bridges, but I must build, even if everything were to be constantly torn down again in this life. I shall build with the courage of faith and a never-ending hope. I know I am often weak and do the wrong thing, but I cannot live without that. And look, I have not

been able to spare you big children the alienation and the bitterness that he feels so deeply and holds me responsible for; he *cannot* view it any differently, either. But as regards the younger children—let me try to ease the discord for them. As for giving in—no, I cannot and will not do that. It would really be untruthful toward him; and once he believes me again, he will learn, to the extent that he is able, to tolerate what moves me inwardly and cannot be stifled. But I must build, if only to make him believe that Christianity means holding on to the love that tolerates and hopes for everything, and that he has to recognize this in me. And therefore let me build, and oh, I beg of you, help me with forbearing love!

But fate took its course. It was not given to the aging man to break through the shell of his own nature. When Helene returned home a few weeks later, he closed himself off from her. By doing so he accomplished the opposite of what he perhaps secretly hoped for. Helene, who ordinarily was always ready to pronounce herself guilty when things went wrong, was not mollified by the unbearable situation but was strengthened in her conviction that there was a higher right which must now finally be fought for. Her husband went traveling with a friend, and she was still able to hope that after a while he would greet her with a changed spirit.

But a short time later, his dead body was brought to her; a gastric hemorrhage had suddenly ended his life. By way of exonerating him, it was learned that the vigorous man had been harboring pathogenic organisms for some time. He had been a man disposed to happiness and enjoyment who, as he felt, had always been vouchsafed much "good fortune," but who was also capable of repressing a sense of growing disharmony; he had finally been overtaken by a truth that was bound to destroy him psychologically unless he humbly searched his soul and learned from it. It was now too late. He was not granted a *Stirb und Werde*[4] on earth.

On a radiant day in August Helene and all her children gathered around the catafalque in the garden. The younger ones were only dimly aware of the tragedy of this conclusion; the older ones understood it with full clarity. But Weber was not shaken by self-reproach. The altercation that had taken place seven weeks previously seemed inescapable even now. Only many years later, with unemotional detachment, did he pronounce himself guilty—in

---

[4]"Death and Rebirth"—from Goethe's poem *Selige Sehnsucht* (Blessed Yearning).—Ed.

form rather than substance. His attitude reassured Helene as well. Later he wrote his youngest brother:

> In those days a great number of mistakes surely were made on all sides, and certainly by me in particular. But in the matter itself Mama could not have done anything but follow *her* nature and her conscience. If she made a mistake, it was that she did not simply *act*—then our father, who, after all, was very much attached to her, would have *accustomed* himself to her different nature and her special interests (religious and social) which he did not share. But it was a necessity for her to have his inner consent. This she did *not* obtain, and since it was not in her nature to assert herself forcefully, she greatly suffered inwardly and finally became completely estranged from him, much more than he suspected, until he finally realized it. He himself did not understand her or his own advantage. He would have been infinitely happier if he had resolved to give her complete freedom of movement in accordance with the saying "Live and let live" . . .

A document that he gave his mother on her seventieth birthday and which will be included in another context presents his unimpassioned interpretation of Helene's matrimonial destiny and his father's personality.

II

Some time after the funeral, toward the end of the summer, the Webers took a trip to Spain. Weber needed mental and emotional relaxation, and he found this only in the new impressions which he again preserved in detailed letters to his mother. First they came under the spell of the lofty Pyrenees and their cool, refreshing atmosphere; in the face of these supraearthly contours, in that light, intoxicating air, all human troubles lost their ominous weight. Then they were fascinated by the strange new world of northern Spain where each day they had to cope with irksome surprises. Weber was irritable and often got annoyed at the lackadaisical transport system, but this time, too, he was eagerly receptive to the new impressions and was flexible enough to discover the most attractive aspects of that unfamiliar world. However, he himself interpreted the restlessness with which he kept grasping for constantly new impressions as a sign of nervous exhaustion:

What you write is correct; under normal circumstances the multiplicity of impressions which we let pass before us might not be beneficial. But as long as work was out of the question for me, I could not have stood it in *one* place. We would, of course, not be in the mood for enjoying nature in the usual unconstrained way. One can simply expose oneself to the whole profusion of the powerful impressions, so that one may, first of all, regain one's full nervous strength and then be capable of objectively processing everything that one has experienced. This, I believe, has now been accomplished.

On the return trip Weber's strained organism reacted by becoming indisposed; he was feverish and felt apprehensive. During the journey home, which could not be postponed, he was not well. But he had to get better, for a course arranged by the leadership of the Evangelical-Social Congress in Karlsruhe called him back to his teaching duties: "Even though we are home, we still travel every day. At 3:00 in the afternoon we go to Karlsruhe and return in the evening; today it will be at 3:00 in the morning, because Max's lecture is to be followed by a discussion. I shall be happy for him when these days are over and we can recover from our pleasure trip."

But when the new semester started, everything seemed to be in order: "Max is better now, he lives sensibly, goes walking a bit, and several times went to bed early; he sleeps a lot." Weber did full justice to his professional duties, perfected his lectures, and devoted himself in particular to the research papers of his students. When he encountered scholarly zeal, he was so carried away that he put off his own production. He also handled a good number of out-of-town lectures—in Mannheim, Frankfurt, and Strasbourg.

Then, at the end of the semester, when he was overloaded with work, an evil thing from the unconscious underground of life stretched out its claws toward him. One evening, after the examination of a student at which he had, as always, worn himself out, he was overcome by total exhaustion, with a feverish head and a strong feeling of tension. The semester was finished, but there was no change in his condition. Weber felt uneasy and consulted a physician. The doctor made light of this disorder in such a robust man, attributed it to constant overwork and emotional excitement, and recommended that he take a trip. The Webers spent a few weeks at Lake Geneva. That year spring was late there. It was cold and the mountain slopes were still dead and brown, unable to nestle against the ground. Weber did a lot of walking, thinking that he could relax his nerves by physical fatigue. When the new semester began, he felt, according to a letter to his mother, revived rather than exhausted:

Glion, April 14, 1898

Our sojourn was really very profitable. Now that I am beginning to work vigorously again I notice its consequences, and in a few weeks I hope to be rid of the last vestiges; they evidently are symptoms of convalescence, because aside from the strain of certain nerves in my head and mild congestions I have been feeling especially well physically and mentally, particularly now . . . Naturally, we all remain nervous Nellies, that cannot be changed, but now that everything capable of oppressing one has gradually been assimilated, our mood is good enough for us not to worry about it.

However, after a few weeks of intellectual labor, sleep—normally a fountain of youth after each busy day—would not come and functional disturbances began to appear. Weber again felt ill. When, during Whitsunweek, he wished to avoid the usually welcome visit of a friend and went walking in the Odenwald by himself, the glory of May was veiled by a dark curtain. He was extremely exhausted, his solid frame was weakened, and tears welled up. Weber felt himself at a turning point. Nature, so long violated, was beginning to take revenge. The doctor did not consider it a serious matter and ordered hydrotherapy. This only increased his excitement and banished sleep completely.

The doctor recommended a stay in a sanatorium during the summer vacation. With childlike faith Weber followed every medical suggestion and spent a few months in an overcrowded, noisy institution on Lake Constance. There he was given the treatments customary at that time and was made to do all kinds of unaccustomed physical exercise. He good-naturedly submitted to everything and watched whatever was done to him with objective curiosity. But when the treatments did not succeed in getting him the only thing he longed for—a regular night's rest and relaxation—he secretly desired, in place of everything else, a prolonged respite from his official duties. But he did not express his desire, for "surely I could not prescribe a leave for myself."

In the fall his condition appeared to be considerably improved; he returned to work seemingly full of physical strength and mentally unchanged. No one would believe he was sick. A few weeks later, however, his nerves broke down again and teaching—every lecture was a free creation—became a torment. He now resigned himself to a long siege of illness: "Theoretically I am fully prepared to suffer for quite a long time from this malady, which must have been in the making for years." But he still had great reserves of strength and probably thought he could already see the bottom of his cup of sorrow. And was not this illness perhaps only a long-gathering cloud whose final discharge could almost be like a liberation from a mysteriously threatening, hostile power? Would it not prepare the way for a greater *harmony* of his vital powers in the future? In this vein he wrote to his wife when he had to be separated from her for a few weeks:

> Such an illness really has its very good points—for me, for instance, it has reopened the purely human side of living, which Mama always somewhat missed in me, to an extent that I had not known before. Like John Gabriel Borkmann[5] I could say "An icy hand has let go of me," for in past years my sickly disposition expressed itself in a convulsive clinging to scholarly work as to a talisman, without my being able to say what it was supposed to ward off. As I look back upon it this is quite clear to me, and I know that, sick or healthy, I shall never be like that again. The *need* to feel myself succumbing to the load of work is extinguished. I want, above all, to live a full personal life with my *Kindele* [baby] and to see her as happy as it is given to me to make her. I do not believe that while doing so I shall accomplish less than I did earlier in my inner treadmill. Of course, this will always depend on my condition, and its real, permanent improvement will, in any case, require a great deal of time and rest. But you are quite right, my sweetheart: earlier I did not even *know how* to live as closely together with someone as I have lived with you these past years.

This period was in fact a particularly happy one for their marriage. Marianne had herself inherited weak nerves and from childhood was used to treating those who suffered in the same way with special consideration. Thus she was able to empathize with her husband's condition completely and to behave in a way that did him good. If Weber's sovereign self-sufficiency had occasionally made her wonder whether he needed her, she now did not doubt it. From the dark crevice that now opened up there sprang a great good fortune for her: her strong husband needed her constant care and presence, and she was privileged to serve him. Their life together was

---

[5] The hero of a play of that title by Henrik Ibsen (1896).—Ed.

filled with an affection and intimacy that even the patient experienced as a new happiness:

> The other day you wrote that recent times *have* been beautiful in some respects—particularly because we have lived together so closely. That is really true, and for me this was, despite everything, especially beautiful and will always live in my memory like this because I had never before been able to experience *in this way* how wonderful the feeling of deep gratitude to a beloved person is, such as I have had toward you.

* * *

However, at that time Weber was only at the beginning of his descent to hell. The metabolic treatment tailored to his vigorous body effected an improvement, and Weber began his lectures in good spirits. After a few weeks there was another breakdown, and around Christmas he was so utterly exhausted that his back and arms failed him when he tried to trim the Christmas tree. Weber suspended his lectures until after the vacation, and then he laboriously struggled through the rest of the semester:

> Max has suspended his lectures for this week, too, and he hopes that he will then be able to get through the three remaining weeks of the semester. Right now this *immediate* future worries us more than the succeeding period, for we hope that his setback will again be completely overcome during the vacation. At present it is especially the mental fatigue that makes Max regard any mental exertion as harmful not only momentarily but to his general condition. *Talking* in particular immediately has a disagreeable effect.
>
> It is a time of sorrow, but we won't let it get us down. Despite occasional anger and impatience, in general Max bears it with stoic objectivity, or rather as something ordained by fate. We also have our humor and are almost always cheerful when we are together. Only, other people should not ask too many questions or give good advice. After all, *I* am well off; the fact that he needs me is a never-ending source of happiness.

How was the sick man, for whom all intellectual activity was poison, to spend his paralyzed hours? Practical activity of any kind was not his style. He had not cultivated any artistic abilities; ever since his adolescence everything had been geared to thinking. This complete halting of the precious

machine which, following the intellect's bidding, had hitherto worked unceasingly seemed unbearable.

It is bad that he has no hobbies whatever and cannot be given any
handicraft or some other mechanical but interesting occupation. I have
thought of trying to persuade him to do some chip carving—but for
the time being he laughs at me. These hours of sitting and *Stumpfen*
[apathizing], as he calls it, just picking at his fingernails, always make me
quite sad. But he claims that this does him a lot of good. These men
with a specialized education are completely at sea when their minds
break down. If he could at least be sent to the kitchen!

All kinds of things occurred to them. Helene sent wax and a little figure
Max had molded as a child. Marianne put out clay for him and was happy
when he goodnaturedly played with it: "Several times he was quite busy
molding. I am quite astonished at his talent; I believe he has much artistic
ability. What is there he *cannot* do? For that very reason it is so hard to
see his strength unused. I am now letting him work with the clay for only
a short time; it is an exertion for him."

For her birthday Helene received his first model, a replica of the Dying
Lion of Lucerne[6]—was it unconsciously symbolic? He wrote her about it
as follows: "This time you are receiving, along with our hearty congratulations and in keeping with the reversal of functions in our household, something handmade in rather tired hours; perhaps you will be able to use it as
a paperweight." But then the handicraft was put aside; it fatigued him.
Marianne made one last attempt and brought him a box of stone blocks;
friends had told her how stimulating this plaything was. To please her, the
patient did build very nicely, but then his hands started to shake and his
back hurt when he piled the blocks up. It was no use; they had to stop
trying to divert him in this manner. So he simply sat by the window of
his apartment in the *Anlage* [park area] and looked out at the tops of the
budding chestnut trees. "What are you thinking about?"—"Preferably nothing, if I can manage it."

" 'Manitou is still in a cloud.' Max's condition is fair to middling. His
whole nervous system is very irritable, and any physical or mental exertion
makes it rebel. Even newspaper reading upsets him, and therefore I read the

---

[6]A colossal statue sculpted in the rock by the Dane Bertel Thorvaldsen (1770–1844) in memory of the Swiss Guards who fell in defense of the Tuileries in 1792.—Ed.

dispatches to him." He was very irritable; a soft sound in the afternoon or evening now became a torment to him, although he had previously been able to fall into a deep sleep after the most intensive work and had been quite insensitive to noise. "Kitty was an annoyance, too, because she sometimes meowed at lunchtime or early in the morning and drove Max out of his mind; so we gave her away, since Bertha now has a fiancé and no longer needs any quadrupeds." Since his condition did not change during the vacation, Weber finally decided to have himself excused from his lectures in the summer semester of 1899 and to continue only with his seminar. He simply could not go through another period like the last weeks of the semester.

The prospect of relief had a liberating effect for a while, as did another medical consultation. Weber wrote to his mother—though, to be sure, in an effort to please her:

> If the government approves of my request for a leave, I have a rather quiet semester ahead of me, and since I am even now considerably improved, as I was in the fall, I expect to take a very substantial step forward. Now that everything I have on me and in me has been examined once more—but for the last time!—with an equally negative result, and since by now I can specify exactly what agrees with me and what does not, I shall be able to arrange the available working time. I only wish you people would now believe that it is not mental apathy if at certain stages of overfatigue I reject all so-called "suggestions," and if I have now gone on leave. My inability to talk is purely physical, the nerves break down, and when I look at my lecture notes, my head simply swims. *Now*, as always when things are decidedly improving, I am in the best mood imaginable, as I have been for some time.

A few lines in this letter indicate that it was hard for Helene to make sense of the mysterious illness. Her own heroic will, constantly and mercilessly exerted, had mastered all psychological and physical exertions. Surely her son could do the same. Of course, life did not demand from her the exertion of intellectual creative energy. But was one really *unable* to do what one wanted if one was sound of limb? Was it not at least possible to attain greater equilibrium by disregarding the individual symptoms of illness? After all, Weber appeared to be unchanged in his basic nature, and although he had now become thin and pale, he still seemed like an elemental force even physically. Sometimes it was possible to regard everything as only an evil phantom that would give way to a decisive act of the will just as quickly as it had appeared. Helene, who was so energetic and who most hated waiting and watching in all situations, suffered greatly because this illness condemned her to do so. On her visits she actually felt that her expectation—which was never expressed, of course, but which was sensed—was making things harder rather than easier for her son. For Weber's sensitive sense of honor became one of the most painful aspects of his condition when people encouragingly indicated that he did not give them the impression of a very sick man and when his friends tried to console him by praising his good appearance.

Now and then Helene and his brothers and sisters made suggestions and plans from a distance, but these were not acceptable. Marianne wrote:

I am very sorry that I reacted with such irritation to your plan which reflects so much love. The real reason may have been that from time to time I seem to perceive that you think Max's condition must be improved by energy, by some act of self-transcendence. And I must defend him against even the appearance of a weak will. Look, the fact that he completely gave up his seminar five weeks ago and even now cancels two lectures a week, although he must feel embarrassed toward his colleagues and students, shows me *how harmful* he now considers any mental effort. And that there is an objective basis for this feeling one can tell each time by looking at him afterward. That is why these past weeks have been an almost unbearable psychological and physical burden, because at present he simply does not feel up to performing his professional duties. You must not imagine that Max is generally apathetic and uninterested in the outside world; it is simply that for the duration of the semester he is imposing restrictions upon himself because his nerves are so very excitable. Nor should you picture our domestic atmosphere as gray and gloomy; no, despite everything we are almost always cheerful.

However, after a few more months of suffering: "For the time being we are very humble people who are allowed to think only of how they can with their slight strength discharge the responsibilities they have assumed and how they can gracefully struggle through the fate currently inflicted upon them." An excerpt from a letter written by Weber years later conveys an idea of the inner attitude with which Weber came to terms with his malady: " 'Adversity teaches one to pray'[7]—always? On the basis of my personal

---

[7]Weber quotes the pithy proverb *Not lehrt beten.* —Ed.

experience I should like to *dispute* this, although I certainly agree with you that very frequently it holds true—all too frequently for man's dignity." (April 5, 1908, from a letter to K. Vossler[8] about his *Dante*)

* * *

Weber was excused from his lectures in the summer of 1899, that is, the second year of his illness, but he still conducted a seminar and directed his students' theses. He and Marianne spent their vacation on the Eibsee[9] and from there went to Venice via the Fernpass.[10] The deliverance from the nightmare of duties and the beauty of the new impressions again had an effect. In the fall, when Weber resumed a small part of his teaching duties, there soon was a new breakdown, which was more severe than all the preceding ones. The patient now no longer doubted that for a long time even the most modest official duties would aggravate his condition and endanger his mind. He felt impelled to escape the spell of all that had gone before. At Christmastime he asked to be dismissed from his position. This was a grave step. In purely practical terms, they would have to endure the years of illness with no salary and depending on contributions from the family.

The Baden educational authorities (Nokk, the minister, and Arnsberger,[11] a department head) found a solution. They wished to relieve Weber but retain his services for the future. The faculty did not wish to see him leave either. His application was rejected, and instead he was given an extended leave of absence with pay. In addition, the second chair in political economy, something Weber had urged for such a long time, was to be established immediately. Weber planned to direct the theses of his students until the arrival of his new colleague, and his actual leave was to start in the fall of 1900.

Arnsberger himself just called on us. In the ministry they had not really understood the subtleties in Max's letter, but wound up thinking

---

[8]Karl Vossler, 1872–1949, Romanist, professor at Heidelberg, Würzburg, and Munich. Among his numerous books are translations from Dante.—Ed.

[9]A mountain lake in a wooded area at the northern foot of the Zugspitze.—Ed.

[10]A mountain pass in the northern Tyrol.—Ed.

[11]Wilhelm Nokk, 1832–1903, since 1881 head of the Baden Ministry of Justice and Education; Dr. Arnsperger was an official in the Baden Ministry of the Interior.—Ed.

that he was planning to do something else and wished to be dismissed for *that* reason!! When A. was told that it was nothing like that, he said that of course he would not be dismissed under any circumstances. I stood behind the door like Sarah [Gen. 18:10], and the civilities of the good old gentleman were like an angelic message to me. Max, of course, acted very "noble," but, thank God, he did not behave like a moralistic prig! He is to be on leave for as long as he needs it. Now we are not entirely uprooted after all, and I believe this is more important for Max's fresh start later than he is now able to fathom.

For a while this generous arrangement was a wonderful relief; for the time being they were able to dismiss worries about the future. Weber, however, secretly doubted that he would ever be able to resume his position. He now mustered all his strength to fight for a satisfactory occupant of the new chair. "The last two weeks were not good; every word was a strain on him. The proposals are ready, and Max did get the faculty to agree to what he wanted. But it took a lot of talking, and as a result he had to spend a week in bed. . . ."

The government refused to appoint Werner Sombart,[12] whom Weber had already proposed as his successor at Freiburg, but Karl Rathgen[13] was accepted.

Weber now was rid of this burden, too, but his condition did not improve. Everything was too much for him; he could not read, write, talk, walk, or sleep without torment. All his mental and some of his physical functions failed him. When he nonetheless forced them to work, chaos threatened him. He felt as though he might fall into the vortex of an overexcitement that would plunge his mind into darkness. "He is a little bit better, but I don't know whether he would be able to supervise his students' work without harm. I have therefore resolved to take him to a nearby sanatorium as soon as I see that he is worse."

That became necessary at the beginning of July. They decided to leave the place of torment for a long time and to break up the household. Weber first entered a small clinic for nervous diseases at Urach in the Rauhe Alb,[14] where he stayed by himself for a few weeks. The nadir had been reached.

[12] 1863–1941, political economist, professor at Breslau and Berlin.—Ed.
[13] 1856–1921, professor of economics at Tokyo, Berlin, Marburg, Heidelberg, and Hamburg; author of books on the economy and culture of Japan.—Ed.
[14] The Rauhe Alb is part of the Schwäbische Alb, which in turn is part of the mountain range known as Deutsche Jura.—Ed.

Max *is* a bit afraid of being alone, and the thought of having to write to me is so horrible to him that I shall prepare self-addressed cards on which he only needs to put a few words. The following example will give you an idea of his condition. A few days ago there came a letter from a colleague who asked for information about a Dr. X. Dr. X is Max's student; he would like to habilitate himself but is encountering difficulties because he is a Jew. Max has always been greatly interested in him, and this matter of *Habilitation*, which put the poor man in a horribly tight spot, was close to his heart. In the afternoon I showed him the letter, and in fifteen minutes he dictated four pages to me; but afterward he was more irritated and excited than I have ever seen him before about the fact that even there he was not being left in peace. For the first time his excitement was directed against me. He said that I failed to see to it that he was left in peace, and that it would take him weeks to overcome this setback; he *had* to have quiet, even if people "croaked" over it; he too had something at stake. In short, he was simply *beside* himself, and I had to give him my solemn promise that in the weeks to come I would not give him a single letter that reminded him of his profession. I should settle everything by myself and return people's letters to them—"even if they think I am crazy."

III

So now they struck tent—who knew for how long. After all, they were up to their necks in the waters of affliction and could not always resist the chilling thought that in the end they might go down together. Most of the time, of course, they were confident that everything would turn out all right and be as before. Marianne believed and hoped; she believed in her husband's unimpaired creative power, and for her he remained even in his present condition the same sovereign person he had always been—a chained titan whom evil, envious gods were plaguing.

In that difficult period hard work on her first publication kept Marianne going. Weber was pleased with this, as he was with all indications that she was leading a life of her own. He always made it possible for her to cultivate her interests. Even in this worst period, when he could hardly do without her presence, he persuaded her to attend a women's convention, because he felt that this would give her pleasure. He was never a slave to selfishness.

An expression of the love and respect of his students gave their departure from Heidelberg a melancholy joy:

Yesterday was an eventful day; at twelve o'clock Leo Wegener[15] appeared in a full-dress suit with a white vest, and with a ceremonious speech which stirred him so much that he almost cried he handed me a scroll from your students. These people are really quite touching. Else said the zeal with which they had devised everything and thought over every word was utterly charming. The scroll is a rather large sepia picture in a handsome brown leather covering. It was made by a Munich woman artist. A man throws firebrands from a steep rock he is climbing; they slide down the thorn-covered rock in which the names of your students are engraved. The background shows golden flashes in the distance. The dedication reads: Highly Honored *Herr Professor* and Teacher! Much luck on your journey! We—not only the undersigned, but *all* whom you have influenced for life—wish you a speedy and joyous return, to the pride and the advancement of scholarship and to the sincere joy of your grateful students.

* * *

Weber now spent a few dull, quiet months in the little Swabian forest town of Urach among good, simple people. Now and then he tested himself in extended walks on the plateau of the Rauhe Alb, but he always found that more vigorous exercise was a source of excitement, and afterward he preferred to lie quietly in the garden again. His life was now reduced to the smallest circle; all problems had to be kept away, and even visits from dear friends meant a strain. Occasionally nature gave him pleasant diversion, particularly when he was able to absorb its shifting images effortlessly on a carriage ride. Many years later a visit to this region stirred a memory:

When I saw the Rauhe Alb with the Neuffen[16] and the Urach Valley lying in the distance, I thought of all the love my lovely *Mädele* [little girl] invested in her really more than strange fellow of a husband in those days. I thought of our trip to the Neuffen on your birthday, the first somewhat joyful day after three quarters of a year of stuporous darkness, and of various things one does not forget—but most of all I thought of my child who is still as warm and as young as she was at that time, when she was my only bond to the world . . .

---

[15]Later the director of the Deutsche Genossenschaftsbank [German Cooperative Bank] in Posen (Poznan).—Ed.

[16]Neuffen is actually the name of a town at the foot of the Hohenneuffen mountain in the Schwäbische Alb.—Ed.

* * *

Weber felt quite ill, and he was sure of one thing: the torment of the last months, when he had been totally exhausted by his few remaining official duties, which he had performed with the greatest of ease as a healthy man, must not repeat itself. Its aftertaste made him wish to break with the past at once, so that he might start from the very beginning at some time in the future:

> I have also had a rather extended conversation with the doctor about my future prospects, about which evidently nothing definite can be said. It is probably almost out of the question that I could do *regular* work tied to *definite hours* in the foreseeable future without running the risk of having the hellish condition of last spring recur soon. That is why our hearts must not be set on the Heidelberg position. I regard it as a gift from heaven that I am not burdened with ambition and am rather *wurschtig* [indifferent]; and for the "world" no one is easier to replace than a docent. Psychologically it might even have been better if conditions had permitted me to resign completely then and there; then I could slowly steer my little ship out to sea when the wind becomes more favorable again, instead of being obliged to be anchored in Heidelberg with my hopes. But a man cannot have everything; how well off we are by comparison with the lot of a thousand others.

In the fall a young cousin of Weber's entered the institution in a severe psychopathic state. The delicate, intelligent young man had been the victim of one of those mysterious "processes" whose nature was at that time not completely clear and was incomprehensible to the layman. He had been tortured a great deal with unspoken appeals to his "willpower." Although his mind was entirely lucid, his actions were under the bondage of severe inhibitions, and being locked up behind invisible but impenetrable glass walls, he experienced his life as something senseless. The question was whether it would be possible to rescue him from this dungeon and restore him to a meaningful life. The doctor held out some hope; it was an alluring challenge.

When the gray veils of November shrouded the autumnal splendor, Weber longed for the bright and cheerful south. He and Marianne could not bring themselves to leave the young man alone for the dreary winter, in an environment devoid of any stimulation; perhaps, too, things would be easier to bear together. When they invited him to come with them, a gleam of joy lit up his always veiled features for the first time. So the three of them

[handwritten margin note: Cousin Otto]

went to Corsica, with Ajaccio, which had been recommended to them as especially mild, as their destination. Their stay began auspiciously. They really found southern clarity, the radiant blue of a high sky which also dominated the sea. The nights were so clear that the great shifting stars filled the gulf with their bright light. Then there was the noble gray green of the olives, eucalyptuses, and cactuses against the background of high, snowy mountains. The brushwood covering the slopes enveloped the island in the fragrance of lavender and thyme. Their beautiful hotel, which faced the mountain-enclosed bay in the south, was almost empty, because the Boer War was keeping the English away. It was all very peaceful.

The landscape and the climate are doing their work on Max and helping him get over his discomfort. In the morning he almost always lies by the mountainside under the olive trees. In the afternoon we take walks together if he is able to do so; the day before yesterday we again went for a nice ride along the gulf shore. He is now trying to get along without sleeping tablets or bromides, and therefore his sleep is restless, but it still is better than when he made similar attempts at Urach. He is much better company; Otto notices this, too, and therefore it pleases me particularly. But his mind still refuses mental nourishment— except for the Frankfurter Zeitung and Figaro.

Weber enjoyed the new impressions and gratefully absorbed the gentle yet magnificent beauty; in good hours he could forget himself and his burden. This was not true of the sick youth, whom a senseless fate had doomed to futility. Otto was able to free himself from his own self only with an effort and for a short time; he had a lucid sense of hopelessness, and even in the face of all the new impressions apathy and stupor would soon descend on him again. When he went on an outing and stayed away a little longer than agreed, his companions had a premonition of his future and feared that he had ended his life. They would not have regretted this for his sake, but they thought of his poor parents.

The melancholy that thus emanated from the incurable young man after a time became a blight on Weber's outlook on life; could it be that he, too, was threatened by such hopelessness? Otto was sensitive and must not notice anything or it would have been his ruin. It was impossible to send him away by himself, so the situation had be be endured. The only thing that could be done was for Marianne to devote herslf completely to Otto and to keep him away from Weber as much as possible. Thus Weber was alone most of the time.

Then the beautiful, empty hotel was closed. They moved into furnished rooms, losing the billiard table and the newspapers. A long rainy period set in, and it was hardly possible to be outdoors. The lonely days now crept by monotonously and colorlessly under overcast skies. There was no pleasant café, no window shopping, no music, nothing to see, and nothing happened. They realized to what extent the life of a civilized person is fed by external stimuli. Weber spent much time lying on the sofa in a semi-conscious state. But he was neither dismayed nor impatient, for despite this tedium he was feeling better. The rebels seemed to be surrendering; harbingers of an improvement were bringing their greeting.

In March they went to Rome, and their protégé accompanied them, for the preparations for this trip had sustained him during all those months. Weber wanted to submerge his illness and his earthbound self in a sea of powerful impressions. In Rome he could transcend his current difficulties and identify with the eternal values. By looking he could palpably experience the greatness of the past with which he was familiar theoretically and expand his being into a vessel of history. Every old stone of the great city spoke to his historical imagination and stimulated him powerfully; this was better than any therapy. But as yet the presence of the other patient inhibited Weber's enthusiasm, which the young man could not share in spite of his interest.

Weber therefore felt Otto's presence as an unbearable pressure; all of Rome would fizzle out as a remedy if he was not liberated at last. On both sides there was a great deal at stake; Otto must not notice anything. Finally they accomplished the separation without upsetting the patient. He parted from them full of confidence and returned to his family, more fit for living for a time. A few years later, after various futile attempts to give his life some meaning, he broke from his prison by a supreme effort of the will and took his own life. Weber was able to transfigure his fate for his parents by means of the following lines:

Dear Uncle:

You know that we are profoundly moved by the end of this life. Each time in Ajaccio that Otto failed to return on time we feared that we would not see him again—*feared* this not for his sake but on account of our responsibility. I have always regarded it as an aberration of our everyday morality, which is ignorant of life, that, in contrast to the much freer and greater sensibility of antiquity, it wants to stamp earthly life as a commodity that a man must never give up, even

if its continuation is devoid of any spiritual *meaning*. He was a man
who, chained to an incurably diseased body, yet had developed—or perhaps developed in part *because* of it—a sensitivity of feeling, a clarity
about himself, and a deeply hidden, proud, and noble height of inner
deportment such as are found among very few healthy people. Only
those can know and judge this who have seen him at close range and
learned to love him as we have, and who at the same time know personally what illness is. His soul, which was locked within the prison
walls of his illness—an impediment everywhere—and yet was so strangely *free*, was as rich and delicate as the substance of his life was poor—
and, as he himself knew all too well, it became *increasingly* poorer as his
fate took its course.

Among my most painful memories is the fact that in those days we
had to stop living together; my fear increased every day that he, being
infinitely sensitive, might notice that my ability to tolerate company, as well as Marianne's strength, were coming to an end. In recent
days we happened to talk about whether we could advise you to let
him go to America with us or to send him to a university here. Perhaps
this would have prolonged his life somewhat . . . but I almost believe
that what has happened is better for *him and you*. For, his future being
what it was, he has done right to go to the unknown land now, ahead
of you, who otherwise would someday have had to leave him behind on
this earth helpless, lonely, and walking toward a dark fate.

Life is a truly heavy burden—and yet no more so than it was when
that Greek mother's prayer was answered with the death of her thriving sons as her only good fortune. To how many of your children has life
given the richest assignments! For this child you yourselves would hardly have begged for anything but that good fortune. He fulfilled what
was demanded of him: a rich inner life, a spiritual refinement of his self,
a strong-willed endurance without complaint. Fate gave him no *external*
assignments, and it deprived him of any opportunity to give some to
himself. It was not cowardly flight when he disposed of himself and gave
up a life that would no longer have been worthy of himself. We shall
never forget him and shall honor and love his memory as you will.

IV

When that problem had been solved, Weber felt impelled to leave Rome
again for a prolonged period in order to cover the agony of the last weeks
with other impressions. He and Marianne went to southern Italy—Naples

and environs, Sorrento, Pompeii, Capri, Paestum [Pesto]. Weber spent a number of days in complete quiet in Sorrento. From a rocky terrace with colorful flagstones which overlooked the sea he enjoyed the view of the blue gulf, the outlines of Ischia, and smoking Vesuvius with its trail of little white houses.

As he surrendered to this radiant splendor, his equilibrium was restored. "For Max nothing is more therapeutic than to have as much enjoyment and to see as many beautiful things as possible. I often think that if we had taken such a trip two years ago and he had gone on leave then, he would have got well more quickly. The doctors failed us there; no one advised us to do so at that time." When he was better, he became absorbed in Pompeii and Paestum, and on a trip to Salerno through the vernal bloom of the [Roman] Campagna, he noticed that the ancient Roman distribution of land had been preserved. "We were in Pompeii for two days. Considering his condition, Max accomplished marvelous things there. Twice a day he spent two and a half hours looking, and he was always very interested and enjoyed himself very much."

In Naples they stayed far out near the Posilipo,[17] directly above the sea. The resplendent scenery, the pure outlines, the clear blue water—all this was for him a fountain of self-forgetfulness. And the more exotic the impressions and the fewer memories they stirred of home, the better it was. "In Max not even the faintest longing for his earlier existence or his homeland is stirring—a sign of *how much* he still is in need of rest. Yet he is strong enough to be able to enjoy the daily impressions." Then they returned to Rome in order to come to terms with the relics of superimposed centuries. The ruins were now flooded by a profusion of summery light which bathed and transfigured every dome and every façade, and even at night there still was blue sky behind the shining stars. The moderate heat of early summer was wonderful. They spent much time lying on the green grass of the Villa Borghese and were delighted when the young clerics divested themselves of their loose cassocks and played ball like other worldlings. Nature and all inanimate things did them good. Only their fellowmen frequently disturbed their precious night's rest: "Fighting for quiet and sleep really is sometimes harder than struggling for a *Weltanschauung;* what couldn't one do if one got seven hours of undisturbed sleep!"

In midsummer they escaped to Switzerland, to Grindelwand, in order to

---

[17]A promontory, southwest of Naples, which is pierced by a grotto.—Ed.

try the mountain air as well. At first it had a bad effect on Weber. The demons that had been kept under control in the south rattled their chains: sleeplessness, excitement, unrest, and other torments broke loose. The ground that had barely been gained became shaky all over again, and this relapse greatly depressed the patient. When his wife returned to him after an absence of a few weeks, she found him in a condition similar to that of the previous year. Could nothing at all be depended upon? Could every idiotic accidental occurrence make everything uncertain again? However, when Weber's brother visited him, he had a more favorable impression.

> I wonder whether Alfred's impression of Max's progress is correct. I'd certainly like to believe it is, but only today he again told me he was still so tired, so tired, and that it did *not* help him if we suggested that he was able to work; he simply felt that the ability was not there. He is still very excitable and can suddenly be quite violent and subjective; however, as soon as one calmly develops one's own point of view, he regains his objectivity.

Finally his unstable system grew accustomed to the mountain climate; when he was at Zermatt looking at the giant ice-covered mountains, Weber was able to believe in an improvement again. He now managed to do a little reading from time to time.

In the fall husband and wife returned to Rome for the third time, this time for the whole winter. A pleasant Italian family provided them with an undisturbed retreat. They lived in complete solitude. When Helene visited her children, she found her son considerably improved. He was accessible to her again, and he was happy to have in the receptive woman an additional mirror of all great things.

In recent years his mother had always been obliged to restrain herself; now it gave him pleasure to show and explain everything to her. Helene was happy; she was seeing Rome for the first time, and although at the age of fifty-seven her outward appearance was that of an old woman, her senses and her heart were young. She was adaptable, capable of shaking off everything that was behind her and surrendering completely to the great new experiences. Everything spoke to her—the self-sufficient perfection of the classical works of art as much as the warm emotional quality of early Christian shrines, the pagan Pantheon as much as the catacombs and the dome of St. Peter's. At the Forum she had to be watched to make sure that she did not put too many pieces of marble into her knitting bag as *Mitbringsel* [souvenir presents]—or, at least, that her "big boy" did not notice it, for it was prohibited, and Weber did not like to break the law. Those weeks in Rome were among the most beautiful she ever spent with her children, and for them her unselfish love was the dearest part of their homeland. After her departure Marianne wrote to her:

> Max sends you his cordial regards, but he was angry about your remark that this time you felt part of us, while at other times you had felt more like an "intruder." He said that was "utter nonsense"; as it is, he is sad that it is so hard for him to show you how much he loves you, and this sadness is heightened when you have such feelings. *So sagt der Patriarch* [So says the Patriarch].[18] So then, dearest Mother, I do know that you had those sad feelings on previous occasions, but that was probably due to Max's hopeless condition and your awareness of your inability to help us, wasn't it? And as for Max's reserve, that was only his instinctive way of protecting himself from any excitement.

Some time after Helene's arrival Weber began to read a real book again—a history of art. He got one volume after another from the library of the artists' association. Helene and Marianne secretly nudged each other: "Look, he's reading!" Toward Weber they acted as though they did not notice it. Only after some time did they dare to make a reference to this progress. Weber said, "Who knows how long I can keep it up?" and "Anything but literature in my own field." But his receptivity continued, and this really marked the beginning of an improvement after three and a half years of illness. Until then he had been convinced that he would never again be able to fill his position; now it seemed to him on good days as though a sufficiently early recovery was not completely out of the question. In any case, to avoid acting prematurely he wanted to announce one lecture course and one seminar for the summer semester. Marianne and Helen became more hopeful.

> Up to now Max's condition has been uniformly good. He has been reading a great deal; one fat tome after another has appeared—now various historical things—and he always finishes them with astonishing speed. If I did not ask him to go out, he would probably not do anything but read; he enjoys reading like a man dying of thirst. . . . All this time

---

[18]"*Sagt der Patriarch*" is the Friar's recurrent phrase in Lessing's drama *Nathan the Wise*, Act I, Scene 5.—Ed.

I have been warmed by a great feeling of gratitude which, to be sure, is still frequently interrupted by timorousness and anxiety; at night my heart pounds between fear and hope. Sometimes hope really runs wild, so that I have to keep struggling to keep resignation in readiness for the immediate future. Too, my spirit must still learn to live without the uniformly heavy pressure. But if Max gradually regains his ability to work, I will sing every day *Mir ist das Los aufs Lieblichste gefallen* [The lines are fallen unto me in pleasant places. (Ps. 16)]. Even when I shall look back to past sorrow, only gratitude will remain.

And now another unexpected thing has happened: A few days ago Max requested Rathgen by letter to announce for him, for the time being, two hours of agrarian policy and a seminar for the summer (1902). To avoid burdening his conscience with an imprudent act and to be able to offer advice when his successor is chosen, he wants to delay his departure until March. Another request for leave appears quite impossible to him. When he asked me "What did *you* have in mind?" I replied "Nothing, because I am not in *your* shoes, although I have recently regained the hope that at some time you will again be able to work." Then we wrote two long letters to R[athgen] and Sch[ellhass]. Thus the decision has been postponed once more. Because it is so very hard to keep my hopes caged up and we still have the step ahead of us, I am sometimes inclined to regret this. But I shall tell myself every day that it is foolish for me to set my heart on the professorship and that if only Max is better, everything else should not matter to me.

His improved condition lasted. He even dared to talk, and occasionally he was able to break through his seclusion and carry on an intellectual conversation with others. He saw Professor Schellhass, the friend of his youth, at the Historical Institute and had discussions with the young historian Haller.[19]

Max is fine! Every day I am full of quiet gratitude. Yesterday he talked with Dr. Haller for almost three hours; he went to the Historical Institute at half past two and did not come back until half past six. He now reads in Conrad's yearbooks,[20] too, as well as Simmel's *Philoso-*

[19]Johannes Haller (1865–1947) was at the Prussian Historical Institute in Rome in 1901 and 1902 before becoming a professor of history at Marburg (1902), Giessen (1904), and Tübingen (1913).—Ed.
[20]Johannes Conrad, 1839–1915, professor of economics at Jena and Halle, edited the *Jahrbücher für Nationalökonomie* from 1872 on.—Ed.

phie des Geldes[21] [Philosophy of Money]. When opportunity offers I may tell him that considering the present state of his health a request for another leave of absence would not seem impudent to me. At present, to be sure, I do not expect to succeed with him; but anyway, one can never tell how his inner attitude toward this question may change if his improvement continues. I do not share your and Sch.'s concerns that Max's lack of influence as a *Privatdozent* may be a source of suffering to him in the future. I believe he has thought over all the consequences of his dismissal from his office and has come to terms with them. In this he is greatly aided by his disposition. As far as his colleagues are concerned, he feels impelled to recognize and tolerate their individuality to the greatest extent. In matters involving his colleagues he is marvelously objective. I always *admire* him in this respect and also for his slight need for self-assertion.

Recovery seemed imminent, and it seemed to be only a matter of time, for—so Marianne secretly thought—he belonged back on the rostrum and among a circle of students. It would be too senseless if such a talent for educating and guiding youth by means of the living word and the other direct emanations of his personality were to be wasted. Yes, she still had reason to hope everything would turn out well, for even the beginning of the new year brought signs of an improvement. However, progress was slow and Marianne constantly worried secretly about whether or not he would reach his goal in time.

"Three days ago the very intelligent Dr. H[aller] visited him. Max talked about the most difficult things for two hours. He drew freely from a wealth of knowledge and spoke as graphically and incisively as ever. That night, to be sure, there were unrest and a sedative [*Trional*]." He now went to the Historical Institute quite frequently to chat with Schellhass and Haller; his need for "life" was increasing. However, any obligation made him as miserable as it had before. A student's essay that required comprehensive rewriting again convinced him that for the time being any duty gave him a feeling of impotence and burdened him inordinately. "We are now living with all sorts of books which one never gets a chance to read otherwise. For example, Max is absorbing a marvelous mixture, all sorts of things about history, the organization and economy of convents, then Aristophanes, Rous-

---

[21]Georg Simmel, 1858–1918, philosopher, sociologist, and psychologist, professor at Berlin and Strasbourg. His *Philosophie des Geldes* appeared in 1900.—Ed.

seau's *Emile*, Voltaire, Montesquieu, Taine's collected works, and English writers."

The high point of this secluded winter in Rome was a visit from Friedrich Naumann, who brought with him present-day German life and a wave of warmth and freshness.

> Now guess what unexpected enjoyment we are having! The day before yesterday there appeared in our quiet hermitage—I almost embraced him in my joyful surprise—*Naumann* in all his splendor! He came from Palermo, is staying only a few days, and we spend a lot of time together. Two days ago, in the afternoon, we were on Monte Pincio[22] with him; yesterday morning we made a three-hour round trip. Max talked like a waterfall, but then he was exhausted at noontime, so I went to the Appian Way with Naumann by myself. We showed him everything, but both of us had the impression that the past speaks to him far less than it does to us. He now feels too "modern," too social, and too economic. Perhaps it was only that he lacked the inward and outward composure. Of course, he cannot be expected to have Max's historical imagination. The stone monuments of the past are to him at first merely empty, broken snail shells; what he needs more are the immediate enchantment of the landscape and the living impressions of the people. For him a prolonged sojourn in Rome would have been far less effective than it has been for Max. Thus we particularly enjoyed the present and his personality against the historical background. What a lovable human being he is! His inner calm and objectivity are comforting, his natural amiability, his personal concern coupled with humor are enchanting, and the indulgence and broadmindedness with which he views people put one to shame. Imagine, he spent all night traveling to Genoa so he would be there on Sunday, in time to send his wife the telegram he had promised her!

However, after those beautiful days of high spirits, the hostile hand again pushed the struggling man back into a state of illness: "Last week our souls once again had to crawl in the dust. Max had several very bad nights in a row, which left him quite kaput and depressed, and I was secretly beside myself. I suppose this was the payment for Naumann's visit. This week he recovered again. I am sure we shall have to experience such disturbances fre-

---

[22]The Pincian Hill, the northernmost hill of Rome on which the Villa Borghese is located.— Ed.

quently, but I cannot say that frequent experience habituates one to them."

V

At Eastertime of 1902 Weber left Rome and started for home, for now his life in Heidelberg was to start anew after an absence of almost two years and an illness of four years. Weber was not recovered—he felt incapable of giving the course he had announced—but he was substantially improved, had accommodated himself to his condition, and was restored to an intellectual existence. Above all, he owed to the sun and to the magnificence of the Eternal City hours impregnated with the past, which had for almost a year made his meager present worth living for. He parted from the south as from a second homeland, and when the long winter weighed upon the lands beyond the Alps, he was often gripped by an irrepressible longing for it. First he spent some time in Florence, and from there he requested for the second time to be relieved of his duties:

> Max has now really asked to be dismissed from his full professorship and to be classified as a titular professor. This also means that the ministry does not have to pension him off. Surely this is the right way; I myself could not have wanted him to apply for another leave of absence and thus put pressure on himself. But I do not find that doing the right thing leaves a pleasant taste. When he dictated his application for dismissal to me, a rather unphilosophical and unchristian rage came over me once more; there were tears, which made Max rather wild. I was ashamed, of course, but not very much. In this matter I am not at all "heroic."

Weber had only passed through the lower circles of hell. His ability to write his mother a rather long birthday letter again, at a time when she was greatly excited about the engagement of her youngest son, struck him and her as a remarkable achievement: "Everything is going quite well. I have managed to write an eight-page letter to Mama, though with some effort!" This letter reads as follows:

Florence, April 14, 1902

It has been a few years, I think, since I wrote you myself on the occasion of your birthday, and this time, too, my back will see to it that

I do not say too much. But in any case, with everything here being in full bloom, my condition is so different from what it was the last two times the trees turned green that I can again present myself as a well-wisher after a fashion. I hope that you have somewhat gotten over the exciting episodes of recent weeks and that at the beginning of a new year in your life you are facing the future more confidently than you were initially able to do. It is only natural that the internal difficulties attendant upon the meeting of two people at entirely different stages of development should continue to loom large. And since it is Arthur in particular who is facing the task of leaping years ahead, a prolonged period of waiting is in store for you, a time that will be inwardly hard. On top of everything else that is inflicted upon mothers, it is also their fate that as soon as the children's drive for independence awakens and while it still is not sure of itself, it is at first directed purely negatively against the parents and specifically against the mother. This is how it was with all of us, and I imagine that it will be similar with Arthur now. And under the influence of this development your new daughter-in-law, too, may not be as open-minded as she will want to be in the long run, according to what you wrote me about her personality.

For the time being you need not make any financial arrangements for us; we can certainly keep above water until fall of next year. By that time an opportunity to make some money may have offered itself to me, provided that I continue to improve. How? I don't really know yet, but at the moment I am not worrying about it. Perhaps by writing articles, etc. Your remark about D[elbrück] only proves that his periodical [Preussische Jahrbücher] is not doing well; something like that is a possibility for later, perhaps together with Alfred. But now my working strength is still much too unsteady and the political situation is not alluring. We simply have to wait and see, and I still have too much to make up to undertake something political now even if it could be done. I have given up my position except for the direction of the seminar. If I had waited any longer, people would have had to assume that I would be able to give major courses in the winter. That can surely not be done, because loud talking is what I cannot do. Whether they will now make me an honorary professor or something similar is really quite unimportant.

In about three weeks I shall go to Bologna, then to Milan and Lugano. I shall pass up Siena, etc., because it would be a detour involving special expenses and I would like to save enough to buy a little work of art for Marianne. After all, we do not know when we shall come here again. Only here in Florence does one realize what a hideous hick town [*grundhässliches Nest*] Rome really is—and yet, I could live the rest of my life there, whereas that would hardly be possible here. A historical imagination is the main thing; those who do not have one should not go there. In your case we have Gervinus and the old Heidelberg atmosphere to thank for this. But now my back, which has stood the strain better than it has in a very long time, definitely refuses to go on. So I am looking forward to seeing you again in the new year of your life which will, I hope, be increasingly beautiful and rich.

On his own thirty-eighth birthday Weber returned home—an eagle with broken wings. His colleagues and friends found him greatly improved and believed that he would be his old self after a while. The warm atmosphere of home enveloped him.

Der Heini von Steier ist wieder im Land! [Heini of Steier is in the country again.][23] He arrived on Sunday evening, coming from Freiburg where he had presented himself to the Baumgartens, the Rickerts, and Papa Baist. Then we moved into our place during a downpour—on foot, because no cab was to be had. Everything had just been finished, decorated, and lighted, and I noticed that he was quite happy with all the comfort and cleanliness of his own home. He finds the apartment very nice, "plays" with his things, and makes himself comfortable at his desk. The friends come and go and rejoice at his vigor.

A short time afterward Marianne reported: "Dietrich Schäfer[24] was just here to tell me that the government wants to induce Max to withdraw his application for dismissal! They wish to keep him in any case." Thus the wavering between resignation and hope started all over again. Weber was pressured so much that, reluctant and yet grateful, he agreed to another temporary arrangement. He was to conduct a seminar and participate in the examination of doctoral candidates. He lived a secluded life, but his old friends—particularly Troeltsch, Hensel, Jellinek, and Neumann—came to see him, and his wife always had to make certain that the lively conversations did not go on for too long.

---

[23]This line is the recurrent refrain of a seven-stanza poem (and song) entitled *Dörpertanzreigen* [Country Dance] and included in Joseph Viktor von Scheffel's extended verse romance *Frau Aventiure* [Dame Adventure] (1863), which evokes the world of the legendary Heinrich von Ofterdingen, here referred to, and other Minnesingers.—Ed.

[24] 1845–1929, historian, professor at Jena, Breslau, Tübingen, Heidelberg, and Berlin.—Ed.

On Sunday afternoons he used to meet—in summer at the Scheffelhaus [inn], in winter at the Stiftsmühle[25] with a rather large and steadily growing group and imperceptibly became its focus again. These gatherings on "neutral" ground were for years the only form of social activity in which he participated. When he was able to live exactly as he wished and had a good day, the level he had reached was maintained. However, any compulsion, pressure or obligation involving a deadline brought the danger of a relapse— as though his body, which had until the outbreak of the illness blindly obeyed his demanding intellect, refused once and for all to bow to any necessity.

* * *

Weber's youngest sister, Lili, who had grown up to be a beautiful and intelligent girl, planned to get married in July of that year. She was engaged to an architect named Hermann Schäfer, a son of the brilliant neo-Gothic architect Karl Schäfer,[26] who was creating considerable excitement at that time with his plan to rebuild the Otto-Heinrichsbau of the Heidelberg Castle[27] and possibly even the whole castle. Helene had her heart set on Weber's participation at the wedding celebration. She secretly hoped that he would consecrate it with one of his sentimental after-dinner speeches and thereby once more impress her own spirit upon the soul of the young woman [Lili] for which she was fighting. But what had come to Weber effortlessly on similar occasions now meant an intolerable imposition:

> Yesterday I cautiously inquired whether he could not participate in the dinner for a half-hour after all; he became very excited and said "Under no circumstances!" The idea of proposing a toast in front of people who were still strangers to him would cost him three nights' rest; he said he did not understand how we could hope for such a thing. He would only go to the church and perhaps stay for half an hour to greet people at the Polterabend [party on the eve of the wedding], but that was definitely all.

---

[25] A hotel and restaurant on the Neckar near the Benedictine abbey Stift Neuburg.—Ed.
[26] 1844–1908, professor at Berlin and Karlsruhe.—Ed.
[27] Erected in 1556 by Count Palatine Otto Heinrich or Ottheinrich on the east side of the courtyard; generally considered to be the finest example of Renaissance architecture in Germany.—Ed.

He would have much preferred staying home to appearing before the sympathetic and questioning eyes of a large gathering. But his mother was to
be certain of his good intentions. For Helene this wedding was another
turning point in her life: She was losing her delicate youngest daughter who
was moving away to a strange family even before she confided fully in her
mother, and she herself was leaving the beautiful big house which was now
to be exchanged for a smaller one. Weber felt so bad in Berlin that he had
to stay away from the celebration, and he felt very much like an invalid.
The aftereffects of those sad days lasted for some time. But a few months
later Marianne reported:

> Max has been in pretty fair condition until now; he works about four
> hours daily. As the first little vernal sign of his returning ability to
> work he wrote a book review at Heinrich Braun's[28] suggestion and
> in just a few days (Lotmar's *Arbeitsvertrag* [Work Contract]). Because of
> its legal character it was really not in his line at all, and he undertook
> to review it only as a favor. But now, I suppose, it secretly gives him
> pleasure that he has accomplished his first literary sign of life in over
> four and a half years, even though with distaste. He is also scribbling
> various things on large sheets of scrap paper; he won't tell me what
> it is going to be—probably a methodological treatise on Knies which
> he had to agree to write, *nolens volens*, for a Festschrift. (October 10,
> 1902)

VI

The new phase of Weber's productivity began. Its nature was entirely different from that of the earlier phase. Its first important work was his essay
about *Roscher und Knies und die logischen Probleme der historischen Nationalökonomie* [Roscher and Knies and the Logical Problems of Historical Political
Economy]. The impulse for this came in part from the outside. The Heidelberg *Philosophische Fakultät* planned to issue a jubilee volume on the occasion
of an anniversary of the university, and Weber was urged to contribute
to it. Otherwise he surely would not have tackled this difficult field first
with his reawakening but very uneven working capacity. Of course, he had
been thinking about these problems for some time. He may have received

---

[28]1854–1927, social reformer, editor of *Neue Zeit, Archiv für soziale Gesetzgebung und Statistik,*
and other publications. The full title of Philipp Lotmar's book is *Der Arbeitsvertrag nach dem
Privatrecht des deutschen Reiches* (1902–08).—Ed.

inspiration from Heinrich Rickert's work about the limits of concept formation in the natural sciences, the second volume of which had appeared
around that time.[29] When he had read it in Florence half a year previously,
he wrote about it to his wife: "I have finished Rickert. He is *very* good;
in large part I find in him the thoughts that I have had myself, though
not in logically finished form. I have reservations about his terminology."

Unfortunately this difficult investigation of the modes of thought of
his discipline and of history expanded as he worked on it, and yet it had
to be ready by a certain date. This soon turned it into a burden and a torment, for his working strength was still unsteady, and only on good days
did his brain stand the great strain in the service of logical problems:

> Our sky has become clouded again. For almost two weeks Max has been
> quite tired; he sleeps badly and has had to interrupt his work, al-
> though he has all ideas ready in his head. He thinks that for the time
> being his energy always suffices only for four weeks; then he really ought
> to go away for four weeks to gather fresh strength for the next four
> weeks in complete inactivity and with a change of scene. It is enough
> to make one despair each time; one always thinks that one should
> finally have a right to a certain constancy in his capacity to work, or
> that one should be able to force it down from heaven. But time and
> time again the watchword is patience.

Now everything again turned on the question of whether a few working
hours could be wrested from a day. He was so modest; if things worked out,
then even a gloomy day had meaning. On a card written in Italian he said:
*La pioggia mi fa molto bene—ho dormito, non bene, neanche molto, ma assai, e pos-
so lavorare, non molto, ma un poco. Dunque sta bene* . . . [The rain is doing me
good; I have slept—not well or much, but deeply—and I can work—not
much, but a little. So things are going well . . .] But three days later he
wrote: "This accursed examination has cost me another bad night. And
there will be three other exams before Christmas! Shall I ever be able to
work? The weather is fine now, warm as on the Riviera; too bad that I cannot go out. Yesterday Troeltsch, Landsberg, His,[30] and Prof. Vossler with

---

[29]The two volumes of *Die Grenzen der naturwissenschaftlichen Begriffsbildung* appeared in 1896 and
1902, respectively.—Ed.
[30]Otto Landsberg, 1869–1957, politician and government official; Wilhelm His, 1863–1934,
professor of medicine at Basel, Göttingen, and Berlin.—Ed.

his charming wife were at the Scheffelhaus, but the conversation did not do me any good."

Weber was unable to keep his promise. This was another drain on his spirits, and combined with the dark winter days it produced a new low. Everything was torture again. He yearned to escape to the south where no *Muss* [compulsion] would reach him, where he would compare himself with no one, not even with his own earlier strength, and where light and warmth made even dull days bearable.

Max's state of health fluctuates from one day to the next; his mood and general condition are a great deal worse than they have been in a *long* time. In the morning he always works one to two hours, but without enjoying it, and then he has to doze on the sofa in the afternoon. Every day he complains that he was not able to get away five weeks ago, when this period began, and thus got into this situation. I am now counting the days until his departure and only hope that he will not go even further downhill before that.

In the meantime he has again expressed himself about what torments him most. It is always the same thing: the psychological pressure of the "unworthy situation" in which he draws a salary and will not be able to accomplish anything in the foreseeable future, combined with the feeling that to all of us—you, I, and everyone—only a person with a *vocation* [*Berufs*mensch] counts fully. In addition to this he remembered all sorts of unpleasant things from previous years. He said that when all of us, including the doctors, always thought that he ought to overcome his illness by an act of will, that was the most horrible burden on his sense of honor. What else is there to tell? Nothing really, dearest Mama. . . . At the Scheffelhaus I meet our acquaintances, but if Max isn't there, it hardly does me any good, for then the tremendous difference between their lives and Max's—the life that he has led for almost five years and is now leading again—strikes me with redoubled clarity. And then the sympathetic questions of the people. I have asked them to stop.

Thus the sun of the year which had had such a promising beginning vanished in a mass of black clouds. Weber escaped to the south. In Nervi, on a rocky terrace above the roaring sea where he spent his days in the mild air even when the skies were cloudy, his agony faded:

My condition is quite tolerable, although my ability to work is only slightly greater than it was in Heidelberg; for *that* I simply left too late. Yet, being here by the sea, always in the open air, is *living*, which really cannot be said of the preceding weeks. Now I shall do nothing for a while. I hope I shall bring home at least the outline of the rest of this *verfl*— [damned] study.

Sometimes he blamed this difficult treatise, whose completion was not in sight, for what was to come—the unavoidable resignation from his position. "If, instead of working on this study, I had calmly prepared my lectures, I would probably have been able to give them in the summer."

At the beginning of March he again escaped to Rome, but this time the city seemed to deny him its curative and uplifting effect. Weber already knew everything there and found nothing new that might have provided an effective distraction; the impact of the impressions was blunted. And he had lost a hope. If only he could go to another world—Constantinople, maybe. But he did not have the means for that. Helene, who could not make enough loving suggestions, wanted to help: since even Rome was still uncomfortable in March, they should go to Africa, to the Biskra oasis;[31] there he *must* find sun!

But Weber probably felt that he could not escape from himself at that point; and now that he no longer *had* to work there was no psychological pressure. One thing was certain: "playing the professor" had to stop. Even Marianne was convinced of that. "So now we are at the point where fate wanted to take us. I hope and believe that this final decision will after a while bring relief to both of us and more uniform strength to Max. However, at present the thousand disappointments of these years, particularly the last few months, are still too vivid in my mind for me to believe in a new future."

To be sure, Marianne's secret desires still made her doubt the necessity of this decision from time to time:

At the Historians' Congress Max listened to only a few papers and did not take part in the discussion. But in recent days various people from out of town have come to visit him, and he has carried on the most intensive conversations with a dialectic adroitness that kept arousing my astonishment. If one listens to him on such occasions, one feels like clutching one's head and asking oneself, "Can it be that this man can-

---

[31]An oasis commune in northeastern Algeria, south of the city of Constantine.—Ed.

not even give a small lecture course?" On our first morning here we had an early visitor: Ministerialrat Böhm[32] from Karlsruhe, who once more asked Max most politely yet most urgently not to take that step. But when Max remained firm, they agreed that his resignation would be effective in October, that he would receive the title of *Honorarprofessor* [adjunct professor] as well as a *Lehrauftrag* [adjunct appointment] to give smaller lectures. Max said that the title as well as the *Lehrauftrag* would mean something to him only if it carried faculty status and a vote at faculty meetings; but this proposal must come *only* from the faculty, not from the government. Thereupon Böhm inserted a passage in his proposal to the faculty which could be interpreted by anyone who so chose to mean that the faculty ought to offer Max membership and voting privileges. However, the dean who circulated the document did *not* understand this passage, whether intentionally or unintentionally. Thus the solution desired by Max was circumvented, though the proper procedure was followed. He got quite excited about it and now wanted to refuse the title and the *Lehrauftrag* too.

He did not do so, but a bitter aftertaste remained with him for a long time, for he felt cut off from his past and the professorial community to a greater extent than he had desired.

Outwardly we are calm and cheerful; I am not quite sure how it looks inside Max, and I would rather not ask him, for we now discuss our affairs as little as possible. It seems to me that by comparison with the sufferings of the last five years the outward resignation is hardly of major importance; after all, it is only the last link in a long chain of resignations. But I believe that simultaneously with the *fait accompli* he began to desire more strongly than ever not to lose all chances to resume his profession again, and he has a slight hope that at some time in the future he will be able to start again where he left off. He is asking himself and me whether he should now limit himself to purely literary projects or work on lecture notes. I am in favor of the latter, mainly because it greatly pains me that otherwise nothing will be preserved of the tremendous labors of past years.

* * *

[32]Franz Böhm, 1861–1915, jurist, Minister of Culture and Education in Karlsruhe from 1911 on.—Ed.

In the prime of life Weber found himself expelled from his kingdom. His career seemed to be behind him; he was at low ebb. But inwardly he towered over his fate. He did not take things seriously: "I simply do not regard my resignation as something tragic, because I have been convinced of its necessity for years and was only oppressed by the fact that no doctor was candid enough to convince Marianne of it as well. My working strength has not reappeared as yet, but otherwise I am passably well." He was angry and sad only when urgent intellectual work was taken out of his hands—something that happened frequently. Otherwise, he spoke words of consolation rather than lamentation—with submission ("What *I* don't do, others will"), or with hope ("Some day I shall find a hole from which I shall zoom upward again").

When his resignation became known, a Berlin physician, a complete stranger, wrote him as follows:

Most Honored Herr Professor:

In today's paper I read that the state of your health has obliged you to give up your teaching activity. This news fills me with sincere regret, for I am proud to acknowledge that I am part of what surely is a large group—those who have had the privilege of sitting at your feet and listening to your words with rapt attention. About ten years ago you gave two series of lectures to the graduating class of the Friedrichswerder Gymnasium here; one was about the history of German law, the other about German constitutional life. I was among these pupils, and I may say that there were as many admirers of the lecturer as there were listeners to his lectures. You not only pleased us by using the unaccustomed form of address *Meine Herren* [Gentlemen], but you also astonished and captivated us by the wealth of knowledge you offered and by an eloquence we had not encountered before. And when we soon thereafter learned of your appointment to the University of Freiburg, we were extremely gratified at this promotion of our teacher and predicted a brilliant career for him. Therefore my former fellow pupils will surely regret it as much as I do when they learn that you have given up your academic office so early in life, and the reason for it. And if I express the wish, in my name and on behalf of my fellow pupils, that the self-imposed leisure may restore your health, I beg you to regard it as a token of my everlasting gratitude for hours that not only were instructive but also lifted us out of the monotony of a schoolboy's existence.

9

THE NEW PHASE _____

I

The benefits of Weber's dismissal from his office were not immediately felt. Being without employment, after years of waiting and secret hoping, now assumed major importance, and his impulse to resume his earlier activity on an informal basis had by now disappeared: "I have the impression that the resumption of his teaching activity *here* holds no attraction for Max— because he was not retained on the faculty and was not given the right to examine doctoral candidates." In addition there was the burden of his incidental methodological study *(Roscher und Knies)*. For the first time it took Weber away from a concrete presentation of material and into extensive logical problems, and it forced him to examine critically already existing and partly obsolete webs of thought. This was not really stimulating, for it did not give rise to any new insights into reality.

For the time being Weber asked nothing of life but an ability to do quiet research. When he was able to get some of the things that had accumulated in his brain, even during the bad years, down on paper, his days were full of meaning. If, however, his mind refused to do his bidding, life under the frequently cloudy northern sky became a burden. During this period, nervous discomfort, annoyance at his surroundings, and a yearning for warmth and light still very frequently crystallized into an urgent desire to leave Germany forever.

> In recent weeks he got annoyed at everything and everyone, even you—a sign that he was again feeling very uncomfortable. Regarding you, I always contradicted him most vigorously, and I called his notion that you no longer had any desire to visit us pathological. His annoyance at X is really nothing serious, although one would think so if one hears Max scolding; fortunately the Xes did not notice anything. It is very convenient that he is almost never angry with me but releases on me all his rage at others. It does him good while it does not hurt me, and this way it does not hurt the others, either.

But despite such occasional violent ill-humor, in moments of quiet introspection he never complained about his destiny, nor did he ever really despair of himself. Presumably he always had the feeling that his basic nature, which harbored the seeds of his creativeness, was unchanged and untouched, that the illness had not penetrated the protective cover. In this he was aided by the security of his personal existence and the profound solidarity of his life's companion, to whom he was always sound and intact, who felt his charisma even during the most difficult period. When her father died around that time, he wrote: "In reviewing the hard life of your father we must always remember how well off we are in our rich life, even if I should be worse than I am now."

In the fall, when his colleagues met at a convention of the *Verein für Sozialpolitik* in Hamburg, Weber felt strong enough to participate again. To be sure, the man who had been a leading light there so early in life was now only a member of the audience. But he spoke with his old acquaintances and enjoyed the substantial gathering so much that afterward he went to Helgoland with a few friends (Sombart, Brentano) and continued their stimulating exchange there—an intellectual excess for which he paid with fresh attacks of insomnia. A simple fisherman who ferried the scholars over the water on a number of occasions did not understand anything of their conversations but sensed something was going on and expressed his admiration and appreciation to them.

Marianne had a much harder time adapting herself to the change than Weber did. When she saw him as a quiet man in a group where his powerful eloquence had once made him one of the masters, she was capable of experiencing excruciating pain:

> But now the longing still burns in me that my star, too, may shine once more, bringing joy to us and benefit to others. Oh my God, how hard it is to watch others working and creating while he is out of action! I wonder whether he does not feel the same way. I don't know, but I am inclined to think that the recent contact with his old group may have brought some of this home to him. Perhaps it is also his illness and his instinct of self-preservation that keep him from these thoughts, which sometimes rage through me.

How topsy-turvy things were! The wife now had to speak in public from time to time, and it was very hard for her. Meanwhile her husband was not permitted to pour out his wealth!

> The other day I attended my first National Socialist [*nationalsoziale*] meeting; educational problems were on the agenda, and willy-nilly I had to present the views of our movement—for the first time before a male audience. Afterward it seemed to me like an irony of fate that I, a wretched little woman, was sitting in a political assembly until 1 A.M., while our "big boy" had had to go to bed at 10 P.M.

When they celebrated their tenth wedding anniversary in the autumn of that year, the couple summed up their personal existence in the following lines:

> *Weber.* Let us hope now that the next ten years will bring as much inner wealth into our lives as the past decade has in unending profusion. Today we are still as new to each other as we were then, except that one of us has found the way to the soul of the other with so much more assurance. Today I think back with gratitude on those days that were complicated, tense, and not without inner danger, and I am thankful that fate has taken me where it did. Compared to this all other things, annoyances and impediments appear so unspeakably small and unimportant . . . (September 19, 1903)

> *Marianne.* We look back on ten years full of love, shared growth, and a harsh human fate. Surely our life together would not have been as deep and rich if we had not been so exclusively dependent upon each other in the last five years. It often seemed to me as though fate had

cast us on an isolated island where all other voices from the world of the living were drowned out by the incessant surf. For what were friends and even our dearest ones able to be to us! We had to bear it and withstand it alone. I believe we would otherwise hardly have been welded together so indissolubly, something that surely is true of few other couples. And this was one of the wishes of my life, my *greatest* wish. Of course, I would never have thought or deemed it necessary that I would have to pay for its fulfillment with your illness. But our love gave us the strength to include even this fate in our will; it did not make us small and wretched, and I hope we shall be able to go on bearing it, hoping and waiting and loving each other.

II

Weber's mind laboriously maintained its dominion over its rebellious vassals. For the time being he was able to work only a few weeks at a time, and then he escaped the dreariness of the dead period by making shorter trips. In 1903 he took no fewer than six of them. At the beginning of the year he was on the Riviera, in March and April in Italy; in June he went to Scheveningen, in August to Ostende, in September to Hamburg and Helgoland, in October to Holland again. New places always brought him the liberation and distraction that familiar places denied him. While staying in Holland and Belgium during the summer Weber was probably less exhausted than usual. He was not only open to new impressions but also felt impelled to preserve in outline form what he had seen and experienced. Almost all the things that he absorbed in this way left traces in his works. The roaring, storm-lashed or sun-drenched sea, or the dreamy mother-of-pearl gleam of The Hague with its imposing works of art immersed his soul in the eternity of beauty. But he was equally fascinated by the changeable behavior of people. Staying at the socialist People's Hotel at Ostende brought him in close touch with types of people he usually did not encounter—workmen, craftsmen, and merchants. He observed them without any academic arrogance; he effortlessly gained contact with them, won their confidence, and learned many things that interested him. From the *Wasserkante* [northern seaboard of Germany] he wrote almost daily, and he explained this need as follows:

I am writing so much for two reasons: First, because I know that you still feel a bit strange when I go away. Later, when you're used to it and you give your hubby the "raspberry" as he leaves [*hinter Deinem "Ol-len" die Zunge herbläkst*], there will be a little less of that. Second, be-cause a bookworm turned pedant has forgotten how to enjoy things in-tuitively and can lay hold of impressions only discursively, so that he can absorb whatever enjoyment of art and nature his ossified condition has left him only by somehow expressing it in words. How I envy those who are better off in this respect—expecially because, with the excep-tion of a very few people, *any company* spoils my pleasure; therefore, when I don't have my *Frauchen* [little woman] with me I am reduced to monologues such as are commonly spoken by characters in Chinese and Indian plays to make it clear to themselves and to the audience what is really going on.

Some excerpts from his letters will show Weber's experiences and atti-tudes around that time:

Scheveningen, June 6, 1903

I slept quite well and am in quite passable condition, having inside me tea with *worst, kaas,* 1 *water-broodge,* 1 *eier-brodge,* 1 *soete brodge und honig-kock*[1] [sausage, cheese, 1 water roll (*sic*), 1 egg roll, 1 sweet roll, and honey cake]. If one goes to the seashore restaurants, life here is about one and two-thirds times as expensive as in Borkum,[2] a guilder goes as far here as a mark does there. But last night I started going to The Hague for 10 Cts. [Dutch cents] where I have discovered an ex-cellent vegetarian restaurant, of the kind established in all cities by the local vegetarian association: no drinks, no tips. For 50–60 Cts. one lives on asparagus, rhubarb, and *sinasappels* (oranges), and thus bilks[3] the gang out of its exorbitant prices. . . .

Scheveningen is grandiose in its way, certainly the best there is in re-gard to luxurious beach facilities. There is a front structure that juts far out into the sea and houses a variety theater seating thousands. It is wonderful to sit out there in the brisk sea breeze looking out upon the endless coast of dunes and, in the evening, on the brilliant lights of the beach as well as the fishing fleet. Behind the dunes there are thousands of little two-story houses that were built as a specula-tive venture and are for rent. Then there is the beautiful dense Schev-

---

[1]Weber's Dutch was faulty. The correct forms are *broodje, zoete, koek,* and (below) *sinaasappels.*— Ed.

[2]German island in the North Sea; a favorite summer resort.—Ed.

[3]Weber uses the word *besch[eisst],* a vulgarism for *betrügt* (cheats).—Ed.

eningen grove, a ten minutes' ride by horse-drawn carriage. But these
people are as much after money as any Neapolitan.

Still, it is a twenty to twenty-five minutes' ride to The Hague.
If I lived there, I might not always decide to come out here; otherwise
I would prefer to live in the city. This town is ridiculously quiet, and
everything is *en miniature*. The museum, public buildings, etc., all have
two floors. At first one feels that one ought to take care not to
knock anything down or to crush it underfoot—like Gulliver when he
returned from Brobdingnag. Our Brobdingnag is the large apartment
houses, and there are very few of them here. Beautiful quiet ponds with
swans on them, surrounded by beautiful lindens and beeches and chestnuts; absolute cleanliness—today they are scrubbing the outside of the
houses, as high as they can reach; all this has a very soothing effect.

June 7, 1903

The whole kit and caboodle [*Pastete*] here—The Hague—has an old-
fashioned bourgeois flavor. Everything is bright and shiny, everyone is
well-to-do, exceedingly ungraceful, and rather untastefully dressed. The
most hideous thing is the national costume of the women—the old
Dutch white kerchief into which the hair as well as the entire top
and back of the head have been stuffed—like the hind part of a spider.
In front the thing is fastened to the tightly parted hair with two
large pins, little curved plates of gilded metal that look like the feelers
of a snail. The women have a horrible shuffling gait. The males are boors
with seamen's faces, as though they had been blinking at a stiff north-
east sea breeze for thirty years. The gray skies we are now having all the
time make the scenery and the city look tired; once the sun comes
out, it must be quite merry.

June 8, 1903

The museum in The Hague has the advantage of being *small*, and one
easily finds what one likes. The most beautiful thing I have found so
far is Rembrandt's *Saul and David* (playing the harp). That two obvious
Jews [*Knalljuden*]—the king, on top of that, as a sultan in a tasteless
costume, David as a real "swinger" [*Schwung*] from the delicatessen
store—could be painted in such a way that one sees only the human
beings and the moving power of the tones is all but incomprehensible.
But the raptness of the musician strongly reminds one of the expression in Giorgione's[4] *Concert*, and the one eye of the king which

---

[4]Giorgio Barbarelli Giorgione de Castelfranco, ca. 1478–1511, Italian painter.—Ed.

can be seen—he tearfully hides the rest of his face—tells us almost dreadfully how he had hoped that the harp playing would make him forget the fact that things were going downhill with him and how this hope had gone unfulfilled. The photos of this painting cannot convey any of this. Next to this picture the others with their "channeled" rays of light mean nothing to me, and even the magnificent *Anatomy* [*The Anatomy Lesson of Dr. Nicolaes Tulp*] shows more that he was a virtuosic portraitist and technician than—as this picture shows—that he was a soulful artist.

June 9, 1903

I could not resist the temptation to buy a print of the Rembrandt painting, although it probably conveys a full impression only to those who know the original. The king's eye has a more powerful effect in the original. Rembrandt painted it after the loss of his Saskia,[5] his property, and his pictures and after he had gone into bankruptcy; he was at the peak of his ability and, living in solitude with his son and his faithful Hendrickje, felt old age approaching.

Yesterday there was a severe storm from the north. The fine sand from the dunes swirled in clouds across the beach and through all the streets. A blue haze shrouded the masts and the lighthouse, and through the white haze over the sea the sun placed a greenish yellow gleam over the monotonous gray mass as through frosted glass. Apart from the dust it was very beautiful. Today there is an offshore wind, and the sky is as blue as it can be here; except in midsummer there is always a haze which gives the sunlit woods and the tree-lined parts of the city a dreamy, eveninglike quality even in broad daylight. Only the highly sober human faces with their extremely this-worldly behavior neutralize this atmosphere again.

Ostende, August 28, 1903 (People's Hotel)

Food quite respectable and ample; they economize only on tablecloths, napkins, towels. Otherwise everything is quite clean and really very reasonable at 4½ francs for room and board (with beer). The people at my table are all Germans from every country under the sun (England, Holland, Belgium, Westphalia, Austria)—some with a little classical education, some without; they are young businessmen and editors. There are also Flemish workers from Belgium. All these people conduct them-

[5]Rembrandt's first wife, Saskia van Uijlenburgh, died in 1642, and several years later Hendrickje Stoffels became his common-law wife.—Ed.

selves *at least* as properly as the German alpine tourists at the Eibsee; most of them are considerably more polite and less puffed up. The conversation is rather stereotyped but quite unconstrained . . .

August 23, 1903

My companions are quite nice fellows who wouldn't harm a cat, let alone a prince. I also enjoy the great mannerliness of the people; it is far better than what one usually finds among Germans abroad. Yet here, in a foreign country, there is a specifically national atmosphere—a strict separation from the Walloons and the French. With regard to *women* they hold absolutely patriarchal views. The discussions about marital *fidelity* are delightful; the wife's right is regarded as the right to her husband's body, that is, its functions. There is a difference of opinion as to whether (in accordance with "natural right") the wife has an absolute monopoly or whether it is enough that a man does not *weaken* himself (while traveling) and thus does not "abridge" her rights (very crude jokes at this point); the married men favor the stricter view.

August 23, 1903

Yesterday I had a very long conversation with one of my companions, a very nice men's custom tailor (cutter) from Paris. Two others from London, a tailor and a shoemaker, always make me think of old Rümelin's[6] classification of people as shoemakers and tailors (do you still remember how we used to divide people accordingly in Freiburg?). Here this once again worked perfectly. I am now paying only 4 francs for the whole day—and yet there are a three-course meal plus soup at lunch, hot meat and a dessert in the evening, and a large, friendly room. The people, to be sure, sometimes eat with their knives—but on the whole they are, as I have said, *extremely* well-mannered, and on the promenade they are fully as elegant as I, and far more elegant than *I* in Papa Sisto's[7] work of art.

August 25, 1903

Yesterday a red flag of giant dimensions waved outside my window, and there was a tremendous festivity, with the workers' "Marseillaise," etc. The musical society of the Brussels trade unions completely filled the

---

[6]Gustav Rümelin, 1815–1888, Württemberg politician and professor of sociology at Tübingen.—Ed.
[7]Max Sisto, Weber's tailor.—Ed.

house. Incidentally, they made excellent amateur music and were also asked to play at the *Kursaal* [casino]. Talking to people one learns many interesting things, for example, about ladies' custom tailoring in Paris. Strange enough that *all* the finest shops should be in the hands of Germans (Austrians), as are *almost* all trained workers. Likewise, half of the highly skilled shoemakers (workers) of *London* are Germans. People told me unanimously that this was due to the fact that the English workingmen's wives are either drunks or bad housekeepers and live in too grand a style, which means that their children have to go out too soon to earn some money, are unable to learn a good trade, and therefore work in the factories. . . . Today my little Paris tailor took my Baedeker and a book about Bruges and went to look at that city. I believe that it would not occur to one in ten of that bunch of show-offs one sees here on the dam that this might be something worthwhile. With my 4 francs for room and board I am now being treated as a "comrade," although the people know, of course, that I am not one and who I am.

August 28, 1903

Yesterday I met Anseele,[8] a leader of the Belgian Socialists and their greatest organizer. He came with 300 children wearing little red bows and red feathers on their hats. Every year the party provides outfits for such children and sends them on a vacation trip to Switzerland or to the seashore. In the evening they sang delightful songs. There is a tremendous enthusiasm in these people. You asked about *women*; there are some here, but they are of no importance. The French are polite toward them, the Germans treat them more patriarchally. The comrades are not interested in women's suffrage and the like.

Domburg, August 29, 1903

The comrades evidently enjoyed being with me and bade me a very cordial farewell. Of course, they *absolutely* associate with everyone on equal terms, because despite their almost superstitious respect for "scholarship," to them a "professor" is only a man whose parents had the money to have him learn something. In *intelligence*, by the way, their average was not below the average of our colleagues. The shyster [*Winkelkonsulent*] from Dortmund, formerly a journeyman butcher, who traveled as far as Middelburg with me, was a fellow of outstanding intelligence.

---

[8]Edouard Anseele, 1856–1938, leader of Belgian trade unions and co-founder of the Belgian Socialist Party.—Ed.

Domburg, August 31, 1903

Today I took a long walk; it is possible to walk for hours through a thick oak forest behind the dunes. The walking went quite well, but it does tire my head quite a bit. It is beautiful here; the old lindens and oaks look into the windows and whisper, and behind the dunes the roaring sea demands the land which by rights has been its property for a long time.

Scheveningen, October 10, 1903

With its pale brown the autumnal sea also is beautiful when the sun for once breaks through the clouds—like an old, old man. There still is little of autumn about the trees. The meadows are now mostly under water, and the numerous big, small, and tiny windmills that pump the water into the canals gesticulate garrulously like deaf-mutes and, being aware of their indispensability, give themselves airs. It is a fabulous day—warm, with a powerful wind and a raging sea. The beach is under a thick cloud of sand dust which whips right into the streets, making one's face red as a lobster and actually sore. One lies down on the sunwarmed black stones of the basalt breakwater and is completely pickled by the fine spray.

Let us add at this point some Dutch impressions from a later trip.

Scheveningen, July 27, 1907

Nothing new. Gray skies, some rain, rather mild. I sit on the beach in my basket chair, eat cheese, fruit, cookies, loll on my bed, and read some Maeterlinck—*Der Schatz der Armen;*[9] I shall send it to you later. For the time being I must wait and see whether my nerves will begin to relax. The wind may be somewhat too strong for this. My sleep has been quantitatively passable (with a lot of bromide), qualitatively not very good. In the evening the people outside and nearby chat until late, while my landlord and his family, from whom I am separated only by a glass door extending over almost the entire width of the room, behave very politely. In the morning a canary whose cage was suspended over my bed shyly chirped for light, and his chirping became joyful when I opened the curtains. The W.C. is out in the open and may be reached

---

[9]*Le trésor des humbles* (1896), a book of essays by the Belgian dramatist and philosopher Maurice Maeterlinck, 1862–1949. An English translation, *The Treasure of the Humble,* appeared in 1903.—Ed.

through the kitchen—really a mysteriously tiny place of business [*Betriebsstätte*] in view of the tremendous size of the old fisherman.

Egmond aan Zee, August 3, 1907

Yesterday I celebrated your birthday by taking a very beautiful steamer ride from Amsterdam to Alkmaar—three hours on the "Noord Hollandsche Canaal," first among the countless little houses, one right next to the other for miles, with doll gardens and flowers in the doll windows, quiet little canals, verandas, tiny boats, then through locks into the endless expanse of the North Holland pasture. Everything yellowish green down to the horizon, but there are countless windmills, some of which pump the water day in, day out from the land that lies below the sea level and also lower than the diked-in canal. The only other break is the beautiful isolated farms that are romantically located among the trees, the trees being a protection against the terrible force of the wind. Two days ago the library in my beloved Leiden was closed, so I took the steamer from there to Katwijk in an effort to become gradually acquainted with all resorts on the coast.

On the return trip I visited Schijnsburg [sic][10] and Spinoza's apartment: two little rooms, each about the size of our toilet, one of them a bit larger; one has a mansard roof. This was in one of the miniature houses which there—as everywhere—are usually located amidst the thickest greenery alongside the canals. The town is quite charming. Yesterday I visited the Rembrandt house in the Jewish quarter of Amsterdam. I spent the night in the vegetarian hotel in Leiden—quite old-fashioned, with a large bathroom, fantastically cheap.

Egmond, August 8, 1907

In the next few days I want to take several excursions to North Holland so I can really get to know the beautiful country. A peculiar calm lies over it, and history seems to be asleep here. Much of it is the way Jan van der Neer[11] [sic] painted it 300 years ago: windmills, little brick houses, canals, clumps of trees, and a limitless panorama of sleepy, fragrant green meadows.

Nidder-Beemster, August 12, 1907

Today I went to Alkmaar by carriage—a most charming little town with green canals, tiny houses, a picturesque church, and a Renaissance

---

[10]Rijnsburg near Leiden was Spinoza's place of residence in the 1660s.—Ed.
[11]Aert (Aernout) van der Neer, 1603–1677, Dutch landscape painter.—Ed.

municipal weigh-house. Then I went to the Beemster polder, the work of Oldenbarneveldt[12] from the beginning of the seventeenth century—a wonderfully fertile grassy plain five miles wide and long, six meters below sea level, which used to be pumped dry constantly by fifty windmills but is now kept dry by three steam engines; the ox is the lord of creation there. Right now I am going by carriage to the old town of Hoorn on the Zuider Zee for the church fair; I am coming back in the evening.

Marken, August 20, 1907

This island swims in the Zuider Zee like a flat plate. The houses on Hümpen are crowded together on sandbanks and are everywhere connected by little canals; inside they are freshly painted, and on the walls there are porcelain plates with colorful glazes. The bedsteads are in a kind of a drawer in the wall. Everywhere water and meadows. The flaxen hair of the women, stiff as straw, sticks out from under their tight caps in front and on the sides; they wear colorful bodices. The men walk around in shapeless plus fours.

III

But was there no fresh breeze at home, in their normal, everyday life, that would come to the aid of the husband and fill his sails for a new voyage? His family made all sorts of plans. Helene wanted very much to brighten their life in Heidelberg by getting them a beautiful apartment in the greenery, out by the Neckar. For a while they eagerly played with this shimmering soap bubble, until the question of expenses made it burst. Considering Weber's need for a change of scenery, he really preferred not to tie himself down by such ownership. Around this time (summer, 1903) Friedrich Naumann suffered his second defeat in an election campaign and liquidated the *National-Soziale Partei*. Perhaps the friends could join together and place their activity on a new footing—perhaps start a political periodical or participate in editing an existing one. But Weber replied to proposals to that effect from his relatives:

The more I think about it, the more it seems to me that a *new* political journal *after* such a failure is equally impossible internally and ex-

---

[12]Jan van Oldenbarneveldt or J. v. O. Barneveldt, 1547–1619, Dutch statesman.—Ed.

ternally. My participation would, in any case, be out of the question; how could I justify it? To deal constantly with those political matters that stir me deeply is something that my body could at best manage for a few months. And what is even more important: If a political matter is not to be bungled, an absolutely cool head is required, and I simply cannot guarantee that now. I have therefore decided to join the staff of Braun's *Archiv* together with Sombart, provided that Jaffé[13] acquires it. It seems that the publisher desires precisely this combination, and since I am right here I can be useful to Jaffé even if my working strength is not great. (July 17, 1903)

So Weber did not feel up to the excitement of political activity. On the other hand, he considered a proposal from his younger colleague and friend, Edgar Jaffé, who had married Else von Richthofen around that time. Jaffé planned to acquire Heinrich Braun's scholarly journal *Archiv für Sozialwissenschaften [und Sozialpolitik*—Archives for Social Science and Social Welfare] and wished to have Sombart and Weber as co-editors. The happy idea of creating a new form of activity for Weber was of some importance in this. He could indeed risk such an activity. At first, of course, he had all sorts of misgivings: "It really is quite doubtful whether I can participate; it is repugnant to me to let the others work and parade my name without always holding out the prospect of a certain quantity of work. Maybe a way could be found that would enable me to participate formally, too. As far as the scholarly aspect is concerned, I would perhaps participate to the best of my ability, that is, I would *only* write for the journal. . . ."

Weber knew that he was overcome by scholarly zeal in *every* assignment, and he was unable to tolerate any façade behind which others were doing the work: "I am not interested in doing *occasional* advising." Also, considering his irritable nerves, he would not find it easy to be even-tempered in the face of the inevitable restraints imposed on his own will by the will of others. However, his friends overcame his misgivings. At that juncture that task seemed to have been made for him, for it did not require an evaluating politician but a thinker who placed himself beyond a Yes or No. It did not tie him to definite hours but left some leeway for the fluctuations of his still unstable strength.

He now reestablished contact with a large circle of scholars and social re-

---

[13]Edgar Jaffé, 1866–1921, from 1910 on professor of economics at Berlin and Munich, minister of finance in Kurt Eisner's Bavarian cabinet after World War I.—Ed.

formers. He started an extensive correspondence to gain new contributors to the *Archiv*, preserve old ones, and distribute varied suggestions for essays. The editors did not just recruit colleagues in their own field but also turned to scholars in adjacent areas. The prefatory note to the first number of the new series, which was drafted by Weber, stated that to expand its former scope (a scholarly investigation of the conditions created by modern capitalism and a critical examination of the course of legislation) the periodical "must regard the historical and theoretical recognition *of the general cultural significance of the capitalistic development* as the problem to which it will devote itself, and it will therefore maintain a close contact with the neighboring disciplines—general political science, the philosophy of law, social ethics, social psychology, and the research usually grouped together as sociology."

The hunger for social data prevalent among the leaders of the preceding generation was followed, as interest in philosophy generally reawakened, by a hunger for social theories. It was to be one of the main future tasks of the *Archiv* to satisfy this hunger as best it could: "We shall have to pay attention both to the discussion of social problems from a philosophical point of view and to the form of research in our special field which in a narrower sense is called 'theory'—the creation of clear concepts. . . . We shall therefore keep abreast of research on the critique of knowledge and on methodology."

This gave the journal such a wide scope that alongside empirical social science and its theory there was also room for scientific philosophy and the philosophical interpretation of social phenomena.

Around Christmas, 1903, Weber's wife wrote:

This year we shall celebrate the festival without the heavy pressure of anxiety and worries, but also without the faint hope of recent years. All in all, Max's present mood is one of such relief and he has been enduring the winter so much better than last year, though it has been very mild thus far, that I can only agree with his views and actions and am thankful that we have overcome the break with the past at least outwardly.

Weber now felt an obligation and an urge to produce for the periodical, and despite all inhibitions and fluctuations various projects soon were completed. In the summer of 1903 he finally completed the first part of his "essay of sighs" (Roscher and Knies) and published it in Schmoller's *Jahrbü-*

cher. At the beginning of 1904 he produced for the first number of the new series an essay entitled *Die Objektivität sozialwissenschaftlicher und sozialpolitischer Erkenntnis* [The Objectivity of Knowledge in Social Science and Social Welfare], which was intended to be programmatic for the area of methodology. "Max's study is almost completed. To be sure, his sleep now leaves a lot to be desired; he again eats a Camembert every night, has to take soporifics, but is quite pleased that he has accomplished this thing." (January 30, 1904).

After a period of inactivity Max began work on another study, for the second number of the *Archiv,* in which he returned to his earlier interest in agrarian policy and concrete problems of legislation: *Agrarstatistische und sozialpolitische Betrachtungen zur Fideikommissfrage in Preussen* [The Fideicommissum Question in Prussia in the Light of Agrarian Statistics and Social Welfare]. "After a few days of rest Max is again very busy, does an awful lot of figuring with all sorts of agrarian statistical stuff; I always have to remind him not to work for too prolonged periods. He is now again able to work longer than I." This treatise was published in the early summer. At the same time he was preparing something greater, namely *The Protestant Ethic and the Spirit of Capitalism.* The first part of this study appeared in the fall issue *of the Archiv.*

Thus Weber managed to produce within a period of nine months in 1904 three major essays in completely different fields as well as an important lecture, which will be discussed shortly. The dark pressure that had been weighing upon Weber during the previous year gradually lifted. From time to time a sky became visible through the shifting clouds in which the star of the productive man shone again.

IV

Midsummer of 1904 again brought an extended break, but this time for pleasant reasons. Hugo Münsterberg, the former Freiburg psychologist and philosopher, who had for years been a professor at Harvard, took the occasion of the Universal Exposition at St. Louis to arrange an international scholarly congress in that city. In doing so he was most concerned with establishing intellectual connections between the United States and Germany. Invitations were issued to German scholars in all fields, including Weber and his Heidelberg friends Troeltsch, Hensel, and others. Each man was to give a lecture in St. Louis for a substantial honorarium. This pros-

pect of the New World was so enticing for Weber that he overcame all inhibitions and misgivings and decided to go out into the world with his wife
for a few months.

The very project and the planning acted as a tonic. The couple embarked
toward the end of August; Ernst Troeltsch and his delightful humor accompanied them. The leisurely voyage gave them a proper preparation for the
new impressions. This was particularly true of Weber, for the swell of the
green and blue ocean obligingly rocked him to sleep, a sleep for which he ordinarily had to struggle. Breathing deeply he enjoyed the relaxing idleness;
watching the play of the clouds, the waves, and the wind, as well as the
crowds of people, offered him ever fresh images. In this floating city which
because of an advanced technology was able to satisfy every desire for comfort, in the delightful freshness of the salt air, he felt truly *well*. The abundance of goods things that surrounded him revived the "merry eater" in him;
there was no seasickness to spoil his enjoyment, though there was Marianne's concern about the increase in his bulk. During the voyage she sent
the following report to Helene:

> The three of us have not been seasick. To be sure, we noticed a ten-
> dency toward asceticism in Troeltsch, but Max has cheerfully eaten his
> way through the whole menu every day, and I have resigned myself to
> seeing his beauty disappear again. He is really fine, or so it seems to me.
> One sign of it is his constant presence at the frightfully long dinners;
> also, he likes to have a chat afterward in the smoking room, where we
> occupy a cozy corner with the nice *Regierungsrat* [privy councillor] and
> a few chief engineers. On the whole, no form of existence is as much
> designed for vegetating absolutely contentedly and unintellectually as
> a voyage. One becomes a mere blank, or a jellyfish that consists only
> of digestive organs. Yet Max usually throws out a few principles of social
> policy and gives the good people some "viewpoints," and again and again
> it is brought home to me that he not only knows a fantastic amount
> but can convey all his knowledge to others so they can understand it,
> which makes him a born teacher.

They entered New York harbor early one September morning and were
much impressed by the view of the skyscrapers towering into the blue atmosphere and by the greenish bronze Statue of Liberty, which waved her powerfully beaming torch with an expansive gesture and daily brought a message
of hope to thousands of wretched arrivals from the classes and races suppressed in Europe, hope for a future shaped by daring and prospects of happi-

ness. Weber could hardly wait for the procedure of landing and the customs
inspection. When they went ashore he darted ahead with long, elastic
strides, leaving his companions behind—like a liberated eagle finally allowed
to move its wings.

They headed for a twenty-story hotel in the middle of the business district of Manhattan Island where the audacious residential towers crowded
together and the "capitalistic spirit" of that country had created its
most impressive symbols. One could virtually smell and taste the dried-up
horse manure of these streets, through which heavy traffic roared. Oh God,
what a contrast to Italy—Rome, Florence, Naples! Everything struck them
as overwhelmingly strange; that loveless barracks for traveling salesmen in
which everyone was only a number! An *"elevator"*[14] took them to the
height of a church steeple and into a room that was distinguished by its
bareness, a telephone, and two enormous spittoons. Looking out of the
window made them shudder and feel dizzy: the street lay far down in an
abyss, and the thirty-story houses opposite them made fun of their small
companion! Were they not cut off from the good earth as though they
were in the tower of a prison? Undoubtedly one could take ill and die without anyone caring!

Most German newcomers who found themselves in such coldly impersonal
quarters so out of keeping with German *Gemütlichkeit* [coziness] felt very uncomfortable at first. The bustle outside, which made an attitude of enjoyment impossible and with which they had no connection by reason of work,
heightened their feeling of forlornness. A few of Weber's colleagues developed
nervous disturbances of all kinds, but not Weber himself: "Incidentally, so
far Max has never been better since his illness, particularly so far as walking
is concerned." His lively interest in the new world almost made him forget
the lack of his accustomed comforts; he was annoyed if anyone made a fuss
about it and wished to appreciate everything and absorb as much of it as
possible. Only when he was bored and wasted time needlessly—as on a
streetcar ride of several hours through New York that was undertaken in
the protective custody of a hospitable American colleague and on which
they say practically nothing but the bottoms of houses—did the lion secretly rage in his cage, and then it was hard to restrain him from breaking
out.

Generally speaking, he rejected for the time being any criticism of the

---

[14]Words (other than place names), phrases, and sentences that are in English in the original
will be italicized and placed between quotation marks.—Ed.

new things which was based on unfamiliarity with them. He was on the side
of the new and empathized with it, as it were, in order to do it justice.
After three days in New York his wife wrote:

> To be sure, we have definitely not decided as yet—at least I have
> not—whether we ought to find this piece of world on which five mil-
> lion people are piled up magnificent and tremendous or crude, hideous,
> and barbaric. The most clearly enthusiastic person is Max, as he always
> is when he travels. Thanks to his temperament and presumably also to
> his comprehensive knowledge and scholarly interest he at first finds
> everything beautiful and better than in our country on principle; his
> criticism does not come until later.

On this Weber remarked: "No one can say that I am especially 'enthusiastic'; I am merely annoyed at my German fellow travelers who groan about
America after a day and a half in New York."

Once again long letters to Helene preserved all important impressions.
Some excerpts from these that best show Weber's way of taking things in
are given here:

> By far the most powerful impressions in New York are the view from
> the middle of the Brooklyn Bridge and the great cemetery in Brooklyn,
> which is reached by taking the *"elevated"* over the bridge. The contrast
> is fabulous. On the Brooklyn Bridge there is a raised footpath in the
> middle; when one walks on it around six o'clock in the evening, the
> roofs of the *"elevated"* trains rush past one on both sides at intervals
> of a quarter of a minute. Still closer to both sides of the bridge there
> are the *"trams,"* with just a few meters between them, all jam-packed
> with people who partly hang from them. There is a constant roaring
> and hissing; the rattling of the trains is punctuated by the tooting
> of the steam whistles of the big ferries far down below. Added to this
> is the magnificent view of the fortresses of capital at the southern
> tip of the island on which the *"City"* of New York is located—nothing
> but towers such as may be seen on the old pictures of Bologna and Flor-
> ence, surrounded everywhere by the light vapor clouds of the freight el-
> evators. This is truly a unique impression, particularly in combination
> with the view of the large outer harbor, the Statue of Liberty, and
> the distant sea. Nor can I find the *"skyscrapers"* ugly: our tenement
> houses [*Mietskasernen*] with their dreary fronts superimposed upon one
> another ten times. The resulting picture is that of a streaked rock
> with a den of thieves on top. This is certainly not "beautiful," but

neither is it the opposite; rather, it is beyond both, and, if it is not viewed from too close, it is the most appropriate symbol that I can imagine of what goes on here.

How great are the works of men, but how small the men themselves appear! When toward evening the fantastic stream surged from the business districts toward the bridge, it was enough to make one shudder; belief in the infinite worth of the individual soul and in immortality seemed absurd.

For the time being the travelers did not see much of the domestic life of the crowds. They were invited to only one of those little one-family houses in the extensive residential districts. Its modest charm was in striking contrast to the citadels of the business world, and what they found there seemed like home to them: the quiet little study of an American professor—"one puff from my long pipe would darken the room permanently."

Among this mass agglomeration any stirring of individualism is expensive—be it in housing or in eating. Thus the home of Professor Hervay [sic],[15] one of the Germanists at Columbia University, was a veritable doll's house. Tiny little rooms, washing and bathing facilities in the same room as the w.c. (as almost always), parties with more than four guests impossible (enviable!), and with all this an hour's ride to the center of the city. The people were almost excessively kind, and both he and she were passionately "German" in their habits. I suppose Marianne will tell you about her. As for him, he told us that a *Deutscher Commers* [German students' party] is now celebrated by the German Department of the university twice a year and attended by the eight German *"teachers,"* the *"graduates,"* and the *"college"* students except the *"freshmen"*—with fencing, songs, and draft beer. Then we were told in the customary way that this was the first university building in America into which a barrel of beer had been brought. This is how seriously the introduction of students to the "spirit" of German culture is taken here.

This time the Webers spent only a few days in New York; they planned a longer stay to end their trip. They now went westward along the woody banks of the Hudson to Niagara Falls. It was really true: everywhere they found *"the greatest of the world"*; the dimensions of human works were only

[15]William Addison Hervey, 1870–1918. Born near New York, he studied at the University of Leipzig in 1896 and taught at Columbia from that year on, publishing a number of textbooks and editions of German classics.—Ed.

the appropriate expression of a nature which was fantastically extensive and tended toward the gigantic. That magnificent river was so wide that the opposite shore could only be dimly glimpsed in the distance. Then came the wide prairie, still barely shaped by human hands, and then that incredible waterfall—not just a lovely, colorfully shimmering spray in a romantic rocky gorge, but something like a captured ocean that frees itself from confinement by a mad leap into the abyss. Weber enjoyed the tremendous spectacle whose roar makes human voices fall silent, but he devoted only a few emotional lines to it, for the products and lives of human beings interested him more than nature:

I am writing you while Hensel and Troeltsch have gone to the green island between the two great falls, where countless quiet spots in thick greenery give one a very special feeling of the profound calm before the storm. Even though the natural beauty is wonderful despite all the shameful disfigurement, the most interesting thing was our visit of two days ago to the little industrial town of North Tonawanda, half an hour from here, with Reverend Haupt,[16] the son-in-law of Professor Conrad in Halle.

There the travelers found a small town that was astonishing in its contrast to New York. Above all, in one day they were able to learn more about the special character of American life from naturalized fellow Germans than they might otherwise have learned in weeks:

The very appearance of the little town is an unparalleled contrast to the skyscrapers of New York. Nothing but little wooden houses of one or two stories along a sidewalk consisting of diagonally placed boards— each with a veranda, flowers, a little garden, trees by the road, infinitely friendly and modest on the outside, tiny on the inside. The houses, like a coat, are cut to order in large saw mills and factories, then transported here and put up. Depending on the size, all of them naturally have the same distribution of space and cost 1000 to 3000 dollars each. The rooms are very small. Six persons plus tables and chairs fill the largest to the bursting point, and one can touch the ceilings

---

[16]John (Hans) Haupt, born in 1869 and married to the former Margaret Conrad, was the minister of the Friedens United Church of Christ (then part of the Evangelical Synod of North America) in North Tonawanda, New York, from 1899 to 1910, and then moved to Cincinnati.—Ed.

with one's hand, but the cheerful decor with the beautiful American hardwood paneling and door frames as well as the single-colored wallpaper make the rooms very pleasant. The kitchen is always next to the dining room; the toilet, the washstand (one for everybody), and the bathtub are squeezed together in one room. The windows are tiny. The parsonage, not substantially larger than the other houses, was next to the small wooden church, which was very cheerfully and cozily furnished (with a kitchen and a *"dining-room"* for the frequent congregational festivities).

Here they also became acquainted with contrasting ways of life within the socially privileged classes. They saw for the first time the unpretentious, heavily encumbered existences of intellectuals who managed to lead cultured lives without support from the state and with an income derived from voluntary contributions made by a working-class community. With four children, and usually no domestic help, the highly educated wife did the cooking, cleaning, washing, and sewing; the husband helped with heavier chores. And yet they remained intellectually alive. The travelers marveled at this tremendous achievement, not suspecting that in the future the intellectual class would have to live in the same way in Germany too.

The next stop was Chicago, the monstrous city which even more than New York was the crystallization of the American spirit. Here they found marked contrasts: ostentatious new wealth which was displayed in sumptuous buildings of marble and gold bronze; unkempt poverty which glared out at them from the opaque window panes and dirty, dark corridors of endless, desolate streets; a mixed population of all races and from all continents in constant flux; a breathless pursuit of loot; a human waste which heedlessly risked the lives of thousands every day; constant building and razing, with torn-up streets, bottomless filth, and deafening overstraining of all voices—and over all this hung a thick smoke which placed a black veil over every stone and every blade of grass and only seldom let through the blue and golden light from the sky and the silvery gleam of the stars. Weber wrote:

Chicago is one of the most incredible cities. By the lake there are a few comfortable and beautiful residential districts, mostly with stone houses of a very heavy and cumbersome style, and right behind them there are little old wooden houses such as one finds in Helgoland. Then come the *"tenements"* of the workingmen and absurdly dirty streets which are unpaved, or there is miserable macadamization outside the better residential districts. In the *"city,"* among the *"skyscrapers,"* the condition of the streets is utterly hair-raising. And they burn soft coal. When the hot, dry wind from the deserts of the southwest blows through the streets, and especially when the dark yellow sun sets, the city looks fantastic. In broad daylight one can see only three blocks ahead—everything is haze and smoke, the whole lake is covered by a huge pall of smoke from which the little steamers suddenly emerge and in which the sails of the ships putting to sea quickly disappear.

It is an endless human desert. From the city one travels on Halsted Street—which, I believe, is twenty English miles long—into the endless distance, past blocks with Greek inscriptions—*Xenodocheion* [Hotel], etc.—and then past others with Chinese taverns, Polish advertisements, German beer parlors, until one gets to the *"stockyards."* For as far as one can see from the clock tower of the firm Armour & Co. there is nothing but herds of cattle, lowing, bleating, endless filth. But on the horizon all around—for the city continues for miles and miles, until it melts into the multitude of suburbs—there are churches and chapels, grain elevators, smoking chimneys (every big hotel here has its steaming elevator), and houses of every size. They are usually small houses, for at most two families each (hence the enormous dimensions of the city), and they are graded in cleanliness according to nationality.

All hell had broken loose in the *"stockyards"*: an unsuccessful strike, masses of Italians and Negroes as strikebreakers; daily shootings with dozens of dead on both sides; a streetcar was overturned and a dozen women were squashed because a *"non-union man"* had sat in it; dynamite threats against the *"Elevated Railway,"* and one of its cars was actually derailed and plunged into the river. Right near our hotel a cigar dealer was murdered in broad daylight; a few streets away three Negroes attacked and robbed a streetcar at dusk, etc.—all in all, a strange flowering of culture.

There is a mad pell-mell of nationalities: Up and down the streets the Greeks shine the Yankees' shoes for 5 cents. The Germans are their waiters, the Irish take care of their politics, and the Italians of their dirtiest ditch digging. With the exception of the better residential districts, the whole tremendous city—more extensive than London!—is like a man whose skin has been peeled off and whose intestines are seen at work. For one can see everything—in the evening, for example, on a side street in the *"city"* the prostitutes are placed in a show window with electric light and the prices are displayed! A characteristic thing here as in New York is the maintenance of a specific Jewish-German culture. Theaters present in Yiddish [*Judendeutsch*] *The Merchant of Venice* (with Shylock prevailing, however) and their own Jewish plays, which we are planning to see in New York. . . .

Everywhere one is struck by the tremendous intensity of work—most of all in the *"stockyards"* with their *"ocean of blood,"* where several thousand cattle and pigs are slaughtered every day. From the moment when the unsuspecting bovine enters the slaughtering area, is hit by a hammer and collapses, whereupon it is immediately gripped by an iron clamp, is hoisted up, and starts on its journey, it is in constant motion—past ever-new workers who eviscerate and skin it, etc., but are always (in the rhythm of work) tied to the machine that pulls the animal past them. One sees an absolutely incredible output in this atmosphere of steam, muck, blood, and hides in which I teetered about together with a *"boy"* who was giving me a guided tour for fifty cents, trying to keep from being buried in the filth. There one can follow a pig from the sty to the sausage and the can.

When they finish work at five o'clock, people often must travel for hours to get home. The streetcar company is bankrupt; as usual it has been administered by a *"receiver"* for years, and he is not interested in expediting the liquidation and hence does not purchase any new cars. The old ones break down every few moments. Around 400 people are killed or crippled in accidents every year. According to law, each death costs the company 5000 dollars (to the widow or the heirs), an injury costs it 10,000 dollars (to the injured party, if the company does not take certain precautionary measures). The company has now calculated that those 400 indemnities cost it less than the required precautions, so it does not bother to introduce them.

The Webers felt as though they were being shaken out of a state of reverie and somnolence: "Look, this is what modern reality is like." But the face of this monster which indifferently swallowed up everything individual stirred them not only with its magnificent wildness but also with its gentle features that bespoke a capacity for love as well as kindness, justice, and a tenacious desire for beauty and spirituality. On the billboards there was a poster proclaiming CHRIST IN CHICAGO. Was this a brazen mockery? No, this eternal spirit dwells there, too—for example, in the work of a woman who has the courage of her convictions. In the dreary streets of a workingmen's district Jane Adams [sic][17] created her famous *"settlement."* There this gentle, refined woman together with a large staff of enthusiastic assistants

---

[17]Jane Addams, the founder of Hull House and the Women's International League for Peace and Freedom, lived from 1860 to 1935.—Ed.

provided the proletarians who were thrown together from all over the world with all the things that they could not provide for themselves. In the hectic struggle for existence it was a place offering beauty, joy, intellectual uplift, physical training, and social service. People looked, marveled, and believed in this "Angel of Chicago."

There were other oases as well: the *"colleges,"* colonies of charming buildings far outside the metropolis set among carefully tended green lawns and in the shade of old trees—worlds by themselves, full of poetry and the happy intellectual life of the young. Here young Americans from a wide social range were taught the tender, beautiful, and profound aspects of life. Weber reported: "The whole magic of youthful memories attaches solely to this period. An abundance of sports, attractive forms of social life, infinite intellectual stimulation, and lasting friendships are the returns, and above all the education includes far more habituation to work than there is among our students." Here he immediately found what so greatly interested him: distinct traces of the organizational strength of the *religious* spirit. Most of the *"colleges"* originally were the work of puritanical sects, and something of the tradition of the Pilgrim fathers was still discernible. It still bound the young men to the ideal of chastity, prohibited smutty stories, and instilled into them a measure of chivalry toward women which was unknown to the average German of the day.

The religious spirit was particularly alive in the Quaker Haverford College near Philadelphia, though even there it was already mixed with uncongenial components. Weber examined the college library for his study of the spirit of capitalism and received unforgettable impressions:

Even these Quakers are still "orthodox" only in that they are not Unitarians. All the other old customs have disappeared. Their *"cricket team"* is regarded as the best in the country, the young rascals [*Bengel*] are rolling in money. In a student's room I found crossed rapiers and a sign saying *Raucher,* which had evidently been pilfered [*stibitzt*] from the smoking compartment of a German train.

But the religious services still are something special. What silence! In the utterly unadorned room—there is no altar, etc.—one heard only the crackling of the fireplace and muffled coughing (it was cold). Finally someone who is being "moved by the spirit" stands up and says whatever he wishes. Usually this is one of the *"elders"* who are designated by the congregation and, men and women alike, sit in somewhat raised pews. This time, unfortunately, it was not a woman, as we had hoped it would be—an aged Quaker woman is said to be the best speaker—but the librarian of the *"college,"* a capable, rather dull philologist. The spirit moved him to supply an initially quite tedious but later rather nice, practically oriented interpretation of the various designations the New Testament gives the Christians—all carefully prepared. Then there was a long silence again, an improvised prayer by another *"elder,"* a long silence, then departure. Singing and organ were unfamiliar.

Otherwise, particularly in the large cities, only the solidly constructed framework was left. The creative initial spirit had disappeared, and this gave rise to those phenomena of Anglo-American life that the Webers judged to be *"cant"*:

It seems incredible if one reads in the statutes of the originally Methodist *"University"* in Chicago[18] that a student must attend either three-fifths of the daily services or one additional hour of lectures in place of three hours of services. If he has a bigger *"chapel record"* (!!) than required, he is given credit for the next academic year, and then he needs that much less *"attendance."* If his *"chapel record"* is inadequate for two years, he is expelled. Yet the "religious service" is peculiar; sometimes it is replaced by lectures, for instance about Harnack's *History of Dogma.*[19] At the conclusion the dates of the next *"foot-ball," "base-ball," "cricket,"* etc., are announced, as the harvesting used to be announced in German villages. The whole thing is utter chaos. It is hard to say how great the indifference is at this time; that it has increased—particularly because of the Germans—is rather certain. But the power of the church communities is still tremendous as compared to our Protestantism.

* * *

On they went, making the long trip over the sweltering plain to St. Louis. There the travelers enjoyed the hospitality of a German-American home. The head of the house, who had immigrated to America as a poor

---

[18]The University of Chicago, succeeding a Baptist institution of the same name that functioned between 1857 and 1886, was founded through the interest of Baptists and opened in 1892.—Ed.

[19]Von Harnack's three-volume *Dogmengeschichte* appeared in 1898 and in English translation a year later.—Ed.

Westphalian peasant boy, now was a well-to-do "*self-made man*" and yet anything but a parvenu. They admired his noble bearing and mentality and saw in him an example of the types favored by a democracy that does not care about a person's upbringing or his diplomas, but as a matter of principle enables everyone with the will and the ability to rise to the class of the "*kaloi kagathoi*". [20]

What delighted the Webers particularly in the brilliant vast panorama of the Exposition was the "German House," distinguishable from a distance by the mighty eagle with its pinions spread wide on the front. Here the achievements of interior decoration and furnishing, and of artistic expression generally, combined in a way that the companions had never before seen, and in the midst of products from all continents these achievements were unequaled. "All products of German arts and crafts are beautiful, and they have been so wonderfully combined into a total picture that it far surpasses every other nation; this is readily acknowledged by everyone." It struck them as strange that the Germans, whose way of life was often so plebeian right up to the leading classes, should attain such perfection in their *plastic* achievement and become in this field the leaders of the West. Viewing these works Weber could be proud of his nation for whose shortcomings he had the painful clear-sightedness of love.

For Marianne the most important thing of all was his obligatory lecture on *Deutsche Agrarverhältnisse in Vergangenheit und Gegenwart* [German Agrarian Conditions, Past and Present.] [21]

You can imagine how I felt when I saw him standing before an attentively listening audience again for the first time in six and a half years! He spoke excellently, very calmly and yet vigorously; in form and substance the lecture was brilliant, and there were many political points that interested the Americans. Unfortunately the audience was very small, as with all foreign speakers who did not have Harnack's international reputation, but all his colleagues were there and he made many valuable acquaintances. And thank God, the lecture was not succeeded by any particularly bad days. On the next day he even had lunch with

---

[20]Those who combine (physical) beauty with (spiritual) goodness—the ancient Greek ideal of education and culture.—Ed.
[21]The English version is entitled "The Relations of the Rural Community to Other Branches of Social Science", *Congress of Arts and Science*, ed. by H. J. Roger, Vol. 7, Boston, 1906.—Ed.

the local representative of the government and dinner with the gover-
nor, but he did do a lot of cursing afterward.

It was to be hoped that Weber's breaking of the spell of silence would have
an important effect on his recovery.

From St. Louis he wanted to go on to the southern states. There he
wished to visit his stepcousins who had been cut off from their fatherland
and their friends. His stepcousins were Grandfather Fallenstein's grandsons
from his first marriage. Their father as an adolescent had left the despotic
pressure of home and secretly escaped overseas. There were many other things
of burning interest to Weber—above all, those which Europe could not offer him: the conquest of the wilderness by civilization, a developing city and
the developing state of Oklahoma in an area that had until recently been reserved for the Indians. Here it was still possible to observe the unarmed subjugation and absorption of an "inferior" race by a "superior," more intelligent one, the transformation of Indian tribal property into private property, and the conquest of the virgin forest by colonists. Weber stayed
with a half-breed. He watched, listened, transformed himself into his surroundings, and thus everywhere penetrated to the heart of things:

Nowhere else does old Indian romanticism blend with the most modern
capitalistic culture as it does here. The newly built railroad from Tulsa
to Mac Alester [McAlester] first runs along the Canadian River
through veritable virgin forest for an hour, although one must not
imagine it as the "Silence in the Forest"[22] with huge tree trunks.
Impenetrable thicket—so dense that except for a few vistas one does
not even notice that one is only a few meters from the Canadian River; dark trees—for the climate is already rather southerly (snow is
rare)—overgrown with climbing plants right up to the top; in between, yellow, quiet forest brooks and little rivers completely covered
with greenery. The larger streams, like the Canadian River, have the
most Leatherstocking romanticism.[23] They are in an utterly wild
state, with enormous sandbanks and thick, dark greenery on their
banks. Their waters roll along in bends and branches, giving the peculiar

[22]A reference to *Das Schweigen im Walde,* the title of a popular novel by Ludwig Ganghofer
(1899), the quintessence of German sylvan sentimentality.—Ed.
[23]James Fenimore Cooper's Leatherstocking novels have been widely read in German-speaking
countries.—Ed.

impression of something mysterious: one does not know whence they come and whither they go. With the exception of a single Indian fishing boat that I saw the streams were empty.

But the virgin forest's hour has struck even here. In the forest one does occasionally see groups of genuine old log cabins—the Indian ones are recognizable by the colorful shawls and the laundry hanging out to dry—but one also sees quite modern wooden houses from the factory, 500 dollars and up, put up on stones; next to these there is a large clearing on which corn and cotton have been planted. The trees were covered with tar at the bottom and ignited. Now they are dying and stretching their pale, smoky fingers upward in a confused tangle; next to the fresh seeds among them this looks strange and by no means attractive. Then there are large stretches of prairie—partly willows, partly cotton again—and corn fields.

And suddenly one begins to smell petroleum; one sees the high, Eiffel Tower-like structures of the drill holes in the middle of the forest and comes to a "town." Such a town is really a crazy thing: the camps of the workers, especially section hands working for the numerous railroads under construction; streets in a primitive state, usually doused with petroleum twice each summer to prevent dust, and smelling accordingly; wooden churches of at least four or five denominations. As an obstacle to traffic on these "streets," wooden houses are placed on rollers and are thus moved along (the owner became rich, sold his house, and built a new one for himself; the old one is taken to the fields where a *"new-comer"* buys it and moves in). In addition, the usual tangle of telegraph and telephone wires, and electrical railways under construction—for the "town" extends into the unbounded distance.

We rode around it in a small carriage pulled by a huge horse: four schools of the various sects as well as *"public schools"* (gratis—compulsory school attendance is in prospect); a hotel with modest rooms but, despite low prices, carpets in all corridors and all *"accommodations"*; interviewers who wished to hear about the greatness of their country, etc. A marvelously attractive—that is, not esthetically attractive—picture of growth which next year will already have assumed the character of Oklahoma City, that is, that of any other western city. The immigrants come from the north and the east, are usually poor wretches and can actually be rich people in a few years. Thus there is a colossal *"boom,"* and despite all laws speculation in land is flourishing. Two *"real-estate men,"* an asphalt man, and two traveling salesmen accosted me. . . .

There is a fabulous bustle here, and I cannot help but find tremendous fascination in it, despite the stench of petroleum and the fumes, the spitting *"Yankees"* and the racket of the numerous trains. Nor can I deny that in general I find the people pleasant. All officials have received me in their shirt sleeves, of course, and together we put our legs on the windowsill. The "lawyers" struck me as somewhat bold; there is a marvelously free-and-easy atmosphere, and yet mutual respect is never lost sight of. You would never believe all the things I have been asked; "How do you cope with the Negroes in Germany?" was not even the craziest question. But the people also tell stories, and I believe I have not been so merry since my first semesters at the university as I have been here with these people, who are as naive as children and yet handle any situation—despite the fact that alcohol is absolutely prohibited here and that this prohibition works in practice. This is a more "civilized" place than Chicago. It would be quite wrong to believe that one can behave as one wishes. In the conversations, which are, to be sure, quite brief, the courtesy lies in the tone and the bearing, and the humor is nothing short of delicious. Too bad; in a year this place will look like Oklahoma [City], that is, like any other American city. With almost lightning speed everything that stands in the way of capitalistic culture is being crushed.

A singular experience that gave Weber much pleasure was a carriage ride up hill and down dale through woodland clearings to a clubhouse at Fort Gibson on the Canadian River:

Fort Gibson is a charming place in the forest, rather high above the river. The clubhouse is a place like all others of its kind: in it there is a form of *Gemütlichkeit* with which we Germans are not familiar. *"Aunt Bessie"* and *"Uncle Tom,"* two very old blacks, are employed as servants. There are beds for people who come to spend the night in the heat of summer as well as simple *"country dinners"* (raw tomatoes, ham, eggs, wild honey, and milk) and, above all, there almost always is jolly company.

The (nonpartisan) club consists of about forty people of various occupations, vacancies are filled by ballot, and it costs each member about 75 dollars per year. In return for this it replaces the tavern, the drink at sundown, and the parties (for the gentlemen; the ladies have their *"receptions"*); and it is an object of pride, because it represents the social exclusiveness of all involved. It is the *symposion*[24] translated in-

[24]Literally, "a drinking together"; in ancient Greece and Rome, a convivial meeting for drinking and intellectual conversation.—Ed.

to American, for there is only conversation and amusement, possibly some sport—but there is no opportunity for this at the Grand River, and there are other associations for it.

The whole thing was very nice. However, my backside had never been subjected to such a bastinado as on these "roads" with the dead-straight *"section lines"* of the surveyor's office. "Holes" would not be the proper word for the valley formation into which the carriage plunges and from which it is pulled out later. Puddles, bogs, tree trunks—all these things leave the horses cold and do not damage the thin wheels made of hickory wood as hard as a rock. We went over a long railroad bridge—at the risk that a train might have the fun of putting us on its *"cow-catcher"*—and then crossed the river at another place on a raftlike ferry. Added to this was the wildness of the cleared areas: charred tree trunks, camps of settlers, an occasional wagon piled high and belonging to small leaseholders on the move, log cabins of earlier vintage, half-finished modern factory buildings, Negro huts crammed with black people—all this scattered over a large area of the prairie and the dense forest by the river, and then suddenly a "town" in the making, like Fort Gibson, with perhaps 100 widely scattered little houses, but including a power plant, a telephone network, etc. Then absolute solitude again. Twice we ran over a cow and once over one of those horrible black Texas pigs. Several times at midnight we had to rouse farmers whom we could hear snoring[25] through the openings of their tents and ask them for directions. I was surprised that these people remained polite. In short, it was a strange drive—first in the darkness, then by moonlight.

Today I watched whole troops of Indians arrive to get their money; the full-blooded ones have peculiar tired facial features and are surely doomed to destruction, but among the others one sees intelligent faces. Their clothes are almost invariably European. I learned many other interesting things from all sorts of people, and I think my host, the Cherokee, will attack the latest Indian policy of the United States in the *Archiv:* his eyes sparkled when he spoke about it. But enough of this trip "to the old, romantic land."[26] The next time I come here, the last remnant of "romanticism" will be gone.

* * *

[25]Apropos of snoring: In my room at the Muskogee Hotel it says on the price list next to the electric bell: *"Frog in your throat?—10 cents."* I have never found such a good expression—or such a deserved treatment—for snoring.

[26]An allusion to the phrase *Ritt in's alte romantische Land,* Christoph Martin Wieland's description of his verse romance *Oberon* (1780).—Ed.

In New Orleans, the southernmost point of their long journey through the tropical forest, the travelers hoped to find the special quality of the originally French foundation. They found paralyzing tropical heat in October, which was too much even for the blacks; withered, dusty vegetation; and a deadly depression over everything. "We were glad to have that accursed hole behind us after two and a half days." Thank God, they were now going north again.

They next landed in the little city of Tuskegee in order to see Booker Washington's famous educational institution for Negroes. What they found probably moved them more than anything else on their trip. The great national problem of all American life, the showdown between the white race and the former slaves, could here be grasped at its roots. They sensed above all the tragedy of the pariahdom of that ever-increasing mixed race of all shades from dark brown to ivory, people who by virtue of their descent and talents belonged to the master race [Herrenrasse] but were excluded from its community as though they bore a stigma. According to law there were no longer any slaves, but the white masters of the southern states took revenge by socially boycotting the slaves' children and children's children. They used them for every kind of work, but anyone who played host to a mulatto thereby permanently removed himself from association with his own race.

Thus the Negro leaders had to strike a counterblow: they had to awaken racial pride in the outcasts and attempt to turn them into cultured persons. This gigantic task involved nothing less than teaching "culture" to a race which in an unmixed state actually seemed to have been relegated to the outer reaches of the human realm. The idealism of the leaders, coupled with sound common sense, attempted to do so by "the gospel of the toothbrush" as well as by training for sensible work of all kinds. Some day, they hoped, even the white man *must* have respect. But the white man tried to protect his own race against degeneration by means of a boycott. The tremendous, irremediable discord of America made the national life of Germany seem on a very small scale. At that time American newspapers were just reporting, with ironic pleasure, all stages of the Lippe struggle for succession.[27] Weber reported:

---

[27]Lippe was an old German principality in northwestern Germany, with Detmold as the capital city. The struggle for succession, from 1897 to 1905, brought the Lippe-Biesterfeld branch to power.—Ed.

At Tuskegee no one is permitted to do only intellectual work. The purpose is the training of farmers; *"conquest of the soil"* is a definite ideal. An enormous amount of enthusiasm is generated among the teachers and students, and Tuskegee is the only place with a socially free atmosphere, particularly for the numerous half-Negroes, quarter-Negroes, and one-hundredth part Negroes whom no non-American can distinguish from whites, who are all barred by law from marrying whites, are in practice excluded from associating with them, and are assigned their own railroad cars, waiting rooms, hotels, and parks (such as in Knoxville). The semi-apes one encounters on the plantations and in the Negro huts of the *"Cotton Belt"* afford a horrible contrast, but so does the intellectual condition of the whites in the south as soon as one looks beyond the humanly attractive surface. Everyone has a different opinion of Booker Washington and his work, ranging from deepest revulsion at any education for Negroes which deprives planters of "hands," to the opinion, not rare among southern whites, that he was the greatest American of all time next to Washington and Jefferson. But without exception they share the view that *"social equality"* and *"social intercourse"* are impossible—even, or particularly, with the educated and often nine-tenths white Negro upper class. Yet the whites are bleeding to death because of this separation intended as "racial protection," and the only enthusiasm in the south may be found among that Negro upper class; among the whites there is only aimless, impotent hatred of the Yankees.

I must have spoken with a hundred white southerners of all parties and social classes, and on the basis of this the problem of what is to become of these people seems absolutely hopeless. In fact, one of these good, proud, but confused people who are lost in today's struggle for existence is Uncle Fritz. He never owned a slave and was a strict abolitionist, but he always fought on the side of the slaveholders, because according to his Jefferson-Calhoun theory his state, Virginia, had the formal right to secede. He always kept too many horses and declined the highest offers, because then his neighbor would have a more beautiful horse than he. He was a Methodist because every day his wife made him fear the torments of hell to which he would otherwise be subjected.

The Webers also met G. F. Fallenstein's descendants, who were leading simple lives with little culture, without the heritage of the Yankee spirit—having, in fact, been raised with an antipathy to it. One of them had been at first a miner and then an elementary-school teacher and was now owner of a law office and associated with a smart Irishman for whom he did the work; he, at any rate, was on his way toward becoming a notable. Two other sons had achieved no more than a few hills—which they had cleared themselves—at the edge of the Blue Ridge Mountains on the border between North Carolina and Virginia, as well as plain farmhouses on a bare elevation with none of the comfortable expansiveness and floral decoration of German farm houses. Unconsciously homesick and with many children, they were struggling for another form of existence. Weber reported:

> We arrived in Mount Airy in the darkness. Jim and his oldest boy picked us up with a carriage, and then we traveled for one and a half hours, in complete darkness and with the moon just coming out, through shrubbery and through the "river" over fords, up and down the valley over horrible roads. Once we seriously thought we had broken all our ribs—the carriage creaked as though it were falling to pieces. We had gone over a thick tree trunk that lay across the road. But the horses remained calm and so did Jim. We were received by Jim's wife. Icy cold—our first frost, and we were dazzled and roasted by the fireplace. In the whole house not a scrap of paper—neither for writing (James writes his letters when he gets to Mount Airy) nor for any other purpose to which civilized persons customarily devote paper. But there were a well, icy water, and very good beds in an upstairs room of the little two-story wooden house.
>
> Let Marianne report about the people; I shall describe more the externals and the outward course of events. The houses of the two brothers, Jefferson and James, are opposite each other and within shouting distance, on two hills that descend rather steeply toward a small brook in the middle. On the low ground below there is the good soil where each raises on his own plot tobacco, corn, and wheat. The cattle graze on the hillside, and besides the tobacco they are the only marketable product. The people eat the corn themselves or feed it to the cattle. The ritual of the overabundant and very good but quite monotonous meals was everywhere the same: boiled beef, pork hash, canned fruit, "hot rolls" (corn cakes baked red-hot), fruit preserves, coffee, and milk—everything three times a day. While one of the teen-age girls stood around waving a huge fly whisk, James and Jeff loaded up our plates, and the women stood and poured coffee or milk. When the old people had eaten, a second set came to the table and sometimes even a third (the children); finally the Negro ate by himself (he lives in a shack with some land, both of which he received from James). In James's house, grace was said briefly before the meal. At Jeff's, whose

children—with the exception of one daughter—belong to no church, there was nothing of the sort. Afterward we sat around the fireplace—sitting outside is not considered comfortable—and everybody chewed tobacco. Jeff spat well-aimed streams of brown sauce into the fire through and over the legs of those sitting in between. We were in quite good humor; only Jeff, who has a profound aversion to *"farming,"* usually remained depressed.

Unexpectedly Weber even here acquired illustrative material for his work: old and new forms of the social stratification of democratic society. In an elemental form he saw the life-forming effect of religious sects as well as their increasing replacement by orders and clubs of all kinds. The result of his observations may be found particularly in his essay on "Churches and Sects."

Sunday morning in church with James, Frank, and Betty. The young Methodist preacher came to James's house for lunch, as did the entirely unchurchly Jeff and his family. In the afternoon everyone attended a Baptist christening. In the open air eight people (three women, several adolescents, two men) were submerged in the icy water of the mountain brook—the only valid form of baptism, according to orthodox Baptist doctrine. The preacher, dressed in a black suit, stands in the water up to his hips; one after another the candidates for baptism get into the brook in their best *"dress,"* grasp his hands, and, after the various vows have been spoken, bend their knees, and, supported by his arm, lean backwards until their face is under water. Then they come out snorting, are *"congratulated,"* and either go home dripping wet or, if they live far away, change clothes in a wooden shack. They do this even in the middle of the winter, chopping a hole in the ice for the purpose. James said that *"faith"* kept them from catching cold. Jeff, who regards all this as nonsense, said that he had asked one of them, *"Didn't you feel pretty cold, Bem?"* The answer: *"I thought of some pretty hot place* (hell, of course), *Sir, and so I didn't care for the cold water."* Betty is an avid churchgoer; *"almost as fanatic as her mother was,"* said Jeff, who, like the others, was driven from any connection with the church by the terrible severity of his mother.

Interest in the church has declined generally—as the young preacher admitted, the old Methodist *"revivals"* and *"class meetings"* (weekly confession by all individuals in the company of their neighbors) have deteriorated. The sermon was good, purely practical, delivered with great excitement. Those who felt "aroused" then stepped forward and knelt by the altar. An old peasant prayed loudly and passionately for all—but the unspeakably horrible singing of the shrill voices kept bringing us back to the prosaicness of the barn in which we were. Naturally there were no vestments. The clergyman spoke in his *"jacket"* and entirely in the manner of a political speaker. On the "altar" (a table) lay his felt hat. The poetry lay in the solitude of the colorful forest all around us, in that baptism afterward, and in the earnestness of the old farmers of the Westphalian-Holstein type. The old social function of these sects has been diminished, too; it is true that everyone, including the clergyman, is introduced as *"brother,"* but James belongs to an "order"— his credit rating is based largely on this—to which one is elected at the suggestion of five members and from which one is expelled for bad conduct. It is a health insurance, a burial fund, and a widows' pension fund; the members are pledged to mutual aid and obligated to grant credit in cases of blameless economic distress; expulsion is the punishment for an unmotivated refusal.

Once this was the most important function of American sects. The tremendous increase in the clubs and orders here is a substitute for the crumbling organization of the sects. Virtually every farmer and a great number of businessmen of medium and lower rank wear their *"badge"* in their buttonhole, the way Frenchmen wear little red ribbons, not primarily out of vanity, but because it immediately identifies the wearer as having been recognized as a *"gentleman"* and accepted by ballot by a certain group of people who have investigated his character and conduct—one automatically thinks of our investigations of reserve officers. This is exactly the same service that 150 years ago was rendered a member of the old sects (Baptists, Quakers, Methodists, etc.) by his *"letter of recommendation,"* which his community gave him for his "brothers" in other cities.

Weber eagerly absorbed all this. He was stimulated to give effortlessly of his own resources what was able to delight these simple people, and thus he unearthed in them the treasures of the experiences of a lifetime. Here, too, he was an equal among equals, a "brother"; everyone felt understood and appreciated by him. Marianne was able to catch only snatches of the conversations that were carried on among the corncobs outside, "for I had to stay inside with the women and had only an occasional chance to pursue a burst of laughter which Max conjured up on the men's side. Of course, he quickly won their hearts with his beautiful *"Nigger-English"* [sic][28] and his

---

[28]The author presumably meant that Weber's English was primitive and perhaps even "exotic" and droll.—Ed.

stories. They often slapped him on the knee and called him a *"mighty jolly fellow."* The good, plain people were sad that they had to let their guests go so soon; they made the parting easier for each other by promising that they would return soon, a promise that could not be kept.

* * *

The Webers then went back to the cultural centers of the eastern states and saw in quick succession Philadelphia, Washington, Baltimore, Boston, and their environs. They could hardly cope with everything. Marianne often felt saturated and wondered what real concern of hers all these strange things were, since they could not be actively drawn into the range of her own existence. Weber, on the other hand, remained intensely receptive; after all, he had the ability to make something of everything by recasting it intellectually.

In Washington they had an opportunity to take an idyllic excursion to Mount Vernon, the birthplace of the great national leader. On an overcast day they traveled on the wide, blackish Potomac; the wooded slopes on the shore had the colors of autumn. They climbed up a slope to little white wooden houses whose Biedermeier modesty had the homey touch of relics from the time of Goethe. There was a profound solitude and quiet everywhere—the quiet of something no longer existing, the exalted melancholy of consummation. The bygone, greatly agitated life now revealed itself only to those who harbored it within themselves. Down below there was the bustle of life again, as though it was of tremendous importance in each individual. They absorbed some very strange things, such as a Negro religious service for the refined Negro world:

Everyone in silk, very elegant black *"ladies,"* fine, intelligent Negroes, and mulatto faces. The preacher was out of town and his place was taken by a layman and an outside visitor. Uncanny how a muffled moaning began as the sermon increased in urgency and finally became impassioned; at first it painfully reminded one of intestinal rumbling, then it was a kind of whispering echo. The last words of each sentence were repeated, first softly, then in a shrill voice—*"Yes, Yes!"* or *"No, No!"* in response to the apostrophizing of the preacher, who was no more impassioned than the young Methodist in Mount Airy and did not begin to compare with Stöcker. We really began to feel uncomfortable and queer. And on the other hand, in back, where we were sitting, there were smiling quadroons and giggling mulatto girls—what contrasts within the Negro group, which we imagine as being uniform!

They had still more surprising experiences of the variety of this competitive American life:

Our departure for Boston was almost fraught with difficulty. You see, the *"football-team"* of the University of Pennsylvania was leaving for Boston to fight against Harvard; all 2000 students saw it off at the railway station, and hundreds took the ten-hour trip here. Consequently, that evening the station was inaccessible for hours. The rascals did not let anyone pass. Everyone missed his train and a lady was badly trampled. We then saw the whole thing from our carriage: The alumni [*alte Herren*] have built a tremendous stone amphitheater for half a million, as big as the Colosseum, with room for 40,000 people. After each *"play"* there was thunderous chanting by whichever team had been victorious, for all of Boston and a good part of Philadelphia were there. The *"City Hall"* and the whole town were decked with flags. And when Harvard lost, a profound depression ensued. The big Boston newspapers had half a page about the war in East Asia, three about the presidential election, and eight about the game. Then there were endless interviews with each of the twenty-two young rascals who had participated. Philadelphia was illuminated and unanimous in its view that this success far outweighed the trampled lady. Incredible goings-on.

In elegant Boston, with its buildings darkened with age, and particularly at Harvard, they again felt that they were on familiar soil. Here the wild adventurousness of colonial life seemed to be settling down in the firmly established old English tradition; things that had ripened now joined together in salutary harmony. This rose to monumental beauty in the marvelous complex of buildings of Harvard College. In this framework of intellectual struggle shared by teachers and students, in which not the state but private patrons proudly expressed their strength, a German scholar, too, could probably feel at home quickly. It seemed admirable that Hugo Münsterberg, whose outstanding ability had not been properly used at home and who was now offering counsel and hospitality to all sorts of illustrious German travelers of the Wilhelminian era, always felt himself as a German first.

The journey concluded with an extended stay in New York. Among other things, Weber wished to inspect the library of Columbia University and get a fuller impression of everything. He met hospitable people and reflected about the country and the people at greater leisure.

> In recent days we have lived extravagantly and met as many new people as we do in a year in Heidelberg. Wonderful that Max was able to endure all this! Sometimes he grumbles a little when he has to put on a clean shirt and his dinner jacket, but he really manages to go out for lunch as well as dinner. To be able to do that we have to busy ourselves with our attire half the afternoon—from polishing shoes to selecting the appropriate tie, and this of course is very relaxing.

Of the Americans the Webers met, a woman, the industrial inspector Florence Kelley,[29] was by far the most outstanding figure. From this impassioned socialist they learned a great deal more about the radically evil things in this world:

> The utter hopelessness of social legislation in a system of state particularism; the corruption of many labor leaders, who incite "*strikes*" and then have the manufacturers pay them for settling them (I had a personal letter of introduction to such a scoundrel); the conditions in Chicago, where despite passionate agitation it was not possible to create a law for the protection of women from the hazards of certain occupations, until a firm was founded which manufactured such protective devices and then managed to have their use legally required by bribing representatives from various states!; etc. Yet the Americans are a wonderful people, and only the Negro question and the terrible immigration constitute the big black clouds.

"A wonderful people"—for there was a youthfully fresh, confident energy, a force for good that was just as powerful as the evil forces. They found the most impressive symbol of this in the Jewish section, that self-contained world in which the wretched Jewish immigrants from Eastern Europe served the God of their fathers and business at the same time. A tremendous project here was the Jewish educational and charitable institution for immigrants, which was built with private funds. Its stone threshold, worn down in a few years, was evidence that thousands of outcast children went in and out every day.

---

[29]1859–1932, chief inspector of factories for Illinois, 1893–97, general secretary of the National Consumers League from 1899 on. American editor of the *Archiv für soziale Gesetzgebung*, 1897–98; lived at Hull House and the Henry Street Settlement.—Ed.

They have everything imaginable here: a library, baths, a gymnasium, instruction in music and drawing, cooking and sewing, courses in handicraft and science, dancing lessons, and even a little theater in which children act to refine their taste. The absolute *"selfgovernment"* of the children, of the clubs, in which they do not allow anyone to interfere and which they do not display to strangers is really the foremost means of Americanization. The young people's freedom from authority in their struggle for existence bears its fruits here. They come in as the children of "schnorrers" who strictly adhere to all religious rituals, and they leave this training institution as *"gentlemen"* and pounce upon the Negroes of the South, on whom they practice a frightful usury.

* * *

It was time to say farewell. The year was drawing to a close, the days were getting shorter, and the Webers wanted to be home for Christmas. Once more they drank in the view from the Brooklyn Bridge. In the winter sunset it was more magnificent than it had been in summer. The sky was dark red, fading into a pale violet. Rising up like rocky mountains with strange contours were the masses of giant buildings at the tip of Manhattan, illuminated by a thousand lights, as though the spirit living in these rocky towers had condensed into red-hot streams of gold. Their last evening was spent in the Jewish section:

First in a "Yiddish" theater, then with our special friend Dr. Blaustein,[30] the head of the reception center for immigrants, an idealist of the first water and an "arch-Jew" [Knalljud] of the craziest physiognomy, and with the author of the play Die emtje Kraft [The True Power],[31] which we saw last night. Two-thirds of the language was incomprehensible to us—a horribly corrupted pronunciation of German, interspersed with Hebrew and some Russian words; at highly tragic moments one gets to hear was is des Läben mies [how lousy life is]—and we were thus largely unable to follow the dialogue. But the acting was so magnificent in its own way that we fully understood the plot, especially since the not unobjectionable play had a few types (particularly a "Socialist" and a rabbinical "Scholar") who were splendidly portrayed

[30]David Blaustein, 1866–1912, from 1898 to 1907 superintendent of the Educational Alliance, then the most important social-educational institution on the East Side of New York.—Ed.
[31]Di emese kraft is a play by Russian-born Jacob Gordin (1853–1908), one of the most prolific writers for the Yiddish stage, who lived in New York from 1891 on.—Ed.

by the actors—the best to be found in America—in absolute self-
caricature. . . .

When Weber was writing this, their boat was already pitching in its uniform rhythm and the bustle of life was silent in the foggy veil of a winter
day. He looked back with gratitude to the country where he had been
granted such happy days. Marianne sometimes had the feeling that she was
bringing home a man restored to health, a man who had again become conscious of the reserves of energy that had slowly accumulated. Weber himself
drew up the following balance sheet:

It cannot be said, of course, that the "scientific" results of the trip
are equal to its expenses. I have secured a considerable number of interesting contributors to our periodical. I am now in a much better position to understand the statistics and the government reports about
the United States. I shall myself write some critiques about Negro literature and the like, and perhaps a few other little things—but for
my work in cultural history I did not see much more than where the
things are that I ought to see, particularly the libraries I would have
to use, which are scattered all over the country in little sects and
"colleges." Under these circumstances the trip can be justified in our
present situation only from the general point of view of a widening of
my scholarly horizon (*and* improving my state of health). Its fruits in
this respect can, of course, not be seen for some time. At any rate,
it is good that I have been able to manage the trip like this; a year
ago it would have been utterly impossible. . . . Stimulation and occupation of the mind without intellectual exertion simply is the only
remedy.

10

THE NEW PHASE OF
HIS PRODUCTION _____

This chapter will attempt to present to nonscholars some aspects of Weber's ideas which may give them a picture of his mind and, above all, add to their knowledge of his personality. Weber's scholarly work is immeasurable, and to assimilate any of it, it is necessary to follow his thought processes and to come to terms with the difficult material. The ideas presented here essentially developed at the point where scientific cognition and life-forming conviction met, where his contemplative faculties were so close to the active ones that his writings illuminate his personality as thinker, teacher, and politician. But this too is only a cup drawn from a gushing fountain: the water comes from it, but it does not contain the essence of the fountain.

* * *

In the first period of his creativity, Max Weber's desire for knowledge and representation was directed at certain aspects of reality itself, that is to say, at events in the history of law and of economics that were significant from the viewpoint of political economy and politics. His first works were primarily the expression of a young historian with an insatiable hunger for material, a man who was so moved by the development and decline of a vanished life that a reflection of that life was resuscitated in him.

He was equally concerned with the political and social problems of his own time. We have seen that he discovered momentous shifts in the governance and property holding of the German rural population and subsumed the results of his research under ideals of a nation-state; guided by these ideals in evaluating existing conditions, he used these conditions to set political goals. The researcher and the politician had fructified each other. The principles guiding Weber in his selection of material were, first and foremost, political passion, then a sense of justice for manual workers, and, further, the conviction that human *happiness* was not the important thing, but that *freedom* and human *dignity* were the ultimate and highest values whose realization should be made possible for everyone. The mastery of facts he had acquired early in life placed an inexhaustible wealth of illustrative material at his disposal for clarifying scientific and theoretical connections or practical and political matters.

Then, in 1902, after the severe crisis that would last for a long time, Weber's creative impulse was directed toward an entirely different intellectual field. From an active life as an academic teacher and politician he was banished to the contemplative atmosphere of his quiet study. Whether for external reasons or because of an inner compulsion, he now withdrew from reality in his capacity of thinker as well and devoted himself to thinking about thought and about the logical and epistemological problem of his science. Undoubtedly an external stimulus was partly responsible for this. His colleagues on the *Philosophische Fakultät* of the University of Heidelberg asked him, in a way that made Weber feel obligated, to contribute an essay to a Festschrift for the celebration of the university's restoration.[1] In the spring of 1902 he began his first methodological treatise, *Roscher und Knies*

---

[1] The University of Heidelberg, established in 1386 by Elector Ruprecht I, was in a state of decline when, in 1803, Grand Duke Friedrich of Baden greatly improved it and named it Ruperto-Carola or Ruprecht-Karl-Universität. The above-mentioned celebration commemorated the centennial of this event.—Ed.

und die Grundlagen der Nationalökonomie. The work expanded as he worked on it. It demanded great mental exertion and therefore tortured the scholar, who was still a sick man, especially since it proved impossible to complete it for the intended purpose. Like several other logical treatises, he finally did not complete it at all, for new tasks came crowding in on him. As he slowly recovered, his ability to work fluctuated for years and he believed that he constantly needed fresh stimuli to overcome his insidious inhibitions. What he did and how things presented themselves did not matter to him as long as he was able to work at all.

Of course, Weber's interest in philosophical and logical problems was not born on this occasion; it was woven into his intellectual life during his entire period of development. In his field, theory had always interested him as much as history. His lectures on theoretical political economy were constructed around a framework of precise concepts. In his Freiburg inaugural address he expressed his views on philosophical problems for the first time.

The factual material of this lecture is arranged around an investigation of the standards of value of economic policy as a doctrine. For this discipline the theoretical questions, about how things were and how things *are*, directly relate to questions about what *should* be and what should happen. It is therefore especially important to have a clear understanding of the guiding principles, because here a scholar has a substantial voice in the social structuring of life. His theses and opinions influence legislation, the property structure, the evaluation of the situation of manual workers, and so on. His thought shares the responsibility for shaping the world.

At that time the orientation within the social sciences was as follows: The grand old men, particularly the English founders of political economy, regarded an increase in pleasure through an increase in wealth—that is, a promotion of the economic production of goods at any price—as a self-evident goal. Then, when under the protection of these ideals "the free play of forces"[2] spawned a ruthless acquisitive drive and the exploitation of the unpropertied became obvious, most younger scholars adopted a different approach. As we have seen, they became "academic socialists" [*Kathedersozialisten*]. A fair distribution of goods—that is, the fulfillment of a moral obligation—was now regarded as the goal of economic policy.

In his inaugural address Weber wished, above all, to point out that it

---

[2]"*Das freie Spiel der Kräfte*"—a phrase from *Von der Weltseele*, a work by the philosopher Friedrich Wilhelm Schelling (1798).—Ed.

was impossible to derive *independent* ideals from the subject matter of political economy: "In truth it is the old general types of human ideals which we bring to the material of our science." He expressed the conviction that political economy ought to be guided neither by ideals of production methods nor eudemonic ideals, not even by ethical ideals, but by "national" ones. To be sure, in dealing for the first time with the main ideas of a specialized discipline, he was as yet concerned not with *logical* problems but with a doctrine with a voluntaristic orientation (to the shaping of life). He was attempting to clarify thought that was to have a voice in economic and political *action.* These were vital questions.

In the first treatise of the new phase, his object of investigation was no longer thought aiming at the orientation of concerned people, but a thinking oriented toward scientific truth—a task without any direct relationship to reality. From then on Weber's concern with logical questions remained with him until his last work. But after he had published the first section of Roscher and Knies, he again relegated it to a secondary place, for in the quiet of his study he was gripped by a desire for universal history—an urge to grasp and present as much as possible of all significant happenings in the world. More will be said about this later. We shall now attempt to convey an idea of the *logical* problems that occupied Weber and thereby find a bridge to that point of his intellectual personality where the perceiving and the desiring man may be comprehended down to his roots.

Most of the essays on the logic of the cultural sciences which Weber published between 1903 and 1918 have a critical and polemical point of departure. Weber develops his own views by pointing out errors and combating them. Again his clear thinking and sense of reality stand him in good stead. The difficult logical analyses are always illustrated by graphic, vivid examples. They unintentionally make these generally difficult and involved writings personal and attractive. For example, Weber uses Goethe's letters to Frau Stein[3] to show the many and extraordinarily different points of view from which one and the same cultural phenomenon may be "historically significant", or he uses the procedure of the game of skat to discuss the fundamental difference in the concept of rules. Elsewhere he draws on concrete happenings—such as a mother slapping a child's face and then giving the reason—to show that even the perception of something one has experi-

---

[3]Charlotte von Stein, 1742–1827, the wife of the ducal Master of the Horse in Weimar, was Goethe's friend and muse for a dozen years, beginning in 1775. His letters to her were published between 1848 and 1851.—Ed.

enced is not a simple repetition of the experience, but is shaped by rules of thinking.

Weber did not care about the systematic presentation of his thinking, for he did not wish to be a professional logician. Even though he valued methodological insights highly, he did not value them for their own sake but appreciated them as indispensable tools that helped to clarify the possibilities of perceiving concrete problems. And he attached no importance whatever to the form in which he presented his wealth of ideas. Once he got going, so much material flowed from the storehouse of his mind that it was often hard to force it into a lucid sentence structure. And yet he wanted to be done with it quickly and express himself as briefly as possible, because new problems from the realm of reality constantly crowded in upon him. For him the great limitation of discursive thought was that it did not permit the simultaneous expression of several correlative lines of thought. Thus a great deal had to be hastily crammed into long, convoluted sentences, and whatever could not be accommodated there had to be put in footnotes. Let the reader "kindly" take as much trouble as he himself did! Weber was a master of speaking without notes, a man who made the most remote things so immediate that he appeared to have just witnessed them himself, and he achieved great effects by simple means, seemingly without effort, art, or rhetoric, although he did have a marvelous voice.

At times it seemed as though he intentionally neglected his scholarly style—in opposition to a current trend to attach undue importance to formal values and to waste time in an endeavor to bestow upon scholarly creations the character of a work of art. In this esthetics of style Weber saw a mixture of intellectual spheres that obeyed different laws, and he particularly hated the "unsimpleness" [Unschlichtheit] of expression that could easily creep in, as well as the straining for a "personal touch." He frequently quoted from Faust: "Es trägt Verstand und rechter Sinn mit wenig Kunst sich selber vor."[4] The diction should be suited to the subject but not blown up beyond its scholarly purpose. The person of the thinker must not intentionally obtrude itself in the realm of scholarship but should withdraw behind the subject.

* * *

[4]"With little art, clear wit and sense suggest their own delivery"—Goethe's Faust, Part I, lines 550–1, in Bayard Taylor's translation.—Ed.

The central problem of logic and epistemology which Weber encountered was the great conflict between the natural sciences and the so-called *Geisteswissenschaften* [humanities]. This occupied most contemporary philosophers and logicians under the leadership of Dilthey,[5] Windelband,[6] Simmel, and Heinrich Rickert. The discussion also extended into the empirical sciences. The enormous successes of the natural sciences had given rise to the conviction that a "rational" perception of all reality was possible, a perception that was free of both metaphysics and individual chance. One universal method could and should predominate in its entire sphere, and only the results of that method could claim to be the valid truth; what this method could not encompass did not belong within the framework of science but was "art." "Naturalism" as a method and *Weltanschauung* claimed dominion in all areas of life and thought. The defense of the "humanities" concentrated on a demonstration of their special character and independence, based on the different subject matters.

In the social sciences the methodological quarrel raged with special vehemence, for their subject matter—human action whose dependence on natural processes is clearly recognizable—seemed to lie on the boundary line between the natural and the intellectual and could with equal justification be judged to be in the realm of "nature" or in the realm of "freedom." Thus the "classical" and the "historical" schools of political economy were irreconcilably opposed. Anton Menger,[7] the leader of the "classical" school, had rejected the division of the objects of perception according to "intellect" and "nature" as logically inadequate and had replaced them with the different *viewpoints* from which the same actualities can be logically processed. But for that very reason he considered political economy to be one of the natural sciences. According to him its task was discovering the *laws* of economic life, and he was convinced that these were analogous to the laws of nature. At the same time, a system of abstract concepts and doctrines from which an idea of reality can be derived appeared to be the only way to achieve a practical and intellectual mastery of social occurrences.

By contrast there was the younger, "historical" school which split off

[5]Wilhelm Dilthey, 1833–1911, philosopher and literary historian, professor at Berlin from 1882 on.—Ed.
[6]Wilhelm Windelband, 1848–1915, neo-Kantian philosopher, professor at Zurich, Freiburg, Strasbourg, and Heidelberg.—Ed.
[7]1841–1906, professor of law at the University of Vienna.—Ed.

from the classical school under the leadership of Gustav Schmoller. It considered the purpose of research in economics and the social sciences, as in history, to be the clear reproduction of the characteristic quality of concrete reality. The problem was complicated by the fact that although distinguished masters of political economy like Roscher and Knies belonged to the historical school, they still believed they could find "natural laws of political economy." Roscher, for example, assumed that events took place among various peoples in accordance with certain laws. Regarding "the people" as a uniform species, as biology regards man, he classified the course of history according to various stages and spoke of the youth, maturity, old age, and death of peoples. What is not explained by such formulas—namely, the actions of specific human beings and their influence—is ascribed to the "freedom of will," which *inexplicably* breaks the laws of nature, or to the mysterious background of divine rule in history.

It is at this stage of the problem in his own field that Weber's logical work began as a process of scholarly self-knowledge. The intellectual tools required for this were supplied him by contemporary logic and epistemology, particularly Heinrich Rickert's theory of knowledge with its separation of practical valuation from theoretical "value relationship," which was particularly important to him. In his essay on Roscher and Knies he said that he wished to test whether Rickert's concepts were applicable to political economy. However, his own methodological ideas soon took him beyond that goal. He took up the logical problems everywhere in order to gain a clear view of the scientific process. Thus, he brought works by Dilthey, Wundt, Simmel, Münsterberg, Gottl, von Kries, Eduard Meyer, Stammler,[8] and others into his discussions. From Rickert's *kulturwissenschaftlich* [cultural-science] logic Weber took a doctrine that he later supplemented with his own sociological method—that the sciences are separated not only by differences in *subject matter*, but also by differences in *interest* in the material and in the formulation of questions.

Thus the natural sciences proceed in a "generalizing" way, because they are interested in the shared, homogeneous aspects of phenomena and cover

---

[8]Wilhelm Wundt, 1832–1920, philosopher, psychologist, and physiologist, professor at Heidelberg, Zurich, and Leipzig; Friedrich von Gottl-Ottlilienfeld, 1868–1958, economist, professor at Brünn (Brno) and Berlin (from 1926 on); Eduard Meyer, 1855–1930, historian, professor at Leipzig, Breslau, Halle, and Berlin; Rudolf Stammler, 1856–1938, neo-Kantian philosopher, professor at Marburg, Giessen, Halle, and Berlin.—Ed.

these aspects with a net of general concepts and laws. Conversely, "individualizing" history and related disciplines are interested in the special character of concrete happenings and objects, specifically those that have "sense and significance" as cultural occurrences. These events, which are determined by human action, are the objects of historical science and other specially constituted sciences based on laws [Gesetzeswissenschaften] that Rickert differentiates from the natural sciences and calls cultural sciences [Kulturwissenschaften].

The social sciences are part of these, for they concern themselves with certain aspects of culturally significant human behavior. Unlike the natural sciences, their cognitive goal is not a system of general concepts and laws, but the special character of concrete phenomena and connections, although in this they also use the concepts and rules of events as means of cognition. Although any object can be given both the generalizing and the individualizing treatment, occurrences of external nature lend themselves more to the former, while the latter is more suitable for human behavior. Moreover, human action is accessible to us through peculiar mental processes that are not applicable to natural phenomena—namely understanding through reliving, which makes it possible to interpret the contexts of meaning [Sinnzusammenhänge].

Weber developed for the social sciences a doctrine of understanding. Its makings may be found in Dilthey and Simmel, it occupied Münsterberg, and Weber's colleague Gottl tried to utilize it comprehensively for political economy and history. Weber first engaged in a critical discussion with Münsterberg and Gottl,[9] and later he presented his own doctrine, which he had derived from this discussion, in a special essay[10] and in the methodological introduction to his major work.[11] According to Weber, "understanding" and "interpreting" are not contrasting but complementary means of cognition.

It is not possible here to go more deeply into the logical analysis by which Weber established this. The doctrine of understanding involves the doctrine of the "meaning" of human behavior and its interpretation. We regard as meaningful those things that can be grasped by understanding, accompanied by the feeling of Evidenz [verifiable proof]. But note well: the meaning that concerns the historical cultural sciences lies in the realm of

---

[9] Cf. Gesammelte Aufsätze zur Wissenschaftslehre, p. 71ff.
[10] Ibid., 16ff.
[11] Ibid, 524ff.

experience. It is the meaning *subjectively meant* by the actor—not a meaning that is objectively "correct" or metaphysically ascertained to be "true." It was very important to Weber that his doctrine of the "subjectively meant meaning" be properly understood and that the "very fine line" between knowledge and faith, the verifiable and the unverifiable, be clearly recognized. Introducing objective interpretations of happenings, such as may occasionally be found in Simmel's ingenious analyses of cultural phenomena, is beyond the scope of the empirical sciences and obscures the purely theoretical validity of their results.

Anyone who makes such a sharp distinction between the verifiable and the unverifiable will be most concerned with the truth content of the cultural sciences. For these sciences are, in the final analysis, anchored to something unverifiable, namely, value ideas. Thus they are empirically tied to subjective and variable premises—subjective premises, because logical argumentation cannot compel recognition of the prevalent values that make a phenomenon culturally significant; variable premises, because ideas of value change slowly with the character of the culture, "for as long as Chinese ossification of intellectual life does not disaccustom mankind to asking ever fresh questions of the always uniformly inexhaustible life."

Weber teaches: the truth content of empirical sciences, whose point of departure is *extra*scientific, is created by subjecting the connections that were at first grasped "understandingly" or "intuitively" to the rules of rigorous thinking—above all, to the rules of "causal attribution." There must be a logically adequate explanation of the causal connection between the processes: "*Only what is causally explained is scientifically treated.*" Basing himself on the ingenious teachings of the physiologist von Kries, Weber analyzed the complicated logical operations by which a valid historical perception of concrete events is created. He came to the conclusion that despite their different points of departure and different cognitive goals, the natural sciences and the historical cultural sciences use the same types of logical tools. For the historical sciences, too, examine not only concrete connections but also *rules* governing the relationship between cause and effect. In addition, each field has its special characteristics. Natural science appeals to our capacity to classify events under "laws" and phenomena as "specimens" under generic concepts; it interprets and comprehends. Cultural science comprehends, interprets, and understands. Of course, unlike natural science it "comprehends" not as an end in itself but only as a means to an end. It seeks the rules governing events and creates general concepts for a better understanding and interpretation of the concrete.

Weber's doctrine of the *general concepts in cultural science* is the most singular point in his logic of history. In almost all of his writings on logic he tried to clarify its special nature, particularly in the area of the social sciences, and later he used it to establish his sociology. He endeavored to show that the theoretical thought structures of these disciplines were not, as traditional political economists believed, generic concepts from the natural sciences, but had different tasks and were derived from a singular treatment of reality. Weber calls such general concepts, which are used in every history, "ideal types"—an expression Georg Jellinek had already used in his *Allgemeine Staatslehre* [General Political Science][12] in the same sense in which Weber used it later. Namely, certain events and relationships of the past are combined into a conflictless cosmos of *imagined* connections "which nowhere exists as imagined, but is a utopia."

Concepts such as economic exchange, *homo oecumenicus* [the economic man], trade, capitalism, church, sect, Christianity, medieval urban economy, and so on are constructs in which certain elements of reality are "intellectually heightened" [*gedanklich gesteigert*] so as to recognize and clarify concrete phenomena and events in which elements of the intellectual mix [*des Zusammengedachten*] are operative.

> The ideal type is not a presentation of reality, but it aims at providing the presentation with clear means of expression . . . It is not a hypothesis, but it aims at directing the formation of hypotheses. It is not historical reality or a scheme into which it is to be integrated, but a *border* concept by which reality is *measured* to elucidate certain significant components of its substance and with which it is *compared.*

As distinct from generic concepts, then, ideal types are *means* of cognition, not goals of cognition. Because "the eternally onward-flowing stream of culture" always gives the eternally youthful historical disciplines ever new ways of formulating problems, new ideal types always have to be created and the existing ones have to be continually corrected. Historical cognition necessarily remains in constant flux. That is why it would be senseless to try to integrate it definitively into a complete system of concepts from which reality is to be derived.

Weber sees a new difficult problem of historical logic in the fact that

---

[12]This book appeared in 1900 as the first volume of Jellinek's *Das Recht des modernen Staates* (The Law of the Modern State).—Ed.

not only certain aspects of phenomena, but also the *ideas* that are active at a certain period in scattered form, are fused into the concepts of ideal types. Concepts with which history operates, such as Christianity, liberalism, socialism, democracy, and imperialism, are ideal types—something like the combination of the basic elements of an economic epoch. But their application is made more difficult by the fact that frequently people read into them not only something that exists but also something that ought to exist—namely, that aspect of theirs which is of permanent value from the standpoint of the *historian* [*Darsteller*]. But as soon as this extrascientific element is present in the application of a concept, this concept loses in cognitive value, for then theoretical "value relatedness" [*Wertbeziehung*] and practical "value judgment" [*Wertbeurteilurg*] intermingle imperceptibly. Then the ideal types change from logical aids to *ideals* by which the extrascientific significance of concrete phenomena is measured. The result is a logically untidy telescoping of the subjective and the objective, of believing and knowing, which diminishes the cognitive value of a historical presentation.

* * *

This brings us to a cluster of problems which continuously occupied Weber: the relationship between the verifiable and the unverifiable in science, between cognition and evaluation, practical value judgment and theoretical value relationship. In other words, it concerns the question of the nature and the limits of verifiable science. Can it teach us not only how to think but also how to act? And can it establish the meaning of existence in an objectively valid, *compelling* way?

This problem is everywhere interwoven with the methodological investigations. It is also discussed in detail in *Der Sinn der "Wertfreiheit" der soziologischen und ökonomischen Wissenschaften*[13] [The Meaning of "Value-Neutrality" in the Sociological and Economic Sciences], a study first written in 1913 for the *Verein für Sozialpolitik* and later published in expanded form in *Logos;* and finally, it is once more put in general terms in the lecture *Wissenschaft als Beruf*[14] [Scholarship as a Vocation], which Weber gave to students. Weber's attitude to these questions should be discussed here, for

---

[13]Cf. *Gesammelte Aufsätze zur Wirtschaftslehre*, Tübingen 1922, pp. 451ff.
[14]*Ibid.*, pp. 524ff.

it not only has scholarly significance but is of great biographical importance; in fact, it takes us right to the center of his intellectual personality. It is of equal interest to the thinker who seeks truth at any cost and to the conscientious teacher, as well as to the prudent politician who realizes that he can bring people under his spell by extraordinary eloquence and demagogic talent.

In Weber's attitude we also see the struggle, lifted onto a suprapersonal plane, between his equally strong active and contemplative tendencies: between an intellect oriented toward an unprejudiced, universal, cerebral mastery of the world and an equally strong ability to form *convictions* and stand up for them at all costs. His logical investigations had shown that the cultural sciences were based on unverifiable premises but that they nevertheless supplied valid insights. Now the question arose how research whose orientation was determined by value relationships would deal with another, extrascientific element, namely, "practical" value judgments.[15]

A value judgment arises when a person "takes an affirmative or a negative stand on the basis of a highly individual feeling or desire, or out of the awareness of a definite obligation." In other words, a "practical" value judgment is a judgment that a phenomenon which may be influenced by our actions is acceptable or objectionable, desirable or undesirable, good or bad. Therefore, in the theoretical value relationship the events and phenomena are "significant" and therefore "worth knowing," and the researcher, observing and perceiving, keeps his distance from the object and thus is in a position to change his standpoint toward it; in the practical value *judgment* the active, desiring side of his nature, the side that is oriented toward his own interest or toward ideals, comes to the fore, breaks through his contemplative relationship to reality, narrows his horizon, possibly clouds his consciousness emotionally, and in this way diminishes the truth in his thinking. Older historians had approached their subjects as judges of the universe and accompanied their presentation of events with personal commentaries. It soon became apparent that their standards were conditioned by their time and were of limited validity.

There is a danger, particularly in the social sciences, that the researcher's vision will be clouded by a desire to maintain the status quo. For the state, being a ruling organization of certain groups of persons, expects of them guidelines for its economic and political conduct and support for its measures. And since the researchers themselves belong to the ruling class

---

[15]Weber's theory applies only to ethical-political value judgments, not to esthetic ones.

and, in fact, in large part derive their livelihood from the state, their interest naturally lies with an order that gives them a privileged position.
It is clear that for them an unconscious interweaving of factual perception
with value judgments, which are prompted by definite practical interests,
is especially natural. Weber observed how often a scholar, without being
aware of it, speaks within his field not only as a servant of truth but also
as a servant of the existing order, thus representing "between the lines"
a policy colored by the interests of his own class; in this respect Karl Marx's
catchword about the "bourgeois science" is not without justification.

But is it possible to separate the two intellectual functions—
theoretical value relationship and practical value judgment, cognition and
volition? It was generally thought to be impossible, and Weber too knew
that he was positing an *ideal* researcher whose complete realization is resisted by the unity of the personality; even in the act of cognition it is
hard to separate the contemplative man from the man of action. But a
researcher should recognize this ideal and come as close to it as possible. Just
as a mystic who wishes to "have" God first curbs every stirring of the will,
a thinker must, if he is to be the mouthpiece of truth, first divest himself
of practical self-interest in what happens. If he does not succeed in doing
so, he should clearly recognize, and make others recognize, "where arguments
are addressed to reason and where they appeal to the emotions."

The important thing, then, is to avoid in scholarly activity an una-
vowed mixture of objective and personal judgments, a mixture that might
give the impression that the thinker is offering objective truth, when he
is in fact suggesting convictions. However, he should never avoid standing
up for his own ideals; on the contrary. "Unprincipledness and scientific objectivity have no inner relationship" The *social scientist* in particular, whose
findings are usable in particular measure for the shaping of *life* and who
therefore shares the responsibility for the course of politics, has a dual task:
the promotion of truth for its own sake and the "guiding of his actions
by clear, consciously chosen convictions."

These postulates are as much addressed to researchers as they are to academic teachers, and Weber reaches even more concrete conclusions for teachers of the social sciences in particular. As has been shown earlier, even as
a young student he had deemed it improper if a professor, who was invested
with scholarly authority and the dignity of his office, forced upon his students from his high rostrum his convictions and views against which they
could not defend themselves and with which they were not able to cope.
Above all, Weber considered the use of this office to form political views

in the lecture hall as thoroughly reprehensible. Inwardly protesting, he had observed in Treitschke's lecture hall the effects of demagogic influence upon young minds. But now hidden suggestion appeared to him to be even worse. He therefore made the following judgment:

> Of those scholars who believe they should *not* deny themselves practical evaluations in empirical discussions, the most passionate ones—such as Treitschke, and in his own way Mommsen as well—were actually the easiest to endure. For the very intensity of the emotional emphasis at least enabled a student *for his part* to gauge the subjectivity of his teacher's evaluations in its influence upon a possible tarnishing of his statements and thus to do for himself what the temperament of his teacher had not been granted.

Combining scientific presentation with personal value judgments struck Weber as dubious for other reasons as well: it accustomed a student to the sensational and spoiled his taste for the practical. The only justifiable pedagogic ideal for an academic teacher in his lectures is the education of his pupils to intellectual integrity and *simple objectivity*. Whatever is not pertinent must be omitted, "but most of all, love and hate." A student should learn from his teacher in the lecture hall to content himself with the simple fulfillment of a given task. Therefore, the teacher should disappear behind his subject and suppress his need "to display his personal taste and other feelings without being asked."

Weber regarded the fact that everyone would like to be a "personality" and to demonstrate it as a sickness of his time, a manifestation of self-importance which must not be encouraged, particularly among young people. "The new generation must again become accustomed to the idea that one cannot intentionally wish to be a personality and that there is only one way to (perhaps) become one: unqualified dedication to a 'cause,' no matter what this cause and the 'demands of the day'[16] proceeding from it may be like." Weber himself acted accordingly. As soon as he spoke in the name of science, he tamed a temperament which in the sphere of volition constantly forced him to select and to reject, to demand and to judge, to love and to hate. While on the job he completely subordinated his person to the subject. Whatever elements of it nevertheless shone through had the attraction of a mystery. In fact, the way he restrained his convictions and concealed his total personality may have had the greatest effect.

---

[16]"*Die Forderung des Tages*"—a phrase from Goethe's *Maximen und Reflexionen*. —Ed.

With his view that the intentional shaping of young people through political, ethical, or other "practical" cultural ideals was not the task of the universities, Max Weber opposed a widespread tendency of his time which sprang from a specific inner "need" of the maturing generation. On the one hand, socialism had shaken the comfortable shell of bourgeois existence by means of political propaganda, particularly Karl Marx's impressive, mind-revolutionizing interpretation of history. Socialism demanded a new social order and undermined the existing order by intellectually emancipating the masses from the domination of the Christian church. On the other hand, Friedrich Nietzsche had a disintegrating effect in that he smashed, in the name of classical-aristocratic ideals of life, the tables of the law of bourgeois society which had been founded upon Christian ideas. All traditional valuations, ideals, concepts, and modes of thought that had seemed unassailable and under whose guidance people had felt so secure for centuries were called in question as nonbinding prejudices of members of the common herd who, in the final analysis, thereby affirmed their own mediocrity. While Marx strove for revolution in the name of democratic ideals, Nietzsche, conversely, demanded the rule of the few and the breeding of a powerful, noble human type which because of its self-affirmation would find full satisfaction in this world. Although the main ideas of these two great modern thinkers pointed in different directions, they had one thing in common: they both tried to destroy the valuations stemming from the diverse and contradictory mixture of "Christian civilization." What, then, was modern man, particularly youth, to rely upon?

The new proclamations of the great poet Stefan George,[17] which in many respects referred back to Nietzsche's range of ideas, also negated all ruling powers of the machine age—rationalism, capitalism, democracy, and socialism. They were addressed to a select few of spiritual nobility and were directed at the *form* of existence, at the aristocratic general attitude toward life; they did not, however, supply norms for action or set new, tangible, substantial goals. Their character-forming effect was limited to small intellectual and artistic circles. Only socialism had wide-ranging, collective ideals and a new faith for *large* numbers of people. Those who had abandoned the old gods without turning to socialism or to the aristocracy of artistry felt that they were in "a freedom's empty space." All the collective ideas that had ruled the lives of individuals for centuries—the Christian religion,

---

[17]1868–1933, poet, essayist, and translator who, together with his exclusive *George-Kreis* or circle of disciples, attempted a poetic regeneration of the world.—Ed.

the bourgeois ethics derived from it, idealistic philosophy, the ethically charged idea of vocation, science, the state, the nation, the family—all forces that had bound and sustained the individual until the turn of the century, were brought into question. This was a situation with which many young people in process of maturing could not cope. They felt forsaken by God and recognized no law that they wanted to obey. When traditional wisdom and instincts failed them, these young people were shaken by the tremendous uncertainty of all standards that guided action.

In this situation the view developed that the universities, as centers of intellectual life as well as educational institutions, must not content themselves with imparting knowledge to the young generation and sharpening their intellectual tools, but that they had additonal tasks: forming the total personality, imparting convictions and ways of thinking, instilling a practical, evaluative stand on all great problems of life, reconstructing an undivided conception of the world, and making ideological proclamations. These tasks did not only concern theology and philosophy. The other cultural sciences seemed to offer a wealth of opportunities as well, and the social sciences and history were primarily charged with instilling *political* ideals. Against the background of an evaluating consciousness and a *Weltanschauung*—which one had not been decided—the fragmented scholarly disciplines would again join forces and be united. That is why, so people thought, a student should find in his university lecturer not only a teacher but also a *leader* who would set goals for him and guide his personal development in the right direction.

Weber, who had been unwillingly and unwittingly venerated by his pupils as a "leader" when he was only a young docent, strongly opposed these tendencies as soon as they appeared. For the qualities that make someone an excellent scholar and teacher do not also qualify him to be a leader in practical life, particularly in politics. Whether he is such a leader or not simply cannot be confirmed by the situation in the lecture hall.

Let the professor who feels called upon to act as a counselor of youth and enjoys their confidence hold his own in a personal relationship between one man and another. And if he feels called upon to intervene in the struggles of world views and partisan opinions, let him do so outside in the marketplace of life: in the press, in meetings, in associations, wherever he wishes. But it surely is all too convenient to demonstrate the courage of one's convictions where the audience and possible dissenters are condemned to silence.

To Weber, suggesting life philosophies [Weltanschauungen] inside the lecture room was just as undesirable as deliberate political indoctrination. Perhaps such suggestion was permissible in an age of a common faith. But in an age characterized by its lack of cohesion and absence of a uniform orientation, forcing subjective truths upon young people would only increase their general inner uncertainty. "Of all kinds of prophecy, *professorial prophecy* which has a personal coloration in this direction is the only one that is utterly unbearable."

All this applies primarily to scholars in the empirical sciences.[18] Values and valuations are for them not objects of proclamation but, of course, objects of cognition and doctrine. They are able to bring both the man of perception and the man of action close to a value and to demonstrate the consequences of a choice. But that is the limit; the *judgment* as to the worth of values, or the selection from among the different values of guiding stars for one's life—that is, the decision as to what values one *should* realize—is left to the individual. "Scientific argumentation forces no one to make a decision in the sphere of values." Such a decision is made with means other than the intellect, and it should not be taken away from anyone.

This is how Weber differentiates the task of the empirical sciences from that of the "dogmatic" ones. But how does he conceive of the task of *philosophy?* Is *it* entitled to make "proclamations" *ex cathedra?* Weber refrains from making a judgment on this point: "I know nothing about that." Basically, he does differentiate between a scientific and an extrascientific philosophy. Logics, epistemology, and a value doctrine that determines the meaning of the various valuations are on this side of the boundary; metaphysical speculation as an attempt to interpret the superempirical meaning of existence and to offer a unified, objective world-view is on the other side. We cannot know, but only believe in, the timeless objective validity of values which are recognized. Anyone who denies the value of scientific truth, art, patriotic feelings, or religion cannot be convinced by any logical arguments. And universally valid instructions for practical action are even

---

[18]Not in the same sense to theologians, estheticians, moral philosophers, jurists.

less possible—if only because an *identification of cultural values with ethical imperatives* is impossible. Speculative philosophy is, to be sure, a science in
method, but it has no object that science can lay hold of. It conveys *unverifiable* knowledge.

This brings us to a point from where we may catch a glimpse of Weber's
ethical *Weltanschauung*. He sees the possible ideals diverge to form two opposite poles of tremendous tension. For one thing, cultural values may be
maintained even if they come into an irreconcilable conflict with all
ethics. And conversely, an ethic that rejects all cultural values is possible
without inner contradiction—like that of Tolstoy. There are areas in
which the values undoubtedly can only be realized by someone who ethically
shoulders "guilt." The sphere of political action in particular belongs there.
(We shall come back to this later.)[19] But it is not the only one.

However, even in its own realm, normative ethics confronts questions
that it cannot decide by itself, where a decision can be made only on the
basis of the aforementioned extraethical values. For example, it cannot settle the question of whether the *intrinsic value* of ethical action—the "pure
will" or the *disposition [Gesinnung]* alone—should suffice for its justification,
or whether the *responsibility* for the foreseeable consequences of the action
must also be considered. And who would be presumptuous enough to attempt a "scientific" refutation of the ethics of the Sermon of the Mount,
such as the sentence, "Resist not evil," or the commandment to turn the
other cheek? And yet it is clear that, from an inner-worldly point of view,
it contains a command to be undignified. A man has to choose between
the *religious* dignity this ethic offers and his *manly* dignity, which preaches
something entirely different: "Resist evil—otherwise you will share the
responsibility for its preponderance." Ultimately, to an individual one
thing is the devil and the other is God, and the individual has to decide
which is God and which is the devil for *him.* "In the final analysis, with
values it is everywhere and always a matter not of alternatives but of an
inevitable *fight to the death,* as between 'God' and 'the devil.' "

What Weber has in mind here is illuminated by the *"Zwischenbetrachtung,"* a section inserted in the writings on the sociology of religion.[20]
Here Weber shows by means of a comprehensive historical survey how the *re-*

---

[19]In Chapter 20.
[20]*Gesammelte Aufsätze zur Religionssoziologie,* pp. 536ff. [An English translation, "Religious Rejections of the World and their Directions," appears as Chapter 13 of Gerth and Mills, *From Max
Weber: Essays in Sociology.* —Ed.]

ligious interpretations of the world, which have been sublimated by rational thought—until now they have all been "religions of salvation"—must be and in fact are in an increasing state of tension in relation to all inner-worldly value spheres that have developed independently, if the various ideals and precepts which result from a religious or a worldly orientation are consistently thought through and deliberately chosen as guidelines for living.

However, the situation does not often arise, for most people cannot bear even a glimpse of this state of affairs, and they manage to live in accordance with very contradictory principles. The superficiality of everyday life consists precisely in the fact that a person does not become aware of this intermixture of bitterly hostile values and, above all, does not *want* to become aware of it; he evades the choice between "God" and "the devil" and his own ultimate decision as to which of the clashing values is dominated by one and which by the other. Even though the attitude of the man of action who is always ready to compromise and adapt may be unavoidable, the *thinking* that gets to the bottom of one's structure must penetrate even the covering by means of which such a person protects himself from insights that are hard to endure.

Thus Weber mercilessly illuminates what most modern Christians, for example, do not want to see. The central ethical postulate of any religion of salvation is *brotherhood* as a force of selfless sacrificial community and of human solidarity generally. An increasing tension develops between it and all kinds of purposive and rational [*zweckrational*] action concerned with the ever richer expanse of cultural values. And beyond this there is even more tension in relation to the irrational forces in life—the economy, the political order, art, and eroticism—for all these inevitably lead to unbrotherly behavior, secret lovelessness, human relationships that may in no way be morally regulated, and to a denial of one's servitude to God. But the most basic and most conscious tension exists between the religions of salvation and the realm of *thinking cognition,* although religion itself constantly enters into new alliances with intellectualism. Progressive empirical knowledge conflicts with the decisive religious claim that the world has been created by God and is therefore a cosmos ordered in an ethically meaningful way. It has once and for all *disenchanted* the world by transforming it into a causal mechanism.

Thus the ultimate formulations of the view of life—by religion on the one hand and empirical science on the other—are at opposite poles. Religion does not claim an ultimate, intellectual knowledge about what exists or is normatively valid; it claims to have an ultimate attitude toward the world, by virtue of grasping its *meaning*—not by the intellect but by an illumination. Science, on the other hand, will see in all efforts of philosophy (and theology) to demonstrate that ultimate meaning and the attitude grasping it nothing but an endeavor of the intellect to escape its inner laws. And finally, not only is there tension between the religions of salvation and the individual value spheres of inner-worldly culture, but the religions reject the world as a whole. They reject a world which leaves the moral claim to a just balance unfulfilled and in which human beings are not only condemned to unjust suffering and senseless death, but evidently have also been created to *sin*. The ethical devaluation of the world is carried to an extreme by the insight that all the highest cultural values are specifically guilt-laden, since they all presuppose forms of existence which are incompatible with the demand for brotherhood. Grave religious *guilt* appears as an integral component of all culture, all action in a cultural world, all of formed life generally.

This exposition is not meant to be a philosophy—Weber expressly said so. It simply aims at uncovering concealed facts and revealing well-considered and meaningful connections. "The theoretically constructed types of conflicting life orders are merely intended to show that at certain points such and such conflicts are internally *possible* and 'adequate.' *But this does not mean that there is no standpoint from which the conflicts could not be considered as having been 'resolved.'* " This may mean that from the standpoint of empirical knowledge there is increasingly a conflict of value spheres which precludes a unified world view. But there is nothing to prevent speculation and faith from bridging this diversity by means of other—albeit unverifiable—interpretations. Weber's own attitude toward such possibilities is reflected by the following excerpt from a letter dated February 19, 1909: "It is true that I am absolutely unmusical religiously and have no need or ability to erect any psychic edifices of a religious character within me. But a thorough self-examination has told me that I am neither antireligious *nor irreligious.*"

Weber remained convinced that a sober *empirical* view of that state of affairs leads to a recognition of "polytheism" as the only metaphysics appropriate to it:

It is like in the ancient world before it lost the magic of its gods and demons, only in another sense. Things are today as they were when the Hellenes sacrificed to Aphrodite and then to Apollo and, above all,

when everyone sacrificed to the gods of his city, though there no longer is any magic or the mythical but inwardly truthful physical quality
of that conduct. And over these gods and their struggle there rules
fate, but certainly not science.

* * *

Weber rejects the interpretation of this standpoint as "relativism" as
a "gross misunderstanding." To him it was self-evident that the absolute-
ness of concrete ideals could not be proved, but with equal certainty he *believed* in it and demanded of himself their realization. There can be different
and equally justified opinions about the nature of moral obligations, but for
him it was an indubitable inner certainty that only the choice and recognition of ideals, tasks, and duties give meaning and dignity to human existence. It is our destiny to know that we cannot derive the meaning of
what happens in the world from the results of our study of history, however
good our research, but that we must be capable of creating this meaning
ourselves. Even though the light of *ratio* may keep advancing, *the realm of
what may be known will still remain shrouded in unfathomable mystery.* That is why
Weltanschauungen can never be the product of progressive experience and why
the highest and most stirring ideals can become effective for all times only
in a struggle with other ideals that are just as sacred to others as our ideals
are to us.

Anyone who cannot cope with this insight should not consult science,
for, if it remains true to itself, it will not give him an answer. Let
him ask a prophet or a savior and let him believe in him and follow him.
And he should know that he will then not be spared the sacrifice of
the intellect (*"Credo non quod sed quia absurdum"*),[21] that distinguishing characteristic of every positively religious person.

II

As we have said, Weber's concern with problems of cultural logic developed
only as a sideline to his new productivity. In 1903, presumably in the second

---

[21]See page 19. *Quod* and *quia* both mean "because," but the latter is the more emphatic
word.—Ed.

half of the year, immediately after finishing the first part of his study on Roscher and Knies, he started his most famous work up to that time, *Die protestantische Ethik und der Geist des Kapitalismus* [The Protestant Ethic and the Spirit of Capitalism]. The first part was completed before the American trip, in early summer of 1904; the second part appeared a year later and reveals the influence of his recent experiences. Not the least reason why these had stirred Weber so much was that in America he had been able to observe everywhere the living traces of the origins of the modern capitalistic spirit and this spirit itself in "ideal-type" purity. He had probably had the idea for this work for some time, in any case since the beginning of his recovery. His intensive study of the history and constitution of the medieval monasteries and orders during his stay in Rome may have been a preliminary for it.

This work was the first in a series of wide-ranging investigations of *universal* history in which diametrically opposed phenomena, namely, elements of *religious* consciousness and everyday economic life, were brought together. Beyond that, the relationship of religion to all important structural forms of social living was investigated. All these essays appeared in the *Archiv für Sozialwissenschaften*. As its co-editor Weber felt primarily obligated to keep it supplied with material. Also, he was always in a hurry to publish, and so unpretentious a publication was the most convenient. That is why none of these writings of his second phase appeared in book form during his lifetime. For the time being, his renewed activities were confined to the narrow sphere of scholarship. True, his very first treatise on the sociology of religion went far beyond the readership of the *Archiv* and aroused a whole series of controversies. The issues in which it appeared were soon sold out, and since Weber nevertheless did not want to bother to issue it in book form, it was unobtainable for more than a decade. More will be said about this later. Only one year before his death did he accede to the urging of many to bring in part of his harvest. It was still given to him to revise the studies contained in the first volume dealing with the sociology of religion, but he did not live to see the publication of the volume.

The problems of cultural logic were not the only ones that interested him. Weber's regained productivity was constantly channeled into several streams that flowed along side by side, and from time to time the needs of others and external stimuli easily forced it into lateral canals. After all, he was interested in everything and had an insatiable thirst for knowledge. We have already discussed his writings on logic. But Weber did not forget his scholarly past either. His old interests in national policy and particularly agrarian policy could flare up at any time. In the fall of 1903, when he was already planning two other studies, there appeared a new bill that was intended to facilitate the expansion and establishment of *fideicommissa*. Part of its ideology was the preservation of the aristocratic tradition and mentality by supporting the landed gentry. This inspired Weber to attack a conservative romanticism behind which material and political class interests were hidden. He took from his desk drawer the agrarian statistics he had worked up in his Berlin and Freiburg periods and tore the bill to shreds in an essay that combined careful scholarly argument with razor-sharp polemics. His pen became a spear again. He showed that the proposed law would promote the accumulation of land and capital in the hands of a few, aggravate the social conflicts in rural regions, inevitably drive out the independent German peasants, and bring Slavic foreigners into the country. And he revealed as the real motives behind this ideology the interest of the dynasty and the ruling class in the expansion of a caste of masters and courtiers that would submit to the authority of the state. The state consolidated its own authority by using laws to gratify vanity interests, namely, the striving of bourgeois capitalists for the "ennoblement" of their profits and a "seigneurial" form of existence. Weber's presentation aroused great anger, but it was effective. Consideration of the bill was postponed and finally dropped. It never became law.

His political interests were again powerfully stirred when the first Russian revolution broke out in 1905. He quickly mastered the Russian language, avidly followed the events of the day in several Russian newspapers, and entered into a lively verbal exchange with T. Kistiakowski, a Russian teacher of constitutional law. This man had been one of the intellectual leaders of the "Cadets" [Constitutional Democratic Party] who had helped prepare the revolution and had fled to Heidelberg. The news of the draft of a democratic constitution by the "Union of Liberation" inspired Weber to publish a few "Remarks" about it in the *Archiv*. These, however, soon expanded into two special issues in small type and became a chronicle-like daily record of the Russian struggle for liberation.

Weber fully empathized with the psyche and civilization of the Russian people, and for months he followed the Russian drama with bated breath. Perhaps the entering of the huge eastern state into the mainstream of European development was one of the last opportunities for building an absolutely libertarian civilization. Perhaps now that "the economic and intellectual 'revolution,' the much-maligned 'anarchy' of production, and the equally maligned 'subjectivism' are still intact," the time had come to secure "inalienable personal rights" for the members of the masses who were thrown upon their own resources because of these and *only because of these.* If the world is economically "full" and intellectually "sated," these rights are closed to them forever. What agitated Weber most was the question of the probable influence of the events in Russia upon German development. Would the eastern colossus, which was because of its very size pressing so hard upon its western neighbor, allow itself to be shaped by western European liberal ideals to such an extent that the dynastic desire for power would no longer be able to rely upon czarism? Would the martyrdom of the Russian "intelligentsia" force through a constitution that would supply energy for the libertarian movements of Weber's own country?

Weber soon realized that the forms wrested from the aristocracy had brought only the *semblance* of freedom, not freedom itself. With typical Asiatic artifice the police state sabotaged the barriers it had imposed upon itself. And political leaders who could have coped with the enormous problems were not allowed to assume the reins. "The situation of Russia does cry out for a statesman—but the dynastic ambitions of the personal regime leave as little room there for a great reformer as they do elsewhere, such as here." The revolution came to naught and new misfortune was in the offing.

All *economic* signs pointed in the direction of increasing bondage; everywhere in an industrially organized life the structures for new serfdom were ready.

> In the face of this, those who live in constant fear that in the future there might be too much "democracy" and "individualism" and too little "authority," "aristocracy," and respect for official positions should finally calm down. It has been arranged all too well for the trees of democratic individualism not to grow into the sky.[22] All experience has shown that history inexorably gives birth to ever new "aristocracies" and "authorities" to which anyone can cling who considers it necessary for himself—or for the people.

* * *

---

[22]An allusion to *"Es ist dafür gesorgt, dass die Bäume nicht in den Himmel wachsen,"* a proverb used by Goethe as the motto for the third part of his autobiography *Dichtung und Wahrheit.*—Ed.

Weber next wrote some essays on logic. But in the autumn of 1908 he was absorbed in a major historical-sociological monograph for the *Handwörterbuch der Staatswissenschaften* [Concise Dictionary of Political Science], *"Agrarverhältnisse im Altertum"* [Agrarian Conditions in Antiquity]. Its very length— 136 two-column folio pages in small print—completely exceeded the bounds of this compilation, and the unpretentious title indicates only a small part of the contents. In reality this study offers a sort of sociology of antiquity—a historical analysis and conceptual penetration of all important structural forms of the social life of classical antiquity. An enormous amount of historical material is here presented in the most concise and precise form. The introduction presents an economic theory of the political world of antiquity. The special character of the various stages of organization is brought out by means of ideal types. Weber shows to what extent the development was determined by elementary geographical conditions— the distribution of water and land—and how the singular character of ancient civilization was based on the fact that it was a coastal and riverbank culture, in contrast to the inland cultures of the Middle Ages and of modern times. A concise survey of the structural forms of the ancient Orient, Mesopotamia, Egypt, and ancient Israel is followed by a detailed analysis of western antiquity: Greece, Hellenism, Rome, the Roman imperial age. All important social phenomena are compared and contrasted with one another and with medieval and modern ones. One thing is explained by another; typical and individual elements are separated; the differences between things bearing the same name is shown; and by means of precise "ideal types" Weber makes it clear where errors arise when historians interpret the past by reading modern phenomena into it.

Around the same time, in 1908–09, Weber once more returned to intensive specialized investigations in his own field. This was occasioned by an inquiry into *"Auslese und Anpassung"* [Selection and Adaptation], the choice of a trade and the vocational fate of workers in heavy industry. This investigation had been planned by the *Verein für Sozialpolitik* and had been suggested mainly by his brother and colleague Alfred Weber. As with the inquiry into farm workers, it was again a matter of collectively investigating as yet obscure areas of modern mass existence with the aid of source materials that had to be laboriously procured through special investigations.

The crux of the problem was this: What kinds of people does modern heavy industry produce and what vocational and other fate does it hold in store for them? In other words, what effect does the machinery to which a great number of modern people are necessarily harnessed have on their character and way of life, what psychophysical qualities are promoted by the various industrial processes? The terms used in the subject of the inquiry—"selection" and "adaptation"—express Alfred Weber's belief that using the methods and insights of the natural sciences is fruitful. Therefore Max Weber was interested not only in the subject, which might furnish· fresh insights into the spirit of modern capitalism, but primarily in the methodological question as well. After all, the result of collective studies, some of which were entrusted to fledgling scholars—doctoral candidates in the various departments—depended on choosing the proper approach and fruitful viewpoints.

Weber prepared a comprehensive exposé for the *Verein* that indicated the great goals of the project and also contained detailed instructions concerning the proper scientific procedure. He even mentioned that self-addressed, stamped envelopes should be enclosed with the questionnaires. One senses the zeal of the teacher who has an equally strong interest in extending a helping hand to others and in making their abilities bear fruit in the service of scholarship. These instructions, however, were only the result of his own intensive work on these problems at that time. Weber examined the research methods of the natural sciences to see whether they were applicable to the projected studies, and himself set the example of a specialized study.

The results appeared in a series of articles in the *Archiv für Sozialwissenschaften* under the title *Zur Psychophysik der industriellen Arbeit* [The Psychophysics of Industrial Work]. The material for the concrete study was supplied by the Oerlinghausen textile mill, which was also the source of much other illustrative material. In the summer of 1908 he spent many weeks with his relatives, studying the wage records and loom records of the factory and assiduously preparing graphs for the hourly, daily, and weekly output of the weavers in order to find the psychophysical causes of fluctuations in performance. But these laborious investigations were not an end in themselves; they were to have only "illustrative" significance for the scientific procedure. His main endeavor, then, was the clarification of the *methodological* problem, particularly of the question of whether the sciences of heredity on the one hand and psychophysical experiments on the other could be of service to sociological analysis. Weber thus studied the most important writings on psychophysics. He concentrated particularly on the studies of Kräpelin[23] and his pupils, analyzed their methods and concepts,

[23]Emil Kräpelin, 1856–1926, psychiatrist, professor at Heidelberg and Munich. The founder of pharmacopsychology, he defined and investigated *dementia praecox* and manic-depressive states as well as studying the effects of fatigue and alcohol upon the intellectual functions.—Ed.

and came to the conclusion that while collaboration between the natural and the social sciences was possible "in principle" and their psychophysical concepts were usable for the projected inquiry, the sociological analysis of mass phenomena could use neither the methods of the "exact" laboratory experiments nor the uncertain results of the theory of heredity.

After all this had been clarified, Weber returned to his general sociological studies. He had two main concerns. He wished to continue his studies on the sociology of religion, and at the same time he was preparing a big collection at the request of his publisher Paul Siebeck:[24] the *Grundriss für Sozialökonomik* [Outline of Political Economy]. He drew up the plan and secured contributors; in addition to doing the organizing he assigned the most important sections to himself. His writings on the sociology of religion were in part drawn from the same sources as the new work and proceeded together with it. We shall now return to them.

According to Weber himself, these writings were intended to be contributions to the characterization of modern Western man and the knowledge of his development and his culture. He originally intended to begin with the Reformation and step back in time in order to analyze also the relationship of medieval and early Christianity to the social and economic forms of existence. But when Ernst Troeltsch began his studies on the social teachings of the Christian churches (the first essay was published in the *Archiv* at the beginning of 1908), Weber suspected that their fields of work were too close to each other, and for the time being he turned to other tasks. When around 1911 he resumed his studies on the sociology of religion, he was attracted to the Orient—to China, Japan, and India, then to Judaism and Islam. He now wanted to investigate the relationship of the five great world religions to economic ethics. His study was to come full circle with an analysis of early Christianity. And while in his first treatise on the spirit of capitalism Weber expressly set out to illuminate only one causal sequence, namely, the influence of religious elements of consciousness upon everyday economic life, he now undertook the larger task as well—namely, the investigation of the influence of the material, economic, and geographical conditions of the various spheres of culture with a view to their religious and ethical ideas. He called this series of studies *Die Wirtschaftsethik der Weltreligionen* [The Economic Ethics of the World Religions]; by economic ethics he meant, as he did in the first study, not ethical and

---

[24]1855–1920. In 1878 Siebeck took over the old Heidelberg publishing house of J.C.B. Mohr and concentrated on the fields of theology, sociology, philosophy, and history. The first edition of Marianne Weber's biography appeared in 1926 under the imprint of J.C.B. Mohr (Paul Siebeck), Tübingen.—Ed.

theological theories but the practical impulses toward action that derive from religion.

These studies of the Asiatic world do not intend to offer any definitive insights in any direction, for in the cases of China, India, and Japan, Weber was dependent on translated sources, and he encountered an almost unmanageable literature on Judaism. Since he had based all his previous professional studies upon a careful study of the sources, he therefore had a very modest opinion of these writings, but he hoped that his presentation of the problems would give a fresh appearance to familiar data. Above all, he hoped that the liberation of scholarly analysis from those religious and ethical value judgments which had, in the nature of things, colored almost all specialized studies on the history of religions would prepare the ground for clearer thinking.

Since it would have been impossible to investigate the multifariously interrelated mutual dependence of religion and economics in all its details, he brought out in each case the *directive* elements of the life-style of those social strata which most strongly influenced the practical ethics of a given religion and gave it the important features from the viewpoint of economic ethics. In China, for example, it was the connection between Confucianism and the life and thought of a group of men with a literary education who received a stipend from the state; in India it was the connection of earlier Hinduism with a hereditary caste of cultured literati, the Brahmins; earlier Buddhism was propagated by itinerant mendicant friars and earlier Islamism by world-conquering warriors; post-Exile Judaism was the religion of civic "pariahs"; and Christianity was propagated by itinerant artisans and by inhabitants of the cities.

However, in this connection Weber expressly resisted the misunderstanding that the special character of a religion was a reflection of material interests or a "function" of the social situation of the stratum that was its bearer. However profound an influence economically and politically determined social factors may have had on a religious ethic, it received its stamp primarily from *religious* sources, from the content of its annunciation and promise, and from the religious needs of its adherents. The causal sequences run back and forth: "Not ideas but interests (material and ideal) directly govern men's conduct. But very often the 'images of the world' that have been created by ideas have, like switchmen, determined the tracks along which action has been moved by the dynamic of interests." In the past, magical and religious forces and the obligatory ideas attached to belief in them were everywhere the most important forces shaping the conduct of life. And everywhere the same process took place: the gradual sublimation of a primitive belief in spirits and demons into a *religion of salvation,* that is, a religiosity that *negates* the world the way it is and strives for a liberation from suffering and sin, which is attainable in this world or in the next.

As soon as a man thinks ahead, he begins to feel that the structure of the world should be, or could become, a meaningfully ordered cosmos. He inquires about the relationship between good fortune and merit, seeks a justification for suffering, sin, and death that satisfies his reason, and creates a "theodicy." In other words, religious feelings and experiences are treated intellectually, the process of *rationalization* dissolves the magical notions and increasingly "disenchants" the world and renders it godless. Religion changes from magic to doctrine. And now, after the disintegration of the primitive image of the world, there appear two tendencies: a tendency toward the *rational* mastery of the world and one toward *mystical* experience. But not only the religions receive their stamp from the increasing development of thought; the process of rationalization moves on several tracks, and its autonomous development encompasses all creations of civilization—the economy, the state, law, science, and art.

All forms of *Western* civilization in particular are decisively determined by a methodical *way of thinking* that was first developed by the Greeks, and this way of thinking was joined in the Age of Reformation by a methodical *conduct of life* that was oriented to certain purposes. It was this union of a theoretical and a practical rationalism that separated modern civilization from ancient civilization, and the special character of both separated modern Western civilization from Asian civilization. To be sure, there were processes of rationalization in the Orient as well, but neither the scientific, the political, the economic, nor the artistic kind took the course that is peculiar to the Occident.

Weber regarded this recognition of the special character of Eastern *rationalism* and the role it was given to play for Western civilization as one of his most important discoveries. As a result, his original inquiry into the relationship between religion and economics expanded into an even more comprehensive inquiry into the *special character of all of Western civilization:* Why is there only in the West a rational science that produces verifiable truths? Why are there only here a rational harmonic music as well as an architecture and plastic art that employ rational constructions? Why only here government by estates [*Ständestaat*], professionally trained organizations of officials, specialists, parliaments, the party system, the state as a political institution with a rational constitution and a rational body of laws? Why only here the most fateful force in modern life, modern capitalism? Why all this only in the West? These questions now occupied him constantly in one form or another and impelled him to transcend the framework of his field—indeed, *any* specialized scholarship—and to recognize worldly [*welthaltig*] reality.

He ascertained, among other things, that the birth of the modern Western state, like the birth of Western churches, was the work of jurists—juridical rationalism, a special achievement of the Romans—and that modern bourgeois "industrial capitalism" [*Betriebskapitalismus*] is in large measure determined by the peculiarity of Western science, which makes possible the exact calculation of its technical factors, etc. And it is one of his most astonishing results that it was *science* which helped determine the character of Western art, at least architecture, the plastic arts, and music. His contemporaries denigrated rationalism, and many artists in particular regarded it as an impediment to their creative power; that is why Weber was especially excited about that discovery. He now also planned to write a sociology of art, and as a first step in this direction he undertook, in addition to his other projects, to investigate the rational and sociological foundations of music as they were around 1910. This study took him into the most remote areas of anthropology and involved the most difficult investigations of tonal arithmetics and symbolism.

However, when this study had been tentatively outlined, he forced himself to go back to the works he had started and promised. The major portions of his new series on the economic ethics of the world religions were finished around 1913, although they did not begin to appear until 1915. Weber first wished to add a scholarly apparatus and make additions to some parts. He was prevented from doing so by the outbreak of the World War and his conscription for duty. Finally, however, he began publication with the section on Confucianism and Taoism, which he prefaced with an introductory essay on the philosophy of history. When he was discharged from military service in 1915, he continued his research. The section on China was revised for the second printing in 1919.

* * *

If we now return to a more detailed discussion of Weber's first study on the sociology of religion, we do so partly because it was the first work to make Weber's star shine again after a serious nervous breakdown had forced upon him a tragic renunciation of the unfolding of his vitality, and also because this work is connected with the deepest roots of his personality and in an undefinable way bears its stamp. It is paradigmatic from a methodological point of view as well. One of its results—and one that was confirmed by all later investigations—was the positive overcoming of the "materialistic" view of history. Weber expressed great admiration for Karl Marx's brilliant constructions and saw in the inquiry into the economic and technical causes of events an exceedingly fruitful, indeed, a specifically new heuristic principle that directed the quest for knowledge [Erkenntnistrieb] into entire areas previously unilluminated. But he not only rejected the elevation of these ideas to a Weltanschauung, but was also against material factors being made absolute and being turned into the common denominator of causal explanations.

Unprejudiced investigation had taught Weber early on that every phenomenon of cultural life is also economically determined, but that none is only so determined. As early as 1892–93, when as a young scholar he inquired into reasons for the flight of farmers from rural regions in eastern Germany, he was struck by the insight that ideological impulses were just as decisive as the "bread-and-butter question." And when he undertook his second inquiry into the situation of farm workers, together with the theologian Göhre, it was from the outset his intention to investigate, in addition to the economic situation of the rural population, the moral and religious situation as well as the interaction of the various factors. Evidently he concerned himself at an early age with the question of the world-shaping significance of ideal forces. Perhaps this tendency of his quest for knowledge—a permanent concern with religion—was the form in which the genuine religiosity of his maternal family lived on in him.

To be sure, he did not intend to replace the materialistic view of history with a spiritualistic one. Both would be equally possible, but "both would be of equally little service to truth." Rather, he wished to illuminate in every significant phenomenon the interplay of the heterogeneous formative forces of existence. One reason why this work is also of methodological interest is that here Weber consciously used for the first time the procedure of a cultural-sociological search for truth—a procedure he simultaneously analyzed in his logical writings. He created central ideal-type concepts such as the "spirit" of capitalism or its opposite, "traditionalism." They are not defined but "composed," that is, their characteristics, which are not deduced but derived from reality, gradually emerge from the historical investigation. What is first presented as an abstract concept acquires an increasingly rich, vivid substance as the presentation progresses. Further, Weber strives for a careful causal attribution of intuitively comprehended connections. After all, he does not wish to offer an ingenious "show" but, as far as possible, verified truths, and so he subjected his brilliant conception to strictly logical revision.

Presumably the unwieldiness of this treatise and its pervasive dualism were largely determined by this. In part the need to save space in the periodical was responsible. The reader must simultaneously absorb the most surprising syntheses above the line and the most painstaking scholarly documentation below the line. Every thesis is buttressed by a reference to the sources. The most important details, including a philological treatise about the origin of the modern conception of vocation, are found as notes in small print. In the second, otherwise unchanged version the "footnote inflation" was considerably increased by arguments with those among his critics, like Brentano and Sombart, whom he had not already refuted specifically, as he had Rachfahl,[25] among others. That it was necessary for this work in particular to present the entire scholarly apparatus and all sources is shown by the controversies that arose mainly from the fact that Weber's points were too surprising and that their careful modifications [Relativisierungen] were at first not completely absorbed.

Finally, anyone who is not convinced by Weber's *logical* arguments that cognition and evaluation can be separated within the framework of a historical presentation may be persuaded by immersing himself in this work, in which the two are consciously separated. Throughout, Weber refrains from making judgments on the value of the various religious and ethical structures he analyzes; nor does he anywhere, directly or indirectly, rank the "gods." And wherever he emphasizes possibilities for future development, as he does at the end, he immediately points out that he has now left the soil of science. The meaningful content [Sinngehalt] of Catholicism and of Protestantism in its various forms is given the same fair presentation by a seeker after truth who was not prejudiced by any of these contents. (The

---

[25]Felix Rachfahl, 1867–1925, historian, professor at Halle, Königsberg, Giessen, Kiel, and Freiburg.—Ed.

same applies to his subsequent studies of Asian religions.) One can probably say that as a matter of principle Weber approached all those manifestations of the human spirit not *sine ira et studio* [without anger or partiality—Tacitus], but with *equal love,* albeit with the disinterested love of a contemplative person who has declined to possess one of these substances himself.

He always preserved a profound reverence for the Gospels and genuine Christian religiosity. The parables of Jesus, the Sermon on the Mount, Paul's Epistles, and, from the Old Testament, particularly the Prophets and the Book of Job were to him incomparable documents of religious inspiration and depth. But, since his maturity, he was not under any particular constraint, and thus he was able, as a thinker, to turn to all religious systems with equal interest. Despite this being "above it all," or perhaps because of it, the plain, artless presentation of ideas in this first essay on the sociology of religion, as in parts of the subsequent ones, has a stirring effect—not only because of its substance, but also because of the personality of the thinker behind it. Weber seems profoundly moved by the course of human destinies which "tugged at his heartstrings" [*"an die Brust branden"*]—moved, above all, by the fact that on its earthly course an idea always and everywhere operates in opposition to its original meaning and thereby destroys itself. And one also seems to detect some of Weber's own features in the magnificent figures of a heroic Puritanism which he presents. For this reason a few points from his treatise will be discussed here.

* * *

Avarice, greed, and an unscrupulous acquisitive drive have existed always and everywhere. The acquisition, in defiance of all norms, of more commodities than are needed to live—the capitalism of adventurers, speculators, profiteers, colonialists, and the like—is indigenous to any economic system that uses money. But affirmation of moneymaking for its own sake, not as an adventure but as a constant *moral duty,* is not a matter of course. It has, rather, existed only since a certain epoch—only in certain strata and only in the West. Before this could come about, Western man, especially the Western bourgeois, had to be taught a certain conduct of life. It was necessary for him to have learned to view rational, methodical work as a moral duty.

How did this orginate, and what was its effect? His investigation surrounds this goal of the inquiry, a goal that reveals itself only gradually, with a flow of ideas that are as bold as they are sensible—until finally all the threads of the argument are revealed. Here we shall proceed to it on the shortest path, and in so doing we can survey only some parts of the wealth of the intellectual world through which Weber leads us. At first he illuminates what is close at hand in the present. With the aid of denominational statistics compiled by a student, he shows that the Catholic population in Germany participated in capitalistic acquisition far less than the Protestants, and that this was determined not by external conditions but by internal ones: the intellectual characteristics the two groups had developed because of their religious surroundings, especially their different conceptions of *vocation* [*Beruf*]. It has long been known that Protestants with a Calvinistic and Baptist stamp have always displayed a peculiar combination of an intense piousness and a pronounced and successful business sense. To discover the causal connection between these striking phenomena, Weber gradually moves away from the present and the familiar and penetrates into the past, going back to the religious intellectual world of the Reformation and the Middle Ages.

Weber begins by analyzing Benjamin Franklin's advice to a young tradesman as one of the characteristic documents of the capitalistic "spirit." Here the ideal of the man of honor deserving of credit is presented, a man to whom the enlargement of his property through tireless work, saving, and the forgoing of pleasures is a *duty*, and who esteems wealth he has acquired himself as a sign of personal proficiency. These religiously indifferent notions, which in antiquity and in the Middle Ages would have been proscribed as utterly undignified sentiments, met with general approval in Franklin's homeland long before capitalism existed as a form of production there. They live on to this day in the modern entrepreneur to whom work is a moral duty and business an end in itself.

The ancestors of this type with its purely ethical and inner-worldly orientation are shown to be the God-imbued, fervently pious, magnificently severe figures of the Age of Reformation: Luther, Calvin, Bunyan, Baxter,[26] Cromwell, the Puritans and Baptists—all people to whom nothing was more important than their relationship to God, the salvation of their souls, their fate in the beyond. And behind them there is Calvin's *deus absconditus*

---

[26]Richard Baxter, 1615–1691, English Puritan minister and church leader, author of *The Saints' Everlasting Rest, The Reformed Pastor,* and more than 150 other volumes.—Ed.

[inscrutable God]—He whose name is not known, no longer the loving Father of the Gospels but the unknown, mysterious God who wants nothing but His own glory. What have these to do with the capitalist spirit that produces mammonism? Is it not overly daring to associate the spirit of world-negation, of the negation of earthly glory, with this "devil"? But link is added to link in the chain of argument until we reach the point at which the forces that by their very nature are eternally hostile to one another become interwoven.

We have seen that the conception of an activity aiming at gain as a binding "vocation" lends ethical dignity to the life of modern entrepreneurs to this day. Where does this conception come from? Neither antiquity nor the Middle Ages knew the word *Beruf* in this sense. Weber's philological analysis shows it to be a creation of Luther. He created it in his translation of the Bible—not from the spirit of the original but from his own spirit. He used it to express the dignity of an inner-worldly fulfillment of duty in *contrast* to the Catholic ideal of asceticism that fled from the world. This word consecrates everyday work and makes it the supreme substance of moral activity. It is one of Luther's most momentous achievements, for all Protestant communities took over his newly created meaning.

Nevertheless, Lutheranism did not create the capitalist "spirit." Its origins were associated with what in *spirit* most strongly conflicted with all earthly business: Calvin's awesome doctrine of predestination and its consequences. By a secret decision the inscrutable God has decreed that some human beings will have eternal life and the others, everlasting death. This predetermined fate can be changed neither by merit nor by guilt, neither by sacraments nor by good works; its meaning is a dark secret. Each individual who believes in it asks with fear and trembling whether he is among the elect or the damned. God has chosen. No one can do anything about it. A person can only surmise what side he belongs on, and the only way he can ascertain his own state of grace is by *standing the test* [Bewährung]—by standing the test in one's vocation, by tireless, successful labor for the glory of God.

This is the basic idea that stamped the completely new religious types—the Puritans, the Quakers, the Mennonites, the Baptists, etc. This new type of man views himself as being entirely dependent upon himself, in terrible solitude, and bereft of all magical powers of salvation. No church, no preacher, no sacrament can help him in the decisive matter of his life. Thus he does not subject himself to any earthly authority and keeps aloof from his fellowmen, mistrustfully and reservedly. In profound inner isolation he communes with a God whom he does not know and from whom he feels separated by an enormous gulf. He is God's tool, not his vessel, and God demands of him *action* rather than feelings and moods. He demands a *rational* shaping of the world in accordance with His commandments. The Puritan avoids all sensual culture and sensual enjoyment. With his eye on eternal life, full of fear for the salvation of his soul, he carries on his earthly activities as a divine service. And since any strong emotional attachment between one human being and another is suspect to him as a deification of living creatures, his community-forming powers are concentrated all the more on *things*: he organizes mundane life with zeal and success.

This disciplined conduct of life which eschews simple enjoyment, this mode of living which is not only God-ordained but God-produced must demonstrate the consecration of the elect. The imperfections of the average Catholic can be compensated for by the means of grace offered by the church. Even Luther left the naturalness of instinctive action and a simple emotional life untouched, but the Calvinists did not. For a Calvinist it is a matter of either God's will or creaturely vanity. He provides himself with the certainty of future bliss only by a systematic self-control aiming to overcome irrational drives, by a methodical conduct of life, by *"inner-worldly asceticism."* This is the decisive ideal of the Puritan "saint." In contrast to a monk, he lives *in* the world, yet, like a monk, he is not *of* it. Luther had rejected asceticism that fled from the world as unbiblical and sanctimonious. That is why the passionately earnest, God-fearing persons of that era had no other choice but to fulfill their ascetic ideals *within* the world. And the idea that it was necessary to *stand the test* became a positive stimulus to asceticism. It linked faith with morality and thus assumed decisive importance for everyday living. It stamped an entirely new type of man, one who knew only an either-or, either God's will or creaturely vanity, who could fulfill himself on earth only by unceasing labor.

But it is still not clear what these ideas—like work in a vocation as moral duty and proving worthy of the state of grace through asceticism in the world—have to do with modern capitalism. It is at this point that the tension of the paradox reaches its climax. For the Puritan religion, *wealth* is a menace and the striving for wealth is meaningless. But wealth is the inevitable result of methodical acquisition and abstinence from enjoyment, and as such it is *a sign of standing the test, indeed, of a state of grace.* Only *repose* in property is reprehensible. Only activity serves the glory of

God; wasting time is the greatest sin, but inactive contemplation, too, is valueless if it is at the expense of vocation. Baxter ordered the pious to work hard in their vocations, and he told them: "You may labor to be rich for God, though not for the flesh and sin."[27]

With this, everything finally comes full circle: Anyone for whom tireless, methodical work is imperative as the most important substance of his life, but to whom enjoyment and rest in success are forbidden, has no other choice but to use a large part of his gain for more and more acquisition. He *has* to become a capitalistic entrepreneur. There we have the sober bourgeois self-made man who thanks God for having produced his faultlessness. The restraints on striving for gain are removed; the acquisition of goods is freed from the traditional inhibitions; and the effect can only be the production of capital through compulsory saving and the accumulation of wealth. God himself visibly blesses the activities of his saints, but he demands an accounting of every penny entrusted to them. "With a chilling impact the idea of a man's obligation toward his property began to weigh upon life."

And with this there began the tragedy of the idea. Puritanism could not withstand the temptations of *acquired* wealth any more than the medieval monastic communities had been able to. The magnificent religious style of life was destroyed by its own consequences. Only when their religious roots withered did the idea of vocation and the ascetic education become fully effective. The modern economic man that had been postulated by Franklin, the man who was "carved from the hard wood of bourgeois righteousness" stands at the end of the succession of figures. Instead of being imbued with religious enthusiasm, he is full of sober vocational virtue; instead of searching for the Kingdom of God he is concerned with this world. As the heir of the religious past he has the specifically bourgeois vocational ethic, and he makes money with a good conscience. Education for work-asceticism places sober, conscientious workers at his disposal and legalizes the exploitation of their willingness.

This cosmos of the modern economic order, which the spirit of Christian asceticism has helped build, today inevitably determines the life-style of all individuals. "The Puritan wanted to work in a calling; we are *forced* to do so . . . The concern with earthly goods was supposed to lie on the shoulders of his saints only like a light cloak that can be thrown off at any time.

[27]From Baxter's *Christian Directory* in *Protestant Ethic*, p. 162.—Ed.

But fate decreed that the cloak should become an iron cage [*ein stahlhartes Gehäuse*]." Today the religious spirit has escaped from the cage, perhaps for good. At the end Weber momentarily reaches for the veil that shrouds the future of this tremendous development, but he does not presume to lift it.

Painting of the balcony facing the castle in Weber's Heidelberg home (Ziegelhäuser Landstrasse 17), showing Emilie Souchay Fallenstein, G. F. Fallenstein, and (leaning against a pillar) G. G. Gervinus. (See page 145.)

343

Max Weber during military training in Strasbourg, 1883.

The Weber family, Berlin, 1887. From left to right: Arthur, Klara, Alfred, Lili, Helene, Karl, Max Sr., Max Jr.

Max Weber, Sr., ca. 1890.

Max Weber as a professor at Heidelberg, 1896 or 1897.

Max and Marianne Weber traveling in Italy, 1900 or 1901.

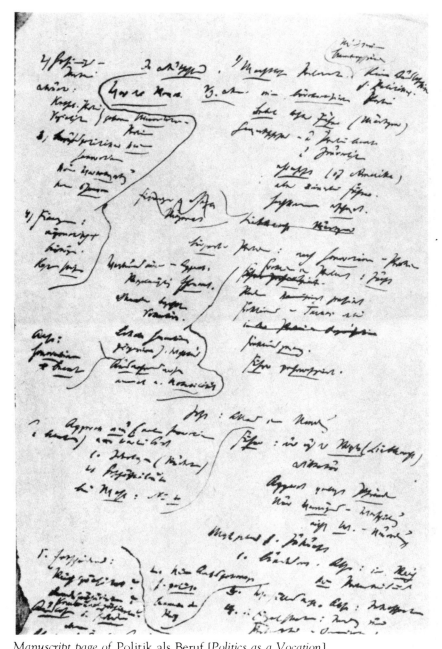

Manuscript page of Politik als Beruf [*Politics as a Vocation*].

Helene Weber, ca. 1914.

Max Weber, 1917 or 1918.

Weber's Heidelberg house on the Neckar (1973 photograph).

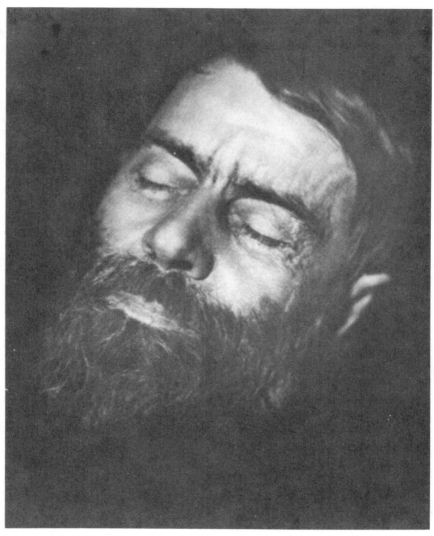

Max Weber on his deathbed.

11

EXPANSION _____

We stopped at Weber's return from America, and now we shall take up the course of his life again. Complete recovery was not the prize of the big trip: "Evidently the two of us have not quite regained our nervous equilibrium. Perhaps it is becoming perceptible that America has not brought us any real relaxation. In any case, Max's sleep is again irregular and he complains about his lack of ability to work. It would certainly be curious if he were less able to bear the steadier life here than he bore the hectic pace in America." However, despite further fluctuations Weber was now accustomed to a more normal way of life. On exceptional occasions the sick lion now left his den in the evening, too. When the Heidelberg Chapter of the *National-Soziale Partei* put on an "American evening" under the direction of A. Deissman,[1] at which Ernst Troeltsch and Marianne Weber gave reports, he was persuaded to attend. His impromptu remarks in the discussion were longer

_____

[1] Adolf Deissmann, 1866–1937, Protestant theologian and leader in the ecumenical movement, professor at Heidelberg (1897) and Berlin (1908).—Ed.

than those of the two main speakers put together; all the impressions he had stored up poured out irresistibly.

He also agreed to give a lecture before a theological discussion group [Kränzchen] newly founded by Deissmann which brought together a small group of outstanding scholars such as Windelband, Jellinek, Gothein, Troeltsch, Neumann, Domaszewski, A. Dieterich, Rathgen, von Duhn,[2] and others. He enjoyed this opportunity for an exchange of ideas which enabled him to be inspired by others and thus to keep reshaping his own knowledge. However, even social obligations of that sort still gave rise to uneasiness: "Tomorrow, Sunday, the 'Eranos,' the scholarly discussion group with ten gentlemen, is in store for us. Max is taking care of 'Protestant asceticism,' I am in charge of 'ham in burgundy.' For Max's sake I wish the thing were over. You see, he has not been feeling well lately."

The treatise about the spirit of capitalism now quickly approached completion. At the end of March, after scarcely three months of work, the second part was finished. Weber wrote to Rickert: "I am working—amidst horrible torments, to be sure, but I do manage to work a few hours each day. In June or July you will receive an essay on cultural history that may be of interest to you: Protestant asceticism as the foundation of modern vocational civilization [Berufskultur]—a sort of 'spiritualistic' construction of the modern economy" (April 2, 1905).

The completion of this work was not followed by exhaustion. A muted happiness about the great accomplishment combined with the grateful enjoyment of a lovely spring. Weber was able to go on working without a break and reported to his mother on the occasion of her birthday: "After all the Puritan oil of the last few months I am now returning to some unfinished writings that are more philosophical in nature. But my head still does not fully cooperate. Here we have full, warm spring in all its splendor. I hope the same is true of you, both outwardly and inwardly."

The sun's magic once again brought an earthly blessing and the confidence of an optimistic outlook on life. The fragments of earlier riches, laboriously joined together, seemed to be coalescing.

---

[2]Eberhard Gothein, 1853–1923, historian, economist, and political scientist, professor at Karlsruhe, Bonn, and Heidelberg; Alfred von Domaszewski, 1856–1927, professor of ancient history at Heidelberg from 1887 on; Albrecht Dieterich, 1866–1908, professor of classical philology and religion at Giessen (1897) and Heidelberg (1903); Friedrich von Duhn, 1851–1930, professor of classical archeology at Heidelberg from 1880 on.—Ed.

I can only say good things about us. Spring with its sunshine and the heavenly green buds that may now be especially seen floating like little green stars on the chestnut trees in the *Anlage* [park] makes our hearts open up in gratitude. Max again goes out more, he rides his beloved mountain railway, and in the late afternoon we sit on our bench up in the *Stückgarten.*[3] At such times I also feel like dancing and singing like the birds because life always rejuvenates itself, rejoicing at all the things we have, and particularly at my having *him.*

How fortunate they were in being able to enjoy the good times gratefully, for such periods of rising strength were soon followed by inexplicable setbacks—a wave rising and falling in a steep upward and downward movement.

In the second half of that year Weber came under the spell of the Russian revolution. He interrupted his scholarly work and learned so much Russian in a short time—studying in bed early in the morning—that he was able to read newspapers and follow the events with the closest attention. He then pursued them with his pen and preserved them in a daily chronicle. What stirred him most profoundly was the question of the possible consequences of the Russian struggle for liberation for his own people. (This was mentioned in the last chapter.) The first book, *Zur Lage der bürgerlichen Demokratie in Russland* [The Situation of Bourgeois Democracy in Russia] was finished by the end of 1905, for the last quarter had been particularly propitious:

Max is very fit and very diligent. I am only surprised that he gives of himself so lavishly, that is, he writes one essay after another, and then these are buried in the *Archiv* and read by only a few people. I am also surprised that he still does not feel impelled to enter public life again. He does not write any topical political articles, nor does he make speeches of any kind. I believe he could make some if he felt impelled to do so, but he declines all requests.

Although his productivity astonished others, Weber continued to feel insecure, and so he refused to incur any obligation with a time limit. The older figures in his field urged him in vain to reestablish himself at one of the

---

[3]A park on the west side of the Heidelberg Castle, originally a "battery garden," made into a park by Frederick V in 1615. Goethe and Marianne von Willemer spent happy hours there in 1814–15.—Ed.

great universities. To such a proposal from L. Brentano, whom Weber particularly respected, he replied:

You again speak in such an exceedingly friendly way of a move to Munich. I cannot do this now; in fact, I have declined a similar suggestion from Schmoller regarding Berlin because I could not do any regular work yet. I stand rather arduous intellectual work quite well, but the *physical* task of speaking gives me sleepless nights and thus makes me unproductive after a short time. It will surely be a year and a half or so before I can seriously consider an academic position in some other city. You know that I would regard working together with you as a piece of great good fortune. The objective question arises whether it would not be more important to have someone who shares my views in *Berlin* at the present time, as a counterweight to that absolute lack of principles that now holds sway there. (February 28, 1906)

Despite his enforced withdrawal, Weber's interest in universities remained as lively as ever. Colleagues and faculties now frequently turned to him for advice when it was a matter of filling chairs, and younger docents made him the advocate of their professional interests. On such occasions he spared no pains and gave liberally of his time, made the causes of others his own, and most conscientiously examined what might be objectively desirable and just. He displayed a profound professional knowledge as well as knowledge of human nature and presented his views firmly but considerately and with great diplomatic tact. If, however, he encountered narrow-mindedness, vanity, and other "human weaknesses" that impeded objective action, he did become troublesome for his colleagues. Then he would unsheath his sword and seek to overcome the resistance through strong moral pressure—a procedure that was sometimes unsuccessful.

What irritated Weber repeatedly on such occasions was the tendency of some professors to prefer for academic appointments mediocre but pleasant colleagues to distinguished scholars with strong personalities. In this he saw a manifestation of a specific occupational disease: professorial vanity. He equally hated the anti-Semitism that denied outstanding intellects—such as Georg Simmel—the sphere of activity they deserved. He never forgave those involved for their failure to bring this philosopher to Heidelberg to supplement Wilhelm Windelband. And, finally, he hated the political servitude and timidity that resisted the appointment of scholars of the Social Democratic persuasion.

A typical case that occupied Weber for a long time was that of the promising young sociologist Robert Michels,[4] to whom the German universities were closed for the last-named reason. Michels had no other choice but to seek an academic appointment abroad. To Weber this situation was "a disgrace for a civilized nation if I compare Italian, French, and, at the moment, even Russian conditions with this; and I am certain that the majority of the best German scholars, regardless of an individual's political affiliation, will applaud me for saying so."

When Max's brother, Alfred, brought this case up at the first convention of university teachers, some professors maintained that there had been decisive personal as well as political reasons for the rejection of Michels—namely, the fact that Michels had not had his children baptized. Upon this Weber published an article in the *Frankfurter Zeitung* on "The So-Called Academic Freedom" in which he said, among other things:

As long as such views prevail, I see no possibility of behaving as though we had such a thing as "academic freedom." . . . And as long as religious communities knowingly and openly allow their sacraments to be used as means for furthering people's careers, on the same level as fraternity ribbons and reserve officers' commissions, they deserve the disdain about which they customarily complain. (September, 1908)

It was one of Weber's principles that in all disciplines based on "values," particularly in the fields of philosophy, history, and political science, representatives of different persuasions should, if at all possible, work side by side. A university as he imagined it must be neither a "church" nor a "sect" nor a state-preserving institution, but a place of intellectual freedom and intellectual struggle.

* * *

The spring of 1906 brought a long-desired change: The Webers moved from the narrow, ugly main street to the south side of the Neckar, the Riviera of Heidelberg. To take this important step they sold the original Klinger etchings, which they still loved but which they had now absorbed completely. It gratified Weber that the Kaiser Friedrich Museum in Posen ac-

---

[4]1876 –1936, professor at Turin, Basel, Perugia, and Rome.—Ed.

quired them and that they would thus help to spread German culture. Their unwieldy modern Renaissance oak furniture with its columns and protuberances was exchanged for plain old furniture. Helene helped, for she was always ready to send a ray of joy her children's way.

Marianne's long-harbored wish for an esthetically unobjectionable environment was fulfilled, and she was as happy as a child: "I am horribly jolly and gratefully dance around the little golden calf, which in this case surely is no wrong." Weber was quite unconcerned with external decorations, and really did not care in what surroundings his desk and his bookshelves stood; when he was able to work he had no eyes for the scenery. He did not require a harmonious setting, and so he was satisfied with the city apartment, too. In fact, in order to enjoy the charm of change, he liked to separate the asceticism of his work from his leisure, and he satisfied his need for beauty primarily on trips. But he was glad that his wife now had her "gem of a house." Besides, he too derived fresh enjoyment from the mountain slope, where delicate greenery was just beginning to appear, and from the merry, sparkling river. For the first time the budding world outside peeked into their own home at all hours of the day; by the house, peach and plum blossoms were opening. Weber wrote to Helene:

> Finally it is spring, and now we are enjoying our new home with a glorious view of the castle and the mountains and the more rural milieu, with the cackling of chickens, with orchards and gardening, and we are wondering whether things are already similar with you and your birthday will light up your room as cheerfully as it will come into ours . . . Every day from 12:00 to 1:00 I sit on our balcony just as God created me and with a long pipe ("sunbaths"); it remains to be seen with what success.

However, in midsummer, a time of year he dearly loved, he was again greatly tormented by the demons. He really should have gone away, but this was prevented by his work on the Russian revolution, which was causing him great annoyance every day. The voluminous second part was printed more slowly than it was written, and in Weber's view it thereby missed its objective. He performed the extraordinary drudgery merely for the sake of the cause and of the *Archiv* and paid for the printing, which was made more difficult by the numerous insertions, out of his own pocket. The fact that despite this the "machinery" ["*Apparat*"] did not keep pace and seemed to offer passive resistance made him furious, as did any resistance of "objects." He resolved to resign his editorship of the *Archiv*:

I have now spent nine months, which I shall never relive, working *exclusively* in the service of the *Archiv*, on things which neither I nor anyone else would regard as scholarly achievements. The functioning of the "machinery" was such that for two and a half months I was occupied with proofreading alone, that is, day after day I waited for the proof sheets without getting them and thus was not able to work on anything else. The result so far: an invoice for 857 marks for the January supplement, which gives one an idea of what the bill for the August issue, which is twice as thick, will be. I don't give a hoot about the money—not because I could afford to be indifferent, but because this is how I wanted it. But the way I have been treated by the "machinery" is anything but a matter of indifference to me. Neither Jaffé nor Siebeck is to blame, and consequently the situation is unalterable. Consequently I do not belong on the *Archiv*. I am half sick with annoyance. Of course, I shall not leave until you and Jaffé have had a chance to look for another associate. (August 20, 1906, to Sombart)

As always in conflicts, Weber staked everything. He was always ready to cut himself off from any group without regard to external interests. This was true not only when his own affairs were involved, but particularly when others dumped their anger on him or appealed to his chivalry. In such cases, too, he risked his own relationships. It could happen that he identified with one party without having heard the other and thus made mistakes. But in such cases he readily let himself be mollified once he was convinced that the cause would suffer if he abandoned it. In this way the quarrel with the *Archiv* was settled.

* * *

But now it was high time to go wandering. In the fall of 1906 Weber, his mother, and his wife traveled to Sicily—once again a strange, wonderful world, new even when compared with Italy. Traveling along a coast fragrant with citrons and garlanded with vineyards, they went first to Taormina. Wide, dry riverbeds containing stones rather than water betrayed the desert in the interior, but at the side of the scorched mountain slopes the sea gleamed dark blue, violet, and green—a sparkling jewel. The waves sparkled round the Lipari Islands with their mysterious clouds of smoke.

Mount Etna rose majestically from the sea as the road climbed along the olive and almond slopes. Its broad base was garlanded with vines and shining evergreens, while farther up it was covered more plainly with deciduous trees and stone pines. Finally, leaving the abodes of men behind, Etna becomes a hermit withdrawn from all earthly beauty and wraps its head in the disembodied universe of perpetual snow. Up there it seemed to belong more to infinity than to earth, and the changing light wonderfully reflected its inaccessibility. A thunderstorm shrouded it in black clouds that later flashed purple; but the white peak had a rose-colored shimmer in the promise of early morning and a pink sheen against the delicate green of the awakening ether. But behold the smoke cloud over the cool peak! No, this miraculous formation does not belong to heaven. The power of earthly fire surges in the solid structure, and any day an unchained primal force may burst forth from the heights, to destroy mercilessly the life on its flanks.

In the semicircle of the theater [at Taormina] in which the heroic landscape and the Greek spirit were combined, Weber read aloud from the *Odyssey*. Hellas enveloped him, and with Homer he viewed the ruby-colored sea. Then they went to Syracuse, once the center of bustling life and the most significant outpost of Greek civilization, now a treeless, silver-gray rocky plateau in whose caves shepherds again lived with their goats. In the morning a shepherd would grab one animal after another for milking at the narrow exit of the dark grotto, like Polyphemus. They felt an infinite melancholy of the past under this glistening sky, whose radiance mercilessly dazzles northern eyes. There is no sylvan shade to invite one for a refreshing rest.

But the sea surges against the rocks as merrily as ever and creates new, colorful caves. The companions rocked in a boat on the agitated crystalline water, whose clearness revealed the wonders at the bottom. Fatigued by the sun's glare they then sat quietly in the *latomiae*,[5] whose wide labyrinth was once carved out of the earth by a whole army of Athenian prisoners. Here thousands spent their lives in unhappy drudgery. Now their suffering had been turned into beauty: a sunken garden with flower beds and clumps of trees. The high stone walls were covered with luxuriant climbing plants; there was quiet whispering far removed from the world. Swarms of bees buzzed about the tartly fragrant ivy blossoms. High on the edge of the upper world, steep garlands of cypresses were outlined against the blue sky and breadfruit trees made shady roofs. Then there was the spring Cyane; in a small boat they followed the meanders of the swiftly flowing source upstream. The water became more blue and narrow; papyrus bushes from the shore bent close together and hid the world. Then the streaming crevice

---

[5] Ancient stone quarries.

suddenly widened into a deep-blue circle where the clear water burst out of the earth.

The trip to Girgenti [Agrigento] took them through treeless, mountainous country. In the autumn there was no grass scar to cover the yellow, sulphurous clay hills in which downpours cut deep furrows. Where once wheat swayed in the breeze and woods provided shade, there now lurked terrifying, deadly desolation. On the inhospitable summits they saw shabby human dwellings, yellow and gray like the mountain clay, and they wondered how the people survived under the mercilessly burning sky. Girgenti, too, stood on a steep summit, but the old Roman installation still supplied it with water, and giant-fingered cactus hedges protected the gardens. Below, toward the sea, where the enormous remains of the temples stood, there were ancient olives, almonds, and breadfruit trees, and the soil was covered with little white blossoms that looked like snow.

From this dreamworld of vanished greatness, bustling Palermo brought them back to the present. There the magnificent bay opened wide, with transparently formed mountains acting as corner pillars. Their clear outlines took on many different hues from the sky and the sea. At midday there was an opalescent blue; when the sirocco was about to bring on a thunderstorm, the colors were a rich dark blue and a somber violet (then the mountains towered darkly over the sea, which was turning green); and in the evening there was mauve and red. On some evenings the sun sank into the sea in clear redness; then its parting kiss glowed over the whole sky. For a long time this kiss preserved the hour's happiness in a more delicate play of all colors.

Here the travelers found Norman-Byzantine works of art. They delighted in the cloisters of the monasteries with their delicately turned marble columns, whose spirals and capitals were adorned with the imperishable gold and motley coloring of the mosaics, and in the oriental splendor of the chapels with their golden background, where the plain figures of legend were entwined by a delicate web of ornaments. In these glittering shrines priests in white brocade performed their age-old magic. Helene refused to regard these genuflections and litanies merely as a spectacle; her Protestant soul shuddered. But the quiet, pensive eyes of a superhuman picture of Christ looked out at her from the golden background of the apse at Monreale and filled her with awe and a sense of the nearness of God. This exalted, commanding look does not desire the world and yet places it under its spell to possess it forever.

However, they saw not only eternal pictures but also the undulations of the temporal at their feet. They could not get their fill of the behavior of the people, who could be seen through the open doors of the windowless apartments and in the streets. In entirely "ancient" fashion the activities of daily life took place in the narrow confines of the streets, and the outrageous filth also struck them as ancient. They enjoyed the tenderness which united the throngs of parents and children, and Helene noticed that even boys were treated by their fathers as comrades. Everywhere she saw a sight not offered by the big cities in the north: families with childlike happiness despite all their poverty. Of course, the travelers could not really feel at home among these people who lived in the present, enjoyed their brief lives unquestioningly, and apparently desired only to be happy. They simply took things as they came and did not seem to struggle or to strive for higher things. No, northern people, who almost always *wanted* things and felt obliged to do things, would find no home here.

* * *

What is it that these people *want*, insofar as they do not live on the hidden basis of their unconscious? Their works? In the final analysis, these probably are not a product of will but of compulsion, the products of talents bestowed by nature. No, to thinking people the realization of the "moral law" in their own actions and in the world appears particularly important—the orientation of life not to formal commandments but to the idea of a moral world-order, to "tasks." Above all others, the *ethical* ideal has an absolute dignity, and the ethical *ideal* is a norm one should obey, even at the expense of one's happiness. Man's dignity demands the shaping of existence by a moral obligation [*Soll*] as well as a readiness to make sacrifices for it. In certain areas of life the moral demand is not just a general form that a person could fill with any substance. In the unending casuistry of concrete ethical possibilities of action it is possible to imagine certain modes of conduct which, independent of circumstances and motives, are in accordance with the norms or, more particularly, in conflict with them. Some ethical ideals, like all cultural ideals, may change in the course of history; in the actions of life an individual step may derive its meaning only from the preceding or the following step—just as in a musical composition a chord receives its justification from the preceding and the subsequent note. But even so, in this process there are eternal and universal guiding principles.

The Webers were aware of such views as a self-evident part of a conscious existence only in their homeland, which had been shaped by the categorical imperative. By comparison with the northern world, the sun-drenched, joyful life of the south seemed like a children's paradise to them. But they could not imagine a *mature* life that did not involve exertion in the service of new tasks, and the overcoming of obstacles.

* * *

Weber concluded his journey with a visit to his young friend and colleague R. Michels, in Turin, and from there he wrote to his mother:

How much good the trip has done me I notice just now by what my body and brain can stand in the way of parties, theater (!), discussions, running around, etc., here in Turin. I would not have thought it possible . . . I sincerely hope that your health did not suffer, as we had reason to fear, and that it was not too much of an emotional strain on you to take that rather hectic trip with such an irritable person as myself. In an unfamiliar country like Sicily we had to go looking for beauty, and that took energy, time, and money and was a great exertion for you. But I hope that among the impressions there were some that you remember with pleasure. Some of the things I saw have made an indelible impression upon me, and, as usual, I shall enjoy the journey fully only in memory. While one is having those great impressions, they strike one dumb. Once more, dear Mother, for us the great outward and inward exertions you imposed upon yourself were a greater boon than you suspect and than one can express during a journey.

* * *

But despite the long period of relaxation, the winter and spring of 1907 were again under the pressure of dark clouds. Weber lacked energy for major work; he felt sterile and thought he had not had such a bad period in years. Oh, what a long, long winter! In those days he sometimes felt very tired of living: "Horrible thought of having to spend so many more sad winters in Germany; we should at least make the autumn of our lives sunny by spending it in the south."

Around that time there were also disagreeable and menacing political developments which will be discussed later and which worried Weber terribly.

Since his muse was failing him, Weber went through his wife's book on marriage,[6] on which she had worked hard for years and which was finally approaching completion.

In March the Webers again escaped to Italy, this time to Lake Como. They stayed on a wooded hill overlooking Bellagio, which is squeezed in between the three arms of the lake, in the Villa Serbelloni, an old mansion that had been converted into a hotel. It was a marvelous place to stay, combining a German sylvan spring with southern splendor. Round the hill, there were continually new visions of the most beautiful things on earth. Toward the north the snowy summits of the Alps were dimly visible; the mountains framing the lake in the south floated in a blue haze, and yet they were clearly outlined in the atmosphere, with every cliff distinctly visible. On the nearby slopes there were pink peach blossoms among the grayish-green olive trees. In the sumptuous gardens along the shore there were luxuriant camellias, pomegranates, and azaleas; in every bay there was a gleaming town.

But the Evil One would not give way. In May, Weber's condition was so poor that his wife, beside herself over the long torment, again consulted a new physician. Weber was not able to produce anything until summer. He then produced the difficult logical dispute with Stammler, the first part of which appeared in the July issue of the *Archiv*. "Rickert thinks the essay is very difficult and says it is too bad that you deposit your entire philosophy in the *Archiv* and make it so hard for readers to get anything out of it. You see, everyone says the same thing."

During the summer there were a number of significant changes. Weber's brother and colleague Alfred, who had been a professor at Prague, received an appointment at Heidelberg. He found it hard to part from Austria and hesitated before making a decision, but Weber was delighted; the brothers had once been very close to each other and were in the same political camp.

Another event was the death at an advanced age of Karl Weber, the patriarch of Oerlinghausen and founder of the textile firm. With age this man, who was accustomed to being in command, had become so gentle and kindly that all awe of him changed to love. He allowed the children to share fully in his prosperity. A flourishing dynasty—a son, a son-in-law, and three grandchildren—had already joined him in running the business. Not

---

[6]*Ehefrau und Mutter in der Rechtsentwicklung* [The Wife and the Mother in the Development of the Law], 1907.—Ed.

without resistance from the patriarch, who at first shrank from the new business methods, the young men changed from cottage-industry weaving to factory production. The business expanded, but the harmony of the working team was preserved.

Helene and her children were amazed at this: three generations managed to be integrated in such a way that the sons, who were more highly trained than their fathers, had freedom of action and yet obeyed and respected the older men loyally. How different this was from what had once happened in their own complicated family! Now death had broken the overripe fruit with a gentle hand. In the pain of parting lay a blessing: when an old tree falls, the young ones can stretch into the light.

The cast-off professor, too, was now freed from financial worries. After his grandfather had been laid to rest, Weber traveled to Holland for a few weeks and then returned to Oerlinghausen for a while. There he thought about the collective project of the *Verein für Sozialpolitik* that the brothers had already discussed in person and wrote about it to Alfred Weber:

> I intend to suggest that the *Verein für Sozialpolitik* start a series of investigations which, in order to have a popular label, one could perhaps call *Lage der geistigen Arbeit in der modernen Grossindustrie* [The Situation of Intellectual Work in Modern Heavy Industry]. I thought of including the inner structure of the various industries in regard to the extent and type of the *skilled* work, the continuity of the work force, *professional opportunities, change of occupation*, etc. From this "morphological" side we might get at the question of the psychophysical selection industry makes, its tendency in the individual industries, and conversely its being conditioned by the psychophysical qualities of the population, be they hereditary or instilled.[7]

As has already been pointed out, this project concerned the other side of the problems that are at the center of the treatise on the spirit of capitalism. There Weber had traced the shaping of those types that are serviceable to modern capitalism by spiritual factors; now their dependency on the technical forms of work was to be investigated. Weber sought to get collaborators and prepared methodological instructions for them. These and the first parts of his own study appeared in 1908.

That year was very productive, even the winter. In the fall of 1908, at

---

[7]Cf. pp. 329ff.

the suggestion of the publisher, Weber began, in addition to the specialized investigations, a sociohistorical treatise for the *Handwörterbuch der Staatswissenschaften*, *"Die Agrarverhältnisse des Altertums."*[8] In three months he produced a work of great importance, processing a vast amount of historical material from various points of view—legal, economic, sociological. This treatise, which by its very length transcended the framework of the compilation, also remained inaccessible to a wider audience. Weber was like the medieval painters who worked to serve God, concealing their works on high walls and in the vaults of dark churches, indifferent as to whether human eyes could see them.

II

Thus important works were completed again. Weber had a right to be satisfied and to give himself a breathing space. He and Marianne had long harbored a desire to enjoy more fully the colorful events of everyday life: "All threads of personal life are being reinforced, and I have the feeling that once again everything is remarkably new—particularly because we intensively share the lives of others. Outwardly, to be sure, everything takes its regular course. Max is still polishing his big essay and has surrounded himself with a barricade of books."

Weber very seldom let himself be lured out of the house, but he always enjoyed the company of stimulating visitors:

Almost every day someone is here; of the scholars, it is particularly Troeltsch, Jellinek, Gothein, Vossler, and Lask.[9] From the intermediate realm between scholarship and art there are Mr. and Mrs. Jaffé and Mr. and Mrs. A. F. Schmid as well as Gruhle, M. Tobler,[10] and others. The friends usually come in the afternoon, but now and then also in the evening. Max retires at nine o'clock, but first he does an enormous amount of talking.

---

[8]Cf. p. 329 in the preceding chapter. [The correct title is *Agrarverhältnisse im Altertum.* —Ed.]
[9]Emil Lask, 1875–1915 (fell on the Galician front); philosopher, professor at Heidelberg.—Ed.
[10]Friedrich Alfred Schmid-Noerr, 1877–1969, professor of philosophy and esthetics at Heidelberg from 1906 to 1918, prolific author of historical works, fiction, poetry, and drama; Hans Walter Gruhle, 1880 –1958, psychiatrist, professor at Heidelberg from 1919 on, director of the psychiatric clinic of the University of Bonn from 1946 to 1952; the Swiss musician Mina Tobler.—Ed.

With the older intellectuals there were important scholarly discussions each time. Enveloped in cigar smoke, one intellect caught fire from another—an attractive spectacle when the knowledge they had acquired in long discipline burst forth as vibrant streams with a personal coloration, and in their union gave birth to new insights.

But Weber also treasured the hours of charming conversation or an animated exchange of ideas with female friends over tea. He was interested in personal experiences and the details of living as much as in scholarly knowledge, and he repeatedly said, "How boring life would be without you little women [Frauchen]; something always happens to you." It was a great loss when Edgar and Else Jaffé left the inner circle of friends and moved to Munich. However, Weber's association with Jaffé continued through their work on the Archiv, and his former student Else—now in the prime of her life and, because of her charm and intellect, the focus of her circle—retained a close spiritual community with her Heidelberg friends.

The philosopher Emil Lask, Rickert's student and close friend, was one of the younger scholars who gradually formed a new circle. He attached himself to the Webers with great loyalty. He had a keen intellect and a brilliant wit which often cathartically broke through his melancholy seriousness. Lask will be discussed at a later point as one of those who died before Weber. He introduced the musician Mina Tobler to the Webers, and she in turn brought a new note into their lives both with the artistic individuality with which she experienced the world and with her noble art. During the many years of their friendship she enriched them humanly and musically.

Then, for esthetic stimulation, there were the manifoldly gifted A. F. Schmid-Noerr and his wife Kläre Schmid-Romberg, a former actress who was at home in every artistic field and brought a breath of the nonacademic world. With A. F. Schmid, the poet-philosopher and connoisseur of the arts, the Webers became particularly interested in the atmospheric religious sculpture of the Middle Ages, while the psychiatrist H. Gruhle, who also was an amateur of the arts, gave them a better understanding of the oddities of modern art.

Sometime later, friendships developed with Friedrich Gundolf, Arthur Salz, and especially Karl and Gertrud Jaspers.[11] The young people stood in

[11]Gundolf, originally F. Gundelfinger, 1880–1931, literary historian and professor at Heidelberg, author of books on Shakespeare, Goethe, and Stefan George; Arthur Salz, 1881–1963, political economist, professor at Heidelberg and Ohio State University (1939–1952); Karl Jaspers, 1883–1969, existentialist philosopher, professor at Heidelberg (1916) and Basel (1948).—Ed.

awe of Weber and always stayed at a respectful distance. He learned of this only from his wife, smilingly rejected the idea, and yet was pleased. After the end of the semester, their friends from outside Heidelberg also frequently came to call: the colleagues Werner Sombart and Robert Michels; Paul Hensel, who now held a professorship in philosophy at Erlangen; and, above all, Georg Simmel, who won everyone's heart not only with his exceptional conversational skill but also with his kindness, warmth, and genuine humanity.

Among the outstanding women who enriched the Webers' house with a shorter or longer stay were Marie Baum,[12] Gertrud Bäumer,[13] and Gertrud Simmel. P. Honigsheim and K. Löwenstein[14] frequently were among the younger men, future scholars who sought stimulation from Weber. In addition, there were often week-long visits from relatives, especially Helene. Now that Weber had opened his storehouses again, the flow of people sometimes became oppressive, although there was a fruitful exchange of ideas between the different age and interest groups.

Around that time the professorial core of Heidelberg intellectual life received a variety of fresh stimulation from young people without an official position and at all stages of development, who either wished to enter the inner academic circle at some time in the future or who desired to live in an intrinsically intellectual atmosphere. Modern currents flowed from the outside to the hospitable shores of the small town. Young people placed a different life-style, one that was beyond convention, alongside the firmly established structures of the older generation. New types of persons, related to the Romantics in their intellectual impulses, once again called in question bourgeois systems of thinking and living. They questioned the validity of universally binding norms of action and either sought an "individual law" or denied any "law" so as to let only *feeling* influence the flow of life.

This assault upon the traditional scales of value was particularly concerned with the liberalization of sexual morality, for it was in this area that "law" and "duty" demanded the most perceptible sacrifices. What was the

---

[12]Marie Baum, 1874 –1964, writer and feminist.—Ed.
[13]Gertrud Bäumer, 1873–1954, writer and feminist, author of works on cultural history and editor of the five-volume *Handbuch der Frauenbewegung* [Handbook of the Women's Movement], 1901 ff.—Ed.
[14]Paul Honigsheim, 1885–1967, sociologist and ethnologist, director of the Volkshochschule in Cologne (1921–1933), professor at Panama (1936) and Michigan State College (from 1938 on); Karl Löwenstein, 1891–1973, political scientist and legal scholar, professor at Munich, Yale (1934), and Amherst (from 1936).—Ed.

value of norms that so often stifled the magnificence of vibrant life, repressed natural drives, and, above all, denied fulfillment to so many women? Law, duty, asceticism—were not all these ideas derived from the demonization of sex by an outgrown Christianity? To shape one's future entirely on the basis of one's own nature, to let the currents of life flow through one and then to bear the consequences, was better than to sneak along on the sterile paths of caution hemmed in by morality.

The Webers had firm convictions and felt that they shared in the responsibility for the general morality. But they were still young enough to be intensely interested in the problems of young people and to allow them to question their own ideals and values. Precisely because they had reached a safe harbor they did not wish to stand aloof. They regarded marriage as one of those "absolute" ideals that had to be constantly defended, provided that it was based upon the power of love and upon faith in its own enduring value. In return for the great happiness bestowed by Eros, there was to be a readiness for serious tasks: a partnership for life and the responsibility of the spouses toward each other and their children. Husband and wife must grant each other the intellectual freedom and independence that will promote inner growth as well as the exploration of the fullness of existence.

In the Webers' view, claims to mutual possession are not justified, but fidelity and exclusiveness in the sexual sphere are a matter of course. Such a marriage is not only an "ideal" from whose realization an individual cannot exempt himself at will; it is also an *ethical norm* of the sexual union. The sacrifices it demands must be made. Anyone who does not strive toward it or who abandons it incurs *guilt,* guilt toward specific human beings or toward an idea of the highest order which presides over all social morality. For an instinct—which in itself is value-neutral—can be either a carrier of precious psychic values or an impediment to them. If it resists ethical molding, it becomes an impediment. Sensual enjoyment therefore must not be an end in itself, not even in the form of esthetically sublimated eroticism. In this area there are no *adiaphora* [things morally indifferent], for no human relationship is as momentous as the sexual kind. The "beautiful moment" imposes an obligation. And nothing stamps a person more decisively than his conduct in this sphere.

Anyone who absolves himself from "duty" here runs the risk of becoming frivolous or brutal. The decisive molding, to be sure, is done not by the "sinful act" [*"Sündenfall"*] itself, but by a person's attitude toward it. A human being can become greater than his guilt if he recognizes it as such, does not minimize it, and takes it seriously. And what is important for civilization is not that everyone should fulfill the norm but that everyone should *acknowledge* it and be guided by it. For only someone who, in succumbing, loses his sensitivity to ethical distinctions approaches the subhuman depths where he is no longer guided by eternal ideals.

These ideals, which Weber had consciously chosen as early as his Strasbourg period, had been a matter of intense public controversy since the turn of the century. From the one side they were given new substance, from the other they were denied. The forces of dissolution were given intellectual ammunition by socialistic theories of marriage, by Nietzsche, Ellen Key,[15] the psychiatrist Sigmund Freud, and others. Both sides fought against certain grave ills. Educators, scholars, clergymen, physicians, idealists, and naturalists strove to conquer the black shadow of marriage: prostitution and its devasting effects. Above all, some courageous women in the face of much hostility began to attack the vice that was sanctioned by the state and the way women alone had to bear the degrading consequences of prostitution, the double standard of morality.

The ethical "idealists" demanded from men, too, greater self-control, a new consecration of marriage, premarital chastity, early marriage, and easier divorces. In addition they demanded marriage reform in general, equality of the sexes, and protection of unwed mothers. Most of these practical demands were also made by the "naturalists," the majority of whom were doctors. But they rejected ethical rigorism as impossible of fulfillment and contrary to nature. They felt that life was short and that it was wrong to suffer by giving up a youthful happiness that was intended by nature. It was better to check the worst evil (prostitution) by means of a lesser one; society should recognize temporary liaisons and give a *positive* value-emphasis [*Wertakzent*] to this necessary supplement to marriage.

Actually, only "laws" brought transgressions into the world; if instincts are given free play, they will not become devils. Only ethical modesty, the *adaptation* of norms to what average persons can achieve, can bridge the gulf between the ideal and reality. Once a healthy young girl with a good reputation is permitted to give herself to a man without a ring on her finger,

---

[15] 1849–1926, Swedish feminist and pedagogue, author of *The Century of the Child* (1900) and *Love and Ethics* (1911).—Ed.

the pernicious consequences of late marriage will be neutralized. Then a young man will not need to waste his vital energy in a brothel, and female blossoms will not have to wither unfruitfully. Marriage with all its obligations is the proper end of the free period of development.

In lectures to students of both sexes, female disciples of this "new ethics" caricatured chastity as the morality of monks, and marriage as the state's compulsory institution for the protection of private property. They demanded the right to "free love" and illegitimate children. Young women who had just been freed from the constraint of their families struggled with the new message, and many welcomed it. Weber remarked about this movement: "This specific *Mutterschutz* [protection of mothers] gang is an utterly confused bunch. After the babble of Miss X I withdrew my support. Crass hedonism and an ethics that would benefit only men as the goal of women . . . that is simply nonsense."

But the controversy over the new morality of happiness was of universal concern. The Webers had to take a stand on it in countless confidential conversations. Even though it was not too difficult to deal with the *theory*, particular cases touched their hearts. These problems were now being discussed in public forums and in print. Marianne shrank from this and viewed it with uneasiness; but she was in the ranks of the women's movement and had written a book in which she had, among other things, refuted the socialistic theories about the development of marriage. At Adolf Harnack's urging she gave a lecture on "Basic Questions of Sexual Ethics" in the midst of the old circle of friends at the Evangelical-Social Congress (Pentecost of 1907, in Strasbourg). Weber stood by her. She stated their shared ethical convictions, casuistically refined by the results of many encounters with the new ideas and various personal impressions.

> Unlike Puritanism and "bourgeois morality," we shall no longer identify the total ethical value of a person with his attitude toward the ideals of sexual ethics and designate a person who does not achieve them as "immoral." We have learned to recognize that human nobility consists of a multiplicity of characteristics and modes of action, and that this nobility is not necessarily destroyed if, despite serious striving, a person falls short of the height of ideals.

These sentences from the lecture were the result of personal experiences and innumerable discussions with young, questing people. A young psychiatrist,[16] a disciple of S. Freud with the magic of a brilliant mind and heart, had gained considerable influence. He interpreted the new insights of the master in his own fashion, drew radical conclusions from them, and proclaimed a sexual communism compared with which the so-called "new ethics" appeared quite harmless. In outline his doctrine went something like this: The life-enhancing value of eroticism is so great that it must remain free from extraneous considerations and laws, and, above all, from any integration into everyday life. If, for the time being, marriage continues to exist as a provision for women and children, love ought to celebrate its ecstasies outside its realm. Husbands and wives should not begrudge each other whatever erotic stimuli may present themselves. Jealousy is something mean. Just as one has several people as friends, one can also have sexual union with several people at any given period and be "faithful" to each one. But any belief in the permanence of feeling for a single human being is an illusion, and therefore exclusiveness of sexual community is a lie. The power of love is necessarily weakened by being constantly directed to the same person. The sexuality on which it is founded requires many-sided satisfaction. Its monogamous limitation "represses" the natural drives and endangers emotional health. Therefore, away with the fetters that prevent a person from fulfilling himself in new experiences; free love will save the world.

The Freudian was successful and his message found believers. Under his influence both men and women dared to risk their own and their companions' spiritual well-being. That this happened while highly-principled, cultured people were struggling for a higher sexual morality shocked the Webers and perturbed them far more than the impersonal public fight. They were profoundly affected by the impact of this message and torn by horror and revulsion at the theory and by a profound sympathy for the unhappy lives that prepared the ground for such misleading teachings. If lonely people who had been denied the blessing of a happy marriage created surrogates for themselves, this might have been a "venial sin." But what was happening now— the desecration of monogamy—was accompanied by the terrors of a grave, destructive guilt: "The killing of something divine!" Nevertheless, they sought to understand the actions of those involved on the basis of their situation. They understood that in a few cases people accepted this dangerous theory in an effort to find the most "fruitful" way out of a very serious

---

[16]Dr. Otto Gross, 1877–1920. See Martin Green, *op. cit.* —Ed.

conflict, and that broken marriages were preserved, not only for the sake of the children but also out of loyal friendship for the partner. They watched the blossoming of beauty and spiritual strength which, at least for a time, kept in check even the natural enmity between erotic competitors. Indeed, they had to admire the courage of those who risked themselves by sinning and then overcame the sin.

In the final analysis, to understand everything means to forgive everything.[17] There is a danger that in empathizing with such adventurism one's own ideals could easily slip away. Where was the ultimate criterion of their truth, anyway? Surely not in their being derivable from a logically demonstrable "law." Not for one moment did the Webers believe in the ennobling effect of sexual freedom. But despite this, they felt they should have further evidence concerning its influence on high-minded people. They had endless discussions with the adherents of the psychiatric "ethos." The restrained scientific disputes concealed a struggle for ideals and for souls. Weber delved into the teachings of Freud. He appreciated their importance, but it was impossible to reach agreement on their interpretation by his apostles. This interpretation endangered the highest values of life. And in this sphere there were no logically compelling arguments, but only the inherent evidence of what was right and the personal choice. A record of these struggles between idea and idea, ideal and destiny, knowledge and fantasy has been preserved in a letter. An essay based on Freud's theories had been submitted to Weber for possible publication in the Archiv. He rejected it with the following explanation:

> I am returning the copy of Dr. X's [Gross's] essay with the suggestion that we do not publish it in the Archiv, although I am ready to be outvoted. I myself cannot vote in favor of it under any circumstances. The obvious thing for me to do would be to inform Dr. X directly, giving him my reasons. However, cui bono? [for whose good?] I know very well that no matter how I may explain myself, in this case, as in all other cases of differences of opinion, he is bound to regard me as limited by convention. My "ethics" must seem to him to be identical with "conventional" ethics or with certain tenets thereof—if only by virtue of the terminology to which I adhere, though I do so on purpose. I cannot change this—even in the case of someone whom I esteem as highly as a human being as I do Dr. X—for this would require extensive verbal

---

[17]An allusion to Tout comprendre c'est tout pardonner (attributed to Mme de Staël).—Ed.

or written discussions, which unfortunately I cannot manage. And I would, moreover, have to be prepared to give offense.

All of us have this in common today: We would much rather be told that we are ethical monsters in our theories than that we are muddle-heads [Konfusionsrat], plain and simple. But the latter applies to Dr. X. And, as far as I can see, wherever he expresses himself beyond the limits of his special field, he indulges in Weltanschauung and thus is a "moralist" and not just a "natural scientist." And I must say this for the sake of truth, even at the risk of being regarded not only as an ethical Pharisee but as an intellectual one as well. I shall, of course, substantiate this, at least briefly.

The theories of S. Freud, with which I am now familiar from his major writings as well, have admittedly changed greatly over the years, and it is my impression as a layman that they have by no means been given definitive form even now. Unfortunately, important concepts—for example, that of abreaction—have recently been disfigured and diluted to the point of utter nebulousness. (May I remark in passing that in the Zeitschrift für Religionspsychologie [Journal for the Psychology of Religion] there was a nauseating concoction of the "holy God" and various unappetizing erotica.) Nevertheless, there is no doubt that Freud's thought can become a very significant source for the interpretation of whole series of phenomena in cultural history, particularly in the history of religion and of manners and morals—although from the viewpoint of a cultural historian its significance is by no means as universal as is assumed by Freud and his disciples in their very understandable zeal and joy of discovery. The prerequisite would be the creation of an exact casuistry of a scope and a certainty that does not exist today—despite all assertions—but may exist in two or three decades. One need only consider all the things that Freud changed in one decade and how alarmingly meager his material is to this day, despite everything; this is very understandable and certainly no reproach.

However, instead of this work, which is of necessity specialized and scholarly, we see Freud's adherents, particularly Dr. X, turn to metaphysical speculations or—and this is worse—to a question which from a strictly scientific standpoint is a simpleminded one: "Can one eat that?"—that is, can't one make a practical Weltanschauung out of it? That certainly is no crime. Until now, after every new scholarly or technical discovery, no matter whether it was meat extract or the highest abstractions of the natural sciences, the inventor has felt called upon to discover new values and to be the reformer of "ethics," just as, for example, the inventors of modern photography feel called upon to be the reformers of painting. But it seems to me that it is not necessary to wash these apparently inescapable diapers in our *Archiv*.

They *are* "diapers." For what else shall one call an "ethics" which, in Dr. X's terminology, is too "cowardly" to admit to itself that its "ideal" ought to be the wholly banal, healthy *nerve-proud person* [*Nervenprotz*], an ethics which believes that it can discredit some "norms" by proving that their observance is not "beneficial" to the dear nerves? And despite all vehement protests that this interpretation would naturally arouse, *this* is the only *ethical* content of the "new" doctrine. There is nothing, nothing *whatever*, concrete behind it other than this philistinism: If *every* suppression of emotion-laden desires and drives leads to "repression" [*Verdrängung*]—and the *wording*, at least, contains this foolish assertion—and if the "repression" as such is the absolute evil (allegedly because it leads to inward untruthfulness, to "error and cowardice," but in reality because from the viewpoint of a *specialist in nervous hygiene* it involves the danger of hysteria, compulsive neurosis, phobias, etc.), *then* this nerve-ethics would, for instance, have to give this message to a Boer fighting for his freedom: Take to your heels, for otherwise you will "repress" your feelings of anxiety and might get the "red laugh" of L. Andreyev.[18] To put it in "technical" terms: "Become a coward" in the *conventional* sense, and, by beating it [*indem du auskneifst*], "abreact" your cowardly feelings so you won't become a "coward" in the hypermodern neurological sense of Dr. X, that is, "repress" those feelings and make them "incapable of consciousness" [*bewusstseinsunfähig*], which would certainly be bad for you and hence is immoral.

The message of this ethics to a husband or a wife—or to a male or female lover—who has twinges of jealousy when there is too quick a change must be this: *Abreact them*—à la Othello, or through a duel, or in whatever form you like, be it ever so philistine; better for you to be "shabby" (from the standpoint of the "new" sexual ethics) than to fight them and thus create a "delusion" formation [*"Wahn" bildung*]. In every situation the ethics must be courageous enough to recommend to me that I give free rein to *every* stirring of my desires and of my instinctual life, no matter how low-down it may be, in order to "abreact" it—which means, to permit this stirring any form of *satisfac-*

---

[18]Leonid Nikolayevich Andreyev (1871–1919) was a Russian storyteller and playwright. His novel *The Red Laugh* (1904), written during the Russo-Japanese War, reflects his revulsion at the horrors of war. A gruesome, mocking "red laugh" symbolizes the deleterious effects of war upon human beings.—Ed.

tion that is adequate to it *in any way*, because otherwise my precious nerves might be injured. This is the typical, familiar standpoint of the medical philistine!

Am I perhaps doing an injustice to Dr. X's "theory"? But on page 9 of his essay I find *expressis verbis* [in so many words] the sentence about the *sacrifices* that the "adaptation" (that is, the suppression of "desires" for the sake of adhering to the norms) *costs*—and these "sacrifices" are sacrifices of *health*. In other words, I am believed capable of being shabby enough to ask, "How much does it cost?" before I act the way I think I owe it to my human dignity to act. And I am supposed to accept the neurologist as an authority as to whether the ethical value of my action is worth the "costs." To be sure, the ridiculous assertion is made that these "costs" (possible "repressions" with their hygienic consequences) arise only as a consequence of a belief in *absolute* values. But I most definitely doubt that Dr. X has any idea of what "a belief in *absolute* values" really means. As we know, this cannot be explained cogently enough in one or two letters or one or two conversations. Yet this is not the main point. The decisive thing is that as soon as a relativistic ethic with "idealistic" pretensions expects a concrete human being to *desire* a value that is valid for him—let us say, *in concreto* only for him—*only* now in *this* situation, thus a "relative" and "subjective" value, it will bring about exactly the *same* hygienic" consequences—unless it be that the "relativism" resides in the idea that an individual should abandon his "relative ideal" wherever striving for it costs him something, that is, perhaps "gets on his nerves." *That*, to be sure, would be a kind of shabby mercenary idealism [*Krämer-Idealismus*] that I, for one, could not accept any more than Dr. X undoubtedly would *in praxi* [in practice].

One can divide all "ethics," regardless of their material contents, into two major groups according to whether they make basic demands on a person to which he can generally *not* live up except for the great high points of his life, which point the way as guideposts in his *striving* in infinity ("hero ethics"), or whether they are modest enough to accept his everyday "nature" as a maximal requirement ("average ethics"). It seems to me that only the first category, the "hero ethics," can be called "idealism," and in this category there belong the ethic of the *early*, undivided Christianity as well as the Kantian ethic.

Both of them proceed from a judgment on the "nature" of the average individual which, measured by their ideals, is so pessimistic that the Freudian disclosures from the realm of the unconscious have, heaven knows, *nothing* "terrible" to add to it. However, since the "psychiatric ethic" only demands, "Admit to yourself what you are like and what you desire," it really makes no new demands of an ethical nature. After all, father confessors and the ministry of the old kind had no task in this respect, and the Freudian treatment involves the restoration of the *confession* with a somewhat different technique. Only, here the purpose is even *less* an "ethical" one than was the case with Tetzel's[19] old indulgences. Anyone who deceives himself, and wants to deceive himself, about himself and has forgotten how to remember the things in his life that he has to be ashamed of, things that he *can* remember very well to a considerable degree if he wants to, will not be helped *ethically* by lying on Freud's couch for months and having Freud bring back into his consciousness "infantile" or other experiences of an embarrassing nature that he has "repressed." Freud's cures may have a *hygienic* value for him, but I do not know, for example, what I would gain ethically if some sexual misconduct in which, say, a servant girl might have engaged with me (Freudian example!), or a dirty impulse I have "repressed" and "forgotten" were brought back. For I make the *en bloc* admission, without having the feeling that I am doing something "terrible," that nothing "human" is and was alien to me. Basically, then, I am certainly not learning anything new.

But this is beside the point, and I am saying it only to make the point that the categorical imperative which reads, "Go to Freud or come to us, his pupils, in order to learn the historical *truth* about yourself and your actions; otherwise you are a coward," not only betrays a somewhat naive "departmental patriotism" [*Ressort-Patriotismus*] on the part of a psychiatrist and professional *directeur de l'âme* [spiritual adviser], but, owing to its unfortunate amalgamation with "hygienic" motives, deprives itself of any ethical value. But, as I have indicated, from this essay, which is moralizing from beginning to end, I cannot derive any other practical postulate but this "duty to know oneself" with psychiatric help. *Where* is there the slightest indication of the *substance* of those new relativistic *and yet ideal (nota bene!)* values that are to serve as the basis of the critique of the "old," "dubious" values? One will look for them in vain, and for good reason: any attempt to outline them would expose them to criticism and show that the problem has not been solved but only put off. An idealistic ethic that demands "sacrifices" and does not eliminate *responsibility* can never produce any other results. But it will not do to criticize an ethic on any *other* basis than that of one's *own* ideals; otherwise one gets into the area of the shabbiest "calculation of costs," and, as I have said before,

---

[19]Johann Tetzel (ca. 1465–1519), Dominican monk, preacher, and purveyor of indulgences who provoked Luther's Wittenberg Theses.—Ed.

the ideal will then inevitably be the normal health snob [*Gesundheits-prot*z] and medically supervised philistine of macrobiotics.

If Dr. X were to see the above lines (I hope he won't, but I leave it up to you. The question is, does he have a sense of humor? I doubt it very much. No moralist has one), he would surely feel that his views have been terribly trivialized. Of course! I have intentionally translated them into our beloved "vulgar" German. That they seem "trivial," then, is his fault, for that is a consequence of his combining his medical research with an utterly confused reformatory zeal. His entire essay fairly bursts with value judgments, and I have simply no respect whatever for allegedly scientific achievements that do not meet the demands of sobriety and objectivity and are not *"value-free."* . . .

For *specialized* scholarship is a technique and teaches technical means. But where there is an argument about values, the problem is projected onto an entirely different level of the intellect, one that is removed from all verifiable "science." Putting it more precisely, there is an entirely heterogeneous *posing of the problem. No* branch of scholarship and no scientific knowledge, be they ever so important—and I certainly number the Freudian discoveries among the scientifically important ones if they stand the test in the long run—provide a *Weltanschauung.* And conversely: in a scholarly journal there is no place for an essay that wants to be a sermon—and is a *bad* sermon. (September 13, 1907)

* * *

It was soon realized that it was a delusion to build up certain psychiatric insights into a world-redeeming prophecy. But that did not prevent people from striving for sexual happiness, to escape gloomy lives of resignation or the burden of unhappy marriages. Things took their course regardless. And to avoid being crushed by self-torment, the people involved initially embraced certain ideas of Freud's disciple which turned all existing ideas upside down. Even though all of this seemed like a delusion to the Webers, they could not turn away in indignation, since they felt deep concern for the noble and lovable human beings involved and wanted to help them as much as they could. They wanted, too, to learn to understand this strange, unbourgeois world of adventurism and to carry on an intellectual dialogue with it.

Some of the ethical casuistry that was inspired by Weber's contact with these currents is reflected in the following excerpts from his letters:

I have taken another soporific especially to be able to write this. You see, I feel that things can't go on like this with Mr. and Mrs. X. . . .

These people, who began their relationship with insincerity, want to mount a campaign against the hypocrisy of convention! But I think that you must not stand by silently. In my estimation you risk your relationship with the Xes by telling them where you stand, and your stand cannot be different from mine, even though it may be milder in form . . .

Achieving depth through erotic adventures is something quite problematical. A woman who harbors some strong, secret affection always *seems* to be "deeper," but she is not always so. All these people are really entangled in a powerful web of gross self-deception, and the esthetic sublimation is only designed to hide the true state of affairs from them. Dr. X has no sensual needs and lives polygamously only out of "philanthropy"? That is nonsense. Anyone with any psychological experience in this field need only hear that statement about the filthiness of unsatisfied eroticism to know what he is dealing with. The counterpoise offered by fanaticism must not deceive one about this. Two poisons counterbalance each other here. . . . This situation is not changed by the alleged "sacrifices," for they only indicate a loss of sensitivity to distinctions and, as every psychiatrist must confirm, are an important symptom of psychic illness. "Theory" or "will" has never overcome a real physical antipathy erotically.

There are "mortal sins" from which a human being rarely recovers. But this is not the situation of K.'s lady friend.[20] Torn away from the roots of morally clear action, she now expends all her energies on keeping her head above water, on remaining "cultivated," on standing her ground against the consequences of her guilt. This undoubtedly *ennobles* her— just as any human being who works on becoming stronger than his sin is purer than an irreproachable "righteous one." But in the final analysis, whether or not she admits this to herself, her behavior is an act of asserting her *self*-esteem in the face of the liberties taken by her *husband*. She could not act any differently; that much is clear. And even if she claims that she and her husband have no *erotic* needs themselves, is surrender *without* the compulsion of love *not* "dirty"? You see, theory everywhere enters into the fractional arithmetic. . . .

A younger friend who had previously had a rigoristic outlook found temporary relief from his hard life in a free erotic relationship. As a consequence he was

---

[20]Presumably a reference to "Karl" and "Dora"; see page 487, notes 9 and 11.—Ed.

converted to the view that one's sexual conduct was in itself a matter of indifference and needed to be controlled only if it pushed into the foreground and endangered other values. To take a "monkish" view, so he said, was to overemphasize it. To this Weber remarked:

> I should like to go into B.'s dicta in more detail. The only thing is, he is fighting against imaginary opponents. *Who* is the "monk" supposed to be? And has *he* been one up to now? The question is precisely when that "pushing into the foreground" at the expense of other values takes place. Surely it *always* does when one does not remain in complete control of one's actions. And undoubtedly it also does when one can perceive "unsatisfied" relationships only as "dirty." Above all, however, any view of the drive "by itself" is an *abstraction*. It is, after all, never found "by itself" but is always bound up with the relationship to a concrete *human being*, and it is from this relationship that it derives its dignity or lack of dignity.

At that time the young people who were concerned with the problems of marriage were constantly agitated by questions such as: Is the ethical "ideal" also the "norm" of action? Do ethical norms apply "unconditionally," and if so, why? Are substantially determined norms or only formal ones universally binding, and are they applicable to concrete actions? Does one owe them obedience even if they inhibit living? Aren't the "gods" permitted what is forbidden to average people? What could one pit against this assault not only upon the norms of sexual ethics but upon the dignity of the "moral law" in general? Adherents of the "old ethics" tried to defend them with logical axioms. Marianne wrote about discussions of this type:

> E. is now so fanatically possessed by the "moral law" that he will talk about nothing else. In general, he regards only what is logically deducible as objectively binding, and he thinks he can derive the validity of ethical norms—the formal, the substantial, and the logical kind—from the proposition of identity, of the unity of a rational being with itself. Feelings, including the feeling of love, must be completely disregarded as a morally constitutive element in marriage, because it is irrational and thus irrelevant as an ethical motive. He also tried to deduce from the concept of the moral law monogamy and the indissolubility of marriage, and in my estimation he completely failed in this. The others took the point of view that ethical norms and valuations are

not logically verifiable and derive their dignity not from logical deductions but are, as it were, "discovered" in practice like the stars and then gain the validity of internal evidence. Thereupon B. was very pleased and declared that he was right; if they are not verifiable, then one need not believe in their universal validity and torment oneself with them any longer!

To this Weber replied with a jocular analogy. On several picture postcards from Monte Carlo he scribbled the following:

Truly, I too believe that the "moral law" which you discuss so much has only a relative content. "How scornfully I once reviled"[21] when someone *won money* in Monte Carlo; now I myself won about 1000 francs (in fifteen minutes)! I feel a bit embarrassed—but if B. enters the area of the "alogical," why shouldn't I enter the area of the absolutely "irrational"? After all, I would have *deserved* 1000 francs for the drudgery of this winter. And it was only this infamous gambling casino that I did out of the money.

Actually I can't see *why* I shouldn't have. Certainly, the company one is in is *low*. At ten o'clock the casino opens; the professional gamblers stand in line and gallop to their tables in order to get seats. A great variety of people: cold, calm calculators who work out their "statistics," who bet on a series of numbers according to a definite plan each time they are told, *"Faites le jeu"* [place your bets], and then with pinched lips calmly pocket their winnings or watch their losses being raked in, with only the redness around their eyes and their hasty, angular movements betraying their inner tension. Next to them there are quiet fanatics, poor devils of both sexes with waxen yellow faces and bad clothes who hold their notebooks in their gently vibrating hands and follow the fate of their five-franc pieces with subdued desperation. Finally, there are corpulent roués with double chins, rolls of fat on their necks, large mustaches, and prominent jaws, peering out from behind the fat bags under their eyes to see what will happen to their stake. These are the main types of those who *sit*. Behind them stand people who are *not* steady customers, who also want to try their luck and in the long run *lose* almost every time.

This is how it went with me, too. I could not resist it, tried a

[21]"*Wie könnt' ich sonst so wacker schmälen*"—a line, slightly misquoted, from Goethe's *Faust*, Part I, lines 3577–78: "How scornfully I once reviled when some poor maiden was beguiled . . ." (Bayard Taylor translation).—Ed.

few more times—the 1000 *francs* are *gone* again! Annoying! No, it's all right! I might have been embarrassed after all. Of course, there is this pointless excitement now—but it is better this way. Perhaps I should not even have started? But only philistines and people without verve do that. Teutons have always gambled! A fellow with verve *cannot* remain passive.

On the last postcard: "But I simply *have* no verve; thus the "moral law" remained intact, so did my purse and the bank, and my money remained in the innkeeper's safe when I came here by streetcar."

Weber's wife acted as though she had not read the last card and granted him absolution for his "apostasy from the moral law." He did not immediately get the joke and became a bit frightened:

What did you read into my cards? I am supposed to have gambled away *someone else's* money?? *Pfui Teufel!* [For shame!] If at all, then my own! Of course, I lost or won *nothing whatever.* After an "intimate acquaintance" of almost fifteen years you believe me capable of fine things, *mein Herz* [my sweetheart]; it is good that I am finally discovering this. *Sieh, sieh!* [What do you know!] I shall put you to the test again with different things. Unfortunately excursions into the "alogical" don't seem plausible to you, so I cannot try that. . . .

* * *

The occasion for these postcards was a prolonged separation of the couple in the spring of 1908. After the hasty completion of his agrarian history of ancient times Weber again needed long weeks of relaxation in the south. This time he found them on the warm, rural lavender coast of Provence. Then he spent a period of intensive sightseeing with Helene in Florence. Marianne was exhausted, too, and went to recuperate elsewhere. They had never been so far apart, but almost every day the distance was bridged by letters reflecting the discussions about the problems that excited young people. Weber worried about his wife and enveloped her with tender care by remote control. During this period of separation a number of anniversaries occurred. On such occasions the treasuries of the soul opened and hidden gems shone forth. The enduring substance of a community based on love triumphantly permeated everyday life.

Lavandou, April, 1908

Spring here is different from what it is at home. One feels this when one walks through these *macchia* [shrubs] and Scotch pine forests. The many dark green, gray green, olive green, and gray hues, which form the background and give a subdued waxen color to everything, carry the atmosphere of late fall with its muted melancholy into the spring, which sits on the forehead of ripe beauty only like a bridal wreath for a silver wedding. But a young soul and a joyful heart in a body that is no longer young and is constrained and inhibited are not without value, and they may be worth more than the mindless bluster of young people, who are nothing but young. . . . We shall never be unhappy, although we are occasionally troubled. You too are greatly troubled, my child; this I know and only now do I realize it fully. God knows that fate has wondrous whims, but there are limits to its power and it will not be able to prevail over the youth of our hearts and cover them with its rust if we do not want it to.

Marianne replied:

Thanks for the wonderful picture of the southern spring landscape! How very rich your soul is, and how you may enjoy your mental powers even in their confinement! We others, almost all of us, walk only in borrowed light, but you harbor this light within yourself. Here things have hardly started budding, and amidst the dark fir treés one does not know whether it is spring or the gentle start of autumn. But what does it matter whether it is one or the other as long as we can enjoy with gratitude and vitality every sunny day fate bestows on us!

To Helene, on her birthday:

How glad I am to know that you are together on this festive day, and how I would like to be with you. But since it cannot be, I kiss you in thoughts, dearest mother, and send you my ever new love and gratitude as well as my profound, reverent admiration for everything that you constantly give and are to us and to others with your great vitality, strength of soul, and capacity for love! May we, your children, also learn to preserve a youth like yours throughout a long and often difficult life such as yours has been.

Weber, from Pisa:

Do you remember how we arrived here from Corsica, half-starved for "culture," and delighted in the marble splendor of this unique little place as we sat in a corner of the quiet greensward by the wall? We took our time and sat in and around the cathedral for over two hours. Then we surrendered to the entire atmosphere of the secluded Campo Santo [cemetery] with its peaceful wild herb-garden amidst the beautiful tracery of the windows of the arcades. To be sure, there is nothing like it in all of Italy. That this was the very first art created in the Middle Ages and turned out so beautiful remains an eternal miracle and a stroke of luck in world history for which one must be grateful to this day. How joyful in a childlike way all this is, and how unpremeditated and unaffected in all its artistic balance.

Florence, April 19, 1908

Unfortunately it is raining buckets. Still, yesterday we first amused ourselves by watching the people amidst the clattering of the *schioppo del carro* [noisy vehicles] (remember?) in front of the cathedral; then, in the afternoon, the graves of the Medici, whose abysmal melancholy and yearning for release from life and eternal sleep had an even more powerful effect under a somewhat gray sky . . .

Florence, April 21, 1908

These big letterheads are really not the proper medium for telling you how very much your kind little birthday letter pleased me—*despite* the "Tower of Babel" you carry on with me there, my good *Mädele* [little girl]. For, as I have probably said before, from this I only see again and again how great your love is, and I shall put up with the humiliation and certainly with the "uncritical attitude" of my *Kerlchen* [little dear]. I am not sure whether my own ever-present critical attitude owes its existence to a weaker heart. But I know that in the midst of all criticism I always yearn for the warming sun, which is greater than all criticism. Life with you, after all, is like the soft light and the warmth of the spring sun, which calmly and surely, *patiens quia aeterna* [patient because it is eternal], dissolves all icebergs of life and melts every snow cover—which is what Tolstoy, with excessive utopianism, hoped the power of abstract *philanthropy* could do—whereas the wild storm of my passion can only shake the snowflakes and icicles from the trees. This day without you is really a terribly strange phenomenon.

Yesterday I also pointed out to Mama that this is the first time in years that we have been apart. Next year we must share something of this sort.

* * *

At home the Webers were concerned with the modern ideas for a long time to come. Weber was greatly interested in the effects of a norm-free eroticism upon the total personality, for the latter now seemed to him what was important in the final analysis. And his empathic contemplation of the destinies of struggling human beings modified his own attitude toward the actions of individuals. The above-cited passages from letters reveal the attitude of a man to whom moralistic narrowness and rigidity were alien, but who reserved the right to measure the conduct of others—with detachment—by universal standards and to judge it accordingly. In discussions of his right to do so he used to emphasize that anyone who was incapable of hating evil was also incapable of loving good and great things properly; the usual judgments about others, based on taste, were far more "unbrotherly" than ethical judgments, for "there is no appeal against the former and one excludes oneself from them, while one always subjects oneself to ethical judgments and thus retains an inward community with that which is judged."

Of course, his view of the nature of people who lived beyond good and evil in the erotic sphere had not changed—his belief in the irreplaceable significance of norms was unshaken—but there *was* a change in his attitude toward the people who had abandoned the norms. He now paid less attention to their actions, which were determined by passion, and concentrated more on their total existence. Whenever he was able to approve of the latter, he was now more interested in its protection and development than in measuring the distance between these individuals' *actions* and the "moral imperative":

The ethical values are not *alone* in the world. If they demand sacrifices, they can make human beings who have incurred guilt *small*. And they can lead to insoluble conflicts where guiltless action is *impossible*. Then (ethically speaking) there must be such action that the people involved suffer the smallest possible losses in their human dignity, in their capacity for kindness and love, in their fulfillment of duty, and in the value of their personality, and this often is a tall order.

His new insight was also crystallized into statements made in conversations. For example, there is a scale of the ethical. If the ethically highest is unattainable in a concrete case, an attempt must be made to attain the second or third best. What that is cannot be decided by any theory but only on the basis of a concrete situation. It can happen that sacrifices imposed from the outside, by convention, psychologically cripple human beings who feel the strong hand of life, that this makes them small, pharisaic, and bitter. In such cases it is better if they sin.

As soon as Weber encountered not only the strong characters who thrived in the new freedom but also the profound sufferings of those who were defeated in the erotic struggle, his attitude changed again, and then there were many things to demand and to reject. In certain cases "the sweet lightheartedness"[22] of varied adventures seemed to Weber to be possibly compatible with a continuation of a marriage for the sake of the children. But if playing around led to the deadly seriousness of a great passion and demanded its due alongside the marriage, then he foresaw with horror the moral destruction of the weaker persons.

The final result of Weber's concern with new views and the lives of others was something like this: The ethical ideal of monogamy as it ought to be, as the highest form of erotic community, remained. But it cannot be forced upon all types of human beings and their lives. And no principles can be formulated for the ethical handling of the manifold concrete situations into which human beings stumble outside and in addition to marriage. But something that remains universally valid is the recognition of *responsibility* in all human relationships as well as the seriousness of the moral endeavor. Also, those who incur guilt under the constraint of powerful vital forces should not make a "theory" or a "right" out of it.

This central imperative—that even if nature and fate compel a transgression, a person should nevertheless humbly submit to the supraindividual norm and acknowledge the distance between it and his own action as *guilt*—was very important to Weber. He expressed it in the following lines:

> What I do not like is that if the fate of a great passion comes over a person, he fashions from it a "right" for himself to act in such and such a way, instead of simply taking it "humanly"—simply as a "fate"

---

[22]". . . *der holde Leichtsinn*"—an allusion to Tasso's speech in Act II, Scene 4 of Goethe's play *Torquato Tasso*: "We human beings are wondrously tried; we could not bear it if Nature had not endowed us with sweet lightheartedness."—Ed.

with which one must cope and often *cannot* cope, because one is only human. Hence the need always to have a "right"—where there is no "right." This I cannot very well have; everything else must be "understood."

Marianne was often touched by his emphatic refusal to be considered sinless by those who were struggling and straying. To be sure, he did not attach great importance to the occasional gruffness and anger that made him awe-inspiring to those not close to him, but he never forgot that he had once unintentionally brought suffering to a delicate girl. Also, he now regarded his hostile outburst against his own father as a guilt never to be expiated. And above all, he wanted to be close to others—a human being among human beings. In this spirit he wrote to a younger friend who had confessed and was shaken by Weber's leniency:

Believe me, there are good reasons for it if I do not make a moralistic attack on someone who knows what "guilt" is! After all, not everything that is a misdeed [*Frevel*] need be in the special area with which we are here concerned. I have been burdened with *extreme* misdeeds—certainly not without profound and lasting aftereffects. But *not* in the sense you mention, as a moral fracture that can never heal again. Such a thing exists only for *very weak people*. What is done is done, and it is a matter of gradually helping *all* those involved to attain to a humanly definitive understanding of how life plays with us. That will come about and work out. For the rest, guilt can become a source of strength, or it cannot, depending on how one takes it. It would be bad if only the *"integer vitae"*[23] made us complete human beings and not also the opposite, properly understood. In that case I, at any rate, would have had to forgo being a complete person.

Weber's wife summed up the experiences of that period in the following lines to Helene:

All the events of the last years involved for us, too, emotional struggles and inner conflicts, which occasionally cost us much strength. For the shocking thing is that human beings of spiritual nobility, with the will to be good and with pronounced, conscientious *motherliness* re-

---

[23]*Integer vitae scelerisque purus:* (the man who is) blameless in life and free from crime—Horace, *Odes*, Book I, XXII, 1.—Ed.

ject our belief in the universal validity of our ideals in practice and theory. But I believe that from this desire to understand, because we *must* love, we have also found inward gain: an increase in freedom, humaneness, and *modesty*. I am infinitely grateful to fate for having spared me entanglement in guilt by bestowing upon me superabundant gifts and satisfying my deepest spiritual needs through a human being whom I love more than anything—and who is *great* beyond all ordinary standards. We still believe in our ideals, although I have been deprived of the courage and the enthusiasm to work for them in public.

12

ACTIVITY IN THE WORLD
AND CONTROVERSIES ⸻

In the summer and fall of 1908, when Weber was so well that he was able to carry forward several major projects in very dissimilar fields, he also mounted his charger again. In the *Frankfurter Zeitung* he published an article in the field of university politics about "The Case of X"[1] as well as a rejoinder to a reply written by the well-known editor of a political journal [H. Delbrück].

The occasion was as follows: Bypassing the faculty, the Prussian ministry had transferred a gifted young political economist to Berlin because it expected him to do some politically desirable work. This prompted Weber to censure the government which, he said, disregarded the faculties and thus bred among young academicians a type of "businessman"—that is, it

---

[1]Ludwig Bernhard (1875–1935), who had taught economics at Posen, Greifswald, and Kiel, was appointed to a professorship at the University of Berlin as a protégé of F. Althoff, but because of opposition from the faculty he could not start teaching until the fall of 1909. See Edward Shils, ed., *Max Weber on Universities,* University of Chicago Press, 1973.—Ed.

tempted young people to facilitate their academic career by doing work for the state. Against the docent who had succumbed to this temptation and whom Weber otherwise esteemed he wrote: "When the present writer was as young as Mr. X is today, it was regarded as the most elementary duty of academic propriety that someone who was offered a professorship by the ministry first of all made sure, before deciding, that he had the scholarly confidence of the faculty or at least of those outstanding colleagues who were supposed to work with him." To this he added a criticism of the way the faculty of political science at the University of Berlin had acted on another occasion. It had recently made a rule that restricted the reaccreditation [Umhabilitierung] of docents and had used this rule to deny admittance to such an outstanding and respected scholar and teacher as Werner Sombart. Weber regarded this as a concession to subjective points of view and a "deviation from the principle of securing as many important scholars as possible—an attitude which in the end will take its toll by weakening the *moral authority* of the faculties. . ." This forceful but considered criticism had an effect. The young scholar submitted himself to the judgment of the faculty, tendered his resignation, and sent word to Weber that he realized his mistake.

On the other hand, Weber's critique of the behavior of the department of political science provoked one of its members [Delbrück] into making remarks that Weber most sharply rejected. The scholar asserted that Weber's criticism of the department had been inspired by personal interests, namely, consideration for his friend Sombart. In this Weber saw not only an inadmissible violation of strict objectivity in public polemics, but also an insinuation that he himself had transgressed a norm that was among the most important to him. His reaction to this was fiery indignation which, however, was cloaked in irony:

I would, of course, judge and label the interpretation that Mr. X in all seriousness presents to his public, namely, that my objective remarks were determined by *personal* motives, simply as a vile act if it had been made by anyone else. However, in the case of this man these things must not be taken *that seriously*—although I would add "unfortunately." It is hardly a matter of conscious and intended indecency toward an opponent, but there are manifestations of a certain insensitivity of feeling on his part. . . . He lacks a professional journalist's sense of responsibility, and therefore one must not get excited if he does things for which one would never forgive a journalist.

* * *

The end of the summer of 1908 brought an interesting intellectual spectacle: the International Congress of Philosophers. Weber saw a great variety of scholars from other places, and the profound and ponderous sociologist F. Tönnies[2] stayed with him during the congress. There were big doings in Heidelberg. The most important philosophers from elsewhere did not attend, but among the younger ones there were many significant figures: Troeltsch, Lask, Driesch, Vossler, and others. The older generation was represented by Wilhelm Windelband and the Nestor of the Hegelians, Lasson.[3] The outsider felt more as though he were at a big public festival than in an "academy." How exciting it was to watch the various personalities presenting themselves! But it seemed impossible to advance truth in this manner, and one gained the impression that philosophy in particular had important insights to offer, but no uniform, comprehensive, compelling truth. Why, almost all of these scholars fought with one another! And each had his own language and a single word had endless different meanings: Nature, Spirit, Truth, Idea, Freedom, God—nothing was unambiguous, and even the concept of philosophy was manifold. The participants ought to have handed one another terminological dictionaries first. As it was, they usually talked past one another fruitlessly in the discussions; basically no one wanted to learn from anyone else and each one thought he was already standing at the throne of the one absolute Truth. For the layman there certainly were no conclusive results. Was one witnessing the building of the Tower of Babel? Were these philosophers not striving with utterly inadequate tools to reveal the secrets of the world? However, their intensive seeking and questioning, and their intellectualization of phenomena and incessant agitation did have an elemental grandeur, like the surging of the sea which never reaches its goal because it is already there.

* * *

In another field, Weber concerned himself with the problems of active people who have to cope with the world directly and practically.

In the autumn of 1908 the Webers again spent a long period sharing the

[2]Ferdinand Tönnies, 1855–1936, sociologist and philosopher, professor at Kiel, head of the German Sociological Association from 1909 to 1933, author of *Gemeinschaft und Gesellschaft* and other works.—Ed.
[3]Hans Driesch, 1867–1941, philosopher and biologist, professor at Cologne (1919) and Leipzig (1921), author of *The Science and Philosophy of the Organism* (London, 1908) and other works. Adolf Lasson, 1832–1917, professor of philosophy at Berlin.—Ed.

beautiful, harmonious, and soulful family life in Oerlinghausen. There Weber continued his research on the psychophysics of industrial labor. In the meantime he had examined the professional literature, particularly the works of Kräpelin and his pupils, to see how applicable the methods and findings of the natural sciences were to these studies. Now he again collected primary material in the family textile mill. The laborious arithmetic went well and he was in good spirits.

The magic of a gentle sun and the fragrance of the ripening year hovered over the magnificent German countryside. Weber was able to relax during rides to the Senne, whose somberness was in places still adorned with the red heather, or walks on the extended ridge of the Tönsberg. He also enjoyed visiting the neighboring Kupferhammer, the patrician country estate of the industrial magnate Karl Möller, which had been built in the barren moors. Möller's wife, Hertha, was Karl Weber's daughter and a native of Oerlinghausen. A giant smokestack of the great factory that the family had founded dominated the peaceful and magnificent park as though it were the reigning prince. However, the restless machines did not monopolize the existence of these people. Their upper-middle-class life was characterized by high principles, and Hertha was an outstanding woman who filled the beautiful framework with intellectual and artistic substance and restless striving. The master of the house, who was really more the scholarly than the entrepreneurial type, devoted a portion of his busy life to the welfare and education of his workers. He was a truly righteous man, stamped by the Puritan ethic. There was a kindly gleam in his eyes, but his manner, which reflected aloofness, reserve, constant self-control, and solemnity and imposed these qualities upon those around him as well, embodied for Weber—as did the patriarch of Oerlinghausen—the typical descendant of those solemn figures whom he discovered at the cradle of modern capitalism.

Weber enjoyed being part of this larger family for a while. He took a warm interest in everything that filled life there, and together with the women, the spiritual focus of the toiling men, he became absorbed in the futures of all their children. He took and gave, and in spite of his intellectuality he was able to come close to the essence of those differently constituted people. By virtue of his descriptive presentation he was able to convey scholarly knowledge even to the uneducated.

The finest thing about the present is that Max almost leads the life of a normal person. He is inexhaustible in the telling of stories as in the distribution of more substantial intellectual fare. He keeps on doing this until about ten o'clock, and the whole family always sits around him as though he were a sage, a saint, and a clow [Paijatz] in one. What they enjoy the most is hard to say. In the evening, when Georg [Müller] also dishes things out, there is virtual Homeric laughter. All the old military and student lore is revived, and it has lost none of its glitter. Sometimes they even unearth something that I had not known. Max's narrative skill pours forth like a dammed-up stream. He works in the morning and dictates in the afternoon—in short, he "lives" as though the illness has left him. And we enjoy the good days although we know that the clouds, the rain, and the cold will come again. It is, as always, lovely here with these good and happy people. The autumn sun lights up the beautiful garden and flashes on the dewy meadow in the morning.

When a few years later death claimed one of the male heads of this circle, Wina's husband Bruno Müller, Weber gave a portrait of this noble figure in a way that sheds light on him as well. Together with Müller's individual character, he portrayed typical features of a pure, high-minded bourgeois. Apart from its political immaturity, he regarded this bourgeoisie as a prized possession of his nation and proudly considered himself part of it.

My dear Wina!

In the same mail I received a business letter that Bruno wrote me yesterday and this shocking, absolutely unexpected news. It is still impossible to imagine that when we enter your house we shall no longer encounter the unpretentious assurance and the noble kindness of the head of your house, who was so infinitely lovable in the subtle pride of his modesty. Such a death without old age, illness, deterioration, and loneliness is *beautiful* for the man who is granted it at the peak of his success and in the awareness that things will continue on the upward grade, that the young generation is standing on the shoulders of the old one and hence will continue to create new life. A life is *beautiful* that is concluded in such a way without ever having had to taste too much misfortune, misunderstanding, disappointment, grief, hardship, and inner conflict—because his own faithful nature and the immeasurable love that surrounded him and grew up around him kept all such specters far from him. And it is *beautiful* to think that here there was a man who could say of himself that all his life, in big things and in small, he never renounced the spirit of *the most genuine, a typically bourgeois chivalry*, a spirit that won him all hearts—and presumably yours as well—as much as thirty-five years ago when he first came to my parental home as a young man.

He was a man of whom one knew that absolutely no one would have ever dared touch on impure and unseemly matters in his presence, not even in the briefest conversation and in any sense whatever, or even to stray to such matters in thought. Such was the atmosphere of purity of heart, of body, and of mind which he radiated. Even though he always strove to keep in the background—quite intentionally and far too much so—it was impossible ever to impress him with spurious means, with poses and clichés, bathos, and vain showing off. All such things evaporated under his reserved and calm but extremely sure glance.

There is no calculating it, of course, but surely that which he gave to the people around him, and particularly your children, in this way is enormous. For how did he gain from them all that unconditional respect and that devotion—something that always impressed me so much in its freedom and naturalness—which was so easy and natural for them to have and which gave happiness to them and pleasure to everyone? Not through "words." No, in his unpretentious way he had certainly not cultivated his expressiveness in words and speeches; he may have disdained this too much, quietly living only for his affairs and his duties. It was not through words that he was effective, that people communicated with him, that his personality asserted itself. Rather, people were close to him through that feeling of complete security and assurance which a human being so rarely inspires. Yet this is the ultimate and the highest thing one can find, for in the final analysis, where else can words, even the best and finest, take one? With him no words were needed, for he was a man one *trusted*, unconditionally trusted, even before he had spoken a word, and no word could have heightened this trust.

There is no calculating what he meant to you, both outwardly and inwardly, and to the proud firm (which one cannot even imagine without him) by virtue of this quality, which is as irreplaceable as any gift from heaven. Georg once told me that an old businessman expressed this wish to him as a summing up of many kindnesses: "All in all—be like your father, that is all I wish for you." One surely envies both the father and the son who has been told something like this, and with full justification. Bruno's imperturbable assurance was the indispensable complement to your father's wonderful "greatness"—one has to use this word—which considered and encompassed everything, and to his son Karl's splendid, irresistible drive. In the unsullied purity of his being he extended from a generation of the German bourgeoisie that contained far more in character and worth than outsiders surmise to a time and a generation that must now lead its own life in its own fashion and inevitably must be different in many ways from what their fathers were. There is no choice, and this is what we all experience.

But if all of us are confident that in their own way these young people will be equally valuable human beings who will make an honorable showing and at the end of their lives will be able to look back upon their life's work as clear-eyed and as joyfully as he and you can, we will not forget that next to the compelling power of the love and the tender understanding which blessedly emanate from you, dear Wina, the profound genuineness and truthfulness in your husband's soul had an equal share in this, and we shall be gladdened by the blessing that will rest on his memory forever. In spirit I press the hands of all of you—yours, Wilhelm's, the children's—in heartfelt loyalty, and I hope to do so in person soon, either during the next few days or shortly thereafter, as soon as the first shock of the great bereavement has worn off.

II

We shall now return to other events of those years.

Since 1905, threatening clouds had been gathering on the political horizon: the Moroccan problem. Dangers surrounded Germany. In the interest of the "open door" policy for its trade, Germany went against French policy in Morocco. The Kaiser's trip to Tangier and his speech to the sultan allayed the danger of war, and it was eliminated by the Conference of Algeciras. Germany was successful and stood its ground, but it had to pay the price. France resented Germany's interference and brought Italy over to its side. In the steadily increasing strength of Germany's fleet, England saw a measure that was directed against British naval supremacy. From that time on Germany was regarded as imperialistic and bellicose, and when it declined to participate in the discussions of the disarmament question at the Hague Conference, it only reinforced that impression.

King Edward's policy of encirclement was successful. England, France, and Russia came to an agreement: Italy and Austria were aroused. At the end of 1906 the dangers of the "personal regime" and the threatening situation were brought up in the Reichstag. In another public address the Kaiser rebuffed those who warned him with this provocative dictum: "I will not tolerate alarmists. Anyone who is not fit for work should drop out and look for a better country." The chancellor backed the actions of the monarch as his constitutional right. Germany, so he said, had no parliamentary government, and the German people did not want a shadow emperor.

When fresh unrest broke out in Morocco in 1907, Germany again thwarted France's policy. But France came to an understanding with England and Italy, and Germany's political defeat became obvious. Nevertheless, there was a temporary relaxation of tensions. Edward and Wilhelm exchanged visits, and there was a meeting between the Kaiser and the Czar. However, at the same time England and Russia reached an agreement on Asian interests, and when the Balkan drama began, Germany and England were in conflict with each other again. The Central Powers sought to support Turkey's independence against Russia and England. Again war threatened, and this time the situation was defused by the Turkish revolution. Soon, however, the Austrian claims to the Balkans furnished fresh grounds for grave conflict. Serbia tried to establish a close relationship with Russia and appealed to the Slavic sense of solidarity. Germany and Austria were isolated.

Thus the German ship of state was tossed back and forth on the high seas. People lived on momentary successes, but the responsible leaders lacked the assurance and the vision to steer their way out of the dangerous zones or to find powerful helpers. From the end of 1906 on there was a severe crisis in domestic politics as well. The Center Party [Zentrum] rejected a request for funds to put down the natives' insurrection in Southwest Africa, and since it was supported by the Social Democrats, this was a welcome occasion for dissolving the Reichstag. Weber's attitude toward these events is reflected in the following letters to Friedrich Naumann, which bespeak great excitement.

December 14, 1906

Dear Friend:

I have neither the authority nor, usually, the slightest desire to interfere with your political decisions, and you would not stand for it if I did so. Permit me, however, to express my *opinion.* You will hear plenty of opinions from other quarters and then make your own decision. *Let us assume* I had "a seat and a vote" on your editorial board and was now supposed to vote on the formulation of the "directive" which must be issued on the part of the staff, which after this utterly *frivolous* dissolution, a dissolution due to pure "power politics" in the interest of the crown (which would like to present the terrible disgrace of the foreign policy as a "domestic victory" by yelling "hurrah")—[4] if we assume, then, that I had a voice in this, then I would advise not to use this awfully facile formulation under *any* circumstances: for the *Kaiser* and against the "power-hungry Center Party." That would take a terrible toll.

The measure of contempt in which we as a nation are by now held abroad (Italy, America, everywhere!)—and rightfully so, this is what really matters—because we stand for *that* regime of *that* man, has become a power factor of the first order and of "world-political" significance for us. Anyone who reads the foreign press for a few months must notice this. We are being "isolated" because that man rules us in that fashion *and we tolerate it and put a good face on it.* No man and no party that in any sense cultivates democratic *and* national-political ideals may assume the responsibility for that regime, whose continuance jeopardizes our entire international position more than all colonial problems of any kind. What the Center Party can be reproached with and what can be held against it is *not* that it questions the "Kaiser's authority to command" or anything like that. *Even less* that, in keeping with its number of deputies, it strove for *power*, for *control* over the colonial administration, for a parliamentary "collateral government," etc. Rather, it is that as the ruling parliamentary party it has promoted and supported the system of *pseudo*constitutionalism. To express it quite concretely, in this case it did *not* make control over the colonial administration by the Reichstag a condition for the acceptance of the colonial budget, but rather insisted only on the maintenance of the "parliamentary *patronage*" that has been going on *behind* the scenes— the lollipop by means of which the ruling parties, the Centrists as well as the Conservatives and the National Liberals, have been attached to the system of the pseudoconstitutional personal regime for the past decade. Therefore, the watchword should be *only* as follows: Against the Center, the *party* of *pseudoconstitutionalism*, the party that has striven, and still strives, not for real power of the representatives of the people *vis-à-vis* the crown, but only for personal bonbons from the hands of the crown, and *for* a strong, open parliamentary administrative control that will then also sweep the dirt of the collateral governments out of its secret corners.

But, for heaven's sake, *no vote of confidence in the Kaiser*—and this not only tacitly, but *expressly* decline such a vote of confidence! Support the oppositional elements among the National Liberals ("Young Liberals"), support the trade-union elements among the Social Democrats—join them *against* the pseudoconstitutional Center Party,

---

[4]This clause is unfinished in the original.—Ed.

but also *against* the dynastic domestic lust for power and, in foreign affairs, the dynastic prestige policy of big words instead of a sensible policy based on interests!

As I have said, this is how I would vote if I had any say. I understand very well why you wish to protect the personal prestige of the Kaiser. But today this is no longer a policy based on realities, either in the domestic or in the foreign sphere. For that prestige is gone. For me and for countless others it is, in all honesty, no longer possible, and above all it is quite pointless and futile, to prolong its semblance for a few more years. If you find it possible to do so, then leave this memorandum outside. Forgive me for bothering you. As ever in cordial friendship,

Your Max Weber

The outcome of the political campaign with the colonial issue was primarily a bad defeat for the Social Democrats. The bourgeoisie was exultant, but Weber made the following remarks about it to L. Brentano:

Wretched results of the Reichstag elections! Strengthening of the agrarian *right*, the possibility that the reactionaries will form a majority together with the Center Party against the National Liberals and the entire left! The only ray of hope: Naumann and the *possibility* that in future the Social Democrats will abandon their braggadocio and pursue practical policies. But will they? (February 6, 1970)

Bülow[5] now formed a national bloc by combining the bourgeois left with the rightist parties. The left-liberal factions united, and for the first time the old *Freisinnige Partei* also supported the world-power policy. A new "national-socialist" [*national-sozial*] era of democratic liberalism seemed to be beginning. But when Naumann and his circle of that time demanded increased political liberties—freedom of association and of assembly, a vigorous social policy, and, above all, the reform of the Prussian system of suffrage— the unnaturalness of that union immediately became apparent. The rightists fought with all their might against the abandonment of traditional privileges. But in the ranks of the liberals, too, the bourgeois and capitalistically minded leaders of the old *Freisinnige Partei* impeded the realization of the democratic ideals. The party leaders gave Naumann a hard time. It became clear that he was a misfit in their company and would not prevail against them with his own policies. That was a bitter disappointment for

---

[5]Bernhard von Bülow, 1849–1928, Federal Chancellor from 1900 to 1909.—Ed.

a man to whom the doors to political activity had finally opened after years of waiting. And when in the spring of 1908 some of his associates, particularly the leaders of the left wing, parted company with the *Freisinnige Volkspartei* [Progressive People's Party] again, Naumann faced a severe conflict. To keep from destroying the laboriously attained union of the left liberals, he did not follow his friends.

At that juncture Weber wrote him as follows:

April 26, 1908

The last few days cannot have been easy for you, and the only purpose of these lines is to assure you of my heartfelt sympathy. Objectively you *could* not have carried on any other policy after you had (justifiably) made your decision last year. Any unbiased person must realize this, even though, like me, he may wish a different policy had been possible. Quite apart from all considerations of pure realpolitik, you also did the right thing by loyally keeping faith with such inferior allies as the *Freisinnige Volkspartei*. *Such* things, too, exist in political life and have their consequences, even though runaways like Barth and Gerlach[6] may not see this. After all, the *Mandat* [seat]—for that is what the affair might cost you—is not the greatest thing on earth, and you alone have the consciousness of having forced through, even at the cost of your seat, what was *possible* in the way of liberal advances (the law concerning associations) and *national* advances (the stock exchange law in the interest of our position of power in the world).

Your position is all the freer now. Surely it is hardly your intention to tie yourself to the parliamentary faction if Bülow *remains the way he is* and then to attach everything to the bloc. *Election* reform in Prussia against financial reform in the Reich—that watchword seems indicated to me, and I am surprised that it was not issued in Frankfurt. And don't you want to use the "tolerance motion" of the Center Party to demand (1) the elimination of *any* compulsory *religious* instruction, and (2) the elimination of *any* privileged status for a *church* (treatment in accordance with the law governing associations!), to demand at least the former as a "basic right"? In this area the Center Party must be democratically trumped.

In the Polish question my position is somewhat *different* from yours; the *compulsory use of a language* is what seems morally and politically im-

---

[6]Theodor Barth, 1849–1909, leader of the *Freisinnige Vereinigung*, editor of the weekly *Nation* until 1907; Hellmut von Gerlach, 1866–1935, pacifist politician, a founder of the *Nationalsoziale Partei* (1896) and the Democratic Party (1918).—Ed.

possible and senseless to me. But the expropriation should in my estimation have been accompanied immediately by this watchword: Annual
expropriation of large estates *everywhere* for the purpose of settling
farmers! "The land for the masses," according to Schulze [-Gävernitz]'s
old slogan, but it would probably be better without this formulation.
In relation to the *Poles* the present law is senseless; only the unlimited
right of expropriation would have made sense there—the sense that
armed with this the Poles could now have been offered a national compromise involving recognition of their "cultural autonomy." But excuse
this "estimable material" from an outsider. The purpose of these lines
was not to lecture you but to greet you cordially.

Faithfully yours,
Max Weber

After the elections to the Prussian diet, on November 5, 1908:

Dear Friend:

The election is now over, and the future of the bloc policy is reasonably clear. Even though honest attempts to achieve a reform of the
system of suffrage in Prussia must definitely continue to be made, it
is evident that *nothing whatever* may be expected. This undoubtedly
means that the bloc policy has *lost* its meaning for you as well, for if
the system of suffrage remains in essence what it is now, everything
else will be petty patchwork without any value. What now? In the
winter you were not able to carry on any policy but the one you pursued. It must be emphasized again and again that the federal regulation
of the right of association meant *only* that the Prussian diet was prevented from doing even *worse* things.

But that is in the past now. Where does the future lie? If you fuse
the organization[7] with the *Freisinnige Volkspartei,* Baden will—as far as
I am able to judge and as I must desire—go its own way. Things cannot
be done any differently here, and the conviction prevails that *you will
not succeed* in influencing the *Freisinnige Volkspartei* to the same degree
as you influenced the *Freisinnige Vereinigung.* (The difference is that the
latter is a group of intellectuals, the former a group of philistines and
people with vested interests.) If possible, retain the option of leaving
the association and leaping *to the left*—that is, get ready for it, so
that you can do so with propriety; it will become necessary. The *Frei-*

---

[7]Presumably the *Nationalverein für das liberale Deutschland* [National Association for a Liberal
Germany].

sinnige Volkspartei is irresistibly moving to the right. *However,* in four years we shall have a *clerical regime* everywhere, in all individual states, including Baden, and in the Reich as a whole. This is definite now. *That* will mark the beginning of the arduous labor to "make a path for freedom."[8] And then *you* must not be dead politically! Do not reply. You have no time now. More another time. Cordial regards—it is a hard time for you!

In the fall of 1908, when the Balkan crisis was becoming critical, Kaiser Wilhelm committed another political indiscretion which dwarfed everything he had done up to then. He published an interview in an English newspaper—with the well-meaning intention of dispelling England's distrust of him. He declared that although public opinion in Germany was anti-English, his own attitude was a friendly one. Thus he had declined France's offer to form an alliance at the beginning of the Boer War. In fact, he had conveyed to his grandmother, Queen Victoria, his own draft of a campaign plan against the Boers, and the plan used by the English commander had coincided with this plan—and other things of this sort.

It really seemed to be the devil's own work. The officials responsible for clearing such things happened to be on vacation. Every single statement turned out to be a disaster. A storm of indignation arose at home and abroad. Foreign countries recalled the Kruger telegram[9] and accused German politicians of lying. England regarded these disclosures as undignified efforts to gain its favor. At home there were cries for safeguards against blunders of the "personal regime." In the Reichstag there was an unprecedentedly heated discussion. Delegates spoke of the tragedy of German policy and proposed constitutional changes in the direction of a parliamentary regime: answerability of ministers, and participation of the Reichstag in the appointment of the Federal Chancellor. But the Reichstag was not unified, and the Prussian Junkers in particular opposed such consequences. Better a monarch by the grace of God who committed foolish acts and then had to lean on his paladins than a limitation of their own privileges by an expansion of the people's rights. And when the Kaiser promised Bülow privately that

---

[8]*"Der Freiheit eine Gasse"*—the libertarian poets Max von Schenkendorf and Theodor Körner used this phrase in 1809 and 1813, respectively. It is sometimes attributed to Arnold von Winkelried (battle of Sempach, 1386).—Ed.

[9]The telegram of January, 1896 in which the German emperor congratulated Paul Krüger, the president of the South African Republic (Transvaal), on defeating Jameson's raiders created an acute crisis in British-German relations.—Ed.

he would exercise greater restraint, the impetus toward sweeping changes dwindled among the bourgeoisie as well.

Weber was outraged not only at the incident, which confirmed all his earlier fears, but also at the slack attitude of his own circles—"a people that never decides to show a monarch the door or at least to impose major curbs upon him sentences itself to political tutelage." More than ever he was convinced that only an extension of parliamentary authority could stave off further disaster, but he foresaw that the Prussian conservatives would impede everything for the Reich as well. In this spirit he wrote to Naumann on November 12, 1908:

> Now everything depends on showing the country in the most graphic terms that the Conservative Party bears the responsibility for the continuation of the "personal regime." There is far too much talk about the "impulsiveness" of the Kaiser and other aspects of his personality. The political structure is to blame for this. Nothing, nothing whatever has improved. Bülow was not able to promise anything, because he did not have the authority that mattered, and in such a position any emperor will fall prey to the same vanity. Wilhelm I and Friedrich III acted, or would have acted, in exactly the same way (in the decisive points), although their style might have been different. Only, Wilhelm I was afraid of Bismarck and, above all, he did not find out what was going on or learned only of the faits accomplis, such as the alliance with Austria in 1879, when he could no longer do anything about them. What has been accomplished now is only that in future we shall no longer find out about all the things which that man perpetrates. The decisive thing is that a dilettante holds the threads of politics in his hand. Any legitimate ruler who is not Friedrich II is a dilettante, and that is what the Conservative Party wants. This is true of the supreme command in wartime and of the direction of policy in peacetime. The consequence: for as long as this goes on, a "world policy" is impossible.

The "romantics" of politics, particularly the bourgeois rabble that adores anything "conservative," naturally admire the infamous coup of the conservative declaration as a "manly deed" and a "historical turning point!" As if that crowd risked anything! In the face of this propagandistic achievement—propaganda directed upward and downward—this romanticism must be destroyed from the start, for as I have just been able to see, it is rather dangerous. It is a pity that one cannot act as the Vorwärts does during the beer boycott, every day printing the well-known "Don't Drink Ring Beer," and publish on the front page of every issue of every independent paper: "The Conservatives do not desire the elimination of the personal regime; *that* is why we *cannot* carry on any global policy, any naval policy, or any policy whatever that could not be carried on by Switzerland or Denmark as well." The king of England has ambition and power, the German emperor has vanity and contents himself with the *semblance* of power—a consequence of the *system*, not of the person. (*Kingdom of influence—Kingdom of prerogative*, [10] as the contrast was once formulated in England). Viewed from a historical vantage point, the *German* emperor, *not* the English king, is the "shadow emperor." . . . The Hohenzollern dynasty knows only the *drill sergeant* form of power: giving commands, following orders, standing at attention, bragging. *That* is what the Conservative Party *wants*. Why it does everyone knows.

* * *

At the end of 1908 another severe crisis rocked domestic politics. The Conservatives and the Centrists reached an understanding on the financial reform of the Reich and of the Prussian suffrage, and the Conservative-Liberal bloc disintegrated. Bülow was replaced by Bethmann-Hollweg,[11] the "chancellor in the philosopher's cloak." The incipient liberal-democratic reforms ran aground. The combative leader of the Conservatives and the farmers even dared to come out against universal suffrage, and this caused enormous excitement. The liberal left established a union with the *Fortschrittliche Volkspartei* [Progressive People's Party]. Naumann coined the slogan "from Bassermann to Bebel."[12] But the Social Democrats declined to participate. The Prussian constitution remained as it was: a shield of agrarian-conservative rule not only in Prussia but throughout the Reich. And the Kaiser soon overcame his shock at the success of his rhetoric. In a public address he referred to the "divine right of kings" [*Gottesgnadentum*]. Weber had long been convinced of the emperor's ineducability and expected only the timely limitation of his authority by an extension of parliamentary rights to prevent further misfortunes. The fact that at that juncture even Naumann did not seem to have a full appreciation of the importance of the political institutions for the future of the nation led Weber to make the following remarks:

---

[10]In English in the original.—Ed.

[11]Theobald von Bethmann-Hollweg, 1856–1921, Imperial Chancellor from 1909 to 1917.—Ed.

[12]The reference is to the Liberal politician Ernst Bassermann (1854–1917) and the Marxist August Bebel (see Chapter 6, footnote 4).—Ed.

After your two excellent articles and the many other good things
that have been said, I would have only little to add about the *emper-
or*. The tenor of what I might have to say now would invariably be
this: Do not overestimate the importance of the quality of a *person*.
It is the *institutions* (not only those formally established by law, of
course!) and your own lack of temperament that are at fault. Both are
the work of Bismarckism and of the political immaturity that was increased by it. The practical effect will probably be that the *Bundesrat*[13] rather than the Reichstag will be strengthened. Hence I can
only repeat again and again: The practical problem is the *parliamentarization of the Bundesrat*—and perhaps the solution will come only in the distant future.

Your letter discouraged me rather thoroughly. You can wait from
now to eternity before Herr v. H. u. d. L.[14] *explicitly* "plays the
part" [*"sich aufspielt"*] of an opponent of the representatives of the people
in *this* matter. These gentlemen have done so, and they have said:
"This does not belong before parliament." Isn't that enough? And you
don't feel capable of showing everyone and making it plausible to all
what that has meant and means for "world policy?" As a "realpolitiker"
you have become discouraged and resigned and let yourself be impressed
by D[elbrück]'s style of politics. This is the issue, and this is what is
so profoundly depressing to others. For there is *nothing* more detrimental to the political education of the nation than this systematic and
oh-so-cheap discreditation of all hopes for the significance of *organizational* changes which we need as badly as our daily bread—a discreditation
that is made impressive by an always self-assured and self-satisfied smile.
See you again at the next "achievement" of the Kaiser! (November 18,
1908)

* * *

During this period of extreme excitement Weber once again allowed himself to be lured to a political assembly. His wife wrote on December 9, 1908:

A week ago a great political experience united us with Alfred. Jellinek

---

[13]Between 1871 and 1918 the *Bundesrat* consisted of the representatives of the twenty-two
federal states under the chairmanship of the imperial chancellor.—Ed.
[14]Ernst von Heydebrand und der Lasa, 1851–1924, Conservative politician, in the Prussian
parliament from 1888 and in the Reichstag from 1903 on; "the uncrowned King of Prussia."—
Ed.

made a brilliant speech about the Kaiser and the Reich: proposals for the promotion of parliamentary government in connection with the recent exciting statements by the Kaiser. Max went along as a favor but assured us that he would keep silent. But when Gothein's remarks had a national-liberal, indeed, an almost conservative tinge, the Weber brothers became infuriated. Max spoke twice with controlled passion and force. Although the people there were much farther to the right than he was, one could see that they were gripped. Afterward there was a cute incident that is now amusing half of Heidelberg. As they were leaving the hall, one petty bourgeois asked another: *"Wer isch denn eigentlich seller Max Weber?"* [Who's that Max Weber, anyway?] The answer: *"Ha das isch halt der Marianne ihrer."* [Oh, he's Marianne's guy.] Isn't that funny, and at the same time grotesque and sad? If only he felt impelled to show himself in public more often; his health would now permit him to do so if he enjoyed it. But evidently he does not deem it worthwhile in relation to his scholarly work.

No, Weber was too unconcerned with presenting himself and with personal success to be tempted to waste his fluctuating energies on impressive occasional speeches that could surely not have changed the course of practical politics. And his nerves were certainly not strong enough for the constant demands of parliament and party activities. Thus, during those eventful years he was able to serve the endangered nation only as Naumann's permanent adviser and by influencing the political judgment of his own circle. But time and again his influence proved to be ineffective. Germany was a powerful country with strong armaments and a flourishing economy. The intellectual leaders of course had no political influence, but their *cultural importance* was duly emphasized and they were well off. They loved their peace and quiet, and as long as they themselves did not feel threatened in their privileged position, the fear of socialism counterbalanced their criticism of the existing regime. They did realize that grave errors were being made, but anything more than passing annoyance did not seem warranted. They wondered whether Weber's constant sharp criticism of the political course was not just a product of his illness. Thus he felt with bitterness that even the most dangerous *faux pas* of the emperor and the severe crises were not able to shake the intellectual leaders of the nation out of their spectator's role. What he desired in those days was the banding together of prominent university teachers for a joint public protest; but there could be no thought of that.

As a document characteristic of the political ineducability of their colleagues, Rickert sent Weber an essay by a Freiburg teacher of constitutional law which opposed parliamentary government. Weber wrote the sender:

Many thanks for sending me Sch——'s[15] political music on a toy trumpet. A horrible, nauseating sound! You had presumably heard that I am supposed to curb my appetite for health reasons and wanted to be kind enough to help me do so! *This* is how the Germans are and *that* is what they call "politics": pouting at "their" emperor, then a Canossa[16] by the latter (on the eve of the Prussian day of penance and prayer, so that everything may harmonize atmospherically), whereupon they again look upon him with pride, and, for heaven's sake, no parliamentary government! As for that nonsense about anarchy and lack of system, look at *our* policy on the one hand and at France, England, Holland, Belgium, etc., on the other. And that is what they call "political" thinking. (November 21, 1908)

Another occasion a few years later showed what he thought about the political attitude of his colleagues and how much he suffered because of it. At a banquet [*Festkommers*] at the inauguration of the new University of Freiburg (fall of 1911), the *Prorektor* [deputy rector] had made some strong value judgments against pacifist "simpletons" and "pacifist daydreaming" [*Friedensduselei*]. This inspired a general who had already achieved some rhetorical prominence to deliver himself of some drastic statements—for example, that pacifists were men who wore pants but had nothing in them and therefore wished to make political eunuchs out of the people. This incident had appeared in the *Frankfurter Zeitung* with disrespectful comments. Since these remarks were also directed against the *Prorektor*, a number of the most distinguished Freiburg professors published an indignant joint declaration in which they reproached the newspaper for undermining national and ethical convictions and claimed it was "the good right and the noble duty of academic teachers to profess at festive occasions that are shared with our students patriotic ideals with that proud and unreserved frankness which young people must expect of us."

---

[15]Richard Schmidt, 1862–1944, professor of law at Freiburg, 1891–1913, later at Leipzig. The reference is probably to an article published in the *Zeitschrift für Politik* which Schmidt had founded together with A. Grabowsky in 1907.—Ed.

[16]Canossa in Northern Italy was the scene of the penance of Emperor Henry IV before Pope Gregory VII in 1077.—Ed.

A co-editor of the newspaper, Dr. H[einrich] S[imon],[17] asked Weber for his private opinion as to the justification of this serious accusation. The following excerpts from Weber's reply, which was also sent to the Freiburg professors, are of political and human interest:

> The reference to the "proud frankness" of academic teachers on an occasion where there was *nothing serious to risk* does not make a good impression. And the prediction that criticisms of speeches made at academic banquets will paralyze the "moral forces" certainly seems like "small-town stuff." . . . The *Frankfurter Zeitung,* among whose traditions there has always been a good sense of humor, will, in my estimation, not take such statements on such an occasion too seriously.
>
> If numerous academic teachers put up with *such* blunders from the author of this declaration so that they might not appear to be bad colleagues before the forum of their own feelings, the ultimate explanation for this probably lies in the feverish excitement which the certainly not brilliant liquidation of our theatrical Morocco policy has created, particularly among large parts of the intellectually highest classes of the nation. I, too, desire increased armaments, and to a greater degree than is emphasized in the *Frankfurter Zeitung,* combined with a foreign policy which is at the same time clearheaded and relentlessly resolute. But I am of the opinion that even with the strongest armaments we *cannot conscientiously risk* a European war *for as long as* we must expect that the leadership of our army would be interfered with by a crowned dilettante who—in diplomacy as on the field of honor—would botch *everything.* All sorts of emotional factors based upon a tradition that has long since become politically harmful are preventing this rage, which is basically justified, from being directed against the *right person.* As a consequence it explodes unexpectedly, on entirely inappropriate occasions and in the wrong direction—in this case against the *Frankfurter Zeitung.* In this sense that declaration also is one of the many symptoms of how the external impotence of the nation is connected with its internal impotence. Because this is so, I permitted myself to discuss it in some detail here.

---

[17]1880–1941, a grandson of Leopold Sonnemann, the founder of the *Frankfurter Zeitung.* After 1933 Simon, who was also a literary critic and a musicologist, emigrated to Palestine and then to the United States. The *Prorektor* mentioned above, was Ernst Fabricius, 1857–1942, professor of history at Freiburg from 1888 to 1926. The general referred to above was Berthold Karl Adolf von Deimling, 1853–1944, commander of the German forces in Southwest Africa, 1904–07, and commanding general at Strasbourg, 1913–14. After serving in World War I, Deimling joined the German Democratic Party in 1918 and became a leader in the peace movement in Germany.—Ed.

When some Freiburg colleagues sought to convince Weber of the unfairness of the newspaper attack on the *Prorektor* and justified the motives of their "declaration," Weber answered them as follows:

Presumably the enclosed letter adequately expresses my view that in this matter a great *injustice* has been done to the motives of the gentlemen involved, as well as my judgment on the correspondent of the paper who is indeed unspeakable. But by now people have become used to the fact that from Freiburg the justified indignation at our political failures has been deflected from the only proper target—for instance, in the well-known "November days" of 1908, when the development of the Reich constitution was brought up for discussion and people in Freiburg made it their business—out of fear of some sort of increase in parliamentary power and thus in the parliament's sense of responsibility—to stab all such proposals in the back. I deem it important that the conclusion of my previous letter not be regarded as a remark that was made lightly.

Everyone, and particularly every general who wants to know it, knows that the aforementioned situation actually exists. And as for the answer usually given privately and confidentially by our leading military men when such fears are expressed—"Don't worry about such interference in an emergency; H[is] M[ajesty] can't stand the smell of gunpowder and leaves things to us"—I shall gladly believe this to be true in case of defeats, but not where victories may be expected and patience is required. *There,* in the politically dangerous *overextension of monarchism,* and not with our handful of pacifist utopians, lies our gravest danger, particularly in our external position. It will probably become necessary to say this in public, ruthlessly and no matter what the risk may be. But where shall we then find the majority of the gentlemen who signed?

But I should like to say also the following about the objective state of affairs as such. It is evident that the statement made by Prof. F.[18] would in itself have hardly inspired a discussion in the press if it had not been followed by the speech of that general who had made drastic remarks in public on a number of previous occasions. The criticism in the press was directed at the latter, although Professor F. was also drawn into it. I happen to regard loquacious generals per se as a phenomenon just as disagreeable as loquacious monarchs. But what especially got on my nerves in the present instance was the fact that *at*

---

[18]Ernst Fabricius.—Ed.

this particular moment the military authorities have after a prolonged hiatus resumed their practice of kicking reserve officers out of the army if they express their political convictions unreservedly. Under these circumstances it is a bit impertinent if a general expresses himself in such a manner. In the letters I have received there is this remark: We simply had to stand up for our "guests" (that is, that general). And although the declaration named only the *Prorektor,* it really backed up that man as well.

Now I permit myself to submit the following question to my colleagues. If I had accepted the kind invitation of the university, I would have secured the floor at all costs and by any means after the general's speech, to say only this: As long as the military authorities try to make political eunuchs out of the officers under their command, officers who, like me, receive their mobilization orders every year, I cannot concede to any general the right to apply that expression to other people. What do you suppose would have been the consequence? Perhaps that I, too, would have enjoyed a guest's rights? You may think so now, but on the basis of years of experience I believe this would have been out of the question. There would have been a general outcry at such an extremely tactless and presumptuous disturbance of a fine celebration and a violation of sacred national feelings, coupled with confidential statements from good friends: Perhaps I was right, but why did *I* always have to be the one to make such a public row? To which I would have replied: Because those who are primarily concerned, whose voice would carry greater weight than mine, don't do it, *never* do it, because they can be set in motion only when it is a matter of so-called national declarations. Although these undoubtedly are made seriously by those involved, they do not convince anyone who thinks differently, but rather can strike him as clichés fully as much as the old ideals of the Enlightenment which are designated by that word.

And I would have you consider further that to characterize a criticism of definite *political* ideals, no matter how highminded, as an undermining of *moral* forces is bound to call forth justified protest in any case. In "ethics" the pacifists are undoubtedly "superior" [*"über"*] to us. In my Freiburg inaugural address, immature though it may have been in many respects, I most outspokenly supported the sovereignty of national ideals in the area of all practical policies, including the so-called social policy, at a time when the great majority of the colleagues in my field were being taken in by the fraud of the so-called social kingdom. But even then I very deliberately emphasized that politics is not and can never be a profession with a moral foundation.

I continue to regard the issuance of this declaration by my colleagues in its present form as anything but beneficial. It is well known that at student banquets the members of uniformed students' associations and corporations usually predominate, even where they are numerically in the minority. The sort of patriotic politics, reminiscent of the *Gartenlaube*, [19] which today fills the pages of the official organs of all these associations—an absolutely hollow, empty, purely zoological nationalism—will, in my estimation, of necessity lead to a lack of principles in the face of all great cultural problems which is as far removed as can be from the view of the meaning of national ideals that we discern and appreciate in Professor F.

Their utter lack of any cultural ideals and the pitiful narrowing of their intellectual horizon in this respect then makes these circles think that they can pay their debts to national culture very inexpensively by greeting statements such as those made by that general at the banquet with tempestuous applause. In my opinion, such speeches as well as the sole tendency [*ausschliessliche Abstellung*] of a collective statement—which, as everyone knows, is an extremely rare thing among professors—namely, the defense of that man, can only widen the gulf between the *emptiness* of the so-called national feelings of large numbers of our students and the fullness of our national cultural needs. This definitely is very much against the intentions of both the author and the signers of this declaration. (November 15, 1911)

From a second letter to Dr. S. the following sentences are significant:

Lest there be any doubts as to my personal views: My personal view of those who are nothing but pacifists is no different from, and if anything more critical than, Professor F.'s—*unless* they not only enjoy the conclusions Leo Tolstoy reached as a literary dessert but carry them out in every respect, at least in domestic policies. Anyone who in the field of foreign policy regards war as the worst of all evils must not get enthusiastic about revolutionaries under any circumstances and must be prepared to turn the other cheek in his personal life as well. Only this could be impressive. Anything else I, too, regard as inconsistent and sentimental fraud . . .

---

[19]An illustrated family weekly published between 1853 and 1943 that catered to popular taste in literature and other aspects of culture.—Ed.

III

To return to the year 1909: Weber's newly burgeoning life became ever more colorful and varied in scholarly as well as personal matters. A new scientific-philosophical group founded by Otto Klebs[20] and Alfred Weber, the *Janus*, assembled young scholars and their wives for festive hours full of wit and charm. Presentations from the most varied fields of knowledge were followed by animated discussions. Results were not the important thing, nor did it matter whether one man or another proved to be right. People gave one another gifts by exchanging ideas and stimulation, and the presence of the women added a particular personal touch.

Max is very productive. Recently he went out on two successive evenings. On Saturday he attended the meeting of the *Janus* at the Onckens' place. The host, who had spent a long time in the United States, gave a very nice and lively talk about Carl Schurz,[21] and afterward, of course, our American traveler spoke for half an hour. On Monday he had a meeting of his especially learned group, the *Eranos*, at Gothein's house, where the host spoke about the possibility of a historical psychology in connection with Simmel. Again Max had a *great* deal to say, for he did not get home until half-past twelve.

But this intensive activity provoked the demons. Toward spring, after the completion of his sociological-historical work, the unpredictable nervous disturbances once again unexpectedly shackled the man, and now that the good periods had lasted longer, he endured these shackles all the more ill-humoredly. The volcanic soil shook, and for months his entire intellectual existence seemed to be in jeopardy. This time even a spring sojourn in the south was incapable of exorcising the evil specter.

Everything he had on his hands now came to a standstill. That summer he had to stop the intellectual machinery and soothe his excited nerves in the country drizzle of the mountainous Black Forest.

Ruhstein, June 25, 1909

Here there is a steady rain and bitter cold. Even though the central

---

[20]Presumably Georg Klebs, 1857–1918, professor of botany at Basel, Halle, and Heidelberg (from 1907 on).—Ed.

[21]1829–1906, German-born American statesman, solider, and journalist. The historian Hermann Oncken lived from 1869–1945.—Ed.

heating is on, I don't think that I shall get my indispensable quota
of heat into my body this year. An hour's comfortable stroll in the
rainy forest was nice, but it cost me three-fourths of my night's sleep.
And only where the firs have hitched up their coats and their dark dignity is answered by the lively lightness of the ferns and bilberries below
is this forest beautiful. Usually the fir is the old maid among the
trees, with drooping or slightly raised coats and one after another
standing on tiptoes on the mountainsides. And the young green
shoots look like a lot of little fingers on a piano that have tinkled
something out for the spring. In winter, when they have taken the
veil, it is something different. But now, in a constant rain and without the odor of resin, there isn't much here. When my room gets too
cold, I usually sit in the drayman's room. All sorts of people pass
through there; yesterday there was a rather nice skilled miller, unemployed, with whom I was able to have a good chat. Or I sit with the
old innkeeper's wife and their daughters, who are just sewing a trousseau. Sixteen children!

* * *

By midsummer he had once more overcome the alarming nervous crisis, and
an increased fruitfulness made up for the unproductive period. There were big
doings in the fall. The *Verein für Sozialpolitik* held its convention in Vienna
to demonstrate its cultural community with the Danube monarchy as well
as its joint efforts with the Austrian scholars. With the magnificent, hospitable city as its setting, the assembly was particularly festive. The Webers participated. A group of important scholars met daily: Knapp, Brentano,
von Schulze-Gävernitz, Sombart, Alfred Weber, Eulenburg,[22] von Gottl,
and others. Naumann was among them. One intellect caught fire from
another; Weber shone and glowed.

He was like a dammed-up stream of intellect that cannot stop flowing
and carrying people away. We always sat among intellectual magnates,
and the men carried on discussions from morning till night. During the
conference one could always see Max in a corner, talking to some individual about the preparation of a great new collective project. Then
he spoke for an hour during the discussion. I sat next to Knapp, who
is always inwardly youthful. He was quite moved and whispered to me:
"How good he looks! We take delight in his fire, but it is consuming

---

[22]Franz Eulenburg, 1867–1943, political economist, professor at Aachen, Kiel, and Berlin.—Ed.

him!" Unfortunately I missed Alfred's speech. The old men were horrified, but the young ones were enthusiastic. They enjoy the temperament and the pathos in which the brothers are so similar. Together
with Naumann we saw *Faust* at the Burgtheater, attended the
banquet at which Sombart proposed a charming toast to
Vienna, and visited Ludo Moritz Hartmann[23] until late at
night.

The struggle for a theoretical and practical solution of modern social
problems was an exciting drama as well. Three generations of scholars had
now been meeting at these conventions. The grand old men of academic socialism [*Kathedersozialismus*]—Wagner, Schmoller, Knapp, Brentano—were
still there. There were also their former pupils—Herkner, Rathgen, Philippovich,[24] Sombart, Schulze-Gävernitz, Eulenburg, Max and Alfred Weber—and
already a third generation was appearing on the scene. Naturally the younger people saw many things differently from the old men, and in opposition
to the political-metaphysical historicism of Gustav von Schmoller in particular they pressed for a more forceful social-political and democratic course.
Sometimes the tensions were strong. But their common search for a compromise among particularistic economic demands and the will to secure for
ideal interests primacy over material interests kept them all together.

In the realm of social policy, the question this time was whether the
right road to social equality and the limitation of the rule of private capitalism was the strengthening of the *power of the state* and the expansion
of the economic activity of the state and the communities, or the *democratization* of all institutions—of businesses as well as parliaments. The fiery
old fighter Adolf Wagner pointed in the direction of state socialism, while
others, especially the Weber brothers, saw in this only a new kind of bondage of the individual to "machinery." For them the ultimate criterion for
a social reformation was the question of what *type of personality* it
promoted—a free, responsible person, or a politically and psychologically dependent one who bows to authorities and superiors for the sake of external
security. Alfred Weber ingeniously suggested the idea that increasing economic activity on the part of the state produces a growth of the bureaucratic machinery and turns an increasing number of people into officials and
servants who have to forgo an independent political judgment for the sake

---

[23]1865–1924, Austrian historian and politician.—Ed.
[24]Heinrich Herkner, 1863–1932, political economist, professor at Freiburg, Karlsruhe, Zurich,
and Berlin; Eugen Freiherr von Philippovich von Philippsberg, 1858–1917, Austrian political
economist, professor at Freiburg and Vienna.—Ed.

of their little jobs. The bureaucratic machinery is necessary for the technical accomplishment of certain tasks, but its political-metaphysical glorification creates servile souls.

Max Weber took the same point of view and added a political point that reflected his profound agitation about the disastrous unsteadiness of the German ship of state. Here are some excerpts from his remarks, which convey something of the flavor of his improvised speech:

> No machinery in the world works as precisely as this human machine (the bureaucracy). From a technical and material point of view it is unsurpassable. But there are other than technical yardsticks. What is its consequence in the area of administration and politics? Everyone who integrates himself becomes a little cog in the machine, just as in a big industrial enterprise, and he is increasingly attuned to feeling like one and to asking himself whether he cannot become a bigger cog. And even though the idea that some day the world might be full of nothing but professors is frightening—one would have to escape to the desert if something like that happened—the idea that the world would be filled with nothing but those little cogs is even more frightening, that is, with people who cling to a small position and strive for a bigger one.
>
> This passion for bureaucratization as we have heard it expressed here is enough to make a man despair! It is as though in politics a charwoman [*Scheuerteufel*], with whose mental horizon a German can get along best anyway, were permitted to run things all by herself, as if we intentionally were to become people who need order and nothing but order, who get nervous and cowardly when this order becomes shaky for a moment, who become helpless when they are torn out of their exclusive adjustment to this order.
>
> The question is what we have as a *counterpoise* to this machinery so as to keep a remnant of humanity free from this parceling out of the soul, from this exclusive rule of bureaucratic ideals of life. . . . And if the state itself becomes more and more of an entrepreneur—for instance, if it participates in coal mining by taking over mines and joins the coal syndicate—this embrace of heavy industry will not find it playing the role of Siegfried but that of King Gunther in relation to Brunhild.[23] The state will be full of the viewpoints of an employer instead of industry being concerned with social welfare. . . .

---

[25]In the *Nibelungenlied*, the heroic Siegfried woos and wins the Amazonlike Brunhild for Gunther by passing various tests of strength in the latter's guise.—Ed.

I am opposing only the uncritical glorification of bureaucracy. Its main driving force is a purely moralistic feeling: faith in the omnipotence of the high moral standards of German officialdom in particular. But I personally consider such questions *also* from the point of view of a country's international political power and its cultural development, and in this regard the "ethical" quality of the machine decidedly plays a decreasing role today. Certainly, to the extent that it promotes the precision with which the machine functions, ethics is valuable for the mechanism. . . . But that "corrupt" officialdom of France, that corrupt officialdom of America, that much-maligned doltish government [*Nachtwächterregierung*] of England—well, how do these countries fare with them? How do they fare in the area of foreign policy? Are *we* the ones who have made progress in this area, or have others?

Democratically ruled countries with an officialdom that undoubtedly is partly corrupt have had considerably more success in the world than our highly moral bureaucracy; and if, in the final analysis, it is a matter of the political standing of the *nations* in the world—and many of us do hold the view that this is the ultimate value—*then* I ask: What kind of organization has the greatest *"efficiency"*[26]—private capitalistic expansion with a pure *business*[27] officialdom that is more prone to corruption, or state control through the highly moral German officialdom, which is transfigured in an authoritarian way? And then, despite my profound respect for the ethically correct mechanism of German bureaucracy, I am for the time being unable to acknowledge that it is still capable of doing as much for the greatness of our nation as is achieved by the foreign officialdom, which may be far below it morally and is divested of its divine aura—coupled with the striving for profit of private capital which, in the view of many of us, is highly reprehensible.

Besides the subject of social policy which occasioned so much evaluating and soul-searching for ultimate practical postulates, a purely theoretical problem was discussed in this circle for the first time: the question of the nature of economic productivity. The treatment of this subject by Philippovich caused Sombart and Weber to press for a clear distinction between scholarly findings and an ethical-political judgment of the recognized relationships. Sombart sought to show that the concept of economic productivity which the main speaker had established was permeated by subjec-

---

[26]In English in the original.—Ed.
[27]In English in the original.—Ed.

tive value-judgments, and he coined this *bon mot*: "We shall not be able to debate this until it has been scientifically established whether blondes or brunettes are prettier."

Max Weber concluded his remarks with the following sentences, which attain a certain solemnity by their restrained ethos:

> The reason why I take every opportunity . . . to attack in such extremely emphatic terms the jumbling of what ought to be with what exists is not that I underestimate the question of what ought to be. On the contrary, it is because I cannot bear it if problems of world-shaking importance—in a certain sense the most exalted problems that can move a human heart—are here changed into a technical-economic problem of production and made the subject of a scholarly discussion. We know no *scientifically* demonstrable ideals. Certainly, in this age of subjectivistic culture it is harder to try to derive them from one's own heart. But we simply cannot promise a land of Cockaigne or a paved road there either in this world or in the next, either in thought or in action. And it is the stigma of our human dignity that the peace of *our* soul cannot be as great as the peace of someone who dreams of such a land of milk and honey.

From that convention on, the discussion of value judgments did not cease in the group, until it was clarified somewhat a few years later in a board meeting called expressly for that purpose. On that occasion Weber submitted to the association a printed opinion which he subsequently published in *Logos* in somewhat altered form.[28]

* * *

In the same year (1909), the publisher of the *Archiv*, Paul Siebeck, began to interest Weber in a large encyclopedia of political economy. It was to replace Schönberg's handbook,[29] which no noted scholar had undertaken to revise. Weber agreed, made an outline, secured contributors, and did the laborious organizing, assigning the most important sections to himself. He

---

[28]Cf. *"Der Sinn der Wertfreiheit der soziologischen und ökonomischen Wissenschaften"* in *Gesammelte Aufsätze zur Wissenschaftslehre*.

[29]The economist Gustav von Schönberg, a professor at Basel, Freiburg, and Tübingen, published his *Handbuch der politischen Ökonomie* in two volumes in 1882. A second edition, in three volumes, appeared in 1896–98.—Ed.

wanted to subordinate himself completely to the cause. The book was to appear under the collective editorship of all contributors. Once again Weber displayed enormous zeal, for the work was meant to appear in two years.

This, of course, proved impossible. The collective project showed once more how hard it was to make scholars accommodate themselves to the requirements of fruitful collaboration. Firm promises were not kept; important authors had to be excused because of illness; others delayed sending in their manuscripts for several years, putting the punctual ones in the annoying position of watching their manuscripts become dated. Finally, a few distinguished colleagues to whom Weber had attached particular importance submitted unexpectedly meager contributions, and yet the editor was unable to refuse them. The original plan had to be postponed. In short, Weber had no end of trouble and annoyance, and in order to make up for the depreciation of the work, he kept setting more and more ambitious goals for his own share. In a letter to his collaborators he wrote:

> It is understandable that a great deal of discord has been created—and *justifiably* so, I don't mind telling you—by the fact that people have had no scruples about carrying forward *other* projects and producing fat tomes while failing to send in the contributions they had promised. I, too, find that this is in no way to be reconciled with the duty of living up to one's contract. . . . The erratic delivery of articles and, above all, the almost complete loss of several particularly important contributions have had disagreeable consequences in other respects as well. Since no replacement could be procured for some of these, I felt that in order to make up for this and enhance the work's special quality I ought to provide a rather comprehensive sociological discussion for the section on economy and society, a task I would otherwise never have undertaken in this form, and in doing so I sacrificed other projects that were far more important to me.

In addition to his other work, Weber now began to pour the stream of his knowledge into this vessel. At last he concentrated on a uniformly great task.

In 1914, three years later than planned, the first two sections appeared. Weber released them with a preface in which he stated the didactic and systematic character of the work and its guiding idea:

> We proceeded from the view that the development of the economy must be investigated primarily as a particular phenomenon of the *gener-*

al rationalization of life. Methodologically and politically, the contributors are in the most diverse camps; therefore no attempt has been made to achieve a uniformity of the methodological or practical viewpoint. The fact that the problems are considered from all sides compensates for this. . . . Professor Max Weber, who edited this edition, is solely responsible for any defects in the conception and the arrangement of the material.

Because of the world war the next volume did not appear until 1918. Weber's own contribution, *Wirtschaft und Gesellschaft,* which grew into his magnum opus as he worked on it, appeared after his death [1925] as a volume of over 800 large-size pages of small type. He saw in print only the conceptual part; he did not live to put the finishing touches to the rest of the work, which remained a fragment. It will be discussed later.

IV

We now return to incidents in Weber's life. In the winter of 1909–10 Weber was particularly active. He participated, among other things, in the board meeting of the *Verein für Sozialpolitik* in Berlin, talked with countless people there, and discussed with Simmel, Sombart, and others the founding of a *sociological society* that could supplement the old *Verein* in the field of purely scholarly discussion. The younger generation of scholars with sociological interests had for some time felt a need for an exchange of ideas about the problems of living in modern society, not only with specialists in political economy but also with philosophers, theologians, jurists, theoretical ethnologists, and so on. They further desired a community whose aim would be to cope with the enormous cluster of problems purely scientifically and without an ethical-political emphasis.

Weber undertook to do the organizational groundwork here as well. He drafted and sent out the promotional material, carried on a huge correspondence, collected money, and made plans for the collective projects that were to be launched. Although he was interested in having a new meeting place for the exchange of ideas, he cared even more about creating a basis for the kind of sociological research which, because of its scope, could produce significant results only through an integrated cooperative effort. Thus he submitted to the committee in charge of preparations a working outline for a sociology of the press [*Zeitungswesen*] and proposed as further projects the investigation of voluntary associations [*Vereinswesen*] and of the relationship between technology and culture. Weber immediately tried to secure individual scholars to run projects particularly suited to them. But here, too, scholarly cooperative action proved to be far more difficult to plan than any other kind. He was not able to order or force people to do things, but could only make suggestions and requests, and many scholars could not be induced to put their individual scholarly interests aside in favor of collective projects.

Weber traveled to Berlin and Leipzig several times to try to imbue the colleagues there with his own zeal, but he was unsuccessful; they were all burdened with professional duties. No one was free to take the initiative and Weber was greatly annoyed: "By now I have finally gathered at least a few of those people who are indispensable for the Sociological Society. But we shall not make any progress; it is enough to make a man despair. Nobody wants to sacrifice any of his time and work and interests, and as for acting, they don't do a thing!" Then there were the questions of etiquette. Weber himself wanted to do the work, but he did not wish to assume the leadership, and it turned out that some scholars who regarded themselves as the creators of modern sociology wanted to have this publicly expressed, particularly because the state was denying them the academic positions that befitted their scholarly stature. Weber now turned the leadership over to a troika. The consequence was that none of them took the initiative and that he continued to be saddled with the work.

In 1909, then, Weber held in his hands at the same time the interweaving threads of three great collective undertakings: the psychophysical project, the preparations for the investigation of the press, and the *Grundriss* [Outline]. With all these different concerns he was in danger of frittering away his strength. For one of his birthdays, therefore, his life's companion wished him concentration on his own work to create enduring things: "Actually, all my wishes boil down to this blasphemous one: The devil take the Sociological Society for which you fritter yourself away on penny-ante stuff, for besides the nice conventions it will remain a machine that runs idle." To this Weber replied:

All right, then, you shall have your will to the extent that this is in my power, even though I don't know what great things this will produce. As it is, I now have to start all sorts of essays which are intended for the *Grundriss*. They will open up problems which may then lead to further things. But everything will go quite *slowly*, for the gestation period should really have been even longer. I am far from having absorbed all the new things and have not yet made them my own.

* * *

In the fall of 1910 the Sociological Society held its first convention in Frankfurt. This was a meeting of men like Gothein, Simmel, Sombart, Tönnies, Troeltsch, von Schulze-Gävernitz, Kantorowicz,[30] Michels, and others—a distinguished group. Sociology was as yet not a specialized discipline but one that aimed at the totality of knowledge [Erkenntnis] and therefore had contact with almost all branches of learning. The subjects of the convention indicated this character: "The Sociology of Sociability," "Technology and Culture," "Economy and Law," "Jurisprudence and Sociology," "Race and Society," and others.

Max Weber participated in the discussion of each subject, and in the modest guise of a "Business Report" he formulated the tasks of the Society as he wished to define them, particularly the purely scientific, "value-neutral" treatment of all problems: "The question shall be asked as to what is and why something is exactly the way it is, but there shall be no judgment as to its desirability or undesirability."

Then he graphically presented those problems of both journalism and voluntary associations that would be worth examining and outlined the possible approach, with all questions ultimately relating to the main one: How do those phenomena influence the character of modern man? Regarding the press, for example, the question was to what extent it brought about a shift in attitudes toward suprapersonal cultural values and what it destroyed and created in the way of mass beliefs and mass hopes, outlooks on life and possible attitudes. For the sociology of associations, too, which would have to range from bowling clubs to political parties and religious sects, the most important question would be the extent to which a person's physical and mental habits are influenced by the various aspects of club activity. Weber uses the political effects of the German men's singing societies to make clear what he means:

A man with the daily habit of letting powerful emotions flow out of his chest through his larynx, without any relationship to his actions

---

[30]Hermann Kantorowicz, 1877–1940, professor of criminal law and legal history at Freiburg (1913) and Kiel (1920); from 1933 on in England.—Ed.

and thus without the adequate abreaction of these powerful expressed feelings taking place in the form of correspondingly powerful actions (and this is the nature of the men's singing societies' art), will become a person who, to put it succinctly, will easily develop into a "good citizen" in the passive sense of the word. No wonder that monarchs have such a great predilection for entertainments of that kind. "Where people sing, you may safely settle.[31] Great, strong passions and strong actions are lacking there. . . .

For a layman who was eager to learn and to whom the general stimulation and intellectual excitement of such meetings were more important than results, those were once again festive days. The intellectual personalities, after all, were at least as interesting as the knowledge they offered. Nowhere did they present themselves in livelier fashion than when they were speaking freely, their gestures and intonation revealing even more about their personalities than their words. Although the group was not without the particular occupational deficiencies of scholars, this was compensated for by the dignity of an intellectuality acquired by long, laborious mental activity. The atmosphere of their intellectual exchange was intoxicating; it was good to be able to understand everything. But Weber applied different standards and had previously had too much annoyance:

Please excuse me for not having been *up to date*[32] toward the end of our conversation. I was too disgusted at that *"Salon des Refusés"* [salon of rejects],[33] with no one recognizing anyone else, everyone begrudging everything to everyone else, and no one making the slightest sacrifice of his individual scholarly interests even for the briefest span of time—and yet these people regard themselves as much more exalted than the evil *Ordinarien* [full professors]. . . . If you cannot stand frankness, tell me. *I* ask you to tell me whenever you are dissatisfied with my behavior (and I shall surely give you frequent occasion for this). That would only strengthen my friendship for you. . . . It is this touchiness of our "great men" that sours me on my work when I would like to do my bounden duty as a simple workhorse.

---

[31]". . . for bad people have no songs" ["*Wo man singt, da lass' dich ruhig nieder; böse Menschen haben keine Lieder*"]: the popular version of the first and last lines, first stanza, of J. G. Seume's poem *Die Gesänge* (1804).—Ed.

[32]In English in the original.—Ed.

[33]*Salon des Refusés* designates an exhibition of works of art by artists refused admission to the French Academy.—Ed.

It turned out that none of the "stars" ["*Grössen*"] wanted to further the collective projects on his own initiative. For that reason Weber was stuck with organizing the investigation of the press. For months he labored to set the project in motion, but on the whole he had to make do with neophytes. A few valuable investigations were finally completed, but because of the difficulty of the material they covered only parts of the field. It was the same with the sociology of voluntary associations. After a year and a half of effort Weber realized that he was wasting his energy disproportionately: "So I am resigning from the executive as of January, 1911, in order to make way for a jurist or someone similar. I now have to get back to scholarly work. Things can't go on like this, since I have remained the *only* one who has sacrificed his individual scientific interests, and yet all I have accomplished thereby is to keep an idling machine barely in motion."

After the second convention Weber completely withdrew from the leadership of the organization for which he had expended so much strength and gave the following explanation of this:

Frankly, I took such an active part in the founding of this organization only because I hoped to find there a place for value-neutral scholarly work and discussion. Therefore I cannot work with a board of directors whose one chairman, Mr. G., thought it appropriate to make a *public* attack on the pertinent statutory principle and later, after I had remonstrated with him by letter, *refused* to acknowledge the impropriety of his conduct.

At the Berlin convention of 1912, with one exception (L. M. Hartmann) *all* official speakers violated the same statutory principle—and this is constantly held up to *me* as "proof" of its unfeasibility. I expressly stated in Berlin *how* I would act if the board of directors did *not* make sure that there was no recurrence of these infractions of statutes. *None* of the members, who have now elected this very Mr. G. as chairman, could have any doubt that I would act accordingly and thereby create a "clean" situation for myself. For such a personality question would be a matter of complete indifference *if* only Mr. G. had the ambition to represent the society purely outwardly. Unfortunately, however, he possesses a so-called *Weltanschauung* and in connection with it makes scholarly pretensions of a kind that makes any collaboration with him impossible for me. It goes without saying that I do not expect anyone else to act likewise.

Will these gentlemen, not *one* of whom can stifle the impulse (for that's just it!) to bother me with his subjective "valuations," all infinitely uninteresting to me, kindly stay in their own circle. I am sick and tired of appearing time and again as a Don Quixote of an allegedly unfeasible principle and of provoking embarrassing "scenes."

* * *

In 1909 the *Heidelberger Akademie der Wissenschaften* [Heidelberg Academy of the Sciences] was established. A Mannheim industrial magnate created a memorial to himself with this foundation. Max Weber was honored with a special membership, but instead of being pleased, he was annoyed. The reason was quite characteristic:

> An academy should include *all* the heads of departments and institutes of the pertinent fields on an equal basis, and it should not be just a combine of bigwigs [*Bonzenkonzern*]. It simply won't do to exclude one's own historian and the younger political economist if all sorts of *out-of-town* historians and *outsiders*[34] like me are included. Even in such basically unimportant matters the academic proprieties ought to be observed, if only for the sake of the students.

Weber was dissatisfied with the arbitrary method of selection, which offended various outstanding younger scholars. Besides, he regarded the academy's organization along traditional lines as old-fashioned. He therefore declined the membership and gave his reasons for this in a very extensive constructive critique that he addressed to W. Windelband, the chairman of the history and philosophy section. Here are a few excerpts from this long, memorandumlike communication:

> The Academy was established in accordance with a traditional scheme that is bound to stint the advancement of the modern systematic political and social sciences. The membership has been selected according to considerations of seniority and notability rather than professional considerations, and only two sections, one for the natural sciences and one for history and philosophy, have been established.
> However, as is indicated by its composition, the Academy does not represent the systematic political and social sciences, nor will it—as I shall demonstrate later—be able to represent these disciplines in the future, even if that should be its intention.

---

[34]In English in the original.—Ed.

MAX WEBER: A BIOGRAPHY

And yet these particular disciplines, in Weber's view, *needed* support from such foundations, for both the utilization of the research material buried in statistical offices and the collective gathering of new data were so expensive that individual scholars could not finance the operations out of their own pockets. It would be much more fruitful if a modern Academy supported such urgently needed investigations, which shed light on the present, rather than spending money on specialized historical and philological investigations, which individuals could carry on so much more easily by themselves.

An Academy that owes its existence solely to those living forces of the present, the investigation of whose conditions of life is among the most important tasks of the systematic political and social sciences, and which nevertheless treats these disciplines as it has treated them—this product of a hypertrophic historicism seems to me such an absurdity that I deem it my duty to call it that in public even though this protest . . . may be condemned to remain completely futile. (August 7, 1909)

Since Windelband indicated to Weber that the rejection of the honor intended for him could be interpreted as an act of disrespect and thus harm the Academy, he withdrew it, but he stuck to his criticism. It did have one result: shortly afterward the Academy gave financial support to the inquiry into the press that had been started under Weber's direction.

* * *

In the fall of 1911 a convention of university teachers took place in Dresden. In a discussion about American universities, Weber once again made extended remarks, and various points created a sensation and led to public controversy that compelled him to engage in extensive argumentation. The disagreement focused in particular on his remarks about business colleges. At a few of these, the most modern institutions of the time, lifelike replicas of the uniformed students' associations flourished. In this Weber saw a danger that the young business student would be distracted from strict academic discipline and instead would be induced to strive for *Satisfaktionsfähigkeit*[35] and social privileges, "all things that suggest the question

---

[35]*Satisfaktionsfähigkeit* refers to the ability (or privilege) to "give satisfaction" in a duel. Jews, who were excluded from participation in the German student corporations, were not regarded as *satisfaktionsfähig.*—Ed.

whether we shall be able to offer competition to the great industrious nations of the world if they are taught to our youth." The form in which the press disseminated Weber's remarks drew spirited protests from the institutions involved, so that Weber took the trouble to submit his views to them in a detailed memorandum, some excerpts from which follow.

The forms cultivated by the student corporations which culminated in the ideal of *Satisfaktionsfähigkeit* seemed to him particularly grotesque and inappropriate for a young businessman and detrimental to the pioneering work of commerce. For the resultant affectation [*Geschwollenheit*] of manners in associating with equals, subordinates, members of other groups, and so forth, was, wherever it appeared, the laughing stock of all foreign countries—and in Weber's view, justifiably so.

> I have no hesitation in saying this quite openly . . .—and anyone who wishes to make jokes about it is welcome to do so—that I have myself experienced the difficulty of getting out of my system the gestures that are instinctively practiced at the university when one is immature. The same thing may be said—and again I speak from my own rather serious experience—about the significant effect of a fraternity student's drinking habits on his productive power. . . . What is cause for concern is not our people's propensity for alcohol as expressed in occasional excesses, but the obligation to drink regularly and in accordance with instructions, which is part of a fraternity brother's *drill*.

Weber also pointed to other dangers arising from the touting of the academically trained businessman as a new type. Weber said that even though he was convinced of the benefits of any intellectual work, particularly that carried on in business colleges, he suspected that among the students there, as in other, similar trade schools, the expectation of social advantages, the so-called *Standeshebung* [upward mobility], frequently was a greater factor than the desire for an extension of knowledge. The new class differentiation of commercial employees through the rise of a diploma aristocracy could disturb the zeal for work and the peace in the offices, particularly if the student fraternity system created a class that claimed a specific prestige for reasons other than its achievement in business.

> Because the life of student corporations today strives everywhere for exclusiveness and drill in a sense previously unknown, there is a danger that membership in a corporation cuts a student off from membership in other clubs . . . and increasingly even from contact with other students, thus locking the member of a uniformed association in the circle

of his companions and making him subject to a narrowing of his intellectual horizon.

* * *

An even greater conflict was aroused by Weber's criticism, at the same
convention, of the relationship between the state bureaucracy and the
German universities, directed mainly against certain practices of the Prussian authorities which had been taken over from Althoff, their great organizer, who had died recently. Weber illustrated the harm and dangers of the
"Althoff system" on the basis of his own experiences as a young docent. He
did full justice to the great importance of the late Althoff, but ethically
disapproved of his system of ends and means:

> It is very hard to talk about him. He was not only a truly good man
> in the specific sense of the word, but also a man of very wide horizons.
> The German universities owe him things that are in a certain sense im-
> mortal. But in dealing with personal matters he proceeded from the
> assumption that everyone with whom he had something to do was
> either a scoundrel or a careerist. This posed a great danger to young do-
> cents who were dependent on him. To make them do his bidding, he
> expected improprieties of them.

By this Weber meant, for example, a teaching post or the like that a docent accepted from the authorities without the approval or against the
wishes of the faculty. "If a highly-placed official of a ministry expects something like that of a young man, I cannot cast a stone at the man who
then falls into the trap." Weber himself had once had to resist such a
temptation; since then others had succumbed to it. In the interest of
the new academic generation, the memory of his personal experience still
weighed on him: "I confess quite frankly that when I left the area of the
Prussian educational administration and came under the jurisdiction of the
Baden authorities, I had the feeling that I was breathing clean air."
These remarks, which were reported in sensational terms by part of the
press and misunderstood by others, created a great stir. One reporter had
even reversed sense completely, so that the *Baden* authorities were presented in an unfavorable light and read a sharp attack on themselves in a
leading Centrist newspaper. Therefore they requested Weber to make a pub-

lic clarification. Weber had to make corrections and additions in many other respects as well, and in doing so it was once again his experience that it was the practice of part of the press "from time to time to yield relentlessly to its need for sensation and then to do everything to deceive its readers about the lack of an occasion for it."

An official of the Prussian Ministry of Education also came forward to refute Weber's remarks by stating that there was no documentation for them. This attempt at a refutation was made in a very matter-of-fact way, and Weber replied in an equally moderate and calm tone with careful statements, hoping, as he put it, to contribute thereby to the shaking of the statement *"Quod non in actis non in mundo"* [What is not in the files does not exist]. The Prussian educational administration then made a further reply. "Very much against my inclinations I must take this as an occasion to state unequivocally once more what I reproach the *present* educational administration with, and this time in a form that will enable a court of law to establish the facts of the matter." (November 10, 1911)

V

We shall now return to the preceding year and deal with some public quarrels that show Weber as a fighter. It will be necessary to discuss them in some detail, because of their intrinsic as well as their biographical significance.

In the fall of 1910 the *Bund deutscher Frauenvereine* [Federation of German Women's Associations] had its convention in Heidelberg. This festive parade of the women's movement was beautiful and encouraging; the women inspired one another. It aroused an unexpected amount of interest. The university and the authorities extended their greetings, and the municipality honored the women by illuminating the castle. Thus authoritative circles now recognized the idealism and the necessity of the women's struggle. The most gratifying thing was that they no longer treated the leaders as caricatures and degenerates of their sex; at last they saw them as new types who rightly strove to make a virtue out of necessity by trying to qualify the millions of women forced to be independent and take outside jobs for their new role and to explain this new role to them. The women thought it was wonderful to feel firm ground under their feet at last, but they knew very well that the hard-won approval could be withdrawn at any moment. This happened soon enough.

The "true German man," insofar as he was a tradition-bound male egotist, felt threatened by the success of the movement and did not wish to give up the hallowed patriarchy in the family and state, a sacrifice that would have been required of him. And as happens in any conflict of interests of this kind, the simple defense mechanisms were concealed by concern for all that was held to be most sacred.

A young docent, who concealed his scholarly insignificance by playing the role of a guardian of a treasure, published a defamatory article about this group of women and won the approval of a large portion of the male population: "At last a bold warrior who dares to take the field even against the ladies of the university." In his lampoon he said, among other things, that the women's movement consisted only of unmarried women, widows, Jewesses, sterile women, and those who were not mothers or did not want to perform the duties of mothers. Weber's wife was childless, she was responsible for the movement in Heidelberg, and thus the most cutting remark was directed against her. Weber grew livid with anger, but he could not act right away. First his wife sent a letter to the reckless writer and demanded that he retract his slanderous remarks. When he refused, a public chastisement appeared under her name, and by its biting tone everyone recognized its co-author. When Weber learned of the young man's complaint that the husband was hiding behind his wife, who could not be challenged to a duel, he decided to give him the opportunity he desired by declaring that he stood behind all statements made by his wife. No challenge was issued, however. The chastised man declared that he was an opponent of dueling and brought a libel suit against Weber which, however, he soon withdrew at the instigation of a third party. A short time afterward there appeared in several newspapers in other towns a vile and sensational article about these occurrences, under the title Alt Heidelberg du Feine. [36] It made reference to the "B[ernhard] Case" which had been much discussed in the press. Excerpts from the article were reprinted everywhere and even entertained readers across the seas. Its special seasoning was the concluding passage: Professor Weber was supposed to have answered in the negative Dr. R.'s [37]

[36]The first line of Joseph Viktor von Scheffel's poem in praise of Old Heidelberg, which has become a popular students' song. The "B. Case" mentioned below presumably was the case of Ludwig Bernhard. See pp. 391 ff.—Ed.

question as to whether he was ready to replace his wife in a duel, saying that his health did not permit it. Dr. R. himself was given as the source of this statement, but he immediately issued a denial.

Weber, who had repeatedly expressed himself in favor of dueling, viewed this gossip as "an unheard-of mean trick." He felt that this was a violation not only of his own interests but of the public interest as well, and for that reason he spared no effort in months of struggle to redress the situation. The history of this affair is not only characteristic of Weber but also of certain practices of a journalism that delighted its readership with sensational disclosures about well-known personalities under the cover of editorial secrecy, and then made it very hard for those involved to defend themselves from the effects of this sensationalism. This time, however, all the participants were to be taught a lesson.

First of all, Weber wrote an extremely polite letter to the newspaper concerned,[38] requesting only the publication of a brief letter in which he made the following statements:

> The article datelined Heidelberg, January 6, 1911, and headed "Alt Heidelberg du Feine" contains in addition to other false statements . . . the concluding assertion that Dr. R. has directed inquiries of a certain nature to me and that I have given him a negative answer. Permit me to remark that these statements are a fabrication from the first word to the last, that nothing even remotely resembling them has actually occurred, and that I would be grateful to your correspondent for informing me where or to whom Dr. R. has made such statements. As for myself, I consider this matter closed, and I see no reason to express myself publicly about what really transpired. With the respectful request for speedy publication of this letter I am, faithfully yours,
>
> Max Weber

If this denial had been published, the case would have been closed. Instead the editors replied as follows:

> Although we should like to honor your request, we regret to say that on the basis of the information supplied by our correspondent, who has

[37]Arnold Ruge (b. 1881), a *Privatdozent* in philosophy at Heidelberg from 1910 to 1920, when he was dismissed from his teaching post.—Ed.
[38]The *Dresdener Neueste Nachrichten*. The author of the article in question was Dr. Bantmann.—Ed.

always proved reliable in the past, we cannot simply give credence to your conflicting statements. If you demand it, we shall, of course, publish your correction in accordance with the press law, but then we would have to reserve for ourselves and our correspondent the right to a reply and a confrontation. We are not in a position to reveal the name of our correspondent, since, as we must candidly confess, on the basis of the evidence we have no reason to mistrust that gentleman and his information.

To this Weber replied:

If you regard a correspondent as reliable who falsely bases himself on statements made by Dr. R., that is your affair. If your sense of professional duty does not impel you to make a public correction of the admittedly false assertion that the gentleman in question has unsuccessfully challenged me to a duel, and if you declare that this assertion, which you printed in spaced type and which was the subject of my denial (in the meantime, the other party has called it a "gross falsification" in the pages of the *Heidelberger Tagblatt*), is "immaterial," this concerns me to the extent that henceforth I shall no longer be interested in having your paper make any corrections about me. You may continue to accept whatever "corrections" you please from here.

When the editors now expressed their readiness to make amends to Weber if he convinced them of the correctness of his statements, he was no longer willing to let them off so easily as with his first denial. He took the trouble to uncover once more, point by point, the misrepresentations of that sensational article, but then he added:

With reference to the statements by your correspondent which I have highlighted above and which he has not withdrawn, and to the conduct of a man whose character a conscientious examination would have revealed to you after I had drawn your attention to what he had stated in public print, I declare to you that you have unscrupulously used the services of a slanderer (I am a former military officer), and I call upon him and upon you to accept the responsibility for your actions, particularly after your informant had the audacity to speak of "proof " even though a local paper had called his conduct an "infamy." If you do not act, I reserve the right to take such action of my own as may seem appropriate to me. What I demand is a public declaration that your "correspondent" deceived you (I insist on that word) after his untrue statements had been challenged and publicly refuted.

However, the editors were not willing to expose their correspondent in that manner, for they knew him to be trustworthy, and they kept countering Weber's statements with the assurance that their man's Heidelberg informant—"a respected person"—was sticking to his guns.

To escape Weber's draconian demand, the editors interpreted Weber's statement that there was not a word of truth to the matter, a statement that was specifically limited to the alleged challenge to a duel, to refer to all statements made in the article, which contained many other errors as well. Some of the information in it was true, they said, and regarding the main point, their correspondent had received that information from a very trustworthy source, namely, a gentleman from Heidelberg *university circles*:

> Therefore, we are prepared to state that according to you no challenge from Dr. R. has been made to you to date. After a minute investigation of the entire matter, we do not know of any misstatement, except for this one significant error, that we might correct. . . . Therefore, you will probably deem it appropriate to withdraw as unfounded your statement that our correspondent wishes to injure your reputation.

This stubborn resistance increasingly provoked Weber, especially since he did not believe in the existence of an informant from university circles. Or was it possible that Dr. R. was the instigator? After all, he had indicated his intention of challenging Weber to a duel. Weber now demanded that he be given the name of the journalist or of his source, or that the instigator be induced to come forward—"which, of course, he would not hesitate to do in the interest of his honor if he belongs to 'university circles' (and exists in the first place!). . . . It goes without saying that, as things stand, a simple or even regretful correction of individual facts without an express disavowal of your correspondent or a disclosure of who that gentleman is and what he can attest will not suffice."

The journalist, who had really been driven into a corner (and had in the meantime been promoted to an editorship on the paper in question), now offered to print clarifications in the form of an advertisement and anonymous letters to the editor. He refused, however, to name either himself or his informant. Weber contemptuously declined that offer, and when his second peremptory demand for publication of his declaration was also refused, he rudely rebuked the editors and thus forced the newspaper and its co-editor to sue him for libel. He now wished to identify the instigator of the intrigue at any cost, but could not believe that it was a colleague who was still hiding.

The trial, which took place in Dresden after several months of correspondence, went through two stages. In the first trial both parties were found guilty, and Weber was fined a higher amount than the two plaintiffs combined. The second trial ended, surprisingly enough, with a settlement. The anonymous instigator was brought to light accidentally; it really was a Heidelberg professor.[39] The journalist had not revealed his identity because he was indebted to him. He was a former student of his, and a short time after the appearance of that interesting article, the professor had recommended him for his new position as "a man of trustworthy character and a skillful journalist." The journalist's patron had denied his repeated request for permission to name him.

Weber now saw the young man's conduct in a different light. He restored his honor to him and in an almost fatherly manner showed him the mistakes he had made. Then he wrote him:

I should like to say it again: What I expect of you is a plain, unvarnished, objective presentation of all facts—of course, only of those which after conscientious reflection you can swear to. After all, I did not leave myself open to a lawsuit in order to expose Prof. X or to be proved right in court at all costs, but so that truth might be established in any case, no matter what the truth might be, and in this you should take a hand. . . . After what has been objectively ascertained, there simply is nothing to justify Prof. X. But none of us may assume the responsibility for charging him wrongfully with anything beyond the guilt that he has actually incurred.

The matter was of importance, for, as a teacher of journalism, X trained future newspapermen, and he boasted of his influence on the press, which gave him a power that people feared. He was not personally acquainted with

---

[39]The man hereafter referred to as "Prof. X" was Adolf Koch (b. 1855), a Jewish teacher of history and journalism at Heidelberg from 1884 on. His appointment was terminated in 1913.—Ed.

Weber. The question was whether he might have induced his protégé to write that article in order to make insinuations against an academic circle that for various reasons did not think highly of him, particularly against Weber who in response to objections from third parties had not invited him to participate in the sociological investigation of the press.

However, neither the motives of his conduct, which might have been harmless, nor the degree to which he was responsible for the article had been demonstrated. After his name had been revealed during the trials, Weber asked him for a clarification. X answered that the rumor about the declined duel had occasionally been discussed in his house, which the journalist frequented as a friend, and he was sorry that it had been spread. If that was so, then the other man bore the sole responsibility. X could simply have repeated an interesting bit of gossip. That would have been a careless thing to do in the presence of a journalist, but it would have been harmless. On the other hand, he might have intentionally changed the rumor to a *fact* and given the young man premeditated information to be used against a colleague. Did he have any interest in getting the matter into the newspapers in sensational form, and if so, what was it? Why had he not revealed himself as the instigator in time? Who was lying, the teacher or his student?

Every nuance in the conduct of both was important, for the behavior of the young man certainly had not been blameless either. After so much unpleasantness Weber now wanted to bring the full truth to light, no matter what the cost. After all, it was no longer a matter of *his* honor but of the public interest—the dignity of the university and the freeing of the press from pernicious practices. If X had really inspired his protégé intentionally and out of base motives, then the education of future journalists could not be allowed to remain in his hands any longer. Weber therefore wrote a long letter to X, in which he remonstrated with him in this manner:

But I must now make a few remarks about your conduct, which caused a trial that fruitlessly troubled the courts and caused both parties considerable expense, loss of time, and all kinds of inconvenience. Even if you had had authentic evidence for the assertion made about me in the article, the following questions would have arisen: What was your *motivation*? How did you propose to reconcile the transmission of such things about a *colleague* to a professional journalist with a position at the university? And after this man, as was to be foreseen, had exploited them journalistically, how could you shroud yourself in *anonymity*

and do nothing to make public and private amends for what had happened (that is, if it was merely an act of carelessness)?

. . . You made that article available to the press quite deliberately
and evidently out of some distasteful motive, then did what you could
to see to it that the newspaper did not make the amends that were
due me. And when this led to legal action, you stayed under the cover
of editorial secrecy, until my inquiry, which was based on facts, blocked
this road for you. . . . You knew full well the importance that is attached to the assertion that a man who has made repeated public declarations in favor of dueling, who maintains his connections with a local uniformed students' corporation of which he used to be a member,
and who as an officer receives his military orders every year has refused
to defend the honor of his wife under the notoriously untrue pretext
that his health does not permit him to bear arms. . . . After the true
state of affairs has been established with considerable sacrifice, I naturally have not the slightest interest in anything bad happening to you,
and even less in a public scandal that might harm the reputation of
the university. If, however, you believe that you can deny the facts
given above, I refer you to the courts or to the appropriate disciplinary
authority. . . . What is decisive for me is that neither your conduct
in the above-mentioned case nor your behavior toward me appears to
be at all compatible with your opinion that you are qualified to train
future journalists at the University of Heidelberg.

Weber still hoped that the unfortunate man would at least forestall
public opprobrium by voluntarily resigning from his teaching appointment,
and he was ready to help him do so. He therefore enclosed the following
lines to the Dean when he sent a copy of the above letter to the faculty:

Privately I wanted to tell you only this: If X were to sever his connections with the university *voluntarily*, I could *guarantee* that the matter
would then be *closed* for me, that no one would find out anything
about it, and that those who are informed would remain silent. After
all, he is married to a wealthy woman, and the matter will then end
without the scandal that can always develop when there is no amicable
settlement, no matter what the judgment of the faculty may be.

However, Professor X did not take this way out; instead he brought a libel
suit against Weber, hoping to place the full responsibility on the journalist.

The press trial had taken place in Dresden where it had, of course, aroused no interest. But with Heidelberg as the scene, things were different. A professorial conflict in court was a spectacle that occasioned as much amusement as disapproval among the citizenry. For Weber a great deal was at stake, for his entire circle dreaded law courts and public fights. Even most of his old friends were against this scandal. They would have deemed it far more "refined" and advantageous to Weber if he had punished the accusations of inferior people by ignoring them rather than making a scene; surely that would not make the world any better. And was Weber really sure of his cause? He was known as a man with a delicate sense of honor who made exaggerated ethical demands on himself and others, and, like old Fallenstein, his grandfather, he was regarded as having a tendency toward immoderation. It would be most embarrassing if he had overreached himself and could not furnish proof of his assertions. Then he would really make a fool of himself and also compromise the university. Even if he received only a symbolic sentence, because of technical libel, it would be embarrassing. People would smile at him, as they had before, as a second Don Quixote who gets bruised by tilting at windmills. Or, in accordance with modern psychiatric practice, they would stamp him as a querulous person—like Michael Kohlhaas.[40] Dissatisfied friends had, in fact already used that term. People secretly resolved to judge Weber's action by its success. If he won, it would meet with subsequent approval; if he lost, his trustworthiness would be severely impaired.

The plaintiff appeared with two attorneys; fifteen witnesses had been summoned. After protracted arguments whereby the plaintiff's attorneys sought to obscure the facts of the case, there was some excitement when the journalist testified under oath about the course of events: X had shown him clippings of R.'s article against the women's movement as well as Mrs. Weber's reply and then told him about R.'s challenge to a duel. Two editors of a respected Heidelberg newspaper had discussed it, and their source was R. himself. Thereupon the young man had asked X: "Wouldn't that be something for the papers? Right now, after the conflict at the University of Berlin, this would be a big thing! But is it a fact? I think I'll first check with Dr. R. or Professor Weber." But X advised him against this: "That wouldn't do you any good, because R. will deny it since he would be committing a punishable act if he issued a challenge to a duel. To Weber it will be displeasing in any case, even if his state of health is sufficient reason for him to decline to fight a duel. R. has said so himself!" "Then I told myself:

---

[40]In Heinrich von Kleist's novella *Michael Kohlhaas* (1810), a horse dealer who has been wronged by a nobleman goes to terrible lengths to achieve justice.—Ed.

If a docent says so and a professor passes it on, with names being named, it *must* be so. So I wrote the article and sent it to five papers, three of which printed it."

After this testimony there was an extremely agitated exchange between the journalist and his patron. Professor X, who had not mustered the courage to mitigate his offense by making a public confession, now saw no other recourse but to brand his protégé as a liar and a dishonorable man. The truth now became more and more evident and the entire web of rancor and resentment was finally exposed. The plaintiff was reduced to the stature of a defendant.[41] Once again Weber had to sit in judgment in behalf of truth. His colleagues, too, now admitted that his personal interest in this matter coincided with public morality. In the final analysis it had proved worthwhile to make an example of a malicious slander.

But the more the wretchedness of his opponent was revealed, the sorrier Weber felt for him. The more the scale of the burden of proof tipped in his favor, the more painful did his judge's function become for him. When those present listened with bated breath to the contradictions between the plaintiff's testimony and that of a member of his family, and when the word "Perjury!" was spoken, the horrified Weber jumped up and cried: "I deeply regret that this word has been spoken! It is entirely possible that in her excitement the witness has said something factually incorrect, but subjectively she was surely convinced of the correctness of what she said." He was profoundly shaken by all this misfortune, and one moment before the decision his opponent's attorneys could surely have persuaded him to agree to a settlement—if his wife had not most resolutely intervened. She knew that too much was at stake as far as Weber's own reputation was concerned. People unacquainted with the details would never believe that he had spared his opponent, who was no match for him, out of chivalry, and they would only see in it a weakness of his own case.

Thus things had to take their course. Just before the sentencing the plaintiff withdrew his suit. When Weber's attorney declared that the evidence bore out all statements made by his client, Weber said: "In the final portion of his arguments my attorney, in guarding my interests, went beyond what I myself would have done." And he added: "I most deeply regret that this trial, with yesterday's horrible scenes and the torment it has

---

[41]This presentation is somewhat one-sided; an examination of the court records does not produce conclusive proof of Koch's guilt.—Ed.

brought Professor X, had to take place. With this I must combine the hope that the academic authorities and the ministry will realize that things cannot go on like this. A court of honor must be created on the pattern of what the doctors and the lawyers have." And in order to divert attention from the personal significance of the events and draw it to their objective meaning, he added a lesson to the press: the abandonment of editorial secrecy in personal affairs.

The unnerving drama was at an end. It was difficult to prevent Weber from helping his crushed opponent. In contradiction to his own original impulse he wrote to the Dean of the *Fakultät* while the trial was still going on: "I shall not be able to do otherwise but ask the faculty, when the time comes, to act leniently toward X. Since the ministry has declined to exercise disciplinary power over me, it would be very embarrassing for me if he were axed [*abgesägt*] on my account." And right after the conclusion of the trial:

Concerning X, I shall submit a petition to the faculty in a week that will state what in *my* estimation has *not* been proved. That seems to me a duty dictated by propriety. I hope he will leave of his own accord. It would be the best thing. But even if he does not, I must now be chivalrous toward him for the sake of his poor wife's highly estimable family. Such a face-to-face struggle is really something horrible! As far as I am concerned, never again!

For a long time the Webers had to live with the insight that moral destruction is more inhuman than physical destruction. Marianne wrote down her feelings in the following lines to Helene:

The trial was gruesome; it is gruesome when things take their own course, detached from the initial impulse of the person who set them in motion, and when the snowball turns into an avalanche that destroys a human being. But for all that, it was glorious how Max succeeded in leading *truth* to victory in every point. Incidentally, don't laugh! We have another suit now. Ella is getting a divorce, and although she has brothers and brothers-in-law, she asked Max for assistance. This again causes him much work and unrest. But his helpfulness knows no bounds; his immoderateness in this respect is at least as great as his immoderateness in anger.

* * *

Shortly after the conclusion of the X trial Weber was again embroiled in a great feud, which he took particularly seriously because it involved in the main an attack on someone else's honor. This cost him almost a year of hard work. In this case he no more took the initiative than he had in the others. The case is recounted here, on the basis of the documents, only insofar as it reveals Weber's personality and conduct. His opponent is illuminated only to the extent that is absolutely required for an understanding of Weber's reactions.

The background was as follows. The publisher Paul Siebeck, whom Weber regarded as a friend after years of harmonious collaboration, had tried for years to produce a new edition of Schönberg's Handbook of Political Economy. It had proved impossible to interest noted scholars in contributing to the project; the handbook had become obsolete. A young scholar (H.)[42] who had been picked by Schönberg to be the co-editor of a new edition had been unsuccessful and had expressly declared that his attempt had failed. About a year later P. Siebeck asked Weber to edit a new collection to serve as a "replacement" ["Ersatz"] for the outdated book. In summer of 1909, Weber drew up an outline for a work which has already been mentioned and which was completely different in purpose, content, and contributors. He also asked the young scholar H. to supply an essay, but H. declined.

Three years later (1912), H. claimed from the publisher an honorarium for Schönberg's impoverished heirs which had been promised them if there was a new edition of the above-mentioned handbook. His intentions were good, but the demand was couched in very defamatory terms, particularly for the publisher, because H. intimated that the new edition of the old work was to be given a different guise in order to evade any obligations toward penniless people. He added the remark that he (H.) had been "removed from his position (as editor of the new edition) under legally peculiar circumstances," but that he fortunately had "proof" that Weber himself had some time previously written him about a "renewal" ["Erneuerung"] of the old handbook.

Weber found the reproaches leveled by his young colleague at the publisher and involving himself as well so outrageous by his ethical standards that he refused to carry to any discussion with the young man until he had unreservedly admitted his error. On the other hand, Weber wished to take up the publisher's cause, because H. was basing his arguments in part on a word by him (Erneuerung rather than Ersatz) for which his frequently unclear hand-

---

[42]In the first edition the author wrote: "Let us call him Z."—Ed.

writing might have been responsible or which might have inadvertently slipped into the letter written by Weber to H. years previously.

He therefore sent P. Siebeck a letter meant for H. which contained in addition to the most detailed factual presentation the following passage:

> With a man who dares to say—and not even to me but to a third party, my publisher—that I have *"kept"* anyone in a false belief (presumably to aid you in the alleged elimination of Schönberg's heirs), who intimates that he has been forced to take a step, under "legally peculiar circumstances . . . the consequences of which he had not foreseen" (supposedly I had something to do with that step), a man who uses phrases like "fortunately" he still has a letter from me, and "I have proof in my hands"—with such a man, of course, I would henceforth only associate via courts of law or, if he prefers, via seconds [in a duel], but *no longer* by personal letter. . . . If you now make any concession to Schönberg's heirs, even the minutest one, I shall sever all my connections with this handbook. You must understand this condition. For *if* the heirs were to base material claims on the circumstance asserted by Mr. H., namely, that I have recruited collaborators for a new edition of Schönberg's handbook, these claims would be made entirely upon *me*, since I had *no authorization whatever from you* for that purpose. If you were to pay debts incurred by me, particularly against my will, my honor would be affected.

Although this trenchant attitude was justified by the facts, it obviously made it difficult for the young man to admit his mistake. He did make a small conciliatory gesture, but in doing so he again used phrases which suggested that he had not abandoned his suspicion. Disregarding the gulf between himself and Weber—among other things, the difference in their ages—he declared that Weber's resistance was the result of a pathological state that had long since led him to regard Weber as being of only limited soundness of mind, "so I shall not go into his insulting invectives which at the most arouse a feeling of sincere pity in me."

In the course of the dispute there were a number of variations on this point. Above all, however, H. made matters worse by submitting the case to a group of older colleagues, who could have no insight into the facts of the matter, and by appealing to their judgment. As Siebeck learned from a member of that group, "from all sides there was a flood of censure for the stinginess of the publisher and his violation of his moral and even legal obligations." On the other hand, H., the man who appeared in that knightly armor in behalf of poor orphans, "everywhere found support for his plan . . . soon to mobilize the public against the publishing firm," if that should prove necessary. Weber answered this threat with twelve typewritten pages explaining the situation for the gentlemen who had sided against the publisher. In conclusion he wrote as follows:

> The facts of the matter being evident, I shall of course completely disregard Mr. H.'s personal rudeness toward me, and I don't mind if he adds to it, as he has said he will do. That people who have not had the moral courage to purge themselves of serious transgressions completely should later harbor "a feeling of sincere pity" for their adversary— evidently "of only limited soundness of mind"—who makes them see the nature of their conduct, is by now such an everyday occurrence that I probably need not waste a word on it.
>
> Regarding the nature of his conduct in this affair I should like to say this: If a young and evidently not very mature man feels called upon to show the aged and experienced head of a great publishing firm with a spotless reputation a "moral obligation" toward a third party which in his subjective view exists, then it is his bounden duty in particular measure . . . to do two things: (1) strictly refrain from irresponsible moral insinuations that render any objective discussion impossible; (2) and this I should like to say most emphatically, because it is the key to everything: strictly avoid jumbling his petty personal hurts with the noble purpose that is claimed, as has been done here. Otherwise things will inevitably take the course they have now taken.

Thereupon H., who had earlier modified his accusations somewhat, though not sufficiently, reaffirmed that the new collection was only a disguised edition of the old one, that it was greatly indebted to Schönberg's ideas and that by means of it the publishing house wished to evade its obligations. This, he said, was a view that he was going to express clearly everywhere in the future as well: neither Weberian sophistry nor his distortion of facts could change this. Weber, so he said, contented himself with words, and where he offered proof, it was a fabrication. Weber had deliberately told untruths, and his remark that H.'s interest in Schönberg's heirs was mixed with petty personal hurts was "shameless slander." However, he wanted to forgo legal proceedings—for one thing, because he conceded extenuating circumstances in that Weber was a sick man, and also to avoid the responsibility for a trial that would damage the reputation of German professors. Nor was he going to issue a challenge to a duel—for reasons that he did not wish to go into. (From the context it became apparent that he meant Weber's illness.)

Weber then challenged him to a duel with sabers "under the most stringent conditions permitted in academic practice." It happened to be Christmas vacation, and Weber insisted that the duel be fought immediately in his opponent's locality. However, when the latter referred to his professional duties and demanded a postponement until the end of the semester, Weber withdrew his challenge in deference to his wife and also because he felt incapable of bearing arms months later: "I shall certainly not fight months from now, cold-bloodedly and without anger and passion, because student custom or a code of honor demands it of me. *Pfui Teufel!* [Disgusting!]" As it was, it would have bordered on the ridiculous if a forty-eight-year-old man had fought a duel with a far younger man for such a reason. But this still did not end the matter. Because H. had asserted that Weber had not offered convincing proof in Siebeck's favor, Weber now submitted all documents to the pertinent forum of colleagues and elucidated them, piece by piece, in a memorandum of sixteen typewritten pages.

This must have made the situation absolutely clear to any impartial observer. Moreover, an impartial observer would probably have admired the amount of work devoted to clearing another man's reputation, and he would have felt sad that all this sagacity could not be applied to other subjects as well and that it finally did *not* accomplish its purpose of making others realize their error. The exposition ends with the following sentences:

> Perhaps the documentary presentation of this particular case will convince the gentlemen that when I treat someone with seemingly unnecessary severity, I usually have *congent reasons* for it, and I stand ready to demonstrate this in the same way on all other cases in which, I realize, this has occasionally appeared to be so. It is always things of the very same nature—and I would rather not characterize it in greater detail here—which make my blood boil. This is not to say that I make no mistakes of any kind. But I am entitled to say this: Whenever I have erred to a person's detriment and done him an injustice—and that has certainly happened more than once—I have been chivalrous enough to act accordingly. . . .

The effort expended on this document was again wasted in that, with one exception, the gentlemen for whose enlightenment it was intended refused to study the documentary material, referring to their "valuable

time." However, it did have the effect of preventing the further public attacks on the publishing firm that had been threatened. After all that,
Weber still offered to give a verbal presentation to his out-of-town colleagues. This, too, was declined by several of them. They were unable to
change their attitude and did not wish to be bothered with things that
no longer concerned them. Thus they withdrew by means of a joint declaration which certified that both H. and Weber, but not the publisher, had
acted "in good faith." Thereupon Weber came forward once more and wrote
them, among other things:

> It is true that in your collective letter you certified that both pro-
> fessors had acted "in good faith," but you reserved judgment on the
> conduct of Mr. Siebeck, although I have given you my most precise as-
> surances on this score and your colleague B., who is familiar with at
> least some of these, has subscribed to my assurances, and even though
> I have never given any of you reason to believe that I would collaborate
> with a publisher in a matter in which anything had been done "unfair-
> ly." It has never been my intention to submit this controversy to you
> as a forum; on the contrary, I meant to tell you to your faces and to
> prove that you have both tolerated injustice and committed an injus-
> tice. I expected that you would regard it as a duty of chivalry to give
> me an opportunity to do so. . . .
>   I have been informed that the time of the gentlemen was too "val-
> uable." If that is true, then your names should have been too valuable
> for you to put them under subjective sentiments. . . . I regret that
> my colleagues did not give me an opportunity to present to them doc-
> umentation of the chivalry and the tact that the publishing house
> displayed in its dealings with Herr Schönberg—and Herr Siebeck is al-
> leged to have violated its obligations to him or his heirs. . . . An out-
> sider is always left with the impression that in a quarrel there must
> have been wrong on both sides. However, in a matter in which I am
> completely certain that I am absolutely right, I cannot give an inch.

This exciting affair had a sequel. Among the out-of-town colleagues who had
let H. induce them to side against the publisher there was an older friend
of Weber's whom he esteemed highly. He was particularly hurt that even
this man seemed to be insensitive to the difference in level between the
participants and their methods of fighting:

> But what strikes me as very strange is this: If you were a seriously ailing
> person like myself, my most elementary feelings of chivalry would rebel
> against a man who dragged your illness into the conflict, in circulars

addressed to third parties, with the expectation and intention of hurting you, and I would not let even someone to whom I was ever so beholden get away with it. This I can guarantee you. But I do not make such a demand upon others, for by now I am used to meeting with incomprehension in this regard. Your whole *Kränzchen* [group] bears the heavy responsibility of not having made it clear to the man that one does not drag slanderous statements like those made against the publisher before a group of outsiders. . . . But I do not make this demand either, for apparently the gentlemen cannot be made to realize the unchivalrousness of this action either. . . .

When the friend still could not see what he had done wrong, Weber considered their friendship at an end and wrote him the following lines:

Your remarks about "the man sustained from his youth by approbation, understanding, success" (myself) show that even though you have been under my roof physically, you have been blind. Otherwise *you* could hardly have written *me*, of all people, in this vein. However, the tragically hard life you have had (I realized this even without your telling me) makes me understand that things which to me are *glass beads* with which one can beguile natives [*Neger*] have dazzled you. But at any rate: I have remained an utter stranger to you. This is no reproach, for it is not your fault, but it is a fact, and we should simply act accordingly, without recriminations or bad blood.

I specifically owe you a debt of gratitude for having acknowledged your shared responsibility in this matter by endeavoring to secure compliance with my request. I confirm that you could not have done any more than that now. But all this cannot dispose of the fact that I did not meet with understanding from you in a matter that concerned my honor—and despite what you think, such matters are not ephemeral. This wretched handbook whose editorship I undertook at the repeated urging of scholars, who then ignominiously left me in the lurch, will, as I have said before, probably cost me not only my scholarly standing (about which I never cared an awful lot) but, thanks to that gentleman, also my spotless reputation. All that did not seem to matter to you, for you were so blindly preoccupied with the belief that "if a professor charges a businessman with something, there must be *something* to it." This I cannot ignore. My outlook remains unchanged, but our relationship cannot remain so. Therefore I wish you all the best for the future with a cordial handshake.

But that was not to be the last word. In response to a gratifying letter from his friend, Weber wrote:

I cannot leave your letter, so full of chivalry and noble sentiments, un-answered. Let us disregard that matter. Perhaps there will be a good hour at some future time. I am not in a position to upbraid you, espe-cially after what you have told me. . . . And if, in my excitement, I have been unjust toward you, as you say I have, I am sincerely sorry. My great respect for you, of which you are aware, was not shaken for a mo-ment, though it seemed to me that we had become estranged from each other. That is all I meant to say, and perhaps even that was too much. You know that I am frequently a very brusque person. The way I see myself, I am generally brusque only where I have reason to be, as I undoubtedly did in the case of Mr. H. Forgive me if in the course of this affair and in accordance with my view of it at the time I fought back more aggressively against you than may have been objectively ap-propriate. At that time I felt as though I were engaged in a struggle for my good name against a wholly unjustified attack. I return your heartfelt wishes with equal cordiality. I need them more than is appar-ent. I hope you don't.

* * *

There was yet another case on which Weber expended time and energy, involving his own reputation for someone else's honor. The first voluminous work of a young scholar from Weber's circle of friends was reviewed by a col-league in a way that gravely insulted the scholar's literary and personal hon-or. Among other things he was accused of plagiarism—not in so many words but by implication, and this seemed to be worse, for it was legally nonac-tionable.

Weber regarded this kind of scientifically unfruitful, personally carping cri-ticism as reprehensible. He therefore accompanied the author's rebuttal with an "Afterword" of his own in which he carefully examined and exposed, point by point, the pettiness and the errors of the review and sought to lay bare what seemed to him the "base motives" underlying it. As a result he was attacked not only by the reviewer but also by the latter's colleagues at his university. The faculty stood behind its member and published a lengthy piece that called Weber's countercritique immoderate and com-pletely unjustified, and showered him with invective into the bargain. It goes without saying that the new "case of the professors" was once again noised abroad [weitergetratscht] with suitable commentaries by a certain type of daily newspaper. Weber now had to take the trouble to refute, point by point, the corporation's document, which had been sent to all faculties in Germany, Austria, and Switzerland, and at the same time to defend himself as well as the insulted author. Almost every paragraph of his complicated but still lucid argument ends with sentences such as, "I stick to my objections," "What I have said stands in its entirety," "I reject the accusations that the faculty makes against me."

This incident showed once more what price Weber was willing to pay for the services he rendered, but it is characteristic in another respect as well. As we know, it was one of Weber's basic ethical demands that a person must be ready to recognize, unreservedly acknowledge, and make amends for errors and mistakes with which he has hurt the feelings of others. It constantly amazed him, however, that people in the wrong rarely recognized this and believed that they would be compromising themselves if they did so. In his disputes Weber was always right as far as the issues were concerned, but in his excitement he unjustly hardened and hurt his opponents on more than one occasion with the vehemence of his attacks and sometimes also by mistaking the motives for their conduct. However, he was quite willing to be convinced otherwise and sought to make amends for his error as soon as the other man was also ready to do so.

When in this case reliable colleagues of the reviewer whom Weber had rebuked assured him that he had not intended to accuse the young scholar of any literary improprieties and that he had not been guided by petty motives in his critique, Weber immediately published the following declaration in a periodical and in a daily:

> With reference to the statement made by Mr. X, I should like to say the following: His declaration that he does not work in the same field as Mr. Y shows that he has undoubtedly been done an *injustice* with the conclusions drawn on the basis of this assumption. *I regret* having trusted a deceptive appearance in this respect. On the other hand, I am glad to be able to revise my original judgment of him.

To be sure, to this withdrawal of his own attacks, which was issued before the publication of the faculty's memorandum, he added the following appeal: "Mr. X sees that it is possible to remove an unjust accusation honestly. It behooves him to do so toward Mr. Y with the unlimited openness that the situation demands. It is not necessary for me to appeal to his "insight," for he does possess this quality. I am appealing to qualities of character [*Gesinnung*]." This appeal was futile, however, because the defense of the reviewer by his faculty now appeared. In his dispute with the faculty,

Weber, as we have already said, did not yield an inch so far as the principle was concerned. But in order to make it easier for Professor X to do his duty toward the insulted author, he once more declared "emphatically . . . that contrary to the appearance that has inevitably arisen, Professor X can henceforth not be reproached by me, at any rate, with having *wanted* to 'defame' ["*die Ehre abschneiden*"] the author. This also goes for the accusation of 'plagiarism-snooping' ["*Plagiatschnüffelei*"] and the other, similar accusations . . . I am pleased to be able to state this herewith."

This by no means completes the chronicle of Weber's chivalrous acts, nor can it be given in its entirety. When it became known how zealously Weber acted on behalf of hard-pressed friends, there was always the danger that he would be dragged into other people's disputes and that his clientele would claim too much of his time. The way in which he assisted women in distress in difficult situations will be illustrated by an example in another context. By applying his keen, legally trained mind and with a solicitude that the average person usually musters only in his own interest, Weber brought several intricate matters to a favorable conclusion as an adviser to the attorneys involved.

There is no doubt that conflict as such stimulated him, conveyed life to him, and offered him relaxation from mere mental activity. The danger in this was that his excitable capacity for emotion sometimes made him side too easily with those seeking protection. After all, they were friends, and at first he uncritically saw everything their way and declared his solidarity with them. And despite all his worldly wisdom and penetrating knowledge of human nature, he occasionally acted like some elemental force of nature that is set in motion by an outside influence: Othello, albeit with a different content, who implicitly believes what is confided in him and acts accordingly.

Almost invariably he was in the right so far as *facts* were concerned, and he finally gained victory for his clients. But the vehemence with which he attacked his adversaries missed the mark in another respect: their attitudes hardened and he did not get them to recognize their injustice. Weber initiated none of his many quarrels. In each instance he was provoked or forced into it by friends who needed help. But in those fights he undoubtedly exercised inherited abilities that he was tragically unable to apply in an appropriately great manner because of his illness and because of political conditions. These qualities were the heroic energy of the old Lützow corpsman Fallenstein and an innate chivalry.

13

THE GOOD LIFE _____

I

Spring of 1910 again brought a change in the framework of the Webers' life. Adolf Hausrath closed his tired eyes forever in August of 1909. His family converted the old family home, built by Friedrich Fallenstein, for renting out. Ernst Troeltsch and Max Weber each moved into one floor. Her children's move into this house meant the fulfillment of a heart's desire for Helene. She always felt homesick for her parental home, which had once contained all the poetry of her youth and, more than that, her idols. When her mother was still living, Helene used to go there to refresh herself with her family during annual vacation weeks, and she always felt restored. Her sister Henriette, who was married to Hausrath, and her children were part of herself. When her son moved into the house, she renewed her claim to it, and she celebrated it like a festival in the fullness of her strength.

Helene was now sixty-six years old. Since her youth her life had been full of tasks and problems. She was now a charming old woman, with a fine but powerful face and brown hair under her black lace kerchief. One could not help admiring her strength and determination as she hurried up and down stairs, busied herself with boxes and chests, and dug in the garden. Oh, if only the spring of her active love could flow forever, like the fountain outside. It was unthinkable that some day she might be no more. She still enjoyed life greatly, but she was always ready for death and wholly surrendered to the hands of her God.

The house had aged, too, having witnessed many difficult times. For Helene it was still filled with the spirit of the departed. The wide staircases, the imposing high ceilings, and the solemn rooms that faced the southern sun surrounded her as beautifully as ever and were to her palpable evidence of the generosity of the builders. Through the windows she could still see the magic outside: the gently sloping wooded mountains, the majestic ruin, the familiar group of houses clustering about the motherly figure of the Gothic church, the glistening river and the bridge spanning it. And when in the morning the sun victoriously chased the mist down the river valley, Helene always regarded it as a profound symbol: the victory of the heavenly light over the earthly darkness.

In the front garden the *Götterbäume*—Chinese ash trees that had been planted by the father—raised their perfectly formed crowns; pinnate foliage with light green clusters of fruit adorned their expressive branches, which now reached to the roof of the house. In the mountain garden in back, the catalpas with their thick trunks were covered each summer with velvety green protective leaves and fragrant, frothy white blossoms. In the wide grotto carved into the mountain slope there still splashed a merry spring, the *Löwenbrunnen* [lion's fountain]. Helene always drank from it when she went away to make sure that she would return. The old trees from her grandfather's day imperiously spread their branches over the entire garden; the roots were no longer able to provide all of them with fresh juices. Boxwood trees of the same age had turned into gnarled shrubs; myrtlelike and evergreen, they gave the garden a southern touch. In front of this shrubbery stood an ancient sacrificial altar on which were inscribed an ode of Horace as well as the names of the former inhabitants of the house: Gervinus, E. W. Benecke, Goldschmidt, and Hausrath—all of them distinguished scholars. Over it bent the branches of a pair of copper beeches planted by Hausrath that were still at the height of their vigor and supplied shade for the spot.

For the first time the Webers owned a piece of land, and they became more deeply attached to the earth, experiencing the sweetness of spring more keenly than before. It was first proclaimed by the delicate green veil of buds over on the castle hill, and this was especially beautiful while the trunks and the branches of the trees and the ground still shone through. Then the magnolia blossoms opened their calyxes in the front garden. From the windows upstairs one could look down into them—what a miracle! The sunlight had drawn such heavenly creations from the mysterious creative powers of the shapeless, dark earth! Then the old fruit trees on the mountain slope near the Philosophenweg gleamed in their bridal finery. Every spring brought such joys. This is what Marianne wrote about it:

> The first green veil lies over the garden. Four weeks earlier than usual. Snowdrops have already crept out and are surprised. One is worried about all this rash lust for life and yet one enjoys it and is oneself young and grateful and ready to blossom. This year there are home-grown fragrant hyacinths at the windows in the living room. . . .
>
> This morning we planted primroses and daisies under the shrubbery on the slope so that it should not be so bare there. But wow, it started to snow! The old gentleman up there, or whoever represents him in worldly government, is once again behaving unreasonably. First he lures out all the blossoms and all the greenery three weeks too early, and then he remembers that we have had no winter this year. Outside it looks sad; the magnolias are black, the tulips droop. If there is another freeze tonight like last night's, the green will turn black too. . . .
>
> In the garden the new seedlings are growing slowly. We bestow much kindness and water on the boxwood tree, and every day we check to see whether it is coming to life. The first leaves of the copper beeches wave their brownish pinnae ·toward the pale blue sky. The mountain slope shimmers with its snowy white blossoms, and now the lilac is coming. . . .
>
> A delightful Easter day! A warm sun and a gentle soughing in the blossomy trees. On the highway outside the dust is already swirling. In our flowerbed yellow and red tulips have opened, just like Easter eggs for good children. If we only could enjoy them together! Do you remember having experienced such a radiant spring in years? I don't. Here there is an intoxication and a profusion. Everything has come at the same time, and by now it is tending toward the brighter hues of summer. I still have real spring fever in my bones; I am always impelled to be outside and go roaming. It was a gratifying gift for me that on his fiftieth birthday Max, whom I had not expected back so soon, went with me on our first real walk in years through the springlike forest.

We took the mountain railway to the Königsstuhl, and from there we walked via the Kohlhof [Sanitarium] to Neckargemünd. Up there we encountered the first delicate green veil over the beech trees, and golden light in the forest. Why are only we human beings not allowed to be renewed each spring like the trees? Max, incidentally, gave the appearance of youthful elasticity. . . .

Here it has been summer since yesterday, and our balcony is becoming a wonderful asylum. At night the nightingale sings enchantingly, the lilac smells sweet, the little fountain splashes; it is lavishly beautiful. We have also started a vegetable garden together, with peas and beans, and each of us has cultivated a bigger piece than the other. . . .

Today Gundolf, Salz, Gruhle, the Radbruchs,[1] and Jaspers came to see us. We sat on rugs in the garden and then up in the vine arbor. Gundolf read poetry to us and was full of ideas. He is capable of imbuing a whole group with his intellect and his charming, happy disposition. We hardly said anything and only enjoyed the spring together.

Weber himself wrote to Helene in early summer: "Under overcast skies we are now having the full splendor of spring; the nightingales sing in the grove. In the evening we sat in the moonlight by the *Löwenbrunnen*; at the tea table the Troeltsches sat with a friend who played the violin and sang—and we were very happy."

In the old-fashioned interior, too, there was beauty. The large living room in particular, with its old furniture and its matching colors—dark green walls, a blue carpet—combined the old and the new to produce unity, and the living figures stood out from the background like *tableaux vivants* [*bewegte Bilder*]. A replica of the Charioteer of Delphi[2] that had been acquired in Rome kept silent watch; presumably it represented a slave, but its initial effect was to make one uneasy, for it reflected so much majesty. Three windows that extended almost to the floor let in almost the entire landscape through undivided panes, and if one stepped through the center door out on the spacious, pillar-supported balcony, one was enfolded by the sun and the smiling wealth of a blessed spot of earth which had been shaped

---

[1]Gustav Radbruch, 1879–1949, legal scholar and statesman, professor at Königsberg, Kiel, and Heidelberg, and his wife Lina.—Ed.
[2]A fragmentary bronze statue, possibly dating from 478 B.C., which depicts a prize-winning charioteer, thought to be a young aristocrat, at the Delphic Games.—Ed.

into a picture by nature and by human hands. Anyone was profoundly moved who saw for the first time how the sun setting over the river poured purple life over the reddish sandstone of the ruin of the castle or how the fragrant veil of September ennobled all colors and outlines. When Georg Simmel had that experience for the first time, he said: "This is *too* beautiful; one can't live with it."

In this environment the Webers were now able to enjoy their daily hours of leisure, and this was all they needed:

Here in the sunny house with this view in front and the shady wilderness in back it is so easy to dream and just vegetate like a plant and stretch toward the sun. But, of course, to be able to do a lot of mental work would be still finer. . . . The hard fate has taught us simply to surrender without a care to the sunshine and the fragrance of the blossoms. Then we no longer need any strong impressions. Oh, how could we ever tear ourselves away from this balcony with the red geraniums and the violet petunias! . . .

You are surprised that I am even more attached to the house than you are? But this is due to our respective natures. With me it is not so much loyalty as captivation by the living beauty with which I am allowed to live and which has poured its sweetness into all my veins. I am simply caught up in the earthly to a greater extent than you are. You are more indifferent to all phenomena; I love them and need them, whereas you are immune to their seduction.

Weber, who was not fond of hiking during his creative periods because it quickly exhausted him, now puttered about in the garden at noon and dreamed away the long summer evenings outdoors.

Max now no longer claims with such assurance that he would have equally enjoyed living on the main street and is remaining in the expensive apartment only for my sake. He gradually grows into the garden. For the past two weeks he has busied himself with the rose arbor for an hour every day. I am surprised that he has not completely shredded it up by now, but fortunately the Dutchman's-pipe [*Pfeifenkraut*] and the boxthorn [*Teufelszwirn*] keep putting out new creepers that have to be cut off or tied. And the roses, too, which are blooming wonderfully, have to be guided in the right direction. I hope he will gradually expand his sphere of activity, but unfortunately I cannot get him to go uphill at this time.

Even in the wintry darkness, when the meaning of existence was shaped by a person's own active strength more than it was in summer, there were hours consecrated by beauty.

The big Christmas tree in the dignity of its quietly glowing decorative lights in the festive room; the fragrant flowers which my dearest had given me; Berta's sensitive spirit and Linchen's happiness—all this was so peaceful and beautiful. Afterward we sat on the sofa together and were edified by *Faust* and the warmth between us. "Those lofty works, uncomprehended, are bright as in Creation's hour."[3]

* * *

Friends and clients of all kinds now came even more frequently than before:

Our life is full to the brim; every day there is a visitor, at least one searching soul. But frequently there are several: women and girls with lonely lives, prospective scholars, the older friends—they all come here. The magnificence of the setting—the cheerful balcony and the shady garden in back—gives pleasure. It is all very beautiful and rich, but some of it must be regarded as work. Yet there are also visitors who are not needy but are givers: of late there has been especially Stephan George, who is still a mystery to us in his human simplicity which is in such contrast to his complicated, solemnly pathos-filled poetry. He evidently feels drawn to Max—who has also acquired a friend in Gundolf, George's most important disciple—as a source of knowledge about the real life of our time. (December, 1910)

Weber himself supplied this humorous description of a day uncommonly rich in impressions:

Yesterday the menu was as follows: Slept well until eight. From 10:30 on: Gottl, who stayed for dinner and until the [male] typist came at 2:00. The latter stayed till 3:45 and left just when Lina Radbruch came. *Tête-à-tête* over tea and cake until 4:30, then + Gundolf and Salz (tea, juice, much cake), thus four of us until 5:15. Then exit Lina R., thus I, Gundolf, and Salz until six, then + Gothein and Honigsheim

---

[3] *"Die unbeschreiblich hohen Werke sind herrlich wie am ersten Tag"* —from the Prologue in Heaven, Goethe's *Faust,* Part I (Bayard Taylor's translation).—Ed.

till 6:45, then exit Gothein, somewhat later also exeunt Gundolf and Salz, thus Honigsheim and I until 7:30, then + Lask (first a tête-à-tête with him, then ensemble) until eight, then exit Lask. Supper with Honigsheim who remained until ten o'clock. Then Berta sent him away: "Frau Professor would really be angry." Then I turned on the electric light in my room to read the newspaper. Berta brought a lamp and turned off the electric light: "Herr Professor would only forget." Then slept tolerably well with a lot of bromide. Talked about the whole world + three villages.

* * *

Among the significant events of their first summer in the old house was the Webers' personal acquaintance with Stephan George. Thirteen years earlier, in the Freiburg period, Heinrich Rickert, one of George's first admirers, had tried to interest Weber in George's literary work. At that time there were the *Hymnen* [Hymns], the *Pilgerfahrten* [Pilgrimages], and the *Lieder der Hirten*.[4] Rickert recited these poems masterfully, but it was in vain; Weber remained completely indifferent toward the early poetry. He saw in it mainly an artistic estheticism that was of no concern to him. On the whole, lyric poetry that subtly depended upon a mood was little suited to the robust man at that time. But this had long since changed. The years of illness had deflected him from his course and had opened secret chambers of his soul that had previously been closed. He was now receptive to these artistic creations, which gave an ever new depth to feeling. He became absorbed in modern works of various kinds, particularly in Rilke[5] and George, and he now read poems aloud very beautifully.

That summer he sent his sister a collection of Rilke and wrote her:

I am sending you herewith one of the well-known collections of Rilke's poetry. Unless I am mistaken, you are not already acquainted with these things. I have marked a few that have especially impressed us—of course, not with the intention of influencing you or in the expectation that these particular poems will appeal to you. On the contrary, I am not sure of that at all and don't even know how much in the little volume will seem worthy of note to you. In R. there are occa-

---

[4]The correct title of George's third volume of poetry (1895) is *Die Bücher der Hirten-und Preisgedichte* [The Books of Eclogues and Eulogies].—Ed.
[5]Rainer Maria Rilke, 1875–1926, the Prague-born German poet.—Ed.

sional things that are downright tasteless, as is the case in some places and in some way with every mystic. And I would by *no* means say that this emotional world is congenial to me. Yet it seems to me that it is certainly worth knowing and that many things could acquire a significance of their own in certain hours. Enough; you will see for yourself! Actually, what do you know from Stephan George's circle, and do you know Maeterlinck's *The Treasure of the Humble?*. . .

I should like to say a few more words about Rilke. What you said about his metrical structure, especially about his letting lines with unstressed words fade away and break off, appears very apt to me. But at the same time it seems to me that this peculiarity, which does immediately strike one as alien and initially disturbing, is very closely connected with the inner meaning and rhythm of the poet and thus is justified to the extent that one accepts this very meaning as subjectively justified. I do not necessarily believe that these things are as "intentional" as they evidently seemed to you; rather, I believe that they reflect a sort of instinctive, subjectively necessary rebellion against that *form* of rhymed verse which is created in us by the need for melodious *completeness* with which we approach this art form. It is an attempt to free poetry with no logical content as far as possible from the requirements of the sonnet and that kind of poetry which directs its inner experience outward into "nature" in order to get it back from there *formed*.

Rilke is a mystic, and in character he is related to Tauler's[6] mysticism rather than to the ecstatic or semierotic (Bernardine)[7] kind. He is altogether not a formed personality *from* which poetry might break forth as its product. "He" does not write poetry, but "it is written" in him. Therein lies his limitation, but it is also his special quality. It seems to me that for this reason *he* regards the rhythmic completeness of the lines of fully formed poetry (Stephan George's, for example) as something that entails too great a loss in atmospheric substance, although any artistic *forming* is based on relinquishments of this kind. Restriction and limitation mark a master of form. And by breaking this metric law and by means of the delicate mood which is created when his verses are read with the proper modulation, Rilke would like to indicate as much as possible of the inexpressible and unformable of the underlying experience, to save it by giving it form,

[6]Johannes Tauler, ca. 1300–1361, Dominican preacher and mystic, associated with his native Strasbourg and with Basel.—Ed.
[7]The reference is to Saint Bernard of Clairvaux, 1090–1153, "the Mellifluous Doctor," a French monk, preacher, and mystical writer.—Ed.

as it were. It seems to me, too, that the question arises whether he is not using a means that is no longer an artistic one (even though it may not be exactly antiartistic). Yet I believe that it is not an "intended" allurement, not a pose or artifice, but the honest consequence of a necessity peculiar to him. (September 20, 1910)

Weber had immersed himself in George's poetry, too, for some time, and he had discussed it with Friedrich Gundolf. He was highly impressed by its great artistry, but he could not find in it the *religious* prophethood that the disciples ascribed to their master—just as he rejected any sort of cult created about a contemporary and any elevation of a human being to the position of an authority on *all* of existence as "deification of a living creature." Also, the poet's negative attitude toward the formative forces of modern culture struck him as alien and unfruitful, though Weber was keenly aware of what was wrong with this culture.

In particular, he regarded the aristocratic stance of the topical poems in *Der siebente Ring* [The Seventh Ring] and their aloofness and contempt for the masses as unbrotherly. He had inherited from his mother a deep reverence for the Gospels, and he resisted the pagan "religiosity" that venerated the highest meaning of existence in the *earthly* embodiment of the divine and that considered formed beauty, the *kalokagathia*[8] of the Greeks, the highest norm of human development. Since he believed in the absolute value of intellectual and moral autonomy, he denied the necessity of new forms of *personal* dominion and *personal* service for him and his kind. He acknowledged service and absolute devotion to a *cause*, an ideal, but not to an earthly, finite human being and its limited aims, no matter how outstanding and venerable that person might be.

In 1910, before his personal acquaintance with George, the work of a gifted woman[9] inspired Weber to make the following remarks:

It is not easy to stop discussing a phenomenon that has aspects of real greatness, like that of Stephan George. Thus I would place, for instance, a considerably higher value on *Das Jahr der Seele* [The Year of the Soul] in relation to his other works and also regard it as less *fahl* [pale] than you seem inclined to do. In many poems of this cycle I tend to

---

[8]The combination of goodness with beauty—the Greek ideal of education.—Ed.
[9]Presumably the writer Margarete Susman, 1872–1966, whose discussion of George in her book *Das Wesen der modernen deutschen Lyrik* (1910) brought her the honor of a visit from the poet.—Ed.

see entire provinces of emotional possibilities captured for expression, an expression that often disintegrates into an affected terseness and sublimation but is an expression nevertheless.

One has to go back to Hölderlin[10] to find this power of the artistic "I will not let thee go. . ."[11] again as it is manifested here and in some other places. It is easy to understand that in these creations George was seized by a feeling that he was saying what had never been said, like what Dante did in his *Vita Nuova*, and in his style generally slipped onto the plane of Dantesque pathos. There seems to be no doubt that a spark of that tremendous fire lives in him too. The enormous, panting labor of compressing things into the briefest, often incomprehensibly concise expression is part of this also. And it seems to me that a few basic reservations concerning his art as it is now developing are derived more from the significance that he attaches to his *"mission"* than from a lack of artistic capacity, although I fully agree with you that in the places where you have noticed such a lack the expression has really lagged behind the intention.

But the really questionable feature seems to me to lie in the following: the longer these poems are, the more they *intend* something. As it is, the George circle has all the characteristics of sect-formation, which includes the specific charisma of a sect, but the way in which the Maximin cult[12] has been carried on is absolutely "absurd," because try as one might, nothing can be said about this incarnation of a redeemer that could in any way make his divinity plausible to anyone but those who knew him personally. The poems of George, Wolfskehl,[13] and Gundolf are the clearest proof of this; I need hardly substantiate it. However, added to this is the fact that all of George's more recent productions demand, proclaim, promise, and propagate *Erlösung* [redemption], that in his collections *Der Teppich des Lebens* [The Tapestry of Life] and *Der siebente Ring* George himself steps out of the esthetic cloister in order to renew and rule the world from which he at first fled as an ascetic with esthetic characteristics, following the pattern of so many other ascetics.

By doing so he gives us the right to ask: "Redemption"—from what? And it seems to me that the only remaining positive goal is the striv-

---

[10]Friedrich Hölderlin, 1770–1843, German poet.—Ed.

[11]". . .except thou bless me" ["*Ich lasse dich nicht (,du segnest mich denn)*"]—Gen. 32:26.—Ed.

[12]George and his circle glorified and even deified a handsome, talented youth named Maximilian Kronberger. "Maximin" died of meninigitis in 1904, at the age of sixteen.—Ed.

[13]Karl Wolfskehl, 1869–1948, German-Jewish poet, essayist, and translator.—Ed.

ing for *self-deification*, for the immediate enjoyment of the divine in his
own soul. The road to this is either through ecstatic rapture or contemplative mysticism. The George school and George himself seem to
have chosen the former, because it is the only way that permits the
application of the Dantesque means of expression which are peculiar to
him. But this road—and this is its misfortune—never leads to a mystical experience (the sort of thing that Rilke undoubtedly knows in
its full purity, no matter what one's general judgment of him may be),
but invariably only to the orgiastic booming of a voice which then appears as an eternal voice. In other words, it never leads to *substance* but
only to the passionate sound of a harp. One promise of an enormous
experience that guarantees redemption is outdone by another, even
greater promise. Always new checks are drawn on what is to come,
although it is obvious that these cannot be honored. And since eventually this purely formal prophethood cannot be topped, the poet is embarked on a constant search for the postulated content of his prophecy, without ever being able to catch it. In my estimation, George has
come to a dead end with his latest cycle. So have his disciples (cf. *Jahrbuch für die geistige Bewegung* [Yearbook for the Intellectual Movement]),
insofar as they are not taking accustomed paths of criticizing rationalism, capitalism, and the like. (May 9, 1910)

In the fall of 1910 a derogatory article about the George circle appeared
in a periodical. It outraged the composer Paul von Klenau[14] who asked
Weber to express his opinion. Weber wrote:

It was with boundless astonishment that I found in this periodical an
article like that of R. B.[15] His views are, of course, his own affair.
In some respects I might be closer to him than I am to his adversaries,
and he also has a perfect right to express himself, no matter how vehement his factual presentation may be. I do not favor pussyfooting polemics. I suppose that in decisive points Stephan George and his pupils
in the final analysis serve "other gods" than I, no matter how highly
I may esteem their art and their intentions. This is not altered by
the fact that I do feel an inner necessity to give my unconditional,
purely *human endorsement* to the unvarnished, genuine seriousness with
which George personally faces his mission and to the sincerity and gen-

---

[14]Paul August von Klenau, 1883–1946, Danish-born musician.—Ed.
[15]"Intermezzo" by the German poet and essayist Rudolf Borchardt (1877–1945) appeared in
the *Süddeutsche Monatshefte*, Munich, VII, 12, December 1910, pp. 694–716.—Ed.

uine devotion with which Gundolf keeps faith with his cause and his master. But this certainly does not mean that I am obliged to or of a mind to subscribe to everything that the *Blätter für die Kunst*[16] and the *Jahrbuch für die geistige Bewegung* print. Anyone who is attacked by them may and should defend himself—with honest weapons, for no matter how one may feel about their position, I do not see any dishonest and unchivalrous means being employed by George's disciples, even where my attitude would have to be one of utter rejection.

However, the article by Mr. R. B., with whose person and intentions I have hitherto had no occasion to be out of sympathy, must be regarded as such a *serious lapse* that I simply cannot understand how it could have been published in the *Süddeutsche Monatshefte*. Even a man with the most passionate feelings had no right to reach for mud as an offensive weapon. Yet this is what has happened here. And that this happened in one of our best periodicals is an irreparable damage, caused not only to this publication. Passion may humanly excuse all sorts of things, but when it appears in public it is an *objective* indecency, an absolutely unpardonable event *for* the public. (Far be it from me to believe Mr. R. B. capable of subjectively indecent intentions.) (November 26, 1910)

* * *

When a visit from the poet was announced to Weber in summer of 1910 he was a bit embarrassed and wondered whether they would be able to communicate at all. But when they actually met, all the inhibitions created by the disciple-cult dissolved immediately. The master was entirely unaffected and behaved with simple dignity and cordiality. For that reason Weber was immediately ready to admire the extraordinary in him and to respond to the commanding weight of an aristocratic humanity grounded in inherent creative powers. Divergences of thought and feeling meant little in the face of the substance of being.

The two men, to be sure, seemed entirely different. They "incorporated" entirely different human possibilities and created their intellectual worlds with completely different tools. Weber did so with his reason, which suffused all material culture, with the help of a direct experience of reality and a graphic creative power. George fashioned his inner world with an in-

---

[16]The journal and publishing house founded in 1892 for the dissemination of George's and his disciples' works.—Ed.

tense strength of vision and plastic representation expressed in a beautiful, controlled, and individual linguistic structure. Both had a profound feeling of responsibility for their time. But while Weber accepted the forces of the present as they were, as material for shaping and as a mission, the other man saw only their devilish aspects and sought to overcome them by rejecting them. He conferred upon himself the office of a prophet and leader in a conversion and a transformation with a backward orientation. This Weber expressly rejected. He was able to appropriate the fruits of a poetic experience of the world and nourish his soul with them. George, on the other hand, had a negative attitude toward the products of scholarly knowledge of the world whose demands on the intellect would only have stifled his creative imagination and the shaping of his spiritual experience. But he presumably wished to derive from contact with the man himself that which he rejected in the strict conceptual language of books. After all, Weber knew how to make his knowledge come to life in the spoken word, and no inner experience was alien to him. Usually their conversations revolved about simple human matters, and in this they had no trouble communicating with each other. Now and then there were also discussions about ultimate values, and there Weber had to be careful not to overwhelm the poet dialectically. That is why he preferred to discuss with Gundolf his objections to the views of the circle. Some of this has been preserved by Marianne:

> Our discussion with Gundolf was occasioned by the programmatic statements in the *Jahrbuch für die geistige Bewegung*. There one of the disciples, at the behest of the master, had hurled an anathema at all of modern culture—rationalism, Protestantism, capitalism. Max's work on the Protestant ethic was adduced as evidence for the mechanizing effect of Protestantism. The modern "emancipated" and godless woman got hers as the "primary sacrilege" that impeded the production of heroes. For days we were engaged in combat with this damnation of everything contemporary that George demanded. In our discussion with Gundolf we immediately established the depth of the various positions. The George circle rejected ethical autonomy as an educational ideal and refused to recognize the value of the individual soul. Their "faith" was subordination to the authority of the hero, and for a woman, subordination to a man. George called for the fundamental subordination of a smaller person to a greater one, and by the latter he meant a person distinguished by greater *cultural* achievements. As Gundolf expressly stated in his essay *Vorbilder* [Models], he sought release from subjectiv-

ism in a *renunciation* of an individual's full potential for development. We, however, affirm the right of the individual to the development that is possible for him and believe that the growth of a soul is impeded if it lets an erring human being prescribe laws for it and sacrifices its convictions even if it feels that the other person is wrong. And the real conflict between the various beliefs begins only at the point where another person starts making improper demands. In our estimation, a person with religious beliefs can subject himself to the commandments of a *god* and become great in this subjection to a divine will. But he cannot do so if he subjects his conscience as a matter of principle to a "hero," no matter how great, who is earthly and who thus errs, let alone to some other mortal.

On Friday, December 1, a long, unintended discussion between Max and Gundolf. The basic questions came up, and at last that degree of sincerity has been created which we have long desired. Gundolf could not feel that he was being attacked, for he had sounded the battle call himself. His modesty, despite his rigid position, was so beautiful, and our enjoyment of him remained quite undiminished. We can go along with George's disciples to a very great extent: with their longing for the integration of the individual into a totality and for a release from the ego-cult, with their endeavor for new forms of inner structure and a new "law." But the cornerstone of the doctrine—the deification of earthly human beings and the founding of a religion centering about George (and, as Gundolf indicated, this already is the intention of the circle)—appears to us like the self-deception of people who are not fully equal to living in the present. . . .

On Monday, then, the master came. I had assumed that he wished to see both of us and was bold enough to be present. And it was beautiful and full of spirit at the end. Conversations about Georg and Gertrud Simmel, about the special sensitivity of women, about women in general—and then there came a moment when George presumably wanted to discuss the "program." But we were not certain, and began talking about Paris, Christianity, Protestantism, and subjectivism. This had brought us to the threshold of the topical, and Max boldly stepped on it, when George wished to use him as a compurgator in his testimony against modern women. George bent his furrowed leonine head quite close to me, his sunken pupils flashed forth, and he asked: "Do you believe that all men can sit in judgment on themselves?" —"Not that all *can* do so, but that it is an ultimate goal to make them ready for it." —"And *you* want to be your own judge?" —"Yes, we do." Then we argued quite intimately, and possibly he did sense some faith behind our "sacrilege." But what was particularly beautiful was that he made a point of taking the sting out of that insult in the *Jahrbuch* and cared about maintaining friendly relations despite our basic opposition. He even went so far as to say that we had misunderstood everything and that he had not meant *us*. This, to be sure, I could take only as an expression of amiable sentiments and not as "truth." He was here for two hours, and when Gundolf came to pick him up, we felt closer to one another than before. Perhaps he can still be kept from becoming rigid. We are still very much under the spell of this man who conceives of his poetic profession as a prophet's office. Justifiably so? But his will is certainly great. (December, 1911)

The day before yesterday Stephan George came to see us again. We had already given him up in thought, since he had been in town for several weeks without letting us hear from him. Can it be that the contact with what is alien to his nature is too much of a shock for him? But then he did come, and by our joy we knew how much we venerate him as a human being. We sat in the ivy grotto by the well, and this time it was quite effortlessly cozy and warm. He opened up more than was his wont and said beautiful and profound things. Some of them derived from Nietzsche, such as his remarks about evil as a universal principle that could not be combatted with weak arms and intellectual weapons, about the blessings of war for a heroic humanity and the meanness of struggle in peacetime, about our enervation through the increasing pacification of the world which even made it impossible for the likes of us to butcher a chicken. He too admitted his incapacity for this heroic act. Then about Othello and Iago and their "cosmic" significance. My view of Othello as very agonizing and frightful, almost a product of an extreme coldness of heart, struck him as a purely psychological, false, and effeminate interpretation. "My child, my child! You must view it as something cosmic, not as an individual fate."

When we spoke of the significance of the steadily increasing intellectual struggles of modern man which perhaps produce *spiritual* heroism rather than the physical kind, he said: "Miscreant, miscreant! You want to keep turning everything into spirit and thereby you destroy the body." He apparently does not realize that he, more than anyone, needs highly refined people as a sounding board, not the intrepid killers of earlier times. But what are "viewpoints"? Warmth, humanity, and vigor flowed from him, and we could not help but love that. There is more to him than his Zarathustrian views. (June, 1912)

But George's liking for the differently constituted Weber and his unaffected attitude toward him did not last. Their divergent interpretations of the World War and different views of the attitude of the Germans may, among other things, have come between them. Despite and beside the fearful, impersonal machinery of murder, Weber saw heroic greatness and self-sacrificing devotion at home and on the battlefield. He experienced at first hand how ordinary men worked for goals they did not fully understand, how obedient they were, and what touching patience they had. The events had a different reflection in the soul of the poet. For him the tragedy of the world and of the German people was the just consequence of accumulated misdeeds. ". . . *Angehäufte Frevel/Von allen Zwang und Glück genannt, verhehlter/Abfall von Mensch zur Larve heischen Busse . . . Das nötige Werk der Pflicht bleibt stumpf und glanzlos/und Opfer steigt nicht in verruchter Zeit. . . .*"[17] He never came again.

* * *

As a counterbalance, each year continued to bring another beloved figure, Friedrich Naumann. By contrast with George, he was among Weber's friends the most significant embodiment of a struggle that was concerned with the present. Marianne wrote:

> They are polarities, and I am glad to have an insight into both. If we had to choose between them as life-shaping forces, we would probably reach for Naumann, because he combines the world-penetrating power of brotherly love with a strong and plastic sense of reality. But fortunately we do not have to choose; in our souls the artistic gospel coexists quite amicably with social concerns. It is certainly inconsistent to give space to two such dissimilar forces, but it is beautiful to feel the wealth of life in the tension between the two.

In 1912 Naumann lost the seat he had won with such great effort. The counterpressure of a materialistic policy of interests in his election district was too great. Once again the people refused to follow one of their best men, possibly the only *humanly* great leader of the time. The Webers were greatly upset and feared that, deprived of a political effectiveness attained

---

[17]". . . Accumulated misdeeds, called compulsion and good fortune by all, stealthy decline from man to ghoul demand atonement . . . The necessary work of duty remains dull and lusterless, and sacrifices do not get off the ground in depraved times . . ."—from George's wartime poem *Der Krieg* [The War], included in the collection *Das Neue Reich* [The Kingdom Come], 1928.— Ed.

so late in life, Naumann would suffer a severe nervous and psychological shock. The entire foundation of his existence seemed endangered. They were all the more surprised and pleased when Naumann called on them right after his defeat, unbroken and calm.

Naumann stayed with us for two days. We have rarely experienced his unpretentious greatness, strength, and fullness as much as we did after this defeat. He came to us from all the leave-taking in Heilbronn. We expected to find him tired and sad, but he completely transcended himself in magnificent nobility. He is a heroic character, and he also has a wonderful greatheartedness for everything human and an abundance created by the mixture of artistic feeling and artistic creative power. Undoubtedly his struggle for existence has brought about certain restrictions in his psyche: he is indifferent to individual destinies. He only sees the economic and political forces, the masses, the people.

* * *

From the opposite pole of the *Weltanschauung* the Webers also met some philosophers from Eastern Europe who were becoming known around that time, particularly the Hungarian, Georg von Lukács,[18] with whom the Webers struck up a close friendship. He was then working on an esthetics that was intended as part of a future system and was to pave the way to an academic career for him. Weber became absorbed in it and remarked about it:

My impression is a very strong one, and I am quite sure that the posing of the problem is the definitively correct one. It is a boon that the "work" as such is now finally given voice after attempts to write esthetics from the standpoint of the receiver and more recently from that of the creator. I am curious to see how it will be when your concept of *form* emerges. After all, not only the value-containing elements [*das Werthafte*] which rise above the experiential are formed life; the *erotic* elements, which dip into deep and outermost corners of the "dungeon," are formed as well. They share the fate of the guilt-burdened with all formed life, and in the quality of their opposition to everything that belongs to the realm of the "form-alien" [*formfrem-*

---

[18]1885–1971, the noted Marxist philosopher and literary critic.—Ed.

den] god they are even close to the esthetic. The topographical position
of the erotic must be determined, and I am anxious to see where it
will be in your work.

Weber was also impressed by Lukács's profound artistic essay about the poor
in spirit[19] in which the creative power of love that brings about salvation is conceded the right to break through the ethical norm.

These young philosophers were moved by eschatological hopes of a new
emissary of the transcendent God, and they saw the basis of salvation in
a socialist social order created by brotherhood. For Lukács the splendor of
inner-worldly culture, particularly its esthetic side, meant the Antichrist,
the "Luciferian" competition against God's effectiveness. But there *was* to
be a full development of this realm, for the individual's choice between it
and the transcendent must not be facilitated. The final struggle between
God and Lucifer is still to come and depends on the decision of mankind.
The ultimate goal is salvation *from* the world, not, as for George and his
circle, fulfillment *in* it.

The intellectual atmosphere provided by these men stimulated Weber's
already strong interest in the Russians. For a long time he had been planning a book about Tolstoy that was to contain the results of his innermost experiences. Helene and Marianne cared greatly about this plan and he
wanted to write the book for them. But the projects that he had already
started left him no time for it. However, now and then he liked to seek
contact with Tolstoy's and Dostoevski's compatriots:

The day before yesterday we sat in the café quite unrespectably until
3 A.M., and it was your son who kept us spellbound and was deaf to all
reasonable governesslike arguments. It happened like this: The Russian
students were celebrating the fiftieth anniversary of their reading
room and got Max, who used to make a lot of use of this room, to
address them on their festive evening. He really wanted to cancel this
engagement on short notice after sleeping badly—but for once I
wanted to break this devilish spell and did not let him do so. It was
a strange celebration. People attired for a ball, then three serious
speeches, an endless musical program, and toward one o'clock the beginning of the dance. Unfortunately Max had to break off his address be-

---

19"*Von der Armut im Geiste,*" a short story written by Lukács in 1912. In the form of a dialogue it reveals the thoughts of a young man who has decided to kill himself following the suicide of his beloved.—Ed.

cause it was getting so late and he also had inhibitions about saying the most profound things in a ballroom. It was the first time that he made a public speech here again that was duly scheduled and contracted for. He was a bit tired, but he did bring himself to produce something that aimed at perfection. The only pity was that he stopped before the decisive point. Then he was alert again and felt like talking; we finally sat in the café with our philosophers until about three o'clock. (December 21, 1912)

* * *

The circle of younger friends, usually young scholars who sought an exchange of ideas with Weber, grew constantly. He therefore tried to think of ways of satisfying their needs without losing too much of his working time. The Webers would have liked to keep the doors of their beautiful home open, but his fluctuating strength meant that he always had to be careful. Thus they decided to have open house for young people on Sunday afternoons during the semester, though not without doubts whether Weber would be able to endure such a constraint. Their young friends were pleased and immediately showed up in large numbers. But they were still strangers to one another, and in the traditional German fashion they were gauche and taciturn. Nor had the Webers mastered the art of social discourse. Weber found only significant intellectual exchange or intimate conversations about personal matters worthwhile. Informal conversation about less weighty matters made him feel almost as awkward as he had once felt at a dance or a flirtation.

Thus the first "Sunday" was hard work; the ice was not broken and the company did not fuse. There was no exchange about substantial matters. Only when half the people had left was there a sparkling, witty, lively conversation between Weber and Gundolf about reverence for the cultural creations of the past. Gundolf approved of their preservation only as a resource for an age without creative power of its own; he would have preferred to destroy them. When the guests had finally left, Weber angrily slammed the door to his room shut behind him: "Never again—having to talk insufferably and immorally for the sake of talking!" However, the second Sunday was quite lively and familylike: "This time we were reassured. This sort of thing works when the people warm up to one another and we don't torture ourselves spreading valuable conversations over larger groups. It seems that our closer friends also come on weekdays anyway."

From that time on these gatherings almost always gave Weber pleasure. After all, they were his only regular opportunity to pour forth his wealth before a larger group. He did not trouble himself with individual guests, but he did deal with the youngest students' questions with as much friendliness and interest as he did with those of important colleagues. He would sit in some corner of the large room, appropriated by the men. Usually everyone wanted to hear what was going on in that corner, so there was general productivity only during Weber's occasional absences. "I simply weigh upon these people," was his interpretation of this. Only a few of the guests, like Gundolf or Lukács, were able to express their ideas well enough to become independent points of interest.

When the style of these gatherings, which were designed for young people, had been established, the Webers also asked friends their own age who were inwardly young enough not to overwhelm the young people. Now all the chords of the intellectuality of the time were struck. Frequently guests from out of town also enriched the Sunday circle. On a few occasions the atmosphere was set by Georg and Gertrud Simmel. Now and then Theodor Heuss and Elly Heuss-Knapp,[20] husband and wife who were active in the political and social fields, came from Heilbronn. Two political economists, Professor Altmann and his wife Elisabeth Gottheiner,[21] frequently came from Mannheim. There also were the physiologist E. J. Lesser[22]—who much admired Weber—and his wife, another daughter of the veteran scholar Friedrich Knapp, who worked in art.

Sometimes disparate patterns were created. Men from various worlds— the common bond seems to have been only the German language—had to deal with one another:

On Sunday Naumann came, and with a bleeding heart I received our other guests by myself. Finally the two men deigned to bestow some of their light upon us, and we succeeded in getting Naumann to tell stories. A new Jewish philosopher happened to be there—a young man with an enormous crown of black hair and an equally enormous self-

[20]Theodor Heuss, 1884–1963, statesman, historian, and author; president of the Federal Republic of Germany, 1949–59. Elly Heuss-Knapp, 1881–1952, social and cultural historian, feminist, and author.—Ed.
[21]S. P. Altmann, 1878–1931, professor of economics and finance at Mannheim and Heidelberg. His wife, who also taught at Mannheim, lived from 1874 to 1930.—Ed.
[22]Edmund J. Lesser, 1852–1918, physiologist, director of the Clinic for Dermatology and Veneral Diseases at the University of Berlin from 1897 on.—Ed.

assurance. He evidently regarded himself as the precursor of a new Messiah and wanted to be recognized as such. From the height of his apocalyptic speculations he directed all sorts of questions to Naumann, who was very amiable but obviously had the impression that he was dealing with someone a bit cracked.

Many of their young friends were Jewish, and there were unconstrained discussions of the problems of Judaism. Echoes of an "important discussion" of Zionism with E. J. Lesser have been preserved in a letter to Lesser in which Weber admits the possibility of a colonization of Palestine but does not see this as a solution for the spiritual problems of Judaism. He formulates the solution as he sees it as follows:

Judaism and especially Zionism has as its inner premise a *highly* concrete "promise." Will a profitable colony, an autonomous small state, hospitals, and good schools ever act as a "fulfillment" of those grandiose promises, or will they to a much greater extent be a critique of them? And even a university? For its *meaning*—which would certainly be a heterogeneous one in relation to the economic purpose of the settlement—would be that the Jews' feeling of *dignity* could be restored by the existence and the intellectual possession of this ancient holy place in this form—just as once the Jewish Diaspora was sustained by the realm of the Maccabees after its war of independence against the world empire of the Seleucids; as the Germans all over the world were sustained by the German Empire; and Islam was sustained by the existence of the caliphate. But Germany is, or at least seems to be, a *powerful* empire and the realm of the caliph still occupies an extensive territory. But what can the Jewish state at best be today? And what about a university that would offer only the same things as the others? It would certainly not be a matter of indifference, but it still could not be compared to the old *temple.*

What, then, is the chief lack? *It is the temple and the high priest.* If *these* existed in Jerusalem, everything else would be of secondary importance. It is true that a devout Catholic also demands a pontifical *state*, though it be of the smallest dimension. But even without one, and even more without one, his feeling of dignity is enhanced by the fact that the politically powerless Pope in Rome, as the purely spiritual ruler of a people of 200 million, is infinitely *more* than the "king" of Italy, and that everyone feels this. A hierarch of 12 million in the world (who mean what the Jews simply are not and do not mean!)—that, of course, *would* be something of really great significance for the

Jews' feeling of dignity, and it does not matter whether they are believers or not. But where is Zadok's stock?[23] Where are there the
Orthodox who would submit to such a hierarch, who would be
permitted—by the law!—to allow him even one-tenth of the importance which the Pope has in every diocese and parish, far more by virtue
of the disciplina morum [discipline of manners] and the universal bishopric
than by virtue of his relatively very insignificant infallibility? Where
is it possible to do anything like that today? It seems to me that the
real problems of Zionism are bound up with the fact that this is where
the values would lie that really concern the Jewish national feeling of
dignity but are closely connected with religious conditions. (August
18, 1913)

* * *

The Webers' circle seemed remarkably free of everyday pressures. They lived
secure lives, with the heady feeling that they were citizens of a flourishing,
respected community. However, far from being sated, they constantly
struggled for greater inner depth and were always fully aware of how deeply
they were indebted to those strata of the people who were underpinning
this high-pitched life with their manual labor. Everyone strove for inner
self-realization or for the completion of his work, and almost every other
person did some writing. Evidently there were too few other forms of expression and creativity for the store of German intelligence. Some of the women, too, wrote or created works of art. And in addition to one's own productivity there was also time to become absorbed in the writings of one's
friends. Lovely ornamentation surrounded the serious creations. In the fall
of 1912 Weber wrote to Helene:

Yesterday we had the Janus group here. Marianne spoke about Greek
matrimony, well and charmingly with a spirited discussion. Today we are
"at home." The old rooms are surprised after such a long solitude, but
I think they are glad, because this is appropriate for them. On the average we have one visitor on each of five weekdays. Naturally this takes
away some of my productive strength, but should we give it up?

---

[23]The house of the priest Zadok (cf. I Chron. 5:34, II Sam. 19:12, 2:35) ruled as high priests
until the time of the Hasmoneans. The "sons of Zadok" are mentioned in the Dead Sea
Scrolls.—Ed.

* * *

In one respect, then, the Sundays did not fulfill their purpose. Visitors continued to come on weekdays; old friends refused to settle for the Sunday gatherings. In fact, by regular attendance on Sundays many acquaintances earned the right to have private audiences, and the Webers themselves could no longer imagine their working days without the adornment of a few hours of an intimate exchange of ideas. Only in the evening did they usually observe complete quiet. But, despite this, it sometimes became too much, especially when dear visiting relatives had to be fitted into their daily schedule for weeks:

> Our life is very unquiet, and sometimes we find the people who make such demands upon us a bit merciless. There has never been such a swarm as this summer. We could no longer absorb all of the various impressions. I have only a blurred recollection of the warm summer evenings under the catalpa trees with ever-changing faces. Now and then there were Chinese lanterns and nice singing to lute accompaniment by Troeltsch's young friend Maag.[24]. . .
>
> The pace of life keeps quickening and threatens to make us breathless and chase us hither and thither, more and more hastily and inexorably. But no, we won't let ourselves be treated this way. Why all this variety that rushes in upon us, why are we wearing ourselves out? Is it not more fruitful to have a deeper relationship with a few, to be a lot to a few rather than being a little to many?

At that time Weber used to get up at about 7:30, if he had spent a restful night. Often, however, he slept until late in the morning in order to get the seven to eight hours of rest that he needed. Marianne protected his morning's sleep, for she never knew what kind of a night he had had. Sometimes he read letters and the newspaper in bed, at other times he read them at the breakfast table. The paper he read "diagonally"— taking in the headlines of a whole page at one glance. Then he leisurely set his work in motion. Once he had become absorbed, particularly in his own production, he paid no attention to external events and was immune to disturbances. His main working hours were from 9:30 to 12:30; before lunch he would be lured outside for a while. After the punctual midday meal,

---

[24]Otto Maag, later a journalist in Basel.—Ed.

which was finished in barely a quarter of an hour—the longer meals in the large family circle used to make him very impatient—he slept a little, refreshed himself with some tea, and then usually worked from 2:30 until company came, or else until evening. Thus he devoted about five to six hours to scholarly work. Business correspondence was usually taken care of on certain days. After the evening meal he generally had to have a complete rest and deliberately turn off his thinking machine.

It seemed incredible that before his illness Weber had been able to work half the night and then sink into a deep sleep. Now he daydreamed outside or on the sofa in his wife's room. They kept quiet and only exchanged occasional warm words. At 10:00 he went to bed. To conserve his productive energy for the next day, he spent his evenings in strict seclusion for many years—except on trips, when he was allowed to live as he pleased. Upon returning home he was then able to attend an occasional concert in the evening or see some friends. After an intellectual exertion he would sit in the room with a cigar for a long time in order to unwind.

* * *

The summer of 1911 was an especially memorable one, marvelously hot, an unparalleled riot of sun. The lawn dried out and shriveled fruit fell from the trees. But the light southern blaze gave people an unreal, blissful existence. Despite full alertness all striving seemed to be stilled and the struggle ended. Weber's constant yearning for warmth was assuaged. He worked during the day and enjoyed the long evenings in the cool, darkening garden. Glowworms, which had slept in the ivy by day, danced a starry roundelay, and the celestial luminaries sparkled through the branches. The sweet harmonies of old folk songs came from the mouth of a youth: *Es ist ein Schnitter, der heisst Tod . . .*[25] Weber would sing the song aloud, pick out the melody on the new piano they had recently acquired, and wait for his soul to be awakened.

For the past ten days it has been quiet—vacation. No people and no pressing duties. Just reading, dreaming, writing, and the radiant sum-

---

[25]"There is a reaper called Death. . ."—the beginning of the old "Harvest Song" which is included in *Des Knaben Wunderhorn*, the celebrated collection of German folk poetry. It has been set to music by Jacobus Balde, Mendelssohn, Schumann, and others, and has been sung in Catholic churches.—Ed.

mer. On the shady lawn under the copper beeches a wreath of begonias is now really gleaming, and fuchsias are blooming under the catalpas. At night, when the storm lantern is on the ground of the grotto and shines a bit from below on the catalpa branches and the arbor roof, when the darkness opens up in back and a yellow gleam of light comes from the windows, then it is as in a deep, dark forest near a fairy-tale house. And deep down strength for new productivity accumulates. . . .

Yesterday was a marvelous quiet Sunday. In the morning a nacreous gleam lay over the familiar things and transported them into a strange stillness. Time held its breath. The bluish phlox swayed dreamily on their tall bushes—a gentle, plentiful bliss. In the afternoon the two of us sat together in the garden. The sun asserted its power and restored everything to reality. But the quenched gratitude remained. Were we happy? I think we were. Happy and contented without anything happening. The beauty of the summer dream was sheer plenitude.

The moonlit nights were dreamed away on the balcony. The fragrance of catalpa blossoms enveloped the house. The silver disc of the moon slowly rose behind the firs on the mountain slope and threw a sparkling ribbon into the dark river, which was now rushing softly. The little fountain babbled. The ruin emerged ghostlike through the veil of night. Earthly weight melted away. The secret of the world whispered in the souls that were anxious about the eternity of all great and beautiful things, that longed for their own eternity. But there was no grasping it. "Alas! Why, ye gods, is all, all eternal, our happiness alone fleeting?"[26]

II

At that time (1911) a highly important member of Weber's older circle of friends, Georg Jellinek, passed away. When soon thereafter his daughter got married, Weber painted a wonderful picture of his friend for the children. Like other documents of this kind that had come into being in solemn hours, it unintentionally revealed some traits of Weber's own personality. The men were very different in structure, but Weber's words about the

---

[26]Ach! warum, ihr Götter, ist unendlich alles, alles, endlich unser Glück nur!—from Goethe's play Pandora. —Ed.

world-conquering humor of his friend could apply to himself as well. This address shall be preserved here as a memorial to both men.

In the discussion of matrimony at the beginning of the Old Testament, the idea is expressed that the partners leave their parents in
order to belong to each other forever. And this is the way it is outwardly, and in the beginning inwardly as well—particularly for a young
woman to whom happiness comes in the bright morning of her unbroken
life, beautiful as a dream, apparently transforming everything and oblit-
erating her whole past. Now the two model themselves for and after
each other, facing entirely new, unexperienced destinies which then,
forming and shaping, lay hold of the young life and turn it into a
human fate that is independent and seems to be detached from the
soil of its own past. And yet: *Nach dem Gesetz, wonach du
angetreten*[27]—something that has once been put into us does not
easily remain lost.

This fate takes different forms with different people, depending on
their individuality. I do not know whether it was the same in our parents' generation as it is with us, and it probably is different with each
individual among us. If I view our young woman correctly, then she, like
so many of us, has inherited, in addition to so many other qualities,
the fine, fateful gift of thoughtful self-contemplation as well as the
inner need to make use of it. And I have often seen in similar people
that during the life and growth of the marriage there came for the
young wife in the midst of the brightest radiance of happiness—sooner,
later, at some time—hours of a peculiar loneliness which her husband's
ardent love for her and her ardent love for him could not eradicate.
It happens this way—or in a different form. Always there is something
that reaches for her with invisible hands: her own nature, her home,
all that the past promised her and imposed upon her. Slowly she seems
to slide back into the paths of her nature and early history: *So musst
du sein, dir kannst du nicht entfliehen.*[28] Have I become what I was able
to become? And what was that? What did the heritage and tradition
of my parental home give me? An outsider is perhaps permitted to remind the daughter of the house that this question will be coming;
but it then behooves him to stop, for he cannot dare to answer it.

---

[27]"In accordance with the law by which you have started out"—from Goethe's *Urworte.
Orphisch.* —Ed.
[28]"This is how you must be; you cannot escape yourself"—from Goethe's *Urworte. Orphisch.*—
Ed.

Instead, however, he may be permitted to acknowledge, to the extent that he is able to do so, what these parents have meant and still mean to him.

Permit me in this gathering to mention first the deep reverence that has for many years bound me to the woman whom we see wearing a widow's veil today. Her passionate desire for clarity and truth, her resolute rejection of all half-way measures and compromises, her striving for unequivocal decisions, the proud assurance of her personality—all this is rooted in a strong, austere sense of dignity that is not at all bound by convention, and in a complete absense of any fear of people, something that has repeatedly comforted me in the midst of all the things that surround us. This has given her an inner sovereignty in the face of life and its dispensations, including pain and death.

At first glance the man who is always and everywhere among us today seemed to be quite different in many ways. When I was called to Heidelberg fourteen years ago, I came from somewhat complicated circumstances. On the basis of some things that had happened here I thought I was getting into a far more difficult situation, and, as things stood, especially as far as my relationship to the man about whom I am talking was concerned. Instead I stand here under the spell of a debt of gratitude for a friendship and loyalty on the part of the older man, who was so much more mature at that time, such as have seldom been offered me, a friendship that truly makes it hard for me to speak about this man, for it may bring his figure too close to my eyes.

I soon realized that this man cultivated lasting close friendships with men of the most diverse personalities and sometimes with extremely difficult men, friendships that meant something to them. To mention only two, there were men of such dissimilar natures as Erwin Rohde[29] and Georg Friedrich Knapp. He was a conciliatory man in the broadest and best sense, always inclined to get along with people and meet them half way, to view things and men from their various sides, to take realities into account, to balance means, results, and all objections carefully one against the other, a man who was averse to one-sided and prejudiced decisions and views. And yet: the temperament, the ways, and the limitations of this born scholar were surely different from those of the very ambitious representative of the interests of her sex—but in the decisive point he was in complete agreement with her.

---

[29] 1845–1898, classical philologist, professor at Kiel, Jena, Tübingen, Leipzig, and Heidelberg.—Ed.

Bismarck spoke of the *Portepée* [sword knot] by which one had to grab his old emperor to get an immediate reaction, and this also applied to this man who seemed to be infinitely obliging and prudent.

We should never forget that he, an impecunious man, at a time when all professors complained—as they still complain—about infringements on the part of ministries, was among the few who flung their professorships in the government's face when he was treated shabbily. That was just it: the decisive point where even his conciliatory attitude changed to relentless unyieldingness lay where matters of personal dignity were involved. He respected the dignity of others. I have heard him talk about outstanding scholars wittily but never nastily (the latter being a bad professorial custom). And thus he demanded that others respect his dignity and he watched over his reputation. He also desired recognition of his accomplishments and made no secret of his claim that he was good at his profession.

This claim was truly well founded. In our present group I need not discuss him as a scholar. But I, in particular, should mention the very substantial stimulation I received from his major works for what fate has granted me to accomplish. To touch on only a few details: the separation of naturalistic and dogmatic thinking in the *System der subjektiven öffentlichen Rechte* [System of the Subjective Public Laws] for problems of methodology; the creation of the concept of "social political science" for the clarification of the blurred tasks of sociology; the demonstration of religious influences in the genesis of the "human rights" for the investigation of the importance of religious elements in areas where one would not expect to find them. And permit me to say also that I, along with many others, have always regarded it as a product of a very specific "stupidity" of people and institutions among us that this man who was among the few with an international reputation in their subject, who represented this subject in an entirely original manner, who year in and year out attracted a large and yet select group of students, nevertheless was excluded from the top positions in which he belonged and that the great artistry of his pedagogical talent was barred from a wide-ranging effectiveness and remained limited to our small university—surely to its benefit and for the enjoyment of us, his local friends.

He got over it, for in the personality of this man, who from his youth on had to contend with various physical and emotional defects, humor, his own kind of humor, was an element of surpassing significance. Let it be understood that it was not a matter of his being "witty," although he surely was that in a high degree. Anyone who ever had the experience of hearing one of his own stories retold by him, prepared for circulation and polished like a gem, fully recognized his great artistry, including the purely formal kind, in this area. Among living men I am acquainted only with the wit of Alfred Dove—and I am told that Joseph Unger's[30] is similiar to his—which is like our friend's in that it manages, by strictly eliminating everything "irrelevant," to extract the substance of genuine humor from a situation or a combination of ideas and to weld it into a unit.

But what is involved here is something entirely different. Humor is not simply wit. Cervantes is not a mocker—and the intellectual quality of our friend that I am talking about was akin to Cervantes' sense for the grotesque as the ineluctable destiny of pure intentions when an attempt is made to realize them in the face of the limitations prevailing in the existing world. But this "humor" in its finest and highest manifestations leads to one of the last possible attitudes of a man toward life in general. After all, our actions and sufferings are woven out of meaningful and meaningless elements and shaped into a "fate." And by seizing this ultimate core of life and placing it before us, genuine humor in its finest sense presents us with hearty, healthy, good, liberating laughter, which is far removed from any mockery. This is precisely what our friend was able to give us in his good hours. And in back of it there was not the attitude of "romantic irony" which is modern again today. For neither in him nor in his wife was there a Romantic vein. In this respect he was not rooted in our foggy, fantastic north, but was in his innermost being a "classical" nature. Filled as he was with that urge for clarity that also stamped the personality of his wife, albeit in a very different form, his home could very well have been in the marketplace of Athens.

One final thing. His descent and the traditions of his family had given him something of that delicate fragrance which comes to us from the gentle and pure emotional world of the Orient. We think here not only of the great purity and goodness in the innermost human core of his being, not only of the way in which the sparkling gem of his intellect was set in the pure gold of his disposition, a quality that gave us profound human pleasure without our being able to express it in words. We think, rather, of that peculiarly sovereign attitude of the spirit toward the world which always returned to its equilibrium and remained in it after all mutations of passing moods, an attitude we may call "worldly wisdom" in the sense of the ancient Orient. When

---

[30]1821–1913, Austrian jurist and government official, professor at Prague and Vienna.—Ed.

he was inwardly quite strong, in his best hours, there was a gentle gleam of that wisdom in him, and this became the source of the best of what I mean by his "humor." Viewed in this light, this humor is not only one of the great masters and conquerors of that humdrum existence [Alltag] whose paralyzing power has already been mentioned, but also one of the forms which enable us to realize that human dignity need not bow even to the strength of the gods.

This kind of humor also contributed to this wonderfully complete, happy marriage which remained at its height from the first day on, until a quick, beautiful, and dignified death ended it at the proper time, before sickness or old age could cloud his wife's image of the sweetheart of her youth. It was a death he saw and accepted, envied by us today who have completely forgotten how to die and to accept another person's departure with dignity. It would not be in his spirit if today we dwelled in mourning and depression on that which we have lost by his passing.

14

TRAVEL PICTURES _____

I

In those years, too, traveling continued to be very necessary for Weber. And if he sometimes in a nervous state threatened to move back into a three-room apartment on the main street, he was probably worried about whether he would have enough money left for his travel needs. The great claims made on his time and energy, and his still fluctuating productive strength, meant that he needed regular relaxation away from home. "The many evenings of gabbing are taking their toll. Max is sleeping badly and is very ill-tempered and depressed. Productivity and an expenditure of personal energy simply are not compatible for us. He has to get away so he can forget about his condition." When the sun went into hiding for a long time, particularly in the spring, Weber still spoke of moving to Italy. Besides the periodic exhaustion of his mental faculties, the reason for his restlessness was probably his need to break up his everyday life—which did not offer him enough responsible action—with new impressions. He regularly celebrated the end of the winter on the other side of the Alps, now usually by himself, and these periods served more for the restoration of his strength than for the garnering of fresh impressions. Sometimes he made physiological experiments: he fasted or went hungry for prolonged periods in order to observe the effect on himself and possibly also to assure himself that he was independent of material requirements and everyday habits.

The following excerpts from letters convey something of his experiences in the south.

Lerci,[1] April 2, 1910

The trip in the *diligenza* [stagecoach] to Sarzana took us through endless olive groves, which cover everything here, to the great bay of the Magra plain.[2] In the old hick town [Nest] there is nothing to see except a Gothic marble church that is beautiful on the inside. But there is a wonderful view, across mulberry fields and vineyards, green vegetable and corn fields, of the Apuanian Alps—which I once saw with Mother from Fiesole—towering as the last thing on the northern side, to the far right. Then we went by carriage to the mouth of the Magra River and back by boat across the foothills. The sea might have been too choppy for you, but the greenish-white crests in their eternal crowding and pushing under low clouds were nice, and so was the coming in of the colorful fishing fleet with its red, yellow, and white sails afterward. Behind it lay the colossal battleships, shapeless and black.
. . .

Yesterday afternoon I went over to Porto Venere in a sailboat—a beautiful trip there through the white lace veil of the little pointed waves, but on the way back the man, fearful because of the stronger wind, tied us to an empty freighter, and now the little boat tossed back and forth, filled up with water, and we got home soaking wet.
. . . Today we have a wild sirocco again, with a roar and pouring rain. At times the sun comes out, and then it is alternately mild and cold. The waves come into the inner harbor and right up to the street, the steamers lurch terrifically, and the battleships lie deep in the dockyard of La Spezia. A beautiful green crest-covered sea. All mountains close enough to touch, all colors with a greenish iridescence. All birds quiet. Green, yellow, violet, and a harsh blue dominate the color scheme, and right now the sea is behaving like mad in the harbor.

* * *

---

[1]Seaport on the Gulf of La Spezia in northwestern Italy.—Ed.
[2]The Magra River flows into the Ligurian Sea near La Spezia.—Ed.

Vevey, April 14, 1911

Many thanks for your two cards. When I take them to bed in the morning, they always bring a little beam of light into the room. Nothing new here, sleep middling. In the room to my right there is a German who goes to bed at 12:30 A.M. after noisily brushing his teeth. In such a situation Tolstoy's mistrust of cleanliness is tempting. To my left there is an English reverend with his wife to whom he reads The Psalms between 10:30 and 11:30 P.M. When this woke me up for the first time, Satan burst forth in me with a tremendous roar. A profound silence. Then the psalmody resumed in muted form, but it was just as disturbing. Wonderful but very cool weather. Early spring, the first greenery. But it is hard to relax here. That lush, blissful, blessed repose of the south simply is missing.

Weber went farther south, and on the way he stopped in Turin to see his younger friend and colleague Robert Michels. He noticed all the human details and described them vividly.

Turin, April 30, 1911

Yesterday afternoon I arrived here and was met by Michels and little, coquettish, nice-looking Manon at the railway station. I am living in a simple hotel and had lunch at the Michels's home. Then a discussion in the afternoon, and various people until eleven o'clock at night. Slept tolerably. Now a few more hours of Turin: art museum and the like. In the afternoon I am going on to the Riviera.

April 22, 1911

You will be indignant at my silence for a day and a half and at my uncommunicativeness. But in Turin I was almost always at the Michels's home. Their apartment is small: three small rooms, another very small room, no guest room; but it is in a nice neighborhood. The children sleep with the servant girl and the oldest boy sleeps on a couch in that very small room. On the first evening three Italians were there; on the second evening we were alone and debated until 1:30. Frau M. has remained pretty and graceful. He: a Chief Forester [*Herr Oberförster*] with *charm.* . . .

When she [Mrs. Michels] shyly raised objections to his playing adultery [*Ehebruchspielen*] with Manon—this was playacted for my benefit, and the little minx is crazy about it—he was acutely embarrassed. Mario, the oldest boy, is very nervous, blinks his eyes and is not very strong, but he is nice and friendly and evidently a very kind soul. Manon is a darling little scamp—high-strung, naively coquettish, behaves like an actress, and splendidly portrayed adultery by gestures, in her manner, and in conversation. But when I said that she was going to be an actress, both parents were morally *outraged*! The smallest girl, about four years old, is a charming, healthy, open, bright, vigorous, and lively child; there is no keeping her down. The children kept jumping all over me, and *he* then discussed with them whether I or Mr. Lagardelle[3] or Mr. Goldscheid[4] were (1) handsomer, (2) gooder [*güter*], (3) pleasanter, etc. *I* received the first prize only for my talent for *playing* and for nothing else. The children are wonderfully open in their judgment. Naturally I had long conversations with the Michelses about eroticism; more about this in person. The awareness of one's ability to make conquests is supposed to keep one young. . . .

Alassio, April 21, 1911

I have found shelter here in a very small Italian tavern, right on the ocean with a very nice beach. This little town is charming. *Haec est Italia, Diis Sacra!* [Here is Italy, sacred to the gods!] One should always come here right away. The Lake of Geneva is really quite northern by comparison. For the past week I have been living quite merrily in tropical heat. Slept well at night. The roaring of the sea came in through my wide open balcony door and the warm wind caressed me. Everything is gay here, as always in Italy. Your old man of forty-seven kisses you with all his might. . . .

Today the weather is glorious. It is getting hot again, but it is not as humid as it was yesterday when I took a carriage ride to the green mountains. Most of the time I lie on the hot sand on the beach in front of the *albergo* [inn]. At night I keep my balcony door wide open. The sunrise over the sea this morning was radiantly beautiful. A magnificent breed of people: the fellows are all so handsome, prettier than the girls. In front of the *osteria* [hostelry] the youngsters bathe in the sea (18 degrees centigrade), particularly a few very graceful little French fellows; there are also women, among them the very pretty innkeeper's wife. Afterward they all roll in the warm sand and lounge about on the beach in their bathing togs for as long as possible. No one seems to have anything important to do.

* * *

---

[3]Possibly Hubert Lagardelle, 1874–1958, the French economist and politician, founder of the French Socialist movement.—Ed.

[4]Rudolf Goldscheid, 1870–1931, Vienna-born sociologist and philosopher, co-founder of the *Deutsche Gesellschaft für Soziologie.*—Ed.

Aiguebelle (Provence), March 9, 1912

All day I lie around either in the pine grove overlooking the ocean or in the wicker chair on my balcony, don't read anything—which means that I sleep passably well, though very restlessly—and eat little. No news about Germany. In the local papers there is not even an indication that it exists. Everything has been dipped into a remote ocean of fog and has disappeared. It is as though I had dropped out of the world, and for a time that is quite salutary. I wonder whether today will bring another dear little card from you. . . .

It continues to be lovely here. Full of sunshine and fresh air. One doesn't see too many flowers, though. Nothing but mountains with plain, low pines, *macchia* [shrubbery], mimosas, etc., everything extremely simple and severe and not at all luxuriant. Incidentally, in the hotel there is a baby who is capable of bawling for a full eighteen hours—I established that when I was sleeping little and stayed in the house all day—the way the phonographic reproduction of an organ with all the stops pulled out must sound. Surely *this* exceeds any performance attainable on the basis of your elocutionary exercises, or could you too do something like that now? I guess you will have another one of those lectures at the end of March. . . .

(March 21, 1912)

If there were any violets or other small flowers here—but strewn in among the mimosas and pines there are only the large, thick-stalked flowers of the south which can't be put into an envelope—I would enclose a few with this letter, which probably will get into your hands on the anniversary of our engagement. This letter is intended to thank you for all the superabundance of love and wealth and happiness that has flowed from you in the nineteen years—would anyone believe the time?—and has made me joyful and free in good times and kept me above water in bad times, and which has, above all, kept me inwardly young. This I feel again and again and I am feeling it here now, although spring usually is not the really beautiful time of year . . . Now let me give you a long embrace and kiss you many, many times. It is so beautiful to reflect now on the *very* complicated way in which life brought us together! It must have intended something unusual—and, well, it accomplished it, too.

I wonder whether you still have spring, or have it again. I must say that there is full summer here. At night one lies down in the sand on the beach in the moonlight, and the warm wind feels like a lover's arm around one's neck . . . Yesterday on Cape Négre till late at night;

it was uncommonly beautiful on those densely covered rocks with their giddy paths over the sea. Just like Villa Serbelloni, only that there you have the Alps in front of yourself in the distance, while here you see the ocean and the Iberian islands. Villa Serbelloni, of course, is more beautiful, but now it is still icy cold there. Around this time of year there is no place where it is as sunny and warm as it is here, except perhaps in southern Spain. From time to time I wish there were a city close by, but suddenly this passes again. . . .

Next I shall go to Marseille and from there, depending on the weather, to Provence: to Arles, Nîmes, Tarascon, and perhaps to one of the old, decayed "love courts" of the troubadours, then to Avignon. Yesterday I took another evening walk along the beautiful coastal road in the warm sirocco air, as on a summer night. The colors here are so discreet in all their severe simplicity, and the warm southern wind, which really "tenderly blows about us," does one good. Then one really enjoys one's isolated location very much. No car—nothing. The only thing is, it is too expensive. I think next year Rome or Athens, and then with you.

* * *

March 26, 1912

Many, many thanks for your good little letter of Saturday, my sweetheart, which came yesterday. But why do you always make such a big shot [grosses Tier] out of me? I bless fate for having meted all this out to me without my deserving it, and I only wish it were also granted to me to muster that much *visible* love.

Aigues-Mortes (Provence), March 31, 1912

The "city of the dead waters"—this piece of the untouched Middle Ages was built by the crusader Saint Louis—lies in utter isolation in the Rhone delta on stagnant marshes. Absolutely straight streets, magnificent, intact walls and towers, a crammed church with a beautifully singing girls' choir and Palm Sunday decorations. All children had laurel and mimosa wreaths. There is a strange, unearthly quiet in this once so important place.

Yesterday afternoon I set out from Arles on a long carriage ride through the alternately gay and serious Provence to the old love court of the Seigneurs de Maurika in Les Baux near Arles, on a wild cone-shaped rock overlooking a green valley enclosed by protruding gray rock walls, exactly like the ones we saw on the trip from Burgos. In the

Middle Ages the place once had 3600 inhabitants; now there are 100, and it is in ruins. The Seigneurs were the greatest in Provence and the center of the troubadours; one of them became emperor of Constantinople.

The wonderful view across Provence with the snowy white streets dusty with chalk and the snowy white limestone walls; the evening ride through the quiet countryside in a strong, warm wind—all this was beautiful. Then Arles itself, the amphitheater and the Rhone by moonlight; the Roman avenue of tombs: for a quarter of an hour one sees one sarcophagus after another right by the roadside—like the graves at Pompeii, remember? They left the dead amidst the flow of life. And then this whole Roman road in the midst of the cheerful yet so much smaller present. All that was beautiful, and I enjoy this sort of thing *very much*. Next spring we shall go to Greece together, shan't we? Tonight Nîmes, tomorrow Montpellier, then Avignon.

Maguelone near Montpellier, April 2, 1912

All right, now the farthest point of this round trip has been reached. One can see the Pyrenees rising in the distance, though but faintly. This little church, founded by Fair Magelone from Schwab's *Volksbücher*,[5] is situated in isolation among pines on a dune by the sea, and it is surrounded by the ocean on one side and broad salt marshes on the other. It is the only remnant of an old harbor town founded by the Greeks which the Carolingians took away from the Saracens. The building is all askew, and it is buffeted by the storms of this region, which next to Holland is the windiest of Europe. But on the dunes the wine grows, fertilized by the contents of the fishermen's chamber pots. The view and mood at night are simply fabulous. Brown, violet, and light green hues, but in the terribly strong sea breeze it is bitter cold.

Montpellier

This morning I saw paintings by Courbet[6] in the museum, the best in France next to the ones in Paris and Lille. Here, too, the landscapes are quite reminiscent of Böcklin.[7] Another particularly notable thing

---

[5] The sentimental story about Fair Magelone and Peter of Provence, of oriental origin, first appeared as a German *Volksbuch* (chapbook) in the sixteenth century. The Swabian Romanticist Gustav Schwab included it in his collection *Deutsche Volksbücher* in 1836.—Ed.

[6] Gustave Courbet, 1819–1877, French painter, founder of Realism.—Ed.

[7] Arnold Böcklin, 1827–1901, Swiss romantic painter, noted for his mythological subjects.—Ed.

in Montpellier is the *château d'eau* [*Wasserschloss*][8] where the aqueduct enters the city; last night I was there in the moonlight—wonderful.

(To Helene) I did bring back some relaxation from southern France, at least enough for me to be able to work passably well, something that went only quite inadequately in winter. And I have also seen many beautiful things in that remarkable country, particularly in the real Provence where I rode and ran around for eight more days. That delta plain of the Rhone must be the windiest place on earth—even Holland is not that windy—and it is as flat as a pancake, just as in Holland. But what a difference! In place of the Dutch meadows and the cattle, salt marshes and heath alternate for miles with vineyards of huge dimensions. And in the middle of that there are the medieval towns, now dead, in the full finery of their fortress walls. Far in back are the mountains, of the most fantastic individual shapes, and there the ruins of the old love courts of the troubadours are on inaccessible cone-shaped rocks on plateaus. A charming population and wonderful illuminations in the afternoon and evening and magnificent artistic monuments from the Roman ruins to the late Gothic period. Only the insane, incessant north wind, against which the fields are protected by thick walls of rushes or cypress hedges, is sometimes enough to make one despair. . . .

II

The springs of 1913 and 1914 Weber spent in a small town on one of the Northern Italian Lakes [Ascona on Lago Maggiore] that provided a refuge to all sorts of strange people who had dropped out of bourgeois society—anarchists, back-to-nature people, vegetarians, and other modern sectarians who wanted to realize their ideals there and form the nucleus of a new world order. Adherents of the disciple of Freud previously mentioned [Otto Gross] had retreated there, as well as anarchists and communists. They lived entirely according to their ideals, free from any traditional norm and in poverty and insecurity. They exchanged the traditional for the unconventional, with psychic adventures and a struggle to hold their own in an existence full of all kinds of afflictions.

---

[8]A *château d'eau* (water castle) is a water tower or cistern, usually with an elaborate architectural setting.—Ed.

This gave rise to grave conflicts—elemental ones rather than those created by convention—particularly for the women involved. There was a complicated trial concerning a child that dragged on for years, and that without Weber's assistance would probably have taken an unfavorable course for the mother. He worked on this case for months with all his energy and skill, instructing several attorneys by means of long memoranda, personally negotiating with them abroad, and securing witnesses. At the same time he aided another hard-pressed woman in a divorce trial that was as difficult as it was protracted. There were piles of documents and letters, and again only because of Weber's energy was the desired goal reached. He acted in a spirit of brotherly helpfulness and because he enjoyed a fight; his rewards were grateful friendship and an enriching insight into the strange world of people with attitudes entirely different from his own and into the consequences of their actions. Some of the emotional residue of his experiences in L[ocarno] shall be preserved here:

When I returned from the post office yesterday, a blonde woman met me at the door of my house here with one blonde and one dark child—Dora,[9] of course. We greeted each other, she told me about the countess[10] and then about her children. So help me, she lives in my house; the children live with the servant girl diagonally across from us by the harbor. Her present "husband," the anarchist,[11] is still in jail in Zurich. She is alone and needs someone to talk to. . . .

Today it is cold, but there is some sun after yesterday's endless rain. Having got up late after a middling night, I am sitting in my large room, three or actually four flights up, with a view of the steeply rising little garden next to the house and of the lake. In the room there are two beds, a small closet, a chest, an old, broken-down *Prahlhans*,[12] a large sofa for sleeping, a large table, a tin washstand, a night table, a few prehistoric easy chairs, an electric lamp, ancient oleographs, a mirror, a clothes tree, and yellow walls. With the room go a small kitchen, a toilet, and a bathroom, and everything is on a

[9]"Dora" was Frieda Schloffer Gross from Graz (b. 1876), a niece of the Freiburg philosophy professor Aloys Riehl. Dr. Otto Gross, whom she had married in 1903, decided that she should live with a Swiss anarchist. She was supporting herself and her three children on a small pension given her by her family on condition that she never return to Austria. See Martin Green, *op. cit.*—Ed.

[10]Franziska (Fanny) Gräfin zu Reventlow, 1871–1918, novelist and bohemian.—Ed.

[11]The painter Ernst Frick, who was serving a two-year term for robbery.—Ed.

[12]*Prahlhans*, meaning "braggart," here indicates a china cabinet, curio cabinet, or chest with a glass front and glass sides for the display of bric-a-brac.—Ed.

locked floor. So it is ideal for "a happy loving pair"[13] of local back-to-nature people who cook nothing more than some occasional oatmeal.

In front of the house there is a highway, then one steps down into a small, luxuriant garden by the lake with an overpowering smell of violets. A poultry yard, a little landing for boats. The owner, *Avvokato e Notajo* [sic][14] is in his office every day. His wife, who must have been beautiful once and is even now very imposing, is the large farmer's wife type. She scrubs the floors together with the *serve* [maids], runs to the post office—in short, in rank she is the same as Signora Q. in the local tavern. It is a real, filthy Italian hick town [*Italienernestchen*], though the tavern has some class because of the Italians living here. The cooking is really too good for me. In the morning I eat biscuits and dried figs. One gets pretty good things in the shop for the nature people. At other times, too, I live on oatmeal cookies, dates, figs, and oranges; every other day I go to Q.'s tavern, but despite all this I haven't lost any weight thus far. . . .

Do send me the Lukács book (*Die Formen der Seele*).[15] I shall be able to read it here. I have read *Marie Donadieu*[16] and have given it to Dora, who gave me in return the latest book of the countess: a Schwabing[17] *roman à clef*[18] with George, Wolfskehl, Count Andrian,[19] and herself. Well written, but only for those interested in Schwabing. *Marie D.* is splendidly written and has depth and refinement, a critique of eroticism on a very high level, but the ending is somewhat contrived; surely traveling in the Gulf of Persia is not a sufficient expression of the wealth and the greatness of an *extra*erotic life. But I shall read the book again. Many details escape me, because my French vocabulary is weak, very weak.

In this bitter cold—I am writing this with blue fingers—I sat with Dora by her fireplace for a few hours yesterday. She has a great need to talk things out. Last week she visited her lover in jail. He, too, has a religious faith in an unjealous future society of truly "free"—inwardly liberated—love. She also did some theorizing about it. But when I said that (1) magnanimous *behavior* in cases of jealousy was a fine thing, *but*

---

[13]"(*Ratum ist in der kleinsten Hütte)/für ein glücklich liebend Paar*"—from Schiller's poem *Der Jüngling am Bache* (1803). "The meanest hut hath space to hold/A happy loving pair"—translation by E. Bulwer Lytton.—Ed.

[14]*Avvocato e Notaio*: Attorney and Notary Public.—Ed.

[15]The correct title is *Die Seele und die Formen* [Soul and Form], 1911.—Ed.

[16]A novel by Charles-Louis Philippe, the story of a complicated *ménage à trois*.—Ed.

[17]The artists' district of Munich.—Ed.

[18]*Herrn Dames Aufzeichnungen*. See page 692, note 11.—Ed.

[19]The Austrian writer Leopold Freiherr von Andrian-Werburg, 1875–1951.—Ed.

I didn't see how one could regard it as chivalrous to accept *everything* from a person to whom one "owed" so much, and (2) when I asked whether an insane waste of emotional energy was not going on here for the sake of a *whim*, she burst out with it: Yes, it was terrible and quite hopeless. . . . There is no helping her, for her relationship to that man decides everything. For as long as this lasts, she will not fit into any bourgeois environment—not because of the thing itself but because of everything that goes with it, and because only things that are out of the ordinary and her varied experiences keep her afloat. . . .

The weather today is cloudy and mild. It is nice to see the outlines of the mountains through the silvery gray, and even nicer to watch the discreet shades of the colors with a steel gray background slowly shifting in the long evening twilight. Perhaps I shall go to L. again today, but I may postpone it until tomorrow as a birthday celebration. For, my God! I am starting my fiftieth year! I still cannot believe it, because I am still so strangely youthful! Or is it only your youth, my sweetheart, that deceives me like this? As a birthday present, let us cap the two cement posts by the bridge leading to the garden with wooden boxes in which we can put nice flower pots. This suddenly occurred to me; I don't know why.

. . . Dora still wants to tell me what I should not think of her—then we shall be finished. Yesterday she blurted out (to her son): "Oh yes, you will notice it when the women won't let their children play with you." Yesterday I again liked her very much for her honesty. I *am* learning a lot—even though these are all things that are self-evident . . .

Your beautiful letter just arrived (for the anniversary of our engagement). My dear, everything you say there about me is a fine "fiction" of your great love. I cannot see myself through such great and beautiful eyes as you see me, and that is why all this is more "given up" [*"aufgegeben"*] than "given" [*"gegeben"*]. But no matter; now is not the time to investigate what is true and what is not, but it is time to enjoy the beauty that enables such "fiction" to come into being. I hope it will always be possible for me at least not to give the lie to it and to keep your soul capable of writing more and more "fiction." Then poems *are* "true" in the sense in which truth is granted to us human beings in this area. . . .

* * *

Yesterday evening and this morning I ate a few oranges, and I have eaten nothing else since Friday evening. Outside of these world-shaking facts there is nothing to report. We are eagerly awaiting news from the attorney and consider the possibility that the judge will tell him, "If she gives up her relationship with Karl [Ernst Frick], she keeps the child." But she will at the most do the former in form only. Yet she realizes with strange clarity that he will not stay here permanently, but she has absolutely no idea what is to become of him later. She says he is always waiting for the moment of great inner enlightenment when he will do something truly great and prophetic. Everything hinges on his sentence; this is almost frightening. Although they are convinced of absolute wickedness as the foundation of society, even Dora found it impossible to explain why he was *so* "obsessed" with these ideas. For the rest, he would like to perfect kindness and brotherly love by taking an acosmistic view of *eroticism*. I had already told Dora why this cannot be done. She admits that the real result would be Tolstoyan asceticism, and he does keep inclining toward that. . . .

Things are still going full blast here. Yesterday I dictated a commentary on the trial letters. Today I shall draft my expert opinion on the anarchist Karl, and the countess will type it up tomorrow. In return, and with the worst conscience, I have manufactured for her a request for legal advice on the possible release of her son from his German citizenship (compulsory military service). I hope that nothing will come of it and that he will have to serve. During the past week I have consumed nothing but four and a half kilos of oranges, two lemonades without sugar, three cups of tea. Today I feel just as I did on the first day—that is, my stomach rumbles often. My condition is not quite normal, but neither is it substantially different from the usual. No change whatever in my figure, no increased nervousness. I walk and read as I always have, only writing is a bit of a strain. Tomorrow morning I shall start my nourishment again with a raw *Finocchi* [sic].[20] . . .

Dora's friend has *depth*. But he lacks the power to express even simple thoughts. Jail has affected him in such a way that he cannot stop meditating on the meaning of goodness. The facts that the *result* of good actions is so often wholly irrational and that "good" behavior has bad consequences have made him doubt that one *ought* to act well—an evaluation of moral action on the basis of *results* rather than intrinsic value. For the time being he does not see that there is a fallacy here. I shall try to obtain *The Brothers Karamazov* for him and at some later time Lukács's dialogue about the poor in spirit, which deals with the problem. . . .

Today I received a fat letter from the attorney which makes it nec-

---

[20]*Finocchio:* fennel.—Ed.

essary for me to go to Zurich. Everything depends on finding persons who can give appropriate testimony on Karl's qualities, his political harmlessness. Then I will see whether I shall, despite the uncertain weather, go to the Ufenau[21] with Tobelchen [Mina Tobler] or whether I shall spend half the day in Zurich with her at the house of her nice sister.

Zurich, April 4, 1914

Now I shall soon be leaving for "home." If I shall be able to use this term for that world full of enchantresses, charm, trickery, and desire for happiness while everything that has to be done still has not been done there, I shall not have labored in vain. I must say: among those fine, in a certain sense also "human" but *backgroundless* impressions of a world based only on sensation, this has been a kind of oasis of purity—it is the only thing one can call it—yesterday this trip to the Ufenau with this girl who is different but seems so "noble" in her reserved and delicately rapturous way. . . .

The weather is glorious, full spring, everything in bloom and green. Last night there was the Easter procession with Chinese lanterns, carried icons of Christ, etc. Everything illuminated by little lights and lamps, living pictures of the Annunciation on the street in front of the café—and with a full moon! It was enchanting. Everything was so different from the Lake of Zurich, where there is "culture." The little houses on the green meadows right up to the mountains, creeping into all the smallest crevices, carrying everywhere human hearts with their sorrows and their joys, and then in the background the giant mountains. Up there the villages are glued on as a piece of nature. The people are as open as these, and just as closed as they are, not transcending themselves, which is *also* beautiful though less human, without intimacy like a painting of a nude, just like the life of the people here. Without background, but not without pride and form. Yes, I certainly have sympathy for Dora because she has remained the way she is, but I could not breathe for long in this atmosphere. The countess is utterly uninteresting to me. A thousand regards to Mother, my darling child; wonder what she would say!! An embrace from your Max, who has been transported to a strange, fabulous world.

. . . Little Walter, incidentally, is a child with a graphic mind. His definitions of people are very nice: "Who was that, Walter?"—"That was Gina."—"Who is Gina?"—"The one whose nose runs when she fetches her milk in a pot." Does one need to know more about a girl?

. . . Today I sent off my response to the complaint. Another long doc-

---

[21]Island on the Lake of Zurich.—Ed.

ument. I hope it is the last of its kind . . . Yesterday Dora had a
long discussion with me about "lies." She simply would not see why
N. could not simply lie on the witness stand; after all, the state is
not a friend, Prof. X [Otto's father, Hanns Gross] is an enemy, so the
two could not really expect her and her lover to tell the truth. Only a
friend was entitled to the truth, no one else. I pointed out to her that I would
never be sure whether someone with this point of view *was* the "friend" that
he claimed to be. Then she demanded to know whether that was the
reason why I remained so aloof from her. I said the reason was to be
sought in my experiences. I could under certain circumstances be quite
fond of specifically "erotic" women, as she herself must have noticed,
but I would never form any inner attachment to one or count on her
friendship. For it had turned out that I was not a suitable friend for
such women, for in truth only an erotic man was of value to them.
I would never rely on the permanence and security of their comradeship,
no matter how strong this subjective feeling might be, for experience
had shown that with the best will in the world all words and feelings
would be invalidated as soon as they were put to the test. Well, she
did not quite like that, but this is how we left it. . . .

Early this morning I went out to the delta; under an overcast sky
and with cloud-covered dark mountains it was incredibly impressive in
its finery. The trees now are no longer merely linear, as on Ernst Gundolf's[22] paintings; the meadows are full of flowers; all around there are
red peach-blossoms, and the lilac is beginning to bloom. But behind me
the nymph Calypso slipped out of the arched grotto of her *palazzo* in
golden garments. To escape her—for she does not fit in there—I walked
faster, went off to the right, then to the left. Finally she must have
seen that Odysseus was not to be had, for she turned around; but now
she angrily pelted me with a thunderstorm that did not leave a dry
stitch on my body, transformed my hat into a tragic mask, and chased
me homeward at a gallop. But it *was* beautiful.

* * *

The way in which Weber helped his lady friend is illustrated by the following excerpts from letters to her.

Whatever you may do, be absolutely certain of one thing: There are

---

[22]The artist and poet Ernst Gundolf, a brother of Friedrich Gundolf, was born in 1881 and
died in London in 1945.—Ed.

expedients to keep your children from being taken away from you, and I, too, shall place every conceivable aid, including *extreme violence*, at your disposal. I am always at your disposal in Basel, and at your friend's as well, to explain the legal situation to you if he should find it useful.

Rest assured that I shall help you exactly the way *you* want me to; that is why you should not be angry if I suggest wrong things, but you can simply say: "You are an ass." I shall then either see it or not see it—but I shall not take it amiss. . . . I think that as far as Karl is concerned Prof. X might demand that he and you with the children live in separate houses. A year and a half ago I made a similar proposal to you, because then your opponent could not take any action. You and he simply have to *choose*. Once you have done so, I shall never tell you, "You have made the wrong choice." I advise you only to choose calmly and with a clear head.

. . . I shall now return to a point that I probably should have emphasized long ago, for it would have saved me much inner turmoil and saved you some scolding on my part. You see, in your letters I keep finding remarks that look as though you think that *I* presumed upon you or that *I* was trying to complicate your relationship with Karl or that I was siding with those who would like to break up this relationship. Dear Frau Dora, this is the *only* point that could endanger our friendship if you believed this after I have associated with both of you in friendship for weeks. But in order to put a stop to this I will express myself quite clearly. You know well that of course it is this relationship that causes the greatest difficulties—not the existence of this kind of relationship as such, nor the "anarchism" by itself, but, above all, Karl's *unemployment*.

I do not need to tell either of you how ugly this situation appears to the cold eyes of outsiders. One simply has to know the persons to judge them correctly. You and Karl—let me tell you this frankly—simply cannot expect an outsider to see things the way I see them and saw them even before I was in L. this year. And this explains *everything* about the attitude of third parties. In the face of this it is possible to say, "We have to be all the more unyielding in small points and matters of secondary importance." Believe me, I understand this. And I also understood that you did not take the simple, purely technical step of effecting, for now, a greater physical separation of each other's living quarters—that is, placing yourself and the children in another house. I can understand that quite well. But *you* for your part, both of you, must understand that I as a friend had to propose to you primarily *prudence* rather than "Catoism" of this kind. That is why I advised you to make that concession—a formal separation of the households, if at all possible. For then the proposals of your father-in-law would immediately have fallen flat. I could not make that suggestion *twice*, for, after all, the most personal affairs of both of you were involved.

Why all this? Because during my entire stay in L. I was in the awkward position of having to *keep silent* about it, and although everything we did—and did very gladly!—involved saving you the choice between your relationship with Karl and your child, I *still* keep getting unsure of myself, and necessarily so: "Could she be thinking, despite everything, that he prefers to have us apart?" But that is unbearable. . . . What I wrote you about the testimony in court also is only a suggestion to be prudent. Do you understand? But there I am on very safe ground. Do things differently—all right, I shall help you as much as I can even then. But you will then be acting *very* imprudently and thoughtlessly; I am sure you will regret it. . . . [There follow detailed instructions.—AUTHOR'S NOTE.] I think everything will go quite well in the end, and I am expecting my summons to Prague.—And now you will get no more "upsetting" [*"verquere"*] letters and no more communications that make you miserable, dear Frau Dora. For I have already said what has weighed upon me and has been hard to express. Now remain well-disposed toward me and retain your friendly feelings for your somewhat clumsy and *not always agreeable*

Max Weber

My dear Frau Dora:

Now everything is in perfect order, and you are seeing ghosts! You have told the *truth* in court and have a chance to supplement it—a clear track, then. Consequently you have done the right thing, objectively speaking, and no one can do the least thing to you. That is simply out of the question, and I am tremendously relieved. You simply are not up to these things now and have to regain your strength. How I wish I could be with you now, and I would like to make a special trip there, but I simply can't. We shall visit you in September, Marianne and I. More very soon. This letter is intended only to ask you to relax. I am glad that you have acted as you did. Everything is in good order now.

III

Weber gratified his need for *cultural* experiences primarily on the trips the Webers took together in late summer. His enjoyment was increased when he could show beautiful things to others. In the summer of 1910 they went to England. They were impressed by the majestic Norman-Gothic cathedrals which, unlike the German cathedrals surrounded by a clutter of houses, rise freely from a level greensward at a solemn distance from everyday things. They thought that the cathedral of Canterbury was one of the most exalted things they had ever seen. Was it the spirit of man that devised this structure, human hands that completed it? Was it the spirit of man which thus concretized the unfathomable, or did God create this place for Himself through His servants? Alas, what poverty, what profound sorrow at being remote from God [Gottferne] lies in this merely artistic exaltation of modern man!

The travelers were shaken in a different way by Shakespeare's birthplace, the little old town where the relics of that genius were so commercialized. The clattering of the automobiles and their hurrying passengers dispelled the mood of absorption and made it impossible to sense the atmosphere of the poet's personal life. But the dark river, winding along under silvery weeping willows, still whispered of Ophelia's sweet sorrow. And in the aisle of the old church, where Shakespeare and his wife and daughters lie buried, the veil seemed to lift a bit. There hung the last depiction of the countenance of a human being who had consciously abandoned his creativity and concluded his work before he departed.

The other aspect of English civilization that most intensively occupied the Webers was, as it had been years ago, the distribution of land. Everywhere the land belonged to aristocratic lords of the manor. If one wanted to enjoy the grandiose view of the Atlantic Ocean from a high point on the rocky coast, one first encountered a garden fence and had to pay an admission fee for certain days and hours. Entire villages, like lovely Clovelly on the west coast, were "private property," and in certain districts there were castles whose game preserves, barred from any kind of economic utilization, had been expanded intp principalities. The proprietors came only for a few weeks during the year to hunt. An area that could have given sustenance to hundreds of thousands provided a livelihood for a few hundred servants. No complaints were to be heard in these empty spaces, for anyone who could have complained had long ago been driven into the slums of the giant city and no longer belonged in the country. The free peasant had been wiped out. Compared with this, the German agrarian system, which Weber was so concerned with, seemed eminently sensible.

After this exhausting multiplicity of impressions the Webers gratefully returned home and were happy to be greeted by so much beauty: "The sun is shining; its soft, blue autumnal light veils the mountains and the river with a mother-of-pearl gleam that wipes away everything trivial and makes the outlines great and quiet. In the garden there already is a trickle of leaves; at the rose arbor the Virginia creepers are beginning to change color, and a few more asters have opened up."

* * *

In winter Weber now usually spent some time in Berlin to further the collective projects, to fan the fire of the Sociological Society, and also to keep abreast of political developments. Each time he also became immersed in art, at the beginning of 1911 especially in music. A few passages from letters deal with these interests, and some artistic impressions from later years are given space here as well.

Beethoven's First Symphony, then *Don Quixote* by [Richard] Strauss (who conducted it himself), a wild thing full of spirit and tone painting, but probably without permanent value [*Ewigkeitswert*]. Then, by way of recuperation, Haydn's Symphony in B-Flat Major. Everything in the morning and then again in the evening—very much to be recommended. The *Königliche Kapelle* [Royal Orchestra], which gives only seven or eight such concerts a year, is a wonderful orchestra. Yesterday Simmel also was in the *Beethovensaal* [Beethoven Room] of the *Philharmonie* [Philharmonic Hall], and the music visibly went through his body in spirals. He is obviously very musical, and his sense of color is also highly developed. His collection of Chinese vases of one color is worth seeing. . . .

Oh, what a pity that we are not here together. Yesterday the five sonatas by Beethoven for piano and cello were very beautiful—opus 5 and then opus 102. All of Beethoven lay in between—from the ingenuous coloratura-happy artist of the Haydn school to the deep, passionate, and controlled man who leans against a rock in solitude and opposes his deep, sonorous, serious voice to all the magnificence of the world: "Yes, it is beautiful, I know what there is to it—but also what there is not to it."

Yesterday *Salome* (Wilde-Strauss). That something like this can be done musically at all is certainly a great achievement, even though the tone painting almost reaches the point of pettiness. But it is brilliant and by no means incomprehensible, some of it really very beautiful, the treatment of the brass instruments simply marvelous. The audience left the hall crushed and as though caught red-handed. The subject has been twisted into something loathsome by Wilde. Now I am eagerly awaiting the last thing I am going to hear: Strauss's *Death and Transfiguration.* . . .

Lancelot[23] in the *Kammerspiele* [Little Theater] of the *Deutsches Theater* was an awful flop [*übler Reinfall*]. Act II, beginning: A disheveled *"double bed"*[24] à la Middle Ages; the knight by the window in the morning sun calls his beloved, the wife of King Arthur, to look at the morning sun with him. A blonde girl in a long nightshirt crawls out of bed and says she was not the one he thought he was kissing; she has been foisted upon him by devoted persons in place of the queen and loves him as the "real one" with a "heavenly love," etc. This is what Reinhard[25] and Stukken [*sic*], the author, call a *Mysterium* [mystery play]! And the oyster-mouthed [*austernschnäuzig*] audience sits in its comfortable club chairs and thinks of Kempinsky's.[26] The ladies were bawling.—Yesterday the Philharmonic Orchestra: Mendelssohn, Liszt, two very modern Russians, then *Death and Transfiguration.* Very beautiful. Not deep everywhere, but with marvelous musical means in an inward sense. . . .

The musical yesterday was *wonderful*—especially the two songs by Ansorge;[27] one in particular, a setting of a Dehmel[28] poem, stood in monumental greatness among the beautiful and interesting but forced and somewhat dragging Hugo Wolf things. The little Tobler girl accompanied splendidly; in between she played Mozart and Chopin, the latter especially wonderfully. Physically, too, she was so graceful and yet so resolutely vigorous that it was a joy. . . .

Yesterday at [*The Marriage of*] *Figaro* with Mother, who was again able to have such a pure enjoyment! It is true: this music ennobles the risqué and partly burlesque subject so much that *everything* is cleansed away and

[23]*Lanzelot* (1909), one of a series of Grail plays by Eduard Stucken, 1865–1936.—Ed.
[24]In English in the original.—Ed.
[25]The noted theatrical director and producer Max Reinhardt (1873–1943).—Ed.
[26]A popular Berlin restaurant.—Ed.
[27]Conrad Ansorge, 1862–1930, German pianist and composer, pupil of Liszt.— Ed.
[28]Richard Dehmel, 1863–1920, German poet.—Ed.

there remains only the *Reigen*, [29] devoid of any substance. Otherwise Mother—and grandmother, who used to sing Cherubino's songs in a thin child's voice—could not enjoy this so much and yet completely reject all erotic music.

May, 1916

Yesterday at the Strindberg play;[30] disagreeable. The daughter of the Hindu god Indra comes down to earth and now experiences all the misery and folly of humans. Many fine individual scenes, but everything is "preachment" and also bad technique and lachrymose, crass methods—a work of his old age. No, there is nothing there. The strangest part of it is that in this day and age the theater is sold out for forty performances of such a thing. This is actually almost incomprehensible and depressing. . . .

Yesterday at Strindberg's *Kameraden* [*Comrades*]. A companionate marriage—a trenchant critique of the women's movement, brilliantly acted, splendid dialogue. One's enjoyment of the unerring artistry made one forget the distortion of the subject. The audience was amusing; many in field gray uniform and many petit bourgeois. *Such* relief and joy on the part of the males when the bad emancipated woman really got the worst of it!

* * *

In summer of 1911 the Webers tried to take in Munich's treasures thoroughly for the first time. They put themselves in the hands of their friend Dr. Gruhle, who was familiar with modern art. He was acquainted with everything and knew how to make even the newest and most unfamiliar things accessible with a few pointers, such as the paintings of the *Scholle*.[31] At that time the plastic arts, which were influenced by Hildebrand,[32] were striving for the calm, architectonically composed lines of classical models, while in painting the dominant trend considered everything objective, in-

---

[29]Probably an allusion to *Reigen* (1903), a once scandalous sequence of erotic scenes by the Austrian writer Arthur Schnitzler (1862–1931). The title has been variously translated as *Round Dance*, *Hands Around*, *Ring Around the Rosy*, and *La Ronde.*—Ed.

[30]*Ein Traumspiel*, 1901 [*A Dream Play*, 1902] by the Swedish writer Johan August Strindberg (1849–1912).—Ed.

[31]*Die Scholle* [The Soil], an artists' association founded in Munich in 1899 by the painters Erler, Jank, and Putz, which aimed at a synthesis between the prevalent *art nouveau* and traditional folkloristic values and themes.—Ed.

[32]Adolf von Hildebrand, 1847–1921, a German sculptor and writer, from 1872 on in Florence.— Ed.

cluding the human figure, only as the bearer of light and color and rejected other meaningful content. In the theater the Webers enjoyed the witty, self-ironic frivolity of a Schnitzler farce and the bacchantic sensuality of an Offenbach operetta bathed in a riot of glowing color by Reinhardt's directing. They were uplifted by the great noble art of *Die Meistersinger*, which made them feel as though they were in a temple of the German spirit. No other country has ever given the world music that is so pregnant with meaning and has managed to such a degree to reveal the special quality of a particular nation's spiritual treasures and at the same time to be comprehensible to the entire civilized world.

Outside it was magnificent summer, with the sun blessing everything. The beautiful buildings bathed their outlines clean in the crystalline air and southern brightness that are granted only to *this* city from time to time. This made the architectural lines taken over from Italy seem appropriate there. The Webers enjoyed the combination of German work and Italian inspiration and were proud that German hands had fashioned such great things. From the journey Weber wrote to his mother:

> We first spent a week in Munich: galleries, art exhibitions, architecture, *Meistersinger*, Offenbach in the Reinhardt cycle; landscape: moors, the Isar valley, lakes together with Dr. Gruhle, who is a sensitive soul and loves this beautiful spot like his native region. We have now had a beautifully quiet week in this little village which is wonderfully situated on the Starnberger See[33] and has been spared all auto traffic, with a view of the Alps across the lake, fine, solemn banks, and wonderful stretches of forests and moors. Now we are going back to Munich and then to Paris.

After the restful days on the Starnberger See real "work" was done in Paris:

> Max is of unlimited receptivity and enthusiasm. Most of the time I had him take me along—for *his* sake, not for the sake of the objects—that is, in order to feel my soul vibrate next to his. He is so very wonderful in his freshness and intellectual voraciousness. But sometimes he is a bit irritated at the *Tücke der Objekte*[34] [the malice of things]:

---

[33] Also known as Würmsee; a lake in Upper Bavaria, south of Munich.—Ed.

[34] *Die Tücke des Objekts* [the malice of inanimate objects] is a recurrent phrase and concept in Friedrich Theodor Vischer's novel *Auch einer* (1879).—Ed.

the streetcar that won't come just when he needs one, the slow service in restaurants, and the like.

Yes, Weber was frequently impatient, for he wanted to see and assimilate
everything: French music, for he was thinking of his treatise on the sociology of
music; modern painting and sculpture, for at some time in the future he was going
to write a sociology embracing all the arts. But even apart from his creative
impulses he was capable of becoming wholly absorbed in this world, animated
only by a will to understand as much of it as possible.

What he had seen in Munich had been the proper prelude for this stranger and
larger world. He and Marianne now quickly adjusted to the masterworks of Monet
and Manet, Degas, Renoir, and all the rest, and after that they turned to Cézanne,
Gauguin, Van Gogh. However, they left it to Americans intent upon the "latest"
to admire a man who was proclaiming a "scientific style of painting"[35] and sought
to capture light in a lot of iridescent dots. They found Van Gogh difficult, but the
most moving. They did not know whether to accept as an expression of the world
the glaring colors, the spaces forced into a flat surface, the branches of trees which
desperately threatened the heavens, the corpselike self-portraits reflecting dark
doom and unspeakable suffering. However, they sensed in Van Gogh the greatness and the passion of a soul under the utmost tension who was engaged in a
lonely struggle to express a transcendent vision in the lines and tones of earthly
phenomena.

All sorts of comparisons came to mind between the cultural forces at work in
the most beautiful German city and the French capital as the center of world
culture. They realized that Munich painting modeled itself on the incomparable
French masters. But despite its artistic perfection, the French theater seemed to
them inferior to the German theater. The moralizing pathos of the classical
tragedy was no longer appropriate; modern actors moved in the plays as in a
masquerade, and the too rapidly delivered speeches spoiled the beautiful and
solemn heroic rhetoric. Then, alongside this, as an expression of modern decay
there was every evening in several theaters the mixture of lust and sentimentality
contained in dramas of adultery; only Maeterlinck's symbolistic fairy-tale plays
were pure and serious. Even in Paris they found that *great* modern art was being
offered only in the works of R. Wagner and other German masters.

In many respects the womb of the city seemed to bring forth nothing new. In an
industrial exhibition, for example, there was no industrial art intended to shape
everyday middle-class life, as in Munich, but only the typical reproductions of the

---

[35]Presumably either Georges Seurat (1859–1891) or his follower Paul Signac, 1863–1935.—Ed.

rococo lines and boudoir colors of the *ancien régime*. Removed from their framework and transplanted in a bourgeois setting, they seemed frivolous and cold. And everywhere, even in the suburbs, the streets were still dominated by the palatial distinction of the boulevard houses and were only occasionally interrupted by ugly imitations of modern foreign styles.

Even though in comparison with this magnificent old vessel of royal and imperial power Munich was relegated to the status of a provincial beauty, it still appeared young and embodied a youthful German evolution and a struggle for new forms. The capital of world culture, in full bloom and overripe, seemed to be holding its own but without offering anything new. To be sure, the wealth and the beauty of this city, a beauty impregnated with the past, were perhaps unsurpassable. How cheerfully the sunlight came through the branches and danced on the pavement of the boulevards, how gaily the old Luxembourg Gardens showed off their crowds of strolling people, how inimitably festive the Bois de Boulogne was in the soft bluish light of autumn with the sumptuous horse-drawn carriages and a graceful elegance that one saw nowhere else! And all the things that could be observed in front of the elegant cafés! Above all, the incomparable taste of Parisian women, which was just then imparting discreet dark hues to the teeming streets and made the colorfulness of the German dresses of the time seem inappropriate there. How the Webers admired the natural grace of the dancing seamstresses in the Moulin de la Galette! The travelers did not belong in that world based upon formal perfection, but they liked to admire it and enjoy it. Weber wrote to Helene about it: "Paris was a feast. The first two nights I still took soporifics, as I had almost every third night at the Starnberger See. Then no more. And yet, all the things we have seen and heard! Yes, loafing and beautiful things—that agrees well with us. But it is good that there are other things, too."

* * *

But Weber did not want to let his trips abroad make him neglect German treasures. When he was reminded of these, he used to say that there would be plenty of time for them in his old age. But he did decide to remain in Germany in the summer of 1912. He and Marianne visited the Bayreuth Festival together with their musician friend M. Tobler, and also took in the beauty of Bamberg and Würzburg. Weber remarked: "I should like to become acquainted with the great wizard [Wagner] once more in as good a performance as possible and in the company of a pianist friend of ours, because I am of two minds about him. Next to great admiration of his ability there is an aversion to many spurious and artificial things. I would not like to see which will prevail."

Bayreuth and *Parsifal* were a disappointment. Playacting remained playacting, and some of the music struck them as empty sweetness or an impure mixture of sensuality and Christian symbolism. Not for a moment did they have the sensation of religious devotion they experienced with the masterpieces of Bach, Beethoven, and Liszt. But the artistic truthfulness and grandeur of *Tristan*, which they saw in Munich, were compelling. This was not the first time they had seen it, for they had attended a performance in Berlin as newlyweds, but they had been deaf then; in the company of an unmusical cousin who suffered visibly they had also been bored stiff. In the meantime they had become far more receptive, and their musical friend had masterfully prepared them for the work. Thus they were completely carried away by its ecstasy and experienced this work of art as the highest transfiguration of the earthly.

The city afforded them many other stimulating joys. An industrial exhibit in a beautiful setting filled them with pride in German ability:

We are feasting on music and paintings; this time we have conquered *Tristan* and Marées.[36] The rest of the world fades away, and only beauty has power. When the sun shines, the festive city is completely bathed in gaiety. On Sunday there was a throng of thousands in the exquisite park where the exhibition is being held. In every corner there was music and something to see for any level of taste and education. It was gratifying also to see the ordinary people there. Max's productive ability is again astonishing. He runs like a hound and looks and cannot get enough; in the evening he always has to be dragged from the cafés, and he is always in a good mood.

Weber himself wrote to Helene as follows:

Würzburg was beautiful, Bamberg incomparable, Bayreuth a strong but not clear impression. *Parsifal* is a work that no longer represents Wagner's full artistic powers, and of course we reject the suggestion that it be regarded as a religious experience; that is simply ridiculous. As compared to this, Mozart's *Cosi fan tutte* two days later here in the Residenztheater was an immersion in pure beauty, despite the frivolous subject. On the other hand, *Tristan* yesterday was the kind of great experience that one very seldom has, a work of great human truthfulness and unparalleled musical beauty. The extrahuman and superhuman additions are simply not there. Together with *Die Meistersinger*, which

---

[36]Hans von Marées, 1837–1887, German painter, from 1875 on in Rome.—Ed.

we heard here last year, *Tristan* is the only truly "eternal" work that
Wagner has created. And then the other things here, the Feuerbachs
at the Schack Gallery, the little Schwind[37] paintings there—and
much else in this blessed city with its incomparable magic.

* * *

In the autumn of 1913 the Webers went on their last joint Italian journey. They visited Assisi, Siena, Perugia, and then Rome again for the first
time in years. On the way they met Adolf Harnack, saw various things
with him, and enjoyed his wisdom, harmony, and intellectual grace. In Perugia they became completely absorbed in the profoundly reverent mood of the
pictures with gold backgrounds. After seeing them, most of what the later
Italian art, with its rich means of expression, offered seemed to them superficial. In Siena they became interested in Saint Catherine. What a miracle of the human spirit—a soul in whom the ecstatic capacity for love was
as strong as the heroic energy, whose political instinct was as sure as the
naive directness of a real woman! They also admired the church that knew
how to preserve the reality of its sacred figures with the same naive sagacity. Did not the mummified head of Saint Catherine, repulsive though it
was, confirm more graphically than any account that she was, is, and will
be?

Assisi was filled with a group of German pilgrims, men and women of various classes. Not all the pilgrims knew why they had been brought there.
A few simple women asked whether it was a bathing resort; others had been
attracted by the opportunity to take an inexpensive trip. One fat pilgrim
who came panting up the steep road was overheard to say in the genuine
Berlin dialect: "My indulgences I can get in Lichterfelde[38] just as good
as I get them in Rome." But many of them reacted to what they saw as
if it were real, and were moved by a beautifully carved, life-size crucifix as
though it were the dead Savior.

The Webers felt that the church was doing good business with Saint
Francis who, having almost been regarded as a heretic, saw his mission in
pitting against the church's increasing earthly glamor the utter poverty,

[37]Anselm Feuerbach, 1829–1880, German painter; the gallery was established by the German
art collector, dramatist, literary historian, and diplomat Adolf Friedrich Graf von Schack,
1815–1894; Moritz von Schwind, 1804–1871, Vienna-born German Romantic painter.—Ed.
[38]A suburb of Berlin.—Ed.

humility, and love of the first disciples of Jesus. As though it were Mephis-to's doing, the giant pilgrims' church, a cold, white building, was built on top of Francis's tiny chapel—a monument to the Counter-Reformation. However, they found that the wonderful pictures of the early masters that adorn the old church, named after Francis, reflected a genuinely religious spirit. The most moving things amidst all this superabundance were the su-pernatural majesty of Cimabue's[39] *Madonna* with the angels and the touch-ing figure of Francis, the lovely majesty of *Saint Clare* by Simone Martini,[40] and the unworldly reverence of Lorenzetti's[41] *Blessed Virgin* being adored by John and Francis. The last-named quiet picture, which reflects a complete absorption in the mystery, moved the Webers profoundly, because it once again brought home to them what was irretrievably lost to their own age. Outdoors, the spirit of Saint Francis was alive as well. The white city was placed around the bare mountain like a lace collar; all elevations were rocky and unfruitful, and only far down in the valley was there a grayish green car-pet of olive trees. In the narrow streets there was ineradicable poverty.

Rome had undergone an ugly transformation. There were obtrusive new buildings, particularly the frosty white and gold marble monument, the ex-pression and symbol of a united Italy. Even the Siegesallee[42] in Berlin was no worse. As though made by a pastry chef, it not only ruined the old Piaz-za Venetia, but—worse yet—by shifting all dimensions it overwhelmed the capitol behind it. The new Rome dared to place itself, parvenulike, along-side the old Rome, and its artists had no taste, although they saw the models they were emulating every day. The grand desolation of the Campag-na had receded as well. The Webers saw ploughed land, tree nurseries, and new little white houses—a gratifying sight for political economists and health inspectors, but an irreplaceable loss for people who, somewhat irre-sponsibly, only wished to enjoy the picturesqueness and the flavor of the past.

But finally the old relics did emerge from the modern everyday surround-ings, and they were almost more moving than ever. This time, too, the Webers were especially impressed by the old avenue of tombs which ran from

[39]Giovanni Cimabue, ca. 1240–1302.—Ed.
[40]Sienese painter, ca. 1284–1344.—Ed.
[41]The Sienese painter Pietro Lorenzetti who, together with his younger brother Ambrogio, was active in the first half of the fourteenth century.—Ed.
[42]The "Victory Avenue" lined (since 1898–1901) with marble monuments of Prussian rulers.—Ed.

the bustle of modern Rome straight as an arrow and endlessly into the silence of the Campagna. Rows of young cypresses accompanied it for a while like a guard of honor, then only umbrella pines stood here and there on the decayed mounds like mute guards, casting blue shadows over the quiet road that no longer served the living. Where did it lead? Its apparent destination was the blue mountains that framed the picture and at the same time pointed to something beyond. Here nature formed a wonderful union with the monumental ruins that were embedded in it. What the Webers saw seemed like a parable; everything near and far was mysteriously fraught with significance. The greatness of the past, although present only in meager fragments, nevertheless had remained effective across the millenia, equally moving as a symbol of transitoriness and as a symbol of eternity.

15

THE MOTHER —————————————————————

In this chapter we return to Helene. Her old age was full of substance and brought her ever new tasks, joys, and sorrows. She now lived alone in her unmetropolitan little house with a tiny garden, and living an unencumbered life became increasingly necessary for her. Yet she did not have many lonely hours, except early in the morning and late at night, when others were asleep. Her children who lived in other cities as well as nieces and nephews often enjoyed her hospitality, and across the way there was the Mommsen house with Klara's large family.

Helene continued her motherly role. She took an active interest in the pregnancies [*Gattungsdienst*] of her two daughters, and she helped deliver almost all of her grandchildren. She was such a skillful and experienced lying-in nurse that even her son-in-law the doctor bowed to the "old school." In this personal service and vigorous activity she was completely in her element, and—uncharacteristically—she had confidence in her ability and enjoyed it. Such quiet weeks full of solicitude and activity in which she could have no other desire but to guard the flames of life were blessed for her by the close, affectionate relationship with her daughters and sons-in-law.

Only now did the young generation fully appreciate Helene's stature and special quality. The daughters, who had sometimes found her annoying while they were growing up, now considered her a paragon. For the growing grandchildren, too, there were always many things to do and to keep in mind—the many birthdays and Christmas, for example. Helene insisted upon giving personal presents to all the big and little children, and whenever she took a trip she tortured herself trying to think of *Mitbringsel* [little gifts] for her entire clientele. She also tried to introduce her grandchildren to her intellectual world by reading with them. Homer, Carlyle's book on Frederick the Great, and Fritz Reuter were brought out again, and she could always make them laugh with Uncle Bräsig's[1] delightfully funny stories. Above all, she helped out when her daughters needed a vacation; then she often took their place for weeks and became an integral part of the newer households. And how very skillful and busy her old hands were! She emptied all mending baskets.

Thus the young lives kept her in constant motion. But her mature sons also desired her services. It almost seemed like a good thing that all of them remained childless; as it was, there was a great deal of life to share with them. This incessant service alone could have filled her days to the brim. And when after the age of sixty all sorts of physical infirmities appeared—particularly in her limbs, on which she had made the greatest demands—her children tried to keep her from performing so many chores away from home. It was in vain, for since becoming a widow she had regarded the social-welfare work that she had started earlier as a "vocation" [*Beruf*].

She took on many commitments in the course of the years. And she always felt an urge to be of direct service to poorer people and never gave up hope of being able to help them morally as well. For example, to counteract the consumption of alcohol, she put a sign saying "HEISSER TEE" [Hot Tea] on the door of her house as soon as the cold weather arrived. In this way she invited mailmen, milkmen, bakers, and whoever else got chilled while working to come in and warm up. Long before there were any organizations for it, she cooked on her own stove for proletarian women in childbed and saw to it that they had domestic help.

Because of the time she had spent helping people, she had gained a profound insight into the problems of the poor, and now that community aid was beginning to be organized, she was able to make all kinds of suggestions.

---

[1] Inspektor Bräsig, a popular character in *Ut mine Stromtid*, the third part of Reuter's autobiographical trilogy (1862–64).—Ed.

She was among the founders of the Charlottenburg Youth Center which aimed to prevent the corruption of proletarian children of all ages in the big city by supervising them outside school hours and giving them loving care. The personal initiative of young people gradually turned this *Jugendheim* into a model institution. She was delighted when the seeds of helpfulness came up and bore such good fruit. It was so important to win new volunteers for service to the community and to instill a feeling of social responsibility in the young women of the propertied classes.

The Charlottenburg *Hauspflegeverein* [Home Care Association], which she helped to found, was also very close to her heart. It gave help of every kind to proletarian women who were having babies, particularly by sending nurses to their homes. It was one of Helene's chief ethical tenets that a man should share the difficult hours of birth with his wife, that the first cry of the baby and all the sorrowful happiness of its first days ought to concern the father as well, for if the delivery was made outside the home, he did not realize the full weight of his responsibility. It often upset her that frequently a proletarian was inconsiderate enough to have sexual relations with a new mother who was in need of rest, or that he replaced her with a "girl friend" while she was in the hospital. She was convinced that such a man would have better control of himself if the burden of the female procreative lot [*Gattungslos*] were deeply impressed upon him and if the shared shock of the life-and-death struggle bound the parents together beyond everyday concerns.

Helene's house was a "collecting center" for all foods and items, from oat cereals to baby carriages, needed by expectant mothers and infants, and this alone meant that there was a constant flow of people. In the course of the years there were many additional projects, particularly the Charlottenburg *Wohlfahrtszentrale* [Social Welfare Center]. It was her idea to coordinate the various scattered charitable activities of certain districts and to direct them from a central point. How varied this task became, and how it snowballed! It was a matter of achieving cooperation among associations bent upon their independence and suspicious of anything new, and of employing trained social workers. Wherever fresh needs became apparent, new institutions were to be created. A cooperative structure of this kind, with a central office and salaried workers in addition to volunteers, was urgently needed—for one thing, because it turned out that many "problem children" of society received care from several places at once, while those ashamed of their poverty stood aside. All the scattered sources of aid were now to be connected to form a network, and they were to be so prudently distributed that, if possible, every needy person could be helped without tempting anyone to become a professional beggar. The experiment inspired by Helene was soon supported by the municipal administration. It was the first of its kind and became the prototype of the central offices in other big cities.

Since Helene was always greatly interested in counteracting the way the welfare system diminished moral energies and self-respect, she always tried to help the weak and those of limited ability by getting them jobs. That was particularly difficult, for it required not only a spirit of enterprise, which she had in abundance, but also business experience, which she lacked. But fortune favors the brave! The women encouraged one another, pooled their talents, and gladly let Helene inspire them. She had so much experience, was always so cheerful and energetic, and placed herself in the background and in the least desirable spots. Thus the general enthusiasm produced results of all kinds. Needy women were given sewing work and trained for it. For unemployed men a *Schreibstube* [writing room] was established.

But Helene's pet project was the scrap collection. She liked the idea of having any broken-down items—which to their owners were only burdensome junk and which were destined for destruction—fixed up in an ingenious fashion and restored to use. In this way many proletarian families acquired new possessions. When no place for this activity could be found, she took the stuff into her own home and personally tackled the unpleasant job of picking the usable items out of the wagonloads of dirty trash.

She did not consider any work too strenuous or too menial for her. Let others work with their heads; she always wanted to serve with her hands and her feet, too. She made many errands in behalf of individuals, and when joint work was done she willingly filled vacancies. She claimed that she particularly enjoyed performing tasks that the younger people found boring. Problems that other people did not feel up to handling, such as reasoning with drunkards, loafers, and brutal husbands, she would solve with ingenuous directness. The vigorous philippics of *Frau Stadtrat* [the city councillor's widow] frequently were successful and inspired respect; many of the sinners she tackled may have thought that she was some kind of official. She finally did become one of sorts: in 1904 the municipal government of Charlottenburg appointed her to the Welfare Board [*Armenverwaltung*] as the first woman so appointed in Prussia. There she soon made understanding friends among the city councillors and was able to show them many things from a new angle, that of a woman.

She strenuously pursued the authorities if it was a matter of breaking through the bureaucratic barrier in the interest of individuals. She was on the board of the *Bürgerhaus* [Citizens House] which was open to impecunious old people as the last stop on their journey through life. No one was permitted to bring his or her own furniture, things to which a human heart is so attached. Helene regarded this regulation as inhuman; how differently women would do things if they had the power! But she fought it in vain. However, on one occasion at least she managed to secure the admission, against all regulations, of an old couple with their belongings. Never was the fate of an individual unimportant to her, never did she grow tired of working in his behalf and keeping his well-being in mind. Indissoluble bonds tied her to a number of her protégés. How it gladdened her to feel the "divine spark" in the souls of the disinherited! But she was not disappointed when she realized that there were countless inferior people who could not be helped permanently. When a sixteen-year-old welfare trainee had once again run away from the master to whom he was apprenticed, she took him into her house, got him out of bed at six o'clock each morning, and planned his daily schedule. Only after a year of this could she be convinced that not even she could keep that boy on the right path.

Each year there was a bit of argument with her children, for in midsummer, when everyone tried to leave the hot city, Helene could not be lured away. Who else would take care of the needy during those months? She was often dismayed when a volunteer's sense of duty broke down at that time of year, and she certainly did not want to set a bad example. Her activities greatly impressed her co-workers and were a constant inspiration to her children as well. Marianne captured it in the following lines:

What is there that one could not do, to which one could not adapt oneself? Only Mama's life has appeared to me to be completely beyond all possibilities. The little house is constantly shaken by the ringing of the telephone. She permits everyone to bother her at any time of day, she is *always* available as a matter of principle and deems it impossible to deny herself to people for even an hour a day. Thus, her house is a dovecote for "poor souls" and "grateful favorites." And what this old woman does purely quantitatively from morning till midnight puts people like us so much to *shame* that I always tell her jokingly that it is impossible to live with her because a person would lose all his self-respect. Yet she does nothing mechanically; she infuses her vibrant life into everything and everything is full of her spirit. And the most astonishing thing is this: Despite all this petty detail that prevents any intellectual concentration and brings her in contact with so much misery, she is still open to everything beautiful and cheerful, so fresh in her receptivity. I experienced this again when we saw *Much Ado About Nothing* together; such youthful delight in the robust, unadulterated gaiety! She really let it relax her. She is a *saint* with both her feet on the ground, and now that her life has an inner harmony, she is so completely life-affirming and healthy.

And to Helene:

> Once again I felt completely surrounded by the inexhaustible ocean of your love—there is only one such mother! To be sure, it is humiliating that we can *never* be like this. And if "we" sometimes grumble a bit about your way of life, we only do it to free ourselves from being crushed by the sense of our own inadequacy. Yes, that is the way it is. Of course, I cannot approve of the telephone running your life; that is barbaric. And that an old woman should stay up until one o'clock in the morning for the amusement of her servant girls is even less acceptable. But I approve of *everything else*!

Helene had to be told repeatedly how much she meant to people, for she was far from satisfied with what she accomplished. As she had done earlier in her life, she constantly overexerted herself. When she was young and it cost her a great effort to keep on an even keel amidst the personal demands and passions crowding in on her, she had often longed for old age as a time of freedom and outward calm. Now her own activity produced ever new struggles and exertions. She was young in spirit, but her tools would not always obey the demands of her will. The receptivity of her memory for all the new things crowding in on her diminished, and this made her suffer almost as if it were her own fault. She said that she was doing everything wrong, that her old head was no longer good for anything, and so on. Physical ailments she shrugged off with a smile—she did not even want to be asked about them—but the decline of her mental powers made her final and hardest relinquishment necessary.

When her family, grief-stricken over Helene's suffering because of herself, implored her to give up part of her work, she refused. It seemed impossible to her while she still had time left. After all, no one would take over *her* work, the unpretentious efforts where the others failed. And she did not want to admit that her very existence and her strength derived from an unselfish love that meant far more than activities. Thus no other way could be found to lighten her load than a new imposition: the temporary move to Hannover, to her unmarried son, Karl, who had been in uncertain health for some time. To leave her home, her work, and her circle and to adapt herself to strange surroundings meant a heavy sacrifice for Helene, but she was ready to make it and moved for an indefinite period in the spring of 1914. But first she had a celebration at home.

In April of 1914 Helene completed her seventieth year. She was now really an old woman with a rather stooped figure. Her bad legs made it increasingly difficult for her to walk on the hard pavement outside, but otherwise she still moved quickly, vigorously, and gracefully. Her smooth hair was still brown, and sometimes a small lock slipped onto her wrinkled forehead—a roguish touch that lightened her seriousness in other respects as well. Her large, nobly formed nose now dominated her narrow oval face and lent it meaning. Her eyes sparkled with kindness, and her mouth, which was often sad when closed, was still capable of hearty laughter. She was excitable, full of temperament, and vigorous in her agreement and disagreement. She still tried to understand the new things that were alien to her nature, and there was room in her even for a Promethean defiance of God. Skepticism toward ideals and exemption from the moral law were the only things she rejected with a silent shaking of her head. When something moved her, a youthful fire glowed through her delicate white skin, and every feature of her animated face expressed a wealth of deep feeling as well as all her sorrow at her own inadequacy or that of others—painful resignation and pious submission.

The celebration that was prepared for her overwhelmed her modesty. After all, for once she had to be shown what she meant to people. From her profuse seeds of love there now bloomed a colorful, miraculous wreath of flowers. It was a pilgrimage. What words could not say was expressed in music and verse. Her friends presented her with a golden heart as a symbol of her own heart. It was filled with gold—now she could make donations! On the day before, in the family circle, there were offerings from children's lips and hands. In the darkness of early morning the nurses sang sacred songs; this was followed by the music of a military band as ordered by her youngest son, the officer, and then there were deputations from the organizations and the city, her protégés and friends. What was expected of this woman celebrating her birthday was almost inhuman, but she could not grow tired; she only thought of how she could do justice to each person with a word of affection and gratitude. Afterward Marianne wrote her about that day:

> It was beautiful to realize that people are just, and the structure of the world makes sense in one respect: love is repaid with love. To be sure, the love that is returned to you is of a lesser metal than your love; I know this only too well. Yours is truly holy in nature, because it never seeks its own interest. What you get back from all of us earthly beings with our more selfish, less pure souls is earthly. But even this has a fine, warm glow, and that we have to love and venerate you so probably leaves its traces in us as well.

Of her children only her oldest son Max was missing on that festive day. He was on his southern journey, and matters of importance kept him away. But he saw the image of his mother all the more clearly. He held out his strong hand to her, and what he was able to express better in writing than in person, his interpretation of her character and her destiny, may have been as generous a gift as his presence.

Ascona, April 12, 1914

Dear Mother:

Of course, it really seems strange to me that I am so far away from you, although it probably would have been hard for me to make any other arrangement than this. And it is anything but easy to say what one means properly in such strange surroundings.

I find it almost incredible that almost half a century should have passed since my earliest Erfurt memories that relate to you—a time when I always took the print of the *Sistine Madonna*[2] (the "artistic showpiece" of our small apartment then) to be you and in characteristic immodesty regarded myself as the Christ child on your arm and my brothers and sisters as the angels; a time when Aunt Monts, the retired railroad director, "Little Sophie," and the Tiedes were the only people other than my parents who existed for me, a time when everything the parents did seemed as comprehensible to the child as the child was to the parents. I wonder how things would have turned out if we had stayed in the old place forever. For a great many of the problems and all the trouble that came later were the consequence of our

---

[2]Raphael's painting for the Church of St. Sixtus at Piacenza, Italy.—Ed.

transplantation in the Berlin atmosphere, particularly after the old
friends of the first period—Fritz Eggers, Julian Schmidt, Friedrich
Knapp—had left one after the other and the Hobrechts[3] had grown
older. For this vanished and forgotten bourgeois generation whose history will never be written was worth knowing and also brought into
our house a way of thinking that constituted a counterpoise to the
alienating elements of the metropolitan atmosphere, an atmosphere
which greatly affects the relationship of children, at least sons, to
their parents if the children, as almost all of us were, are nervous, impressionable boys with a tendency toward introversion. The first difficult things in your life, including Helenchen's [little Helen's] death,
I did not even share with you, for as you know, I matured early intellectually but very late in every other respect. On the contrary, that
was the beginning of the years in which children, particularly sons,
usually cause their parents, especially their mother, trouble and worry
and are quite inaccessible to her. I did so to a degree far greater than
the usual, and, as I often notice, to a far greater extent than you
remember today. But it is perhaps a good thing that all this has been
buried! Then came my student days, and, as I well know, these brought
more great worries about me, worries to which my only response was estrangement.

In those years it probably happens often that growing sons are
particularly averse to opening up to their mothers, because they now
feel a need to be "independent" and yet are aware of their insufficiency
and know that their mother is so very *right* to worry and admonish,
because the fact that she *is* right is what is most unbearable to them.
I know well that during the first years of the hard period that now
began it was a great disappointment to you that your son, who had
returned home after student years that were certainly not pleasant in
every respect, was a support for you to only a *very* slight extent, and
at first no support at all. This changed only very gradually—and even
then I bore the blame for needlessly exacerbating the situation, in
minor and major instances, and I very often aggravated things for you
rather than easing them, until the very last.

But anyway, things finally did improve; and even if you did not, *I*
experienced in a decisive measure the whole splendor and warmth this
created inside me, and I not only carried the *memory* of this into my
life, but something else too: That which has been flourishing between

[3]Artur Hobrecht, 1824–1912, mayor of Berlin (from 1872), Prussian minister of finance (from
1878), and Reichstag member (1881–1890). His brother James Friedrich Ludolf, 1825–1902, was
a construction engineer and expert on canalization.—Ed.

Marianne and me would never have come into being and grown if I had not recognized your life—hard on the outside, beautiful on the inside—the way I did at that time. For I could very easily have become a *very* different person. Accept the thanks for this especially from Marianne. And with my brothers and sisters it did not happen immediately, because they were younger and did not immediately experience many things with the same awareness. But sooner or later it did happen with all of them, in a different way with each, and despite the very dissimilar problems they faced, it pointed each person in the same direction. I suppose that very seldom has a mother had to raise children who were more dissimilar and more difficult, children for whom it was made so extraordinarily hard to harmonize with one another. But if you disregard a few tensions that still have not been entirely removed but really mean *nothing,* and if one subtracts what fates that were inevitable or that a person brought upon himself have done to individuals, well, you have to say in retrospect: All of them have led, are leading, and will continue to lead lives that are worth living.

That is why this day, with all our memories of hard times of the past and our awareness of external and inner difficulties, such as are inevitably and repeatedly brought about by circumstances and the somewhat complex nature of all concerned, is really a day of *very* great *joy*—at least for me, and I hope for you as well. "She did what she could"—these words apply to your relations with our father, which were frequently difficult and particularly so at the end. Certainly all of us have a fair view of him today, and now that all the difficult tensions have been forgotten, we can rejoice at what he was in his surely uncommon, solid, and pure bourgeois mentality. We know that the rifts in his life were the tragedy of his entire generation, which never quite came into its own with its political and other ideals, never saw its own hopes fulfilled and carried on by the young generation, which had lost its old faith in authority and yet still took an authoritarian view of matters where *we* could no longer take such a view. His life would have been a hard one without your love, which was ever awake despite all conflicts. And even though he had—happened to have—some grievous experiences toward the end of his life (actually it was more a specific awareness of them), I believe that he would think the same way today, and he knew it even in those days.

But the years since then have brought a great deal of immeasurable wealth, both in your life with your daughters and grandchildren and in your immense amount of public service. If you now interrupt this for some time for the sake of human duties and turn some of it over permanently to others, I know that this will be very hard for you and that on this day you are not so much looking back with joy as looking *ahead* into the future with some uneasiness. But consider what it means that you have brought yourself to make such a decision in the first place and that we found it possible to expect you to make it! What other woman your age would be strong enough to do this? Compared to this the details and everything else are trifles; the decisive thing is that you had the *will power* and exerted it. But one thing is certain: You will have been to this son, too, what you have been to the two older sons and to the younger children as well, and he will be as eternally grateful to you as the others.

Here everything is a most luxuriant green and in full bloom. I once wrote Marianne why I love the *southern* spring so much. It is not the impetuous boy who roars through fields and forests, making everything rejoice, releasing torrents, and reawakening all impulses. It comes to the stylized landscape in severe forms, and what it brings to it in the way of fresh greenery and flowers is like someone putting a light wreath on the head of a mature woman. It is the kind of spring that can be in the hearts even of people who have half a century on their backs, as I do now, or who are a bit older still (it is not much more, for you were only a young girl when you gave birth to me). I am thinking of the fact that one can always have this spring, and I *bless* you, dear Mother, with an old, strong love from the bottom of my heart.

Your Max

16

SERVICE

I

Despite periodic exhaustion, Weber's productive power and his agility were now so steady that sometimes only the dark memories of his grave illness still kept him from being in good health. Those who were close to him frequently thought, "Oh, if only some great wave came and carried him into the mainstream of life!"

The summer of 1914 reigned in splendor. In the mountain forest, students had a festival on warm Midsummer Eve. The clearing overarched by giant trees was illuminated by torches. The students performed a Shakespeare comedy with artistic perfection and then jumped through the fire. The spectators nestled against the warm sylvan soil. In July the deputy rector of the university, Eberhard Gothein, gave a party in the castle park at Schwetzingen. Once more the relaxed gaiety and the finely honed wit of the world's poet spoke through the mouths and the gestures of radiant young people. In the festive afternoon sun and with the Greek temple as a background, everything almost seemed even more beautiful than it had been by torchlight, and the festive hours went by undisturbed in the avenues of the princely park. Delighting in the artistic spirit of their class, people moved easily and freely in the summery blue; the earth was fair.

Soon thereafter, on the last Sunday in July, Weber's *Saal* [parlor] was filled, with some of the same people—young and old friends, but now under a different constellation. They crowded together and no one paid any attention to the others. An evil thing—the murder at Sarajevo—had begotten other evil things; what significance would it have? A misfortune that had been threatening for a decade was now upon them. But they still argued back and forth about the various courses that world history might take. The war clouds had been just as low before and they had always been scattered, so perhaps that would happen this time too. They did not even totally reject the horror of war, for they felt that the release of tensions, the raging of the elements, the adventures, and the breakdown of the world order might somehow be great and inspiring and would release previously confined energies. Whatever presentiments may have filled people's souls with horror, *an abyss separated possibilities from realities,* and no acuity of perception was able to bridge it.

That afternoon all the tense people clustered about Weber. Their questions took him around the globe, and hour after hour they hung on his every word. He had had his most important childhood experience, the outbreak of the war of 1870, in that very room and at the same time of year. Thinking back it seemed to him that the mood had been different then, more serious and more solemn. But the die was not yet cast; it was still possible to play with fate. One thing, however, had already become apparent: These young people, who had previously searched for a form of existence away from the community, were now ready to sacrifice themselves in service to the community. No one desecrated his intentions by expressing them in words, but it could be sensed that no member of this group of intellectuals and aesthetes would regard himself as too good to serve. There were no farewells, but one week later they were scattered over the face of the earth.

* * *

The hour had come, and it was of undreamed-of sublimity. Outward events, to be sure, did not loom large in the small town. In the marketplace between the church and the city hall, the people who gathered to receive the news were almost entirely from the older part of town. There were no speeches of consecration or rhetoric. People listened quietly and then went away quietly. Yet it was an hour of the greatest solemnity—the hour of *depersonalization* [*Entselbstung*], of integration into the community. An ardent love of community spread among people, and they felt power-fully united with one another. Having formed a brotherhood they were ready to destroy their individual identities by serving.

On their way home the Webers paused at the upper end of the old bridge for a moment; a radiant summer evening lent perfection to everything around them. The setting sun glowed like a firebrand on the windows of the houses on the mountain slope, and the soaring sky imparted its delicate blue to the river. The earth rested blissfully in its beauty. Soon it would drink in the blood of thousands. It was going to shroud in darkness the eyes of the young people who delighted in it, still ignorant of its full wealth, and dim the summery splendor of mature manhood. With a shudder, human beings now stood on the edge of reality. And even more touching than the fate of the youth was the fate of the men who now moved knowingly and soberly from the height of life into the darkness.

* * *

But what about action? Where would it show itself? All earlier life paled. What had still been meaningful and important yesterday was now no longer so. Everyone was looking for new forms of activity and service. Would they find them? Weber had long since left the military service; he was now fifty years old. His figure was towering and vigorous, but he was by no means fit to bear arms. That he was not able to march into the field at the head of a company was acutely painful to him: "I may be the most martially dis-posed of your sons. That the fate and the experience of this—despite everything—great and wonderful war finds me here in the office and passes me by like this, I shall add to many other things. Even so, life keeps bring-ing many things that make it worth living."

However, Weber immediately reported to the garrison command; he was given the post of a disciplinary officer on the Military Hospitals Commis-sion of the Reserve Corps, and since for the time being no other men were available, he was put in charge of establishing reserve hospitals in Heidelberg. He accepted these assignments without hesitation, and on the first day of mobilization he sat in the office from 8 A.M. on: "I am on duty for thir-teen hours. Perhaps I shall still be transferred to a fortress or something similar. Unfortunately I cannot march and thus cannot be used at the front, and this is really very hard for me."

Several large hospitals had to be ready in ten days. The plans and direc-tions that he found were very disorganized, and nothing had been prepared. The supply contracts drawn up twenty years earlier were unusable. For days

Weber negotiated with indignant tradesmen who were unable to supply things at the agreed-upon prices. He had to start everything all over again, and he plunged into feverish activity over concerns completely new to him. A thousand items for the care of wounded men had to be conjured up as quickly and inexpensively as possible, and local suppliers had to be favored. All the anonymous things whose duty it is to be there quietly and as a matter of course when they are needed, down to ladles and the cooks using them, now assumed great importance. Weber even procured the kitchen furnishings in a hurry—things that normally did not concern him and about which he knew nothing.

The hectic pace of the first weeks really wore him out, and the question was whether he would be able to stand it. He was very irritable, and when superiors or authorities placed obstacles in his path he was disagreeable. When, for instance, the commissariat in Karlsruhe asked why a telephone had to be installed, he sent the inquiry back with this handwritten note: "Normal people know why a telephone is needed, and I cannot explain it to others." When in a case of the greatest urgency the same administrative authority first demanded a list of all items necessary for an unscheduled hospital, Weber punished the bureaucrats by sending them a meter-long telegram. He was equally annoyed by unnecessary disturbances, particularly telephone calls from persons who were too far away to compel him to be courteous. Once there was a long-distance call from the *Hofmarschallamt* [chamberlain's office] in Karlsruhe: "How are the wounded men?" Weber: "Which ones?" —"Well, *all* of them." Weber (ironically): "Oh, very well." —"Her Royal Highness the Grand Duchess would like to know whether a visit from Her Highness would be welcome." —"I have no objection, but *I* have no time to take anyone around." End of conversation. The chief medical officer, Weber's military co-worker, was horrified when he heard of this incident and immediately got on the line to assure the caller ever so humbly that a visit from Her Royal Highness would be appreciated by everyone as a great favor and honor.

But if Weber was not exactly cut out to be a "subordinate," he was all the more suited to being a superior. In this position he had full control over himself. His staff tried to win his approval; they loved and respected him. The university was on vacation. The anatomist Hermann Braus,[1] a friend of Weber's, offered himself as a personal aide and came to the office every day. The prudent man acted as a beneficial buffer between the outside

---

[1]1868–1925, professor of anatomy at Heidelberg and Würzburg.—Ed.

world and Weber. Other friendly colleagues also offered their services. Scholarly work was impossible, and everyone scrambled for a chance to lend a hand in some way. Weber let them supervise the setting up of the hospitals. Together with their own staff of helpers they could now see to it not only that mangled limbs were healed for fresh combat, but also that souls benumbed by horror thawed out in the love of the homeland. The helpers were on hand when the first transports of wounded soldiers arrived. The soldiers were embraced and kissed, everyone was moved to tears, and as the aides helped to cut the bloody pieces of uniform from their bodies, they saw frightful things. "This was done for you"—this knowledge inspired any amount of loving strength in the souls of those who had stayed at home.

A military hospital now was a world that obeyed its own laws. Everyone who was washed ashore in a mutilated condition by the waves of fate became a new gift and a precious treasure worth saving from destruction with the utmost effort of all healthy forces. Every person who had recently been mercilessly sacrificed to the common good was here reinstated into his right to live. Here compassionate love atoned for the offense against the individual. Countless simple people had never before experienced as much love as they did there, and to many of them the hospital became a new home. From the outside, too, enthusiastic gratitude penetrated all crevices of the military system. Almost daily the citizens of the small town saw long processions of seriously wounded men being carried through the streets on stretchers. Every wounded soldier appeared to them as a hero and was showered with gifts. How rich Germany was! The baker, the butcher, the grocer—they all made donations. Senseless? Unreasonable? Certainly; a limit had to be set to this pampering. But it *was* magnificent that such effusiveness was possible, that the well-ordered *amour-propre* of the citizens was so generous. In those marvelous first months, all inner life was reduced to its simple, shared outlines and everything unimportant crumbled away. Everyone was full of goodwill and each day brought action and tension. Personal considerations were suspended in the superpersonal. It was the acme of existence.

From the moment that England sided with the enemy, Weber took a very serious view of Germany's situation. Yet when the German flags waved over Namur and Liège, a happy end did seem possible to him. But come what might, this attitude of the entire people, this strength for fighting, suffering, sacrificing, and loving seemed to be sublime in itself. Now that war had proved to be inevitable, Weber thanked his lucky stars for having let him live to see the war: "For *no matter* what the outcome—*this war is great*

and wonderful" (August 28, 1914). "Despite its hideousness this war is great
and wonderful and worth experiencing. It would be even more worthwhile
to participate in it, but unfortunately they cannot use me in the field
as they would have used me if it had been waged in time, twenty-five years
ago. My brothers are all serving in the field or in garrisons; my brother-in-law
[Hermann Schäfer] fell at Tannenberg."[2]

Weber, who normally was isolated at his desk, now navigated in the middle of a stream of the most intensive communal labor. He controlled an expanding network, and under his administration nine new hospitals came into being in the town. When they were ready and in use, he became involved
in another and disagreeable task, the disciplining of men who had committed offenses. Weber's jurisdiction as a disciplinary officer extended to
the approximately forty military hospitals of the district, and there was
a wide radius of human impressions and experiences. These showed the other,
more commonplace side of the exaltation.

> Max is now frequently bothered by the monotony of his daily work, since it
> consists of countless punishments for minor infractions of discipline commit-
> ted by hospital inmates. The whole prison is overcrowded, and the poor
> sinners often wait for a week before they can serve their sentences. This often
> puts him in a bad humor, but his devotion to his duty is admirable. His
> "comrade" gladly turns all unpleasant tasks over to him and says that *he* has
> not been blessed with the patience for it.

Despite Weber's sensitivity toward the faults of his equals, the recalcitrance and the vices of the simple people he had to discipline did not diminish his appreciation of them:

> The impressions that I am having here among our people are part of
> what—again and again—makes life worth living, despite the fact that
> as organizer and disciplinary officer of the reserve military hospitals in
> the Heidelberg district I really get to see virtually *all* their disagreeable
> sides. We have demonstrated that we are a great civilized nation.
> People who live in a highly refined civilization and then nevertheless
> are equal to the horrors of war out there (which is no achievement for

---

[2]Town in East Prussia where the German Eighth Army under General Paul von Hindenburg
defeated the Russian second army under General Alexander Samsonov between August 26 and
30, 1914.—Ed.

a Senegalese Negro![3]), who *despite this* come back like that, as *thoroughly decent* as the great majority of our people—such people are genuine human beings, and this must *certainly* not be overlooked amidst all the obtrusive activities of a disagreeable kind. This experience will definitely last, no matter what the outcome may be. (January 13, 1915)

In addition to dealing with patients and staff in the hospitals, Weber came into contact with all kinds of people: doctors, Red Cross officials, nurses, orderlies, and cooks. And whenever something happened—which, of course, was every day in these makeshift groups—Weber was sought out as a Solomonic judge. There were all kinds of things to be settled—when the medical potentates had got into one another's hair or had made unauthorized arrangements, when the inspector had treated the nurses in an unseemly manner, when the mistress. [*Favoritin*] of a senior medical officer had committed some infringement, when a nurse had let an unparliamentary expression against some ruffian slip out, when eggs and bottles of wine had been pilfered, or when a hysterical cook had washed her hair in the stewpot. Or His Honor the Mayor of some place in the district might personally appear in the office declaring that it was high time to fill the beautiful hospital that had been ready for so long; the inhabitants of the village urgently demanded their wounded. The mayor was told that unfortunately it was impossible to have the requisite number of men in field uniforms shot especially for M. Or it turned out that the mayor of another town had taken the law into his own hands by uncoupling a few cars from a passing hospital train at night and bringing his loot home triumphantly. Thus all sorts of amusing things were added to the Webers' store of anecdotes. Weber traveled a great deal. His automobile whizzed through the area every day; people called it "The Yellow Peril" and him "The Flying Dutchman."

Some serious problems arose as well, for instance, the attitude toward wounded enemies, particularly the French. Weber wished the disabled prisoners to be regarded simply as fellow human beings in need of care. He thought it politically prudent to treat enemies as humanely and carefully as one's own fellow nationals; surely that was bound to ease the lot of Germans in enemy countries. That is why he permitted his Alsatian colleague Sch———[4] who was married to a Frenchwoman, and the Swiss professor F. to visit the

---

[3]A reference to the military use by the French of natives from the colonies.—Ed.
[4]Heinrich Schneegans, 1863–1914, professor of Romance philology at Würzburg and Heidelberg.—Ed.

French patients and cheer them with small gifts. This, however, aroused great excitement in certain circles; people suspected the Alsatian in particular and notified the district command. But Weber managed to secure the continued admission of his colleagues by appealing to his excellent superior's military honor and pointing out that it was unmanly to bow to public opinion. A different view was held by another professor, a friend of Weber's,[5] in whose hospital there were members of a French unit. Without Weber's knowledge he had a military man accompany the Alsatian colleague on his visit. The latter, who was already aware of the increasingly hostile atmosphere, took this as a sign of distrust. He was deeply hurt and stopped his visits. This incident so enraged Weber that he brusquely broke with his friend. As so often in such cases, cause and effect were disproportionate to each other. Weber later apologized for his vehemence, but he expected the other man to admit his mistake. When he failed to do so, the break remained, and not until five years later were the stubborn men brought together again by their wives.

For Professor Sch—— it became impossible to remain in Heidelberg. He resigned from his teaching position and planned to move to Switzerland. But the district office refused to provide him and his wife with passports. Weber now made a lengthy petition to the authorities in which he called the insinuations circulating about Sch—— an expression of a war psychosis and pointed particularly to the political imprudence of such a measure. A hostile reaction could be expected not only from enemy countries but from neutral countries as well, and there would be tremendous repercussions in Alsace if a "Sch—— Case" were created. The passports were issued.

Even though Weber felt impelled to defend people with dual nationality who were experiencing a grave inner conflict, he harshly turned his back on such people if, instead of keeping quiet, they joined in the national strife. For example, it was equally repugnant to him when the half-Englishman H. S. Chamberlain[6] made pro-German remarks and when half-Germans abroad criticized their hard-pressed native country. When an old friend did criticize Germany, he seriously remonstrated with him, and when this produced no results, he broke with him with the following words:

---

[5]Ernst Troeltsch.—Ed.

[6]Houston Stewart Chamberlain, 1855–1927, Anglo-German writer, biographer of his father-in-law Richard Wagner and author of *Die Grundlagen des 19. Jahrhunderts* [Foundations of the Nineteenth Century] (1899–1901), a work containing racist theories of Teutonic superiority.—Ed.

You have a dual fatherland. That is your fate. It is not your fault, and you would not want it any other way. This situation gives you certain rights. In many respects you can feel differently from the way we others are permitted to feel at a time when our country—*only* ours among the Great Powers—is fighting for its very existence. This, to be sure, also imposes upon you certain obligations toward the land of your birth . . . particularly the duty to be able to *keep silent* under certain circumstances. No German can concede to you the right to have a say in the shaping of the peace, and certainly not in a way that is certain to meet with the approval of our enemies . . . *We* could have an honorable peace at any time? Not that I know of. Oh yes, we could! Perhaps from Italy, if we were scoundrels enough to break our alliance, that is, if we were not Germans . . . Enough. We evidently shall have no meeting of the minds. I regret this, for as you know, I have always been rather fond of you. Everyone has his faults, myself included. But at the moment yours are the more disastrous faults. You do not rise to the occasion, and in such serious matters everyone should clearly realize what is *not* given to him.

* * *

The hectic activity of the first months often took Weber to the limits of his strength, particularly since the man who had been used to sleeping in the morning now considered it important to be the first and the last in the office. He expected his organism to break down at Christmastime, but it did not. On the contrary, it got more and more accustomed to the service and seemed to derive its equilibrium from it. It seemed like a miracle. Had Weber's frequent feeling of sickness over the last few years been imaginary? No, because even the most intensive activity of an official evidently is not nearly so much of a nervous strain as *creative* mental activity. The only pathological emotional residue was Weber's fear of any task with a deadline. Fresh experience now covered up the deeply engraved memories which continued to cause that fear. Weber had recovered.

Life was much simpler now; every person was single-minded, and the days rushed by like a torrential stream. The Webers derived much satisfaction from their ability to help and counsel others. Weber was on duty on Sundays as well; he was home only afternoons, and many friends came to call then. Even during vacations Sundays were now very busy, for people wanted Weber to interpret the war news of the day for them and given them his judgment of the situation. There were no conversations about anything else, for this topic was inexhaustible.

Often friends who had been wounded at the front came and spent some time at home. They were the focus of attention and could never tell enough, for each man saw events differently and reflected the good fortune of a life that had been spared and the happiness of devotion to a lofty goal. Their erect figures were magnificent to behold. Some who had been youths a short time before now appeared in their uniforms as men. For the most part the features of the soldiers on leave were curiously drawn; they bespoke constant inner alertness, heavy responsibility, and their experiences at death's door. They were confident, but they knew that they could survey only a small segment of the enormous battle lines and were experiencing only their own actions. Now they were anxious to hear how the total situation was viewed at home. The soldiers usually agreed with Weber's views, for despite all successes they felt the growing superiority of the enemies.

On the other hand, in the eyes of many of those who had stayed home and now liked to talk politics, Weber was a "pessimist," for from the beginning he conceived of the war as a defensive war only and wanted to bring it to a conclusion as quickly as possible. Any aspirations to the permanent possession of captured territories, whether in the east or in the west, seemed pernicious to him. The pealing of bells, the waving banners, the inspiring victories at no time closed his eyes to the threatening difficulties of the situation or to the insight that time was not on Germany's side but was working against it. As early as September, 1914, he demanded that the government designate Belgium as a "security" [*Faustpfand*] and hold out the prospect of its future release. And in October he wrote:

> How should one imagine a peace? And when? Hundreds of thousands are bleeding because of the horrible incompetence of our diplomacy; unfortunately there is no denying that, and therefore I have no hope of a lasting peace even if there is a favorable conclusion to the war. If everything were as good as the leadership of the army surprisingly is—well, then things would be different with us.

How gladly he would have let himself be proved wrong!

* * *

Service on the homefront constantly brought new assignments: the organization of care for invalids, then the provision of occupations for those
slowly recovering, men for whom the tedium of the military hospital was
so dangerous. Weber organized adult education classes and training in manual
skills for the wounded—new and attractive work for his voluntary helpers.
The tiered semicircular rows of a lecture hall for clinical medicine were full
of people in light-colored hospital clothes, and there were many boyish faces
among the men. Weber himself mounted the rostrum in simple field gray,
the garb suited to his noble figure. He explained the nature of money, and
on another occasion he talked about the differences between the Russian
and the German agrarian constitutions.

Strange things are happening. Max gave two lectures [Kolleg] to
wounded men in the evening *after* hours. You see, adult education
classes are being organized in the military hospitals so the convalescents
may have something to do and a chance to advance themselves. So Max
gave two trial lectures, and he was fresh and lively, even though he had
been silent for sixteen years! And it did not do him any harm. So the
war had to come to outwit his inhibitions.

The atmosphere of the first wartime Christmas was everywhere loving and
romantic, yet solemn. Giving and receiving were blessed. The eyes of ordinary
men grew moist; they were as happy as children. Many had never before been
gifted in such a charming way. Among those who spoke to them was Weber.
When he stood before the tall Christmas tree and looked into the eyes
that were upon him, his emotion shone through his reserve. He knew that
these men would have to return to the front. His voice was like the sound
of an organ as he spoke of the greatness of death in battle: In everyday life
death comes to us as something uncomprehended, as an irrational fate from
which no meaning can be derived. We simply have to accept it. But every
one of you knows why and for what he dies if it falls to his lot. Those who
do not come back will be seed corn of the future. A hero's death for the
freedom and honor of our people is a supreme achievement that will affect
our children and children's children. There is no greater glory, no worthier
end than to die this way. And to many death gives a perfection that life
would have denied him.

What were the emotions of those who listened to Weber's words? Each
man had the right to hope that death would not find him, but there were

some who managed to say quite simply at parting: "And even if I don't return—so long as Germany remains."

II

The family suffered a grievous loss in the very first weeks of the war. Hermann Schäfer, the husband of Weber's youngest sister Lili, fell in one of the skirmishes near Tannenberg. He was a prince among men, full of kindness and noble-mindedness, an artist who made great demands upon himself. That is why he found the intellectual heritage of his brilliant father, the neo-Gothic architect Karl Schäfer, hard to handle; everyday pressures, too, often weighed heavily upon him. When the war broke out, he immediately left his office in high spirits and joined the army as an officer. He dedicated himself with enthusiasm, and his delicate wife had no doubt that she had to let him go, although she had a premonition that she would not see him again. Now death had quickly taken him in his prime, and he left a young widow with four young children. Yet Weber was able to find in this sacrifice a meaning not only for the common good but for the dead man as well. He wrote his sister, among other things:

> He would surely have liked to go on living with you, for you brought him all the happiness he had been created for, and yet, since all of us will have to die some day, this death in this war is not something that he would have wanted to evade. For no matter what the outcome may be, this war really is great and wonderful beyond all expectations. Not the successes but the spirit of the soldiers which we have been able to see here and can see every day in the military hospitals exceeds all expectations, and on the whole, so does the spirit of the population, at least here. I would never have hoped for this, and come what may, this shall remain unforgotten. To have fallen on these battlefields is worth even a beautiful and rich life. This is what *he* would think. Then, to be sure, he would think of you and the children, as we do.

* * *

The year 1915 brought two further painful losses: their old friend Emil Lask and Weber's brother Karl fell in action. Both of these successful university teachers had volunteered for service and both died at the height of their careers. Gratitude bids us preserve their pictures here.

Emil Lask, a Jew, was a philosopher and a stranger in the world of action. His home was on the cold, snowy peaks of contemplation. There he knew all paths and walked with a sure step; there he was able to be a guide to others. With a compelling hand he gave universal form to the bewildering profusion of individual phenomena. Universal truths were sacred to him; since they were unshakable, he regarded them as guarantors of the absolute truth he thirsted for. However, his ardent soul loved not only supernatural forms of beauty but earthly forms as well. His keen intellect moved over everything human like lightning, and his flashes of wit liked to sparkle over human weaknesses. But he also bowed full of reverence to everything great and good, and whenever these qualities moved him in someone, he henceforth viewed them as the essential thing. When he was gripped by the magic of love for living beauty, his entire being glowed and his surrender turned into self-effacement. Even the gentler emanations of friendship inspired sacrifice and loyalty in him. Yet he was always a lonely man, for he found it difficult to cope with things and human beings. When he needed to make a quick decision, he always became caught up in melancholy reflection and doubts. If good fortune came along, he always saw that it was transitory, and his clearsightedness always kept him from taking decisive action.

However, he immediately made the decision to offer himself for his country. He did not want to preserve himself by tending the temple while the earth was becoming saturated with the blood of his brothers. He was not young or strong and knew that the joyous spurt of vital energies out on the battlefield was denied him. He had no prospects of good fortune, heroism, or leadership. He went as one of the mass of people who are there to obey and to hold out. After long, tedious service at home he was finally sent to the front as a noncommissioned officer. Because of his poor eyesight he was unable to shoot. Fate let him go to the end of the line. The fatal bullet hit him immediately. Viewed intellectually, it was a *senseless* sacrifice. But did anyone have a right to prevent him from acting nobly in defiance of his nature or to keep him from a fulfillment he had never dreamed of?

Weber wrote to his family:

It is not easy to find the proper attitude toward the passing of such an exceptional and uncommon human being, particularly in view of his "mass death" on the Galician heath in a fight against barbarians. At first one is absolutely embittered at what has happened. One thing, to be sure, may be said: It is *not* entirely senseless if a man validates what he has taught his students by the manner of his death. Inwardly without illusions as he was, he saw in his departure for the front *nothing* but his *"bounden"* duty ["verdammte" *Pflicht und Schuldigkeit*]. It would have been utterly alien to his nature to waste any words on it. But to do it in this particular way was in keeping with those views he espoused from the rostrum, knowing full well how often all of us human beings are unable to live up to these ideals. Though he would have liked to go on living—this we know—he would be equally in tune with himself if he were able to look back on his end. That is quite a lot. If he had acted differently, he would always have been unsure of himself and never have admitted to himself that it would have been more appropriate for a man who was so courageous by nature but simply was *un*warlike to devote himself to his profession. That, of course, is our view as well. But we know that later it would have been impossible to save him from the stinging thought, "You should have acted as the others did." In his profound honesty with himself he knew this quite well, and that is why, after a brief period of indecision, he went.

* * *

Karl Weber's death appeared in a different light. He was martial by nature, and soldiering was in his blood. He rushed to his death intoxicated with life and the cause. The brothers Karl and Max, who had been estranged from each other in their youth, had grown together only a year before the outbreak of the war. At that time the younger man found a support in his older brother at a period of great inner distress. Weber lost a great deal, but he took a positive view of Karl's death, too, and wrote to Helene:

He had reached his fulfillment. How very hard it was for him to develop in himself the consistent simplicity, the refined inner objectivity, the ability to deal with things in silence, the relinquishment of "recognition"—in short, all those qualities we found so delightful in him. In his younger years he was so very differently constituted. The vigor and seriousness of his personality were something that only fate and his own inner work on himself gave him. What a problem child he was for you right up to his manhood, and how absolutely secure was the trust his personality inspired in all of us for years. And in the end he gained a complete understanding of you, which he once found so difficult. And one of our last conversations—carried on by him with fine and touching emotion—showed what it meant to him *to have completely understood and grasped you.* And finally, he had a beautiful death in the only place where it is worthy of a human being to be at the moment. (September 4, 1915)

Karl Weber (1870–1915) had after a problematic youth become an outstanding person—kind, dependable, and capable of great sacrifice. When he finally left school, which he had hated so much, he began a life of disciplined work in Karlsruhe under the direction of his brilliant master, Karl Schäfer, to whom he was utterly devoted. He had outstanding artistic and didactic gifts, and he was enthusiastic about his profession. As a government architect he received important assignments at an early age, and these included the restoration of churches at Dobrilugk and Oliva.[7] As a professor at Danzig and later at Hannover he gathered a large circle of students around himself, who admired him as much as he and his circle had once admired Schäfer.

Helene's seeds of love bore rich fruit. None of her children admired and loved her more dearly than Karl. In his youth he had not heeded her and had gone astray. When he had fought his way to clarity and purity, he credited this to her influence. He was convinced that her example and her teachings had now taken hold. When the war broke out he immediately went to the front, but after a short time he came down with a serious physical ailment. After months of being gravely ill, he recovered somewhat and against the advice of his doctors managed to rejoin his regiment in the east. He seemed to have recovered for nothing else. He tore himself away from the arms of loved ones, and his family did not dare restrain him, for he had never looked so radiant. He went away intoxicated with the sacrifice for a great cause; victory still beckoned, and a divine power still seemed to be guiding Germany's armies. It was toward the end of the summer that he saw his old mother for the last time. A bullet hit him during the first battles on the eastward advance. He had expected it. Helene approved of this sacrifice for a great cause. A long time after his brother's death Weber described him for Karl's fiancée in the following lines:

[7]Dobrilugk, now known as Doberlug-Kirchhain, town on the Kleine Elster in the Cottbus district. Oliva, a former commune of the Free City of Danzig.—Ed.

June 20, 1917

My Dear Martha:

I once read Karl's letters during a lonely train ride, and now I have reread them at leisure—with my most heartfelt gratitude for this great and very touching demonstration of confidence on your part and with profound emotion. The great genuineness and depth, the delicacy of feeling which these letters so touchingly reflect make me regret it all the more acutely that the bonds of understanding which had been fashioned in his last years did not have the time or the opportunity to develop further. We saw each other so seldom, and the estrangement of our youth, the many independent experiences each of us had had since then without the other man's knowledge, first had to recede into the background in favor of the newly shared things [Gemeinsamkeiten].

The great injustice we older brothers—or at least myself—committed toward Karl when we were still young lay essentially in our failure to realize that his outward behavior in those days, his style and gestures were *not* theatrics or something of the sort, as it appeared to my more sober self, but the entirely genuine and justified behavior of an *artist*. What did I know about such things at that time? His enthusiasm for working with his magnificent teacher Schäfer made a deep impression upon me, but since we did not see each other, this hardly brought us closer together. Karl's hard fate, of which I had only a partial knowledge, the disappearance of his youthfully unconstrained surrender to life, the great seriousness that took hold of him changed his outward personality in many respects, and I saw only that when we became closer to each other again. It made such a strong and favorable impression on me that I completely forgot to ask how dearly bought it might have been. But in the meantime I had seen enough of life and people to know how complete our misconceptions about young Karl had been and that we had done him an injustice in those days. There never was a good opportunity to discuss all this. And now he is no longer around.

But I see with great joy and emotion to what a great extent his ardent love for you restored to him what had been deeply buried under resignation—particularly toward the end, after the bad experience that wounded his heart—and those entirely immoderate self-reproaches which in his relentless honesty he leveled at himself because he had been as guileless as a child toward himself and human beings that he trusted. Thank fate for completely eradicating that and giving him this magnificent, mature, and at the same time enchanting youthful second bloom as the *fulfillment* of a life that was longingly reaching for the highest things. The alternation of exultant certainty with despondency in the letters from the period that was decisive for your relationship is as humanly genuine as his honest avowal of his religious attitude, an attitude that is in keeping with the fate of our time. This is particularly valuable to me, because it shows me that there too he did not delude himself, which is what so many people are doing today, particularly artists, weak souls who cannot bear the face of today's life. That he was strong enough not to do this and did not lose himself in the harshness of his fate and all his harsh self-criticism is evidence of such great inner strength that one has to love him for this alone.

And that is why we thank *Ihnen* [you]—or, rather, dear Martha, after this proof of trust I cannot bring myself to say anything but this— we thank *Dir*[8] for this wonderful flowering which you gave to the man who was already marked for death in such beauty, something that is expressed in every line of these touchingly beautiful last letters. *If you remain open to the splendor of this life, which was great despite everything, you will live a life that will be most nearly in his spirit.*

* * *

This death created a new close relationship. After the death of her husband, Weber's sister Lili had moved with her children to the home of Karl, who had been closest to her when they were young. When this home, which had barely become hers, was dissolved again, she built a nest for her boys in Heidelberg, and Weber now had the task of giving her brotherly support. He gladly laid hold of his new duties and told his sister how much having his blood relations near him meant to him. And as though by chance he revealed his own character a little:

It needs saying that I shall probably continue to be a more reserved and perhaps a more lonely person that I appear to be. Nature did not make me an open person, and this has often made many people whose love I had and still have suffer, and some may be suffering still. And because I very emphatically say what I think about *objective* matters— for I can bring myself to talk about personal matters only in rare, good hours—people who do not see this correctly easily feel outraged. You

---

[8]Weber switches in midsentence from the formal *Ihnen* and *Sie* to the familiar *Dir* and *Du.*— Ed.

are not afraid of people, so never be surprised at this either. Then everything will be all right.

As his time allowed, he devoted himself to the fatherless family and soon was deeply involved with their interests.

This morning the children serenaded me—very cute [*niedlich*] under Klärchen's direction. Finding myself the object of a "celebration" was somewhat embarrassing to me, as I have always been embarrassed on similar occasions. To think that even Lili broke into verse [*sich auf den Pegasus geschwungen hatte*]! However, it was very nice, and this perceptibly placed me in the circle of the "old" uncles that are mentioned in *Max und Moritz* and *Die fromme Helene*.[9] Give Lili my warmest thanks. Her children are very likeable.

In the spring of 1916 he accompanied his sister to the remote warrior's grave of her husband in that same eastern frontier district [*Ostmark*] whose Polonization he had always opposed so vigorously. The following lines to Helene indicate how deeply moved he was on this journey by the fate of individuals and of the community:

Our trip from and to East Prussia was good, even for my mind which has become very dull and tired, not because of work but because of unsatisfying semiwork. But, as always of late, I was inclined to be taciturn. That impression up there—the grave on the newly ploughed land, the strange little "aristocratic village" that has completely gone to pieces because of economy measures [*Abbau*], the "*Weltferne*" [seclusion] in which this peculiarly burdened life came to a beautiful and meaningful end here in a last liberation from the pressure of excessive tasks—all this and many memories stirred me more deeply than I could express in words and had the inclination to do. To the children the impression would have meant nothing now . . . I found Marianne in very good spirits. Her inexhaustible store of profound spiritual serenity helps her again and again and will continue to help her, come what may.

* * *

---

[9]*Max and Moritz*, a tale of boyish mischief, and *Hypocritical Helena: The Perils of a Pious and Passionate Pilgrim* (in the translation of H. A. and M. C. Klein)—two picture stories by Wilhelm Busch (1832–1908), the father of the comic strip.—Ed.

At the end of 1914—by then the war seemed endless, because all earlier experiences were so far removed—Weber submitted his resignation from the service, not because he was tired of working but because his military associate had himself reactivated and thus became his superior. For Weber, who was doing the bulk of the work, such a relationship would have been unseemly. However, the authorities did not wish to do without his services and found an expedient, so Weber worked without a break for nine more months. When E. Jaffé tried to lure him to Brussels for a few days to discuss a possible project in the field of social policy, he replied:

> As you know, I volunteered for duty, for I was no longer subject to service, and am active here as a captain and military member of the Heidelberg Reserve Military Hospitals Commission. There are forty-two hospitals in the district, nine of which I had to organize and am administering disciplinarily and economically largely by myself. My duties here do not permit me to get away for any great length of time. Since the beginning of the war I have had two Sundays off and I am in the office or in the hospitals from 8 A.M. to 7 or 8 P.M. every day. If I receive orders or am sent for with the consent of the military authorities, I am of course ready to do *anything* or go to *any place* where I can be of service, but I am not "applying" for anything. It weighs too heavily upon me that I am not fit for military duty at the front because I am unable to march and ride. Therefore I only want to prove to myself *that I am not too good for any work.*

In the fall of 1915, however, the Reserve Hospitals Commission, which had long since become illegal, had to be dissolved. Military men who were unfit for field duty were supposed to take over its functions. When Weber learned that the high command was racking its brains over where and how to "take care" ["*versorgen*"] of him, he requested his discharge.

Although he had basically had enough of his nonstop office duty, his predominant feeling at first was one of sadness at not being able to be of direct help any longer. Having performed the increasingly dull work with a touching devotion to duty, he was again out of a job. His subordinates regretted his departure for a long time. They revered him and felt secure because of his humane approach. That he always stood behind them as far as the "higher-ups" were concerned [*gegen "oben" deckt*] had made work under his direction a pleasure for them. When he left he was presented with a very thoughtful gift, a souvenir album with the pictures of all the doctors, civil servants, and hospitals in his charge. Weber was sincerely pleased.

Where should he help now? For a time the social-policy project in Belgium beckoned again. He went there to discuss it, but it was only a temporary assignment that came to nothing.

In Brussels there is a strange phantom life. There is the undercover *Nebenregierung* [collateral government] of the American Relief Fund which provides the Belgians with food and thus has more power than the mayors. The Belgian ministries (with the exception of the war ministry, the colonial ministry, etc.) work with German chiefs and Belgian officials. Next to this there is the German administration, each section of which proceeds on its own course. The life of Brussels is changed because of the absence of all refinements, carriages, and elegant clothes. The shutters of the "fine" houses are down. Otherwise things look exactly as they do at home, and only the big guns atop the Palace of Justice and the machine guns at the ministries remind one that the front is close by. So do the sentries in the park and in front of all ministries, etc. The large, swanky restaurants are almost empty and close very early. The attitude and the intentions of the German officials evidently vary greatly. Those with a university education are *against* annexation. But people holding such views are not influential now. *Every victory removes us farther from peace; that is the peculiar thing about the situation* . . . (August 24, 1915)

Before Weber became engrossed in his neglected manuscripts, he quickly wrote a report, intended for the authorities, about his military activities and what he had learned from them. This report is characteristic in many respects. It shows with what a loving eye for detail Weber observed all the little wheels of the huge military machine and indicates his desire to pass on insights that might prevent defects and promote useful practices in the future. Many of his experiences easily fitted into the scheme of his sociological types and added fresh illustrative material to them, for example, the special character of the administration, from sheer necessity, by amateurs [*Dilettanten*] in contrast to the later administration by civil servants and the transition from one to the other. He describes the integration of the volunteer aides into the military structure, their achievements and their indispensability, assesses the work of the "free lance" ["*freien*"] nurses and discusses their advantages and disadvantages over the professional nurses. He traces the reasons for the increasing criminality among the hospital inmates and draws practical conclusions from all of them. The almost illegible, hastily written draft remained in Weber's desk. Perhaps its submission to the authorities would have been regarded as evidence of self-satisfaction. However, some of it is given here as documentation of unglamorous service on the home front.[10]

General Remarks

The local hospital administration in the beginning consisted almost entirely of *amateurs*. It did not lose this character definitively until the erstwhile Reserve Hospitals Commission, which at the end consisted of two noncareer military men, was replaced by the appointment of a military physician-in-chief. This presentation of the development of the military hospitals will therefore cover the transition from a loose administration by amateurs to an ordered bureaucratic administration.

When the undersigned reported to the office of the garrison hospital, only the following experienced military men were there in addition to the medical officer: Sergeant L., who had been transferred there the week before. He was supposed to serve at the same time as the office manager, clerk, and inspector of the garrison hospital, for there were no clerical workers or orderlies. Chief Inspector H. had been designated as the economic member of the Commission, and he did show up after a few days. However, his state of health at the time was such that he was able to work only with a great effort. On top of that, the administration of the garrison kept him so busy that at first he was available to us only for hours at a time. The gentlemen who had been drafted to be inspectors of hospitals that were to be established did not arrive until the hospitals, which were to be opened according to plan on the tenth day after the mobilization, had been in full operation for some time. It took much longer, of course, for these gentlemen to become even minimally acquainted with the workings of hospitals such as the ones here. Their services could really be put to effective use and halfway normal opeations could be started only after the

---

[10]In the 1950 edition of her book, which abridges this section considerably, the author makes the following prefatory remark: "Because of the initial shortage of civil servants Weber had no choice but to establish peculiar 'amateur administrations' in the widely scattered reserve hospitals, that is, he gave a great deal of authority under his direction to his colleagues from the university who offered themselves as voluntary helpers. This collaboration was very fruitful for the hospitals. Without the roundabout way via the Red Cross, this administration channeled to the wounded the plentiful gift packages from the citizenry as well as streams of helpful warmth."—Ed.

definitive organization of the office of the central administration and
the assignment of officials to the hospitals as inspectors; this was done
about six weeks after the outbreak of the war. But even these men
had in civilian life been civil servants, administrative officials, manufacturers, etc., and had in any case not concerned themselves with problems of military administration. What were the bodies with which the
operation and, above all, the establishment of the hospitals were accomplished until then?

1. In addition to the undersigned, who is quite inferior as a calli-
grapher, the clerical work had to be done by the civil servants when
they arrived and until then by Sergeant L., the bookkeeper. Without
exception, all orders and the entire correspondence with the numerous
contractors were handled by the undersigned and were not entered in
a daybook. All important letters from the contractors were collected
and arranged by firms by the undersigned, so they are available. Everything else was, if necessary, preserved in penciled notations by the undersigned. Any other method was unthinkable, for I do not see who
could have written these letters and kept a daily record of them.

2. All duties of an orderly—particularly the delivery of local letters,
which could not be sent postage-free at that time—were performed by
volunteer schoolchildren who used either bicycles or electric streetcars,
on which everyone who had an identity card could ride free. Later, to
be sure, in a quest for popularity [*Popularitätshascherei*] which is typical
of Heidelberg, the company concerned gave thousands of free rides to
wounded soldiers, which meant that they pointlessly rode around the
city and its environs, although the company had at first completely
denied such passes to our hard-working civil servants and orderlies and
then limited them to a few dozen. The delivery of letters in this manner naturally resulted in the nonexistence of a postal record or receipts
for letters, and some letters were not even properly delivered. When
school started again, the pupils no longer showed up and now we had
to use male nurses as orderlies until the district command was in a position to supply some (albeit in *very* modest and absolutely inadequate
numbers). Yet in the very first days the number of the brief written
communications, which increased daily, may be estimated to have been
about 500 per day.

The undersigned personally went to see the suppliers and visited the
hospitals, unless he was able to get the former to come to the hospitals; because of the tremendous press of business this happened only in

very exceptional cases. During the first days vehicles were utterly unobtainable, and later their availability was very doubtful, until Mr. R. Sch—— placed his automobile at the disposal of the Commission.

3. The setting up of the hospitals, which were at a distance of 3 kilometers from one another, could only be accomplished by bringing in voluntary helpers, since the civil servants either had not arrived or had to learn their jobs first. Consequently a volunteer "civilian inspector" was appointed for each hospital. These gentlemen were mostly professors, and in collaboration with the undersigned, schoolchildren, other voluntary helpers, and the gradually arriving male nurses and police officers they accepted the deliveries and made provisional decisions about the placement of the beds and the equipment. If the undersigned could not be present, they used their own judgment or did things in accordance with the specifications made by the undersigned. Since the first trains with wounded soldiers arrived when the hospitals were barely ready, they helped the doctors to find places for them, and by collecting gifts [Liebesgaben] of all kinds they saw to it that all imaginable needs of the soldiers were met. In the early days these unofficial, voluntary "civil inspectors" were in effective charge; the personnel obeyed them because there simply was no other authority and the undersigned stood behind them. They were given formal authorization only to the extent that this was unavoidable in practical terms; they were authorized to give receipts for deliveries that were to be made. This clearly ran counter to regulations, but it was unavoidable if the hospitals were to be finished. But it did have the great disadvantage that in large part there was no proper record of the deliveries, and since wounded men arrived while such deliveries were still being made—they were invariably delayed because of the shortage of raw materials and workmen—other arrangements frequently had to be made over the telephone. These were then quickly carried out by all sorts of volunteer helpers (schoolchildren), and thus there was no way of bringing some order into our linen lists. The undersigned, who was called to this post as an amateur, takes the full and sole responsibility for the discrepancies of these lists which, despite all efforts, could never be straightened out afterward. It should be particularly emphasized that the civil servants should not be held responsible for this. They were not even there when the first deliveries were made; later they were in no position to check on the purchases, and given the daily rearrangements concerning the linens they never had an opportunity to keep an effective check on their whereabouts.

Gradually this unofficial and irresponsible administration was replaced by an administration of officials that was organized in accordance with regulations. However, it was around November before this was really accomplished in all departments. After that the "civil inspectors" who had been active until then either left together with their helpers or transformed themselves into *Liebesgabenverwalter* [administrators of gifts]. We gave them only (1) modest space, and (2) the *exclusive* right to accept gifts and issue receipts for them in accordance with a prescribed pattern. For if gifts are delivered by the public to the hospitals at random and are accepted by unauthorized persons who are not traceable afterward—and this is what happened at first—this leads to the most serious abuses. It seemed definitely advisable not to involve the official administration of the hospitals in these gifts of money and merchandise and thus burden it with a responsibility that it was unable to bear.

These administrations of gifts performed indispensable services for the hospitals, and given the nature of other tasks, the official administration could never have rendered these. On the one hand there were the purely human aspects—the personal encouragement, the procurement of reading material and job opportunities, the private employment service for the wounded men. The practical significance of this is demonstrated by the fact that there was a very obvious relationship between the *number of those subject to confinement* and the presence or absence of such a *Liebesgabenverwaltung*. The greatest number of prisoners was found where there was none and people had nothing but the tedium and the idleness of the hospitals. Another important factor was the collection of funds for needs which the administration of a hospital either could not meet at all or not in such quality and quantity. The funds that were raised by these *freiwillige Lazarettverwaltungen* [voluntary hospital administrations] *(Liebesgabenverwaltungen)* were modest compared to the total military budget and the resources of the Red Cross. But the total amount of over 20,000 marks which was made available to the gifts administrations of the various hospitals in the course of one year, mainly by faculty members of the university but also by local private citizens, carried far greater weight than, say, the resources of the Red Cross. There was absolutely no chance to gratify any personal vanity in this way, something to which the Red Cross is often obliged to appeal in its fund raising. For no one but the head of the *Liebesgabenverwaltung* ever knew anything about these donors, who had to remain in the background. These funds—which, incidentally, were supplemented by plentiful gifts in kind that were inestimable in value—not only paid for cigarettes, ordinary foods, games, entertainments, material for weaving, decorations to make the rooms more livable, books, tonics of all kinds, and better wines for convalescents as well as for the expenses of instruction and lectures, but also defrayed the costs of lounges and chairs for rest cures, the latest medical equipment, therapeutic items, linens, and articles for personal use that were not provided for in the budget and which, in accordance with the usual practice, the Royal Commissariat would hardly have been in a position to approve. It was also possible to put on beautiful Christmas celebrations and distribute gifts in the hospitals without becoming indebted to the Red Cross. Any financial dependence of the reserve hospitals on the ample funds of the Red Cross—which, incidentally, it did not hesitate to dispense—would not have seemed quite proper to us; as far as possible, then, we avoided turning to this source more than was absolutely necessary. This was done to a considerable extent by a few hospitals only during the last months of the administration of the undersigned, and even then merchandise rather than money was requested.

The gifts administrations further participated to a great degree in the organization of *instruction* for the wounded. The instruction given them in basket weaving, the cutting and gluing of sheets of cardboard, in braiding; the hourly employment of the men under the supervision of master craftsmen which was organized on as large a scale as possible after the qualifications and terms of the masters had been investigated; the highly meritorious attempts of the Red Cross to find employment for wounded men in workshops; or simply entertainments of all kinds—all this remained modest in value. Only a few people availed themselves of the opportunity to work, even for good wages.

While a considerable number of the men had no intellectual interests of any kind and requested only trashy reading matter, there was also a considerable and valuable minority that could not stand the enforced idleness in the hospitals and was receptive to stimulation and intellectual pursuits, which also meant that these men were in danger of committing disciplinary infractions if they were denied this opportunity. It was for the sake of these men that the classes were organized. In a few of the hospitals the head of the gifts administration was in full charge. The instruction was partly specialized (stenography, French, bookkeeping), partly general education (history, geopolitics [*Kriegsgeographie*], economic conditions). For reasons of discipline this latter kind of instruction was made obligatory as *military instruction* and scheduled for definite hours under the supervision of noncommissioned officers, who were present in the classrooms. In the main this involved a large number of gentlemen, particularly university professors and teachers in the public schools; occasionally members of the *Reservelazarettkommission* [Reserve Hospitals Commission], and qualified and interested hospital inmates participated in an auxiliary capacity. On the whole, the men's attentiveness on the long evenings of the winter months was commendable. Upon the recommendation of the hospitals the instruction was suspended for the summer, because the good weather on summer evenings was too much of a competition and the teachers were bothered by the perceptible disinclination of the students. The optional courses were usually given in the afternoon. The obligatory instruction amounted to four to six and a half hours a week and was given in the evening, usually after supper, so as not to interfere with doctors' visits and the hygienically necessary outings. From the point of view of discipline this instruction had a *very beneficial* effect, as was evidenced by the decrease of confinement, which had experienced a sharp rise in the fall, and this was really all that had been intended.

It was inevitable that with the increasing training of the drafted civil servants, the increasing supply of military personnel, and the gradual change of the hospital administration from an improvised transitional state of the first few months to a normal permanent operation the regular officials, particularly the hospital inspectors, increasingly claimed their rights and regarded the voluntary helpers and their influence as bothersome competition. There was no lack of friction. On the whole, however, the tactful attitude of both sides permitted a smooth, gradual withdrawal of the volunteer workers from positions which had at first dominated the entire operation to the activities carried on by the *Liebesgabenverwaltungen.*

As the administration became more and more monotonous, one "unofficial" figure after another disappeared, until finally the undersigned— who, being tied to his study in civilian life, has the slightest imaginable talent for management and order—remained as a last vestige of what had initially been an amateur operation only.

At first a considerable portion of the patient care depended upon the work of amateurs.[11] At the beginning of the war the view pre-

---

[11]In the 1950 edition the author prefaces this (abridged) section as follows: "Weber also considered it worthwhile to preserve his experiences with the various kinds of female attendants, the professional nurses and what he called *Dilettantenschwestern* [amateur nurses]. He was particularly interested in the latter. They were girls and women who almost exclusively belonged to the educated classes and had turned to nursing only under the impression of the war, out of patriotic enthusiasm. Weber fashions the following garland for them."—Ed.

vailed here that nurses were not appropriate. Hence, professional nurses were at first not employed here; instead, it was suggested that doctors help themselves as best they could, although they emphatically declared that they could under no circumstances entrust wounded and suffering men to the unpracticed hands of any old attendant. Insofar as the doctors followed that suggestion, they used volunteer helpers drawn from the population of the town. Their number varied in the different hospitals. After the professional nurses had successfully campaigned for the employment of a minimum of six to eight nurses per hundred beds and it was decided to hire trained nurses, if possible those accredited by the state, the undersigned applied to the various organizations with the request that such nurses be supplied. It turned out that quantitatively and qualitatively this request could not be met. Almost all the available nurses were already being used elsewhere, particularly in the field and in base hospitals. The number of nurses supplied was by no means in keeping with the officially established minimal requirement (90 to 120 nurses for 1500 beds). Therefore we had to content ourselves with amateur nurses in many instances. Extensive experience with these could be gathered particularly in Reserve Hospital II; they worked there without pay for seven months and received the regular rates only after passing the state's emergency examination in the spring. The following can be said about this.

Undoubtedly, membership in an established organization that continues to exist in peacetime and practicing nursing as a permanent profession offer a certain guarantee for the efficiency and standard of conduct of the nurses. When there are transgressions against tact and slackness in the performance of duty, the nurses' association takes action in the interest of its reputation, and it is to a nurse's material advantage to avoid a conflict with her organization. As a substitute for this, the typical amateur who had taken up nursing only during wartime had only her personal idealism to offer as well as what was on the average a superior education because of a better family background and a higher cultural level. For it goes without saying that primarily, though by no means exclusively, only girls of a considerable educational level had a chance to be given equal rating with the professional nurses when a volunteer nursing staff was selected. In general it can be stated with absolute assurance that *in the long run* here as anywhere else mere idealism and devotion to the nursing profession are *not* an adequate substitute for professional training in the prosaic specialized work. One important practical factor that partly makes up for this is the fact that it is much easier to discipline an inefficient amateur nurse than a professional one, because this could easily lead to a conflict with the association (this applies particularly to religious orders and other associations with highly placed protectors). In individual cases this advantage was neutralized by the fact that doctors were reluctant to deal as relentlessly and objectively with amateur nurses as they did with professionals. Generally speaking, to be sure, this danger is not very significant, because compared to doctors in other countries German doctors attach considerable importance to emphasizing their authority, formally and otherwise.

Among those who wished to serve as amateur nurses, two kinds of personalities can be rather clearly distinguished. On the one hand there was the typical "young German girl" with her usually very genuine enthusiasm, her sentimentality, and her unconscious hunger for sensationalism. This type was unsuitable for nursing in a military hospital, was always inclined to pamper the patients, and not infrequently was in danger of committing grave improprieties. On the other hand there were the girls and women with either intellectual or professional training. On the average they were highly qualified, very often equally so and not infrequently more so than the average professional nurse who had in wartime remained on the homefront. And apparently it mattered very little in what occupations or by what means these girls and women had become accustomed to being *matter-of-fact* in the comprehension of such tasks, something that was very important.

Our most favorable experience, both as to performance and assurance in dealing with patients, was undoubtedly that with more mature, that is, those of about twenty-five to thirty-five years of age, well-educated girls who had worked at quite heterogeneous occupations (as violinists or writers, for example), had had strictly professional training of some kind (physiotherapy [*hygienisches Turnen*], massage), or had overcome a hard life and had resolutely struggled against difficult circumstances. What such personalities were able to achieve in the way of uninterrupted labor during a year and a quarter of war was wholly unexpected, and after the initial difficulties had been overcome it was surely on *at least* the same level as the performance of an especially well-trained professional nurse. But it surpassed the average performance of such a nurse by virtue of the amateur's usually far less cut-and-dried and more individual manner of dealing with a patient, her attempt to satisfy not only their hygienic and physical interests but also their purely human and intellectual ones without failing to keep her required distance. This presupposes a rather considerable educational level as well as prudence and a sense of responsibility.

If the performance of the amateur nurses was in general quite satisfactory, their personal conduct was so almost without exception. Of the nurses secured by the doctors as helpers only two were without any doubt failures, and these bad choices were appropriately rectified. Understandably, there was no lack of professional nurses whose conduct was open to criticism. Something that seemed particularly noteworthy was the extraordinary perseverance of the amateur nurses. In the course of the observation period of fourteen months, only a very small fraction of them left their jobs, and even those did so only because of pressing obligations elsewhere. The zest and love of their work which this indicates would surely *not* have been present in equal measure if the amateur nurses had been employed only as helpers subordinate to the professional nurses to whom, after all, they were on the average superior in education—something that would have had to be done if the regulations had been interpreted literally.

Finally, it should be mentioned that the employment of these helpers meant a considerable savings. At first, until they became state employees, there was a saving of 100 marks per quarter over the salary of each professional nurse that was replaced, which amounted to 7500 marks in the nine months of this situation for twenty-five to twenty-six nurses so replaced. Further, since the care of patients did not require all regularly employed nurses to sleep in the hospitals, which is the regular practice of professional nurses, there was a permanent saving of twenty beds and bedding to the amount of about 1500 marks. Food and dishes amounted to about 8000 marks in nine months (figuring board at cost at 1.40 marks). The total savings up to the date of the examination (May 1, 1915) was approximately 16,000 marks. The beds saved could be used as sickbeds, and the available space could be put to fuller use. After the nurses were fully accredited by the state, the savings in beds and bedding continued, but now a considerably larger number of the nurses took their meals in the hospitals, so that the total savings until October 1, 1915, may be estimated at about 18,000 marks without figuring in the better use of hospital space. It should be noted, however, that on the basis of experience it seems highly desirable in the future to give *proven* helpers at least their meals during their working hours. All of them should be entitled to a noonday meal and afternoon coffee, but those on duty should be given full board. It is to be hoped that the present regulations will be changed accordingly.

It was in the nature of things that the internal developments in our hospitals increasingly pushed the volunteer nurses, who at first had been the only ones, into the background. This happened in accordance with the directions of higher authorities and also because many doctors found it more convenient to work with head nurses and other professionals, having neither the time nor the energy to train volunteer workers. Then, too, the supply of volunteers from among the townspeople gradually diminished.

This amateur system certainly had a few other advantages as well. It helped shape the individual character of the military hospitals in this area, and the *Liebesgabenverwaltungen* in particular did so to their great benefit. Its weaknesses lay mainly in the field of the not insignificant economic order. None of those involved, and least of all the undersigned, was familiar with the pertinent regulations or, considering the very heavy work load, had the time and the energy to familiarize himself with them in the evening, after working hours which continued for seven days a week. Above all, no one had the faintest notion of how to keep records, make reports, and so forth. But there is a good reason for the regulations governing such things, no matter how imperfect and obsolete they may be in places. They are the result of long experience and are not neglected with impunity.

Discipline in the Military Hospitals

Punishments. The incidence of punishable acts was generally very high and served as an outward indication of the soldierly quality of the patients. There were weeks on end when there was an average of one confinement per day—a figure that would have been unheard of in an active troop of 3000 to 4000 men. This figure underwent characteristic fluctuations. The discipline of the first two months or so was good. A considerable period of time passed before the first punishments had to be meted out. Then, in late fall of 1914, criminality increased. It declined perceptibly in the second half of the winter, increased again in the spring of 1915, decreased somewhat during the summer, and rose again with the advent of fall. The reasons for these fluctuations may be found in the following circumstances:

1. First of all, discipline grew worse because of the progressive recovery of the patients. As a patient's strength returned, so did his ability and inclination to commit transgressions, and he increasingly resisted detention in the tedium of the hospital.

The most central problem of all military hospital care next to the health problem is without a doubt the protection of the inmates from the psychological consequences of the enforced idleness of convalescents in a hospital. It seriously endangers military discipline as well as the future employability of the patients. Many of the endless orthopedic cures of five to six months, ordered for people who feel almost well but are fed in the hospital while they use exercise equipment for half an hour a few times a day, surely do at least as much damage to a patient's psychological qualifications for a job as they—possibly!—increase his physical qualifications. Despite all our efforts we did *not* succeed in bringing these people really effective relief. The daily medical schedule makes it very difficult to employ hospital patients *outside* the hospital, and such employment also poses some knotty disciplinary problems. Also, local commerce does not flourish enough to create plentiful employment opportunities. Efforts to create jobs inside the hospitals were stymied by the difficulty of effective supervision, which is indispensable if entrepreneurs are to give the hospital materials for processing—and besides there were space problems. The problem of employment in the hospitals hardly permits a completely satisfactory solution. One thing could be done, though: a far more extensive transfer of convalescents to *convalescent companies* of reserve units. Each unit has work that needs to be done, while in the military hospital any work is under the unavoidable odium of being demanded only for the sake of employment and without any objective need for it. A unit also has military men for supervising the work, while a hospital has none. As soon as *daily* medical treatment is no longer needed, a stay in the hospital is definitely inadvisable and should, wherever possible, be reduced. Any attempt to introduce anything that corresponds to drill is hardly feasible, and even real military instruction presupposes a *senior officer* [*Vorgesetzter*] who has time for it. A noncommissioned officer who is a patient in the hospital is no substitute.

2. Added to the effects of idleness as such there was the foolish behavior of the local citizenry. In these people a natural feeling of gratitude combined with a hunger for sensationalism and the desire to gratify cheaply both it and their own "pseudopatriotism." The soldiers were invited out by families and were treated to food and drink in homes as well as inns. They were in particular tempted to drink alcohol, something they were no longer used to and could not handle. They were encouraged to gab and brag; their pitiable situation in the hospitals was criticized and thus their dissatisfaction and obstinacy were aroused. While in the early months the patients had been full of praise for the hospital food, there now began constant grumbling about it. Anonymous letters and complaints of all kinds piled up, and yet, as was established without any doubt, there had been no change in the

quality of what was offered. Since it has turned out that both the Royal General Command and the civilian authorities are not sure about the competence in this matter, it is highly desirable that for the duration of the war and during the assumption of the executive power by the military it should be clearly established by law that the military authorities have the right to prohibit innkeepers and, what is equally important, private persons on pain of punishment from dispensing alcohol and other stimulants to soldiers. Because the competence is not clear, a request by the undersigned that this be done had to be declined. As experience showed, an ordinance which was issued by the Heidelberg garrison command and applied also to out-of-town reserve hospitals, stating that taverns were off limits, did not suffice.

3. At first the hospitals housed almost exclusively North Germans and Bavarians rather than people whose homes were here. This changed partly because of numerous transfers to hospitals near the patients' homes and also because of increasing transfers of wounded men from Baden to hospitals in this region. A rapid decline of discipline went hand in hand with this, and this was quite understandable: a patient who was in an unfamiliar area felt he was part of the army, not of the local population, just as he had felt at the front, and conducted himself accordingly. Natives of the area felt like deserving members of the local population who were entitled to special consideration, and naturally they became prime objects of the citizenry's pampering proclivities. It is unmistakable that these serious disadvantages for military discipline can be irreconcilably opposed to other considerations. Even if he has no family of his own, a patient in a military hospital in general satisfies his sexual needs in a more human, less brutalizing, and hygienically less harmful way in his home region than in strange places, where he is dependent on prostitutes. At home he is able to help his family economically at least by offering advice and possibly also by doing a certain amount of work. If he is expected to be permanently disabled, he can more easily take the necessary steps to find a suitable occupation. However, military discipline and such considerations of bourgeois morality and welfare are basically irreconcilable. By now it is generally recognized that a man with minor injuries who will presumably soon be fit for duty again should be kept as close to the front lines as possible and should perhaps receive only a brief home leave before he returns to duty, and all those who will probably be permanently disabled should return to their home region and their families as soon as possible. For the cases that lie in between it is not possible to give a clear answer.

Two categories were particularly troublesome as far as discipline was concerned and explain the resurgence of criminality in the spring of 1915: those with venereal diseases, who had to be quarantined for hygienic reasons (some 200), and the *orthopedic* patients (about 400 to 500). Both categories included young people who either were strong or felt strong, but were extremely difficult from the viewpoint of discipline. Some remarks about the orthopedic patients in particular seem indicated here.

As is generally known, the extraordinary prestige of orthopedic medicine is closely connected with the increasing importance of *pensions*, and this is due primarily to our social legislation. Even very considerable expenditures for orthopedics are an excellent investment for the authorities who have to pay pensions, if such expenditures result in a general reduction of the enormous number of pensions by 10 to 15 percent. An orthopedist who works with mechanical aids performs this service, and by virtue of the position he thus attains he is enabled to include among his activities more and more operations, at first nerve sutures and other things within his speciality, but then others as well, and finally almost all of limb surgery. Not only economic but also ideal interests suggest this to him; the mere control of the prosthetic devices and the patient's handling of them is rather tedious, and experience has shown that it seldom satisfies the doctor. Hence the actual supervision and direction of the orthopedic exercises was here, too, in the hands of younger doctors without orthopedic training and of the staff. The large number of orthopedic patients, the travels, the problems of artificial limbs, and the general interests of orthopedics as a specialty made it impossible for the orthopedist who was initially in charge to give intensive personal care to the patients. It was the unanimous complaint of all educated orthopedic patients who were personally known to the undersigned that they were essentially on their own with the appliances and, in contrast to the massage treatment, felt no real progress. A check of the central medical records confirmed the observation that the treatment often dragged on endlessly and detained people who would long since have been qualified to do at least garrison duty. It is perhaps worth considering whether in future it would not be more practical to assign a large number of such people to units stationed locally and have them do orthopedic exercises after hours (in addition to their duty), and whether in many other cases it would not be more appropriate to get them started on some physical, gainful employment. At any rate, these people were not hospital patients in the ordinary sense, nor could they feel that they were. Instead, they felt that they were quartered in a boardinghouse, as it were, and if an attempt was made to hold them to hospital regulations, they gave us the greatest disciplinary trouble. Thus, the punishable practices increased with the number of orthopedic patients.

4. The decrease in punishments in winter probably was connected with the courses of instruction which could be organized at that time. Their increase in spring was due to both the above-mentioned circumstances and the increased emotional (sexual) excitement and the necessary suspension of instruction.

5. The increase in the patients' pay in the fall of 1915 made discipline worse. In many cases the people used the money only to get alcohol. From a disciplinary point of view the question arises whether it would not have been more sensible to make this raise in pay, which for 3000 patients per year entailed an additional expense of around 200,000 marks, available in the form of a fund for communal purposes (materially, the improvement of the evening meal; ideally, the providing of suitable occupations).

6. Finally, the mounting disciplinary difficulties were also caused by the ongoing review of the draft status of police sergeants, which meant that in the end the hospitals were deprived of almost all physically strong and resolute personalities, not to mention the inordinate overburdening of these officers by record-keeping of all kinds. [There follow detailed expositions about the granting of leaves as well as a section about the relationship of the military authorities to the Red Cross, but these remarks remained fragmentary.—AUTHOR'S NOTE.]

17

THE PREREVOLUTIONARY
POLITICIAN ────────────────────

I

After leaving the service Weber became absorbed in work on the sociology
of religion. Even in the last months of his service he had saved an hour a
day for this. His series of articles on *Die Wirtschaftsethik der Weltreligionen* [The
Economic Ethic of the World Religions] began in the September, 1915, issue of the *Archiv für Sozialforschung* with an *Einleitung* [Introduction] on the
philosophy of history and the first chapters about Confucianism. The plan
was that this material, which had been written down two years earlier,
would appear simultaneously with the systematic treatment of the sociology of religion that was intended for *Wirtschaft und Gesellschaft* [*Economy and
Society*]; the two works were supposed to illuminate and supplement each
other. Weber now abandoned this plan. The November issue of the periodical carried the conclusion of his study on China and the *Zwischenbetrachtung*
[*Religious Rejections of the World and Their Directions*], the above-
mentioned typology of the various religions of redemption and their atti-

551

tude toward the "world." These sections, too, had been written before the war. Weber now wanted to explore the economic-ethical significance of the other Asian religions, first of all Hinduism and Buddhism. For that he needed the English census reports in the Berlin library. He therefore traveled to Charlottenburg in November and became engrossed in mountains of research material. But his scholarly work was not the only thing that attracted him to the capital of the Reich; he primarily wanted to be in a political atmosphere, feel the pulse of world events, and see whether he could be of any help.

What was Germany's situation at that time? It was the end of the second year of the war, and in late summer there had been inspiring successes, one victory after another against the Russians. They had been pushed out of Lithuania and Courland, Poland, Western Galicia, and Hungary. Turkey was holding the Dardanelles against the Franco-English onslaught, and Bulgaria, having been victorious against Serbia, had sided with the Central Powers. But the scale of the enemy, too, was heavy with weighty events: Italy, the former member of the Triple Alliance, was fighting against Austria; in large sections of the Western front the advance had long since been halted in exhausting positional warfare, and in Flanders and a few other hotly contested areas the Germans had even lost ground. Then, too, the blockade was making itself felt; the most important foodstuffs had to be rationed. And finally, since the sinking of the *Lusitania*, relations with the United States had been strained.

Weber was beside himself when Austria permitted the break with Italy to arise; as he saw it, this should have been prevented by timely concessions. "Yes, the situation is *bad*; the entire statesmanship of the last twenty-five years is now breaking down, and it is a very poor satisfaction to have 'always said so.' The war could now last forever." He also regarded the torpedoing of the *Lusitania* as a major misfortune, for a great neutral nation with a sense of honor might permit the destruction of property but not the destruction of its citizens. Weber was of the opinion that wherever there was an opportunity to make peace on the basis of the status quo, without any loss of territory but with no expansion either, this opportunity must be taken immediately; given the preponderance of the enemy, time would work against Germany rather than for her. And then, the war, which was *magnificent* as an extraordinary exertion of all heroic forces and loving readiness for sacrifice, would become satanical in every respect if it lasted for years, and it would wear away the hard-pressed people's moral as well as physical power of resistance.

Around that time Weber wrote down his thoughts about the question of making a peace in a treatise that was evidently intended as a memorandum for the government and the members of parliament, although he kept it in his desk. Public discussion of war aims was forbidden in those days, but the secret agitation by large pressure groups for annexations in the west and the east was all the more powerful. To this Weber opposed a "cool head" and unfailing clairvoyance. He demonstrated that Germany had only one choice: to carry on a global policy based on a policy of alliances or to pursue a policy of expansion in Europe which would unite all world powers against her. A colonial world policy presupposed, above all, an understanding with England, but that would be out of the question if the areas occupied in the west were annexed or "incorporated" [Angliederungen]. And these would not even broaden the maritime base of operations against England, but would instead gain Germany new enemies and, above all, increase the threat from Russia, for in any conflict not only France but England as well would side with Russia. "It is against German interests to force a peace of which the main result would be that the heel of the German boot would stand on everyone's toes in Europe." Weber saw a further danger of any policy of annexation in its indefinite prolongation of the war. No matter what the outcome, such a prolongation would in itself bring *industrial* supremacy to the non-European nations, particularly the Americans: "We shall slide into a paper economy, use up our domestic capital, paralyze our industry by decreasing the resources at its disposal, and lose our economic power to expand."

Another highly political problem in which Weber had a burning interest was created by Germany's and Austria's joint conquest of Russian Poland. He had always regarded the permanent protection of the eastern flank against the pressure of the Russian colossus as a most important national task. From his military period he knew the Polish areas that Germany had incorporated, and he had closely followed Prussia's Polish policy, frequently criticizing it sharply. As a young professor he had encouraged several students to make economic studies of this area. One who was particularly devoted to him, Leo Wegener, became the director of the *Deutsche Genossenschaftsbank* [German Cooperative Bank] and made the Germanization of Posen his great task in life. Now the question was whether it would be possible to create a Polish state that would be freed from its attachment to Russia and would become an ally of the Central Powers as their "protectorate" ["Schutzstaat"]. But first a whole skein of difficulties would have to be untangled. Would Polish industry be able to exist without any connection with the Russian hinterland? Would Germany and Austria be able to agree on each other's sovereign rights and on tariff questions? Above all, how would the reestablished state react if it was not given back Posen and Western Galicia, areas that had long been in the possession of Germany and Austria? The conquerors postponed a definitive settlement, first assumed joint control over the occupied territories, helped to rebuild the devastated land, and opened the University of Warsaw with Polish as the language of instruction. By means of this and other "cultural" deeds they hoped to gain the friendship of the Poles.

Weber regarded these as rash actions, for he surveyed the entire complex of difficulties and foresaw that the military command would make further political mistakes. What he desired most of all in those days was a chance to help and counsel on this point through personal contact with the Poles. In December of 1915 he published two eminently political articles in which he derived his own guidelines for the Belgian and Polish problems from an analysis of *Bismarck's* foreign policy. The nub of the Polish problem was the following: The restoration of Poland's political independence required a completely new orientation of the Polish policy. The force of the realities was now pointing both nations toward each other, and protection against Russia was a vital question for both. Consequently the Poles should no longer be treated as enemies but must be gained as allies. Therefore, Prussia's policy toward the incorporated areas must take a new course as well. Only by coming to an understanding with the Prussian Poles could a tolerable solution be found for all the difficult conflicts of interests now arising. However, people in Prussia were still far from this insight.

"I shall try to learn Polish and then seek to make contact with the Poles." But his discussions with Naumann and other politician friends soon led him to doubt that the authorities would make use of him. Many other political thinkers of his persuasion who were ready to cooperate remained untapped.

It is highly unlikely that there will be anything for me *here*, and Naumann agrees. Well, in the next few days I shall start to visit a few people at least. But everything is "all sewed up" [*"in festen Händen"*]. They have more than enough voluntary advisers and are very uncritical in this; they let everyone have his say, and whoever happens to be there "is right." They really don't know how to make progress; their hands are tied because of the Austrians whose situation seems to be quite difficult, as is understandable.

Dernburg[1] and all those who signed that declaration opposing the annexation of Belgium have absolutely no contact with the government and don't know about *anything*. The government *must* not have any contact with them because of the fanatical interest groups. Sering[2] is mentally colonizing Lithuania, but he does not ask where the people and the money are to come from or what Germans are supposed to do in that hopeless location. And so everyone is doing his thing [*So macht jeder seinen Kram*]. There is no one—a statesman!—to pull things together. Such a man does not exist, and no one can replace him. (November 26, 1915)

Naumann, who was not put to use by the government either, was planning to do some private political work and sought to interest Weber in helping him prepare an economic, and later a political, union with the allies: *Mitteleuropa* [Central Europe]. Weber thought this plan presented many problems—in the industrial field, for one thing—but he still understood his friend's intentions and kept himself available.

Dear Friend:

You overestimate my collaboration. I shall be available in the office all day, weekdays and Sundays, from early until late and do whatever is wanted. But I am absolutely *un*acquainted with things, and work on trade policy requires training. During the first two weeks I shall only listen. In twenty years I have not concerned myself with trade policy and I have absolutely heterogeneous things to do here. It is a great pity that I don't get a chance to deal with *political* questions (Poland, Lithuania) instead. But one does whatever comes along, and gladly. But not a word about my collaborating in any way on a matter where representatives of the government may be present. I shall soon tell you a story about Belgium. I am telling everybody that it is absolutely private work with "party politicians."

Weber still hoped that this would also bring him closer to the Polish problem as part of the Central European problem, and on this basis he tried to win his colleague Franz Eulenburg, whom he esteemed highly, for Naumann's committee.

---

[1]Bernhard Dernburg, 1865–1937, official in the German Colonial Office from 1907 to 1910, Minister of Finance in 1919.—Ed.

[2]Max Sering, 1857–1939, professor of economics at Bonn and Berlin, founder (in 1922) of the *Deutsches Forschungsinstitut für Agrar- und Siedlungswesen.*—Ed.

The central problem at the moment is *Poland*. It seems that the Foreign Office has *already offered* Congress Poland to the Austrians and asked them under what conditions Austria is ready to accept it. This politically (Upper Silesia!) highly dangerous situation requires one to consider what our relationship to Austria-Hungary would *then* be. It is clear that we could then not avoid making *very firm* commitments, including economic ties and a customs union. Which ones? [There follows a detailed discussion of this.—AUTHOR'S NOTE.] If incorporation by Austria is out of the question and incorporation by Prussia even more so (freedom of *those Jews* to come here!!), it must be considered what the proper customs policy toward Poland will be if it becomes the protectorate of both powers. This presupposes an understanding and agreement between both beyond this specific problem; otherwise it cannot be done. The question is *what* this understanding should include.

I think that despite my great skepticism it is tactically prudent for me to *collaborate* with Naumann, Jäckh, and Somary[3] for the time being under the assumption that it will lead to something—perhaps something *entirely* different and outwardly very much more modest than what they are hoping for—and to keep these capable people from being driven into the arms of the visionaries. Please do likewise if necessary.

Here and there the opportunities Weber hoped for did arise.

Today discussions with a German Pole about the Polish question (only about the—almost insoluble—problem of the *economic* consequences of the separation from Russia, which will mean the ruin of industry in Lodz and Warsaw). Factually quite interesting, since the man is intelligent and has invested his money in a large factory in Lodz. I am learning something factual, even though, heaven knows, it unfortunately has nothing to do with "eternal values."

However, he was denied a task he had desired for himself and his colleagues: a visit to Poland merely as a private person, but with the consent of the government and with access to official material.

Yesterday I managed to obtain an interview with the Undersecretary of State about whether someone could go to *Poland* or establish con-

---

[3]Ernst Jäckh, 1875–1959, journalist and political scientist, founder of the *Hochschule für Politik* in 1920, after 1933 in England and the United States; Felix Somary, 1881–1956, Viennese-born economist and banker.—Ed.

tact with Polish industrialists in some other way. For in this specific case failure is certain if the authorities obstruct such efforts directly. *Unfortunately they are doing so,* as the interview, which was exceedingly annoying to me, showed—even though I cited the support of a deputy of the Center Party who has rank and influence. I was told that (1) *any* negotiation with the Poles was *undesirable,* (2) such discussions were being carried on *officially,* and (3) the official material was *inaccessible* to us. A thousand reasons were given, and all of them were pretexts. The truth is that the gentlemen do not *want* anyone to stick his nose in this political matter and are afraid of "competition." This whole Berlin atmosphere in which all *talented* people are incapacitated by the resentful stupidity which prevails in the Reich offices is highly disgusting, and I am staying on *only* for Naumann's sake in order to help with what can be done.[4] (March 28, 1916)

Once again, then, it was hopeless, and Weber had to watch while the military men pursued a completely wrong policy. In the fall of 1916—in his view, much too early—the government proclaimed the new Kingdom of Poland without having made decisions on the most important problems. In return the Germans expected their own fighting forces against Russia to be strengthened by Polish volunteers. But their recruiting drive right after the proclamation was unsuccessful. They had miscalculated and played their trump cards in vain.

* * *

At the beginning of December, 1915, the Left asked in the Reichstag under what conditions Germany was ready to enter into peace negotiations. The Chancellor declared that Germany was ready to discuss peace offers but would not make one herself: "The German people's confidence in its strength cannot be shaken and it is invincible. In our calculations there is no weak point, no uncertain factor that could shake our confidence, which is firm as a rock . . . For the German government the war has remained what it was from the outset: a defensive war of the German people." Under pressure from the Rightist parties the Chancellor was vague about the war aims: "I cannot say what guarantees the imperial govern-

---

[4]Wolfgang J. Mommsen (*op. cit,* p. 236) points out that the last sentence is from another letter, probably one to Marianne.—Ed.

ment will demand, for example in the Belgian question, what bases of power it will deem necessary for these guarantees."

Weber rejected this conflicting and ambiguous attitude, saying that the situation demanded clear statements and firmness. What he regarded as important is indicated by the following lines he addressed to the editors of the *Frankfurter Zeitung*:

I am against *any* annexation, including the East. Instead, if it can be accomplished militarily, I am *for* the creation of autonomous Polish, Little Russian, Lithuanian, and Latvian national states giving us the right to build and *staff* military bases north of Warsaw and to the Austrians the right to do the same south of Warsaw. Then only a customs union with Poland, Lithuania, and the Lettish state, otherwise *full* autonomy. *No official German* settlement policy *outside* our borders. In the West, military occupation—permanent occupation of Luxembourg, twenty years of Namur and Liège with a guarantee that the troops will be evacuated and as a pledge that Belgium will fortify and defend Ostende and its southern border. *Nothing* else (in Europe). Thus only what is indispensable *militarily*, no "annexations" of any kind.

The impression I gained in Berlin as well as very simple political considerations lead me to advocate this. But I shall completely stop polemicizing against differing views. I suppose that what is attainable will be less than these "optimal" demands. (December, 1915)

Above all, it is a matter of scaling down our "expectations" and "appetites." Peace must not fall short of the expectations that have been aroused, at least not overly so. And that is the result of the government's attitude thus far. As early as September, 1914, I demanded that the expression *Faustpfand* [pawn] be used for Belgium. (December 25, 1915)

Wherever he could, Weber tried to counteract the annexationist desires privately by influencing the circles accessible to him. One opportunity to do so presented itself in the *Gesellschaft von 1914* [Society of 1914], a Berlin political club in which practicing politicians of all persuasions met politically-minded scholars and civil servants for discussions.

This evening I listened to a speech by Sering about the occupation of Courland (!). Fantasies as though we were all alone in the world.

Last night in the *Deutsche Gesellschaft*. As usual, wrangling with the Pan-Germans, although it was fairly amicable. But the horribly big mouths of that tribe evidently can't be cut down to size. I offered to give a lecture on democracy in America. But since I am regarded as a "defeatist" ["*Flaumacher*"], the gentlemen, despite all their courtesy, showed little inclination to be in a great rush about it. (March 13, 1916)

On Monday I am giving my talk on democracy in American life before the *Deutsche Gesellschaft* after all, having been asked suddenly with little notice to substitute for Göhre, who is unable to appear. Until now the gentlemen have always been "afraid" of what I might say.

I don't know whether people liked the talk I gave two evenings ago. It was *very* "realistic," for I was thoroughly fed up with all those clichés of the "ideas of 1914." Anyway, they paid attention for two hours and had to listen to a lot of things which most of them certainly did *not* like to hear. (The position of women, German sexual morality, international law, etc.) Well, I said what I wanted to say, and that's that.

II

In February, 1916, a new misfortune threatened which overshadowed all other problems and filled Weber with extreme concern: the break with America because of the intensified submarine warfare. The governments were still negotiating about the torpedoing of the *Lusitania* without warning. The United States demanded that Germany expressly acknowledge the illegality of this sinking. This was rejected by the German government, and both the Secretary of State and the Chancellor told representatives of the American press that they would rather risk a break than face such a humiliation. Weber was *beside himself* over these events and wrote to Naumann:

If the Wilhelmstrasse[5] does *not* succeed in disposing of this American matter *at any—any!—cost*, our work will make no more sense than any other efforts. Then we shall have *entirely* different "problems" in nine months or a year. It is to be hoped that your party, or its serious-minded politicians as individuals, will decline *all* responsibility in no un-

[5]The seat of the German government in Berlin.—Ed.

certain terms. That *no one* in Germany knew what an American election campaign is and what its consequences are, despite all the examples furnished by history, is an unparalleled scandal.

And on the same day:

> My worst fears are exceeded by the Zimmermann[6] interview. How is it possible to do this sort of thing and to commit oneself *publicly* like that instead of answering that of course the attack was *völkerrechtswidrig* [a breach of international law], but it was an act of *retribution* for equally serious breaches of international law by the *other* side. As a result of our great appreciation of America's friendship we have given our U-boats entirely new instructions, and in this we should like to be as considerate as possible. In future, then, such an unannounced attack *would* be illegal, and for what happened in the past we have promised to make amends. With this we consider the incident as closed to our mutual satisfaction.—Finished! *Quem Deus perdere vult, dementat prius* [Whom God wishes to destroy, he first makes mad]. What point is there to *our* work if this break comes about? It will mean two more years of war and the ruin of our economy—*what* will "Central Europe" matter then? What is the *party* doing? (February 2, 1916)

When Weber, who had concerned himself with his scholarly work at home for a few weeks after Christmas, returned to Berlin in February of 1916 at Naumann's request, he found there an extremely confused situation over the continuing tension with America. With regard to the *Lusitania*, the two governments had in the meantime agreed on a formula. But the resumption of the "intensified" ["*verschärfte*"] submarine warfare against armed merchant ships, that is, their torpedoing without warning, immediately created new grounds for conflict. And when America demanded that in accordance with international law enemy merchant vessels that were armed to defend themselves should not be treated like battleships, a vehement agitation began in Germany under the leadership of Grand Admiral von Tirpitz[7] not only for intensified but for *unlimited* submarine warfare, that is,

---

[6]Arthur von Zimmermann, 1864–1940, the German Secretary for Foreign Affairs in 1916–1917, was the author of the "Zimmermann telegram" to the German ambassador in Mexico which was deciphered by British Intelligence and revealed Germany's plans against the United States.—Ed.

[7]Alfred von Tirpitz, 1849–1930, the architect of the German navy.—Ed.

the torpedoing of all enemy and neutral ships encountered in the war zone. Tirpitz and his adherents believed that in this way England could be blockaded and starved out and the peace could be won by force. They refused to see that war with America would then be inevitable and that it would be a great misfortune for Germany. The Grand Admiral won the army command for his plans, against the wishes of the Chancellor. Weber wrote on February 20, 1916:

> Politically everything here inspires *little* confidence; no one knows what is to become of Poland. People are still harboring the very dubious hope that there will be a separate peace with Russia. And above all, the situation with America is *quite* serious. They hope that in case of "foreseeable fresh incidents" they will manage with delays and lies—in short, "small steps." In this they will be mistaken. But the navy is obsessed with trying out its new U-boats and it doesn't "give a hoot" [*ihr ist alles "Wurst"*]. No one knows how much longer the Turks will hold out, particularly regarding food, which is greatly in jeopardy. There is great optimism concerning Rumania, and *I hope* it is not entirely unjustified. Well, *qui vivra verra* [those who will live will see].

And on February 23, 1916 he wrote:

> If only those crazy Pan-Germans and navy people don't get us into trouble with America! The result will be (1) that *half* our merchant marine will be confiscated, one-quarter in American ports, one-quarter in Italian (!) harbors and used *against* us, so that at first there will be an *increase* in the number of English ships, something that these asses are not taking into account; (2) that we shall have 500,000 American *sportsmen*,[8] splendidly equipped volunteers, fighting against our tired troops, something that these asses don't believe; (3) that there will be 40 billion in cash for our opponents; (4) that there will be three more years of war, which means certain ruin; (5) that Rumania, Greece, etc., will be *against* us. And everything so that Herr von Tirpitz "can show what he can do." No one has ever thought of anything more stupid.

Now we are really facing a break with America! Just as I predicted it. And always because objective questions are always treated as a *point d'honneur* at public rallies, there is talk of "humiliation" and things like

---

[8] In English in the original.—Ed.

that, and then there is no road back. The whole thing is horrible and a crime. And especially now when one would like to rejoice at Verdun and almost everything is going well. It is as though we were being ruled by madmen. You ask what we should do? *In any event*, not make any big public speeches if we plan to do something like that, avoid "pathos," keep a cool head, and calculate rationally. The arming of merchant vessels *is* permitted "for defense," that cannot be changed, and our repeated actions against this international law which is "sacred" to the Americans would be pardonable only if we were *certain* of success. But there simply is *no* such certainty. On the contrary! In case of a break *our* ships (which are in American ports) will be torpedoed by our U-boats, for they will then be used *against* us. And then half a million *additional* sportsmen fighters [*Sportsmitkämpfer*], splendidly equipped, on the enemy side against our increasingly worn-out poor fellows, 40 billion in gold more, etc. And all this because of a few dozen U-boats! England can be "starved out" even less than we can be. We can't even manage a serious disruption of the *troop* transports! But enough. It is too horrible to contemplate. The war may simply last *years* longer. And this the Turks, for example, will not be able to stand. They would *have* to desert us. (February 27, 1916)

In the meantime the dangerous situation with America has reached its climax, and I feel as if a mob of madmen were ruling us. All the people who shared my views two weeks ago have given in. Those who two weeks ago said, "Oh, the Americans will *never* attack," are now saying, "Oh, the Americans *want* war in any case"—just the way people talked in the case of Italy. The few calm people here *know* that the war will be lost if America comes in—financially, because our war bonds will then not be bought, and economically, because we are still getting a lot of indispensable raw material from abroad which we shall then not get. Also, because Rumania will then attack us and the Turks will make a separate peace in half a year when our money is exhausted. It is enough to drive one crazy. And there is something uncanny about the terrible rage one arouses if one tries to convince such a warmonger with *objective* arguments.

The agrarians know that *bread* must be bought even if we are defeated; industry and shipping will then be ruined and we shall be rid of *those* competitors for power. The discouragement of some workers and the revolutionary despair of others see to it that the landed proprietors stay in power, and then the monarch is in their hands. And therefore: *va banque* [all or nothing]. I hope the faint hope will not

THE PREREVOLUTIONARY POLITICIAN

be extinguished that considerations of the *bond sales* will exert pressure on the German government. That is the only chance today, and I hope it will be utilized. (March 5, 1916)

The optimism of the military men and politicians regarding a war with America is incredible. It is an *entirely* different story if you have a private conversation with those people who are responsible for the economy—the supply of raw materials. It is the same with the representatives of industry, *except* for the manufacturers of grenades and the agrarians, to whom any prolongation of the war brings higher prices. (March 7, 1916)

* * *

Weber did what he could to fight against the impending doom. Together with Somary he wrote a memorandum that was intended to inform the party leaders and support the Chancellor against the Grand Admiral.[9] Its arguments were not in apodictic form, but took the form of relentless references to the innumerable and unfulfillable conditions on which a decisive success of the submarine warfare depended, and each of the finely chiseled sentences included the question: Have you considered all this and calculated it soberly and correctly? If you have made a miscalculation in even one point, then even the greatest bravery cannot save Germany from defeat and economic agony.

At the beginning of March the memorandum was submitted to the Foreign Office, and around the tenth of the month it was delivered to the party leaders. The decision had been made on March 4 under the influence of Bethmann and Helfferich. The unlimited submarine warfare was postponed and Tirpitz was dismissed, but the "intensified" action against merchant ships was resumed. Weber's memorandum, which also opposed intensified commercial warfare, can hardly have had any effect, but it was able to strengthen the Chancellor's position against the onslaught of the Rightist parties which was now beginning, and to spread enlightenment. The fanatics, to be sure, did not let themselves be convinced by anything.

Tomorrow I am sending a memorandum about America to the party heads. The Foreign Office, to which I had sent it earlier, wrote me

---

[9]Published in *Gesammelte politische Schriften*.

immediately (by messenger) that I should *definitely* send it out, it was
highly desirable, and it would be submitted to the Chancellor right
away. Yet it contains only ordinary things! So they must be in hot
water up to their necks. The situation is still quite serious, and it
is these damned "accidents," which after all anyone can foresee, that
give one the feeling that one is sitting on a volcano. And on top of
that, Turkey desires to make a separate peace, and who could blame
her? We want to make annexations, and what do we have to offer the
Turks in this line? And there is the bad attitude of Rumania. Well,
perhaps everything is going better than one thinks. If only they do
not sacrifice too many men in the west! Our special work is being
greatly obstructed by the authorities, just as I foresaw it, and my mission to Poland seems to be out of the question. . .

I am anxiously awaiting the Chancellor's speech in the Reichstag, and
on the basis of all my earlier experiences I am worried. All these people
are so "upright" ["*brav*"] and none of them is a statesman. That is why
we can win the war with a vengeance and still not get anything out
of it. Well, perhaps things will be better some day. With that "memorandum" I shall incur all the rage of the firebrands [*Scharfmacher*] and
be regarded as a defeatist archcoward. So much the better. (March 11,
1916)

I am enclosing the memorandum whose distribution to all the conservative hotheads will probably bring an enormous amount of anger down
on my head. It won't do any good—although the Foreign Office requests that it be sent to the Bavarian prime minister and all sorts
of big shots [*hohe Tiere*]—but I have done my duty. Of course, once
again *no one* would have cared to *participate!* (Undated)

You have received the memorandum, haven't you? Now, after Tirpitz's
downfall, there will probably be a reaction. We are said to have ten
new U-boats. And with those they want to blockade England! And my
colleague L.[10] as the Pythia of the admiralty! That man made such *utter*
miscalculations in the question of the grain supply that he is now completely
discredited with the grain-buying association. What makes me shiver with
fright is whether these people can really make dependable *calculations.*
(March 14, 1916)

---

[10]Hermann Levy, 1881–1949, from 1914 on professor of economics at Heidelberg. Upon Tirpitz's
request Levy made an assessment of England's prospects in the face of U-boat warfare, basing himself
on the pessimistic 1905 report of the British House of Commons.—Ed.

The danger of war, which was at its height on Friday and Saturday, is over for the time being. The Reich Chancellor won a victory over Tirpitz, and we shall *give in*. But how are we to do this without compromising our dignity and without spoiling the *effect* of our tractability by braggadocio [*grosse Protzen-Worte*]? That is the question. Tirpitz played an irresponsible game. He must have *known* that he *cannot* torpedo enough ships in the course of a year to "starve out" the English *if* they adopt our standard of living and introduce *our* measures. That is simply nonsense. But now he kept raising his stake, like a desperate gambler, and declared that he could "guarantee" success only if he torpedoed all ships approaching the English coast, including Dutch, Scandinavian, Spanish ones, etc. *That* is what he had in mind. Thus, war with Holland, Denmark, etc. *This* is what brought the turning point. Just as a hysterical collapse of this "heroic" emperor—"think of some way to bring the war to an end"—created the crisis, an attack of fear of war with America, where things are far more serious than our newspapers lead us to believe, brought about another turning point. Whether it has come too late remains to be seen. The way we are being governed at a moment when our entire existence is at stake is disastrous. (March 15, 1916)

I have surely told the *government* nothing new; I have only rendered it a service. The memorandum went to the deputies. *Perhaps* it influenced Deputy Sch——[11] and a few others, and it may have had *some* effect on the Center people, but they are intelligent anyway and are No. 1 with the government. But it surely had a real *effect* in only a very small measure, if indeed it had any; the government had already made up its mind on the matter. (March 19, 1916)

In those days the Grand Admiral's power of suggestion seemed pernicious to Weber, and he fought it passionately. But the downfall of the patriotic man filled Weber with indignation:

The rude way in which Tirpitz was expelled—a public announcement of his "sudden illness" just when he was being ordered to tender his resignation. On the same day the herculean man stood in front of the Foreign Office on Wilhelmstrasse and yelled at Privy Councillor Kiliani, who had asked him a question, in a voice loud enough for everyone to hear: "Did I *request* my dismissal? I was ordered!—ordered!!—(in a thun-

---

[11]Presumably Gustav Stresemann, 1878–1929, a member of the Reichstag from 1907 to 1912 and 1914 to 1918, from 1923 on Chancellor and Foreign Minister of the Reich.—Ed.

derous voice) *ordered!!!* to leave." That arouses an awful lot of ill will and is bound to have a depressing effect on our friends and to encourage our enemies. It is highly imprudent, not to mention the human hideousness which always remains the same in *this* monarch. That he yielded the point ought to have sufficed; that was a kind of acknowledgment of defeat. Peace with America will now probably remain assured, but for that they did not have to send him away with a kick in the pants. (March 16, 1916)

Tirpitz's *forced* resignation amounts to a lost battle, to judge from the impression at home and abroad. He was prepared to stay on. Instead of acting in the *matter* itself in such a way as to eliminate the danger of complications and retaining the *person*, they torpedoed a Dutch ship and gave the only popular minister a kick in full view of the entire world. The result: at least 2 billion less in bond subscriptions than was normally to be expected. Whenever H. M. does anything, it is sure to be wrong. This unreliability and these sudden shifts depress everyone here, and the morale in the Reich offices is evidently *quite* low at present. (March 17, 1916)

On March 17 the Rightist parties, together with the Center, attempted to score against the Chancellor by again proposing unlimited use of submarines, but the matter was settled in favor of the Chancellor in the Budget Committee of the Reichstag.

We have now learned the following about the committee meeting of the Reichstag: (1) The admiralty declared point-blank that the isolation of England was not *possible*. (The number of U-boats available for duty at any given time is even smaller than I assumed.) By *next January* we might have enough U-boats to cut England off (in my estimation not even then). (2) Helfferich *declined* to take the responsibility for the financial consequences of America's intervention. The effect of all this was such that the wicked conservative Fronde collapsed—forever, I hope. It is a scandal that the Reich naval office could have played with fire like that, and even though the Chancellor exposed only the "Press Bureau," entirely different people were meant in reality. Everything was *bluff*. The way matters stand now it has to appear as though the submarine war is being waged in an intensified manner, for it must not look as though we had "erred." And that is why we go ahead and torpedo and then slowly let things die down. But this could—"by accident"—bring us war with America! That is what is so unspeakable about it! Well, I hope it will not happen, although the mobilization of Holland—which, it seems, is not directed against us—is *bound* to have an inflammatory effect over there in Washington. I must say, the world is being directed with *little* intelligence! (April 1, 1916)

On April 5 the Chancellor discussed the foreign situation in the Reichstag, and again from the standpoint of an undefeated and undefeatable people whose war aims would in future be determined by the expected success: "We are not motivated by a desire for conquest and a greed for territory . . . we have gone to war in self-defense. But that which *was* is no more . . . after such enormous events history does not know a status quo ante." About this Weber remarked:

The political atmosphere is a bit clearer now. *This* speech by the Chancellor is possible and defensible only if he is sure that in the foreseeable future there is *no* hope of serious peace negotiations. And presumably that is the way it is. Even so, I certainly did not find it skillful and politically prudent, though it was better than his earlier speech, particularly from an oratorical point of view. The mistake that it was not stated *at the outset* that Belgium was *not* to be kept simply can no longer be rectified, and in the East the hopes of the Courlanders, etc., have been aroused. No one has any judgment of what is possible and useful. And above all, these things are treated purely as *domestic* affairs. The Chancellor had to show that he was the "strong man," just as "strong" as Tirpitz, otherwise he would have been lost because of the Fronde of the Conservatives. And the policy of the Conservatives and industrial magnates is quite simple: The *longer* the war lasts, the *more* Social Democrats swing to the "left," the better for us, the pillars of the throne and of the altar. No compromise peace, for then concessions would have to be made in the question of suffrage. This was what was behind the whole U-boat agitation. Since we have given in, the danger with America has now decreased, but it could flare up at any moment for as long as the war lasts. A great deal depends on the harvest. If it is good, the English might abandon the matter; if it is not, they are not likely to do so. There is enough coffee for only a brief period. The sugar situation will improve again; the meat rations are going to be very, very meager. (April 7, 1916)

In the meantime new material for conflict with America had been created: the inadvertent torpedoing of the *Sussex,* a French passenger steamer which had on board many members of neutral nations, mainly women and children. In mid-April the United States categorically demanded the "immediate" cessation of attacks without warning on merchant ships.

> Yes, the torpedoing of the *Sussex* admittedly was an unparalleled dirty trick [*Schweinerei*], the most stupid thing that could have been done. Outstanding people from *all* neutral countries—Spain, etc.—were on it with their families, and mostly women and children were killed. If things go on like this—I hope not!—we are certain to be at war with the whole world. And there is *no one* in the parties who declined the responsibility in high places and protested against this action. Everybody feels the matter has been very nicely taken care of by the resignation of Tirpitz and the resolution, which was a bad defeat for the U-boat screamers. (April 5, 1916)

> So we are yielding in the case of America—but again we are not doing so courageously and openly and without reservation, but with "face saving"; this is what is regrettable. These people have neither vision nor a sense of dignity. It is bad enough. And that they saddled us with this bad *échec* [failure] is certainly incomprehensible and very sad. When those accursed interviews came, anyone was able to see what was bound to happen. Why were these people the only ones who didn't? In truth, it was because of a craven fear of the Conservatives. When matters got serious, all the braggarts crawled into their mouse holes. It will be hard to mitigate the depressing impression this is bound to make after all this twaddle about the "only road" that is supposed to lead to an honorable peace! (May 2, 1916)

The unavoidable German concession was tied to the condition that America ask England for "freedom of the seas," which meant the lifting of the blockade, and *achieve* it. Weber regarded this as another political mistake:

> Now the note given to America is here. One can tell that it was a forceps delivery. In addition to very good individual points there is, *in general*, again only the desire to save face. Everyone *knows* that once a concession has been made, it *cannot* be withdrawn without the immediate danger of war. Everyone knows that the more time elapses, the more *impossible* it becomes to risk this war (with A.). Everyone knows that in the meantime the English are laying in provisions. What good, then, are all these provisos when the *only* thing worthy of us would have been this honest statement: "All right, we are giving in. Now

it is a matter of your honor to make England accept the 'international law' too." And then—"extreme concession." Always tying ourselves
down like that! It is quite doubtful whether this matter will get us
ahead in any way. The Chancellor's nerves are in very bad shape and he
is not up to these things. Least of all is he a match for his *domestic*
opponents, who are absolutely unscrupulous. Well, we shall see. (May 7,
1916)

This criticism proved to be correct. The result was a fresh diplomatic defeat. The United States government refused even to consider, let alone
discuss, that respect on the part of the German naval authorities for the
rights of American citizens on the high seas should in any way or to the
slightest degree be made dependent on the conduct of any other government. It said that responsibility in these matters was separate rather
than joint, absolute rather than relative. Weber commented on this as
follows:

Yes, the American note has now disposed of the matter. But we remain saddled with the defeat. We have staged things with a great to-
do, talked about "humiliation," etc.—and now Wilson's note can
confirm that we are exactly where we were before and have achieved
nothing, except that now any "incident" can still mean war and England is taking the opportunity to intensify its blockade. And our
stupid proviso that we might again torpedo without warning gives
Wilson a chance to say, "I am doing *nothing*, but I shall wait and see
whether you behave well, and then—we shall see." And then the *Sussex* affair; these stupid denials and the subsequent obligation to confess
are extremely unfortunate. I have not doubted this for a moment.
And what a bad light in our disfavor this throws on the *Tubantia*[12]—in
short, this entire matter is extremely sad, and the people should have
known whether they could risk a war with America or not, and if not
they should have left things alone. In his pedantry, which is so unfortunate for us, Wilson has remained absolutely true to himself. That
is just what people here cannot understand, that someone should carry
on a *purely* formalistic policy, like a jurist in a lecture course or a doctoral examination, and conclude even his note with a sentence that
surely came out of his notebook on responsibility in international law.
We, on the other hand, are so proud of our Realpolitik, which we have

---

[12]On March 16, 1916 the Dutch ship Tubantia was sunk by U-boats off the Dutch coast on a voyage
from Amsterdam to Buenos Aires.—Ed.

turned into a theory. This president pursues policies like a *juristic* discussion in a scholarly dispute. (May 10, 1916)

III

After these extremely exciting events, Weber, despite all his efforts, could not find anything important to do in Berlin. The offices and authorities continued to deny him any opportunities, and in the face of official obstruction his work on a trade policy for Central Europe was fruitless.

My work—if one can call it that—is coming along sluggishly. Perhaps things will be livelier in May, for that is when the interested people plan to get together. But it is tedious to be "superfluous." I almost preferred the military hospital! I am awfully homesick; working against official obstruction and in an area strange to me is anything but easy. And the people are so inordinately timid. If they don't let even the *Dezernent* [department head] of the *Reichsamt des Innern* [Ministry of the Interior] go to Poland, then I as a private person really cannot complain. This Polish matter is the only thing that interests me, and in general I care only about the political aspects; everything else is only a means to an end.

Fortunately he made progress with his scholarly work.

I feel so well and able to work as soon as I deal with Chinese and Indian matters, and I am very eager to do this work. Being half-occupied is unbearable. Now things are finally starting to roll and to get interesting. I have waited for three months, and that's enough. I am very homesick for Heidelberg and think I am doing the right thing to get out of here now and leave the project to others. In any case, I have an *extremely* "good conscience."

His Heidelberg friends had long thought it was time for him to return to his work with undivided energy. His wife wrote Weber:

Two evenings ago K. Jaspers came to see me, and as so often we spoke a lot about you. He has such an exalted view of you [*er sieht Dich mit so "grossen Augen"*]—as a new type that, so he says, is strong enough to control and rise above enormous inner tensions and conflicts of outside life, even though he is completely free of illusions, a man who could even afford to be ill or possibly even to make a fool of himself. I am impressed by the fact that Jaspers, who regards a striving for knowledge and truth as the highest value in life, should have said: "It is a pity about every day which this Max Weber wastes on political things instead of objectivizing himself." I am writing you this because right now you must again consider how you could most fruitfully use the talents you have been given. You know how gladly I now give you to our fatherland. But if the machinery of government is so rigid and the people in control are so small that no really *suitable* task is found for someone like you, then you must not fritter your energies away on petty projects. Perhaps fate wants to save you for more important things.

Because of his futile wait for an opportunity to employ his political talents, life in Berlin had become rather *ungetröst* [cheerless] for Weber. Helene often found her son quiet and ill-humored, and when she thought that she herself was the reason for this, he opened up to her in the following lines written during the period of utmost tension between Germany and America:

You again speak of that which you could not "offer" me. How strange, considering that it is just the other way around. It was I who was not capable of giving much intellectually and emotionally, and this was due to circumstances. I believe that of all your sons I had the strongest innate "martial" instincts, and in the light of this it is an unnatural and unsatisfactory situation to be of no use now for what is primarily needed—and then to be unable even to find some other occupation that would be fulfilling and of undoubted usefulness. Basically, I share Maeterlinck's belief in getting close to others by keeping silent. But, even though it is a serious breach of taste to talk about it in the face of the terrible sacrifices others are making, this somewhat difficult situation, too, seals one's lips, especially when one is under the pressure of an imminent serious danger to one's country. Now that this danger has become an actuality, for a peaceful compromise with America hardly seems conceivable and probably would be only a postponement, the situation has changed. There no longer is any point in ruminating about these things and their unavoidability. And since I am now determined to be realistic and, if I am not needed, not wanted for something *necessary*, simply to call it quits and wait quietly until I might some day be useful after all, I shall return far less depressed than I used to be.

Naturally, I felt better—very good, in fact—working in the military

hospitals, although any inspector really could have done that work—
but that did not matter. This Berlin project was a waste of time and
a lot of gabbing with all sorts of people without my having the feeling
that I was accomplishing anything . . . One has to be "on duty" to
be able to achieve something. I cannot bring myself to beat down the
doors of the harassed people in the offices in order to be able to "do
something." Everyone here knows that I shall be available again at any
time. (April 17, 1916)

On the whole he did not take the fact that he could not be used politically too much to heart; after all, other "brilliant" ["*grundgescheit*"] minds
were suffering the same fate. He was just as annoyed for the sake of some
of these as he was on his own account:

May you finally find the employment that is your due and is definitely
indicated from a pragmatic point of view! Does one really have to be
either an ass or a careerist to be deemed acceptable by the authorities?
What should one say to the following conversation? General X in the
General Staff here: "Lieutenant Y. You write here about the production costs of industry *and* agriculture. Only industry has production
costs; agriculture doesn't have anything like that. Change that, will
you!" Lieutenant in the *Landwehr* [Reserve], a professor of economics
(employed in the General Staff): "Yes, sir, Your Excellency!" May God
improve things!

* * *

Before Weber returned home for a long period, an attractive assignment
did arise unexpectedly in the middle of May: a trip to Vienna and Budapest
in the interest of "Central Europe" in order to discuss questions of tariff
policy with the industrialists. This extended trip, something that he had
been without for two years now, brought him the stimulation he had
always desired as well as giving him a respite from his worries about Germany's fate. Weber's letters from the trip not only sound cheerful but, in
contrast to his earlier expressions of grave concern, are full of political confidence. Their bright tone was intentional; they were supposed to lift the
spirits of the censorship authorities. However, at that time Austria was
penetrating through the Southern Tyrol onto Italian soil, and in June,
1916, the German naval victory in the Skagerrak filled everyone with joyful
pride. Besides, whenever there was any ray of hope, Weber, despite every-

thing, always welcomed it. In Vienna he enjoyed the hospitality of his friend, the historian L. M. Hartmann, and found much to stimulate him:

Have been here for two and a half days already. Being on the go all day and meeting people of all kinds, I hardly get a breathing space to send as much as a greeting. It is interesting—and this is the purpose of my stay here—to get an impression of the *mood*. It is *splendid*, quite different from the way we imagine it. People here are afraid that *we* are going to starve, just as we fear for the Austrians. And actually a great many things are already better organized than they are in our country. The magnificent successes in the Southern Tyrol are making themselves felt. At any rate, I am very pleased about these impressions; the Austrians are going to see it through. Since I am only a private person who is gathering information for himself, I see only private persons, of course. But the winning charm and openness of the Austrians certainly are extremely attractive. (May 26, 1916)

Vienna is working its full old magic, and it is so gratifying to take along these impressions of a period of such honor for Austrian arms, a time when even the many pessimists here are changing their tune. Despite all the talk about it, peace evidently still is quite far away, but people *are* confident that everything will turn out all right. And it is also good and important that for once the Austrians have *indubitably* done something by themselves and have splendidly prepared it . . . What am I doing here? I am seeing old and new acquaintances of all kinds at all hours of the day, from afternoon coffee in a café to midnight. Yesterday I met a considerable number of rather intelligent industrialists. I admit: the intellectual level is high; even with businessmen one could not easily carry on such conversations in Germany. (May 29, 1916)

The beautiful long flags that are waving down from the city hall please me, for that they should signal a German naval victory surely is the most astounding of all the miracles of this war. How very glad I am for our navy people! If everything goes well in the east now, as is to be expected, the war will be finished internally because of Austria's successes in Italy. The Austrians have taught that gang there the lesson they deserved. Who would have thought it possible? Tomorrow morning I shall return to Germany, and then I can be in Heidelberg soon. I am now completely superfluous in Berlin and shall return home for good; I am inordinately looking forward to it. Here I have seen and spoken with many additional pleasant people. They all had the same relaxed and refined manner which is so comforting as well as that "cosmopolitanism" [*"Weltmännische"*] which we completely lack. The weather has been heavenly, and my whole love of Vienna has reemerged. Next to Munich it is the most beautiful German-speaking city! But still, one likes to go home again. (June 5, 1916)

* * *

Weber now spent a few quiet summer weeks at home and immediately became absorbed in his scholarly work, enjoying the regularity and quiet harmony of a contemplative existence. But at the end of August he went to Berlin again for a short time—at Naumann's request, for another discussion of Central European affairs. In the meantime the situation there had worsened again. The Austrians had long since lost the positions in the Southern Tyrol which they had captured in May, and now the Italians were standing on Austrian soil. The eastern front, too, had caved in under the Russian onslaught, and in the west the German lines were slowly being pushed back by the English. At the end of August, Rumania sided with the Entente. Peace negotiations broke down. Things were not going well. As a talisman against the incipient demoralization, Hindenburg,[13] the most admired man of all, was appointed commander-in-chief of the allied armies and chief of the General Staff. He was the hero of the nation, and the belief in his military and human greatness united all. Weber wrote:

There is a widespread feeling that Bethmann "cannot be retained" [*"nicht zu halten"*] because he is said to have suffered defeats in the peace negotiations with Russia and in the Polish matter vis-à-vis Austria and is supposed to be incapable of making *decisions*. That really seems to be the case. The poor fellow simply is not a "statesman," no more than the younger Moltke[14] was a strategist. But *if* he goes, then only *Hindenburg* could keep the nation together. I see no other personality who could then make peace. And he is no "statesman" either. All in all, things don't look good here. Everybody is so disoriented; it is strange—and then again it is not. It's this endless war! (August 22, 1916)

---

[13]Paul von Beneckendorff und von Hindenburg, 1847–1934, became president of the Reich in 1925.—Ed.

[14]Helmuth von Moltke, 1848–1916, Prussian military leader and chief of the General Staff from 1906 to 1914.—Ed.

People here are now thinking more about the *economic* situation than about the war situation. The latter, so it seems, will gradually stabilize. But if after the war income *and* property taxes of 40, 45, 50 percent have to be levied—and this will be necessary *if* the war lasts until next summer—then *all* of us will have to change our standard of living. Well, we shall do so undauntedly. I hope that at least a decent peace will make these insane sacrifices of both life and property worthwhile! But this is still quite in the dark and far away. (August 23, 1916)

We cannot know as yet what Rumania's entrance into the war signifies. The quality of its army is unknown and untested. The situation is certainly serious, and the wanton talk of people like Dietrich Schäfer ought to stop at last. But I believe today as I always have that we shall come out of this thing with *honor*. To be sure, there is no doubt that our future will be affected, as in the case of Italy. We are becoming ever more isolated diplomatically and more and more limited in our choice of alliances and friendships. Next to the unknown military aspect, this seems to me to be an important political aspect which severely limits the scope of our global policy. That Hindenburg should be called only now when the dynasty is up to its neck in difficulties is regrettable. But the peace he is going to conclude will be accepted by the nation no matter what it looks like. That is the meaning of this thing. (September 8, 1916)

* * *

From Berlin Weber went to Lake Constance, there to permit himself at last a few days of shared enjoyment of nature with his wife after two years of uninterrupted work. How beautiful it was on the large lake! The changing light constantly imparted new magic to the gentle outlines of the shore. The lake reflected the soft blue of the September sky; the landscape enveloped in autumnal fragrance was cleansed of the petty works of man— unearthly. But dark memories obtruded themselves upon the harmonious images. It was on this lake that Weber had vainly sought recovery eighteen years before and had had a premonition of his long suffering. The Webers saw the old places for the first time in years—Konstanz and the Konstanzer Hof. The past emerged from the shadows like an uncannily threatening figure, but it could no longer harm Weber. He had stood the test and was not worried about himself. If he suffered again *deeply*, it was because of Germany. And now that, despite everything, he was experiencing a second

flowering of his strength, he might well have felt that the deprivations
of those years had not been too high a price to pay for the scope and the
substance of his intellect.

I believe that the old memories affected you far more strongly than
they affected me. They certainly did not oppress me as much as you
thought; rather, I was troubled by the *"mass fate"* that goes on without the end being in sight. After peace is concluded—when do you suppose that will be?—we shall immediately consider a sojourn down there.
It was, despite everything, lovely [*wunderschön*], and it did me good to
be in the woods together with you. In the future this sort of thing
must happen much more frequently. *Hab Dank!* [Thank you!]

IV

At the end of August, agitation for unlimited submarine warfare started
again. The people became more and more disunited. Societies and committees with no party affiliation sought to influence political opinion. Some
worked for a quick negotiated peace; others, who emphasized confidence in
victory, urged the dismissal of the Chancellor and demanded the ruthless
employment of all weapons and instruments of power, particularly the U-
boats. Generals and the admiralty staff constituted a collateral government [*Nebenregierung*]. Weber again opposed it and regarded the public discussion of this question as political folly. He wrote to Naumann:

The resumption of the U-boat agitation suggests the question
whether those in the highest places have so lost their heads or their
courage that they continue to tolerate *this* wretchedness—agitation
about *military* measures—for which there is no analogy in any of the enemy countries. Let us assume—although I don't believe it—that the
use of the U-boats will become unobjectionable or less objectionable
militarily, economically, and politically. Then it would be the height
of madness to let this be noticed *beforehand* and thus give our enemies
a chance to *lay in the proper supplies*. Especially then would the government have to make this clear public announcement: "That is out of
the question in any probable circumstances!" The government ought
to tell the leaders of the rightist parties confidentially but plainly
that the efficient military use of the U-boats is being rendered *impossi-*

ble by their own talk, and it should unconditionally *prohibit* and re-strict any discussion of this in the press and in speeches. All this is so simple that one is ashamed to make a point of writing and saying it. But today the simplest things seem to be forgotten. I no longer understand the Reich Chancellor—unless he is *unable* to do what he thinks right. But in that case—he ought to resign. (September 18, 1916)

When Lloyd George's statements—to a representative of the press to the effect that the fight would be continued until Germany's knock-out—were beginning to make themselves felt, Weber again turned to his politician friends. He wrote to G. von Schulze-Gävernitz:

Dear Friend:

I hope that at least no one in your party will let himself be confused by what Lloyd George says. He is a fanatic—but *these* things are said with calculation: in the hope *that the U-boat hysteria* (for that's what it is) of the people who cannot stick it out will be so increased by these insane threats that we shall commit the U-boat folly and thus bring the Americans and other neutrals down on our heads. This is the only way in which these speeches can be understood. But England's real conditions for peace are sufficiently known from the English conserva-tive press. No foolish things, then. Naturally, that foolish speech must be exploited as a bugaboo for the weak-kneed peace lovers in our country. But one has to give it the correct political evaluation *pro foro interno* [for domestic consumption]. *I hope* that this time the only decisive calculation has been made correctly: *How much* tonnage does England need to "stick it out" in case of U-boat blockade if (a) it po-sitions its cotton and wool ships favorably, (b) it imports flour instead of grain, canned and frozen meat instead of cattle, etc.

This calculation had *not* been made when I saw the memoranda, all of them bad, in the spring. And yet everything depends only on that. With the four million tons that Tirpitz wants to torpedo, nothing will be gained. Let the gentlemen realize that! Who is the man who makes these calculations? Forgive me for these hasty lines! But this utterly senseless and shameful uproar about the U-boats is doing us un-told harm. It is irresponsible to make the troops out there and the people at home believe that there is a way of *shortening* the war. Amer-ica's entrance will prolong it by two to three years. If Germany decided to carry on U-boat warfare, it would be irresponsible to let the enemy

notice it so that he can *lay in supplies*! Bethmann must either secure
a prohibition of any and all direct or indirect discussion of military
measures—or *go*.

Ceterum censeo [In my opinion]: It is *necessary* to crack down on this
U-boat demagoguery with *club blows* from the top—otherwise I don't
know why we are called a "monarchy." The main thing! (October 2,
1916)

* * *

Toward the end of the year German arms again made the impossible possible: the western front held firm, in the east Hindenburg advanced again,
and, above all, Rumania was conquered and a new source of food for the army
and the people opened up. The annual statistics listed millions of prisoners
and several hundred thousand square kilometers of occupied territory. The
propitious moment for holding out the hand of peace finally seemed to have
come. An offer was made to the enemy the middle of December, and hopes
were raised at Christmastime. But the government regarded a victor's
stance as appropriate. Its note made reference to "the invincible strength"
and the tremendous successes of the Central Powers. On the other hand,
the concrete war aims were still shrouded in silence. The government still
thought that it could obtain territorial concessions in the east and the
west as well as war indemnities—and those responsible political leaders who
did not believe this still acted as though they did, so as not to be regarded
as bad patriots.

The Entente responded in scornful and hostile terms. Lloyd George named
as English conditions the complete "restoration" of and "satisfaction" for
the occupied territories. Now the government yielded to pressure from the
Supreme Command and the admiralty. It was decided to engage in unlimited submarine warfare as of the first of February, 1917. There seemed to be
no other expedient than this extremely risky undertaking. There still was
hope that America would remain neutral. Weber again regarded the note
sent there as quite inept, like most diplomatic actions. He wrote about
it to Naumann on February 3, 1917:

Why does the note for America (a declaration about the intensified
submarine warfare that was intended to make an "impression" there
and make it *easier* for Wilson perhaps to keep the peace after all—and
for this it was a well-chosen opportunity) not contain this one deci-

sive sentence: "The measure will be rescinded *immediately* after our adversaries have acceded to the suggestion for a reconciliation of conflicting interests on the basis of equal rights and an avoidance of threats in the future"—that is, after the meeting of a peace conference? After all, it is clear that this would have aggravated the situation of the opposition and cost us *very* little. If the sentence "We are not waging a war of conquest" could have been added rather than allowing only the Austrians to say it, this would not have cost us anything either, and would have produced a good effect. Was this omitted for fear of the Pan-Germans? That would be regrettable! Our situation has been such that it was and still is advisable.

However, once the decision had been made, Weber, too, backed the government—both out of political discipline and in the faint hope that the *others* might have been right and he could have been wrong. In this vein he wrote an encouraging letter to a young friend who was in despair over the threatening doom. After presenting all the reasons that made the dangerous action appear less hopeless now than it had seemed in the spring, he added:

It nevertheless *is va banque* [an all-out gamble], if you will. We are holding some important trump cards, and a number of factors that are quite unknown to me are working against us. It is very difficult to evaluate these, Certainly, it was similar at the beginning of August, 1914, and also when Italy and when Rumania struck. It may be that things will go wrong this time. Well, then we shall say, as Prometheus did, *"Meinst Du, ich soll in die Wüste gehen, weil nicht alle Blütenträume reiften?"* [Do you think I should go to the desert because not all blossom dreams ripened?][15] The world's *hatred* of us will be better than its cold contempt up to now, a contempt that will not recur. I hope that we shall then find the "detachment" we so badly lack now. We are suffering because we are not "in it" [*"dabei"*], that's it, for otherwise why should the political sun always smile only on *us*? I am now suffering less than I did during the past twenty-five years when I watched the hysterical vanity of this monarch spoil everything that was sacred and dear to me. Now that which human stupidity used to perpetrate has

---

[15]The correct quotation from Goethe's poem "Prometheus" is as follows: *Wähntest du etwa,/ ich sollte das Leben hassen,/in Wüsten fliehen,/weil nicht alle Blütenträume reiften?* [Did you fancy perchance that I should hate life and flee into wildernesses because not all my dreams blossomed to maturity?]—Ed.

become "destiny," and with "destiny" one can cope. Later it will be worthwhile to be a German and nothing else—even *if* things should turn out badly, which is really quite doubtful. The worst thing is the *prolongation* of the war, which will be the probable consequence. But: we must see things through abroad and consequently also at home.

* * *

Weber had already resumed giving talks before small groups on a number of occasions. At the end of October, 1916, Dr. Haussmann,[16] the head of the Progressive People's Party [*Fortschrittliche Volkspartei*] in Munich, had succeeded in luring him onto the rostrum for the first time in nineteen years. What were Weber's feelings when he noticed that he was again able to speak extemporaneously and that he held the souls of his audience in his hands? He probably was too preoccupied with his subject for any conscious reflection about this. His subject was "Germany Among the European World Powers." Weber did not wish to speak as a member of any party, for *"I have always regarded politics from a national point of view—not only foreign policy, but all policy"*—exactly the same view that he had already held as a young man. Accordingly, the ultimate yardstick was not domestic policy but *foreign interests*: Germany's special situation as a state based on power, which like no other was surrounded by large powerful states. This geographical location demanded a *realistic* policy, not one based on emotion, a policy of silent action rather than one of boastful vanity, a policy of alliances rather than or:e of conquest.

As for the substance of this policy, Weber was particularly in favor of an understanding with England, for in his opinion Russia was the most dangerous foe and he regarded the threat from there—because of the pressure of a growing population and the land hunger of the Russian peasants—as the only one that was directed against Germany's *existence* as a national state based on power. England could take maritime trade away from Germany, France could deprive it of land, but a victorious Russia would endanger its independence and national culture. The development in the east would henceforth appear as a bagatelle. At the end of his speech, Weber interpreted the historical meaning of the war in a few sentences. The real reason for the war was Germany's development into a state based on *power*. And why had the Germans become a people organized along such lines? Not out of vanity, but for the sake of their responsibility to history.

---

[16]Conrad Haussmann, 1857–1922, a member of the Reichstag from 1890 to 1922.—Ed.

Future generations, particularly our own descendants, will not hold the Danes, the Swiss, the Norwegians, and the Dutch responsible if world power—in the final analysis this means *the determination of the character of the civilization of the future*—is divided without a fight between the decrees of Russian officials on the one hand and the conventions of Anglo-Saxon "society"[17] on the other, perhaps with an admixture of Latin *"raison."* They will hold *us* responsible, and rightly so. Because we are a people of seventy and not seven million, because by contrast with those small nations we therefore tip the scales of history with our weight, it is our bounden duty, and not the duty of those nations, to history—and that means to posterity—to pit ourselves against the swamping of the entire world by those two powers. The *honor* of our people bade us not to shirk this duty in a cowardly and slothful manner; this war is being fought for *honor*, not for changes in the map and economic gain.

* * *

In spring of 1917, when the last card—unrestricted submarine warfare—was played, all the energies of the nation were strained to the utmost. The rift had been healed and the members of the nation were united. The Kaiser's *Ostererlass* [Easter message] promised the speedy elimination of class suffrage in Prussia; steps were to be taken to democratize the political system [*Staatswesen*]. At first the success of the submarines seemed to justify the venture. People were thrilled by the enormous amount of enemy tonnage that was sunk. And then the Central Powers were even aided by a *miracle*: the overthrow of Czarism, the Russian Revolution. The revolutionary government declared that the Russian war aim was peace without annexations and indemnities on the basis of the nation's right of self-determination. But the new cabinet was disunited: the imperialistic Milyukov against Tscheidsee and Kerensky.[18] Weber therefore recommended the utmost caution and again made quite *concrete* proposals to Naumann.

Only after Milyukov's overthrow did he want comprehensive, if cautious cooperation:

[17]In English in the original.—Ed.
[18]Pavel Nikolayevitch Milyukov or Miliukov, 1859–1943, co-founder of the Cadets, foreign minister of the provisional government March-May 1917, exiled to France. Nikolai Semenovitch Chkheidze, 1864–1926, leader of the Social Democrats in the Duma and minister of labor in the provisional government, émigré in Paris after 1921. Alexander Fyodorovitch Kerensky, 1881–1970, minister of justice and later prime minister in the provisional government, exiled in France and the United States. See Paul Miliukov, *Political Memoirs, 1905–17* (Ann Arbor, 1967).—Ed.

In view of the declarations made by those in power in Russia and no matter how one evaluates these statements (for reasons that you know, my estimate of them is not high), the Reich government cannot possibly avoid expressing a *very* obliging attitude toward Russia. Otherwise we shall not only stimulate the Russian zeal for war and arouse the neutral nations (Scandinavia) against us, but we shall increase Austria's ill-humor in what may be a dangerous fashion and particularly harden the attitude of our Social Democrats, who are greatly influenced by Russia. Also, precisely *if* we are convinced that *nothing* will come of peace negotiations at the moment, it may be wise to base ourselves on the Russian declaration and therefore to declare in any case:

(1) That we are ready to make an immediate peace with Russia on the basis of no annexation, no indemnity, mutual guarantees by eliminating any military measures that may be a threat to either side, and a treaty drawn up by a court of arbitration; (2) that we are no more inclined to "subjugate" Poland than the Russian government has declared it wishes to do; (3) that we cannot make any further declaration regarding the western powers *for so long as* they espouse war aims that are indiscussable and incompatible with the declaration made by the Russian government.

I would consider it prudent not to add *anything* further and above all to *omit* any moralizing, any unfriendly references to the English as "warmongers," as well as any regrets that Russia "must bleed for England." No nation likes to have its back slapped and to be pitied, and all such phrases in our earlier declarations have *only* done us harm (in contrast to Austria, which avoided them). [There follow details.—AUTHOR'S NOTE.]

If the war continued, then, of course, in view of the enemy's openly avowed intention of conquest and enrichment at our expense, we would have to reserve the right to act accordingly in the future. I am convinced that the war will be *continued* now, but that the effect of such a declaration at home and abroad would be the more considerable the more soberly and matter-of-factly it was made. In the Boer War, Lord Salisbury[19] said that they did not want *any* diamond fields and gold mines. This declaration made a very favorable impression. When the military and diplomatic situation later was such that he had them and could keep them without any danger, he *kept* them. So far we have done exactly the opposite, and this is what we regard as "hon-

---

[19]Robert Arthur Talbot Gascoyne-Cecil, third Marquis of Salisbury, Lord Cranborne, 1830–1903, British prime minister and foreign secretary during the Boer War (1899–1902).—Ed.

est.'' But it ought to be possible to make it clear to the military men and the sensible leaders of the Center Party and the Right privately that Lord Salisbury's procedure was the *smarter* of the two. And in our case it is honest in a higher sense, too. For we *do not know* the outcome of the war. If next year we are in the same position diplomatically and perhaps are on even somewhat shorter rations as far as food and coal are concerned, the war will in all probability be completely lost, because then (1) conditions *at home* will simply be out of control, and (2) we shall inevitably be *financially bankrupt* and thus, no matter how favorable the conditions for a peace may be, we shall for generations be utterly incapable of carrying on any sort of global and colonial policy or of concluding a *financial* treaty, while the American subsidies will tide our adversaries over the catastrophe and keep them capable of political action.

These cogent reasons certainly militate against doing anything that will prolong the war, and any declaration that is *even less* obliging than the above or a similar one involves this danger. The worst thing would be if *no* declaration were issued, or one that was vague in regard to Russia. It would be well if any "annexation" and "subjugation" could be expressly disavowed in relation to France and Belgium as well.

Even the splendid submarine successes in no way make up for those financial and economic consequences of a prolongation of the war until next year, not to mention the fact that the possibility of one technical tool being immobilized by another can never be ruled out. I am always worried that the Reich Chancellor will let himself be intimidated by the Pan-Germans. This crowd will definitely be beaten to the ground *if* a peace is concluded in the foreseeable future and if at the same time, or even earlier, the government announces with regard to Prussia *that the right to vote of any man who has served at the front must not be inferior to that of any man who stayed at home.* (To Naumann, May 8, 1917)

V

Weber lived in constant political excitement and could not bear concentrating exclusively on scholarly work. Since he was denied any opportunity for military service or practical work, he again attempted to act as a political educator from his writing desk. From the beginning of 1917 on he repeatedly expressed himself on questions of foreign policy in the pages of the *Frank-*

furter Zeitung, and in the early summer he started a series of important treatises on constitutional questions. After all, the domestic reorganization—
which to Weber was basically a problem of the second order—became more
important as the war dragged on endlessly. For the readiness of the masses
to go on suffering for unclear and remote goals appeared to be guaranteed
only if all of them were conceded an equal influence, at least formally, in
the political decision-making process and if the authoritarian state were
transformed into a people's state. This required the elimination of bureaucracy in politics and of the Prussian class suffrage, the parliamentarization
of the governments, and the democratization of all state institutions.

The tone of these essays,[20] which aimed at highly controversial and
long overdue changes in the constitution, is very different from the tone
of Weber's essays on foreign policy. The latter are matter-of-fact and very
even-tempered, and their effectiveness derives solely from their prudent argumentation and mastery of history. Although the former also draw on a
comprehensive statesmanlike knowledge, they are polemical in character.
They contain caustic criticism of the accumulated political sins of the Wilhelminian age, although they do not incriminate the individuals responsible
as much as they do the *system*, the structure of the state and of the government. They also attack "the literati"—those irresponsible writers with
no training in practical politics, some of them professors, "who are always
the claque [*Beifallssalve*] of the ruling class" and are never available when it
is a matter of jointly censuring the mistakes of the government. Instead—
because it is much cheaper—these men scold the parties in the Reichstag,
oppose democratic development in the unconscious interest of their own
privileged position, and are not aware that "their will to powerlessness"[21]
at home is in strange contrast to their boastfully proclaimed "will to power" abroad. Among other things, they make a business of manufacturing all
sorts of "ideas of 1914" for which the war supposedly was being waged, and
thus are "good people but bad musicians."[22] "It has been said that now
is not the time to touch domestic problems, that we have other things
to do now. We? Who? Surely those who have stayed home. And what must
we do? Scold the enemy? One doesn't win a war that way . . . Or: Speeches

---

[20]*Gesammelte politische Schriften*, pp. 126ff.

[21]*"Ihr Wille zur Ohnmacht"*—a reference to the Nietzschean phrase *Der Wille zur Macht* [the
will to power].—Ed.

[22]*Gute Leute aber schlechte Musikanten*—a phrase used by Clemens Brentano in his play *Ponce
de Leon* (1804); also used by E. T. A. Hoffmann and Heinrich Heine.—Ed.

and resolutions about all the things that 'we' ought to annex before 'we' can make peace?"

Basically, Weber regarded the *monarchic* form of government as the most appropriate, because it removed the head of the government from political competition and guaranteed a certain steadiness of course and the government's independence of the parties. Then, too, he deemed the continuation of the individual German dynasties desirable for reasons of cultural policy. To be sure, for him the *nation* and its future in the world "towered" over all questions of the form of government, and for generations the nation had been staked by its political leaders:

I would not fire one shot or buy one penny's worth of war bonds if this war were anything other than a national war, if it involved the *form* of government or if it were being fought for the sake of retaining this inept dynasty and the apolitical officialdom. I don't care a fig about the form of government *if* only politicians and not dilettante cox-. combs [*Fatzkes*] such as Wilhelm II rule the country. I now see no other way of removing these people from power but relentless, wholesale parliamentarization *quand même* [come what may]. The civil servants shall be responsible to the parliament. They are *technicians*. In the purely parliamentary state their power will remain just as great as ever, but it will be where it *belongs*. In Germany they presume to play "politics," and we have seen with what results and with what unprincipledness [*Charakterlosigkeit*] toward the crowned dilettante! To me, forms of government are something technical, like any other machinery. I would equally strike out against the parliament and for the monarch if he were a *politician* or showed promise of becoming one.

This excerpt from a letter compresses into a few sentences the question of the form of government discussed in the above-mentioned treatises. Bismarck, the master of foreign policy, left as his domestic legacy a nation without any political education and any political will, a nation that was accustomed to having a great statesman take care of its politics. He smashed strong parties and did not tolerate independent political personalities. The negative result of his tremendous prestige was a powerless parliament with a greatly diminished intellectual level. And the consequence of this was the exclusive rule of the officialdom.

The effect on politics was that the "bureaucratic spirit" ["*Beamtengeist*"] prevailed where another spirit—namely, the guiding spirit of the politician—should have been. The two are very different, and they ought to be, for very different demands are made of them. For example, a civil servant has to give up his own will and obey the orders of a superior authority even if he regards these orders as wrong. The *political* leader who acts thus deserves contempt. A civil servant should be *above* the parties—which means, however, *outside* the struggle for his own power. And this—the struggle for his own power and his *own responsibility* for his affairs, which stems from this power—is the politician's element. Wherever it was a matter of the conscientious completion of clearly defined tasks, German officialdom stood the test splendidly, but it failed completely whenever it had to deal with political problems. Weber proved these theses by showing the disastrous result of all the blunders in foreign policy since the fall of Bismarck. What he had feared for decades had come true, and his indignation at "the personal rule" had turned out to be justified. "In all these cases the behavior of the leading statesmen was irresponsible and unparalleled in the politics of all great states." They tolerated the public statements of the monarch and their publication, whereas political prudence would have required obtaining the leading statesman's advice beforehand, and the stateman's resignation if his advice was not taken. That this was not done was due to the faulty structure of the state, which places people with a bureaucratic spirit in positions where men with a sense of their own political responsibility belong.

The only counterweight to bureaucracy within the framework of the monarchy would be a *vigorous parliament* that can pursue positive policies. Only the parliamentary system, according to which the administrative heads either are drawn from the popularly elected deputies or require the confidence of the majority, will educate the nation to think politically. And, above all, only then will born *leaders* [Führernaturen] find political activity worthwhile.

The proper selection of the political leaders was to Weber the most important problem of parliamentarianism and democratization. For neither of these means the "rule of the masses"; political action is always controlled by the manueverability of small groups or by an individual acting "Caesar-like" [*"cäsaristisch"*] as someone who has the confidence of the people. The mass of the deputies should always be only the followers of those leaders involved in the government. Only if the existence of the parties is dependent upon their representatives rising into that circle will the party system be upgraded too. Then those with political talents will more easily prevail against the party functionaries and local bigwigs.

Weber formulated precise proposals for constitutional reform intended to facilitate a better selection of leaders, and illustrated their effects in all ramifications of political life. He demanded above all the elimination of the legal impediments which kept political leaders from being at the same time members of parliament and of the government, thus preventing the elected representatives of the people from participating in the leadership of the state. But this alone would not assure the proper selection of leadership; a politician must acquire sufficient expert knowledge, for the Reichstag must no longer "remain condemned to dilettante stupidity." Therefore it is important that it be given the right to exercise continuous and effective control over the administration. A means to this end is the *right of inquiry* that will make it possible to know the facts and be familiar with administration. Only such an experience with the realities will produce a powerful parliament as a place for the selection of leadership—not of mere demagogues but of competent professional politicians. The model for this proposal was the committee system of the British parliament.

What was quite new and of great importance, however, was Weber's demand for the right of inquiry for the *minorities;* this will be discussed shortly. Another innovation in the discussion of problems of constitutional law was the fact that Weber did not base his proposals on ideological political theories but presented them, explicitly and intentionally, as something practical and utilitarian, the need of the moment. He regarded the state only as the framework for the life of the *nation;* people had to be free to change it if its structure led to large numbers of people losing their sense of belonging to the nation. And Weber suspected all political metaphysics up to that time as a kind of mimicry by which the privileged classes protected themselves against a rearrangement of the spheres of power. In this respect he shared Karl Marx's conception of the state and its ideology.

The needs of the hour, and not absolute norms, were *parliamentarization* as the guarantee of a better foreign policy by removing uncontrollable and irresponsible influences, as well as *democratization* for the preservation of domestic peace and as the inevitable consequence of the war. The latter was also dictated by justice, for if the modern state offered every citizen a certain equality of fate and in particular death on the battlefield, it also owed him that minimum of political influence through universal suffrage.

Weber discussed all sorts of objections to democracy; above all, it would destroy the refined traditions and the political sagacity of the "aristocratic" strata that had hitherto dominated the state. He asked:

Where is the German aristocracy with its refined tradition? If it existed, one could talk about it, but outside a few princely courts it simply is not there. For aristocracy in the *political* sense requires an economically unassailable existence. An aristocrat must be able to live *for* the state instead of having to live on it. He must be economically independent so that he may be available for political purposes at home and abroad. Only a person living on large private means and a very great nobleman [*Standesherr*] have sufficient detachment from the economic struggle of interests. Such persons do exist here and there in Germany, but they are not a *political class* as in England. The Prussian Junkers have long since become agricultural entrepreneurs and are thus involved in the struggle of interests. If this class of entrepreneurs, which is bourgeois by nature, gives itself the stamp of the aristocracy by making feudal gestures, there arises a parvenu physiognomy. The pillars of the old Prussian political system and of German culture, whether aristocrats or not, have, economically and socially, an eminently *bourgeois* character.

In Weber's view, then, there was no German aristocratic class of sufficient depth and political tradition that might be destroyed, nor any refined social forms. The typical social education of the young members of the leading classes and the bureaucracy—the uniformed students' associations—was not suitable for molding the entire nation into a self-assured *Herrenvolk*. [23] The specifically German concept of *Satisfaktionsfähigkeit* [worthiness to fight a duel] which opens the door to society cannot be democratized; rather, it formally constitutes a caste convention which, materially speaking, is not aristocratic but *plebeian* in nature. "The Germans are a *plebeian* people—or, if one prefers, a *bourgeois* people of workingmen, and only on this basis can a specifically German form come into being that will be appropriate to our bourgeois social and economic structure and thus will be genuine and refined."

* * *

Denied access to practical political action, Weber did not content himself with his treatises and letters. At the beginning of May, 1917, he transmitted to Conrad Haussmann, a member of the parliament's constitu-

---

[23] The author presumably did not intend to use this word in the later Nazi sense of "master race," but probably meant to indicate a nation of lords.—Ed.

tional committee, two detailed drafts of bills to change the constitution. One of these concerned the elimination of Article 9, an obstacle to a parliamentary form of government, according to which the Reich Chancellor could not be a member of the Reichstag, and it called for the formation of a *Reichskronrat* [imperial privy council] whose task it would be to put a stop to the dissemination of impulsive political utterances on the part of the monarch. The other bill, which consisted of sixteen sections, outlines the introduction of a right of the parliament to make investigations through special commissions. This so-called *Enqueterecht* was to extend to all matters which according to the constitution were subject to the legislation, the administration, or the supervision of the parliament. On the basis of the proposed law, administrative control and fact-finding were to be accomplished through an examination of records, subpoenas, cross-examination, and testimony under oath from witnesses and experts. The Reichstag was to be obliged to appoint such commissions at the request of one-quarter of its members—which made it an *Enqueterecht* of the minorities. Weber's rationale for these proposals was, above all, the necessity to control the power of the bureaucracy which inevitably increases in any modern commonwealth, no matter what its form—a power that is based not only on specialized professional training and expert knowledge but also on the *inside knowledge* [Dienstwissen] which is carefully guarded as an "official secret." In the face of these privileges, mere parliamentary rights fizzle. The right of inquiry would be the most appropriate corrective. It was a way of forcing the administration to submit to public scrutiny if there were no cogent reasons for secrecy.

Moreover, in the form that was envisaged the parliamentary minorities would have been given an influence on the government and the administration. The proposal thus constituted an effective protection against the encroachments and dangers of "majority management," a protection that was still lacking in other countries with a parliamentary government.

* * *

Weber's political essays appeared at a time of fresh grave tension and caused a stir. He received communications expressing agreement and rejection. His proposals for constitutional change became points in the program of the leftist parties. One article that held the political leaders responsible for tolerating the political blunders of the monarch caused the military authorities to impose censorship upon the *Frankfurter Zeitung*. Around that time Germany was split into several camps again. People felt less confident that the U-boats would, as promised, force peace by the end of summer at the latest. The first American troops landed. Prospects of a separate peace with Russia vanished. The socialist left propagated a "peace of reconciliation" ["*Versöhnungsfrieden*"] without annexations and indemnities; the right advocated a "peace based on power" ["*Machtfrieden*"], and a moderate group came out for a "German peace"—no annexations in Europe, but reacquisition of the colonies. Both the right and the left pressed the Chancellor for a clear formulation of war aims and decisions in domestic policy. Even at that stage, however, he did not want to tie himself down to either a program of conquest or of relinquishment, and he postponed the implementation of the Easter message. Only insignificant reforms were achieved; the parliamentary system did not get a majority. In Prussia the Conservatives prevented the elimination of the three-class system of election. Neither the Kaiser nor the Chancellor dared take decisive action.

The tension developed into an unprecedented internal crisis when the deputy Erzberger[24] uncovered the errors in the calculations of the effectiveness of the submarines and demanded a proclamation of peace on the basis of the policy of August 4, 1914.[25] There was tremendous excitement among the parties. The rightists opposed it with everything at their disposal, but in the middle of July the centrists and the leftists forced through a peace resolution that renounced the annexations. At the same time the left demanded the immediate introduction of the parliamentary system. In Prussia the king ordered that a bill be drafted calling for the introduction of the right to vote for representatives to the Reichstag. The Chancellor, who had been unsuccessful in uniting the nation regarding the war aims, in carrying on a skillful foreign policy, and in satisfying people by making generous changes in the constitution, was overthrown. Weber learned from Conrad Haussmann that the crisis had been due in large measure to his writings. But he regarded the amalgamation of domestic reforms with the peace resolution as most unfortunate:

One notices the excitement that has been caused by the prospect of an endless war and financial ruin of the country as well as by the horribly unskillful way in which both Erzberger and the government are dealing with this crisis. First the sensation in the Reichstag, then the watchword: The parliamentary system will bring peace! This is nothing

---

[24]Mathias Erzberger, 1875–1921 (assassinated), member of the Reichstag since 1903, became finance minister in 1919.—Ed.

[25]During the night of August 4, 1914, the German army invaded Belgium.—Ed.

short of outrageous, for who wants to hear of that? That democratization is connected with the *hopes for peace* is a very grave error. Foreign
countries will gain the impression that we are at the end of our
strength and will hope for revolution. This would prolong the war. And
at home it will now be said that these concessions were made under
pressure from abroad. It is a wretched business. The new man (Michaelis)[26] certainly is an excellent official, but is he also a statesman? His first
speech supplies no evidence of this; on the contrary, he seems to be a
Bethmann with more willpower. That is an advantage, but it is not
enough.[27] (July 21, 1917)

The new Chancellor, again a man appointed without the participation
of the parties, soon demonstrated his political ineptness. When Weber revised his essays, he analyzed these incidents as an instructive example of how
the absence of parliamentary leadership manifested itself in cases of internal
crisis:

> When a strong majority in the Reichstag insisted on a positive deci-
> sion by the government, the system immediately broke down in all
> parts. The perplexed representatives of the government had to slacken
> the reins because they had no footing in the party organizations. In
> its political lack of leadership the Reichstag itself presented a picture
> of complete anarchy, because the so-called party leaders had never had
> a place at the government table and even then were not under consid-
> eration as future leaders of the government. The parties were con-
> fronted with a task that had never before appeared on their horizon,
> and to which they were not equal as far as their organization or their
> personnel were concerned—namely, to form a government from their
> ranks. Of course, they proved utterly incapable of doing so; they did
> not even make the attempt and were quite unable to make it. For
> from the extreme right to the extreme left not a single party had
> a politician who might have been recognized as a leader—no more than
> did the officialdom itself.

When Weber wanted to publish his collected political essays, the military censors requested the Baden ministry of education to persuade the author to omit the publication of certain sections. The ministry sent a very

---

[26]Georg Michaelis, 1857–1936, became Reich chancellor and Prussian prime minister in 1918.—
Ed.

[27]Wolfgang J. Mommsen (*op. cit.,* p. 265) points out that this is a pastiche of several
letters.—Ed.

tactful letter, so Weber answered very obligingly that he had already reworked the essays in a more academic fashion but now could not willingly
forgo their publication. He gave the following reasons for his attitude:

> I am probably not wrong if I regard my remarks about the publication
> of political statements by the Kaiser as objectionable to the military
> point of view. From numerous approving communications I gather that
> people read them as a concealed polemic against the monarch, and this
> very assumption has caused me to make comprehensive changes. If a
> polemic against the monarch himself became inevitable, I would defi-
> nitely engage in it *openly*. What is involved here, however, is the serious-
> ly faulty conduct of the responsible political leaders, the civil cabinet,
> and court circles. The Kaiser himself can be involved only insofar as he
> did not fully realize what the consequences of the publication of his
> statements, which not infrequently were very justified, would be. For
> the past twenty years there has been *no difference of opinion whatsoever*
> about these matters in Germany, irrespective of parties and social stra-
> ta and demonstrably down to the circles of the ruling German princes.
> That there should be a change here is incomparably more important for
> German politics than any electoral provisions of the constitution.
> Proceeding from entirely different points of departure, my political at-
> titude has changed solely under the impression that here no other au-
> thority took the necessary steps to bring about such a change. Having
> been occupied with purely scholarly work, I would surely not have con-
> sidered it my business and appropriate to the situation to point to
> this worst defect in our system by taking "refuge in public exposure"[28] if the
> *utter inability* of the monarch's circle *to listen to reason* had not manifested
> itself *during the war.* . . . [There follow the familiar exam-
> ples.—AUTHOR'S NOTE.]

It is most deplorable that in Germany both indispensable reforms and
unavoidable changes in political customs always appear to be accomplished only under pressure either from the outside or from below, and
that this invariably happens only when it is too late in the interest
of the cause. But since this is so, we must act accordingly.

Even though I was aware that the grand-ducal ministry might not
regard all my statements as correct, I still thought that I should
make them in order to counteract the impression that this was a case

---

[28]*"Flucht in die Öffentlichkeit"*—a phrase from a statement made by Adolf Freiherr Marschall von
Bieberstein as a witness in a trial in 1896. Cf. "She fled for refuge to the public exposure"
in Hawthorne's *The Scarlet Letter.*—Ed.

of a journalistic occasional polemic. The grand-ducal ministry is aware that I am planning to devote myself to purely scholarly work and at some future date perhaps to teaching, that I do not wish to participate in active politics and as a matter of *principle* avoid bringing political value judgments into my *teaching* far more strictly than many other professors. (August 8, 1917)

VI

Amidst all the unrest of the Berlin scene and his own political excitement Weber had, as already mentioned, been working on his treatises on Hinduism and Buddhism since the end of 1915 and had done research on ancient Judaism in the fall of 1916. His Hebrew was adequate for him to work from the sources. "Max now is almost 'skinny,' but he is very industrious and, on the whole, fresh. He is studying the Old Testament, analyzing the Prophets, The Psalms, and The Book of Job, and in the evening he sometimes reads me some of his latest writings." But since he wrote political essays in addition and also reworked individual sections of *Wirtschaft und Gesellschaft,* the studies in the sociology of religion extended over a longer period and were not completed as planned. Weber intended to analyze also The Psalms and The Book of Job in this context and then the Judaism of the Talmud. He had already made preliminary studies before the war for the sections on the sociology of religion in *Wirtschaft und Gesellschaft.*

In the extant, self-contained part about ancient Judaism, the old Israelite prophets in particular are viewed in an original way as a special type. They are impressively presented as the first historically accredited "political demagogues," and their prophecies are described as "the earliest immediately topical literature of political polemics." Weber shows that the prophets always appeared when great powers threatened the homeland and when it was a question of the existence or nonexistence of the Jewish national state. Then they were caught up in the maelstrom of political divisions and struggles of interests, particularly with regard to foreign policy. Whether or not they so desired, they had to be partisans of those who pursued the foreign policy of the moment. When Weber had a few years previously concerned himself with the type of the old Hebrew prophet in the framework of his systematic sociology of religion, he had not yet employed these concepts. Evidently, only the experience of the war and political activity had suggested them to him. He was particularly moved by the figure of Jeremiah, the prophet of doom, and Weber's analysis of him, like his analysis of the Puritans, betrays great inner involvement. When he read excerpts from his manuscript to Marianne in the evening, she saw his own fate expressed in many passages.

Jeremiah implores God to relieve him of prophesying. He does not wish to speak, but he *must*, and he regards the compulsion to speak as a terrible ordeal. By order of Yahweh, he speaks publicly in the streets, and he always speaks against the rulers of his own people, the king and his family. Yahweh speaks through him and forces him to prophesy misfortune and to curse the king because he has not kept his covenant with Yahweh and is making concessions to other gods. The glowing passion of the prophet bursts forth unrestrained; however, this "titan of holy invective" is dominated not by his own person but by Yahweh's cause. And after he has been proved right, he is not at all triumphant, nor does he feel dull despair, as before. Next to profound grief there is hope for God's grace and better times. And despite all his wild rage at the obdurateness of his listeners, he heeds Yahweh's admonition not to forfeit the right to be his voice by using ignoble words. The prophet of doom is feared, hated, and frequently persecuted. He gets no support from the king, because the latter has no political use for his advice and admonitions. Counterprophets appear and seek to invalidate his speeches by using force, trickery, and mockery. Jeremiah wrestles with his visions in solitude, and after he has proclaimed them, the man whom the others regard with horror and fear returns to his house. Charisma is his privilege; it is never his aim to let his listeners, too, be seized by the "spirit." That is why, unlike a Christian prophet, he does not depend upon a spiritual fellowship. On the contrary; uncomprehended and hated by the masses, he never has the feeling of being supported and nurtured by like-minded companions, as the Christian apostles were. Instead, the pathos of inner loneliness engulfs him. Not swarms of ecstatics but one or a few disciples share his lonely ecstasy and his equally lonely torment. He never claims to be a savior, an exemplary religious virtuoso, or a man without sin. Nor does he offer any original means of salvation. He urges the people to be moral and obey God, yet he proclaims neither a new conception of God nor new ways of achieving salvation, nor even new commandments, but only religious depth [*Verinnerlichung*]. He is the mouthpiece of the God who is known to all.

18

INTERLUDE _____

The summer of 1917 also brought periods of relaxation from the mounting burden of cares. For a prolonged period Weber immersed himself in the quiet harmony of life at Oerlinghausen. He received good care and was spoiled there, and he took a close interest in all that everyday life brought. He enjoyed playing with Wina's grandchild, who used to run through the high arch of his legs. In the afternoon, when the women were doing needlework, he would read to them poems by Stefan George and excerpts from Gundolf's book on Goethe. Even though they did not fully understand everything, the music of his voice soothed their souls. Now and then they persuaded him to give a lecture before a larger audience, perhaps on the Indian castes, the Jewish prophets, or the sociological foundations of music. As yet there was no destruction there; time seemed to be standing still and to envelop the countryside in the dream that everything was as it had been before. Friendly images hovered about his soul:

I sleep in the customary beautiful room and write on the old desk. Here, too, everything calls out "Home, home!" and the cloudy-sunny

weather goes marvelously with this infinitely German countryside. It
is a great pity that you are not here as well, because we imagine your
presence everywhere. At the Scheerenkrug [restaurant] at Whitsuntide
twenty-four years ago—do you remember?—with the little cap on your
short thick hair, all red like a little rose. And then the wedding in
the hall over there and in the adjoining room. It is quiet and homey;
I think it will do me good and it was probably the right thing. Prophets, Wilhelm II, the *Frankfurter Zeitung*—all that is quite far away.

This countryside is really incredibly beautiful. The *Senne* [heath] is now
gradually losing its former oceanlike loneliness; instead of the reddish
heath one sees more dark forest nurseries on the one side and wheat
fields on the other. But the view remains quite enchanting, and on
the other side of the Porta Westfalika[1] it is unchanged, giving the
impression of inexhaustible fertility and homey, nonconformist coziness.
But on both sides it is immeasurably peaceful; it seems incomprehensible
and unimaginable that this land should be engaged in a struggle for existence.

It is now heavenly beautiful again, especially on this early morning; the
sun is gentle and warm, the view over the fertile plain from the window of the study [*Herrenstube*] is as wonderful as ever . . . They are doing a fabulous job of "fattening" ["*nudeln*"] me up. I am afraid I am losing
in spiritual beauty and gaining in corpulence, but it seems that you
little women [*Weiberchen*] do have that ambition, and in any case, it
does one good now and then. For the winter and the first part of next
summer will be bad.

The early summer and the autumn brought days crammed with intellectual exchange and combat at Lauenstein Castle.[2] The castle towered in
solitude on a bare peak over Thuringia's sober fir forests, and its gray walls
were outlined against the sky. For a long time proletarian families had
dwelled there, and then a fancier had acquired it. After he had staked all
his means on its stylish restoration, he opened it as an inn. This is where
the Jena publisher and book dealer Eugen Diederichs[3] convened a colorful
group of scholars, artists, political writers, *Lebenspraktiker* [men in practical

---

[1] A mountain gap south of Minden. The Weser River flows through it—Ed.

[2] A castle in the Franconian forest between Ludwigstadt and Probstzella; destroyed in 1290,
restored in the fourteenth century, expanded in the sixteenth century, and remodeled in
1896.—Ed.

[3] 1867–1930, established in Jena from 1904 on.—Ed.

life] and *Freideutsche Jugend* [Free German Youth][4] for an exchange of ideas about the meaning and the mission of the age.

Some of the well-known scholars who participated were Crusius, Meinecke,[5] Jaffé, Sombart, Tönnies, and Weber. Among the literary artists were R. Dehmel, P. Ernst, J. Winckler, Vershofen, W. v. Molo;[6] the writers on politics and *Lebenspraktiker* included G. Bäumer, T. Heuss, Grabowsky, Kampffmeyer, Scheffler,[7] Maurenbrecher, and others. Among the younger men were Bröger, Kroner, Uphoff, and Toller[8]—young artists who were not only concerned with their work but also wished to bring a new social epoch into being. The basic theme of the discussions was to be the linking of cultural questions with political ones. The main organizer hoped for more—namely, that the meetings would promote the evolution of a new German spirit, one that was anchored in religion.

The setting was full of atmosphere. The rooms with their old-fashioned furnishings had windows looking onto wooded mountain slopes and offering a view of several valleys. The meetings took place in the *Rittersaal* [hall of the knights] or in the castle yard. The colorful tendrils of Virginia creepers covered the walls. From the roof the German flag waved—a symbol of superpersonal community. The old things surrounding them that had defied the tempests of the times also spoke of the common roots of German civilization, of a past in which everything and everyone had a predetermined place and meaning. By contrast, the feeling and thinking of that group of *modern* Germans were anything but unified; they spoke the same language but had difficulty understanding one another. The older men were divided primarily by their different political convictions, and the younger ones were separated

---

[4]A youth organization founded in 1913 and aiming at the development of young people according to their own desires and capabilities.—Ed.

[5]Presumably Otto Crusius, 1857–1918, professor of classical philology at Tübingen, Heidelberg, and Munich; Friedrich Meinecke, professor of history at Strasbourg, Freiburg, and Berlin.—Ed.

[6]The dramatists and novelists Paul Ernst, 1866–1933, and Josef Winckler, 1881–1966; Wilhelm Vershofen, 1878–1960, economist and novelist, professor at Nürnberg from 1923 on; the novelist Walter von Molo, 1880–1958.—Ed.

[7]Adolf Grabowsky, 1880–, jurist and writer on politics, editor of *Das neue Deutschland* (1912–23), founder of *Weltpolitisches Archiv* in Basel (1937); Hans Kampffmeyer, b.1874, took his doctorate at Heidelberg under Weber in 1910 and published a number of books on industrial housing, garden cities, and similar subjects; Karl Scheffler, 1869–1951, art historian, editor of *Kunst und Künstler* in Berlin (1906–33).—Ed.

[8]Karl Bröger, 1886–1944, workingman-poet and storyteller; Richard Jacob Kroner, 1884–, philosopher, professor at Freiburg, Dresden, Kiel, Union Theological Seminary, and Temple University, author of *Von Kant bis Hegel* (1912–24) and other works; either or both of the Uphoff brothers (Carl Emil, b.1885; Fritz, b.1890), artists and members of the Worpswede group; the dramatist, poet, storyteller, and revolutionary Ernst Toller, 1893–1939.—Ed.

from the older men by their rejection of all traditional values, especially of
a political and social order that led to wars. They longed for a simpler existence, a new community, and a new faith. That ungodly [gottfremd] world appeared to them to be ripe for destruction. They awaited the birth of a
new world, a world of supernational union in which peace, brotherhood, solidarity, and socialism would finally reign.

The older men were also profoundly shaken by the European catastrophe,
but they were tied to their personal tasks in life and set in their values.
Most of them knew that a revolution in the external order could not
change basic human nature—and it was human nature that thwarted the
hopes of the young. Among the older people, the writer Max Maurenbrecher, a man of mercurial opinions and at that time of a "Pan-German" orientation, tried to convert people to his conservative political ideas. He presented them as specifically German and opposed them to the "democratic
individualism" of Western Europe; the state as "idea," as objectivization of
the "absolute," was to overarch subjectivism.

At a time when everything depended upon pushing through the necessary
domestic reforms, Weber hated this political romanticism. He vehemently
opposed it, and the political duel between the two men threatened to
stifle all other discussion. Weber was keenly aware of the countless political
blunders of the Wilhelminian age. It irritated him that even in that group
of intellectuals so many opposed the necessary internal transformation of
the faulty political structure. Were these people *still* unable or unwilling to
see the light? Could they *never* be induced to give up their illusions? To
Theodor Heuss, who shared his views, he said passionately: "As soon as the
war is over, I shall insult the Kaiser until he sues me, and then the responsible statesmen—Bülow, Tirpitz, Bethmann-Hollweg—shall be obliged to
make statements under oath."

In the quieter evening hours the young people also came into their own
in an intimate exchange of ideas. They would meet outside in the bright
moonlight under the high walls of the old castle—with what ghostlike un-
reality that poetry projected into the strife-torn present!—or in one of
the dark-paneled chambers with its ancient furnishings where one of the
Freideutsche would reveal the young people's longing for a new prophecy.
What they were saying seemed to come like chaotic bombast and the expression of an exaggerated sense of self-importance. These self-confessions
were alien to Weber's reserved nature, and he was impatient with romantic
notions that were an escape from the hard fights of everyday life to
another world of atmosphere. But he did manage to empathize with these

young people, and then he worked with them for clarity and objectivity. He sought to make them understand why at that particular moment national self-assertion [Selbstbehauptung]—*the saving of Germany*—was the order of the day, beside which everything else paled into insignificance. What would it avail to gain one's own soul if the nation deteriorated? He rejected as a serious aberration the attempt to awaken feelings of religious community during the first session by means of a medieval mystery play. And he found all the talk about the world-secret and the obligation to confess in a larger group, as the young people wanted it, impossible. His views are expressed in the following lines to one of the younger participants:

Naturally a great deal can be said about your wishes, provided that it is definite *what* is really to become "known." So-called "final standpoints"? That will give rise to gabbing and sensationalism and *nothing* else. And above all, on the basis of much experience and also of fundamental convictions my viewpoint is that an individual sees his own real desires clearly *only* if he tests his supposed "final" attitude by reacting to *very concrete* problems that have come to a head. So make the proposal that, for example, "pacifism" (this is only a suggestion; I think I feel how very close this is to all of you) or anything else you want be discussed in an unreservedly "confessional" manner. If I continue to attend the meetings, I shall be the very last one not to participate in *that*. But I have one thing to say about this. Not only this question but—although I know that *all* of you do not believe or see this— all cultural questions are influenced by what appears to be a purely superficial preliminary question: *How will this war come to an end?* For this will determine the specific future tasks of the German character [*Wesen*] within this world. *All* final questions without exception are affected by purely political events, external though these may seem. That is why everything that is said now, and particularly by us nonparticipants in the war, is so very nonbinding. Yet, such a subject is possible. To me the limit of "confessing" is where things are involved that are "sacred." They belong in what is humanly a "good hour" in the highest sense and within a circle of people who are personally very close to one another, but not in a "meeting" of an "audience," no matter what that meeting may be like. By "audience" I mean anyone I do not know well as a human being. Only a prophet or a saint and (in his language) an artist acts differently and is allowed to act differently.

During the days at Lauenstein, Weber was greatly stimulated intellec-

600 MAX WEBER: A BIOGRAPHY

tually. It took little for his accumulated knowledge and experience to burst forth. He talked all day and half the night. Several small photographs show him engaged in lively conversation, surrounded by a group of attentive listeners. During the fall session, which was devoted to discussing the "Problem of Leaders in the State and in Culture," he gave the opening lecture on "Personality and Life Order" [*Die Persönlichkeit und die Lebensordnungen*].

The wealth of material that crowded in upon him was tremendous and his knowledge was overwhelming, particularly for the young artists striving for expressionistic primitiveness; their mental capacity was too limited for them to absorb this flow. Inwardly they rebelled against it. They regarded it as the hated scientific mind that showed no simple way to solve practical problems because it surveyed a whole web of interconnected processes, and asked in connection with every social "ideal" by what means and at what price it was attainable, thereby impeding choice and action. This sober incorruptibility deprived them of the courage to be visionaries. They felt repelled and magnetically attracted at the same time, for the man who was behind that intellectuality and acted as its mouthpiece was so mysteriously alive and anything but a mere scholar. When he expressed himself through words and gestures, was he not an artist as well? To some he appeared as Satan, to others as their conscience. At night, when Weber walked across the castle yard, he overheard some young people in a corner dramatizing him. He had not only stimulated their thinking but stirred their imagination as well. Most of them sensed his controlled ethos. If they could only secure him as their leader and prophet for the future! But he refused. He had no new salvation to proclaim of the kind they desired, and so long as Germany was at stake and thousands were dying out there every day, he was not interested in a new world order. He was willing to be their teacher, in scholarship as in politics, *if they wanted to crack hard nuts* [*wenn sie harte Bretter bohren wollen*]. "I believe I know my business there." But anyone who wished to learn from him had to realize first that intellectual probity is the simple virtue of scholarship, that it is a vocation practiced professionally in the service of self-knowledge and the recognition of factual connections, not the gift of seers and prophets which produces salvation and revelations. The prophet for whom so many of the new generation yearned simply was not there. It was their fate to live in an ungodly, prophetless time: "He calleth to me out of Seir, 'Watchman, what of the night? Watchman, what of the night?' The watchman said, 'The morning cometh, and also the night: if ye will enquire, enquire ye: return, come.' " [Isa. 21:11]

* * *

From Lauenstein Weber went to Schwarzburg, to the quiet Thuringian forest, for a few days. Images from his childhood came back to him. There he had gone hiking with his father and younger brothers forty years before and had written his mother his first travel letters. He liked to look back on that period and still remembered many details. In general, he had vivid memories of his childhood and youth and liked to tell stories about them. From the gentle mountain ridges the Webers looked down into green valleys and at slopes that were acquiring various colors. They lay down on a soft bed of golden brown leaves that the wind had blown into the gutter. The ripeness and peace of autumn streamed forth. For a while they forgot the threatening doom, happily ignorant of the future.

* * *

As a result of the days at Lauenstein Castle, in the winter of 1917–18 some socialist and pacifist students attended Weber's Sunday open house. The experience of the war had shaken them profoundly. Among them was Ernst Toller. He began to feel at home, brought some of his poems, and read them aloud. His listeners were stirred by the breath of a pure soul that had faith in the original goodness and solidarity of human beings and believed that it was possible to get the peoples that were murdering one another, at the behest of their governments, to throw away their arms. Weber said that the time for pacifist propaganda had not yet come for the Germans, that their will to national self-preservation must not be broken, and that the fighting men's duty must not be made loathsome to them. But the peace movement, he said, would prevail if the war destroyed itself without a positive result for any nation.

However, Toller tried to make converts to his belief among the students. A group was organized that hoped for Weber's leadership and for his approval of a proclamation which called, among other things, for the rule of Eros in the world and for the abolition of poverty. Weber was aghast at this confused and unrealistic program. Yet he was ready to discuss it with the young people; however, they refused. When Toller and his adherents began to agitate for a general strike, Toller was arrested. Thereupon Weber requested that he be allowed to testify; he secured Toller's release, but was not able to prevent the young people's expulsion from the university.

In the late fall of 1918, shortly before the outbreak of the revolution, Weber again debated about pacifism in a small group in Frankfurt. Now, too, he denied the young people his leadership and revealed himself as their opponent if they did not take their ideals seriously and subject themselves to *all* commandments of the Christian ethic of brotherhood. As he saw it, either they must adhere to the principle of the Sermon of the Mount and turn the other cheek in personal as well as public life, that is, they must renounce *any* form of violence, or they must recognize the fact that in a world which cannot be shaped by that law, war is only one of a number of forms of struggle and perhaps not the meanest. This displeased the young people, for they wanted revolution. In the aftermath of this discussion an older pacifist, Professor G[oldstein], presented his convictions to Weber in a letter and censured him for having deserted the Heidelberg students in their distress and having put them off with sophistries by asking them the "Tempter" question: whether they were ready to fashion their entire lives in accordance with the teachings of the Sermon of the Mount. As a precondition for the moral regeneration of man, G. demanded, among other things, that each individual, and particularly the intellectuals, acknowledge guilt for the war. To this Weber replied:

Dear Colleague:

Thank you very much for your friendly, detailed, and serious letter which I would like to answer in greater detail than conditions here permit. I must categorically reject your statement that I left the students here "in the lurch" in 1917. When the highly immature young people, some of whom were serious-minded, submitted their "proclamation" to me, I offered to discuss the matter with them in detail. That offer was declined, and the reasons do not concern me. Thereupon I wrote to the leader, Herr Toller, and declined to take responsibility for that sort of thing. When he was arrested after his speech calling for a general strike, I immediately secured a hearing as a witness before the court-martial. What I said there is a chapter by itself. He was released from prison. Thus, you are falsely informed. Nor can I, of course, go along with your assertion that my reminder of revolution, strike, and so on is "tempter's work" [*versucherisch*]. I simply don't understand you. Either—or! Either resist evil with force *nowhere* and then live like Saint Francis or Saint Clare or an Indian monk or a Russian navordnik (?).[9]

---

[9]The *norodniki* were adherents of a populist movement in Russia (ca. 1860–95) who desired to bring about a social regeneration of the country through the peasantry, using ideas of utopian socialism.—Ed.

Anything else is fraud or self-deception. For this *absolute* demand there is only an *absolute* way, the way of the *saint*. Or else, desire to resist evil by force, because otherwise you *share the responsibility* for it. But it simply is and will continue to be a mystery to me why civil war or some other form of violence—such as any revolution employs at least, at the *very* least, as a "means" toward an end—is supposed to be "holy," while just self-defense in war is *not*. If Poles were now to invade Danzig and Thorn, or if Czechs moved into Reichenberg, the first thing to do would be to establish a German irredenta. I shall not be the one to do this, because for reasons of health I am incapacitated, but every nationalist will have to do it and particularly the students. Irredenta means nationalism with revolutionary instruments of force. Perhaps you will like it better that way than "war." But it is the same thing, and of course this is what I meant, and I shall say so in public.

I have kept silent about the "guilt" of the *others* in wartime, and I have not participated in the disgusting moralizing, which is equally loathsome on both sides. This gives me the right to say now that this wallowing in guilt feelings which I encounter in a number of places is a *sickness*—just as flagellantism is one in the religious area and masochism in the sexual sphere. The policy of the past two years was an outrage—not because it was a war policy, but because it was *frivolous* and *mendacious*. Our policy before the war was *stupid*, not morally reprehensible—it certainly cannot be called that. This is my judgment. Whether or not we come to an understanding, I thank you for your letter and the seriousness of your convictions. (November 13, 1918)

To return to the chronological narrative, in the late fall of 1917 Weber went to Vienna again, this time on personal business. The university there wished to secure him as a teacher. When colleagues in Munich had asked him, shortly before the outbreak of the war, whether he would be interested in a lectureship, he had rejected the idea and reacted strongly when he noticed that his wife regarded it as worth trying: "Terrible that you should still entertain the notion that I could get on a lecture platform!" By now his attitude had changed; bad memories had receded and he knew that he could now work more steadily than before. He was very tempted to exert himself in the beautiful city, and in any case he would have to seek a steady source of income after the war. Personal negotiations showed that both sides were extremely eager to oblige, for the University of Vienna needed distinguished teachers and was willing to do everything he wanted. He himself was to determine the scope and the manner of his teaching activity; the important thing was that he came. He was touched, decided to try it, and accepted a full professorship [*Ordinariat*] on a trial basis for the summer term of 1918.

But from the outset he felt that he would not permanently leave Germany and that he could not burden himself with full-time official duties. In April, a few weeks before the beginning of the semester, Weber moved to Vienna. The early spring gently spread over the magnificent city. Despite the heavy pressure that weighed upon it, joy and beauty still seemed to be the meaning of its existence. Everything smiled upon him: the gentle landscape, reminiscent of the south; the obliging attitude of his colleagues; and the friendliness and open-mindedness of the others. He met the politicians and statesmen he knew, and, in contrast to the Berliners, he found them free from the insolence of office, open and communicative even then. By day he worked undisturbed in the library, in the evening he occasionally went to the theater. The high-protein diet he had been without for so long made him feel strong and well. Once again it was a fresh start.

However, soon burdensome "duties"—visits to his colleagues—obtruded themselves upon this gratefully enjoyed holiday existence. Weber, who had always attached importance to observing academic and social etiquette, did not exempt himself from these. Now the seamy side of the big city became apparent. Every visit meant a trip by inadequate means of transportation, followed by many stairs and trivial conversations. Through the years he had become unaccustomed to such tedious and superfluous formalities: "I am terribly worn out by walking and standing in the electric streetcars. If it goes on like this, the question of my being able to lecture will soon be completely pointless. These visits are a frightful burden; I cannot stand it."

The chores of daily living, of which no one relieved him there, cost him a great deal of energy, and he loathed the slow bureaucratic pace. Even before the semester began, the feeling came over him that it would not work. His first lectures after an interruption of almost nineteen years took a tremendous effort. Under the title "A Positive Critique of the Materialistic View of History," he presented his research on the sociology of religion as well as his sociology of the state. It was a matter of getting accustomed to lecturing again, and he evaluated his performance as "middling" [*"mittelgut"*]. Soon, however, the steadily increasing number of his students showed him that he had not lost his charisma as a teacher. After some time he lectured in the largest auditorium to an overflow audience, and about one-third of it consisted of mature people: politicians, civil servants, university teachers. His lectures were "events."

After Pentecost Marianne also was among those in attendance. She listened with rapt attention and was moved. Weber usually lectured about the sociology of religion for two and a half hours without pause, until it became dark in the beautiful paneled room. He had not yet regained the customary lecturing style. What he offered instead was usually an enchanting artistic achievement. The overabundant material was perfectly organized, everything was vividly presented, and the most remote civilization— the Orient—was related to the Occident. He would invariably present his ideas in such a way that the remote material suddenly threw new light on the current problems that were familiar to all—for example, when he explained the religious ideas by which the Indian caste system produced an antirevolutionary frame of mind and then juxtaposed with it the antithetical religious background of modern European socialism.

Weber's approach was purely scientific and he conveyed value-free empirical knowledge, yet one could tell that deep down he was excited. If he was asked for the reason, he would say only, "It's just that the facts themselves are so fabulously interesting." As he put it in the prefatory note to the first volume of his essays on the sociology of religion: *The course of human fates powerfully tugged at his heartstrings.* Each of these high-powered lectures, delivered without notes, required concentrated ready knowledge and imagination and diminished his reserve of energy. Marianne's enthusiasm was tempered with worry. Naturally, he could not stand *that* for long. After each of these long lectures Weber was completely drained, and having patiently satisfied the questioners who surrounded him in the corridor, he would quietly slip off to the *Silberner Brunnen* [Silver Well Restaurant]. A good meal and a cigar gradually restored him and gave him confidence that he would get through the next day as well. But then he said, making inordinate demands upon himself: "This is how I would have to be able to lecture every day if I wanted to be a professor." Marianne reminded him that a man could not sing the role of Tristan every day either, that his talks were quite unacademic and an excessive pampering of his students.

Weber's colleagues and the authorities tried in many ways to persuade him to stay in Vienna permanently. It was hardest to resist the entreaties of young people, including young scholars, who wanted him as an intellectual focus. He hesitated and referred the requests to another authority: "My wife manages me." Marianne, however, from the beginning thought that the stay in Vienna should remain an "adventure," since Weber definitely belonged in Germany. And in the meantime the schools of philosophy and of jurisprudence in Heidelberg had urgently requested him to teach there for at least part of the year. If he only got through that semester! Another breakdown would be a disaster. That he was in danger is shown, among other things, by the following experience.

On a holiday the Webers made a pleasant excursion to the Kahlenberg.[10] Weber enjoyed the magnificent view of the city, the broad Danube River, and the circle of gently sloping, wooded heights behind which the high mountains gleamed in the distance. He was in good spirits and praised the "gentle beauty" and German quality of this sight. Toward evening they walked down over the ripening, corn-bearing hills to the streetcar line in one of the suburbs. But before they got there Weber was exhausted and suddenly became annoyed. Then it occurred to him that he had forgotten to send his prescription for sleeping tablets to the pharmacy. Fortunately he had it with him. But it was Sunday evening and his usual store was closed. They trudged on and finally found one that was open, but the druggist refused to refill the prescription without authorization from a physician. Weber did not know any doctors, and by that time it was very late. Exhausted and excited as he was, he began to despair. A big lecture was imminent; the night would of course be a bad one and he would be utterly unfit tomorrow, but he still could not cancel the lecture. "If we had only not gone on that accursed excursion! And then this foolish idea of walking; now I shall surely get sick again!" All attempts to calm him failed; he refused to go to bed in the first place. After midnight his wife left him, at her wit's end and in despair. Then she unexpectedly found a few tablets of her own soporific. The relief was enormous. Weber was immediately freed from the spell of his anxiety. His features relaxed and he smiled; now he would get some rest. And he did sleep and was up to par the following day.

But his decision had been made. In the middle of the semester Weber handed in his resignation, but he promised to come to Vienna as a visiting teacher for a semester at a time. He was now relieved of the psychological pressure, and his lecturing experience also made itself felt. But he received many invitations, and in the expectation of important political conversations he did not turn them down. These visits and the other hardships of city life took him to the verge of serious nervous strain a few more times. In the end he did accomplish everything; in fact, he did something additional. He gave a lecture on socialism before an audience of officers, and

---

[10]One of several small mountains that frame Vienna.—Ed.

in his final week he taught and debated every day. The cultural section of a Viennese newspaper described his personality as a teacher. He angrily rejected the "drama review," but the following excerpts from it are of interest as the reaction of an outsider:

> The tall, bearded scholar resembles one of the German stonemasons from the Renaissance period. Only his eyes do not have the directness and the sensual joy of the artist. His gaze comes from deep down inside, from hidden passageways, and strays way off into the distance. The man's mode of expression is in keeping with his exterior. There is something infinitely graphic about it. What is revealed here is an almost Hellenic way of viewing things. His words are simply shaped. In their quiet simplicity they are reminiscent of cyclopean stones. But when the focus of the presentation is on a person, it immediately becomes monumental. Each feature is as though chiseled in marble and it is most brightly illuminated. Now and then his speech is supported by a gentle movement of his hand. Delicately structured and narrow, with pointed fingers and a somewhat willful thumb, this hand would seem to indicate a Petronius[11] type rather than a scholar. Since the days of Unger, Lorenz von Stein,[12] and Ihering, no professor at the law school of the University of Vienna has attracted as many students as Max Weber. But this extraordinary power of attraction is by no means due only to the rhetorical mastery of this man, nor is it the original and strictly objective nature of his argumentation. Rather, it is primarily his ability to arouse feelings that have lain dormant in the souls of others. Each word clearly demonstrates that he regards himself as an heir of the German past and is dominated by a consciousness of his responsibility to posterity. . . .

In the course of that summer the pressure weighed more heavily upon Vienna. Things were going badly on the Austrian front, and the offensive against Italy had failed. On the battlefield and at home people went hungry. Among them were the families of many professors. These people were fed in communal kitchens and regarded their worn clothes as a badge of honor. Undernourished civil servants fell asleep at their desks. Beggars stalked the streets. There was a sense of impending catastrophe. What Weber himself

---

[11]Gaius Petronius ("Arbiter Elegantiae"), Roman satirist in the first century A.D.—Ed.
[12]1815–1890, professor of constitutional law and economics at Kiel and Vienna (from 1855 on).—Ed.

thought about his Viennese period is shown in these excerpts from his letters.

I have now been in this city, which is enchanting in its spring finery, for eight days. I have just been to the Hofoper [opera house], at a faculty meeting, and in the Prater [nature and amusement park], spend many hours each day in the library, and am trying to see how I can manage for the time being. In any case, I am very *lonely*. "Social intercourse" is stagnant here as well. In the evening everyone goes to bed early, only toward evening are the cafés as alluring as ever. My stomach is glad to have escaped the German potatoes, for there is nothing like that here; I haven't seen any yet. People who can afford it eat eggs, also meat and now spring vegetables. I always eat my fill; my body enjoys all the albumen. The prices, to be sure, are fantastic! My apartment is all right, and above all, it is *clean*. What bothers me is a young couple next door with the usual vices of such a pair, especially after dinner. Otherwise it would be almost "ideal." For in front of my window the trees are blooming, and they almost completely cover the prosaic façades of the rear buildings. Everything is still as death. The weather is warm; I can hardly stand wearing an overcoat when I am out walking, and always have my window open. This noon or tomorrow I shall start paying calls, and considering the distances I dread this somewhat. I am fine, there is no denying that. For the time being my brain is on the job and I like everything; whether I shall continue to do so is questionable, but I do now. (Pension Baltic, Skodagasse 15, April 14, 1918)

The city continues to be enchantingly beautiful, both the early spring and the old elegance of the streets and yards with their massive baroque quality. The other conditions are burdensome only where one has to deal with the "state." For example, *to this day* I have received no *money*, despite all my tricks and ruses. In the meantime I had to get a loan from Frau Hartmann![13] It is almost incredible. Likewise, my lecture was, of course, announced incorrectly—scheduled for one hour instead of two, etc. Things like that are par for the course. None of the libraries has any proper card catalogues, which greatly diminishes their general convenience of use. And there are many other things. Still—it is beautiful here, but one should not lecture for five hours or more, *that* can *not* be done without greatly burdening a nervous person. But this semester will go quite

---

[13]The wife of the historian Ludo M. Hartmann.—Ed.

nicely. Klenau is here, and we spent an evening together. On Tuesday his symphony will be performed, and on Monday I want to see *Elektra,* for the "great Richard" [Strauss] is here and will conduct it himself. After that, on Wednesday or Thursday, I may see Moissy.[14] You can see that I am not denying myself anything, and right now I can still do all this. Later, when my lectures have started, I shall no longer manage so well.

Otherwise, I am living *very* well. Saturday is "breadless day" in the boarding house; then people eat eggs and are glad about the pretext, for the corn bread is miserable stuff. My daily schedule is like this: In the morning, after tea, I go to the library until 12:30, then to dinner, then half an hour's rest during which that damned young couple seems determined not to let me sleep. Then library from 3 to 6 o'clock, then to the café or a walk, then library again until 8 o'clock, then to Klomser's Restaurant or some other eating place for supper, then a cigar at home (a rare treasure obtained through someone's "good offices"!), then to bed. (April 19, 1918)

(To Helene Weber on her birthday) In front of my window I have a large inner court with a thick growth of old trees; there are birds in them, otherwise there is dead silence. This sort of thing exists only in the center of Vienna. I live ten minutes from the university, which is located on the Ring opposite the Hofburgtheater, and in front of my door there is a streetcar that goes to the Prater, etc. I hear the roar of the city noise only in the distance, and if a young married couple were not carrying on next door, this would be nothing short of "ideal." In any case, I am living under the most favorable sanitary conditions imaginable. I have just returned from the Vienna Woods, which are enveloped in early spring. It is warm and there is a tendency toward spring showers. My lectures don't start until two weeks from now.

You know what we want from you and what we wish you. Stay as beautiful and strong and vibrant in your love as you have always been and have been just now, and preserve your enjoyment of life. This period is as great as it is terrible. Certainly, during this offensive one thinks every day of the people there, particularly of Klara's son who is right in the thick of it, and every morning there is this thought of "still" all over again. It is often too much to bear and one is all choked up and incapable of saying anything. You must have noticed this when I was in Heidelberg. And yet, if it had to be, one is grateful to be living through it. (April 14, 1918)

---

[14]The actor Alexander Moissi, 1880–1935.—Ed.

(To the mother) Thank you for your affectionate letter. Things are starting out nicely here, that is, we shall not begin to lecture until next week, and in the meantime there is a lot of drudgery with the visits, which take a lot out of me considering the endless distances, and the accursed Austrian treasury which in its infinite *Gemütlichkeit* [easygoingness] has now taken two and a half weeks to decide to pay me my money. But other than that everything is *very* enchanting—the old city in its spring finery. In the morning I am awakened by the thrushes in the large, parklike yard with old trees outside my window. One finds this sort of thing in the heart of a big city only in Vienna. . . .

People are feasting on eggs, meat, shortcake, wonderful coffee, and excellent cuisine generally, provided they can pay for it. In the morning I can always eat two eggs in the café opposite the university, and surely that would be unthinkable in Germany! I am quite close to the theater and the opera; the other day I heard the *Entführung*[15] and I shall soon see [*King*] *Lear*. The excursions to the Vienna Woods are heavenly, though I haven't had much time for them so far, but I shall catch up on that with Marianne. Of course, this cannot turn into a "home," and I can already predict with certainty that under the conditions of a big city I shall not be able to accomplish things to the full extent.

Yes, our policy in Estonia and Livonia is *not* pleasing, but rather dangerous and irresponsible as far as the future is concerned. As for domestic policy, it is highly uncertain. Then the people from the battlefield will have to build their state the way *they* want it. But if one considers what we have been saved from, it is almost a miracle, and then one simply casts aside all "pessimism." (April 22, 1918)

(To a sister) Here the thrushes are warbling in the beautiful, old, very large Viennese inner court with a park of old trees which my window faces, and the old city is adorning its enchanting elegance with the most wonderful spring of all stages, depending on whether one takes the cog railway up the Kahlenberg, which is enveloped in early spring, or stays in the midst of the fruit trees, which have just stopped blooming, or enjoys the luxuriance of the Prater with its meadows, tree-lined avenues, and spring *Korso*.[16] Persons with *means* notice almost too little of the war. The theater and the opera, to which I am quite close, have most seductive programs and are always sold out

---

[15]Mozart's opera *The Abduction from the Seraglio.*—Ed.
[16]A festive parade of flower-bedecked carriages.—Ed.

a week in advance. The general elegance is fabulous. For fantastic prices one eats fantastically well, as in peacetime; feasts one's eyes on the astonishingly beautiful girls; sees very beautiful carriages, although the advent of the automobile has caused the gentleman fiacre-coachman to become extinct; and enjoys the culture-laden human atmosphere, which in the bourgeois strata takes the form of a massive but charming *joie de vivre* and among the upper classes is of a nonchalant refinement and a rather comfortable lassitude.

This cannot offer me a "homeland." But to spend half a year here every other year would be fine with me. Organizationally speaking, everything is mildly *schlampig* [sloppy] and *gemütlich* [easygoing]. They simply forget to pay you your money until you tell them off, and they print announcements of lectures wrong. In the seminars and institutes there is naive dawdling, and it is all incurable. To have to take the responsibility for this would be impossible, but it is quite attractive to experience this once—*provided* that it agrees with me. I could never fill a full-time post as a full professor here under big-city conditions; I already realize this—half resignedly, half relieved that I have good reason to return home. . . .

What I find "strenuous" here is life in the *big city*. Those visits! There is no end to them. In the morning I don't get a chance to work and in the afternoon I am worn out, for on the streetcar I *stand* in a tight squeeze. And everybody lives four flights up and a half-hour away. All this *walking*! That is just what I am simply unable to do. And that's why it won't work, despite all the attractiveness. An "apartment" for us would be hard to get. The moving expenses would be fabulous, the prices are fantastic, and it will be impossible to do any building. In short, nothing will come of it, I can see that, because I *cannot* do it. But we shall have a good time together at Whitsuntide. Two evenings ago I visited Hammerschlag, the director of the *Kreditanstalt* [bank]. As usual at 8:30, dinner at 8:45, around ten o'clock the "after-dinner guests" came: two excellencies, Dr. Friedjung,[17] the famous historian, and others. Relaxed and stimulated as always. Only, *those* things last a bit late: you don't get to bed until two o'clock, whereas there are no "cafés" after eleven o'clock. Tuesday, then, is the first lecture; today and tomorrow visits, Wednesday and Thursday the same. . . .

Well, the first lecture is over. I now lecture two hours Monday evening

---

[17]Heinrich Friedjung, 1851–1920, Austrian historian with a Pan-German orientation, author of *Das Zeitalter des Imperialismus* (1919–22).—Ed.

(6–8), one on Tuesday (7–8), one on Wednesday (7–8), the last two starting next week. About sixty to seventy students who will probably dwindle down to thirty or forty (judging from the number of those who took notes). It "drains" ["*schlaucht*"] me terrifically! I'd rather give ten impromptu "talks" than a two-hour academic lecture! I'll have to see whether I can endure it. In any case, full-time teaching is unthinkable; my physical condition today shows me this. The students are quite attentive; I have no complaints on that score. This running around—visits and so forth—is what simply cannot be done. It gets my head in miserable shape, and I need sleeping pills. And then this necessity to speak *formally* in a *loud* voice and the feeling that the people don't understand me. In short, it is an exertion that cannot go on. My lecture was "middling"; a week ago it would have been *very* good. But running to twenty different districts, almost always climbing four flights of stairs, and the *annoyance* had made me half dead. It was crazy that I didn't get my money until Monday! And only after I had submitted a petition to the authorities, telling them that I would not stand for this disgraceful situation and would *resign* immediately!

Otherwise everything is beautiful: the spring—on Monday evening I went up to the Vienna Woods—the beauty of the old city, the people, the academic offices, and the like. But I am a *scholar* and—for reasons of health—unfortunately no longer a *teacher*. We have to resign ourselves to that. . . .

Well, the second lecture (i.e., two hours, from 6–8) is over, too; the third follows right away, and tomorrow is the seminar. Attendance has picked up; in particular a number of *colleagues* came and busily took notes. My God, what an *exertion* that is! Ten informal talks are nothing compared to a two-hour academic lecture. Merely being tied down to an outline and making allowance for those taking notes—it is fantastic. I shall never be able to manage more than two to three hours a week. And yet I know exactly that my lecturing is middling *at best*—despite, or perhaps *because* of, the preparation, which is indispensable after all. No—I was born for the pen and for the speaker's platform, not for an academic rostrum. This experience is a bit painful for me, but it is quite obvious.

Well, two more teaching days are behind me; rather strenuous, because the number of students has again increased, this time to considerably more than 300, with some of the people standing by the walls, because there is no longer hall. But as usual after such a long respite from bad nights, I am significantly improved. The day after tomorrow is a holiday, but the young people want to have their colloquium, and so I shall have to give it tomorrow evening. Tomorrow afternoon I shall see Baron von Plener at [His] Exc[ellency] Sieghart's[18] house, and on Saturday evening I shall go to the Rohrerhütte[19] with Section Head Riedl[20] and ministry officials. I cannot tell as yet when I shall conclude my lectures. The serious students have requested me to lecture until August, but I shall not do so, if only because my money won't last until then. Meanwhile, goddamn nonsense has been spoken in the Reichstag and the poor fellows from here have had their usual bad luck at the Piave.[21] Two disagreeable developments.

In the last few days I have of necessity led a rather domestic life. The great overexcitement affected my digestion and my stomach kept turning, so I had to take Friday off and slept almost twenty-four hours on several days. Now that is just about over and I am restored to my old condition, somewhat improved. Tomorrow I shall lecture again, also on Tuesday, then there are five more lectures and five colloquia. Naturally, I am only counting how many more days I have to do this, but I think I shall see it through.

My stomach nerves having calmed down, my head is much clearer, and if I can now manage to avoid bad nights, I think I shall endure this thing until July 17 or 18. Today I spoke before an officers corps (combatting of peace propaganda) about "Socialism"—rather pleasant people (300), about one and a half hours, then "questions." Tomorrow is colloquium, the day after that I shall dine with His Exc. Sieghart. The lectures on Monday and Tuesday were somewhat difficult, but they seem to have met with applause; the attendance, at any rate, was good, as usual.

My condition is more tolerable. My lectures continue to be overcrowded and strenuous, especially because I must hurry to cover the ma-

---

[18]The Liberal Austrian statesman Ernst Edler von Plener, 1841–1923; Rudolf Sieghart (Singer), 1866–1934, banker and financial adviser to the Austrian government, longtime head of the *Bodencreditanstalt.*—Ed.

[19]An inn in the Vienna Woods.—Ed.

[20]Richard Riedl, 1865–1944, undersecretary for commerce and industry, after the war Austrian ambassador in Berlin.—Ed.

[21]In the Battle of the Piave River in Italy (June 15–24, 1918) the Austrians lost some 100,000 men.—Ed.

terial. Yesterday I visited the Saxon ambassador (von Nostitz) with H. von Hofmannsthal,[22] an intelligent, refined Viennese, but not of such cultural sophistication [*raffiniert kultiviert*] as *Der Tod des Tizian*[23] might lead one to suppose. He spoke in an agreeable way about George and Gundolf, although he is aware of the disdain in which they hold him.[24] This evening at a lecture by the very pleasant Herr von Rosthorn[25] (ambassador to Peking) about China. If I only knew when the university closes. Some say on July 22! Well, everything comes to an end some time. I really wish it were already over, for it is no pleasure always to be on the *qui vive* as regards one's health. However, I do intend to stick it out for the remaining four weeks. . . .

Yesterday, Saturday, a quite nice dinner at His Exc. Sieghart's house with the German ambassador and a few politicians, then with members of the *Freideutsche Jugend* until eleven o'clock. Today tea with the Saxon ambassador. Tomorrow another lecture! I don't know how it will go; a "head cold" has completely addled me and made me kaput. There simply *always* is some symptom of overexcitement—now one thing, now another. If I have to do it for *money*, I shall gladly lead this half-animal existence of giving academic lectures, for then it will have to be. But for "ideal" purposes and from "ideal" points of view—no! For that the sacrifice of all enjoyment of life is too terrible. For there has been no change, no change whatever, compared to the period of twenty years ago.

Again two lecturing days have passed; now it is only two plus two and two to three seminar evenings, then I shall have survived this thing. I hope I shall stick it out. Yesterday, too, attendance was such that the people stood along the walls in that large lecture hall.

During the past week I lectured every day; attendance is still considerable, although everything is closed and examinations are being held. In

[22]Alfred von Nostitz-Wallwitz, 1870–1953, German diplomat, Saxon ambassador and minister plenipotentiary in Vienna; the Austrian poet, dramatist, essayist, and storyteller Hugo von Hofmannsthal, 1874–1929.—Ed.

[23]*The Death of Titian*, fragmentary verse drama by Hofmannsthal (1892).—Ed.

[24]George wooed the young Hofmannsthal and attempted to add him to his circle, but the Austrian declined.—Ed.

[25]Arthur Edler von Rosthorn, 1862–1945, Austrian diplomat, ambassador extraordinary and minister plenipotentiary in Teheran (1905) and Peking (1911), later professor of Chinese language and history at Vienna.—Ed.

reply to the letters from the Heidelberg jurists and philosophers I wrote that I *might* want to give a small lecture course in Heidelberg next summer. The gentlemen here want to do something with me; I asked them not to do it under any circumstances now, *before* the full professorship is filled. . . .

(Marianne to Helene) Imagine, last night Max returned home—still alive but incredibly skinny, although he ate meat twice daily and about four eggs a day. But I hope that the quiet and the beauty of summer here will make up for the gastric joys [*Magenfreuden*] which, as he claims, were in the final analysis the only compensations for the terrible mental exertion in Vienna. In his last week there, you see, he lectured *every day*, and in his colloquium he frequently had three-hour discussions. The people could not get enough of him. Thank God he did not have a breakdown, but now he will have to learn again to exist without soporifics and also without the stimulating nutrition. He does not like to discuss war and politics; it would not do him good. But last night he was so happy to have returned "home" that none of the disagreeable things mattered.

* * *

For a time, of course, Weber was very tired, but the expected exhaustion did not materialize. He was soon able to work again and had a beautiful period of quiet. In September he and Marianne went to Oerlinghausen and there met Helene and other members of the family. In the place where they had once had their "green" wedding, their silver wedding anniversary was now to be celebrated. Wina had been preparing for her guests for a long time. Months before, a large roast goose had been sealed in a tin container and buried; this had become the talk of the town. With such preparations it was possible to have a beautiful feast even in those hard times. The autumn sun shone on the gardens, the foliage was already discoloring, but the red geranium beds still gleamed. In the morning everyone went to the garden to gather a bunch of beech nuts for oil. The group was smaller than it had been before, for many beloved persons had long since passed away. One of Wina's fine sons was not there; he had laid down his life on the general hill of sacrifice in the flower of his youth.

But the two branches of the Weber family, Helene's and Wina's offspring, were still flourishing and the two mothers were still active. In the early morning, "Praise the Lord, O My Soul"[26] was sung again. Once more the sisters' hands offered gifts and a silver wreath, and they recited verses composed by Helene. During the meal those assembled for the celebration exchanged addresses and responses. Their words contained a breath of all the loveliness and all the hardships of their past lives, just as delicate bubbles rise from the bottom of a wine glass. They had *so much* for which to thank one another. Marianne thanked her husband for placing her beside him in full freedom and allowing her to develop in accordance with her own law; Weber thanked his wife for blessing his daily life; all thanked the mothers for their inexhaustible love, and fate for giving them, together with its trials, the strength to bear these trials. But the Webers felt that they were not at a peaceful end but at the beginning of a new, difficult phase that would require them to stand the test again. Weber's ship of life was again being tossed about on a choppy sea. Who knew whether there would be new shores?[27] And even the harmonious happiness of their marriage did not seem like a comfortably safeguarded property; instead, they knew that it had to be wrested anew each day from the humdrum of everyday life.

One week after that celebration came Bulgaria's collapse. It was a bad omen, and hope for a tolerable end to the war faded. Now they would hardly have been able to celebrate. Weber became very quiet and withdrawn; "there is an iron ring around one's heart now." He suffered greatly and now and then reviled the one who was directing the world [*Weltenlenker*].

---

[26]*"Lobe den Herrn, o meine Seele"*—the beginning of a paraphrase of Psalm 146 by the pietist Johann Daniel Herrnschmidt, 1675–1723, which became a popular Protestant hymn after 1714.—Ed.

[27]*Ob zu neuen Ufern*—a reference to Goethe's *Faust*, Part I, line 701.—Ed.

19

THE POSTREVOLUTIONARY
POLITICIAN

I

We now go back to the end of 1917 and take up the political thread again. By that time the hopes placed in the submarines had long since faded, and although the German armies were still on enemy territory, they were being pushed more and more into a defensive position. The domestic conflicts again intensified. The same things were always involved: the question of making peace and constitutional reforms. The "Independents" split off from the Social Democrats, whose national outlook had stood the test during all those years, as a radical pacifist and revolutionary wing. The opposite was desired by the *Vaterlandspartei* [Fatherland Party], which was organized in the fall of 1917 and in which Tirpitz and Kapp[1] gathered Pan-German and conservative elements. This party fought the peace resolution and domestic re-

---

[1]Wolfgang Kapp, 1858–1922, the rightist politician who attempted to overthrow the government in March, 1920 (the so-called Kapp Putsch).—Ed.

forms, demanded that Belgium and other occupied territories be kept permanently, and advocated political indoctrination of the troops against a negotiated peace and against the government. These tactics poisoned the atmosphere of the domestic political struggle particularly in that this party boasted about the special quality of its patriotism as compared to all other parties. This party was opposed by the *Volksbund für Freiheit und Vaterland* [People's Association for Freedom and Fatherland], a group outside the party system which demanded a *Verständigungsfrieden* [negotiated peace] and the immediate free development of all political institutions. A proclamation published at the end of December was signed by Max Weber in addition to Brentano, G. Bäumer, H. Delbrück, Naumann, Oncken, Troeltsch, and others. The feeling of national community which had united and uplifted all at the outbreak of the war was now completely destroyed. The fellow countrymen who now faced a common danger hated and fought one another.

For example, at a meeting of the *Volksbund* in December, 1917, Weber criticized the methods of agitation of the *Vaterlandspartei*, particularly the politicization of the army, which seemed highly questionable to him. He used a statement made by Blücher at the Congress of Vienna,[2] but his words were changed into their exact opposite in the mind of a listener—a welcome subject for a demonstration on the part of the opponents on the extreme right who therefore made no attempt to assure themselves of the accuracy of the assertion. Weber fought back with the following declaration:

That there should be "citizens" in Heidelberg who delude themselves into thinking that they heard the sentence *Die Feder macht wieder gut, was das Schwert verdorben hat* [The pen restores what the sword has ruined] from *my mouth* surpasses even those expectations that my very low estimate of the intelligence of the so-called *Vaterlandspartei* caused me to have. That a similar alleged statement should then be repeated at

---

[2]Prince Gebhard Leberecht Blücher, 1742–1819, the Prussian field marshal, is reputed to have said after the Battle of Waterloo: *"Mögen die Federn der Diplomaten nicht wieder verderben, was das Volk mit so grossen Anstrengungen errungen"* [May the pens of the diplomats not ruin again what the people have attained with such exertions]. According to another source, K. A. Varnhagen von Ense, Blücher said at a banquet in Paris in July, 1815, responding to a toast: *"Mögen die Federn der Diplomaten nicht wieder verderben, was durch die Schwerter der Heere mit so vieler Anstrengung erworben worden"* [May the pens of the diplomats not ruin again what has been achieved with so much effort by the swords of the armies].—Ed.

a public assembly in the large auditorium of the university and made the object of a telegram to the Reichstag is regrettable, because such nonsense is designed to hold the citizens of Heidelberg up to ridicule. I gladly make use of the obligation to set the record straight and to state publicly what I really said, and did not say for the first time there: The politicizing of the army in general and the involvement of the Supreme Command in factional strife through telegrams and expressions of allegiance by parties in particular must lead us to make this request of our great military leaders: See to it that no one can say some day that you have allowed that which you have achieved with the sword to be ruined by letting yourselves be dragged into the bustle and onto the thin ice of domestic party struggles. For the officer who goes into an area that he does not master stakes his authority with his men and with the nation even where this authority is his rightful due.[3]

Around that time an outside event came miraculously to Germany's aid: the breakdown of revolutionary Russia, which had already been foreshadowed in the spring, was complete. In the middle of December the Bolshevik state requested an armistice and offered a negotiated peace on the basis of a national "right to self-determination," which was to apply particularly to the peoples of the border states. Germany was in principle ready to accept this formula, but she refused to abandon the Baltic provinces to Bolshevism before a general peace was concluded. In other points, too, the negotiating general adopted the posture of a victor, and this made the negotiations break down. The Russians hoped that the revolutionary spark would spread to Germany. The result was a separate peace with the Ukraine but an uncertain relationship with Russia, which ceased all acts of war but did not make peace. The German troops again advanced eastward, and Weber commented: "This thing in Brest-Litovsk does not impress me favorably. The results will show what can be expected from this needlessly gruff tone, but I think Trotsky is smarter than our people." And a few weeks later, when the negotiations were at an impasse:

Without absolute force no Russian can deliver Riga to Germany. Any peace on this basis would be an absolutely phony peace, which will last only for as long as Russia is unable to stir. Since there is no chance for us to occupy substantial parts of the country, Trotsky has no really

---

[3]Letter to the editor of the *Heidelberger Tageblatt*, 12/10/17.

compelling interest in peace, and we should have realized that. *If*, therefore, we wanted to make progress, the formulation demanded by the military should not have been chosen. And the Hoffmann incident[4] was a scandal; it could have cost us the treaty. It was the pessimism regarding our *leadership* that caused Scheidemann[5] and associates to adopt their pessimistic policies—in other words, it was their firm conviction that things would turn out badly despite everything, *so* they simply let them take their course. (February 7, 1918)

The offensive in the west has been decided upon (the calculated losses are fantastic and ghastly!). All their hopes are pinned on the sorties [*Ausfall*]. Justifiably so? I am betting two to one that there will be peace in the *autumn*; but I am *not* giving *higher* odds, for our military is plumb crazy. If something goes wrong with the suffrage bill and there is a general strike, then bad things could happen. Rathenau[6] is betting that there will be three more years of war. That cannot be; there would certainly be a revolution. But everything is uncertain. (January 17, 1918)

The emergence of the *Vaterlandspartei* caused the German radical left to take threatening counteraction. In Berlin and other large cities they organized the first *political* strike in Germany, several days of work stoppage by the munition workers. This strike was intended to bring about world peace and force through the democratization that was still being delayed. On this occasion, too, the Reich government acted like masters and refused to enter into discussions with the leaders of the strike. Yet a great misfortune was averted, because the unions opposed the strike and the leaders of the socialist majority regained control over the workers. Weber wrote about this to Oncken:

The political events in Berlin are enough to make one despair. But anyone who saw that political madhouse two weeks ago could not have

---

[4]General Max Hoffmann, 1869–1927, chief of staff on the eastern front since August 1916, was one of the German representatives at the conference of Brest-Litovsk. Weber is presumably referring to the crisis precipitated by Hoffmann on January 18, 1918, when he presented the Russians with a map detailing the territories they would have to cede if they did not want to risk a resumption of the war with Germany.—Ed.

[5]Philipp Scheidemann, 1865–1939, Social Democratic politician, proclaimed the republic on November 9, 1918, as state secretary in Prince Max's cabinet.—Ed.

[6]Walther Rathenau, 1867–1922, German-Jewish industrialist, philanthropist, author, and politician; assassinated while serving as Foreign Minister in the Weimar Republic.—Ed.

been surprised. The behavior of the war press bureau—feeding the juris-
dictional dispute with the military regarding Brest-Litovsk to the
press—and General Hoffmann's speech ruined everything in Vienna and
consequently in Berlin as well. Not a soul on the left believes in equality of suffrage (nor does Naumann), and it was a foregone conclusion
that then the Social Democrats would no longer be able to restrain
the workers (they had always said so and pointed to the consequences).
Their position is not an easy one, for after the recent events everyone
is moving left toward the Independents. (February 1, 1918)

Despite all this there was reason for fresh hope. Russia, the most dangerous enemy, was incapable of fighting, and at the end of March it had to
accept a dictated peace that brought large parts of the country under German control. Without the steady supply of the well-nourished and excellently equipped American troops in the west an acceptable peace would
probably have been assured. But now all victories seemed to be leading further away from victory. The great spring offensive, for which frightful casual-
ty figures had been "calculated" in advance, was supposed to force the end
of the war. For months on end it did bring wonderful successes. German
troops were deep into France; Paris was shelled by long-range guns, and young
officers already indulged in the hope that they would soon occupy the city.
When at the end of July the secretary of state in the Foreign Office, von
Kühlmann,[7] declared in the Reichstag that the war could not be ended
by force of arms alone and indicated that the government was ready to negotiate, he had to give way to the attacks of the Pan-Germans. But in
mid-July the great counteroffensive started in the west, and from August
on the superior forces of the enemy forced the Germans to retreat on all
fronts. It finally could no longer be concealed that the supply of manpower,
foodstuffs, and especially matériel had been exhausted and Austria had broken down. At the military headquarters it was ascertained that the Central Powers were incapable of breaking the enemy's will to make war by military means.

Now the German oratorical "peace offensive" began. But the advancing
enemy was not prepared to negotiate. The statesmen carried on their dialogues across the ocean, and Germany always heard the same demands: Belgium was to be restored again, all occupied territories were to be surren-

---

[7]Richard von Kühlmann, 1873–1948, diplomat and writer, concluded the treaties of Brest-
Litovsk with Russia and of Bucharest with Rumania.—Ed.

dered, restitution was to be made for all damages, and Alsace-Lorraine and Poland were to be given free access to the sea. These demands were now also incorporated in Wilson's world peace program, his so-called Fourteen Points. He held the balance of Europe's fate, and he was still the hope of the Germans. In Germany the parties favoring a "power peace" and a "negotiated peace" opposed one another more vehemently than ever. But all agreed that Germany could not be truncated in the west and in the east. The government admitted the failure of the offensive: "The situation is serious, but we have no reason to be despondent." The majority parties now pressed for parliamentarization. The Reich Chancellor (von Hertling),[8] who, like his predecessors, was under the political influence of the military, declared his opposition to it and resigned. Constitutional reform now had a clear track. But Germany was in extreme danger. Who was to take the helm now? Many who had read his political essays and had heard him speak thought that Max Weber could be the man. One of his Berlin school friends wrote to Helene Weber on October 2, 1918:

In recent days I have thought a great deal about you, and I feel impelled to write you a few lines. You see, I cannot rid myself of the feeling that the domestic political crisis in which we find ourselves could be resolved only by one man, and that man is your son Max. The more I think about it, the more it seems to me that he may be destined to be our leader in these difficult times. Today a few Social Democratic leaders from Saxony came to see me on business, but since they had just attended a party meeting, we naturally came to speak of politics, and they told me that a chancellor still has not been found. They did not like Max of Baden[9] at all. Then I told them: "Why don't you send for the other Max of Baden, Max Weber; he is the proper person, perhaps the only one we need." This idea made a lot of sense to them, and they were going to bring up his name in tonight's party meeting. I have great hopes once his name comes up for discussion, and I don't doubt that all members of the majority parties would agree on him. I frankly admit that I did not always agree with Max's earlier political activities, that, for instance, I did not really understand his warm support of Bethmann. But his political genius, his profound knowledge, his

[8]Georg Graf von Hertling, 1843–1919, Catholic philosopher and statesman, professor at Bonn and Munich, Bavarian Prime Minister from 1912 on, Prussian Prime Minister and Reich Chancellor from November 1917 to September 1918.—Ed.

[9]Prince Max of Baden, 1867–1929, became Reich Chancellor on October 3, 1918.—Ed.

superb eloquence, the enormous wealth of his intellect predestine him like no one else to take a leading role precisely in times like these when only the best men are good enough for us. . . .

In those days this was the thinking of many who were remote from the party system and did not know its driving forces.

But for the professional politicians a man who stood aloof from active politics and the bustle of party life was out of the question. And the gentle, prudent ways of a noble potentate, Prince Max of Baden, seemed acceptable to the conservatives as well. He became Chancellor and decided in favor of the program of the majority parties, that is, for a negotiated peace and for the parliamentary system and the democratization of Prussia. At last the endangered state seemed to have been guided onto the paths of reason by a new harmony between the people and its government. Representatives of the left entered the cabinet. It was still possible to hope that democracy would be capable of saving Germany. After all, the front was unbroken, and German armies still stood on enemy soil. Then, right at the beginning of the new course, the Supreme Command of the army—Ludendorff[10]—demanded that a peace offer, and above all an armistice offer, be made to Wilson. The Reich Chancellor opposed it, but in vain; the generals insisted on it. The general consternation in Germany was enormous, and abroad this was interpreted as a sign of imminent breakdown. Weber commented on it to Naumann on October 11:

In view of its fearful responsibility the government will have to make sure that it gives an *accounting* to the country immediately after the conclusion of peace and the demobilization and *before* the elections. The groundwork for this important and difficult task must be laid *now*, because *this* is the time to start *ascertaining the facts* which led to the major decisions—*in detail*, with full documentation regarding dates and persons and including statements from all individuals responsible for the situation. It does not matter who takes care of this, but it must be done *without fail*, otherwise the failure to do so will be a cause for great regret.

If I have so far made no public statements whatever, the reason for it is that I, like all of us outsiders, am absolutely uninformed and fear

---

[10]The general and politician Erich Friedrich Wilhelm Ludendorff (1865–1937) became quartermaster general in 1914 and two years later joined Paul von Hindenburg in directing Germany's war strategy.—Ed.

that I would be disavowed by events and steps taken. I confess that everything we hear from Berlin gives us the impression of a *boundless lack of nerve.* The nation might pay terribly dearly for this. I hope this is not the case. Now that misfortune is here, I am keeping absolutely calm. I hope you are, too.

Once again Weber foresaw everything that was going to come. The very next day he pointed out to his politician friends G. von Schulze-Gävernitz, H. Delbrück, and Naumann that only the immediate voluntary abdication of the Kaiser could possibly still save the monarchy and the dynasty. On October 11, 1918, he wrote to Professor von Schulze-Gävernitz:

As a sincere adherent of monarchical though parliamentarily limited in-stitutions, particularly of the German dynasty, it is my firm convic-tion that the present emperor must resign in the interest of the Reich and the dynasty. He can do so with complete dignity if he in-sists that he had to act the way he did in accordance with justice and his conscience, that fate has been against him, and that he did not want to be an impediment to the new future of his people. It would be *unworthy* of him and the imperial office to eat the "bread of charity" in a dismembered Germany—and this is what would happen. If he leaves *now, without* any pressure from the outside, he will go in honor, and the chivalrous sympathy of the nation will be with him. But, above all, the position of the dynasty will be preserved. If he stays, then the inevitable judgment of the serious blunders made by the politicians will turn against him as well. Some suitable person would have to come forward to explain the situation to the monarch if he does not understand it. I openly confess that I have observed his style of government with pronounced distaste. But in the interest of the *imperial office* I cannot desire an emperor to come to a *dishonorable* end, whether he goes later under outside pressure or whether he con-tinues to vegetate on his throne. That we shall get better terms if he leaves is only a secondary consideration, although it is not an unim-portant one. But imagine the horrible humiliations the monarch will face if he remains! The very thought is terrible! And the aftereffect will last for generations! I also wrote this to Naumann and to Hans Delbrück.

When nothing of the sort happened, Weber kept writing urgent letters:

The abdication of the Kaiser is and will remain the central question. If he had only abdicated *immediately*! Now everything is more difficult,

I admit, but it *must* be done. It will not constitute an acknowledgment of *moral* guilt on his part or on ours. But he *must* face up to the fact that he has made *political* blunders of the most serious kind, so that both he and the nation can live in dignity. . . . It would be of fundamental importance for men on the *right* to recognize the absolutely decisive importance of this step for the future of the dynasty— above all, the Center, the National Liberals, and the Free Conservatives, for I do not believe the extreme right to be capable of such vision. . . . Everyone here agrees with me, but no one has the courage to act accordingly.

That step was not taken, and later it was made more difficult by the fact that Wilson, who had been requested to mediate, now *demanded* it: "The United States does not want to negotiate with the military rulers and monarchical autocrats of Germany. From them it would demand *surrender* rather than peace negotiations."

Now the military leaders pressed for an all-out continuation of the war. Many were ready to do so, but their demands did not gain a majority in the Reichstag. Not only the exhaustion of the masses but other problems as well decided against it; particularly the threatening disintegration of the Reich. Thus, for example, Weber received the following impressions in Munich: "If there is a call for 'national defense,' the defection of Bavaria from the Reich will automatically take place. *None* of the authorities here and *not one* of the local parties is of a different opinion, and the king will have no other choice for the sake of preserving his crown" (October 6, 1918). And four weeks later to H. Oncken:

The following information about *Bavaria* is *strictly confidential* for now: Two weeks ago the Center Party deputy H.,[11] who has in the meantime become minister, said to the chairman of the Liberal Party in the *House of Deputies* before several witnesses that the slogan *Treue zum Reich* [Loyalty to the Reich] in the proclamations of the left had better be *avoided*, because one did not know what would become of the Reich and it might be advantageous to abandon it to its fate and go with *Deutsch-Österreich* [German-speaking Austria], financially as well (Reich debts). Unfortunately at least a hundred people are already

---

[11]Heinrich Held, 1868–1938, head of the Bavarian Center Party (1914) and co-founder of the Bavarian People's Party (1918), was to have become a minister in the new government to be formed in November, 1918, in line with the parliamentarization of Bavaria, but this government was never formed. Held served as premier of Bavaria from 1924 to 1933.—Ed.

privy to the incident, because it was announced "in confidence" and
discussed at a meeting of the deputies of the *Fortschrittliche Partei* [Pro-
gressive Party] in Nuremberg—which was highly inopportune. After a
public meeting in which I had ridiculed the idea of secession and had
reminded people of the dissolution of the *Zollverein* [customs union] and
the consequences of that customs separation, I received a telephone
call from an engineer who declared that these arguments were completely irrelevant now. When I said, "Go ahead and try it," he replied
only, "We will." That the court would not be averse to the whole
thing everyone knows. *Only* the left is "loyal to the Reich," but the
Social Democrats attach the proviso that Wilhelm II must *go*, otherwise they will not believe in anything.

For the rest, the general mood even among the best men was without exception *so* radically in favor of peace in *any* case—since any attempt to organize resistance would lead to immediate anarchy—that
it was enough to make a man despair. (November 6, 1918)

* * *

When the military forces were subordinated to the Reichstag, Ludendorff
resigned his command of the army. Hindenburg, however, remained at his
post, and everything he did at that time increased the general reverence
for him. The Kaiser escaped to General Headquarters. The left demanded his
abdication. Wilson held the fate of the world in his hands. In those days
Weber warned him—in a brief letter to the editor of the *Frankfurter
Zeitung*—against making his conditions any harsher:

If we accede to his demand that the German government accept conditions for an armistice that make further military resistance impossible, this would eliminate not only Germany but in very large measure
him as well from the factors determining the peace terms. His own position as arbiter of the world was and is based *only* on the fact that the
importance of the German military power is at least such that without the participation of the American troops it could by no means
be compelled to surrender. If this situation changed, then the absolutely intransigent elements of the other enemy states, which undoubtedly are present, would gain the upper hand and would be in a position to shove the president aside with polite thanks for all his help.
His influence would then be at an end. . . . [12]

---

[12]Cf. *Gesammelte politische Aufsätze,* p. 340.

But the misfortune was already on the way: On the third of November the sailors on the fleet lying in the harbor of Kiel mutinied. On November 4 Weber made a political speech in Munich at the invitation of the *Fortschrittliche Volkspartei.* In that city assemblies of the radical left and processions were already taking place around the clock. His subject was *"Deutschlands politische Neuordnung"* [Germany's Political New Order]. In the opinion of several listeners it was one of his most passionate speeches, "with his passion, aware of itself, trying to subdue itself during his analysis of the situation, but bursting forth again and again." He appealed to instincts of manly self-preservation in the face of the enemy and to the will for the preservation of the Reich: The slogan "Away from Prussia" is criminal folly. It is the peculiar fate of the world that the first real ruler of the world should be a professor [Woodrow Wilson]. How much of a professor he is may be seen from the great folly that he has committed: his terms for an armistice. If he does not keep Germany from entering into peace negotiations unarmed, his own rule will be at an end. Then the French generals will say, "Thank you very much, now we can cope with Germany without you." There are two roads to peace—that of the politician and that of the Sermon on the Mount. A politician must make peace in such a way that all concerned can sincerely live up to it. The other way is called "Peace at any price!" One can have the greatest respect for those who make this demand if they are ready to put the ethic of the Sermon on the Mount into practice in other ways as well. The question of whether the national war of self-defense shall be resumed if the terms are intolerable must be decided by the soldiers at the front. Revolution does not lead to peace. Bolshevism is a military dictatorship like any other and will break down like any other. And the bourgeois society can by no means be changed into a socialistic utopia by a revolution. The consequence of such a revolution would be invasion by the enemy and, later, reactionary rule.

Some of the audience were bourgeois intellectuals and members of the *Freideutsche Jugend,* others were on the radical left: communists, aroused by chiliastic hopes, and anarchists, among them the Russian Bolshevist M. Levien,[13] and Erich Mühsam,[14] who had until then been known as a typical bohemian figure from Schwabing. When Weber came out against peace at any price and against the revolution, Levien heckled him and Weber replied more and more sarcastically. The excitement was great even as Weber spoke, and he sensed an air of hostility. These people could and would

---

[13]See Chapter 20, footnote 3.—Ed.
[14]1878–1934, poet, dramatist, and essayist.—Ed.

no longer understand him. During the discussion they mouthed communist slogans and Weber's arguments fell flat. The middle-class members of the audience kept silent. For the first time, hostile mass instincts were directed against him and he could not control them. These demagogic doings struck him as "ugly" and a pernicious portent.

After his talk Weber met some of the audience at the home of E. Katzenstein, who a few days later led the occupation of the Munich police headquarters. At that point none of those present seemed determined to make a revolution. Weber sat among them "like an old knight" and passionately spoke about the failure of the Kaiser, who did not take the only dignified and proper step to save the monarchy. Weber was plied with questions about what could be done now. To these he again answered, "The soldiers at the front must decide." The young people would not recognize this; they had been out there themselves for a time and were convinced that only freedom from the military gave one the proper perspective.

What members of the *Freideutsche Jugend*, who were still uncertain whether to adopt a revolutionary or a national-patriotic attitude, thought about Weber's remarks and what they desired and expected him to do is expressed in a characteristic way by a letter from a very intelligent young man, G. W. Klein:

> On you, Herr Professor, the political hopes of the best people are pinned, as far as I can tell. And, to put it plainly, my greatest desire would have been to see you in the post of the Reich Chancellor. Among all politically active people I really see no one whom I would trust, as I would trust you, to know for certain what he wants and to desire what is definitely the most manly and the best thing to do. Besides, what seems important to me, and of great urgency today, is not only what is done but *how* it is done. We now simply need an educator who can teach the entire nation to assimilate these things in such a way that it makes something out of them. I am deeply sorry that I did not succeed in getting close enough to you in Heidelberg to discuss these very important matters with you, and therefore I don't know whether you will concede me the right to draw your attention to a few objections that are being raised by young people known to me and also by myself. . . .

> People say primarily that you are not moving with the times. Permit me to tell you that I do not go along with this reproach, least of all with those from whom it originates—ideologues. I have already heard this said in Heidelberg and again at your recent speech. Regarding

this speech, I beg to confess that it contained little that was new to me. But what really inspired me was your attitude and the enormous vitality with which you spoke. It is my belief that it was not possible or permissible for you to make the adaptation that has become necessary even for us very liberal people with the same speed as we young people, who have not yet solidified and can adapt to circumstances far more easily. I therefore had the impression that, without talking about it, you were content to let the things that have changed change and that basically you may have cared most about trying to define clearly and incisively the attitude of a serious, chivalrous, and absolutely decent person in this revaluation of all values, which is threatening to become a devaluation of all values. I used these explanations to meet the reproaches of the others. . . .

We badly need you as a leader—not to settle the question whether one should turn the other cheek or not tolerate any injustice, but to articulate the glaring contradiction inherent in a quantitative or qualitative socialism. It is an urgent task and every minute counts. It is now a question of whether we shall surrender to crowds and numbers or whether we shall make a quick attempt to channel the unleashed energies into paths where they will create valuable work and bring beauty and movement into our lives. . . .

It is psychologically understandable that after a period of such unprecedented misfortune and such extraordinary universal sadness as this war has produced and after the miserable existence that workingmen have had to lead, the only thought should be of happiness, happiness, happiness! If we now get civil war, misery will mount so sky-high that the only feeling left will be this: Let us stop this at last and have some happiness in this miserable existence! You brought this out in your lecture here. In your whole attitude you represented a *high standard* and talked to listeners who wanted nothing but some joy and to whom the thought of even one additional sacrifice for what is to them some hypothetical standard is an abomination. The audience simply did not understand you and probably felt in large measure that you had come from another planet . . . Who still understands today if someone like you exclaims, "Germany, which we love more than ever!" To these people that was a cliché which no longer conveyed any feeling to them. Everybody thinks of himself and his own advantage. . . . (Munich, November 6 and 7, 1918)

No sooner had Weber returned from Munich than the revolution broke out there. Bavaria was declared a free state, and the "people's government"

of the workers' and soldiers' councils constituted itself after the Russian
pattern. The Berlin government still hoped that it could control the
movement. The Kaiser still believed that he could restore order at home
at the head of the army. The Reich Chancellor still hoped that the general revolution could be impeded by the monarch's abdication. But now it was
once again too late. On the day on which the Kaiser abdicated, the "German Republic" was proclaimed in Berlin as well. At the same time the communists proclaimed the "Free Socialist Republic" after the Bolshevist pattern. One day after that the armistice terms, frightful beyond measure,
were accepted. Many repressed their despair by engaging in intoxicating revolutionary activities. They imagined themselves on the threshold of a more
perfect social order; finally the road seemed to be clear to the realm of
peace, reconciliation among peoples, community, and human solidarity. The
others, to be sure, the pillars of the old regime, blamed the revolution for
the dimensions of the national misfortune. They created the stab-in-the-
back legend and vilified the "unfaithful nation" that was incapable of rous-
ing itself for the last desperate struggle.

Wherever Weber encountered this judgment he was indignant, particularly when colleagues made it from the protected height of their academic
rostrum. But he rejected the revolution and the hopes pinned on it with
equal vigor. Under the impression of the Munich events and the sad spectacle of young lads tearing the epaulets from the uniforms of returned officers,
he called it "a bloody carnival that does not deserve the honorable name
of a revolution." And even though he understood that it had to happen
that way, he foresaw at the same time that the revolution at *that* point
would worsen Germany's chances for peace and bring about her financial collapse, without being able to lend permanence to socialistic institutions.
His sympathy for the struggle of the proletariat for an existence worthy
of human beings had been so great for decades that he had often considered
joining their ranks as a member of the Socialist Party, although he had
always decided against it. One could be a "Socialist"—as well as a
"Christian"—in all honesty only if one was prepared to share the way of life
of the propertyless, at least to give up a cultured existence based on *their*
labor. Since Weber's illness that had been impossible for him, and his scholar's existence simply depended on unearned income. Besides, basically he remained an *individualist*. At some other time he would have been greatly interested in an attempt at a revolutionary transformation of the economy,
in its "socialization," but at that particular moment he felt that all ex-

periments of that nature would further weaken the structure of the state
and aggravate the national catastrophe.

A new order that is the product of this terrible defeat and disgrace
will hardly take root. Certainly, one can enjoy the "faith" (in a socialistic future) even if one does not share it. *But I simply do not share it,*
although my own faith in our future as such is quite firm. And I fear
that once it becomes apparent that faith can move mountains but
not remedy ruined finances and lack of capital, the disappointment—
after everything that has already been taken from people—for many of
the most faithful will become unbearable and make them inwardly bankrupt. I shall not be affected, provided that I remain healthy and am
able to work, for I can live without faith—in *this* sense. (November,
1918)

* * *

In those weeks Weber was ready to do anything for the nation and to
assume the leadership of youth, but there was no one to follow him. It was
not really surprising that his national ethic fell flat with the young pacifists and communists, who were hoping for a turning point in world history in accordance with their beliefs. But that there was no reaction from
the young people with traditional attitudes had to be taken as a crushing
symptom of a complete moral exhaustion caused by the war. A friend made
the following notes on what happened at a meeting of students in Heidelberg:

Weber gave an unvarnished and unsparing presentation of the political
hopelessness of the situation for the present generation, but in his national faith this very hopelessness led him to certain conclusions,
which were uncomprehended at the time. "You know," he said, "what
it means to stand up to an invading enemy who can no longer be offered military resistance. You know the methods of the Russian revolution of 1905. Then the watchword was: Have every faith in the future,
abandon all personal hopes. The lot of the living is only incarceration
and a drumhead court-martial. When you have reached the point where
you have decided not to make any grand speeches but silently to see
to it that the first Polish official who dares to enter Danzig is hit
by a bullet—when you have decided to take the course that will then
be inevitable, then I am at your disposal, then *come to me!*"

These last words, which he spoke with a sweeping motion of his arm, as though he wanted to pull his comrades toward himself, were followed by an icy, uncomprehending silence. This silence could have had another meaning, but what followed showed that it did not. Weber continued by outlining the present possibilities, spoke about the honor of the students and about the hope that Germany, which, as Treitschke once put it, had been the only one among the European nations that had had a second youth, would now be granted a third. Then he closed by saying: "But anyone who belongs to a uniformed corporation while Germany lies prostrate is a *Hundsfott* [son of a bitch]!" The silence continued, but in this case the lack of comprehension soon turned into indignation. Students wearing the colors of the corporations ostentatiously walked up and down in front of Weber's house. Some time after that he courteously returned his ribbon to his own corporation. He never again spoke of the will of that moment to resist the enemy in the knowledge of certain doom.

II

Weber did not surrender to bitterness and despair but tried to be of help again. Wherever he encountered honest goodwill, he was pleased. This was true particularly of the prudent sense of responsibility and the unassuming efficiency of the Majority Socialists who tried to stand their ground against the unwanted revolution in the face of the Bolshevists. At their request he joined the Heidelberg council of workers and soldiers for a time, believing that his knowledge might be useful to it. He got along well with the labor leaders. It seemed that real unreason could not prevail in that blessed Baden region. Thus his faith in the Germans and in Germany was always given fresh sustenance. None of his illusions were destroyed, for he had had none. For that reason he was a strong support for his environment, which had often regarded him as a political pessimist and had "repressed" his insights.

"About the difficult times we are going through I shall tell you another time. The years of quiet worry were even more difficult! Chin up! After the peace there will be things to do. Happy the man who can participate with full vigor. I can do so with half strength at best." And a few weeks later:

The collapse of Ludendorff, the demoralization of the army: consequences of the constant whipping up of "morale" by promises that could not possibly be kept. The shortsightedness and lack of vision for what was possible, the lack of dignity on the part of the Kaiser, and the thoughtlessness of the dilettante government—all that was painful. What was done to our honor will weigh upon us for a long time, and only the headiness of the "revolution" is now a kind of narcotic against it for the people before the great distress comes. All the phrasemongering is horrible, too, and the vague hopes and quite dilettantish playing with a "happier future," something that is as remote as ever, are depressing.

What *pleases* me is the simple realism of the plain people in the unions and of many soldiers, for instance in the local "Council of Workers and Soldiers" to which I am attached. I must say that they have done things splendidly and without any idle talk. The nation as such simply is disciplined; of course, it is plain to see that once this discipline is shaken, so is everything, even what is deep inside these people. What is decisive now is whether the crazy Liebknecht gang[15] will be kept down. They are going to make their putsch; that cannot be changed. But what matters is that it be put down quickly and that it be followed by levelheaded policies rather than wildly reactionary ones. This is what we must hope for; we cannot know for sure. If it goes badly, then we shall have to let the Americans put things in order, whether we want to or not. I hope we shall be spared the disgrace of having to let the enemy take charge. All this almost makes one forget the loss of Metz and Strasbourg! Who would have thought this possible? . . . (November 18, 1918)

* * *

At the end of November, Weber went to Frankfurt for a few weeks in answer to a request by the editors of the *Frankfurter Zeitung* that he act as their political adviser. There he wrote his essays about *Die neue Staatsform* [The New Form of Government] in preparation for the new constitution. On December 12 he witnessed the arrival of the unbeaten army, something that profoundly moved him. All houses were decked with garlands and people crowded the windows and roofs. Ringing cheers greeted the men who had done and endured such superhuman things. How trim they still looked! Every steel helmet was decorated with a little wreath and every gun barrel

[15]Karl Liebknecht, 1871–1919, politician and revolutionary, Social Democratic member of the Reichstag from 1912 to 1916, later one of the leaders of the radical Spartacists (*Spartakusbund*). —Ed.

sported a bouquet of flowers. From the opera house, where the army's leader and his staff stopped, there waved a red flag. Opposite it stood the old emperor in bronze, high on a horse, the symbol of the united Reich. An ordinary man in field-gray uniform, a member of the soldiers' council, offered the first greeting to the general. At that moment everything that had happened on the front and at home coalesced. The high officers kept their mouths shut tight and stared fixedly into space. Gray-haired men wept.

The domestic situation worsened daily. Communist fanatics—Liebknecht and Rosa Luxemburg[16]—tried to wrest the leadership of the bloodless revolution away from the socialists and to force through, in place of a democratic republic, a socialistic one, that is, a proletarian dictatorship with a Soviet system. The Munich leader K. Eisner,[17] prime minister of Bavaria, published documents that supplied the enemy with material for his "war-guilt lie." The pacifists hoped that such "confessions" would lead to more lenient peace terms. At the beginning of December the first bloody uprisings took place in Berlin and Munich. Invasion by the enemy threatened.

In those days Weber wrote from Frankfurt:

Everyone here believes that civil war in Berlin is inevitable and that Germany will then go to pieces; it is enough to make one despair. To be sure, Wilson will probably state emphatically once more that he will not supply socialists with bread or give them a peace. That was announced today. But that will not cut any ice with Liebknecht's gangs. They are going to plunder, and what happens afterward doesn't matter, for they are going to clear out [verduften] in a hurry. It is not certain whether Frankfurt will be an unoccupied area after all; some of the cowardly local rabble [Bürgerpack] even want it to be! Out of fear of the reds [Sozen]! The devil take them. (November 22, 1918)

Haussmann writes he has proposed me as ambassador to Vienna. Nothing will come of it, that much is certain. For these people, too, only want to be deceived, in a pacifistic sense. Yet the presumptuousness of our opponents is boundless and the very worst is to be feared. To them Erzberger is not spineless [schlapp] enough! Oh for this untalented peace commission! (November 25, 1918)

---

[16]Rosa Luxemburg, 1871–1919, Polish-born revolutionary, co-leader of the Spartacus League.— Ed.

[17]Kurt Eisner, 1867–1919, Berlin-born journalist, theater critic, and pacifist, proclaimer of the Free State of Bavaria.—Ed.

For the time being there is a mess [Kuddelmuddel], and the whole thing is rapidly moving toward a catastrophe. The people in Munich are quite mad and without dignity. But there is nothing to be done, and in my opinion an invasion by the Entente is rather certain. Well, everything comes to an end, and we shall rise again some day. If only the dregs were disposed of at last! This government will never need me and I shall never serve it. Herr Haase[18] and company, in contrast to the trade unionists and Ebert,[19] need only flatterers, flunkies, and people without character, just as the princes do. The talkers and the screamers are on top, and so is hate. (November 29, 1918)

Everything in reality is so *terrible* and disgraceful that one is grateful for having work to do; otherwise one would almost have to go out of one's mind. How much longer is this carnival going to last? Our economy is rapidly going downhill. Everything is becoming insanely disorganized, all reserves are being used up, and I believe the end will be putsch and occupation. But the most horrible thing we are experiencing is the lack of *backbone*, the lack of dignity. And those conversations of lieutenants that one overhears at the next table! An incredible insipidity and matter-of-fact[20] attitude.

Weber saw everything clearsightedly, yet he sensed in the people, of which he was part, indestructible energies and qualities. He *believed* in the nation as he did in himself, in the sense that no external fate and no burden, no matter how heavy, could destroy its intellectual substance. Thus he was able to write in those terrible days to Friedrich [Otto] Crusius, who had asked him for an evaluation of the situation, present and future:

If I have kept silent for a long time, this was because I am rather certain that we have still not drained this terrible cup of degradation to the dregs. Ludendorff's insane gambles, then as now a reaction this "revolution," have dissolved all orderly authorities, especially in Berlin. The government does not have *really* loyal, organized troops to send against Liebknecht's gangs; hence its unavoidable weakness. If this ochlocracy persists, as must be expected, or, rather, if it gains a (temporary) victory through a putsch (which will surely come), then the enemy will

---

[18]Hugo Haase, 1863–1919 (assassinated), politician, leader of the Independent Social Democrats in the Reichstag.—Ed.

[19]Friedrich Ebert, 1871–1925, Social Democratic member of the Reichstag from 1912, became the first president of the German Republic in 1919.—Ed.

[20]In English in the original.—Ed.

come to the "rescue" and occupy the country, whether he is called in or not. As long as we are facing this prospect, it is hard to make any public statement.

In the meantime I am trying to discuss more *formal* questions in the *Frankfurter Zeitung*. As long as such massive technical and economic problems are on one's mind, which is the case now and will continue to be—it is a question of the bare existence of the masses—one cannot really concern oneself inwardly with cultural problems. Foremost among these, too, is the restoration of that very prosaic moral "decency" which, on the whole, we had and which we *lost* in the war—our most grievous loss. Massive problems of education, then. The method: only the American club system, *no matter* for what purpose. The makings of it may be found among the *Freideutsche Jugend*. I know no other methods, since authoritarianism, against which I am not at all prejudiced, is now failing completely—with the exception of the *church*. Rejection of intellectual narcotics of all kinds, from mysticism to "expressionism": *Sachlichkeit* [matter-of-factness] as the only means of genuineness and the development of a *sense of shame*—in the face of the loathsome exhibitionism of those inwardly broken down—which is the only thing that can give one *Haltung* [backbone].

At present our "face" is destroyed as no other nation's has ever been in a similar situation, neither that of Athens after Aigospotamoi and Chaironaia[21] nor that of France in 1871. But the cheap judgments which—naturally—are being based on this by the adherents of the broken-down game of chance are vile, unfair, and unkind. More than four years of starvation and especially more than four years of propaganda shots of camphor and morphine—no other nation has ever had to endure such things. We are once more starting *from scratch*, as in 1648 and 1807;[22] this is the plain state of affairs. The only thing is that today the pace of life is faster and people work more quickly and with more initiative. We shall not live to see the beginning of the reconstruction, but the next generation will.

Of course, the self-discipline of truthfulness bids us say that Germany's role in *world* politics is over; Anglo-Saxon world rule—*ah c'est*

---

[21]Aigospotamoi: Small tributary of the Dardanelles, site of a victory of the Spartan fleet under Lysander over Athens in the Peloponnesian War (405 B.C.). Chaironeia or Chaeronea: Town in Boeotia, site of a victory of Philip II of Macedon over the Greeks in 338 B.C.—Ed.
[22]The end of the Thirty Years' War and the conquest of Prussia by Napoleon, respectively.—Ed.

nous qui l'avons faite [oh, we're the ones who did it], as Thiers[23] said to Bismarck about our unity—*is* a fact. It is most disagreeable, but we have averted far worse things—the *Russian* knout! No one can take that glory away from us. America's world rule was as inevitable as that of Rome after the Punic Wars in ancient times. I hope it will *continue* not to be shared with Russia. To me *that* is the goal of our future global policy, for the Russian danger has been averted only for now, not forever. At the moment, of course, the hysterical, loathsome hatred of the French is the main danger. Like [Till] Eulenspiegel on the uphill road, I am an *absolute* optimist (but only at long range) as far as our own nation is concerned. We have now seen all its weaknesses, but if one wishes one can also see its fabulous efficiency, simplicity, objectivity, its *capacity*—not the attainment!—for the "beauty of everyday life," in contrast to the intoxication or the playacting of the others. The next ten years will still be horrible. As for the political-social masochism of those shameless pacifists who are now voluptuously wallowing in "guilt" feelings, as though *success* in war were inner proof of anything, like a divine judgment, and as if the God of battles were not "with the bigger batallions"[24] (*we* have shown: not *always!*)—our enemies will see to it that this sort of thing disappears. We have to let the raging class struggle run its course, and during the terrible inner exhaustion that is going to come we must only take care that it does not turn itself into a theory but that it honestly owns up to its nature. *Honesty* in general is now the primary consideration.

One hundred and ten years ago we showed the world that we—*only* we—were capable of being one of the very great civilized nations under foreign rule. *That* we shall now do once more! Then history, which has already given us—*only* us—a second youth, will give us a third. I have no doubt of it and neither have you—*quand même* [despite everything]! What one now says in public is, of course, always *"rebus sic stantibus"* [in the present state of things], not *"pour jamais"* [forever]. *Toujours y penser* [Always keep that in mind]. Cordial greetings and a handshake.

Your old Max Weber (November 24, 1918)

---

[23]Adolphe Thiers, 1797–1877, French statesman and historian, author of a history of the French Revolution.—Ed.

[24]Cf. Marshal de la Ferté-Sennetere's remark to Anne of Austria (ca. 1652): "I have always noticed that God is on the side of the big battalions." (Quoted by Madame de Sévigné, Voltaire, Frederick the Great, Napoleon, and others).—Ed.

At the end of December, when the Spartacus rebellions were assuming ever more menacing forms, he wrote to Crusius once more:

> I fear we shall get civil war and an invasion in any case. As hard and as terrible as it is, we shall have to go through that, too. For *I believe in the indestructibility of this Germany, and never before have I regarded my being a German as such a gift from heaven as I do in these darkest days of Germany's disgrace.* Have some patience, difficult though it is. (December 26, 1918)

III

By means of his essays about the *new form of government*, which were published in the *Frankfurter Zeitung* in November, Weber joined the ranks of those who were working on Germany's political reconstruction. Here are some of his basic ideas: Bismarck's work is gone. What now? A parliamentary monarchy or a republic? Even now the former would be preferable, for it is "the technically most adaptable and in that sense the strongest form of government." It would not necessarily prevent a radical social democratization. But recent events have made it impossible to advocate it. "Therefore, support of the republic has been dictated to us." Of course, not only the present political situation but also arguments of lasting significance speak for it: the instilling into the middle class of a new political sense of duty and self-assurance. What has prevailed for decades is the spirit of security under the protection of the authorities, and thus fear of any innovation—in short, the cowardly will to domestic political impotence. The republic is putting an end to this. Like the working class, the middle class is now thrown on its own resources. For the first time it has to realize that "the umbrella of the divine right of kings that had been spread over its divine-right pocketbooks [Gottesgnaden-Portemonnaies] is closed."

Weber discusses the various constitutions that are possible within the framework of a republic. Bound by no preconceived constitutional theory, he proceeds solely from historical actualities and the demands of the day. The German Reich is a federal state consisting of many parts. Therefore the question is, above all, whether it should have a unitary or a federalistic structure. A socialistic organization of the economy would promote a unitary state. But in this impoverished country, which needs foreign credits for its reconstruction, such an organization is impossible. On republican soil, too, there must be room for federalism. The *unitary* solution would really be desirable to Weber, but he regards it as unattainable for the time being.

What, then, shall be the nature of the federative state which is indicated by what exists? The old hegemonic Greater Prussian structure is eliminated, particularly the connection between the highest leader of the Reich and the top man in Prussia. But then the question arises whether the organ to be created in addition to the parliament shall consist of delegates from the individual states, in the manner of the old *Bundesrat* [upper house] or whether it is to become a *Staatenhaus* [house of the states], that is, a house of representatives chosen by the parliaments of the individual states. In principle Weber preferred the *Staatenhaus* as the more democratic institution, but he nevertheless recommended the delegate organ, because it alone would assure the individual states a measure of participation in the central government, which would tone down their particularistic striving for power.

A matter of great importance, especially for the way in which leaders were to be selected, was the question of whether the country should strive for a purely parliamentary structure of the republic or a structure that was based on plebiscites. As long as the German state had been led by a monarch, Weber had advocated the selection of leaders by the parliament. Now that the monarch was being eliminated, he demanded that the top man, the president of the Reich, be *popularly elected* and thus given an independent authority vis-à-vis the parliament. He was to be the head of the executive branch of the government, and in case of a conflict between the parliament and the government he was to be able to appeal directly to the people. Popular election of the president also meant limiting the influence of the parties in the selection of the ministers as well as a limitation of political patronage in general. This would please opponents of the parliamentary system, for democracy and this system are not identical.

At the same time that Weber's constitutional essays appeared, the new Minister [*Staatssekretär*] of the Interior, Dr. H. Preuss,[25] undertook to draft a constitution for the Reich. He invited a small group of experts, among them Weber, for a confidential conference. This was the kind of task Weber had wished for.

Yesterday, then, the meeting. Preuss is doing his job very well; he is

---

[25]Hugo Preuss, 1860–1925, German-Jewish politician and teacher of constitutional law, author of the Weimar Constitution.—Ed.

a *very* smart man. Everything is to be ready tomorrow; a "constitution" has probably never before been made so fast. What makes the situation so spooky is that everything may wind up as scrap paper; it is even *likely* to do so, for the wheels of history will pass over things and all of us—unless a dictatorship by Ebert is coming, which is possible.

All right, the Reich constitution is ready in principle, and it is *very* similar to my proposals. But it was hot work all day with *very* smart people; it was a pleasure, Monday to Thursday evening. Today I slept my fill for the first time. (December 13, 1918)

On many points Weber agreed with the leader of the conference. However, he could not go along with his basic idea, the dissolution of Prussia into individual free states for the relief of the unitary state. For he was convinced from the outset that this plan was not feasible—not only because of tradition-bound opposition but also for technical reasons of administration and economics. He, too, would have preferred a unitary state, but he foresaw that for the time being historical realities demanded the preservation of the *federalistic* system. Thus it was a question of building as much unitarianism as possible into a basically federalistic constitution, and not the other way around, which is what Preuss desired.

The latter's point of view prevailed in the draft, but in the working committees it was already substantially modified and received no majority in the National Assembly. The federative character of the Reich was preserved, although the *Länder* [states] were subordinated to the Reich in important regards. In one respect Weber's work left demonstrable traces in the constitution. His wholly original contribution to the Preuss draft was the introduction of a constitutional *right of inquiry* which also applied to the minorities. As we have seen, he had already demanded this in his prerevolutionary political treatises and had formulated concrete proposals for legislation. The constitutional assembly accepted his proposal. This new control organ within the parliament was not only able to prevent parliamentary corruption but also made it possible for the minorities, which otherwise would have been forced into mere opposition, to take positive action. Through both of these functions it became an instrument of balance between the conflicting parliamentary forces, thus a regulative principle of the parliamentary system in general, "an intellectualization of the parliamentary form . . . its liberation from the absolutism of the majorities."[26] This innovation (Section 51 of the Reich Constitution) was also taken over by the states and subsequently was incorporated into the constitutions of Danzig and Latvia.

The other corrective of parliamentary rule demanded by Weber, the *popular election of the Reich president* and his authoritarian position, was formulated in the draft and incorporated into the constitution. When despite this the National Assembly made the first election, Weber once more published an urgent plea in a Berlin newspaper that the second election be made by the people: "Just as those monarchs acted not only most nobly but also most prudently who limited their power early in favor of parliamentary institutions, the parliament should voluntarily recognize the Magna Charta of democracy, the right to a direct election of leaders."

* * *

Would Weber now find employment as a *practical* politician as well? A great many people expected it, and for a time it seemed as though it would happen. In the middle of November the *Deutsche Demokratische Partei* [German Democratic Party] was founded, mainly at the suggestion of Alfred Weber. The powerful wave of events united large parts of the old "National Liberal" bourgeoisie with the "Progressives" into this timely new formation. It strove to be a connecting link, made up of all strata of society, between the social democratic and the bourgeois parties, just as Naumann's National Social Party had once been. Many intellectual leaders joined it who supported genuine democracy just as resolutely as the socialist workers did, but in contrast to the workers they rejected experimentation with the economic system and placed the *national* idea above international considerations.

Weber did not sign the founding proclamation. After all, a short time previously he had still advocated the preservation of the parliamentary monarchy, and he was unable to change into a republican overnight. Now the times called for a decision in favor of the republican principle. At first he could muster no more enthusiasm for it than he had for the revolution. But he saw no other way to save Germany, and therefore he resolutely sided with the new party. At the end of November, the beginning of December,

---

[26]W. Lewald, *"Enqueterecht und Aufsichtsrecht,"* in *Archiv des Öffentlichen Rechts* No. 3, pp. 315ff.

and in January he gave major political speeches in its behalf at Wiesbaden, Hanau, Heidelberg, Frankfurt, Karlsruhe, and Fürth. He now attacked the left more sharply than before, for the irresoluteness of the Majority Socialists in the face of the communists, the resulting danger of a Spartacist dictatorship, the bloody uprisings in Berlin and Munich, and especially the terrible mismanagement of the Berlin councils of workers and soldiers appeared to him to be a grave national misfortune. And then, "this stupid hatred of the domestic entrepreneurs, the only result of which will be that *foreign* capital will control the German economy that is to be rebuilt."

These speeches, whose wealth of material was carefully structured and at the same time full of passion, always made a great impression, although Weber refrained from demagogic rhetoric and always did justice to his political opponents. Thus he was able to appreciate both Ludendorff's military brilliance and Liebknecht's and Rosa Luxemburg's idealism:

The dictatorship of the mob has come to the kind of end that I did not desire. Liebknecht undoubtedly was an honest man. He called upon the mob to fight, and the mob killed him. The councils of workers and soldiers were honest as well. The bourgeoisie must not forget what it owes to their honest, upright labors. But their headquarters in Berlin was politically beneath contempt and an amateurish operation of the worst kind. It ruined the discipline of the army.

Sweeping socialization is impossible at the present time. Our situation does not permit the elimination of the private entrepreneur. Credit is granted only to brains. Never will a government be given credit behind which there are no independent bourgeois and no independent entrepreneurs with equal rights.

If the economic ruin continues like this, we shall in effect have foreign rule, and then our businessmen will be mere employees of the Americans in their own factories. If the peace turns out the way we must fear that it will—and the untimely outbreak of the revolution will have been partly responsible for this—then an unprecedented chauvinism will arise in Germany for a few years. And if foreign rule comes, we shall experience an enormous awakening of national feeling.

Weber was still a charismatic figure, and the vigor of his youth seemed to have returned. The organizers of the evening in Fürth, where at the end the communists threateningly moved toward him with chair legs in their hands but were kept in check by his composure, wrote him a letter in which they said, among other things: "Never before has a man of scholarship, who has recognized that now scholarship, too, must serve politics and thereby the German cause, revealed our situation so openly, clearly, and fearlessly and carried the torch of knowledge as the leader of the people as you have. . ."

On the evening after the speech in Fürth, Weber also mounted the podium in Heidelberg. He was very pale but in full control of his intellectual powers. At the end an old man bowed down by Germany's disgrace and disunity rose in the audience and thanked him for restoring his faith in the fatherland.

* * *

On December 1 Weber gave a speech for the Democratic Party in Frankfurt am Main. When he had finished, the party members in attendance spontaneously demanded that his name head the slate of the Hesse-Nassau election district. The closed membership meeting of the Frankfurt chapter of the party, which took place on December 19, went against the proposal of its executive committee and again placed him at the head, with only two dissenting votes. After all, the party's slogan was "All available strong and leading personalities belong in the National Assembly."

Under these circumstances Weber was ready to be a candidate. He would not have taken the initiative in entering practical politics, for he was not certain whether his nerves would be equal to its demands and whether he would be able to act coolly when passions arose in him. He also knew that he would find it hard to integrate himself into groups that were less knowledgeable then he. Under no circumstances was he parpared to "work his way up" to a seat by making the usual efforts within the political associations; that would have been unseemly. But if he was now *chosen* to be a political leader without further ado, he would recognize this as the "call" ["*Berufung*"] for which he was, deep down, waiting.

The Frankfurt party members were proud of their unusual action, and the newspaper praised it as an exemplary way of choosing leaders. This established Weber's Frankfurt candidacy in public, so that no other election district nominated him. Everything seemed to be a matter of course. Weber did not concern himself further with the matter; activity for its own sake was contrary to his nature. Then, after Christmas, a few days before the final slates were due, it became known in Heidelberg purely by accident that the Wetzlar conference for the nineteenth election district had corrected the will of the voters behind closed doors. A Frankfurt local bigwig now headed the ticket, and Weber's name had been moved far down. There was great indignation, particularly among the Heidelberg party members, for if Weber had not been tied up by Frankfurt the whole time, they could perhaps have put him on the slate for Baden.

On January 2, 1919, Weber spoke in Heidelberg about Germany's reconstruction. When he mounted the platform, he was greeted by a roar of applause, but he stopped it with a vigorous gesture. He once more pointed out all the errors of the Wilhelminian epoch down to recent days, and his thought was clearly expressed in gripping images that were comprehensible to all. He also managed to raise people's national pride; "The war was unavoidable; it had to be fought to the end because honor demanded it. And some day history will extol Germany because it freed the world from Czarism." At the end the audience tempestuously demanded that the party leadership of Baden be urged to place him at the head of the Baden ticket at the last moment. A delegation went to Karlsruhe, but it was too late. The slate was complete and none of the candidates was ready to resign in favor of Weber. Now the Heidelbergers requested his consent to an action over the heads of the party executive. But Weber refused, saying that such a breach of discipline was impossible.

Weber took the whole affair very calmly; he knew the party machinery and the eagerness for seats, and he conceded to the professional politicians the right to occupy them. Only when a well-meaning fellow party member, who was a candidate in a safe district, told him that he was going to try to put him on the Reich slate at the last moment did Weber's blood boil. His sense of honor was outraged, and he angrily objected to being forced into the role of a seat-hunter backed by others. The fellow party member thought he had done his duty and was aghast at receiving this moral slap in the face for it. On January 5, 1919, Weber declared in the *Frankfurter Zeitung*:

> In the interest of discipline, the continued public discussion of my noninclusion on the slate of candidates for the province of Hesse-Nassau is disagreeable to me. Since I am not a professional politician, this is not a matter of importance to me, and I hope that in the National Assembly there will be sufficient persons who are able to work toward a usable constitution just as well as anyone else. Regarding your intimation that some other election district could have nominated me, I shall say that I accepted the Frankfurt nomination *only* because

it was made in a strictly *democratic* way, and of course I disdained *to make any concessions* to the party notables—whose power, incidentally, turns out to be only increased by the supposedly so democratic election by proportional representation, something that leads to *bargaining*.

This decided Weber's renunciation of political leadership and practical political effectiveness on a large scale. For the second time his talent as a statesman was excluded from the active sphere, this time not by causes inherent in himself but by the servility of the political organizations and the ambition of mediocre men. At a time when everyone clamored for leaders, the nation had no use for him.

IV

Weber now had all sorts of different offers to choose from. He had already rejected an inquiry from the University of Göttingen the previous summer. He was being urged to accept a chair at the *Handelshochschule* [Business College] in Berlin; that would also have meant an opportunity for indirect political activity. His friends in Frankfurt sought to interest him in the directorship of the *Institut für Gemeinwohl* [Institute for Public Welfare] in connection with a lectureship at the university and a position on the editorial staff of the newspaper. At the same time the universities of Munich and Bonn negotiated with him about the acceptance of a chair. Despite all the intense emotional excitement, Weber felt that his nerves were more stable than they had been in Vienna half a year before, and now that a new world had to be built from the ruins of the old, he was not content to work only with his pen. He needed some form of direct influence upon people and a new source from which he could draw strength.

An offer from Becker,[27] the Prussian secretary for higher education and former Heidelberg colleague, was particularly generous. He offered Weber a high-salaried position in Bonn, a professorship in the political and social sciences fashioned especially for him and calling for only two hours of teaching per week. This position would, in any case, have been in keeping with his energy and compatible with the advancement of his work. However, for quite some time there had been negotiations with two friends who were professors in Munich, L. Brentano and

---

[27]The orientalist Carl Heinrich Becker (1876–1933), author of *Gedanken zur Hochschulreform* (1919), served as Prussian Minister of Culture in 1921 and from 1925 to 1930.—Ed.

W. Lotz. Brentano's famous chair was to be filled. The wonderful, familiar city and the close friends there beckoned. But Weber did not want to commit himself again to teaching political economy and finance, two subjects he had outgrown. It was a difficult decision. When the university administration and the government agreed to his lecturing primarily on sociology, this tipped the scale in favor of Munich. In the summer semester Weber planned to give only a one-hour lecture course as well as seminars; his normal teaching activity was not to begin until winter, for until the peace was concluded, politics did not quite relinguish its hold upon him.

In January he published an essay on the war-guilt question[28] and included in the discussion proposals for a future League of Nations statute governing the conduct of war. In it he rejects the "confessing" of German pacifists as downright undignified behavior of people who cannot bear the face of reality and thus fashion for themselves a world order in which defeat necessarily is a consequence of guilt. However, the way the war ended was not a divine judgment. As countless corpse-strewn battlefields of history show, success simply proves nothing about right or wrong. To be sure, mistakes were made, and the most disastrous was the naval policy carried on by Tirpitz. England could not but feel threatened by the extent of German shipbuilding. But the decisive responsibility is borne by Russian imperialism, Czarism as a system, which desired war for its own sake and under any circumstances and was bound to do so in accordance with its political aims.

Around that time Prince Max of Baden, who had returned to private life, established contact with Weber. The two men took a great liking to each other. Their collaboration in responsible positions could no doubt have been extremely effective at another time. What they were now able to do as private persons came to nothing. The all-important thing was to wring a bearable peace from the Entente. Prince Max and his staff had connections with British and American politicians: Colonel House, Trevyglian [sic], Morel,[29] and others. With their aid an attempt was to be made to eradicate the guilt dogma and to interest England in objective negotiations.

---

[28]*Politische Schriften*, pp. 381ff.

[29]Edward Mandell House, 1858–1938, American statesman, Woodrow Wilson's closest adviser from 1911 to 1919. Edmund D. Morel and Charles Philips Trevelyan (1870–1958) were pacifist members of the British Labour Party. Morel served as secretary of the Union of Democratic Control which worked for the termination of the war. Trevelyan, later Sir Charles Philips Trevelyan of Wallington, was a founding member of the UDC.—Ed.

But it was known, and confirmation came from across the seas, that nothing could be done unless the German people pulled themselves together and
a stable and undivided government tightened the reins. Above all, the restoration of a *Wehrmacht* [army] was required.

> Today another Englishman came to see me. I told him in essence: We
> can either talk as *gentlemen* or as *"Old Maids."* In the latter even-
> tuality, the talk would have to be about "guilt" and the like, and
> that would be undignified for both parties. Or else I would say, *"We
> lost the match, your sake is [sic], what is to be done to face the responsibility
> in history?"*[30] and in the face of this treatment, the only one
> worthy of England and Germany, I must confess that I don't under-
> stand the British statesmen. Without a fundamental change of heart
> on *their* part everything is hopeless, for we could forgive them for violat-
> ing our interests but not for violating our *honor*. I would not sit down
> at the negotiating table with *"Pfaffen."*[31] I also told him: As long
> as the German government is not in *sole* possession of all *stockpiles of
> arms,* I do not regard it as capable of negotiating. I would understand
> the *rationale* for it if *this* condition were imposed by the allies, but
> other conditions currently under discussion (limitation of the *Wehr-
> macht,* etc.) are an insulting interference in our internal affairs and—
> because they are utterly pointless and dictated by no *rational*
> interest—highly imprudent. (To Oncken, February 19, 1919)

At the initiative of Prince Max, the *Heidelberger Vereinigung für eine Politik
des Rechts* [Heidelberg Association for a Policy Based on Justice] was founded
in Weber's house at the beginning of February. The first conference was attended, among others, by Professors L. Brentano, Alfred Weber, A.
Mendelssohn-Bartholdy, and R. Thoma, also by General (ret.) Count
Max Montgelas, Captain Colin Ross,[32] and General von Holzing—almost

---

[30]Italicized words here and above are in English in the original.—Ed.

[31]A derogatory term for narrow, hidebound clergymen or dogmatic, intolerant people
generally.—Ed.

[32]Albert Mendelssohn-Bartholdy, 1874–1936, a grandson of the composer, professor of international law at Würzburg, Hamburg, and Oxford; Richard Thoma, 1874–1957, professor of constitutional law at Hamburg, Tübingen, Heidelberg, and Bonn; Maximilian von Montgelas, 1860–1938,
army general until 1915, co-editor of a collection of German war documents and author of historical
works; Colin Ross, 1885–1945, military agitator, world traveler, and high-class international spy
between the two world wars, author of books on South America, the United States, etc. Committed
suicide upon the downfall of the Third Reich, which he had served as a geopolitician.—Ed.

exclusively patriots who had throughout the war opposed the policy of annexation and worked for a negotiated peace. Count Montgelas had been dismissed from the service as an opponent of the invasion of Belgium. The men
resolved to offer continuous systematic opposition to the dogma of guilt
abroad as well as to combat the enemy's *Greuel-Kampagne* [campaign of atroc-
ity stories], and they discussed the various possibilities for reconstituting
an army. For the time being Colin Ross regarded only the formation of a
recruited army of mercenaries as possible, and von Holzing hoped for the speedy
introduction of a militia system after the Swiss pattern.

In public the association demanded the appointment of an international
neutral commission for the investigation of the war causes, and at the
same time it appealed to the people to help the government lay the foundation for a new *Wehrmacht*. The British reply to an offer to that effect
by the German government was negative: *"because it is long since established,
that the German government is responsible for the outbreak of the war."* [33] Now
Weber, at the suggestion of Prince Max, called upon the Foreign Office to open
the German archives and to arrange for the personal testimony of those involved
before some body whose composition would offer to any unprejudiced observer,
and particularly to future generations, every guarantee that the truth would be
brought to light.

The Foreign Office, which had desired such a public request, thereupon
charged first K. Kautsky, then Count Montgelas and Professor W. Schücking[34]
with the publication of all official documents. When a parliamentary commission of inquiry was constituted later for the personal interrogation of the
statesmen and military leaders accused by the Entente, Weber branded it as
a great blunder that one-third of that commission—before which men like
Hindenburg, Ludendorff, Bethmann-Hollweg, and others had to give an accounting of themselves—consisted of politicians of Jewish origin.

Weber despised anti-Semitism, but he regretted the fact that in those
days there were so many Jews among the revolutionary leaders. If he was
asked whether he too was now becoming an anti-Semite, he indignantly denied such a possibility. He said that on the basis of the historical situation
of the Jews it was understandable that they in particular produced these
revolutionary natures. But given the prevailing ways of thinking, it was
politically imprudent for Jews to be admitted to leadership and for them

---

[33] In English in the original.—Ed.
[34] Karl Kautsky, 1854–1938, Prague-born politician and author, a leading Marxist theoretician;
Walter Schücking, 1875–1935, professor of international law at Breslau, Marburg, Berlin, and
Kiel.—Ed.

to appear as leaders. He thought in terms of Realpolitik and saw the danger that basically desirable political talents would thereby be discredited in the minds of the public. In these aspects of the Jewish problem, too, he was in complete agreement with his Jewish friends with whom he always associated with human candor and without ulterior motives.

* * *

At the suggestion of Prince Max, Weber was invited to attend the conferences of the *Ausschuss für Friedensverhandlungen* [Committee for Peace Negotiations] which took place under the direction of Count Bernstorff,[35] and to accompany the delegation to Versailles. The idea of being among the many who were urging themselves on the government for this exciting project was extremely embarrassing to Weber. For any German patriot the journey to Versailles must surely be one of the hardest tasks he could face. How could the men of the new republican era flock to *this* governmental undertaking as if it were a sensational event, with the same eagerness with which the monarchists had once flocked to court functions? He did not, of course, wish to shirk this opportunity. With mixed emotions he wrote the following lines to Count Bernstorff:

In view of the general vain and bustling inclination to participate in everything, a tendency which is a gift of our so-called revolution, it seems proper to ask oneself in each case whether there really is a cogent reason for it. I could judge this only if some concrete political or scholarly *services*, no matter of what kind, were asked of me, which could possibly not be performed as well or better by someone else. Since I am told that Prince Max of Baden is interested in having me take part in the Paris negotiations, I should like to state expressly that in my opinion there are already far too many personalities present in Versailles, although these include, gratifyingly enough, a number of outstanding experts such as Herr Warburg, Herr Melchior,[36] and many others with whom I could not compete in expert knowledge. Although I have held, and still hold, certain views—though hardly singular

[35]Johann-Heinrich Graf von Bernstorff, 1862–1939, German diplomat, ambassador to the United States from 1908 to 1917, later head of the German Association for the League of Nations and the German representative at the Disarmament Conference (from 1926 on)—Ed.
[36]Max Warburg, 1867–1946, German-Jewish banker, emigrated to the United States in 1938; the German-Jewish banker Carl Melchior (1871–1934).—Ed.

ones—as to *what, when,* and *how* certain things should be stated *politically*—in public or possibly privately—*these* questions will have been disposed of by the time negotiations begin, and that is one reason why my going along to Paris could hardly be justified, especially since these very things are reserved for the leading statesmen.

Finally his reservations were dispelled; perhaps he would have a welcome opportunity to help after all. In Berlin his fears of the uselessness of deliberations by people who did not rightfully have the responsibility were confirmed.

We had our first session here yesterday. A horribly pointless, futile activity: long "reports" about the state of the problems which usually contained little that was new, almost *no* discussion. I participated at two points, but everything remained "academic" and there is no assurance that what one says will not fall on deaf ears. It is utterly useless *this way;* I regard myself as *completely* superfluous and told them so emphatically. On Wednesday is the second—and last!—session with the rest of the reports. No one was able to enlighten me as to *why* we are really here. Therefore, I shall go tomorrow to see Count Bernstorff, who is presiding, and shall ask him. I shall stay here till Wednesday, but then I shall leave and *not* go along to Paris unless very definite answers can be given. This is nothing but a supernumerary's role. (March 30, 1919)

Today I spoke with Count Bernstorff, the chairman of our conference. The *purpose* of the whole thing is that we give an expert opinion about the terms—"acceptance or rejection"—as soon as they are made known. For this, two to three weeks in Versailles have been set aside. *This* I can participate in, but then I shall have enough and will return—and I shall not take part in the "definitive negotiations," because I don't belong there. But it is possible that the Entente will say, "No more than twenty people," and in that case I shall not even go there. The composition of the "experts" ["*Gutachter*"]—purely on the basis of *party* politics!—is a grave mistake and will have dire consequences. Stinnes,[37] for example, should certainly have been among them, but he was turned down. At first there were supposed to be

---

[37]Hugo Stinnes, 1870–1924, industrialist, mining and shipping magnate.—Ed.

twelve of us, then there were seventeen. What nonsense! As I have said, I think the number will be reduced. (April 2, 1919)

At the urging of his politician friends Weber decided to accompany the peace delegation to Versailles. Again he went by way of Berlin. In the meantime it had become known that the Entente really was making the extradition of the army leaders, the statesmen, and the Kaiser a condition for peace. Weber was beside himself. He saw in this a devilish desire to destroy the honor of a great nation. In those weeks he once mentioned his longing for the blue southern sea into which one goes—farther and farther—forever. "But I can't do that to Marianne."

Was there no way of averting that ultimate disgrace? Oh yes, he knew what *he* would do if he were one of the responsible leaders: immediately cross the Rhine voluntarily, surrender to the American authorities, and demand a hearing before an international court of law. Such an act of sovereign ethical self-assertion would perhaps free the nation from this outrageous demand, make a moral impression upon the world, and also restore the domestic reputation of those responsible for the outcome of the war.

When immediately after the collapse the accusations against Ludendorff started, Weber planned to write an essay to rehabilitate him. As already mentioned, he also made positive statements about him in his political speech in Heidelberg at the beginning of January. The ethics of a great military leader should not be measured by yardsticks other than those appropriate to them; a general must have confidence and daring. If he loses, he must not be judged only on the basis of success. The dignity of heroic greatness must not be encroached upon.

Later, to be sure, when facts became known that for the first time clarified the full extent of the commander-in-chief's responsibility for the policy toward the Poles and Czechs, Weber was outraged: Such infringements destroy the ethical value of a military leader. His law is limitation. A general must subordinate himself to the responsible statesman. He must not carry on policies about which he knows nothing, let alone use his military indispensability at a time of danger for extortions in the political area. Weber now abandoned his planned justification. But he believed in Ludendorff's personal dignity and greatness despite everything; he simply *wanted* to believe in it.

Now there was a situation in which the general could prove it. He had a chance to head off the disgraceful demand of the Entente, which created fresh, insoluble complications for Germany, by giving himself up, thus demonstrating his own clean record, saving the honor of the nation, and causing the enemy the greatest difficulties. Above all, such a heroic and chivalrous act would strengthen the nation's faith in itself and at the same time enhance its moral reputation abroad.

In this vein Weber wrote to Ludendorff shortly before his departure for Versailles. He told his sister about it in a few hasty lines:

> I am now leaving for Versailles, having been urgently requested to go. For what purpose I do not know, and I have no hope for myself or for the cause. But I am going just the same. I have written a letter of advice to Ludendorff. In view of the enemy's demand for extradition, he, Tirpitz, Capelle,[38] Bethmann, etc., have to *know* what they should do *immediately*. The officer corps can be gloriously resurrected some day only if they voluntarily "offer their heads" to the enemy. Wait and see what they will do!

* * *

The general's brief and negative answer had not yet reached Weber when he returned from Versailles by way of Berlin. That is why he felt impelled to meet the man face to face and to present his viewpoint in person. Through the good offices of a few German-National deputies, a conversation of several hours took place. The two men were united in their heroic patriotism, but it was hard for them to reach intellectual agreement. Weber reproached Ludendorff with the political blunders committed by the army command, and Ludendorff blamed Weber for the sins of the revolution and the new regime. Finally they did agree in their ardent will for Germany's reconstruction, though they had very dissimilar views on the methods. Weber remembered that conversation for a long time; he frequently described it with all the gestures and emphases. When he was alone in his study, the profound political excitement of those weeks sometimes erupted in loud dialogues. He reasoned with his opponents and let them answer him. Some of the things that Weber told friends about his conversation with the army leader were preserved by them later on.

---

[38]Eduard von Capelle, 1855–1931, admiral, from 1916 to 1918 state secretary in the Reich Naval Office as the successor of Tirpitz.—Ed.

Ludendorff (who knew about Weber's desire from his letter). Why do you come to me with this? How can you expect me to do a thing like that?

Weber. The honor of the nation can be saved only if you give yourself up.

Ludendorff. The nation can go jump in the lake! *Such* ingratitude!

Weber. Nevertheless, you must render us this last service.

Ludendorff. I hope to be able to render more important services to the nation.

Weber. Well, then your remarks are probably not meant so seriously either. Incidentally, it is not only a matter of the German people but one of restoring the honor of the *officer corps* and of the army.

Ludendorff. Why don't you go and see Hindenburg? After all, *he* was the General Field Marshal.

Weber. Hindenburg is seventy years old—and besides, every child knows that at the time *you* were Number One in Germany.

Ludendorff. Thank goodness!

The conversation soon turned to political matters, to the reasons for the collapse and the interference of the army's Supreme Command in politics.

Ludendorff (driven into a corner, and evading the issue). There you have your highly praised democracy! You and the *Frankfurter Zeitung* are to blame for it! *What* has improved now?

Weber. Do you think that I regard the *Schweinerei* [unholy mess] that we now have as *democracy*?

Ludendorff. If you talk that way, maybe we can have a meeting of the minds.

Weber. But the *Schweinerei* that preceded it was not a monarchy either.

Ludendorff. What is your idea of a democracy, then?

Weber. In a democracy the people choose a leader whom they trust. Then the chosen man says, "Now shut your mouths and obey me. The people and the parties are no longer free to interfere in the leader's business."

Ludendorff. I could like such a "democracy"!

Weber. Later the people can sit in judgment. If the leader has made mistakes—to the gallows with him! . . .

The two men's conversation was very excited at first, but then it became quite calm and friendly, though they talked past each other. But Weber was profoundly disappointed—not so much because the general rejected his request (he was not afraid of dying, of course), but because of what he had learned about Ludendorff the man. He summed it up as follows:

> Perhaps it is better for Germany that he does not give himself up. He would make an unfavorable personal impression. The enemy would find *once again* that the sacrifices of a war which put this type out of commission have been worthwhile. Now I understand why the world resists the attempts of men like him to place their heels upon the necks of others. If he should again meddle with politics, he must be fought remorselessly.

* * *

The peace delegation, which was led by Count Brockdorff-Rantzau[39] as the Foreign Minister of the Reich, finally consisted of eighty persons, among them important politicians, scholars with an interest in politics, organizers of the economy like Rathenau, Warburg, H. Delbrück, Count M. Montgelas, and Professor A. Mendelssohn-Bartholdy—a selection of German intellectuals from the spheres of action and thought. The men were taken into protective custody, as it were; the hotels at the edge of the Versailles park to which they were assigned were closed off from the outside world by palisades. Their hopes for a verbal discussion with the "Supreme Council" were not realized. When they handed over the peace documents, they were told that only short-term written negotiations were permitted. The frightfulness of the treaty surpassed their worst expectations. From their charge of war guilt the victors had derived the right to force unfulfillable conditions upon the disarmed nation as an aid to further destruction. In addition, the Germans were supposed to sign a confession of guilt that was included in the treaty. An outcry of horror united the German people. The government and all parties, including the extreme left, declared that the peace terms were unacceptable. The idea of a general people's war arose. But there was still hope that more moderate terms could be wrung from the enemy by this joint pressure.

---

[39]Ulrich Graf von Brockdorff-Rantzau, 1869–1928, diplomat, became Foreign Minister in February of 1919.—Ed.

The German delegation handed in note after note as well as a counter-proposal. The "Supreme Council" based its demands on a committee report about "the responsibility of the instigators of the war." They refused to make this report public, but substantial portions of it found their way into the French press. The reply was entrusted to Professor H. Delbrück, Count Max Montgelas, Professor A. Mendelssohn-Bartholdy, and Max Weber. Weber wrote:

> I arrived here on Friday morning after traveling two nights and one day. Through Paris by car, along the boulevards, the Arc de Triomphe, the Bois de Boulogne, and St. Cloud to this enclosure. There is space for walking in the park, but the rooms are uncomfortable and there are no proper facilities, least of all for writing. Tomorrow H. Delbrück is coming, the day after that Count Montgelas will arrive; then the *"guilt"* note, for which I have been brought here, is to be edited. I have already made some proposals regarding the *east* note, and I hope with success. In any case, I shall not work on the *guilt* note if any discreditable things are intended or permitted. The day before yesterday Simons[40] and I had dinner at Brockdorff's place. Brockdorff makes a good impression; I am anxious to see whether he is also *firm*. The *fragmentation* of work is very great here and editing skills are very slight. Morale is *quite* low. The more closely one looks at the *economic* terms, the worse they seem. They are so terrible and so artful that even if only half of them are accepted one will actually be looking into a dark hole without even the most distant shimmer of light. It is very uncertain *what* can be attained. The government and the delegates are resolved to *reject* the terms if nothing is achieved in the territorial and the decisive economic questions. (Middle of May, from Versailles)

The memorandum *Zur Prüfung der Schuldfrage* [An Examination of the Guilt Question] was presented on May 28. It comprised six sections of text as well as documentation consisting of eleven appendices with notes. The document, which ran to about 150 printed pages, was officially published as a German White Book (about the responsibility of the instigators of the war). Very factual expositions attempt to refute the enemy's assertions point by point; nothing is covered up. Austria's conduct appears in an un-

---

[40]Walter Simons, 1861–1937, jurist and statesman, with the Foreign Office since 1911, Foreign Minister 1920–21, later holder of high judgeships.—Ed.

favorable light; her short-term ultimatum to Serbia, her rejection of the British attempt at mediation, and her refusal to engage in any exchange of opinion with St. Petersburg are described as grave blunders. But the main responsibility is borne by the imperialistic Russian policy whose goal was Pan-Slavism, the smashing of Austria-Hungary, expansion in the Balkans, and the conquest of the Turkish straits. "The German people took up battle in 1914 single-mindedly and resolutely only as a defensive war against czarism."

The exposition and documentation did not change the enemy's attitude. The reply of the Supreme Council again called the war with theatrical pathos "the greatest crime against mankind . . . that has ever been consciously committed by a nation claiming to be civilized." The German counterproposals were rejected. The opponents dictated restitution to the outermost limits of Germany's capacity, the dissolution of the army, the surrender of the guilty men, the exclusion of Germany from the League of Nations, etc. A few concessions were obtained, to be sure. Above all, a future revision of the treaty was promised.

There was only a short time until the signing of the treaty. The enemy army stood at the western border, yearning for a victory march through Germany. What was to be done? Weber wrote:

Oh, it was horrible in Versailles. I was not consulted on *anything*, that is, *authoritatively* consulted, and in the end they did make this unreasonable demand of me: "Now *you* write the introduction to this draft." I did it in such a way that I knew they could not accept. For how can one do it if one does not know how these incredible demands (100 billion! dissolution of the army!) arose and—is given three hours?? And how shall I answer Count Brockdorff's question, "What shall we do?" if he can *not* tell me what the *Cabinet* plans to do in case there is a *rejection*, whether it will remain firm?

For a moment it seemed as though they were all united in their heroic attitude. But when the enemy persisted in his demand for unconditional acceptance, a rift opened once again between Germans and Germans. The rightist parties *and* the Democrats voted for unconditional rejection—not only out of heroism, but because they foresaw that the unfulfillability of the treaty would offer France a pretext for further incalculable repression. But in addition to the "Independents," Erzberger and some of his party came out in favor of acceptance. They pulled along the Majority Socialists who expected that otherwise there would be fresh Bolshevist chaos. "To save what could be saved" the Center Party and the Social Democrats decided to sign. Whether they did the right thing, history will decide. Weber was among those who refused to accept the treaty.

His opinion was that the people and the government ought to offer no resistance to invasion by the enemy armies and turn over the administration of the Reich to them. They probably would soon convince themselves that there was not much to be gained there and would agree to new negotiations. However, he was also able to appreciate the opposite standpoint:

I confess that I am at a complete loss politically. Personally I would favor *rejection*, no matter what the danger. But I suppose that there will then be a plebiscite that will accept the peace, and this I regard as the worst thing, because it *ties us down* so much internally. The whole thing can make one absolutely sick with rage and despair. (June 20, 1919)

So now it has happened. Oh, it is awful! For the harassment will now start in earnest, a long series of humiliations and torments, because the conditions *cannot* be fulfilled; in this the French are masters. Actual brutal, quite open foreign rule and a clear *goal* for us would be a thousand times better! But of course, *this* mean trick on the part of the U.S.P. [Independent Social Democrats] meant that everything was placed in doubt, and I understand those who are of a different opinion. Let us wait and see what will now happen in the East.

Only now does one feel physically and emotionally what these last months have meant and *how great* were our secret hopes for some "miracle"—or for a vindication of our honor such as was accomplished by the good seamen at Scapa Flow.[41] If only Ludendorff had made the right decision in those days, a decision that the others would have followed! He could have *saved* us this ultimate disgrace of the "duty to surrender," or at least forestalled it. Now it is too late for that. What good was his declaration that he was willing to appear before an "unprejudiced" tribunal? That did not do any good. (Munich, June 26, 1919)

I fear this peace means only the *beginning* of our misery. For it is absolutely unfulfillable, and the French will now start to give us a bad

---

[41]An expanse of sea in the southern part of the Orkney Islands off the Scottish mainland where the German crews scuttled their surrendered ships in 1919.—Ed.

time, to harass us, to cut off the Rhineland, etc. I fear there will be a "terror without end"[42] and we shall witness a partial occupation and dismemberment of the Reich after all. Well, it does not *have* to happen, and let us hope for the best. I have the impression here that failure to sign would have led in a short time to the defection of Bavaria and to a revolution of the "Independents" [Social Democrats] and of the clericals. That argument against it I understand. For the rest, I still do not have a clear view of the situation. The peace delegation *and* all experts were unanimously *against* acceptance, surely on the basis of the impressions they had received from sources in Paris and elsewhere. Well—it is done, and now we have to pursue positive policies. For that reason it is, of course, utterly wrong to refrain from action (as the Democrats in parliament did), but that will surely not last long. The only ray of hope is Scapa Flow, and I hope that Ludendorff and the others will, even though it is too late, find some dignified way of sparing us their extradition. As for the Kaiser, well, he is safe—at the cost of his dynasty. (June 28, 1919)

You say that I have not written anything about this peace. Oh, I was so tired and "indifferent" [*wurstig*] that I *understood* the exhaustion of the nation. The "rejection" should, of course, not have been a turning down [*Ablehnung*] but a dissolution [*Auflösung*] of the governments and the transfer of their sovereignty to the League of Nations—such or similar actions that would have made war measures impossible. *That* at least could have been done. To be sure, if I reflect about the mood here in Bavaria, I also ask myself whether there was any chance of anything good—awakening of the inner national resistance—coming from it. . . I think I shall now become quite unpolitical—for the time being, at any rate. (July 1, 1919)

Pitiful that the Kaiser *never* makes the right decision. And Hindenburg's letter, too, is simply two months too *late*. All these people should *immediately* have gone there in person and given themselves up *as soon as* the surrender was demanded. But they simply have no feeling for this sort of thing! (July 9, 1919)

---

[42]"*Lieber ein Ende mit Schrecken als ein Schrecken ohne Ende*" [Better an end with terror than a terror without end] is what Ferdinand von Schill, 1776–1809, a Prussian officer in the Wars of Liberation, said shortly before his death, referring in part to Psalm 73:19.—Ed.

20

THE TEACHER
AND THINKER _____

I

Weber's remarks about the peace treaty were written down in the Isar valley. After his return from Versailles he needed a period of complete rest in
order to overcome his spiritual and nervous exhaustion. His lectures were
not going to start until June, for a spring semester had been added for
those who had been in the service. The transfer of the Webers' household
was planned for the fall. Weber withdrew to Wolfratshausen, and for a time
he lived as though he were on a trip.

I have three full days of loafing behind me—that is, after I had slept,
simply slept, almost all day Friday and for two nights and had still been
quite addled on Saturday, I walked for hours yesterday and today—
perhaps a bit too much. For a quite senseless fatigue now makes itself
felt, inhibiting all thought and activity. Only the absolutely glorious
weather and the heavenly mild air of this plateau induce me to go out
after all, and then I lose my way in the forests along the Isar or up

on the plateau and thus get to do forced marches. I can't wait to see what the condition of my head will be when the "work" is supposed to begin. I just sent off an announcement of my course and shall start on Tuesday ("The Most General Categories of Sociology"). I think I shall have seminar discussions with older, mature students every other week; this is not as strenuous as it is with unpracticed people. But I am anxious to see what my body is going to do.

The atmosphere in Munich was still very tense because of the most recent and bloodiest unrest. Unlike what happened in Berlin, the moderate socialists there had not succeeded in forcing the revolution into channels of justice and order. The machinations of foreign communists were greater here than elsewhere, and Eisner had already desired to replace "the parliamentary swamp" with a soviet government [Räteregierung]. His assassination radicalized the moderates. The three socialist parties combined and proclaimed a soviet republic at the end of February. The proletariat was armed, and the popularly elected parliament was pressured into making socialistic experiments. The young Austrian economist O. Neurath[1] was entrusted with the "full socialization" of Bavaria in order to keep the ever-growing Communist movement in check, but this was unsuccessful.

In April the Bolshevists seized power; for the second time a soviet republic was proclaimed, this time with a red army. The government was headed first by a demented political adventurer,[2] then by the student Ernst Toller and by the bohemian Erich Mühsam, and finally by the radical Bolshevists Levien, Leviné-Nissen, and Axelrod;[3] these three were foreigners and belonged to another ethnic group [Stamm-und Landfremde]. Reich troops had to march on Munich. Toller commanded a section of the red army; almost all decrees of the soviet government were signed by him. Now the bloody carnival really triumphed. For a few days Munich was frightened by the dictatorship of the red army, and some hostages were murdered. Finally, in the first days of May the government troops won a victory after heavy street

---

[1]Otto Neurath, 1882–1945, Vienna-born economist, sociologist, and philosopher, author of *Modern Man in the Making* (1939); emigrated to Holland in 1934 and England in 1940.—Ed.

[2]Dr. Franz Lipp, the foreign minister of the soviet republic.—Ed.

[3]Eugen Leviné-Nissen, 1883–1919, a native of St. Petersburg, took part in the Russian Revolution of 1905 and subsequently studied economics in Germany. He was executed for high treason on June 5, 1919. Max Levien, a biologist, also participated in the Revolution of 1905. He returned to Russia in 1919 and was liquidated in the Stalin era. Leviné and Towia Axelrod were Jews, but Levien—despite his name and propagandistic reports to the contrary—was not; he came from a German family that had emigrated to Russia.—Ed.

fighting. There was great outrage among the population at the revolutionaries and their foreign Jewish leaders, and the result was an increase in xenophobia, anti-Semitism, and Pan-German nationalism. The pendulum now swung in the other direction; Bavaria wanted to be the "cell of order" of the German Reich and strove for the restoration of the monarchy. If it succeeded here, the hour of the counterrevolution would probably come for the rest of the Reich, or there might be an opportunity to detach Bavaria from the Reich and thus shake off the North German hegemony at last. Blue-and-white [Bavarian] and black-white-and-red associations and endeavors sought followers. Some of these opposed other groups, while others had the common goal of turning back the wheel of history.

In university circles, too, the outrage at the attempts at socialization during the soviet period and the temporary threat to academic freedom had left deep traces. The will to restoration predominated; the students were politicized, and teachers and students were divided into hostile camps.

One trial for high treason succeeded another. Weber again had an opportunity to help people in distress. He testified to the political integrity of O. Neurath, the commissar in charge of socialization, and particularly spoke in behalf of E. Toller, of whose idealistic thinking he was as certain as he was of his political immaturity. It was one of the grotesque aspects of the Bavarian revolution that young people like Toller had actually ruled for a time and made the masses follow them. During the court hearing Weber characterized Toller as a *Gesinnungsethiker* [man guided by an ethic of ultimate ends] who was a visionary [*weltfremd*] in the face of political realities and had unconsciously appealed to the hysterical instincts of the masses: "In a fit of anger, God made him a politician."

In those weeks he wrote:

The city still looks rather warlike; the trenches are being deepened, the barbed wire is being reinforced, and so forth, probably because the government is planning to move back here. Arrests are made constantly. Yesterday a whole Bolshevik cell, complete with communications and Russian money, was cleared out at Ansbach[4] on the Starnberger See [Lake Starnberg]. I am still too tired and numb to be entirely "above" these things. Well, everything will work out, and better than we think, though *right now* things look horrible . . . This letter is a bit weary because of the dreadful political situation and the

---

[4]Presumably a slip for Ambach. Ansbach is a city in Franconia, near Nuremberg.—Ed.

exhaustion that is coming now. But otherwise things are going quite well.

* * *

At the end of June, Weber moved to Munich. He had a pleasant place to live, as well as L. Brentano's fine study at the university. When he read his name on that door, he was secretly pleased; who would have thought that one day he would occupy a distinguished chair in that city after all! He opened his first lecture with a survey of the political situation. In his lecture hall, so he said, these would be his first and his last words about politics, for politics did not belong on the rostrum and in scholarship but, rather, where there was the fresh air of criticism. He spoke passionately of Germany's tragedy: We are, for all practical purposes, under foreign rule. Like the Jews we have been turned into a people of pariahs. The German government is the lackey of foreign interests, and it is forced to take vengeful action against its own nationals. We can have only one common goal: to turn the peace treaty into a scrap of paper. At the moment this is not possible, but the right to revolt against foreign rule cannot be done away with. What is needed now is the art of silence and a return to plain everyday work.

Soon Weber's students flocked to see him during his office hours; he counseled them and gave them assignments. They regarded him with awe and found that he looked "majestic" and "like a lion." He could inspire fear when his brow wrinkled to produce deep furrows and when his eyes flashed. But his expression became kind and relaxed when the students came to him for advice. Many of the young men who now had close contact with Weber as members of his seminar saw more than a teacher in him—although he wished to be nothing else. They secretly venerated him the way the Hindus worship their gurus, those teachers of wisdom who are expected to be at once helpers in need, counselors, and spiritual advisers. But they felt that they could gain access to him only through devotion to scholarship; his interest was aroused only when he sensed scholarly zeal. One of his most mature and most noble-minded students, Jörg von Kapher, a penetrating critical intellect, who, however, desired nothing but an affectionate understanding of Weber, summed up the young people's impression of their teacher:

He was realistic [sachlich] through and through. The full heroism of realism which presumably is the heroism of our age, came alive in him. And that is why his *Sachlichkeit* was such an inexhaustible experience. That is why his practical discussions, his lectures were like works of art—not in form, but in their essence. . . . The important thing was not what he said about a subject, but the subject itself seemed to come before us in its inexhaustibility, and he was its interpreter. . . . His personal relationship with us was based on *Sachlichkeit* as well, and for that very reason it was infinitely valuable to us. Just as no subject of investigation seemed uninteresting to him, he managed to show interest in all of our ideas. And his interest was never half-hearted. He treated our work with all the seriousness that informed his own work. He examined and rejected it—not lightly, for he understood. He rejected relentlessly, but when he found something that seemed valuable to him, he supported it wholeheartedly in order to help it develop, and again nothing was too small for him. He was capable of tending such a germ with infinite kindness and love. The entire warmth of his personality shone upon anyone in whom he thought he had found an idea or a valuable impulse. This warmth was enlivening, invigorating, and hope-giving. Thus working under his direction meant not only scholarly enrichment, but an increase in strength and joyfulness.

The young man's inner nobility prevented him from requesting his beloved teacher to take special notice of him. The result of such self-restraint is reflected in the following words:

Perhaps this depersonalized relationship is the only possibility of sharing a person's capacity for devotion and enjoying his gifts once we leave the community of common blood [*Blutsgemeinschaft*]. Perhaps it is a law of this strength that it cannot be directly aimed at those whom it ultimately enlivens. Presumably, someone who cannot offer us anything but his goodwill and a readiness to love us is never a help but sometimes a burden. Those who have given people the most and whose love appears to us as immeasurable were servants of something alien, of a god, of a cause. In the name of this they were able to demand what was hardest for human beings: "Take your cross and follow me."[5] They do not comfort, but they give strength.

* * *

—————————

[5] Mat. 10:38—Ed.

In the midst of his students Weber seemed to have been vouchsafed a second youth; his professional life came full circle. But he was still quite worn out, and teaching was a strain. Also, he had to further his writings. *The Protestant Ethic*, long out of print, was finally to appear in a new edition together with other writings on the sociology of religion, and much work still had to be done on it. The two addresses, "Scholarship as a Vocation" and "Politics as a Vocation," were in press. The latter had grown into a voluminous treatise. The intellectual distance between him and most of his students was very great, and it almost seemed inappropriate for him to continue to serve their purposes instead of his own work. On the other hand, he noticed that the need to express his theory of sociological categories orally a number of times helped him to formulate it more precisely. His mood fluctuated greatly depending on his capacity for work, and it was well that devoted friends took care of him and diverted him. Among the newcomers who did him good was his younger colleague Karl Rothenbücher,[6] a teacher of political science, to whom he felt close because of their common political outlook.

I am bone-tired; I noticed this in yesterday's first meeting of my lecture course. *Far* too many people; a number of them were standing. But *this* time they *will* drop out soon; I speak abstractly, purely conceptually—intentionally. Lots of registrations for the seminar, which I shall start very slowly. For the winter semester I have announced two hours of Economic History, two hours of "States, Classes, Estates," and "Introduction to Scholarly Work," the latter in informal individual conferences or possibly an hour's lecture every other week. I hope it will work out; very odd that *this* kind of *physical* activity should be such a strain on me.

So my second lecture is over, too. Again so terribly overcrowded that I had to *shout*. This is the most strenuous thing of all, and I feel that it really exhausts me tremendously, *more* so than at the beginning in Vienna (probably because I am more worn out [*zermürbter*] by that demagogy and by Versailles, for I can feel this). And then, the *climate* here is really not beneficial. I miss the relaxation in the strong mountain air, and yet this is something I especially need in this kind of work. For that reason I accomplish almost *nothing* aside from my lectures; one to two hours a day, then it doesn't go anymore.

---

[6]1880–1932, professor of constitutional and church law and of sociology at Munich.—Ed.

"Work" is coming along very modestly—one to two hours a day. I am astonishingly worn out, my head is in bad shape. But it will work out, and getting used to it slowly is probably the only way of regaining my ability. I am now preparing the "Protestant Ethic" for publication, then I shall take up the "Economic Ethic." After that the Sociology, the introduction to which is identical with my course. Wait and see how things will go! I am now a man of the *pen, not* of the rostrum. But what must be, must be. There is no *joy* in it; it was different in the beginning in Vienna. It's no use; I'll manage. I am splendidly taken care of. In addition to Else Jaffé, whose [servant] Anna brings me eggs, Sascha Salz[7] supplies me with butter; so what should happen to me? I do think we *could* feel at home here. Everything is so cheerful—the city and the people—only the climate is *horrible.* I should say so. Rain for the past three and a half weeks and no end in sight!

I am slowly working away on the edition of "The Protestant Ethic" and the other articles, and I shall see things through. I think I shall manage in the winter, too, after a good rest and the fading of all the depression that is weighing me down. If you can, bring along the black briefcase with the "Sociology of Music." When you are here, I will present this thing in my seminar, and then you can listen if you like; all right? For the rest, we will have a *really* good time together and listen to music, too (Mozart, Wagner Festival), won't we? I hope the *miserable* weather will stop; this climate is really disgusting and so *cold.* Otherwise I am quite all right—the consequence of absolute *laziness* for which your and Else's advice bear the responsibility before heaven. Everything has remained quiet here and it will continue to be quiet, but what about winter, considering *this* unemployment and *this* shortage of coal? I shudder a little. Despite all the "mad rush" [*"Hetze"*] your dear little letters always sound generally cheerful; I hope you are *really* doing tolerably well.

After I had been a bit industrious on Thursday, I was just about to go to the Englischer Garten[8] yesterday when Else Jaffé telephoned from Irschenhausen to say that Brentano has announced his visit out here, and would I help entertain him. Well, I was glad to do so, and since the weather turned beautiful—*at last,* at long last—I stayed here, missed the train, and was then put up here by squeezing kith and kin together. This morning the sun was beautiful and hot on the bal-

---

[7]The wife of Professor Artur Salz.—Ed.
[8]A large Munich park, patterned after London's Hyde Park.—Ed.

cony as early as six o'clock—you know the little house—and I walked around in a bath of sunlight while everyone in the house was still fast asleep. After this "escapade" I am going to the city again at noontime. The *forest* is so wonderful in the early morning, calm and as if expecting something.

From all this you can see that I am tolerably well again, though it is true that this is at the cost of tremendous laziness; the "Spirit of Capitalism" is hardly making any progress in addition to the lectures! Well, you gave me the *permesso* [permission].

So Mother is coming on Tuesday. Unfortunately I shall then have not only the seminar but also the Neurath trial, in which I am a witness, having already testified in the case of Toller, who received five years confinement in a fortress. My account of that strange Lauenstein affair put the court in a good humor, and that is always beneficial. Many thanks for your nice little letter; despite all the melancholy it sounded quite cheerful. Yes, it is a chapter in our lives, and some things here simply cannot be made as beautiful as what we had in Heidelberg. Let us wait and see what may develop here if, as I hope, I can cope with things.

* * *

By the end of the short semester Weber had already adjusted tolerably well; he felt part of the community that revolved about the university and participated in it with his characteristic zeal. When his wife came for a while in August, he took time out to enjoy all sorts of beautiful things with her: they saw the altar executed by Matthias Grünewald before he went wandering,[9] then made a summery excursion to the Roseninsel [Rose Island]. This gave them a chance to appreciate the magnificent expanse of the mountain country that was to become their home. They dreamed all sorts of pleasant dreams; how beautiful it would be to have a summer retreat out there by the lake with a view of the mountain chain, as did so many other inhabitants of Munich!

In the theater they saw Ibsen's *Brand.* Its profound symbolism stirred

---

[9]Since little is known about the life (ca. 1470–1528) of this painter, whose real name was Mathis Gothardt Neithardt, this reference is not clear. The Alte Pinakothek in Munich houses a later work, the high altar painting of St. Erasmus conversing with St. Mauritius, executed for the collegiate church at Halle, as well as Grünewald's early *Verspottung Christi* [Mockery of Christ] (1503).—Ed.

them deeply, though they did not express it. Brand, who was filled with an exacting God, put his obedience toward the absolute into radical practice. He not only demanded every sacrifice of himself but also wished to bring other mortals up to the level he had attained. However, they were not made to follow him; they wanted to live happily first and serve God afterward. Therefore, they drove the leader who constantly made inordinate demands upon them into an icy solitude. And only in the hour of his death did he experience the God whose mercy was higher than His law.

At some time in his life Weber might have become a man of "all or nothing." But again and again he opened himself up to the full earthly lives of others with all their wealth and conflicts, again and again he concerned himself with *everything* human, loving and investigating. He measured *himself* by absolute standards, but he did not force these on anyone else, and he definitely preferred being numbered among the sinners to being part of the "just."

* * *

After the end of the first semester Weber returned once more to the old house in Heidelberg for a few mild autumn weeks. He had the feeling that he was already detached from the place, but he wrote to his sister Lili, who had moved to the Odenwaldschule[10] with her children: "Later we shall all get together again here." The Heidelberg friends gave the Webers a farewell party; it took place exactly a year after the celebration of their silver wedding.

Weber had lived so aloof from the university that the young people called him "the myth of Heidelberg," and he was known to many colleagues only as a difficult, excitable man whose intellectual superiority was a burden, whose ethical standards were inordinate, and whose constant criticism of the political conduct of his own group was disquieting. But many came to his farewell party to be with him once more. The women celebrated the departing couple in music and verse, the men in toasts and responses. When the nymph of the *Löwenbrunnen* [Lion Fountain] conjured up Weber's youth, he and Marianne secretly nudged each other: "Like at the *Polterabend.*"[11]

---

[10]An innovative country boarding school founded by Paul Geheeb in 1910 at Oberhambach on the Bergstrasse.—Ed.

[11]A boisterous party on the eve of a wedding at which it is the custom to break dishes for good luck in front of the bridal home.—Ed.

Eberhard Gothein and Hermann Braus made clever speeches, which the latter wrote down later. As a medical man he jocularly compared Weber's effect
upon the organism of the university with the effect of the newly discovered
"hormones" on the body: Their removal causes dangerous deficiencies, but if
a prudent doctor transplants them in a different place, they continue to
benefit the entire organism. Similarly, the departing scholar would continue to have an effect on Heidelberg even while he was in Munich. And then
he found still other images:

> I am thinking of the time when I worked under you as a wartime com-
> panion and experienced many serious, cheerful, and strange things to-
> gether with you. They were small things, but we viewed them in the
> mirror of that great period. There are many who have lived through
> weightier things while near you. But no matter what it was, everyone
> who was close to you saw your chivalry and upright manliness and re-
> garded your incorruptible loyalty to your convictions as a modern incar-
> nation of Dürer's knight between death and the devil.[12] I remember
> also your tenacious energy, which did not deem even the smallest
> things too unimportant when it was a matter of serving a great cause.
> The great experience, however, which no one who has ever known you
> will ever forget is this: to have experienced the highest measure of
> human wealth, a profusion of capabilities drawing on the deepest roots,
> the faith that Dionysus is not dead.

Weber's words of thanks embraced everyone, bound together as they were
by their common, superpersonal fate. He affirmed his unshakable faith in
Germany and his affection for the beauty of this country whose soul could
be felt in its forests. He also lifted the veil a bit as far as his own life was
concerned and spoke of the years of his illness and of what Heidelberg's gentleness had meant to him when he was slowly awakening to a new life. He
said he felt as though he were leaving his homeland to go to strange places
that were beautiful but cold. However, at that time no one had a right
to lead a luxurious existence. And since it was now impossible to engage in
politics fruitfully, the simple practice of one's profession remained one's first
obligation.

* * *

---

[12]A reference to Albrecht Dürer's celebrated engraving "Knight, Death, and the Devil"
(1513).—Ed.

Munich was beset by an early winter. One morning the full, fresh foliage of the proud poplars, which gave the avenue beyond the Siegestor[13] such an air of grandeur, was frozen. The dead leaves rustled sadly when the wind moved through them. But soon the trees were resplendent with a coat of hoarfrost. It was wonderful to stand at the gate and watch the white guardians outlined against the blue sky. And in the clear, cold air the elegant yellowish houses around the university exuded courage and strength. Weber was now ready to build a new life for himself once more. He and Marianne first had temporary lodging in the familiar rooms of their friends and then moved into Helene Böhlau's[14] little house, which was close to the Englischer Garten. These quarters were cramped in comparison with the spaciousness of the house in Heidelberg, but they were homey and satisfied Weber's desire to live modestly in keeping with the meager times. And the small Seestrasse was a cozy spot. Here the metropolis merged with the little village of Schwabing, which had once been far outside its gates. Little village houses, whose roofs could be touched if one stretched out one's arms and behind whose window panes old-fashioned plants stood dreaming, still stood their ground next to their proud city sisters.

Weber's den, smaller than the one in Heidelberg but similar in form, faced a tiny garden, and two white birch trunks and a young copper beech covered the ugly wall opposite. On the street side there was a view of a grove of firs and birches, the children of the tableland. At the end of the street, where the Englischer Garten began, a tributary of the Isar rushed by, and a little further on there was a large lake populated by ducks and seagulls. The discovery of little Biederstein Castle which stood there dreamily, just as it had in the time of Goethe, gave the Webers great pleasure. What a boon it was not to be confined to the cold stone prisons of the city streets!

* * *

Just before Weber began his winter course, Helene came to the end of her road. The vibrant woman had always wished for a slow expiration in order to *experience* her end. Now death came to her instantly, without granting her a gentle farewell. During the summer she had spent months in Heidel-

---

[13]The "Victory Gate" which was built 1844–50 in the style of a Roman triumphal arch.—Ed.
[14]1856–1940, novelist.—Ed.

berg with Marianne and had also visited her son Max in Munich. She was small and stooped, and she grew short of breath when she walked. She frequently said that presumably her end would come soon, and that she belonged at home, for she wanted to spare her children the burden. Of course, she would have liked to live a while longer to see the recovery of Germany, and she had all sorts of other plans. Her last surviving sister, the widow of the geologist E. W. Benecke, was among those who had been driven out of Strasbourg. She had returned to her paternal house in Heidelberg as an invalid—paralyzed for years and mentally handicapped, but unchanged in the last mysterious core of her being. She had now moved into Weber's apartment. Helene wanted to spend the winter with her and envelop her in love and shared memories. Then she planned to move into the Mommsen house to live with her children.

She devoted the energy of her last day to a typical act of kindness. For quite some time her heart had been failing; walking and climbing stairs were a severe strain on her. She lived on the fourth floor, and going downstairs and upstairs once a day was the most she could do. But that day she managed to climb the stairs twice. A lady friend of hers, a co-worker who lived alone in an apartment several flights up, was returning from her vacation, and she was to have a "warm" welcome by her friend the *Grude* stove[15] which required much time and care to heat. Helene left in the morning, carrying a heavy bag. She was lugging some briquettes and her own lunch; someone saw her bowed figure creeping along. With a great effort she negotiated the numerous stairs, but then she accomplished what she had set out to do and was very satisfied; the dead ashes were red-hot. That evening, when her heart began to fail, a baby jacket fell from her busy hands. Her death struggle was very hard; her daughter Klara was with her.

All her children assembled at her bier; they had no idea that it would be their last reunion. The beloved face of their mother bore the painful traces of what she had been through. And that she now lay there so closed up [*in sich beschlossen*] and inaccessible was not at all suited to her, for she had exemplified an ever-active, creative, fighting life. But her influence on the hearts of her loving children and through them could not be at an end. The children bade her farewell now, but they were going to return to her. Her eldest son made a speech at her open coffin and evoked her person-

---

[15]*Grude* is a combustible by-product of the burning of lignite in paraffin factories that was formerly used as a household fuel.—Ed.

ality for them. He particularly praised her love of life, her fiery strength, and the inexhaustible humor that she preserved through all vicissitudes of fortune.

Ida's son Otto, who had always been close to her heart, officiated at the funeral. He spoke of her active ethical religiosity, "her hunger and thirst for justice," the absolute nature of the demands she made upon herself, and the constant tension under which she lived because she was always painfully aware of the distance between the highest human striving and its ultimate goal. This was not the whole story so far as the women were concerned. Just as for a man only a man is a standard and a model, for a woman only a woman can serve as such, and that is why a woman is moved most deeply by the specific values of a woman's nature. What the worshipful women felt to be Helene's charisma was interpreted for them by Marianne: that creative, *absolute* love whose fullness is independent of what it is offered, a love that is never satisfied with a blessed upsurge of feeling but hastens to perform a helpful deed and has an enriching effect all around.

* * *

Weber's winter work then began. Entirely against his original intentions he had yielded to the urging of the students, who found his theory of categories too difficult, and agreed to give them an outline of universal social and economic history, which meant a new course of enormous scope and substance. Most of the knowledge for this was at his disposal, but the material had to be organized and the results of recent research had to be considered. The course was given in the *auditorium maximum* [largest lecture hall] before about 600 people. It required a great deal of work from one lecture to the next. In addition, Weber conducted a sociological seminar as well as a colloquium for junior faculty, which a number of his colleagues had requested. This scholarly exchange gave him a great deal of pleasure.

These duties absorbed all his energies, and he had to live very carefully. In fact, in the first weeks he was again worried that he would not permanently be equal to full official duties. Then, too, it offended his sense of honor that he was not able to relieve his colleague W. Lotz, who would be overburdened until someone could be appointed to an additional chair in economics. He considered exchanging his full professorship [*Ordinariat*] for an associate professorship [*ausserordentliche Professur*] that was about to be created, and he made the proper application for it. He felt relieved, but he did not receive a response. And by Christmas he had adjusted; he managed his teaching duties without an effort, and felt increasingly secure, in contrast to his experience in Vienna.

Weber regarded his renewed strength as miraculous, but he wondered whether it would last. At the annual celebration of the university, Weber wore the ruby-colored robes of the faculty of political science; the tall man walked with a regal stride and quickly glanced at his wife with a gentle smile. He knew that the sight of him stirred her. But they asked themselves whether a teaching position was to be his final form of activity. Earlier it had appeared to be an incomparable pinnacle; now that the reconstruction of Germany would need every person with political talent for an indefinite period to come, it looked different. When Marianne at that time said that in a few years, when he was even older and healthier, the nation would call him after all—"and then you will go no matter what the risk"—he nodded and said solemnly: "Yes, I have the feeling that life is still keeping something in reserve for me."

* * *

In the middle of January, 1920, political passions were again inflamed by the pardoning of Count Arco-Valley,[16] Kurt Eisner's young assassin. Weber disapproved of the judgment despite his sympathy for the murderer, for it was not only unjust but also portentous: "Political murders will become the fashion." Nationalistic students, who regarded Arco as one of theirs, celebrated the verdict by holding a rally in the halls of the university—in the presence of the Rector, a man with Pan-German sympathies.[17] During this meeting they revealed that if Arco's sentence had been carried out, they would have staged a putsch with the aid of a *Reichswehr* [army] detachment. When a socialistic fellow student expressed the opposite viewpoint, he was vilified by a member of the student committee. His Magnificence [the Rector] made no objections to this. The offended minority now excitedly complained to Weber. He contacted the Rector on their behalf, requested him to remedy the situation soon, and asked him "not to underestimate my relentlessness if need be." When nothing had been done two days later, he began his lecture with approximately the following words:

---

[16]Anton Graf von Arco (auf) Valley, 1897–1947, an Austrian-born aristocrat, shot the Bavarian prime minister in Munich on February 21, 1919. He was sentenced to death on January 16, 1920, but his sentence was commuted to lifelong imprisonment, and in 1924 he was released on grounds of ill-health.—Ed.
[17]Friedrich von Müller, 1858–1941, professor of internal medicine.—Ed.

Contrary to my usual practice in political matters, I feel impelled to make a remark about what happened here last Saturday. And you have the right to demand that I show my true colors in actual *cases* as well. You have extolled Count Arco because—and this is my conviction, too—his conduct in court was chivalrous and manly in every way. His action was born of the conviction that Kurt Eisner brought disgrace after disgrace upon Germany. I share this opinion.

Yet it was a bad thing to pardon him so long as the law is in force, and if *I* had been the minister I would have had him shot. Your demonstration would not have prevented me; on the contrary! But the ministry yielded to you. Arco's tombstone would also have exorcised Kurt Eisner's ghost, which is still haunting us; now he will live on in people's hearts as a martyr, because Arco is alive. That is to the detriment of the country. And what will your demonstrations turn Arco into? Make no mistake about it: a coffeehouse celebrity! I would have wished something better for him! On Saturday accusations were made here, accusations that have not been withdrawn to this day. Anyone who fails to do so is a *Hundsfott* [son of a bitch]!

And another thing: It has been mentioned that the *Reichswehr* was ready to stage a putsch in association with the students. Gentlemen, I am not impressed with conspirators whose vanity is so great that they have to blab [*ausplaudern*] such things in public. There is no need to say anything about the plan as such.

But let me tell you this. To restore Germany to her old glory, I would surely ally myself with any power on earth, even with the devil incarnate, but not with the force of stupidity. So long as madmen carry on in politics from the right to the left, I shall stay away from it. (January 19, 1920)

Two days later the vilification of the socialist students was redressed. Thereupon Weber withdrew his hypothetical "*Hundsfott*" at the beginning of his next lecture. Nevertheless, when he was about to proceed with the lecture, there was a riot of hissing and hooting. Students of the School of Veterinary Medicine who had been sent there by the Pan-Germans, as well as other youths of the radical right who did not know Weber and had not heard his earlier statements, applied what they had learned in election meetings. When Weber calmly remained on the rostrum and laughed at them, they became even wilder. His students were just about to hit the others when the lights were turned out and the hall was cleared. Immediately afterward Weber attended a rather large social gathering, was very animated, and then slept splendidly. Political strife obviously had a refreshing effect on him.

* * *

Around that time there was a discussion in Weber's seminar of Oswald Spengler's work *Der Untergang des Abendlandes* [*The Decline of the West*],[18] which was attracting universal attention. Weber saw in it a conception of the philosophy of history by a very clever and scholarly "dilettante" who had squeezed the results of historical research into his speculative constructions. Some members of the seminar who knew the author personally desired a debate between him, Weber, and a few other thinkers. The men were prepared to cross swords. On a cold, clear winter day they met at the city hall. The young people, sitting in several rows, clustered about the small group of scholars; they consisted predominantly of *Freideutsche Jugend*, but young communists and sectarians of all kinds were also present. The intellectual tournament lasted for a day and a half and was extremely exciting. Weber attacked very cautiously and with the most chivalrous weapons. His respect for the other man's dissimilar intellect made his critique bearable. Others proceeded more ruthlessly. Spengler maintained his gentlemanly self-control as his intellectual structure was gradually demolished. The men found it impossible to convince one another with regard to Spengler's basic thesis. Once again the young listeners were overwhelmed by an enormous amount of knowledge which, however, gave them no answer to their question, "But what shall we do?"

Afterward, some of the young people drew Weber, along with the writer Paul Ernst and the socialist Otto Neurath, into their company so as to get a chance finally to express themselves. In one of the tiny village houses on the Seestrasse they had a retreat whose sole furnishings were chairs, a table, and a large, brown tiled stove. It was a bitterly cold winter afternoon. The stove heated up slowly, because it was getting little fuel. But poverty and the trenches had accustomed these young men and women to hardship, and they were proud of their frugality. Weber sat on the bench by the stove. His expressive head was outlined against the tiles; his straight hair was youthfully thick and brown, but his beard was interlaced with many silver threads, and he frequently smoothed its unruly tips into place with his delicately jointed hand. His kind eyes reflected his complete readiness to empathize with the young people.

What agitated them was, among other things, the belief that by means

---

[18]The first volume of this work by Spengler, 1880–1936, appeared in 1918, the second volume in 1922.—Ed.

of communistic oases (rural settlements and the like) the natural cells of a new, higher world order could be created—the peaceful overcoming of capitalism, or at least liberation from it for those who seriously *wanted* to be free from it. And by living off the soil together they hoped to remain free from specialization in working for a living, for in this they saw a soul-destroying compulsion. But they wished to remain men of culture nevertheless. "*Landwirtschaft mit Kunstgewerbe*" [agriculture plus arts and crafts] was Spengler's ironic remark.

The writer Paul Ernst, who had been working a farm for a few years with the help of his extremely efficient and intelligent wife in order to create for himself a basis for his intellectual existence, knew what it took in the way of industry and energy and issued a warning. A few of the young men had already made some practical attempts but had failed. One particularly daring young man wished to lead a large group of intellectuals and proletarians to Siberia, an area he knew from the war, and to create with them a model communistic community there. He had in mind not only communal living and working but also the anarchistic ideal, liberation from the political forms of domination.

Weber endeavored to make it clear to them that only small, familylike communities but not larger ones can be organized without laws and without force. But he was impressed by their chiliastic enthusiasm; he did not want to destroy their faith or paralyze their energies, and so he told them that he was ready to advise them in practical economic matters. The young settlers, however, felt that he could not become one of them. They were disappointed and threw him on the scrap heap.

At home the exchange with Paul Ernst and his wife continued until midnight; these were hours of great intellectual excitement. Soon thereafter Spengler came to the house, and again one intellect caught fire from another. When the scholar was questioned regarding his constructs in the philosophy of history [*geschichtsphilosophische Konstruktionen*], he confessed that he was a "poet" ["*Dichter*"].

II

For the rest, the winter was spent with unceasing concentrated work. The demands of his course were great. In addition Weber read the galleys of the first volume of his writings on the sociology of religion and worked particularly on his theory of sociological categories in *Wirtschaft und Gesell-*

schaft [*Economy and Society*], the first proof sheets of which had been ready for some time. The volume was to appear in the spring. At this point we shall make some remarks about the form and *method* of this work, the product of Weber's scholarly life work, which may help laymen to understand it.

The *"understanding sociology"* consists of two methodologically different parts, both of which have remained incomplete: a systematic theory of types and the treatises that correspond to it in part, and in which the concrete historical data are connected and arranged by means of the concepts of types. In other words, the conceptual constructs used in the descriptive parts for the penetration of historical processes are in the first part arranged systematically and presented as unambiguously as possible. The theory of concepts, then, presupposes a comprehensive mastery of history, because it is not deduced from major terms or principles, as speculative intellectual systems [*Denkgebilde*] are, but is directly evolved from the concrete factual material and *composed* inductively. That is why Weber wrote his historically analytical and descriptive treatises before the war and "from memory"—without notes. He did not need any material or *apparatus criticus*, for he had universal knowledge at his disposal. Only later did he set down his theory of categories. He had to do this for the lectures he gave in Vienna in 1918 and in Munich a year later. Now, a few months before his death, it was given its final form. He kept remolding the difficult concepts and made many changes in the proof sheets.

Weber finally achieved a concision of expression which satisfied him. To be sure, "People are going to shake their heads." He realized that his method, which was filling well-known historical, economic, juridical, and theological systems with a completely new substance, would at first not only be hard to understand but would also strike people as strange. The reasons for this will be discussed shortly, but first a few more remarks about the form are needed.

The language of the entire work, particularly of the theory of concepts, is very different from that of his other writings. The sentences are almost always short, subjects and predicates are close together, and there are no encapsulations. Arranged by numbers and letters, sentence follows upon sentence, blow upon blow, as it were. The definitions are expressed pithily according to a peculiar formula: *"Soziologie soll heissen," "Soziales Handeln soll . . . heissen," "Betrieb soll . . . heissen," "Herrschaft soll . . . heissen,"* etc. ["Sociology shall mean . . .," "Social action shall mean . . .," "Organization

shall mean . . .," "Domination shall mean . . .,"]. These imperatives, however, are not a claim to the validity of the new constructs outside the
framework of this special sociology; on the contrary, their meaning is this:
"In *my* theory of concepts this shall be the meaning, this is what *I* call
these structures for certain methodological purposes, and only the scholarly
yield shall justify my procedure; let other sociologies and, above all, other
disciplines proceed differently for their cognitive purposes." The illustrations
and interpretations that are inserted between the definitions and that
break up the substance that has just been compressed are usually couched
in sentences with a transparent construction. The thought process moves
at a brisk pace, a rhythmic pace, as it were, and anyone who has the capacity to understand it is swept along through the material by this logical
verve. It is true that at first not many will have this experience, for each
of the concise sentences is a symbol for conceptual sequences that span
time and space and are filled with a rich substance. For anyone who does
not master much of it they remain empty.

The following remarks about the method and the scholarly thinking behind it presuppose familiarity with the exposition in Chapter 10 of this
book.

Weber concerns himself with "understanding sociology" as an empirical
science—"a delimitation that shall not and cannot be forced on anyone."
Its object is the only *understandable* factor of history—namely, the meaningfully oriented action of individuals and groups of people, that is, their actions that relate to one another and are therefore called "social action."
As this sociology understands such action interpretatively, it explains it
causally at the same time. What Weber wants to determine as the meaning of the action is, as we know from earlier remarks, the *subjective* meaning,
the meaning "intended" by the actor himself as an ultimate, concrete, empirically graspable reality, not some thought structure that is speculatively
superimposed upon reality.

With this, understanding sociology sunders itself from all normative
sciences such as jurisprudence, logics, ethics, and esthetics, sciences that desire to determine a "valid," "correct," or "true" meaning in their objects.
It is closest to history, sharing with it the *extrascientific* factor, namely,
the selection of culturally significant events from an unlimited variety of
matters of little importance, as well as the *scientific* factor, causal attribution, and interpretive understanding as a means of cognition. But while
history is primarily interested in fathoming important individual connec-

tions, sociology is concerned with the *typical*, creates typal concepts and seeks *universal rules* for the ever-recurring and ubiquitous "course" ["*Abäufe*"] of social action. In this interest in the universal it is related to the natural sciences; yet it differs from them, not only in its object but also in the different logical meaning of its general concepts, with which we are already acquainted.

But since in this work Weber restructures and systematically arranges such "ideal types," it is well to bear in mind that he could have no use for their arrangement into a system for the sake of an integrated conception of the world. For these types were not intended to be definitive fixations but only temporary stopping places in the flow of a constantly changing process of historical cognition. Besides, *empirical* research does not of itself supply any uniform principle in accordance with which culturally significant components of reality could be given a definite, scientifically compelling arrangement. Rather, it always leads only to a multiplicity of ultimate ideas of value and forces of life—"gods"—which vie with one another for the domination of existence. It is self-evident, of course, that this intentionally self-limiting empirical science always is aware of its own extraempirical *premises* and indeed recognizes them as its condition. One such condition is the general ideas of cultural values by means of which the important is sifted from the unimportant, and furthermore, there is the specific personal "idea" of the investigator, as clear, as objective, as universal a recognition as possible of what was and what is, and above all, the greatest possible penetration of the forces of modern life. One day, when Weber was asked what his scholarship meant to him, he replied: "I want to see how much I can stand." What did he mean by that? Perhaps that he regarded it as his task to endure the *antinomies* of existence and, further, to exert to the utmost his freedom from illusions and yet to keep his ideals inviolate and preserve his ability to devote himself to them.

These ideas are *behind* empirical research and its concepts. Speculative thought structures are banished from concrete cognition itself, and the idea of something supernatural or of a realm of compelling objective validities is expressly and intentionally avoided as a task that does not belong in empirical science. The specific quality of this understanding sociology—for example, something that might appear to be a logical paradox: the rational construction of typal concepts that are removed from reality—derives from its intention of freeing the *kernel of reality* of typical social action from all value-speculative casings. Weber traces the regularities of social action all over the globe and subsumes them under concepts that imagine the course of action as though it took place without disturbance by irrational, that is, incalculable, influences—something that never happens in reality. By means of these abstractions the irrational components of concrete action are to be seen all the more clearly as "deviations." Thus there arises for empirical sociology, too, the strange situation where the nature of what *exists* is recognized through confrontation with something that does not exist— rational abstraction. But here it is a matter of bringing logical thought structures to bear on reality. The abstraction serves *scientific* truth, while the application of ethical, political, and metaphysical constructs to actualities serves extrascientific, "practical" purposes that have been selected by the subjectivity of the researcher.

Furthermore, the empirical recognition of reality which Weber aimed for required not only that "normative" ["*dogmatische*"] ideas of any kind be kept out of the thinking process, but also demanded the removal of a *logical* veil of a certain kind which other sciences, such as jurisprudence, history, and economics, justifiably employ. The concepts of these sciences are based on the idea that there are acting *collective personalities*. Consequently they think of complex structures such as state, nation, community, joint-stock company, family, and so on, as *individuals*. Understanding sociology proceeds differently. It *breaks through* these logical fictions in order to penetrate to the last comprehensible reality, the meaning-oriented action of an individual or individuals. A few examples of this will be given presently. Its method may therefore be called "rationalistic" and "individualistic," although it would be just as misleading to think of individualistic *valuations* as it would be to believe that "the rationalistic character of the formation of concepts means a belief in the *predominance* of rational motives or even a *positive* valuation of rationalism." For once, nothing but the kernel of reality is to be brought out without any illusions.

Simple, self-evident, and even banal as this may seem, the appropriate reconstitution of generally known concepts was in the nature of a *logical revolution*. In particular, Weber's definitions relating to political and legal sociology seemed so odd to jurisprudence and his definitions in the area of the sociology of religion struck the theologians as so strange that at first they presumably did not have much use for them. The deliberate elimination of all their customary overtones of value gives to concepts—such as legitimate order, law, corporate group [*Verband*], domination [*Herrschaft*], power, state, nation, church, and the like—an entirely new and purely logical meaning, a meaning that is, of course, strangely cold and devoid of pathos. And even though Weber rejects any claim to their exclusive validity, they nevertheless are uncomfortable for the accustomed thinking and feeling, for their very existence brings the extrascientific components of the other, equivalent intellectual systems into focus, thereby showing indirectly which of their aspects were *not* logically compelling and could not be forced on anyone. Besides, it is possible that with many people the inevitable by-product of this *logical* disenchantment of historical structures will be another *valuation*. For instance, the kernel of reality shared by all the above-mentioned social collective structures consists "entirely and exclusively in the *chance* that there will be action in a way that can be meaningfully stated, and it does not matter what this chance derives from, whether it is based on psychologically compelling ideas or on actual external compulsion or on both at the same time . . . Viewed sociologically, those structures consist of nothing else but the *chance* that the action which is oriented in such a way will take place."

If "chance," something that in its everyday usage seems shadowy, is here raised to the rank of a category for the sake of grasping logically what is common to all social action, it really is, as Weber put it, as though the cold hands of a skeleton reached for warm life. A similar peculiar sobriety also attaches to those further conceptual definitions by which the specific substance of the various kinds of "chances" is expressed. For example, "An order shall be called 'law' if it is outwardly guaranteed by the *chance* of physical or psychological compulsion . . . by a group of men specifically equipped for it . . . A compulsory political association [*Anstaltsbetrieb*] shall be called a 'state' if, and to the extent that, its administrative staff successfully claims a monopoly on legitimate physical compulsion for the enforcement of its regulations," etc. The law, the state, the church—all of them structures which seem to be indissolubly bound up with metaphysical notions and which are impregnated with claims to objective validity—are in such definitions really freed of these. Through them, it appears, the idea of value-free science is given a more comprehensive meaning than the idea of excluding the subjective judgments that something is worthy of approval or objectionable, desirable or undesirable, good or bad. What is beyond this deliberate elimination is the unprovable proposition not only of all "normative" sciences but of almost all history that the *empirical* validities—that is, all those conceptions of value which actually determine action as psychological contents—are due an "objective" validity *transcending* the consciousness of individuals, that they constitute a supernatural realm that is beyond question, a realm of the correct or "true" meaning that rightly dominates real existence.

In his sociology Weber keeps *these* notions of an empirically graspable, objectively supernatural realm away from his cognition of reality. Nevertheless, norm valuations and ideologies of all kinds have their full significance for this sociology—namely, as actualities, as important, "rational value-oriented" [*"wertrationale"*] series of motivations which are present in almost all meaningfully oriented action and indeed frequently have a decisive influence on it. Thus, in all parts of his sociology the causal weight of specific valuations and interpretations which are determined by the contents is investigated. But the investigator always directs his attention, as far as the content is concerned, only to their empirical realization, not to the metaphysical significance that is also due them. As he develops his concepts, Weber repeatedly explains the manner in which he separates *actual* validities from their value [*Werthaftigkeit*] as *objective* validities. If, for example, in his theory of the types of domination he calls charisma "a quality that is *regarded* as being . . . out of the ordinary," this very formulation indicates that the question of whether in a concrete case this quality is *justly* evaluated as charisma is something that does not concern him within the framework of sociology: "So the recognition of a personality as a charismatic leader is based upon the *subjective* evaluation of his qualities as extraordinary and superhuman by a group of disciples or followers who are ready to obey him . . . What the 'objectively' correct evaluation of the extraordinary quality in question would be from any ethical, esthetic, or other point of view is, of course, a matter of complete indifference."

The methodical result is that a "berserker endowed with the charisma of martial frenzy," a war lord, a political demagogue, a founder of a sect, a prophet, and a savior are all charismatic leaders. This is bound to be not only strange but also annoying both to everyday thinking and to thought accustomed from other sciences to cover actualities with claims to objective validity, and it must often seem like a senseless deprivation. And only those who join Weber in this thought process will be compensated for the radical "disenchantment" of those value-covered structures by a new truth-content. In his quest for truth, Weber everywhere "removed magic from his path."

But a nonscholarly [*ausserwissenschaflich*] person expects of a new *logical* treatment of reality new guidelines for his entire existence. In the face of

Weber's intellectual system, too, he will involuntarily ask, *"Cui bono?* [For whose benefit?] Can I derive guidelines for the conduct of my life from this?" And he will be disappointed if he cannot. Understanding sociology, which expressly refrains from promulgating norms, demands, and practical valuations, naturally does not satisfy this demand within its realm, at least not in a direct way. But perhaps the treatise *Politics as a Vocation* will permit us to draw certain conclusions regarding the usefulness of this thought for human action. In this work, which developed out of a lecture given before Munich students in the revolutionary winter of 1918–19, Weber relates his insights into political sociology to an important sphere of practical action—namely, *politics,* politics as a vocation, that is, the form of activity of actual people. The background of this treatise is the collapse of Germany, Russian bolshevism, the chiliastic excitement of youth. Young people felt called upon to build a new world and hoped to succeed in establishing, with pure motives, an unprecedented social order whose structure would be very different from any previous kind and would be filled with ethical and religious ideals of justice and brotherhood. But events in Russia soon showed that the road there was long and ran through the utmost inhumanity, without any guarantee that the goal would be reached.

Weber forced his listeners, first of all, to recognize without illusions all the socio-political [*staatssoziologisch*] processes and phenomena which, typically, determined political activity. He showed them the various forms of government and their historical development as well as the different types of political domination, and presented a typology of political figures from all ages and all countries. From the vantage point of historical universality he showed that the *specific,* though not the only, resource of the state has been at all times domination based on legitimate physical violence and that politics always means the striving for a share in political power. Anyone who engages in politics, then, strives for *power,* be it for its own sake or in the service of idealistic or egotistic goals, and in order to attain this power a person will, if need be, employ against others the physical or psychological force that is behind him. All these are scientific observations gained by a logical treatment of historical experience. But in the context under discussion here, Weber uses them as the basis for discussion of one of the most significant "existential" problems, namely, for illuminating the relationship between politics and ethics, something that greatly concerned young people.

The Christian churches had not only acquiesced in the war as an inevitable evil, but in all countries they had even glorified it in the name of the Gospels and fomented nationalistic hatred. To religious persons this was bound to appear as an aberration, as something painfully absurd and untrue. And now the revolution was creating an analogous paradox. The communistic adherents of pacifism regarded themselves as entitled to realize their ideals through the worst form of violence: civil war. In the face of this, the much discussed question of whether politics and ethics had anything to do with each other, whether or not there was such a thing as a specific political ethic, was once again a burning question. Some denied it, while others maintained that the same absolute ethic must apply to political action as to everything else.

Weber denied this, as he had already done earlier, but at the same time he showed that nevertheless it certainly did not belong in the realm of *adiaphora* [matters of moral indifference]. Precisely because the specific method of politics is the use of force it needs an ethical orientation—namely, the weighing of ends and means, and responsible reflection on whether the desired end is valuable enough to "sanctify" the means and compensate for the undesirable secondary effects. On the other hand, because political action is inevitably tied to force and compulsion, the ethic that governs other things does not apply to it any more than identical ethical commandments can be formulated for the other highly dissimilar relationships in which a person is involved. Under certain circumstances every holder of political power is forced to do harm to others for the sake of his goals. That is why he cannot be subject to any absolute ethic, and least of all to that of the Gospels. The unconditional demand, "Give up *everything* that you own," is a senseless demand for him as long as it cannot be enforced from everyone. And the other demand, "Turn the other cheek," unconditionally, without asking why the other man has a right to strike him, is "an ethic of dishonor—except for a saint." Or if the ethic of love commands, "Do not resist evil" [Mat. 5:39], the opposite applies to a politician: Resist it, and by using force, otherwise you will be responsible for its prevalence. This is the decisive point where the Christian and the political ethics diverge, where two lines of ethically oriented action diverge, although in practice, of course, they are often intertwined.

Fundamentally, ethical conduct is determined either by the *ethic of ultimate ends* [Gesinnung] or the *ethic of responsibility* [Verantwortung]. As a believer in the ethic of ultimate ends, a true Christian "does the right thing and leaves the results up to God"—that is, his goodwill and his life in the absolute ennoble his actions. God commands him, and that is why he does not ask about the consequences and does not take the credit for them. If they are bad, he blames the world or God Himself. Magnificent though this attitude be as an expression of an inward life aiming at the salvation of an individual's own soul and those of others, a *politician* obeys a different law. He wishes to be effective in the world and therefore is obliged to deal with the world as it is, taking the weaknesses of people into account and even placing them in the service of his purposes. His specific ethic is passion, responsibility, and a good eye [*Augenmass*]—passion in the sense of unreserved devotion to a *cause*, "to the god or the demon that is its ruler," responsibility as the will to calculate the consequences of his action coolly and calmly and to stand behind them, and a good eye as that detachment from things and people which makes the right judgment possible. And above all, no matter what goals he may serve, he must always have *faith* in them if he is to escape the curse of creatural futility. But the success of his work is determined not only by his own motives but also by those of his followers, which often are predominantly base in nature.

That is why pure ends are often reached only by morally questionable means. In all violence there are diabolical forces. It is at this point that the polarity of the two sets of laws manifests itself clearly. Logically speaking, a believer in the ethic of ultimate ends would have to reject any action that employs morally dangerous means. Conversely, a politician must be ready to take this upon himself and thereby risk his own soul. A believer in the ethic of ultimate ends denies the ethical irrationality of the world, according to which evil frequently arises from good and good sometimes comes from evil. A politician must be able to bear this irrationality. "Only he has the 'calling' for politics who is sure that he will not be shattered if the world, from his point of view, is too obtuse or too mean for what he wants to offer it."

If on the basis of his sociological insights Weber calls our attention to the ideal forces that determine action in an important area, he does so both for the sake of truth and in order to give young people greater clarity in their choice of a road to take. This illusion-free illumination of the various roots of existence may mean a new deprivation for many—for those whose capacity for devotion to a cause is fed by influences that arouse enthusiasm. Others, who do not need such aid, will find that "the trained relentlessness of vision" for the world as it is will give them greater strength to endure it and be equal to its everyday manifestations.

21

THE FINAL CHAPTER _____

Weber's work absorbed him a great deal, almost as much as in the first years of his teaching activity. He had little time left for "living," but his capacity for work became steadier, and his sleep, too, hardly needed to be induced by drugs any longer. Only political events frequently disturbed his equilibrium. When in the middle of March the Kapp Putsch showed that destructive forces were still at work in the country, he became extremely excited. Did these fools want to ruin everything that the lost war had left? In those days he once hummed Herwegh's old *Reiterlied:* [1] *Die bange Nacht ist nun herum, / wir reiten still, wir reiten stumm, / wir [und] reiten ins Verderben* [The anxious night is over now; we are riding quietly, we are riding silently, we are riding to perdition].

Then came the vacation, followed in the early days of April by Easter. The women wished to celebrate the feast and lured Weber out to Irschenhausen, to the log cabin at the edge of the forest, where he had spent

---

[1] The "Cavalryman's Song" by Georg Herwegh, 1817–1875, set to music by Justus Wilhelm Lyra, 1822–1882.—Ed.

such beautiful hours in the summer. This time, however, it cost him a great effort; he really did not want to go away, and when the train was overcrowded he became very ill-humored: "I wish you had left me at my desk!" In the pure mountain air he changed and began to enjoy himself. Spring was still holding back, but the open earth exuded the delicious fragrance that proclaimed its newly awakened fruitfulness. The forest was still wearing its brown winter garb; the meadows were still gray, but the bushes were budding, and deep blue gentian gleamed in sunny valleys. Their eyes roamed over undulating land interwoven with forests and meadows; the Isar flowed in its deep bed. The lines of the soil were reminiscent of the Westphalian homeland, although here the magnificent lines of the Karwendel mountains added a lofty note.

Bathed in a soft light, the days passed in perfect harmony. Despite the shortages of the times, the children were allowed to hunt for eggs, and at night they played around the Easter fire. For hours the family sat outside in the sunshine. On Easter morning Weber read aloud the text of *Die Walküre* which contained many profundities; they were going to see the opera together at the end of the holidays. In the afternoon, while a gentle rain was falling, they all sat in the little wood-paneled room and told tales from their youth. Outside everything vanished behind a wall of white fog. As Weber later told them, a strange feeling came over him, like the atmosphere of some Russian work of literature; toward the people crowded together on a height moved a black something, an abyss that was going to swallow them up.

Die Walküre was very impressive, although the meaning of the work did not fully emerge from the bonds of reflection in artistic form. Weber particularly loved Siegfried's[2] spiritual struggle with the herald of death who promises him Valhalla, though it is a hero's heaven without his beloved. And he replies to her: *Von Walhalls spröden Wonnen sprich Du mir wahrlich nicht.*[3]

* * *

On the morning following these holidays, a brief message announced the death of Weber's sister Lili. She was not yet forty years old, refined, ani-

---

[2]It is *Siegmund* to whom the Valkyrie Brünnhilde appears.—Ed.
[3]"Of Valhall's brittle raptures/ vaunt no vauntings of them" (Stewart Robb's translation).—Ed.

mated, charming, and self-assured [souverän], with that absolute nobility of mind which nothing petty can touch. Of all of Helene's children, Lili's features most closely resembled those of her mother: the aristocratic, boldly shaped nose in the narrow, delicate, oval-shaped face with the finely formed mouth. In many other ways she was different; in particular she lacked her mother's unshakable vitality, and she never had any illusions. Everyday life with its tasks was often a great burden for her, as it was for many of the women descended from Emilie Souchay Fallenstein. But for some time she had seemed safely settled in the beautiful, love-filled country boarding school on the slopes of the Bergstrasse. Her fatherless children were happy there, and Lili was surrounded by tender friendship. She was absorbed in a new, rich life in which everything revolved about young people.

And now, suddenly, an accident[4] had plunged her into the mysterious abyss! She left four young children. Her death was a terrible, shattering blow. The Webers immediately went to Heidelberg, where the misfortune had occurred. There they were greeted by a resplendent sea of blossoms. Oh for this first reunion after a half-year's absence! What was now to be done with the orphans? Quite unexpectedly, as though by chance, the Webers had a revelation: "These children are yours." Their friends thought their decision was too hasty, and they tried to warn them with many arguments: "You are too old, too set in your ways." However, no scruple or consideration of the difficulties could dispel their certainty. The Webers were ecstatic. And even though Lili's death had shattered them, this momentous decision gave them new strength and security. Weber was profoundly moved, yet overjoyed; it seemed to him as though Marianne's becoming a mother was the crowning of her woman's life, its real fulfillment, a fulfillment hitherto denied her. She, of course, would not hear of that, for in her eyes *he* was the blessing of her existence. Weber forced himself to extract a meaning from his sister's death. On their trip to the Odenwaldschule he said mysteriously: "Wonderful if one experiences a rise once more and then goes." The thought of *him* flashed through Marianne like the brief beating of black wings.

In Heidelberg Weber greeted all his closer friends; they found him so open and alive, so lavishly kind. He said, "I am working the way I did thirty years ago, I have an abundance of ideas [es strömt mir zu]," and he assured them that Heidelberg would remain his home and that he would come again soon.

---

[4]Weber's sister died of gas poisoning by her own hand.—Ed.

Lili and the question of the children were the main topics of conversation. His friends had the impression that "no fate can harm this man any more."

Then he went back to Munich—alone, for his wife had to make a lecture tour that had been arranged for some time to the "occupied territory." It was a very arduous duty, for she was constantly thinking about what had just happened. And she was also worried about the effect on her husband's nervous system. He was too overwrought. On the other hand, she knew that he now needed to be alone to do his work. However, great political excitement was in store for him in Munich. The Bavarian prime minister, Herr von K.,[5] was said to have hinted in a conference that Bavaria might detach itself from the Reich. The rumor also made its way into the foreign press. The report was denied, but Weber and his political friends did not trust the policies of that blue-and-white man. Weber inserted the following notice in the paper:

> According to published reports, the Bavarian prime minister is said to have made statements that would be tantamount to an incitement to commit high treason. These statements have been denied so conclusively that among men of honor there can be no doubt about the actual state of affairs. The prime minister would surely be glad to affirm them under oath, if need be. Therefore I should like to observe that the person who falsely attributed these statements to him must be regarded by any decent person as a *Hundsfott*. I now expect this gentleman at least to come forward publicly and in a *court of law*. I am making this declaration because the false impression that was bound to be created among the French was really designed to promote their plans and confirm them in their intentions. (April 13, 1920)

This notice was intended to force the presumed slanderer of Herr von K. to bring suit against Weber for defamation of character and thus bring about a complete clarification of the matter. However, the newspaper refused to print the challenge, saying that the interrogation of a participant in that conference had shown that there was insufficient evidence and that the trial would therefore end with a defeat. To this Weber replied: "If the reason you have is the *real* reason—and I have no doubt that it is—you should not have let *my* heart sink into your boots (pardon the

---

[5]Gustav Ritter von Kahr, 1862–1934, served in that office from 1920 to 1921. He was later murdered by the Nazis.—Ed.

expression!). I would have won the suit for calling someone a *Hundsfott* who had *falsely* put words in Herr von K.'s mouth—*if* that *Hundsfott* had brought it. For a minute I thought you had reasons of high politics. This would have been open to discussion." But Weber now let the matter drop.

In those days, when the cohesion of the German Reich mattered more to him than anything else, Weber seems to have intended to free himself from any party ties again. In a letter addressed to his sister Klara Mommsen in the middle of May, there is the following passage:

Since the [German Democratic] party is presuming upon me to help with the *"socialization,"* which I regard as nonsense at the present time, I shall resign. A politician *must* make compromises; a scholar *must not* cover them. You, too, should leave *this* German-National Party—*es tut mir weh, wenn ich Dich in der Gesellschaft seh*[6] [it hurts me when I see you in such company] and take a look at it. The prime minister here is supposed to have spoken about "separation from the Reich," because the fat bourgeois [*Mastbürger*] are afraid of the Spartacists. If the Reich breaks up, then it will have been the work of these people (Kapp, Lüttwitz,[7] and I fear I must add Ludendorff). I am afraid they will *not* be shot and *not* be sentenced to hard labor as any working-man would be in the same circumstances, a worker who does *not* have their "education."

* * *

Now Weber had to pay for his extraordinary intensity during the days in Heidelberg with a period of great nervous exhaustion. He realized how difficult it would be to reorder his life completely, and he sometimes worried about whether he would manage being a father. Friends who visited him were frightened by his appearance. He also told about a cardiac spasm: "The machine wouldn't work anymore." He said he had lain on his sofa, unable to work, and occupied himself with thoughts of death. "What death is no one can say—is it *das dunkle Reich der Nacht, aus dem die Mutter mich gebracht* [the

---

[6]*"Es tut mir lang schon weh,/Dass ich dich in der Gesellschaft seh"*—Margarete to Faust (about Mephisto) in Goethe's *Faust* I, lines 3469–70. In Bayard Taylor's translation, "I've long been grieved to see/That thou art in such company."—Ed.
[7]Walter Freiherr von Lüttwitz, 1859–1942, the general who participated in the Kapp Putsch of 1920.—Ed.

dark realm of night from which my mother brought me]?"[8] Then, with a vigorous gesture of rejection and full of lust for life: "But enough of that now, we are *still* alive!" His depression gradually left him. Marianne was absent and learned nothing of this at the time. A short time afterward, when his friend Frau Else Jaffé, who had diverted him with her charming and witty chatter, said to him, "It was as if a cold hand had touched you," he said seriously: "Yes, Else, that's how it was." One moonlit night, when he sat with her on a bench by an Isar weir, watching for a long time how one quick wave gave way to another, he said softly: "Yes, that's the way it is; one quickly follows another, but the stream is always the same." Not what he said, but his tone of voice suggested that ultimate secrets had been unveiled to him for a moment.

By the end of April the shock had abated and the clock was again ticking evenly. Weber became absorbed in his work with his full strength. He once said that the scholarly tasks he saw before him would suffice him for a hundred years. When he was handed the first dissertation that had been produced under his direction, he put his hand over it with obvious satisfaction: "It is the first one, and it is good." Now and then he was even tempted to be sociable. Next to his work, he was most occupied with the children.

Finally spring came to Munich, too. The young copper beech outside his window shook its brownish plumage; occasionally he took a rest down in the little garden in the evening. Sometimes the smell of a stable came over the wooden fence of the neighbor's garden, and this gave him the idea that they could get rabbits for the children. The two younger ones were supposed to come to Munich soon, and he wanted to see his wife become a "real" ["*effektive*"] mother. One day he said, "Then she will not be so alone if anything should happen to me." Later he had all sorts of fears again: that the children would have a hard time adjusting, that their financial means would not suffice, and so on. The problems of the past mingled with those of the present, but they could not paralyze him. Instead, in that extraordinary period all the psychic forces that had shaped his life combined once more to produce a full chord: creative productivity, political passion, tender friendship and faithful love, readiness for new, responsible, human tasks, enjoyment of the concrete details of existence, and vigorous humor.

---

[8]An adaptation of Tristan's line in Act II, Scene 3 of Richard Wagner's *Tristan und Isolde:* *"Es ist das dunkel nächtge Land, daraus die Mutter einst mich sandt' "* [It is the dark nocturnal land from which my mother sent me one day].—Ed.

In those weeks Weber wrote his wife almost daily in order to make their separation easier for her. His letters, for which he took time out from his most pressing work, express with a directness shared by few others his deep concern and his enthusiastic acceptance of life; they also reflect his fluctuation between his newfound happiness and his worries about the limits of his own strength, which, however, he repeatedly managed to overcome so that Marianne might do as she desired. Here are some excerpts from these last letters.

As you see, *everything* is working out. Dear heart, I can't find K.'s address, and I have also lost *your* address! *Vater werden ist nicht schwer,* but after this performance you will add, "*Vater sein dagegen sehr.*"[9] I am eating myself fat again—quickly, quickly, before your other children come. You will disapprove of this. But I am also smoking "*zum Abgewöhnen*" [like someone breaking himself of the habit], and that you did approve of. My dearest heart, I wonder how you are doing. How angry you will be not to find anything from me in Kreuznach, that is, the children are now necessarily a hundred times more important to you than this constantly "working," grumpy *Ehemann* [husband]. Otherwise everything is going well. "Otherwise"?? *Everything* is going well. Except work: nothing doing. That'll come, too. It has to! My dear child, things will be hard, including all that "money-making"—but everything is "easy" *nevertheless.* And Bavaria seems to be *staying* in the Reich.

I wonder how you are doing in your burgeoning motherhood. Again the joy is for me and the burden for you. Are you still *that* open-minded? For the "ecstasy" that they talked about gave way on the very next day to sunny clarity, which *also* delighted me. Here it is *heavenly* spring; in the evening it is cool, and the leaves are just opening. But in the future this will not "impress" the little children when they think of the Odenwaldschule. There will be *great* inward difficulties. At first they will be thoroughly miserable here. A great ordeal for you. The main problem is how you will cope with that. Work is starting now. All right, then! Give my regards to everyone there and continue to be kindly disposed toward your "old papa" Max.

So you really landed in Cologne and are "thinking of the twenty-first of April" [Weber's birthday] in the midst of all your drudgery and over-

---

[9]"Becoming a father is easy enough,/ But being one is very tough"—from Wilhelm Busch's *Julchen* (1887).—Ed.

work? That is very kind, and I hope you believe that I too am thinking of "some things." For a few days I was *quite* tired, but now things are going well; I work a lot, and when that is possible, it does me good. This *absurd* political situation makes me absolutely *sick* every time I think of it or am reminded of it. I still do not feel like giving my lecture course—it is drawing closer; only two more weeks! But: plenty of proofreading; the first volume of the "Sociology of Religion" is finished in manuscript and two-thirds completed in galleys. So things are making progress.

Oh, how much I enjoyed your birthday letter! And the book by M. L. Enckendorf[10] (though I cannot read it just now). And "Herr Dahme."[11] And the chocolate—gulped it down immediately. Else sent me a wonderful cake with her daughter; Lisbeth [a servant] also baked one. It was just right for a "papa." So, darling, *give some thought* to when you are going to bring the children here. Whether we shall get another apartment is uncertain. Who knows whether we shall not be obliged to keep this one? G.'s scruples about a *big city* are certainly weighty. In any case, let us not be *hasty*. If something should happen to me— and it is *conceivable*—the situation of the children here would be very bad. I am in favor of waiting a *while*, until the spring of '21 perhaps, and having them come *then*. That is what you thought, too. I am working rather snappily, though I haven't been able to bring myself to work on my lectures. But that will come. Am sleeping all right again; for a time I was able to sleep only with Nirvanol [brand of sleeping tablets]. After some debility I am "up" again. Day in, day out I read proofs; almost everything is finished, but my lecture course makes me shudder a bit. Well, last summer Else managed to work all kinds of hocus-pocus on me—that sorceress can really do this!—so that I got over it. She should do it this time, too, and if it works *now*, it always will.

   Oh, my heart, if I could only see you as a real mother, with the children around you! This is what heaven created you for—not to take care of a big lug [*Schlagetot*], a big sick child such as I used to be. But— careful! "*Make money*"? Yes, but how? That is the question for me. Instead of playing professor, I would have to go to work for a newspaper

---

[10]Marie Luise Enckendorf was the pen name of Gertrud (Mrs. Georg) Simmel.—Ed.
[11]*Herrn Dames Aufzeichnungen oder Begebenheiten aus einem merkwürdigen Stadtteil* [The Notebooks of Herr Dame or Occurrences in a Strange District], an autobiographical, satirical *roman à clef* about Schwabing by Franziska von Reventlow (1913). Figures in this novel represent Stefan George and members of his circle (Klages, Wolfskehl, Schuler, Schmitz, etc.)—Ed.

or a publisher *here*, and to this I would have no objection. After all, I can do such administrative work better than this academic gabbing [*Kolleg-Schwätzerei*], which *never* gives me spiritual satisfaction.

Thank God, the semester doesn't start until May 11. Suits me quite well, because so far it has been all proof sheets (just kilograms of them!), and as for work on the course: *niente*. I am starting it now and will have to continue during Whitsuntide. *Utter* nervous exhaustion did set in, and only now is everything all right again, so I am awaiting future events with equanimity—*all* of them, particularly if you should decide to bring the children here as early as the fall, on account of school (although that is not "compelling"). Of course, no one can make me believe that I am a "born papa." No, I am not. I enjoy children, but God knows I am not a "pedagogue"—and my real enjoyment is of *you* in the beauty of your awakened motherhood. The main thing is for my *health* to hold out. And when this summer has passed well, I shall be sure of it. . . .

Here comes Else; she is sitting down with a little book and wants to eat here afterward: I don't have much time for her now. We have now discussed the question of the children again, as you asked her to do. In the main she shares our view, but she is very keenly aware of the drawbacks [*Bedenken*]. In one respect she may be right, and she very "strongly" ["*scharf*"] emphasized it: It is certainly true that I cannot "vouch" for myself as far as my health (despite everything) and my temperament are concerned, and that, as she says, I may not be very qualified to be a "papa." Consider this, too; the best thing will be if you make no definitive decisions in the *near* future, but make them in about a year, as you planned to do. . . . Once you have decided, all doubts will cease. I shall manage and shall then be happy. . . .

In her "costume" with the little red apron Lisbeth is round like a bowling ball; I must say she is happy as a lark and very willing. And these invitations of hers to Director P. and his wife, for *dinner*, once together with a painter, the next time by herself; she said that there was only music-making. Everything *a conto* [on account] of their Lower Saxon background! That really is fabulous and may already be called "democracy"! Besides, every few days some festivity or a walk in the moonlight. Yes, *her* life is a full one, and that despite this *I* should be doing so splendidly—for she takes *good* care of me—is almost a miracle.

I resisted the beautiful weather, and now that I am completely well and normal again, I have made notes and prepared my lectures, for things are starting on Tuesday. . . . Everything in the garden and elsewhere is now fully green—late by our standards, early by the local ones. A delicate copper beech in my little garden is turning out especially charming. Yesterday I was invited at the home of the Salzes; in addition to me, the guests were Dr. K. from Heidelberg and Else. The Salzes are being *deported.* I have set everything in motion to prevent this absurdity, but the "Upper Bavarian Government" finds Salz "suspicious." Sascha is sick and tired of this treatment—after all, she is a proud, splendid woman—and although the matter still rests with the ministry, they will probably leave voluntarily and buy some property somewhere. Their apartment (in one of the courtiers' houses that belong to Nymphenburg Castle) is *heavenly!* Those round rooms! The lilac was in bloom—the white bushes that they gave me are still in front of me—and Nymphenburg *Park* is quite close by. I looked in for a minute; the paths are neglected and covered with grass, but all the chestnut trees are in their full blossomy splendor, and yet there are many trees still in the very first stage of early spring, still brown instead of green! *Our* little garden is now quite densely green and brownish. The birch and the little beech shield us from the neighbors. Eduard Baumgarten,[12] who is happy about the scholarship donated by an anonymous American, was here for a short time, having carried on passionate conversations about religion with his Uncle Otto; he is going to be in my seminar. My lecture course starts on Tuesday. Naturally the *auditorium maximum* again for *both* lectures; as of two days ago, almost 600 students had registered for Socialism and almost 400 for Political Science. It is going to be a *physical* strain. But by the time you come, I shall be acclimated; things are going quite *well* now.

That Lisbeth! What a *Lebewesen* [high liver]! Always with Anna and especially with Herr von Bethmann-Hollweg, or rather, Herr Hollweg, who is passive and dreamy like that statesman, but seems to love *das Rundliche* [curves]. . . . The ball at the home of the Lower Saxons is said to have been fabulous. So! Frida, she said, had only two dances (she never learned how); as to how many Lisbeth had, *darüber schweigt der Sängerin Höflichkeit*[13] [the singer's discretion is silent on that]. But

[12]Born in 1898, sociologist and philosopher, professor at Göttingen, Königsberg, and Mannheim, lives at Ebnet near Freiburg.—Ed.

[13]"*Darüber schweigt des Sängers Höflichkeit*" is the refrain of two anonymous Berlin ditties (first decade of the nineteenth century), one of which begins with the lines "*Als der liebe Gott die Welt erschaffen,/Schuf er Fische, Vögel, Löwen, Affen*" [When the good Lord created the world, he made fishes, birds, lions, monkeys]—Ed.

she is greatly satisfied: every month a ball! Today she was sick. As the "papa" I sent her to bed, boiled three eggs for her, and ate bread and butter myself. . . .

Yesterday the *auditorium maximum* was overcrowded for Political Science (two-thirds of the people were "visitors"). Today is the start of "Socialism." Otherwise everything is fine, but I must now work on the lecture course. Have a good rest in Heidelberg! Don't rush things. Have a quiet talk with Gruhle and Jaspers. Traveling is impossible at Pentecost, so I shall expect you toward the end of Whit Week. By then I shall be ahead on my lectures and we shall have a day of "rest" and "heart-to-heart talks," you *Mütterle* [mummy]. Did I have stage fright before my lecture? I felt *koddrig* [nauseous], and thousands of marks were at stake if I was *not* able to start. After all, that is something. . . .

Today Political Science, the second lecture, still a lot of students; I "managed." Now two days of rest, then a week with *six* hours and one hour of seminar. Am curious. But it is going well; only, I am costing so much for *food!* What will be left for the poor children? Our income will approximate that of a locksmith (six marks per hour!). . . . So now you are giving a talk in Karlsruhe.[14] But that is the *end!* And *rest*, a Whitsuntide rest with relatives and friends. So far I am doing better than I *dared* hope. A little bit of diversion through Else; such an utterly escapist [*weltfern*] chat was *good*. But now that is finished. At Whitsuntide I must do an "awful" lot of work. Wild political activity of the right here, among the students, too. . . . Jörg von Kapher wants to organize the leftist students. I shall keep away from it.

Yesterday a lecture and a very lively seminar—three hours in all, and that is why I did not write. Now: rest and bad weather. Countless proof sheets to be taken care of, of course! Yes, our income will *never* again be what it has been this year. Once the third full professor is here, I can count on a thousand marks in lecture fees [*Kolleggeld*] at most—*at most!* Otherwise I would have to give money-making courses [*Gelderwerbs-Kollegs*]; disgusting, and I couldn't do it. . . . Do you suppose Tobelchen [Mina Tobler] will come? She would like to. But I don't have much time for anyone. During Whitsuntide I shall work hard. But between times it can be done, and I wrote her in this vein.

---

[14]Marianne Weber had been elected to the Baden legislature.—Ed.

* * *

On the last day of May, the Saturday after Pentecost, Marianne finally
returned. A magnificent early summer sun poured its light over the streets,
and for the first time the city seemed like home. She was immensely grateful to be coming home. Weber welcomed her with roses in his hands; he
looked well and was cheerful and receptive. The first lectures he had so
dreaded were already behind him, and, above all, the first part of his theory
of sociological categories was finished and satisfied him: "I shall probably not
have this acuity of conceptual thinking when I am older. Of course, people
are going to shake their heads, and at first they won't be able to make
head nor tail of it."

The Webers spent the afternoon and the evening conversing. Marianne
had decided that it would be better to postpone moving the children for
a while, until a larger apartment had been found and she had given up her
office in the women's movement. Also, she had gathered from Weber's letters that it would be some time before he was able to add the duties of
a father to his professional obligations. At first Weber seemed a bit
disappointed—he was looking forward to the new experience—but then he
was probably relieved. In the late afternoon they went for a walk through
the fresh greenery of the Englischer Garten. Everything was so joyful; the
surface of the lake reflected the blue of the sky onto the dark earth like
a softly shimmering opal. They stopped where the Seestrasse ran into the
tributary of the Isar and thought that the grassy slope by the shore, as
yet not cultivated, on which a white goat was tending her kids, would
be a nice playground for the children.

At night there was a change in the weather; the next day was nasty,
cold and rainy. In the afternoon the Webers took tea with a neighbor. In
the evening Weber, as a treat, read to his wife from the *Hasenroman* by
Jammes,[15] which he had given her as a Pentecost present. He enjoyed the
deeply felt figure of Saint Francis and the animals that followed him into
death. But he was particularly moved by the fact that the hare, the only
animal that had slipped into the animal paradise without having suffered
death first, was not happy there. It yearned for its dearly beloved earth
with its unrest, its danger, and its fears. As he was reading, Weber's voice

---

[15]*Le Roman du Lièvre* (1903), a prose romance by the French writer Francis Jammes, 1868–
1938.—Ed.

became slightly husky, and the next morning he was a bit hoarse. Marianne anxiously implored him to cancel his lecture, but he vigorously refused, and during the lecture he managed to shake off his hoarseness. The thought flashed through his wife that it might be his last one. So it went for three days. Thursday was Corpus Christi and the university was closed. Weber was pleased about that. It was warm again, and in the evening they sat in the garden with their lady friend and chatted animatedly.

The next morning Weber felt ill. During the night he had had an attack of chills; was it the grippe? His lecture was canceled. He had a high fever. However, the doctor found nothing but bronchitis; straining his voice in the lecture might have made the throat infection spread to the bronchia. "There is absolutely no cause for concern." The election to the Reichstag was to be held on Sunday, June 6. It was important, for democracy was in danger. The doctor had no objection to Weber going out and voting, but he did not want to do so. He felt dizzy and dozed in his bed. He would not hear of politics; it was too disagreeable. His temperature remained high, and the doctor said that this was better than a fluctuation.

At the beginning of the second week of his illness Weber was in a euphoric state, full of love and delighted gratitude. Every glass of milk and every strawberry were delicious. But it would probably cost him the semester, and the lecturing fees would have to be returned. His first doctoral candidate in particular must not wait; it was urgent that he receive his degree. Weber wanted the examination to take place at his bedside. When the dean sent word that his colleagues would fill in for him, he was very relieved. On Monday, June 7, he discussed with his lady friend [Else] the dedications of his books that were in press; one of them was to be dedicated to Helene, the other to Marianne. This was to be a surprise for his wife.

On Wednesday a mild state of delirium set in, with fantasies which at first were not recognized as such. He told about all sorts of adventures that he had never had and was full of charm and amiability. On Thursday morning he received the doctor with a loud and clear rendition of Figaro's aria *Will der Herr Graf ein Tänzchen [nun] wagen*[16]—as a sign that he was completely recovered. But later someone overheard him sing a different song: *Grabt mir ein Gräbelein auf grüner Heide* [Dig me a little grave on the green heath]. He said: "Next week I shall lecture again. But my heart is beating

---

[16]"*Se vuol ballare, signor Contino . . .*" [If the Count wishes to dance . . .], from Act I, Scene 2 of Mozart's *The Marriage of Figaro.* —Ed.

so slowly and my brain is *so* small." During his nervous illness, he said, he had also lain like this and examined the pattern of the wallpaper, "but at that time I was able to think and I struggled with the good Lord. With *this* illness he can't impress me. Oh, if it were a real pneumonia, then I would draw up the balance sheet of my life." Did he feel remorse or have any feelings of guilt? He thought it over and said first hesitantly and then definitely: No.

The patient was now coughing a great deal, and the doctor finally diagnosed a deep-seated pneumonia. His delirium became more severe. Two nights before the end he thought his student was at his bedside; he tested him and praised him in a touching tone of voice. Scholarly and human matters occupied him equally. Sometimes he debated in various languages, evidently carrying on political conversations with Germany's enemies. But despite the thick haze he was in, he recognized all who were around him and had kind and affectionate words for them. He no longer was in control of his tormented body or his dimmed intellect, but he was still himself, with the same greatness, grace, and humor.

He did not resist the dark force. Several times he said a veiled farewell. Once he said with inexpressible authority: *"Das ist mir ja nun ganz gleichgültig"* [That is a matter of complete indifference to me now]. Another time he said, as though with calm expectancy: *"Wir werden ja sehen, was nun kommt"* [Well, we shall see what comes now]. During his last night he mentioned the name of Cato and said, with an unfathomable mystery in his voice: *"Das Wahre ist die Wahrheit"* [The true is the truth]. All that human strength could do to wrest him from death was done. He patiently put up with everything—but then he said: *"Ach Kinder, nun lasst es nur, es hilft ja doch nichts"* [Oh, children, don't bother anymore; it won't do any good, anyway]. His heart could no longer withstand his high fever.

On Monday, June 14, the world outside became quite still; only a thrush sang incessantly its song of yearning. Time stopped. Toward evening Weber breathed his last. As he lay dying, there was a thunderstorm and lightning flashed over his paling head. He became the picture of a departed knight. His face bespoke gentleness and exalted renunciation. He had moved to some distant, inaccessible place. The earth had changed.

A GENEALOGY OF MARIANNE AND MAX WEBER

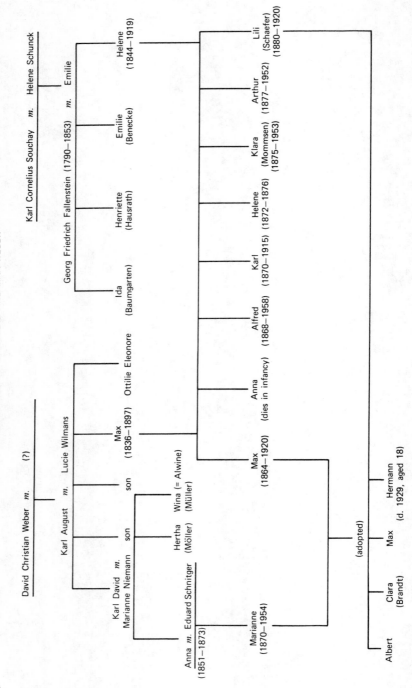

CHRONOLOGY OF
MAX WEBER'S LIFE _____

1864

Born at Erfurt on April 21, the first child of Helene Fallenstein and Max Weber.

1866

The child becomes ill with meningitis.

1869

The Weber family settles at Berlin-Charlottenburg.

1877

Max Weber writes precociously learned essays on the position of emperor and pope in German history and on Roman emperors from Constantine to the migration of the peoples.

1882

In the spring Weber graduates from secondary school in Berlin and begins law studies at the University of Heidelberg, where he joins the Alemannen dueling fraternity.

1883–84

Spends a year of military service in Strasbourg where he has close relations with the family of his uncle, Hermann Baumgarten.

1885–86

Studies in Berlin and prepares for the law examination qualifying him to be a *Referendar* (at Göttingen).

1887–88

Military service at Strasbourg and Posen. Falls in love with his cousin Emmy. Joins the *Verein für Sozialpolitik.*

1889

Awarded a doctorate of laws *magna cum laude* for a dissertation on the history of trading companies in the Middle Ages.

1890

Participates in the first Evangelical-Social Congress and accepts an assignment from the *Verein für Sozialpolitik* to investigate the situation of farm workers east of the Elbe.

1891

Completes his *Habilitation* thesis on the agrarian history of Rome.

1892

Substitutes for his teacher Goldschmidt at the University of Berlin. In the spring he completes his final period of military service. Becomes engaged to Marianne Schnitger.

1893

Weber is considered for appointment to a professorship of economics at the University of Freiburg and to a professorship of commercial law at the University of Berlin. Joins the Pan-German Union and lectures on the Polish question. His uncle Hermann Baumgarten (b. 1825) dies. In the early fall, Weber marries Marianne Schnitger.

1894

At the Evangelical-Social Congress in Frankfurt, Weber reports on his investigation of farm workers. There is a breach between the leftist Christian Socialists (Weber, Schulze-Gävernitz, Naumann, Göhre) and the Conservatives (Stöcker). In the fall Weber moves to Freiburg as a professor of economics.

1895

In May Weber gives his inaugural lecture at Freiburg. Travels in England and Scotland (August-October).

1896

Appointed to a professorship of political science at the University of Heidelberg as the successor of Knies. Participates in the seventh Evangelical-Social Congress.

1897

Declines to run for election to the Reichstag from Saarbrücken. In July he has a showdown with his father, who dies the following month.

1898

In a state of nervous exhaustion, Weber seeks relaxation on Lake Geneva in the spring and in a sanatorium on Lake Constance in the summer. He suffers another breakdown at Christmastime.

1899

In April Weber resigns from the Pan-German Union. For reasons of health

he asks to be excused from teaching in the summer semester. In the fall
he resumes his lectures, but he suffers another breakdown, and in the winter
he offers his resignation.

1900

Seeks to recuperate at Urach in the Swabian Alps in the summer. Spends
the fall and winter on Corsica.

1901

In March Weber travels to Rome and Southern Italy. After spending the
summer in Switzerland, he returns to Rome for the fall and winter.

1902

Leaves Rome at Eastertime and goes to Florence, from where he again sub-
mits his resignation. In April he returns to Heidelberg and resumes his writing. In December he travels to Nervi on the Riviera.

1903

Trips to Rome in March and to Holland and Belgium in the summer. In October Weber resigns from his teaching post and becomes a *Honorarprofessor*.
He completes the first part of his essay on Roscher and Knies and starts
work on *The Protestant Ethic and the Spirit of Capitalism*.

1904

In August the Webers travel to the United States to attend a scholarly
congress in conjunction with the Universal Exposition in St. Louis, returning to Germany in the winter. Weber takes over the direction of the *Archiv für Sozialwissenschaft und Sozialpolitik*.

1905

Studies Russian and hails the Russian Revolution in hopes of a liberalization
of the czarist regime.

1906

Attends the convention of the Socialist Party and concludes that its petit-bourgeois nature makes it unfit for revolutionary or dynamic action. Travels to Sicily in the fall.

1907

Marianne Weber publishes a book on the legal status of wives and mothers (*Ehefrau und Mutter in der Rechtsentwicklung*). In March Weber travels to Lake Como. He participates in a convention of the *Verein für Sozialpolitik* and criticizes both the Kaiser and the Social Democrats.

1908

In the spring Weber goes to Provence and Florence. In the fall he has a lengthy sojourn with his relatives at Oerlinghausen where he studies the psychophysics of work in his cousin's textile factory. Participates in the congress of the National-Liberal Party and attacks Gothein, who had polemicized against parliamentarianism. In the *Frankfurter Zeitung* Weber inveighs against the practice of German universities of refusing advancement to Social Democrats.

1909

Accepts the editorship of the *Grundriss der Sozialökonomik* and joins the newly founded Heidelberg Academy of the Sciences. Spends the summer in the Black Forest and attends a convention of the *Verein für Sozialpolitik* in Vienna.

1910

The Webers and Ernst Troeltsch move into the old Fallenstein house on Ziegelhäuser Landstrasse, Heidelberg. Weber wins suits against a journalist and a Heidelberg professor. In the spring he travels to Italy with Else and Edgar Jaffé, and in the summer he takes a trip to England. Stefan George, Georg Lukács, and Ernst Bloch are among those who frequent his home.

1911

Polemicizes against the educational and personnel policies of Prussia, fraternity practices at schools of business, and the military tone of an academic banquet at Freiburg. Travels to Italy (spring) and Munich and Paris (summer).

1912

Travels to Provence (spring) and Bayreuth and Munich (summer). Participates in a Berlin convention of sociologists and expounds his value-free conception of nationalism.

1913

Trips to Italy (spring and fall).

1914

Travels to Italy in the spring. In April his mother celebrates her seventieth birthday and he sends her his congratulations from Ascona, where he is helping Frieda Gross defend her maternal rights against her husband's father and counseling Fanny Reventlow on how to save her son from military service. After the outbreak of the war, Weber accepts a post with the *Reservelazarettkommission* in Heidelberg and organizes nine military hospitals.

1915

Karl Weber, Max's second youngest brother, falls in the war. At the suggestion of Edgar Jaffé, Weber goes to Brussels but fails to get an appointment in the military government. He fails in his endeavor to obtain a political post in Berlin and to be consulted on the Polish question. Works on his sociology of religion.

1916

Writes a memorandum opposing stepped-up U-boat warfare and involves himself in public debates about pacifism. Goes to Berlin, Vienna, and Budapest for talks with economists. In the fall he takes a trip to Lake Constance and lectures in Munich on Germany's position among the world powers. Publishes his studies of Confucianism, Taoism, Hinduism, and Buddhism.

1917

Publishes several articles on political and economic problems in the *Frankfurter Zeitung* and polemicizes against censorship. At a meeting in Heidelberg he calls upon the military to keep out of political struggles. At the invitation of the publisher Eugen Diederichs, Weber participates in the Lauenstein congresses in May and October where he meets socialists and pacifists such as Ernst Toller and Erich Mühsam. In the summer he goes to Oerlinghausen and in October to Vienna, where his appointment to a professorship of economics is under consideration.

1918

Weber accepts a professorship of economics at the University of Vienna on a trial basis and lectures there on the sociology of religion during the summer semester. He attempts to induce the Kaiser to abdicate in time to save the honor of his dynasty. In a stormy lecture in Munich on November 4 he warns against revolution and "peace at any price." At a meeting in Mannheim later that month, Weber defends the German generals. In Heidelberg he is made a member of the workers' and soldiers' council. Weber joins the founding committee of the German Democratic Party and actively campaigns for it. In December he is nominated for election to the Reichstag from the Frankfurt district, but his unfavorable place on the candidates' list assures his defeat. Weber is proposed for appointment as Secretary of the Interior and ambassador to Austria.

1919

Gives lectures on "Scholarship as a Vocation" and "Politics as a Vocation" in Munich (January–February). Continues to campaign for the German Democratic Party and publishes an article on the war-guilt question in the *Frankfurter Zeitung*. At a rally at the university of Heidelberg in March he calls for a national revolution against an imposed peace settlement. On May 13 he goes to Versailles as part of a delegation charged with the drafting of the German reply to the Allies' memorandum on war guilt. Afterward he visits Ludendorff in Berlin and tries to persuade him to surrender to Allied justice. In June Weber moves to Munich and starts his lectures at the university. In August he is elected to the executive committee of the German Democratic Party. His mother dies in October.

1920

On January 22 rightist students demonstrate against Weber's uncompromising stand on the Arco-Valley case. On April 7 Weber's youngest sister, Lili Schaefer, dies by her own hand; Max and Marianne plan to adopt her four orphaned children. In the summer semester Weber gives courses on Socialism and Political Science in Munich. He works on his collected writings on the sociology of religion, and the first part of *Wirtschaft und Gesellschaft* goes to press. On June 14 Weber succumbs to pneumonia.

INDEX